Statistical Handbook on Aging Americans

Statistical Handbook on Aging Americans

Edited by
Frank L. Schick

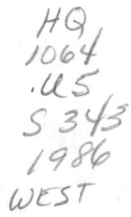

ORYX PRESS
1986

The rare Arabian Oryx is believed to have inspired the myth of the unicorn. This desert antelope became virtually extinct in the early 1960s. At that time several groups of international conservationists arranged to have 9 animals sent to the Phoenix Zoo to be the nucleus of a captive breeding herd. Today the Oryx population is over 400, and herds have been returned to reserves in Israel, Jordan, and Oman.

Copyright © 1986 by
The Oryx Press
2214 North Central at Encanto
Phoenix, AZ 85004-1483

Published simultaneously in Canada

Printed and Bound in the United States of America

∞ The paper used in this publication meets the minimum requirements of American National Standard for Information Science—Permanence of Paper for Printed Library Materials, ANSI Z39.48, 1984.

Library of Congress Cataloging-in-Publication Data

Schick, Frank Leopold, 1918–
    Statistical handbook on aging Americans.

    Bibliography: p.
    Includes index.
    1. Aged—United States—Statistics—Handbooks, manuals, etc. I. Title.
HQ1064.U5S343 1986   305.2′6′0973021   85-43607
ISBN 0-89774-259-1

*The oldest hath borne most: we that are young
shall never see so much nor live so long.*

Shakespeare, *King Lear,* Act V, Scene 3, line 325.

*To the twelve younger members of my family who
made me forget about aging.*

Contents

Introduction

The United States stands today at a significant demographic turning point. For the first time in our history, there are as many Americans aged 65 or over as teenagers. In 1776, the total population of the American colonies was approximately 2.5 million and only one out of 50 persons was 65 years old or older. At that time, Thomas Paine proposed a nationally funded pension system to prevent poverty among the elderly. During the twentieth century, the Social Security System, Medicare, Medicaid, the National Institute on Aging, and many other federal, state, local, and private agencies concerned with the aging were established. By the year 2000, every fifth American will be in the over 65 age group.

Today we can assume that a majority of us can look forward to 10 to 20 years of life after work, in relatively good health with adequate and secure retirement income. The most severe problems such as chronic illness, poverty, and social isolation persist, but for many, they are being delayed beyond the age of 75.

This publication provides recent statistical data about the aging population in the United States. Regarding the value of statistics, I agree with Robert J. Samuelson who recently wrote: "Good statistics are rarely the end of knowledge but they are often the beginning. Properly used, they can lead to truth and protect from falsehood." He also stated that "wrongly used, statistics are a plague because they project a false air of authority." ("The Joys of Statistics," *The Washington Post*, October 30, 1985, p. F1+)

With this caveat in mind, readers can proceed to locate specific information from the tables and charts in this book. If they need more data they should consult the references given for each table and chart (see List of Sources) and the Guide to Related Information Sources, which is arranged by agency or publisher. The data presented here are the most recent available as of December 1985. In a few cases, late 1970 data are given because no later figures could be obtained. Whenever the term "elderly" is used, it refers to the population of 65 years and older. The tables and charts were collected from over 120 publications, most of which were produced by the government. In many instances, they are related to the Decennial Census and its derivative surveys. Few other countries have the same constitutional mandate regarding statistical information, which gives the US Census its dominant position and provides us with better, more reliable, and more frequent information on the essential aspects of our culture than found elsewhere.

Other government agencies such as the Bureau of Labor Statistics and the National Center for Health Statistics are legally mandated to undertake their own data collections and analyses. Private research organizations usually concentrate on further analysis of government surveys rather than collect their own data because of time and costs involved.

When using statistical tables, one must keep in mind the reliability of the sources of information. The British economist Sir Josiah Stamp (1880–1941) said about the government that it "is very keen on amassing statistics. They collect them, raise them to the nth power, take the cube root and prepare wonderful diagrams. But you must never forget that every one of these figures comes in the first instance from the village watchman who just puts down what he damn well pleases." Having spent over two decades with the development of government and other statistics, I feel confident that the data presented here are reliable. The titles of all charts and tables and the original data were used without editorial changes.

This book was published because certain conditions relating to the aging population can only be fully understood through quantitative information. To assemble this information, the appropriate agencies in the Washington area were contacted for their newest publications and work in progress. These contacts were followed by a thorough literature review, using printed bibliographies as well as online databases. The National Gerontology Resource Center of the American Association of Retired People (AARP) was the ideal resource facility for this work because of its unique combination of a supportive administration, a superb and dedicated staff headed by Ms. Paula M. Lovas, and an excellent up-to-date collection of materials on aging. Without the help, guidance, and support of my wife Renée, this publication would not have seen the light of day.

I am also very grateful to Ms. Dorothy M. Gilford, senior research associate of the National Research Council, for giving me access to her project concerned with an inventory of data sets relating to the health of the elderly; to Mr. Herman B. Brotman, formerly with the Administration on Aging; and to Dr. Carol Allan, consultant, for sharing their extensive knowledge of the subject field with me. To these experts I am sincerely indebted for their advice and assistance.

List of Tables and Charts

A. Demographics

AGE AND SEX DISTRIBUTION

The elderly are increasing far more rapidly than the rest of the population and are living significantly longer and in better health than previously. At the beginning of the century, only one in 25 Americans was over 65; in 1984, one in nine was at least 65, and by 2050, one in five will fall into this age group. In the last two decades, the 65+ population increased twice as fast as the under-65 population. While in 1980 only 40 percent of the elderly were over the age of 75, 50 percent are expected to be in the 75+ group by the year 2000.

In 1984, the ratio of women to men aged 65 and over was three to two; for the 85+ group, this ratio increased to five to two.

LIFE EXPECTANCY, NUMBER OF BIRTHS

During this century, life expectancy in the United States has changed dramatically. In 1900, the average person could expect to live 47.3 years; by 1950, this figure had increased to 68.2, and in 1983, the average life expectancy for women had risen to 78.3 and for men to 71 years. The shifts in life expectancy explain the upward movement of the median age of the population, which reached 31 in 1984 and is expected to have risen to 36 by the year 2000.

RACE AND ETHNICITY

In 1984, 15 percent of the entire population was black; of those 65 years and older, only 9 percent were black. Fertility and mortality rates are such that this proportion is expected to remain fairly constant until 2025; after that time, the proportion of elderly black people will increase more rapidly than that of whites. During the first half of the century, life expectancy for the white population was considerably longer than for blacks; these differences have narrowed, and today, life expectancy is longest now for white women, followed by black women, white men, and black men.

GEOGRAPHIC DISTRIBUTION, MOBILITY AND MIGRATION

Today, over half of the elderly live in eight states: California, New York, Florida, Pennsylvania, Texas, Illinois, Ohio, and Michigan. Between 1975 and 1980, one-fifth of the older population moved; this mobility rate was only half that of the younger population. The number of those who changed their residence nearly doubled since 1950. During the last 10 to 15 years, a pattern of "countermigration" has developed, indicating that a substantial number of retirees who had moved to warmer climates returned after a few years to their home states, families, and friends.

VETERANS

The total number of veterans is directly related to the US participation in twentieth-century armed conflicts. Provided that the US does not engage in additional military conflicts, the number of veterans is projected to decrease from 28.6 million in 1980 to 20.7 million in 2010, but the number of aged veterans will increase from 3 million to 8.1 million during the same period. Currently, one-quarter of the male population over 65 are veterans; of these, over 95 percent are male. Due to the longevity of women they will constitute about 10 percent of the aged veteran population in 2010.

AGING IN OTHER COUNTRIES, USE OF OTHER LANGUAGES

The proportion of the aging is increasing the world over. In 1980, there were about 376 million people over the age of 65 in the world. By 2025, this number is projected to increase to approximately 1.1 billion. The proportion of this age group in the total world population is expected to rise during that period from 8.5 percent to 13.7 percent.

A1. AGE AND SEX DISTRIBUTION

A1-1. Percentage of the Total Population 65 Years and Over, for States: 1980

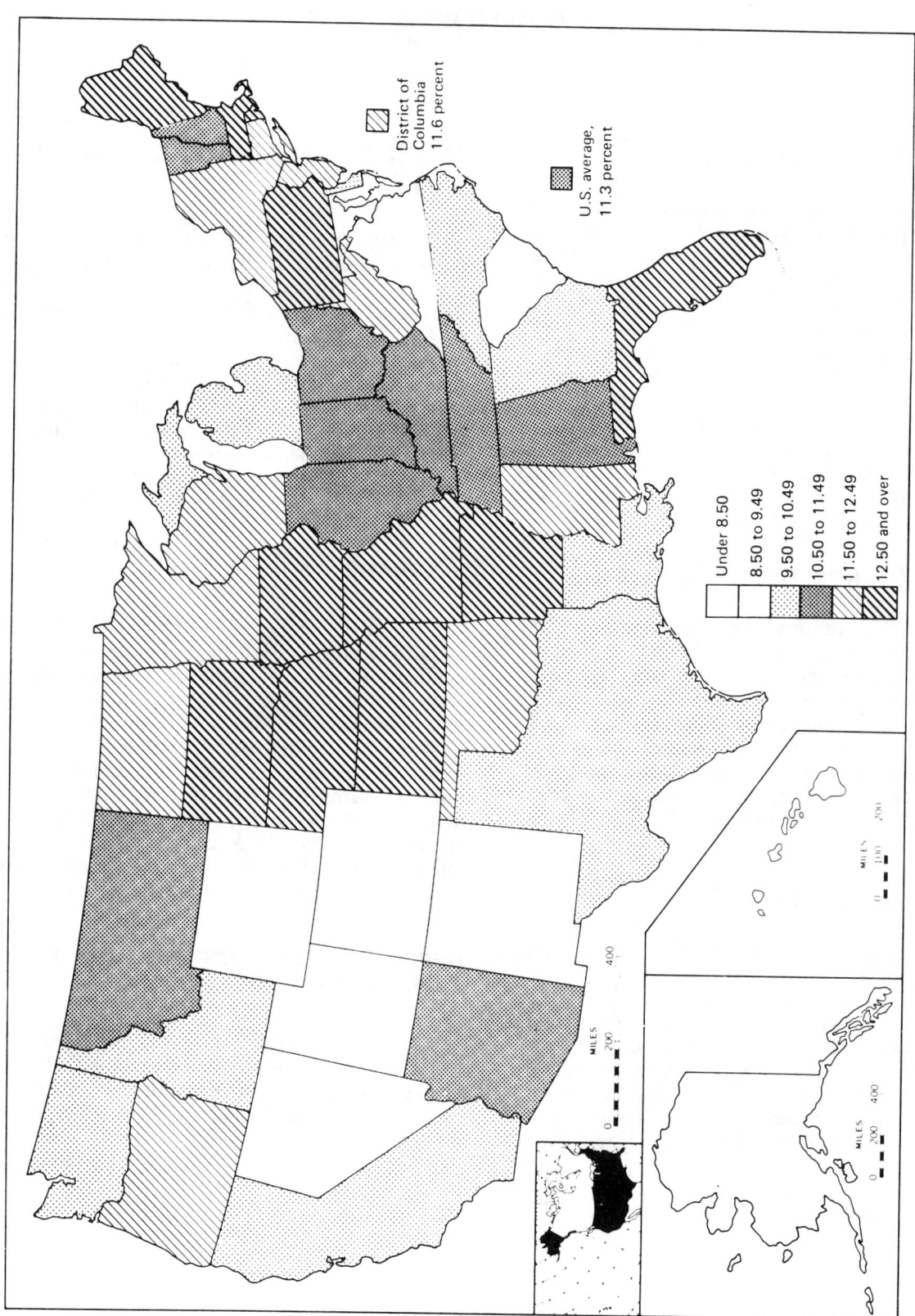

District of Columbia
11.6 percent

U.S. average,
11.3 percent

Under 8.50
8.50 to 9.49
9.50 to 10.49
10.50 to 11.49
11.50 to 12.49
12.50 and over

A1–2. Resident Population

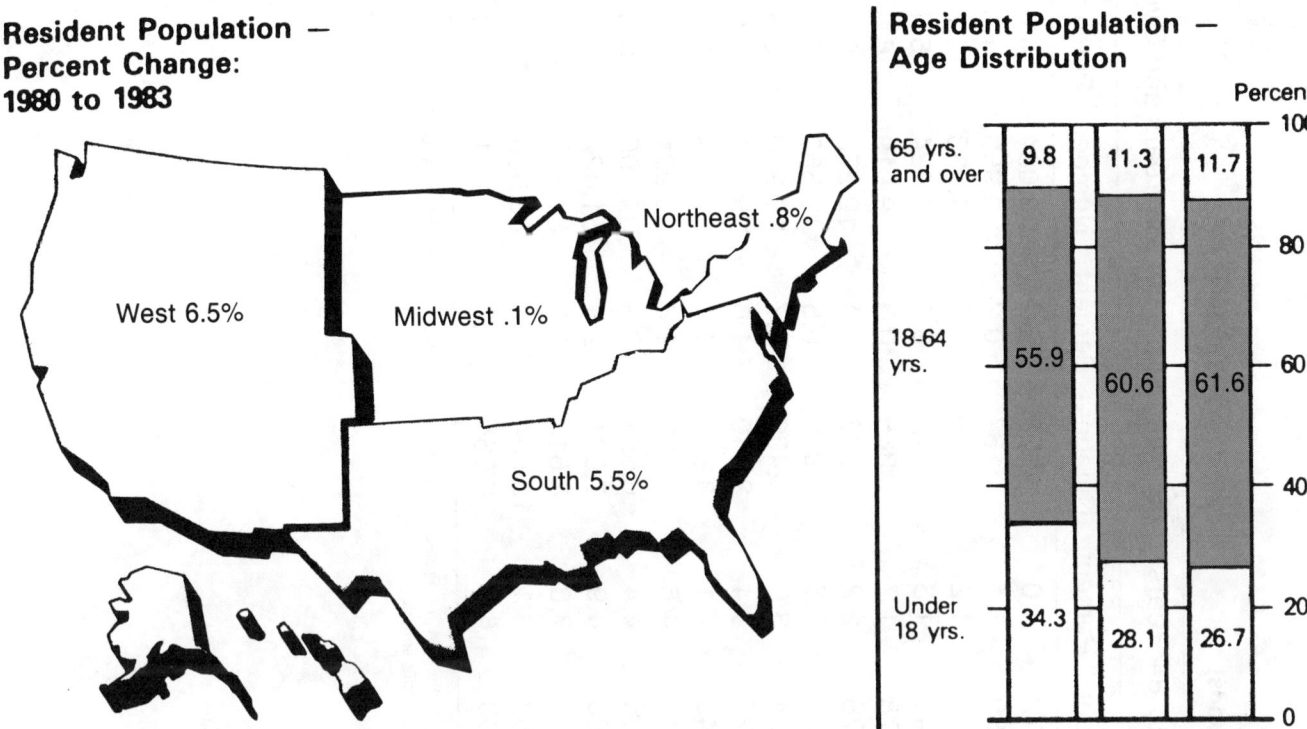

**Resident Population —
Percent Change:
1980 to 1983**

Northeast .8%

West 6.5%

Midwest .1%

South 5.5%

**Resident Population —
Age Distribution**

Population	Unit of measure	1970	1975	1980	1982	1983	Average annual percent change		
							1970-80	80-82	82-83
Resident population, total	Millions	203.3	215.5	226.5	231.8	234.0	1.1	1.0	.9
Northeast	Millions	49.1	49.4	49.1	49.3	49.5	(Z)	.2	.4
Midwest	Millions	56.6	57.8	58.9	58.9	59.0	.4	(Z)	(Z)
South	Millions	62.8	69.6	75.4	78.4	79.5	1.8	1.8	1.4
West	Millions	34.8	38.6	43.2	45.2	46.0	2.2	2.0	1.8
In metropolitan areas [1]	Millions	155.5	(NA)	172.0	(NA)	177.9	1.0	[2] 1.1	(NA)
In nonmetropolitan areas	Millions	47.8	(NA)	54.6	(NA)	56.1	1.3	[2] .8	(NA)
Under 5 years	Millions	17.2	16.1	16.3	17.4	17.8	−.5	2.8	2.6
5-17 years	Millions	52.5	51.0	47.4	45.4	44.7	−1.0	−1.9	−1.5
18-24 years	Millions	23.7	27.7	30.0	30.2	29.9	2.4	.2	−.8
25-44 years	Millions	48.0	54.1	62.7	67.5	69.6	2.7	3.3	3.1
45-64 years	Millions	41.8	43.8	44.5	44.5	44.6	.6	(Z)	.1
65 years and over	Millions	20.0	22.7	25.6	26.8	27.4	2.5	2.2	2.1
Median age	Years	28.0	28.7	30.0	30.6	30.9	.7	.9	1.0
White	Millions	178.1	187.2	194.7	198.1	199.5	.9	.8	.7
Black	Millions	22.6	24.7	26.7	27.7	28.1	1.7	1.6	1.6
Persons of Spanish origin [3]	Millions	9.1	(NA)	14.6	(NA)	(NA)	4.8	(NA)	(NA)

NA Not available   Z Less than .05 percent   [1] Metropolitan statistical areas as defined June 30, 1984.
[2] Percent change, 1980–1983.   [3] Persons of Spanish origin may be of any race.

A1–3. Actual and Projected Growth of the Older Population, 1900–2050

(Numbers in thousands)

Year	Total population all ages	55 to 64 Years Number	55 to 64 Years Percent	65 to 74 Years Number	65 to 74 Years Percent	75 to 84 Years Number	75 to 84 Years Percent	85 Years and Over Number	85 Years and Over Percent	65 Years and Over Number	65 Years and Over Percent
1900	76,303	4,009	5.3	2,189	2.9	772	1.0	123	0.2	3,084	4.0
1910	91,972	5,054	5.5	2,793	3.0	989	1.1	167	0.2	3,950	4.3
1920	105,711	6,532	6.2	3,464	3.3	1,259	1.2	210	0.2	4.933	4.7
1930	122,775	8,397	6.8	4,721	3.8	1,641	1.3	272	0.2	6,634	5.4
1940	131,669	10,572	8.0	6,375	4.8	2,278	1.7	365	0.3	9,019	6.8
1950	150,967	13,295	8.8	8,415	5.6	3,278	2.2	577	0.4	12,270	8.1
1960	179,323	15,572	8.7	10,997	6.1	4,633	2.6	929	0.5	16,560	9.2
1970	203,302	18,608	9.2	12,447	6.1	6,124	3.0	1,409	0.7	19,980	9.8
1980	226,505	21,700	9.6	15,578	6.9	7,727	3.4	2,240	1.0	25,544	11.3
1990	249,657	21,051	8.4	18,035	7.2	10,349	4.1	3,313	1.3	31,697	12.7
2000	267,955	23,767	8.9	17,677	6.6	12,318	4.6	4,926	1.8	34,921	13.0
2010	283,238	34,848	12.3	20,318	7.2	12,326	4.4	6,551	2.3	39,195	13.8
2020	296,597	40,298	13.6	29,855	10.1	14,486	4.9	7,081	2.4	51,422	17.3
2030	304,807	34,025	11.2	34,535	11.3	21,434	7.0	8,612	2.8	64,581	21.2
2040	308,559	34,717	11.3	29,272	9.5	24,882	8.1	12,834	4.2	66,988	21.7
2050	309,488	37,327	12.1	30,114	9.7	21,263	6.9	16,034	5.2	67,411	21.8

SOURCES: 1900–80: U.S. Bureau of the Census, Decennial Censuses of Population. 1990–2050: U.S. Bureau of the Census, Projections of the Population of the United States, by Age, Sex, and Race: 1983 to 2080. Current Population Reports, Series P–25, No. 952, May 1984. Projections are middle series.

A1-4. Civilian Noninstitutional Population, by Age, 1948-83

(In thousands)

Year, sex, and race	16 years and over	16 to 19 years			20 years and over						
		Total	16 to 17 years	18 to 19 years	Total	20 to 24 years	25 to 34 years	35 to 44 years	45 to 54 years	55 to 64 years	65 years and over
TOTAL											
1048	103,068	8,449	4,265	4,185	94,618	11,530	22,610	20,097	16,771	12,885	10,720
1949	103,994	8,215	4,139	4,079	95,778	11,312	22,822	20,401	17,002	13,201	11,035
1950	104,995	8,143	4,076	4,068	96,851	11,080	23,013	20,681	17,240	13,469	11,363
1951	104,621	7,865	4,096	3,771	96,755	10,167	22,843	20,863	17,464	13,692	11,724
1952	105,231	7,922	4,234	3,689	97,305	9,389	23,044	21,137	17,716	13,889	12,126
1953	107,056	8,014	4,241	3,773	99,041	8,960	23,266	21,922	17,991	13,830	13,075
1954	108,321	8,224	4,336	3,889	100,095	8,885	23,304	22,135	18,305	14,085	13,375
1955	109,683	8,364	4,440	3,925	101,318	9,036	23,249	22,348	18,643	14,309	13,728
1956	110,954	8,434	4,482	3,953	102,518	9,271	23,072	22,567	19,012	14,516	14,075
1957	112,265	8,612	4,587	4,026	103,653	9,486	22,849	22,786	19,424	14,727	14,376
1958	113,727	8,986	4,872	4,114	104,737	9,733	22,563	23,025	19,832	14,923	14,657
1959	115,329	9,618	5,337	4,282	105,711	9,975	22,201	23,207	20,203	15,134	14,985
1960	117,245	10,187	5,573	4,615	107,056	10,273	21,998	23,437	20,601	15,409	15,336
1961	118,771	10,513	5,462	5,052	108,255	10,583	21,829	23,585	20,893	15,675	15,685
1962	120,153	10,652	5,503	5,150	109,500	10,852	21,503	23,797	20,916	15,874	16,554
1963	122,416	11,370	6,301	5,070	111,045	11,464	21,400	23,948	21,144	16,138	16,945
1964	124,485	12,111	6,974	5,139	112,372	12,017	21,367	23,940	21,452	16,442	17,150
1965	126,513	12,930	6,936	5,995	113,582	12,442	21,417	23,832	21,728	16,727	17,432
1966	128,058	13,592	6,914	6,679	114,463	12,638	21,543	23,579	21,977	17,007	17,715
1967	129,874	13,480	7,003	6,480	116,391	13,421	22,057	23,313	22,256	17,310	18,029
1968	132,028	13,698	7,200	6,499	118,328	13,891	22,912	23,036	22,534	17,614	18,338
1969	134,335	14,095	7,422	6,673	120,238	14,488	23,645	22,709	22,806	17,930	18,657
1970	137,085	14,519	7,643	6,876	122,566	15,323	24,435	22,489	23,059	18,250	19,007
1971	140,216	15,022	7,849	7,173	125,193	16,345	25,337	22,274	23,244	18,581	19,406
1972	144,126	15,510	8,076	7,435	128,614	17,143	26,740	22,358	23,338	19,007	20,023
1973	147,096	15,840	8,227	7,613	131,253	17,692	28,172	22,287	23,431	19,281	20,389
1974	150,120	16,180	8,373	7,809	133,938	17,994	29,439	22,461	23,578	19,517	20,945
1975	153,153	16,418	8,419	7,999	136,733	18,595	30,710	22,526	23,535	19,844	21,525
1976	156,150	16,614	8,442	8,171	139,536	19,109	31,953	22,796	23,409	20,185	22,083
1977	159,033	16,688	8,482	8,206	142,345	19,582	33,117	23,296	23,197	20,557	22,597
1978	161,910	16,695	8,484	8,211	145,216	20,007	34,091	24,099	22,977	20,875	23,166
1979	164,863	16,657	8,389	8,268	148,205	20,353	35,261	24,861	22,752	21,210	23,767
1980	167,745	16,543	8,279	8,264	151,202	20,635	36,558	25,578	22,563	21,520	24,350
1981	170,130	16,214	8,068	8,145	153,916	20,820	37,777	26,291	22,422	21,756	24,850
1982	172,271	15,763	7,714	8,049	156,508	20,845	38,492	27,611	22,264	21,909	25,387
1983	174,215	15,274	7,385	7,889	158,941	20,799	39,147	28,932	22,167	22,003	25,892

A1-5. Distribution of the Population by Older Age Groups, 1984

Age group	Number	Percent
All ages	236,416	100
0 to 54	186,220	79
55 to 64	22,210	9
65 to 74	16,596	7
75 to 84	8,793	4
85 plus	2,596	1
55 plus	50,195	21
65 plus	27,985	12

A1-6. Actual and Projected Growth of the Older Population, 1900–2050

[Numbers in thousands]

Year	Total population all ages	55 to 64 Years Number	55 to 64 Years Percent	65 to 74 Years Number	65 to 74 Years Percent	75 to 84 Years Number	75 to 84 Years Percent	85 Years and Over Number	85 Years and Over Percent	65 Years and Over Number	65 Years and Over Percent
1900	76,303	4,009	5.3	2,189	2.9	772	1.0	123	0.2	3,084	4.0
1910	91,972	5,054	5.5	2,793	3.0	989	1.1	167	0.2	3,950	4.3
1920	105,711	6,532	6.2	3,464	3.3	1,259	1.2	210	0.2	4,933	4.7
1930	122,775	8,397	6.8	4,721	3.8	1,641	1.3	272	0.2	6,634	5.4
1940	131,669	10,572	8.0	6,375	4.8	2,278	1.7	365	0.3	9,019	6.8
1950	150,967	13,295	8.8	8,415	5.6	3,278	2.2	577	0.4	12,270	8.1
1960	179,323	15,572	8.7	10,997	6.1	4,633	2.6	929	0.5	16,560	9.2
1970	203,302	18,608	9.2	12,447	6.1	6,124	3.0	1,409	0.7	19,980	9.8
1980	226,505	21,700	9.6	15,578	6.9	7,727	3.4	2,240	1.0	25,544	11.3
1990	249,657	21,051	8.4	18,035	7.2	10,349	4.1	3,313	1.3	31,697	12.7
2000	267,955	23,767	8.9	17,677	6.6	12,318	4.6	4,926	1.8	34,921	13.0
2010	283,238	34,848	12.3	20,318	7.2	12,326	4.4	6,551	2.3	39,195	13.8
2020	296,597	40,298	13.6	29,855	10.1	14,486	4.9	7,081	2.4	51,422	17.3
2030	304,807	34,025	11.2	34,535	11.3	21,434	7.0	8,612	2.8	64,581	21.2
2040	308,559	34,717	11.3	29,272	9.5	24,882	8.1	12,834	4.2	66,988	21.7
2050	309,488	37,327	12.1	30,114	9.7	21,263	6.9	16,034	5.2	67,411	21.8

Sources 1900–80: U.S. Bureau of the Census, Decennial Censuses of Population. 1990–2050: U.S. Bureau of the Census, Projections of the Population of the United States, by Age, Sex, and Race: 1983 to 2080. Current Population Reports, Series P-25, No. 952, May 1984. Projections are middle series.

A1-7. Projected Demographic Trends for the Elderly 1980–2050

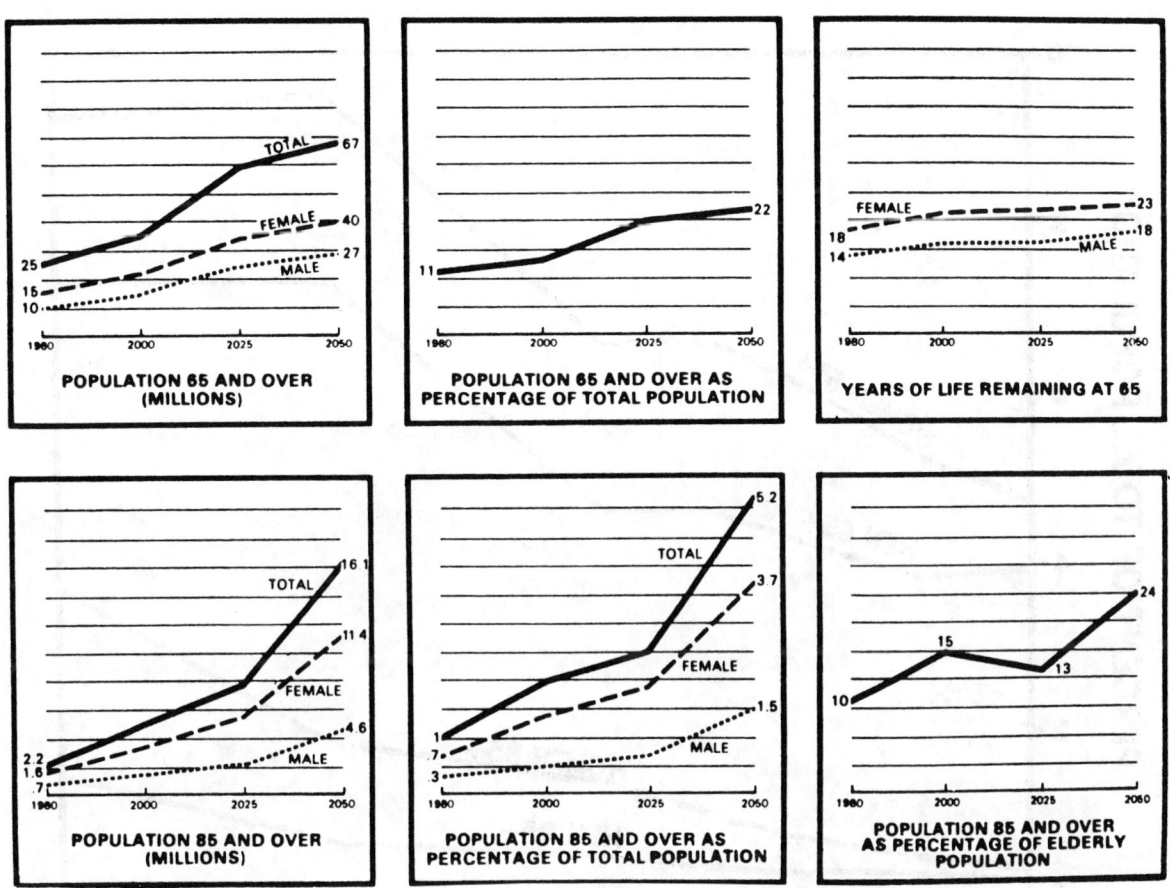

A1-8. Historic and Projected Trends in Social and Economic Characteristics of the Elderly 1960–2000

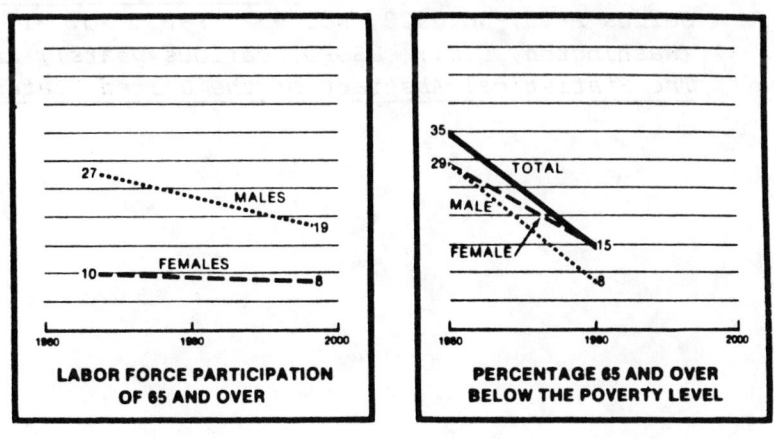

A1–9. Proportion of the Population 65 and Over and 85 and Over by Sex 1960–2050

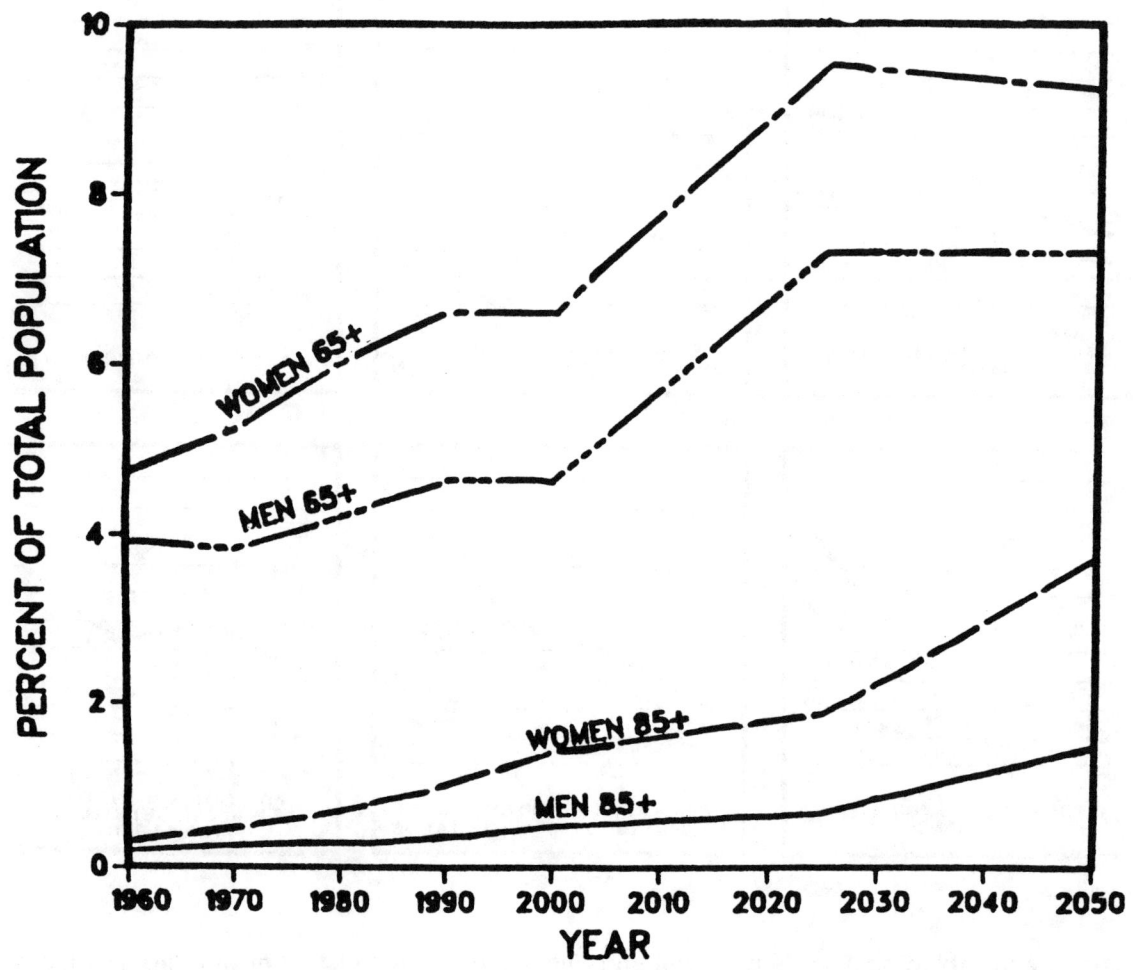

Source: US Bureau of the Census, *Current Population Reports*,
          Series P-25, No. 922, No. 937; P-25, No. 917
          (Washington, D.C.: USGPO, various years); and
          The Statistical Abstract of the United States, 1963.

A1–10. Civilian Noninstitutional Population by Sex and Age, 1948–83

(In thousands)

Year, sex, and race	16 years and over	16 to 19 years			20 years and over						
		Total	16 to 17 years	18 to 19 years	Total	20 to 24 years	25 to 34 years	35 to 44 years	45 to 54 years	55 to 64 years	65 years and over
Men											
1948	49,996	4,078	2,128	1,951	45,918	5,527	10,767	9,798	8,290	6,441	5,093
1949	50,321	3,946	2,062	1,884	46,379	5,405	10,871	9,926	8,379	6,568	5,228
1950	50,725	3,962	2,043	1,920	46,763	5,270	10,963	10,034	8,472	6,664	5,357
1951	49,727	3,725	2,039	1,687	46,001	4,451	10,709	10,049	8,551	6,737	5,503
1952	49,700	3,767	2,121	1,647	45,932	3,788	10,855	10,164	8,655	6,798	5,670
1953	50,750	3,823	2,122	1,701	46,927	3,482	11,020	10,632	8,878	6,798	6,119
1954	51,395	3,953	2,174	1,780	47,441	3,509	11,067	10,718	9,018	6,885	6,241
1955	52,109	4,022	2,225	1,798	48,086	3,708	11,068	10,804	9,164	6,960	6,380
1956	52,723	4,020	2,238	1,783	48,704	3,970	10,983	10,889	9,322	7,032	6,505
1957	53,315	4,083	2,284	1,800	49,231	4,166	10,889	10,965	9,499	7,109	6,602
1958	54,033	4,293	2,435	1,858	49,740	4,339	10,787	11,076	9,675	7,179	6,683
1959	54,793	4,652	2,681	1,971	50,140	4,488	10,625	11,149	9,832	7,259	6,785
1960	55,662	4,963	2,805	2,159	50,698	4,679	10,514	11,230	10,000	7,373	6,901
1961	56,286	5,112	2,742	2,371	51,173	4,844	10,440	11,286	10,112	7,483	7,006
1962	56,831	5,150	2,764	2,386	51,681	4,925	10,207	11,389	10,162	7,610	7,386
1963	57,921	5,496	3,162	2,334	52,425	5,240	10,165	11,476	10,274	7,740	7,526
1964	58,847	5,866	3,503	2,364	52,981	5,520	10,144	11,466	10,402	7,873	7,574
1965	59,782	6,318	3,488	2,831	53,463	5,701	10,182	11,427	10,512	7,990	7,649
1966	60,262	6,658	3,478	3,180	53,603	5,663	10,224	11,294	10,598	8,099	7,723
1967	60,905	6,537	3,528	3,010	54,367	5,977	10,495	11,161	10,705	8,218	7,809
1968	61,847	6,683	3,634	3,049	55,165	6,127	10,944	11,040	10,819	8,336	7,897
1969	62,898	6,928	3,741	3,187	55,969	6,379	11,309	10,890	10,935	8,464	7,990
1970	64,304	7,145	3,848	3,299	57,157	6,861	11,750	10,810	11,052	8,590	8,093
1971	65,942	7,430	3,954	3,477	58,511	7,511	12,227	10,721	11,129	8,711	8,208
1972	67,835	7,705	4,081	3,624	60,130	8,061	12,911	10,762	11,167	8,895	8,330
1973	69,292	7,855	4,152	3,703	61,436	8,429	13,641	10,746	11,202	8,990	8,426
1974	70,808	8,012	4,231	3,781	62,796	8,600	14,262	10,834	11,315	9,140	8,641
1975	72,291	8,134	4,252	3,882	64,158	8,950	14,899	10,874	11,298	9,286	8,852
1976	73,759	8,244	4,266	3,978	65,515	9,237	15,528	11,010	11,243	9,444	9,053
1977	75,193	8,288	4,290	4,000	66,904	9,477	16,108	11,260	11,144	9,616	9,297
1978	76,576	8,309	4,295	4,014	68,268	9,693	16,598	11,665	11,045	9,758	9,509
1979	78,020	8,310	4,251	4,060	69,709	9,873	17,193	12,046	10,944	9,907	9,746
1980	79,398	8,260	4,195	4,064	71,138	10,023	17,833	12,400	10,861	10,042	9,979
1981	80,511	8,092	4,087	4,005	72,419	10,116	18,427	12,758	10,797	10,151	10,170
1982	81,523	7,879	3,911	3,968	73,644	10,136	18,787	13,410	10,726	10,215	10,371
1983	82,531	7,659	3,750	3,908	74,872	10,140	19,143	14,067	10,689	10,261	10,573
Women											
1948	53,071	4,371	2,137	2,234	48,700	6,003	11,843	10,299	8,481	6,444	5,627
1949	53,670	4,269	2,077	2,195	49,400	5,907	11,951	10,475	8,623	6,633	5,809
1950	54,270	4,181	2,033	2,148	50,088	5,810	12,050	10,647	8,768	6,805	6,006
1951	54,895	4,140	2,057	2,084	50,754	5,716	12,134	10,814	8,913	6,955	6,221
1952	55,529	4,155	2,113	2,042	51,373	5,601	12,189	10,973	9,061	7,091	6,456
1953	56,305	4,191	2,119	2,072	52,114	5,478	12,246	11,290	9,113	7,032	6,956
1954	56,925	4,271	2,162	2,109	52,654	5,376	12,237	11,417	9,287	7,200	7,134
1955	57,574	4,342	2,215	2,127	53,232	5,328	12,181	11,544	9,479	7,349	7,348
1956	58,228	4,414	2,244	2,170	53,814	5,301	12,089	11,678	9,690	7,484	7,570
1957	58,951	4,529	2,303	2,226	54,421	5,320	11,960	11,821	9,925	7,618	7,774
1958	59,690	4,693	2,437	2,256	54,997	5,394	11,776	11,949	10,157	7,744	7,974
1959	60,534	4,966	2,656	2,311	55,570	5,487	11,576	12,058	10,371	7,875	8,200
1960	61,582	5,224	2,768	2,456	56,358	5,594	11,484	12,207	10,601	8,036	8,435
1961	62,484	5,401	2,720	2,681	57,082	5,739	11,389	12,299	10,781	8,192	8,679
1962	63,321	5,502	2,739	2,764	57,819	5,927	11,296	12,408	10,754	8,264	9,168
1963	64,494	5,874	3,139	2,736	58,620	6,224	11,235	12,472	10,870	8,398	9,419
1964	65,637	6,245	3,471	2,775	59,391	6,497	11,223	12,474	11,050	8,569	9,576
1965	66,731	6,612	3,448	3,164	60,119	6,741	11,235	12,405	11,216	8,737	9,783
1966	67,795	6,934	3,436	3,499	60,860	6,975	11,319	12,285	11,379	8,908	9,992
1967	68,968	6,943	3,475	3,470	62,026	7,445	11,562	12,152	11,551	9,092	10,220
1968	70,179	7,015	3,566	3,450	63,164	7,764	11,968	11,996	11,715	9,278	10,441
1969	71,436	7,167	3,681	3,486	64,269	8,109	12,336	11,819	11,871	9,466	10,667
1970	72,782	7,373	3,796	3,578	65,408	8,462	12,684	11,679	12,008	9,659	10,914
1971	74,274	7,591	3,895	3,697	66,682	8,834	13,110	11,553	12,115	9,870	11,198
1972	76,290	7,805	3,994	3,811	68,484	9,082	13,829	11,597	12,171	10,113	11,693
1973	77,804	7,985	4,076	3,909	69,819	9,263	14,531	11,541	12,229	10,290	11,963
1974	79,312	8,168	4,142	4,028	71,144	9,393	15,177	11,627	12,263	10,377	12,304
1975	80,860	8,285	4,168	4,117	72,576	9,645	15,811	11,652	12,237	10,558	12,673
1976	82,390	8,370	4,176	4,194	74,020	9,872	16,425	11,786	12,166	10,742	13,030
1977	83,840	8,400	4,193	4,206	75,441	10,103	17,008	12,036	12,053	10,940	13,300
1978	85,334	8,386	4,189	4,197	76,948	10,315	17,493	12,435	11,932	11,118	13,658
1979	86,843	8,347	4,139	4,208	78,496	10,480	18,070	12,815	11,808	11,303	14,021
1980	88,348	8,283	4,083	4,200	80,065	10,612	18,725	13,177	11,701	11,478	14,372
1981	89,618	8,121	3,981	4,140	81,497	10,705	19,350	13,533	11,625	11,605	14,680
1982	90,748	7,884	3,804	4,081	82,864	10,709	19,705	14,201	11,538	11,694	15,017
1983	91,684	7,616	3,635	3,981	84,069	10,660	20,004	14,865	11,478	11,742	15,319

A1–11. Characteristics of Population Aged 65 and Over, by Various Characteristics, 1982

Characteristics	Male			Female		
	Ages 65 and Over	Ages 65-74	Ages 75 and Over	Ages 65 and Over	Ages 65-74	Ages 75 and Over
	Numbers in Thousands					
Population	10,310	6,770	3,540	14,920	8,927	5,993
	Percent Distribution					
Race	100.0	100.0	100.0	100.0	100.0	100.0
White	90.0	89.7	90.6	90.5	90.1	91.2
All other	10.0	10.3	9.4	9.5	9.9	8.8
Marital Status	100.0	100.0	100.0	100.0	100.0	100.0
Single	4.4	4.9	3.3	5.6	5.3	6.1
Married	80.0	84.0	72.5	40.2	51.3	23.6
Widowed	12.4	7.5	21.8	50.4	38.3	68.5
Divorced	3.2	3.6	2.4	3.8	5.1	1.8
Family Status	100.0	100.0	100.0	100.0	100.0	100.0
In families	83.7	86.6	78.0	56.8	63.0	47.5
Householder	76.8	80.3	70.1	10.0	10.0	10.0
Married, spouse present	73.9	78.0	66.1	1.7	2.3	.9
Spouse of householder	3.1	3.0	3.2	36.4	46.7	21.2
Other	3.8	3.3	4.9	10.4	6.3	16.3
Not in families	16.3	13.4	22.0	43.2	37.0	52.5
Householder	15.3	12.4	21.1	42.4	36.1	51.8
Other	1.0	1.0	.9	.8	.9	.7
Labor Force Status*	100.0	100.0†	100.0‡	100.0	100.0†	100.0‡
In labor force	17.8	26.9	12.2	7.9	14.9	4.5
Employed	17.1	25.8	11.8	7.6	14.4	4.4
Unemployed	.7	1.1	.4	.3	.5	.1
Not in labor force	82.2	73.1	87.8	92.1	85.1	95.5

*Based on 1982 annual average.   † Refers to ages 65-69.   ‡ Refers to ages 70 and over.

Note: Data relate to the noninstitutionalized population.

Source of basic data: Reports of the Bureau of the Census and the Department of Labor.

A1–12. Sex Ratio of the Population in Selected Age Groups: July 1, 1984, and April 1, 1980

(Numbers in thousands. Total population including Armed Forces overseas)

Age	July 1, 1984		April 1, 1980		Sex ratio[1]	
	Male	Female	Male	Female	July 1, 1984	April 1, 1980
All ages.................	115,236	121,446	110,528	116,533	94.9	94.8
Under 5 years.................	9,115	8,702	8,362	7,986	104.7	104.7
5 to 13 years.................	15,438	14,727	15,923	15,237	104.8	104.5
14 to 17 years.................	7,525	7,182	8,299	7,950	104.8	104.4
18 to 24 years.................	14,855	14,520	15,295	14,995	102.3	102.0
25 to 34 years.................	20,505	20,603	18,545	18,713	99.5	99.1
35 to 44 years.................	15,129	15,589	12,632	13,066	97.1	96.7
45 to 54 years.................	10,895	11,541	11,015	11,791	94.4	93.4
55 to 64 years.................	10,474	11,842	10,152	11,551	88.4	87.9
65 years and over.............	11,299	16,741	10,305	15,245	67.5	67.6

[1]Males per 100 females.

A2. LIFE EXPECTANCY, NUMBER OF BIRTHS

A2–1. Annual Number of Births (U.S. Census Projections Middle Series): 50 States and D.C., 1940 to 1992
(In thousands)

Year (July 1 - June 30)	Births	Year (July 1 - June 30)	Births
1940-41	2.631	1966-67	3,608
1941-42	2.789	1967-68	3.520
1942-43	3,168	1968-69	3,583
1943-44	2,989	1969-70	3,676
1944-45	2,937	1970-71	3,713
1945-46	2,873	1971-72	3,393
1946-47	3,948	1972-73	3,195
1947-48	3,658	1973-74	3,111
1948-49	3,660	1974-75	3,185
1949-50	3,638	1975-76	3,126
1950-51	3,771	1976-77	3,274
1951-52	3,859	1977-78	3,304
1952-53	3,951	1978-79	3.384
1953-54	4,045	1979-80	3,543
1954-55	4,119	1980-81	3,628
1955-56	4,167	1981-82	3,677
1956-57	4,312	1982-83	3,694
1957-58	4,313	Projected	
1958-59	4,298	1983-84	3,788
1959-60	4,279	1984-85	3,826
1960-61	4,350	1985-86	3,855
1961-62	4,259	1986-87	3,873
1962-63	4,185	1987-88	3,879
1963-64	4,119	1988-89	3,871
1964-65	3,940	1989-90	3,849
1965-66	3,716	1990-91	3,815
		1991-92	3,772
		1992-93	3,725

SOURCE: U.S. Department of Commerce, Bureau of the Census, *Current Population Reports*, "Population Estimates and Projections," Series P-25.

A2–2. Number of Births, by Year, 1910 to 1984, and Relationship to 1984 Age Groups

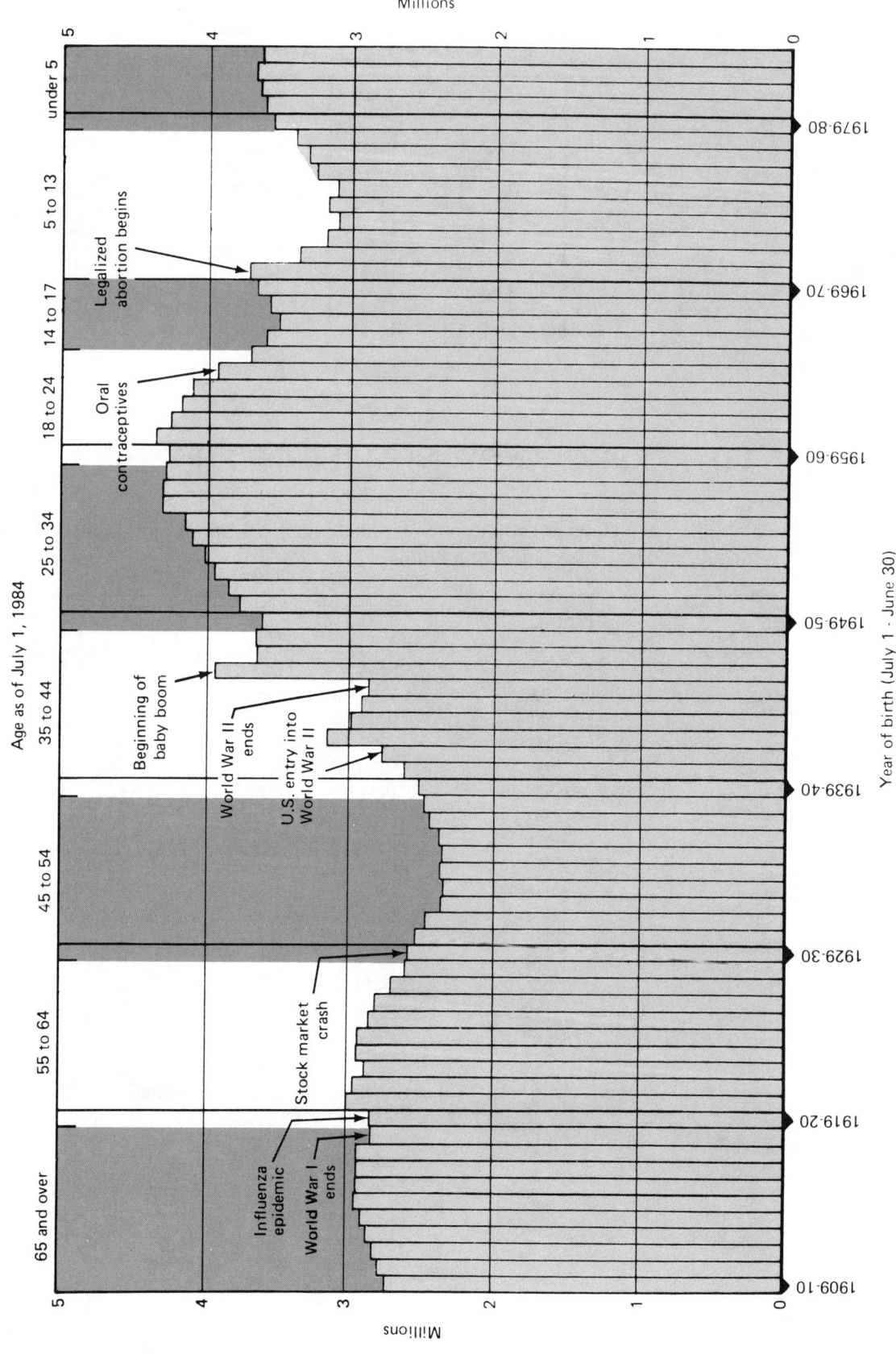

A2–3. Life Expectancy at Birth and Age 65 by Sex and Calendar Year, 1900–2050

	Male		Female	
	At birth	At age 65	At birth	At age 65
1900	46.4	11.3	49.0	12.0
1910	50.1	11.4	53.6	12.1
1920	54.5	11.8	56.3	12.3
1930	58.0	11.8	61.3	12.9
1940	61.4	11.9	65.7	13.4
1950	65.6	12.8	71.1	15.1
1960	66.7	12.9	73.2	15.9
1970	67.1	13.1	74.9	17.1
1980	69.9	14.0	77.5	18.4
1990	71.4	14.5	78.9	19.2
2000	72.1	14.8	79.5	19.5
2010	72.4	15.0	79.8	19.8
2020	72.7	15.2	80.1	20.1
2030	73.0	15.4	80.4	20.3
2040	73.3	15.6	80.7	20.6
2050	73.6	15.8	81.0	20.8

SOURCE: Social Security Administration; Social Security Area Population Projections, 1984; Actuarial Study No. 92, Alternative I.

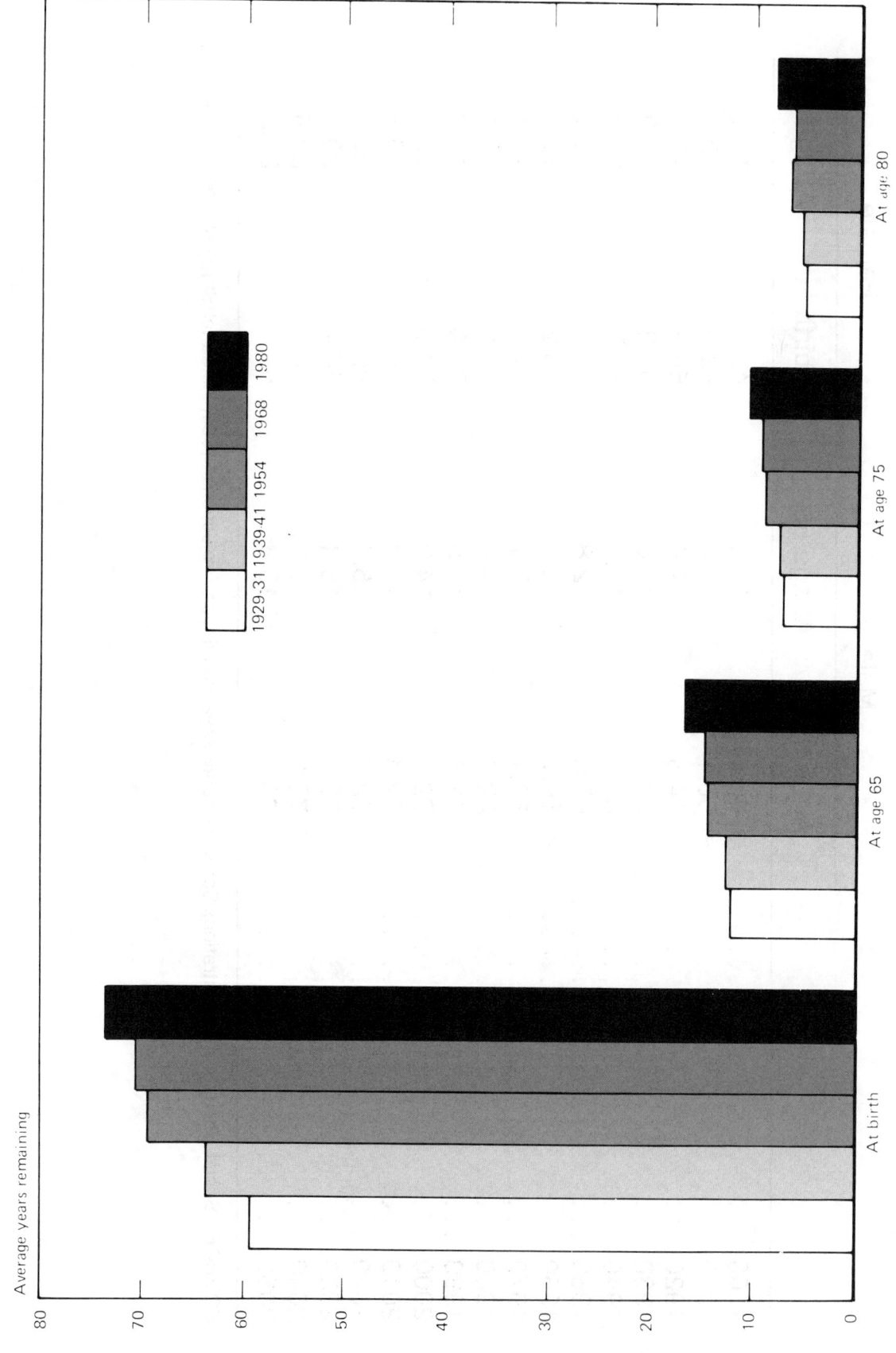

A2–4. Average Remaining Lifetime at Birth, Age 65, Age 75, and Age 80: 1929–31, 1939–41, 1954, 1968, 1980

A2-5. Expectation of Life at Selected Ages, by Color and Sex: Death-Registration States, 1900-1902, and United States, 1959-61, 1969-71, and 1977

Life table value and age	Total	WHITE Male	WHITE Female	ALL OTHER Male	ALL OTHER Female
Expectation of life:					
At birth					
1977	73.2	70.0	77.7	64.6	73.1
1969–71	70.75	67.94	75.49	60.98	69.05
1959–61	69.89	67.55	74.19	61.48	66.47
1900–1902[a]	49.24	48.23	51.08	32.54	35.04
At age 1 year					
1977	73.2	70.0	77.6	65.2	73.6
1969–71	71.19	68.33	75.66	62.13	70.01
1959–61	70.75	68.34	74.68	63.50	68.10
1900–1902[a]	55.20	54.61	56.39	42.46	43.54
At age 20 years					
1977	54.9	51.9	59.1	47.2	55.2
1969–71	53.00	50.22	57.24	44.37	51.85
1959–61	52.58	50.25	56.29	45.78	50.07
1900–1902[a]	42.79	42.19	43.77	35.11	36.89
At age 65 years					
1977	16.3	13.9	18.4	14.0	17.8
1969–71	15.00	13.02	16.93	12.87	15.99
1959–61	14.39	12.97	15.88	12.84	15.12
1900–1902[a]	11.86	11.51	12.23	10.38	11.38

a. For 1900-1902 figures for "All other male" and "All other female" include only the black population, which comprised 95 percent or more of the "All other" population.

Source: Vital Statistics of the U.S, 1977. Vol 11-Sec 5, Life Tables DHEW Publication No. (PHS)80-1104, page 5-4.

A2-6. Life Expectancy at Birth, According to Sex: Selected Countries, Selected Periods

(Data are based on reporting by countries)

Male

Country	Period	Life expectancy in years	Period	Life expectancy in years
Japan	1974	71.2	1980	73.3
Sweden	1971-75	72.1	1980	72.8
Netherlands	1971-75	71.2	1979	72.4
Norway	1973-74	71.5	1979-80	72.3
Israel	1975	70.3	1980	72.1
Denmark	1972-73	70.8	1979-80	71.2
Australia	1965-67	67.6	1979	70.8
Spain	1970	69.7	1975	70.4
Switzerland	1968-73	70.3	1968-73	70.3
England and Wales	1970-72	68.9	1977-79	70.2
Canada	1970-72	69.3	1975-77	70.2
Greece	1960-62	67.5	1970	70.1
France	1972	68.6	1978-80	70.1
United States	1975	68.8	1979	70.0
Italy	1970-72	69.0	1974-77	69.7
Federal Republic of Germany	1973-75	68.0	1978-80	69.6
Finland	1974	66.9	1980	69.2
New Zealand	1970-72	68.6	1975-77	69.0
Austria	1975	67.7	1980	69.0
Singapore	1970	65.1	1980	68.9
German Democratic Republic	1969-70	68.9	1978	68.8
Ireland	1965-67	68.6	1970-72	68.8
Bulgaria	1969-71	68.6	1974-76	68.7
Belgium	1968-72	67.8	1972-76	68.6
Cuba	1970	68.5	1970	68.5

Female

Country	Period	Life expectancy in years	Period	Life expectancy in years
Norway	1973-74	77.8	1979-80	79.0
Netherlands	1971-75	77.2	1979	78.9
Japan	1974	76.3	1980	78.8
Sweden	1971-75	77.7	1980	78.8
France	1972	76.4	1978-80	78.2
United States	1975	76.6	1979	77.8
Australia	1965-67	74.2	1979	77.8
Finland	1974	75.4	1980	77.6
Canada	1970-72	76.4	1975-77	77.5
Denmark	1972-73	76.3	1979-80	77.3
England and Wales	1970-72	75.1	1977-79	76.4
Federal Republic of Germany	1973-75	74.5	1978-80	76.4
Switzerland	1968-73	76.2	1968-73	76.2
Spain	1970	75.0	1975	76.2
Austria	1975	74.9	1980	76.2
Italy	1970-72	74.9	1974-77	75.9
Israel	1975	73.9	1980	75.7
New Zealand	1970-72	74.6	1975-77	75.5
Belgium	1968-72	74.2	1972-76	75.1
German Democratic Republic	1969-70	74.2	1978	74.7
Poland	1975	74.3	1980	74.4
Scotland	1971-73	73.6	1976-78	74.4
Singapore	1970	70.0	1980	74.2
Northern Ireland	1973-75	73.6	1976-78	74.1
U.S.S.R.	1971-72	74.0	1971-72	74.0

NOTE: Rankings are from highest to lowest life expectancy based on the latest available data for countries or geographic areas with at least 1 million population and most recent data for 1970 or later. This table is based only on data from the official life tables of the country concerned, consistent with the data presented in the United Nations Demographic Yearbook, 1981. In Health, United States, 1983 more recent estimates prepared in the Population Division of the United Nations were shown for certain countries.

SOURCES: United Nations: Demographic Yearbook, 1976 and 1981. Pub. Nos. ST/ESA/STAT/SER.R/5 and ST/ESA/STAT/SER.R/11. New York. United Nations, 1977 and 1983; Unpublished data from the Division of Vital Statistics.

A3. RACE AND ETHNICITY

A3–1. Percent Distribution of the White and Black Populations, by Age and Sex: July 1, 1984

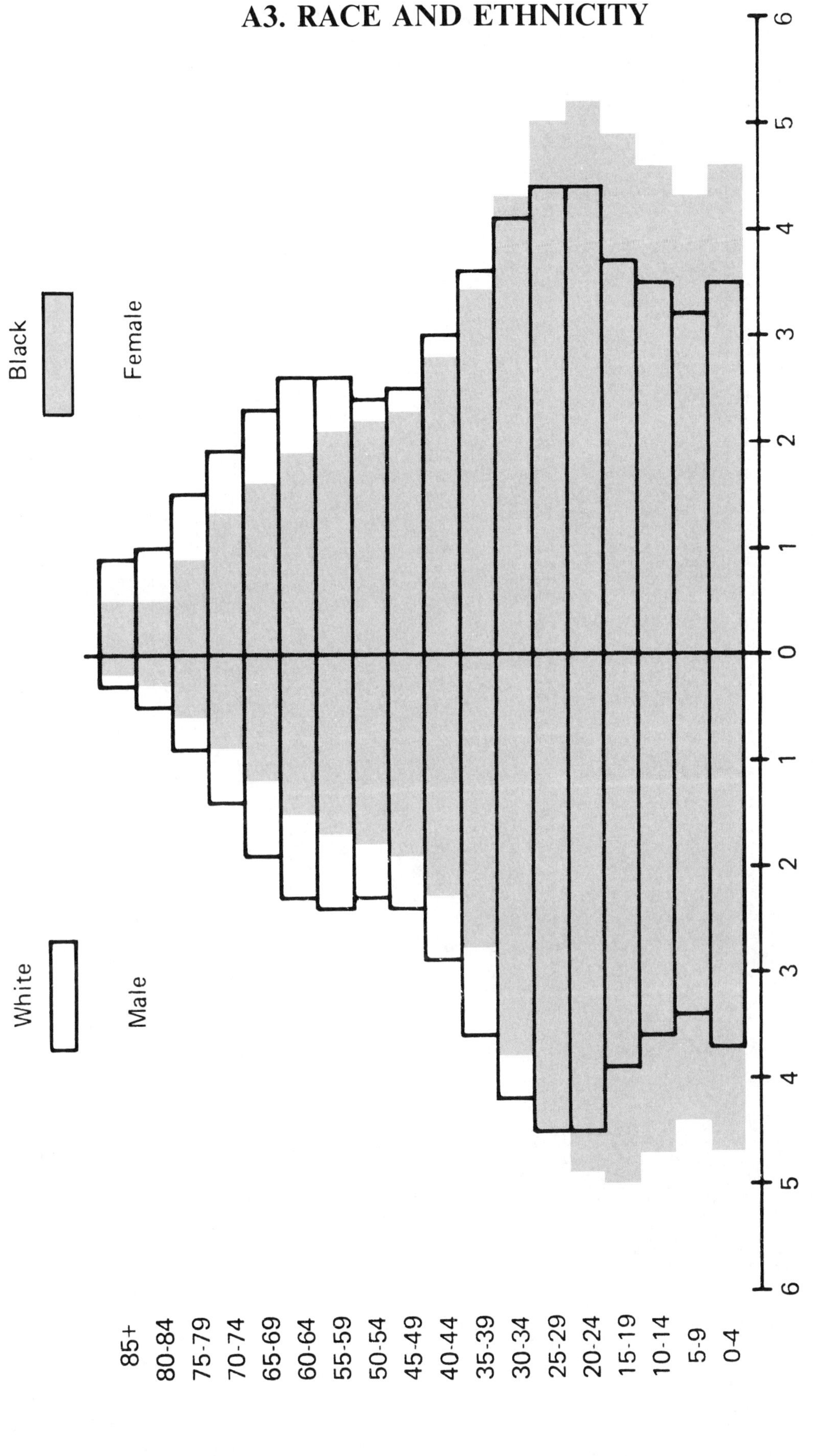

White

Male

Black

Female

85+
80-84
75-79
70-74
65-69
60-64
55-59
50-54
45-49
40-44
35-39
30-34
25-29
20-24
15-19
10-14
5-9
0-4

6 5 4 3 2 1 0 1 2 3 4 5 6

Percent

A3–2. Distribution of the White, Black, and Hispanic Populations 65 Years and Over by Metropolitan Residence and Size of Metropolitan Area, and Percent 65 Years and Over of Total Population: 1980, 1975, and 1970

(Numbers in thousands. Data exclude inmates of institutions. Data pertain to the 1970 definition of metropolitan areas)

Race and Spanish origin	Total	All metropolitan areas			Metropolitan areas of 1 million or more		Metropolitan areas of less than 1 million		Nonmetropolitan areas[1]			
		Total	Central cities	Outside central cities	In central cities	Outside central cities	In central cities	Outside central cities	Total	In counties with a place of 25,000 or more	In counties with a place of 2,500 to 24,999	In counties with a place of less than 2,500
1980												
Number												
Total.....................	23,743	15,085	7,162	7,922	3,760	4,680	3,402	3,242	8,658	1,956	5,553	1,150
White.....................	21,446	13,495	5,970	7,525	3,027	4,479	2,943	3,046	7,951	1,801	5,124	1,026
Black.....................	2,019	1,377	1,055	321	643	170	413	151	643	133	394	115
Hispanic[2]...............	563	460	291	170	168	115	123	55	102	20	71	11
Percent of All Ages												
Total.....................	10.9	10.2	11.8	9.1	12.0	8.9	11.6	9.3	12.3	11.3	12.5	13.5
White.....................	11.4	10.8	13.4	9.4	14.2	9.4	12.6	9.5	12.5	11.5	12.8	13.4
Black.....................	7.9	7.0	7.4	5.9	7.1	4.9	7.8	7.9	11.1	9.4	10.8	15.7
Hispanic[2]...............	4.2	4.2	4.6	3.7	4.3	3.6	4.9	3.8	4.6	3.1	4.9	8.3
Percent of All Areas												
Total.....................	100.0	63.5	30.2	33.4	15.8	19.7	14.3	13.7	36.5	8.2	23.4	4.8
White.....................	100.0	62.9	27.8	35.1	14.1	20.9	13.7	14.2	37.1	8.4	23.9	4.8
Black.....................	100.0	68.2	52.3	15.9	31.8	8.4	20.5	7.5	31.8	6.6	19.5	5.7
Hispanic[2]...............	100.0	81.7	51.7	30.2	29.8	20.4	21.8	9.8	18.1	3.6	12.6	2.0
1975												
Number												
Total.....................	21,127	13,445	6,737	6,707	3,782	4,053	2,955	2,654	7,682	1,926	4,730	1,026
White.....................	19,206	12,091	5,701	6,390	3,117	3,877	2,585	2,513	7,115	1,770	4,387	958
Black.....................	1,721	1,176	919	257	601	145	318	112	544	152	324	68
Hispanic[2]...............	405	323	198	125	125	84	73	41	83	23	45	15
Percent of All Ages												
Total.....................	10.1	9.4	11.0	8.2	11.6	8.4	10.3	8.1	11.4	10.3	11.7	13.1
White.....................	10.5	9.9	12.4	8.4	13.7	8.6	11.2	8.2	11.7	10.3	12.0	13.8
Black.....................	7.2	6.6	6.7	6.3	6.7	5.8	6.6	7.0	9.2	9.8	9.4	7.5
Hispanic[2]...............	3.6	3.5	3.7	3.3	3.5	3.2	4.0	3.5	4.0	3.3	3.6	12.8
Percent of All Areas												
Total.....................	100.0	63.6	31.9	31.7	17.9	19.2	14.0	12.6	36.4	9.1	22.4	4.9
White.....................	100.0	63.0	29.7	33.3	16.2	20.2	13.5	13.1	37.0	9.2	22.8	5.0
Black.....................	100.0	68.3	53.4	14.9	34.9	8.4	18.5	6.5	31.6	8.8	18.8	4.0
Hispanic[2]...............	100.0	79.8	48.9	30.9	30.9	20.7	18.0	10.1	20.5	5.7	11.1	3.7
1970												
Number												
Total.....................	19,235	12,344	6,640	5,704	3,816	3,484	2,825	2,220	6,891	1,511	4,479	902
White.....................	17,532	11,207	5,751	5,457	3,251	3,348	2,500	2,108	6,324	1,411	4,095	818
Black.....................	1,549	1,027	815	212	519	117	296	95	522	90	357	75
Hispanic[2]...............	405	317	216	101	134	64	82	37	89	16	63	11
Percent of All Ages												
Total.....................	9.6	9.0	10.6	7.7	11.1	7.7	9.9	7.7	11.0	9.5	11.3	12.5
White.....................	10.0	9.4	11.8	7.8	13.0	7.8	10.5	7.7	11.2	9.7	11.5	13.1
Black.....................	7.0	6.3	6.3	6.2	6.0	5.7	7.0	6.9	9.1	8.1	9.4	9.6
Hispanic[2]...............	4.5	4.3	4.6	3.7	4.5	3.6	4.8	3.8	5.6	4.0	6.0	8.5
Percent of All Areas												
Total.....................	100.0	64.2	34.5	29.7	19.8	18.1	14.7	11.5	35.8	7.9	23.3	4.7
White.....................	100.0	63.9	32.8	31.1	18.5	19.1	14.3	12.0	36.1	8.0	23.4	4.7
Black.....................	100.0	66.3	52.6	13.7	33.5	7.6	19.1	6.1	33.7	5.8	23.0	4.8
Hispanic[2]...............	100.0	78.3	53.3	24.9	33.1	15.8	20.2	9.1	22.0	4.0	15.6	2.7

[1]Includes areas which gained metropolitan status between 1970 and 1977.
[2]Hispanics may be of any race.

Source: U.S. Bureau of the Census, Current Population Reports, Special Studies P-23, No. 75, for 1970 data; data for 1970 are based on 1-in-100 sample of the 1970 Census of Population. Data for 1980 and 1975 are unpublished data based on the Current Population Survey; they have been adjusted to current independent estimates for age, sex, and race based on the 1970 census.

A3-3. Age Structure of the Population, by Race: July 1, 1984, and April 1, 1980

(Numbers in thousands. Total population including Armed Forces overseas)

Age	Population		Percent distribution		Population change: 1980-84	
	July 1, 1984	April 1, 1980	July 1, 1984	April 1, 1980	Number	Percent
ALL RACES						
All ages..............	236,681	227,061	100.0	100.0	9,620	4.2
Under 5 years...............	17,816	16,348	7.5	7.2	1,468	9.0
5 to 13 years...............	30,165	31,159	12.7	13.7	-994	-3.2
14 to 17 years..............	14,707	16,249	6.2	7.2	-1,541	-9.5
18 to 24 years..............	29,375	30,289	12.4	13.3	-915	-3.0
25 to 34 years..............	41,107	37,259	17.4	16.4	3,849	10.3
35 to 44 years..............	30,718	25,698	13.0	11.3	5,020	19.5
45 to 54 years..............	22,437	22,806	9.5	10.0	-370	-1.6
55 to 64 years..............	22,316	21,703	9.4	9.6	613	2.8
65 to 74 years..............	16,746	15,581	7.1	6.9	1,165	7.5
75 to 84 years..............	8,620	7,729	3.6	3.4	891	11.5
85 years and over...........	2,674	2,240	1.1	1.0	434	19.4
WHITE						
All ages..............	201,358	195,086	100.0	100.0	6,272	3.2
Under 5 years...............	14,485	13,414	7.2	6.9	1,071	8.0
5 to 13 years...............	24,470	25,691	12.2	13.2	-1,221	-4.8
14 to 17 years..............	12,061	13,493	6.0	6.9	-1,432	-10.6
18 to 24 years..............	24,412	25,567	12.1	13.1	-1,155	-4.5
25 to 34 years..............	34,750	31,945	17.3	16.4	2,805	8.8
35 to 44 years..............	26,543	22,282	13.2	11.4	4,261	19.1
45 to 54 years..............	19,492	20,059	9.7	10.3	-567	-2.8
55 to 64 years..............	19,824	19,473	9.8	10.0	351	1.8
65 to 74 years..............	15,046	14,045	7.5	7.2	1,000	7.1
75 to 84 years..............	7,837	7,057	3.9	3.6	780	11.1
85 years and over...........	2,439	2,060	1.2	1.1	379	18.4
BLACK						
All ages..............	28,609	26,803	100.0	100.0	1,806	6.7
Under 5 years...............	2,682	2,459	9.4	9.2	222	9.0
5 to 13 years...............	4,656	4,629	16.3	17.3	27	0.6
14 to 17 years..............	2,194	2,380	7.7	8.9	-186	-7.8
18 to 24 years..............	4,070	4,019	14.2	15.0	51	1.3
25 to 34 years..............	5,043	4,284	17.6	16.0	760	17.7
35 to 44 years..............	3,235	2,739	11.3	10.2	497	18.1
45 to 54 years..............	2,365	2,286	8.3	8.5	79	3.4
55 to 64 years..............	2,060	1,916	7.2	7 1	145	7.6
65 to 74 years..............	1,439	1,344	5.0	5.0	95	7.0
75 to 84 years..............	663	589	2.3	2.2	74	12.6
85 years and over...........	202	159	0.7	0.6	43	26.9

Note: This table should not be compared with the comparable table in Current Population Reports, Series P-25, No. 949 (last year's report). See text for details.

A3–4. Civilian Noninstitutional Population by Race and Age, [1954]

(In thousands)

Year, sex, and race	16 years and over	16 to 19 years			20 years and over						
		Total	16 to 17 years	18 to 19 years	Total	20 to 24 years	25 to 34 years	35 to 44 years	45 to 54 years	55 to 64 years	65 years and over
WHITE											
1954	97,705	7,180	3,786	3,394	90,524	7,794	20,818	19,915	16,569	12,993	12,438
1955	98,880	7,292	3,874	3,419	91,586	7,912	20,742	20,110	16,869	13,169	12,785
1956	99,976	7,346	3,908	3,438	92,629	8,106	20,564	20,314	17,198	13,341	13,105
1957	101,119	7,505	4,007	3,498	93,612	8,293	20,342	20,514	17,562	13,518	13,383
1958	102,392	7,843	4,271	3,573	94,547	8,498	20,063	20,734	17,924	13,681	13,645
1959	103,803	8,430	4,707	3,725	95,370	8,697	19,715	20,893	18,257	13,858	13,951
1960	105,282	8,924	4,909	4,016	96,355	8,927	19,470	21,049	18,578	14,070	14,260
1961	106,604	9,211	4,785	4,427	97,390	9,203	19,289	21,169	18,845	14,304	14,581
1962	107,715	9,343	4,818	4,526	98,371	9,484	18,974	21,293	18,872	14,450	15,297
1963	109,705	9,978	5,549	4,430	99,725	10,069	18,867	21,398	19,082	14,681	15,629
1964	111,534	10,616	6,137	4,481	100,916	10,568	18,838	21,375	19,360	14,957	15,816
1965	113,284	11,319	6,049	5,271	101,963	10,935	18,882	21,258	19,604	15,215	16,070
1966	114,566	11,862	5,993	5,870	102,702	11,094	18,989	21,005	19,822	15,469	16,322
1967	116,100	11,682	6,051	5,632	104,396	11,797	19,464	20,745	20,067	15,745	16,602
1968	117,948	11,840	6,225	5,616	106,107	12,184	20,245	20,474	20,310	16,018	16,875
1969	119,913	12,179	6,418	5,761	107,733	12,677	20,892	20,156	20,546	16,305	17,156
1970	122,174	12,521	6,591	5,931	109,652	13,359	21,546	19,929	20,760	16,591	17,469
1971	124,758	12,937	6,750	6,189	111,821	14,208	22,295	19,694	20,907	16,884	17,833
1972	127,906	13,301	6,910	6,392	114,603	14,897	23,555	19,673	20,950	17,250	18,278
1973	130,097	13,533	7,021	6,512	116,563	15,264	24,685	19,532	20,991	17,484	18,607
1974	132,417	13,784	7,114	6,671	118,632	15,502	25,711	19,628	21,061	17,645	19,085
1975	134,790	13,941	7,132	6,808	120,849	15,980	26,746	19,641	20,981	17,918	19,587
1976	137,106	14,055	7,125	6,930	123,050	16,368	27,757	19,827	20,816	18,220	20,064
1977	139,380	14,095	7,150	6,944	125,285	16,728	28,703	20,231	20,575	18,540	20,508
1978	141,612	14,060	7,132	6,928	127,552	17,038	29,453	20,932	20,322	18,799	21,007
1979	143,894	13,994	7,029	6,964	129,900	17,284	30,371	21,579	20,058	19,071	21,538
1980	146,122	13,854	6,912	6,943	132,268	17,484	31,407	22,174	19,837	19,316	22,050
1981	147,908	13,516	6,704	6,813	134,392	17,609	32,367	22,778	19,666	19,485	22,487
1982	149,441	13,076	6,383	6,693	136,366	17,579	32,863	23,910	19,478	19,591	22,945
1983	150,805	12,623	6,089	6,534	138,183	17,492	33,286	25,027	19,349	19,625	23,403
BLACK											
1972	14,526	2,018	1,061	956	12,508	2,027	2,809	2,329	2,139	1,601	1,605
1973	14,917	2,095	1,095	1,000	12,823	2,132	2,957	2,333	2,156	1,616	1,628
1974	15,336	2,137	1,122	1,014	13,199	2,137	3,103	2,382	2,202	1,679	1,689
1975	15,751	2,191	1,146	1,046	13,560	2,228	3,258	2,395	2,211	1,717	1,755
1976	16,196	2,264	1,165	1,098	13,932	2,303	3,412	2,435	2,220	1,736	1,826
1977	16,605	2,273	1,175	1,097	14,332	2,400	3,566	2,493	2,225	1,765	1,883
1978	16,970	2,270	1,169	1,101	14,701	2,483	3,717	2,547	2,226	1,794	1,932
1979	17,397	2,276	1,167	1,109	15,121	2,556	3,899	2,615	2,240	1,831	1,980
1980	17,824	2,289	1,171	1,119	15,535	2,606	4,095	2,687	2,249	1,870	2,030
1981	18,219	2,288	1,161	1,127	15,931	2,642	4,290	2,758	2,260	1,913	2,069
1982	18,584	2,252	1,119	1,134	16,332	2,697	4,438	2,887	2,263	1,935	2,113
1983	18,925	2,225	1,092	1,133	16,700	2,734	4,607	2,999	2,260	1,964	2,135

A3-5. Resident Population Aged 65 Years and Over in the United States, by Race and Spanish Origin: April 1, 1980

RACE

Age	Total	White	Black	American Indian, Eskimo, and Aleut	Asian and Pacific Islander[a]	Other	Persons of Spanish Origin
65 years and over	25,544,133	22,944,033	2,085,826	74,788	211,834	227,652	708,785
65 to 74 years	15,577,586	13,905,249	1,339,974	48,142	137,765	146,456	457,114
75 to 84 years	7,726,826	6,994,079	586,991	20,794	60,215	64,747	202,841
85 years and over	2,239,721	2,044,705	158,861	5,852	13,854	16,449	48,830
Percent Distribution of the total 65+	89.8	8.1	.3	.8	1.0	2.77	

a. Asian and Pacific Islander groups such as Cambodian, Laotian, and Thai are included in the "other" race category. In sample tabulations, these Asian and Pacific Islander groups will be included in the Asian and Pacific Islander category.

Source: Adapted from Population Profile of the United States: 1980, Bureau of the Census, Series P-20, No. 363, Table 5, p. 10.

A3–6. Percent of Population Aged 65 and Over in Each Color and Race Group, 1980

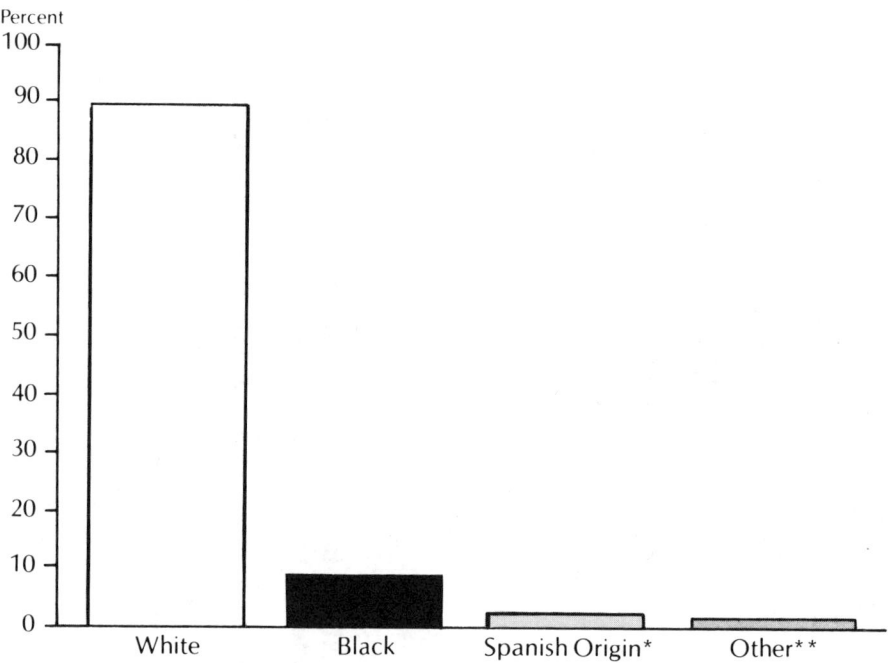

A3–7. Percent of Population of All Ages in Each Race/Color Group Aged 65 and Older, 1980

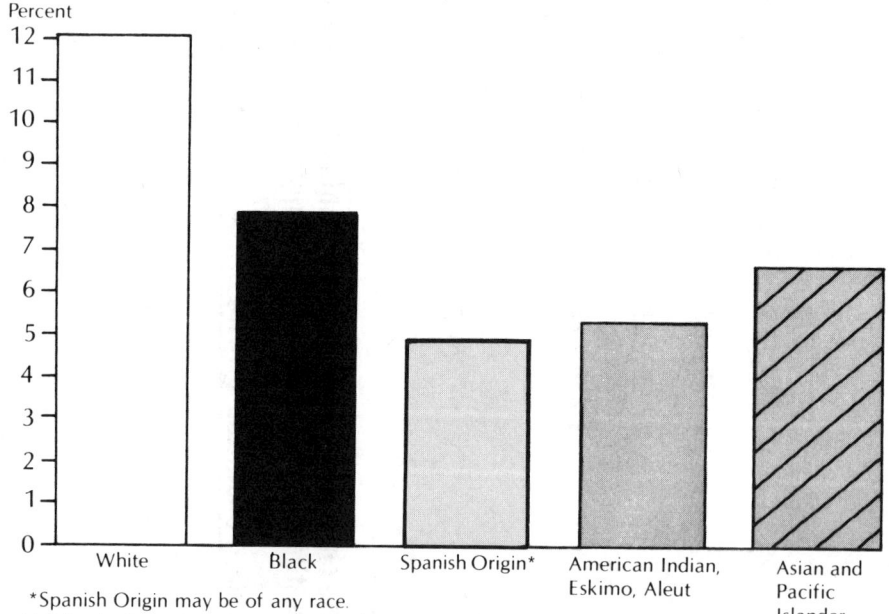

*Spanish Origin may be of any race.

**Other includes American Indians, Eskimos, Aleuts, Asians and Pacific Islanders.

Source: Bureau of the Census

A3-8. Population of Blacks 65 or Older (in Thousands) in the Top 20 States in 1980

New York	164	Mississippi	94
Texas	143	Virginia	87
Georgia	119	Ohio	84
California	115	Michigan	83
North Carolina	114	South Carolina	77
Illinois	109	Tennessee	71
Louisiana	108	New Jersey	58
Alabama	106	Maryland	58
Florida	101	Missouri	46
Pennsylvania	96	Arkansas	46

Source: Bureau of the Census, Department of Commerce

A3-9. Population of Blacks 65 or Older (in Thousands) by States in 1980

Alabama	106	Nevada	2
Alaska	0.2	New Hampshire	0.1
Arizona	5	New Jersey	58
Arkansas	46	New Mexico	1
California	115	New York	164
Colorado	5	North Carolina	114
Connecticut	11	North Dakota	*
Delaware	7	Ohio	84
		Oklahoma	220
District of Columbia	43	Oregon	2
Florida	101	Pennsylvania	96
Georgia	119	Rhode Island	2

A3-9. Population of Blacks 65 or Older (in Thousands) by States in 1980 (Continued)

State		State	
Hawaii	.0.2	South Carolina	77
Idaho	.0.1	South Dakota	0.1
Illinois	109	Tennessee	71
Indiana	30	Texas	143
Iowa	3	Utah	0.4
Kansas	10	Vermont	0.1
Kentucky	26	Virginia	87
Louisiana	108	Washington	5
Maine	0.1	West Virginia	10
Maryland	58	Wisconsin	7
Massachusetts	13	Wyoming	0.2
Michigan	83		
Minnesota	3		
Mississippi	94		
Missouri	46		
Montana	0.1		
Nebraska	3		

* Less than 50 Blacks 65 or older.

Source: Bureau of the Census, Department of Commerce

A3–10. Largest Single-Ancestry, by State

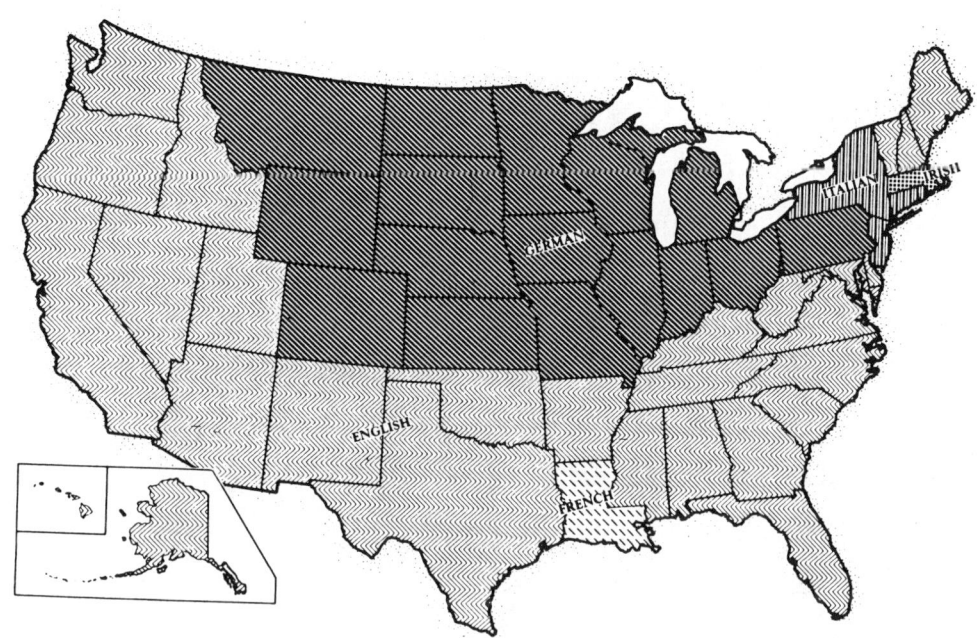

A3–11. Second-Largest Single-Ancestry, by State

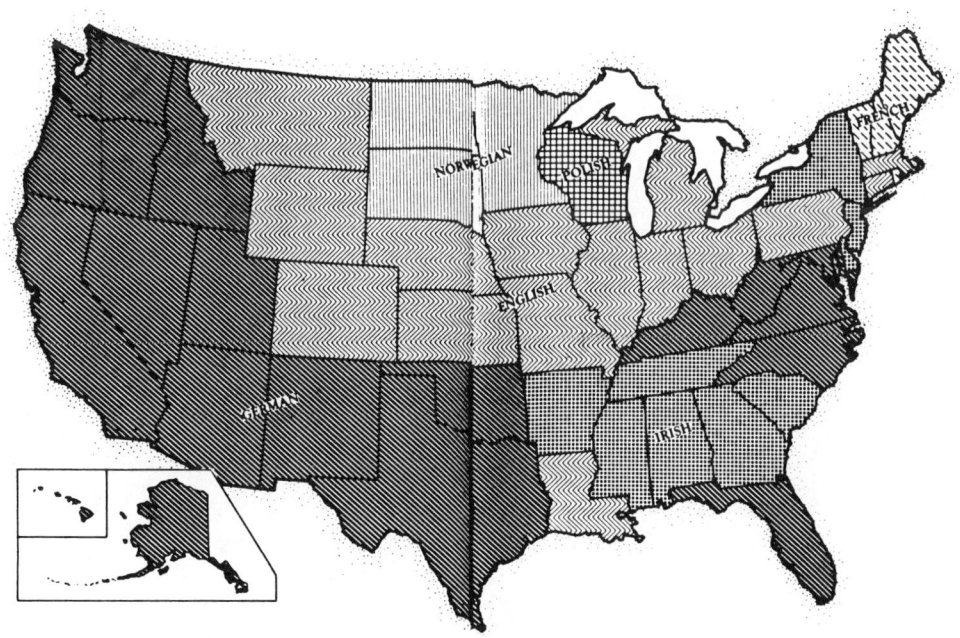

A3–12. Third-Largest Single-Ancestry, by State

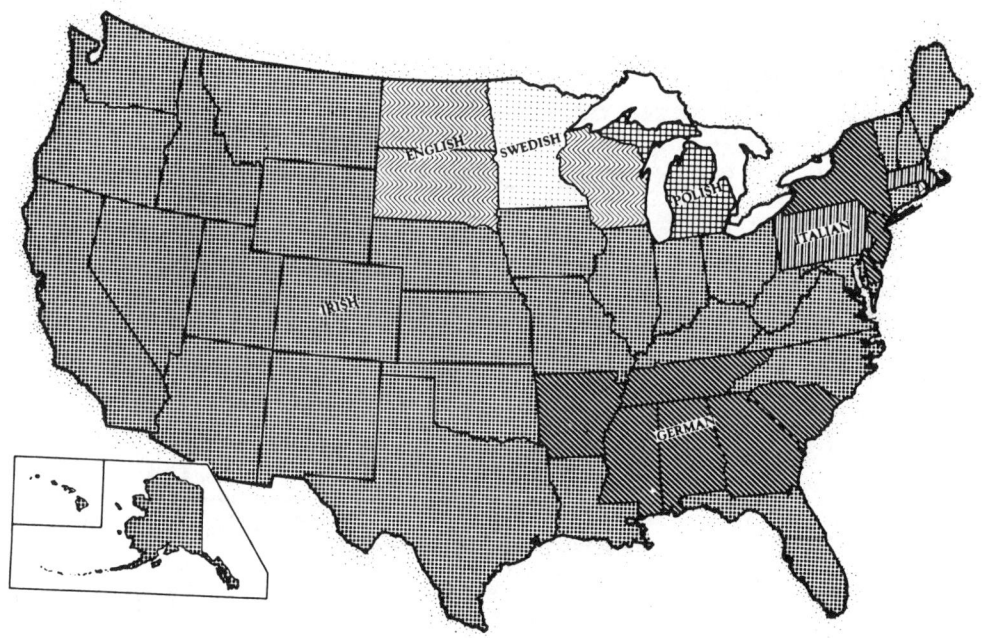

A4. GEOGRAPHIC DISTRIBUTION, PLACE OF RESIDENCE

A4–1. Growth of Each State's Elderly Population 1970–80 and 1980–84

(Numbers in thousands)

State	1980 all ages		1980 65 plus					1984 65 plus		
	Number	Rank	Number	Rank	Percent	Rank	Percent increase, 1970–80	Number	Percent	Percent increase, 1980–84
Alabama	3,894	22	440	19	11.3	24	35.0	476	11.9	8.3
Alaska	402	51	12	51	2.9	51	67.7	15	3.1	32.6
Arizona	2,718	29	307	28	11.3	25	90.4	375	12.3	21.9
Arkansas	2,286	33	312	27	13.7	2	31.4	336	14.3	7.4
California	23,668	1	2,414	1	10.2	34	34.1	2,693	10.5	11.5
Colorado	2,890	28	247	33	8.6	46	31.6	280	8.8	13.4
Connecticut	3,108	25	365	26	11.7	18	26.3	407	12.9	11.6
Delaware	594	48	59	48	10.0	36	35.0	67	11.0	13.8
D.C.	638	47	74	46	11.6	20	4.9	75	12.1	1.5
Florida	9,746	7	1,688	3	17.3	1	70.6	1,931	17.6	14.4
Georgia	5,463	13	517	16	9.5	41	40.6	577	9.9	11.7
Hawaii	965	39	76	45	7.9	49	72.4	94	9.0	22.9
Idaho	944	41	94	41	9.9	37	38.2	108	10.8	14.9
Illinois	11,427	5	1,262	6	11.0	29	15.4	1,356	11.8	7.5
Indiana	5,490	12	585	13	10.7	31	18.5	638	11.6	8.9
Iowa	2,913	27	388	24	13.3	4	10.7	410	14.1	5.9
Kansas	2,364	32	306	29	13.0	8	15.1	323	13.3	5.6
Kentucky	3,661	23	410	21	11.2	27	21.5	438	11.8	6.8
Louisiana	4,206	19	404	22	9.6	39	31.8	435	9.7	7.5
Maine	1,125	38	141	36	12.5	11	23.0	152	13.1	7.6
Maryland	4,217	18	396	23	9.4	42	32.0	447	10.3	13.0
Massachusetts	5,737	11	727	10	12.7	10	14.2	777	13.4	6.9
Michigan	9,262	8	912	8	9.9	38	21.2	1,007	11.1	10.3
Minnesota	4,076	21	480	18	11.8	17	17.3	517	12.4	7.7
Mississippi	2,521	31	289	31	11.5	21	30.1	306	11.8	5.9
Missouri	4,917	15	648	11	13.2	5	15.6	682	13.6	5.3
Montana	787	44	85	43	10.8	32	23.0	96	11.6	13.2
Nebraska	1,570	35	206	35	13.1	7	12.1	216	13.4	4.8
Nevada	800	43	66	47	8.2	47	112.3	87	9.5	32.2
New Hampshire	921	42	103	40	11.2	28	31.3	114	11.7	10.6
New Jersey	7,365	9	860	9	11.7	19	23.4	942	12.5	9.6
New Mexico	1,303	37	116	38	8.9	45	64.2	135	9.5	16.6
New York	17,558	2	2,161	2	12.3	13	10.2	2,247	12.7	4.0
North Carolina	5,882	10	603	12	10.2	35	45.7	688	11.2	14.1
North Dakota	653	46	80	44	12.3	14	21.2	87	12.6	7.6
Ohio	10,798	6	1,169	7	10.8	30	17.2	1,280	11.9	9.5
Oklahoma	3,025	26	376	25	12.4	12	25.5	401	12.1	6.5
Oregon	2,633	30	303	30	11.5	22	33.8	344	12.9	13.4
Pennsylvania	11,864	4	1,531	4	12.9	9	20.3	1,676	14.1	9.5
Rhode Island	947	40	127	37	13.4	3	22.1	138	14.3	8.7
South Carolina	3,122	24	287	32	9.2	44	50.5	331	10.0	15.1
South Dakota	691	45	91	42	13.2	6	13.1	96	13.6	5.8
Tennessee	4,591	17	518	15	11.3	26	34.8	566	12.0	9.4
Texas	14,229	3	1,371	5	9.6	40	38.2	1,514	9.5	10.4
Utah	1,461	36	109	39	7.5	50	40.8	128	7.7	16.9
Vermont	511	49	58	49	11.4	23	22.5	63	11.8	7.8
Virginia	5,346	14	505	17	9.5	43	38.1	572	10.2	13.2
Washington	4,132	20	432	20	10.4	33	34.0	492	11.3	14.0
West Virginia	1,950	34	238	34	12.2	15	22.3	255	13.0	7.1
Wisconsin	4,705	16	564	14	12.0	16	19.3	611	12.8	8.4
Wyoming	470	50	37	50	7.9	48	23.1	42	8.2	12.3

SOURCE: U.S. Bureau of the Census, Decennial Census of the Population "Estimates of Population of States, by Age: July 1, 1981-83," Current Population Reports, Series P-25, No. 95, and "State Population Estimates, by Age and Components of Change: 1980-1984," Current Population Reports, Series P-25, No. 970.

A4-2. Provisional Estimates of the Resident Population of States, by Age: July 1, 1984

(In thousands. Includes Armed Forces residing in each State)

Region, division, and State	Resident population	Under 5 years	5 to 14 years	15 to 24 years	25 to 34 years	35 to 44 years	45 to 54 years	55 to 64 years	65 years and over
United States......................	236,158	17,816	33,917	40,078	40,912	30,649	22,430	22,316	28,040
Northeast.........................	49,728	3,253	6,597	8,362	8,267	6,526	4,958	5,249	6,515
New England......................	12,577	806	1,634	2,197	2,160	1,669	1,197	1,263	1,650
Middle Atlantic...................	37,151	2,446	4,963	6,165	6,107	4,856	3,762	3,987	4,865
Midwest[1]........................	59,117	4,483	8,705	10,076	10,189	7,393	5,529	5,518	7,223
East North Central...............	41,601	3,103	6,157	7,147	7,206	5,259	3,924	3,912	4,892
West North Central...............	17,515	1,380	2,548	2,929	2,983	2,134	1,605	1,607	2,331
South............................	80,576	6,169	11,886	13,821	13,806	10,393	7,639	7,448	9,414
South Atlantic...................	39,450	2,744	5,451	6,739	6,706	5,191	3,819	3,857	4,943
East South Central...............	15,028	1,123	2,329	2,581	2,511	1,897	1,434	1,367	1,787
West South Central...............	26,098	2,303	4,107	4,500	4,590	3,304	2,386	2,223	2,684
West.............................	46,738	3,911	6,729	7,819	8,649	6,337	4,304	4,100	4,888
Mountain.........................	12,553	1,153	1,993	2,109	2,281	1,622	1,114	1,030	1,250
Pacific..........................	34,184	2,758	4,736	5,710	6,368	4,715	3,190	3,070	3,638
New England:									
Maine............................	1,156	82	168	195	189	149	111	111	152
New Hampshire....................	977	68	137	169	173	137	91	88	114
Vermont..........................	530	39	75	92	96	72	47	44	63
Massachusetts....................	5,798	362	729	1,032	1,015	759	542	582	777
Rhode Island.....................	962	60	121	169	161	119	89	105	138
Connecticut......................	3,154	195	403	540	526	433	317	333	407
Middle Atlantic:									
New York.........................	17,735	1,183	2,370	2,993	2,916	2,364	1,812	1,851	2,247
New Jersey.......................	7,515	485	1,010	1,238	1,226	1,024	778	811	942
Pennsylvania.....................	11,901	778	1,583	1,935	1,965	1,469	1,171	1,325	1,676
East North Central:									
Ohio.............................	10,752	788	1,583	1,814	1,840	1,354	1,037	1,055	1,280
Indiana..........................	5,498	409	841	947	940	695	519	510	638
Illinois.........................	11,511	885	1,672	1,955	1,989	1,472	1,097	1,085	1,356
Michigan.........................	9,075	664	1,371	1,600	1,612	1,154	836	831	1,007
Wisconsin........................	4,766	358	691	831	825	584	434	431	611
West North Central:									
Minnesota........................	4,162	330	600	718	744	527	371	355	517
Iowa.............................	2,910	220	428	474	491	345	267	274	410
Missouri.........................	5,008	374	714	837	824	621	477	478	682
North Dakota.....................	686	61	106	115	121	78	59	60	87
South Dakota.....................	706	63	110	116	114	78	62	66	96
Nebraska.........................	1,606	131	240	266	272	192	145	144	216
Kansas...........................	2,438	199	350	402	418	293	223	230	323
South Atlantic:									
Delaware.........................	613	43	84	113	108	79	60	60	67
Maryland.........................	4,349	301	576	784	775	620	433	414	447
District of Columbia.............	623	42	68	112	121	87	58	59	75
Virginia.........................	5,636	391	775	1,025	1,006	797	554	516	572
West Virginia....................	1,952	136	302	302	328	244	187	199	255
North Carolina...................	6,165	416	891	1,092	1,072	816	608	581	688
South Carolina...................	3,300	252	512	601	579	429	305	290	331
Georgia..........................	5,837	443	902	1,055	1,022	797	553	488	577
Florida..........................	10,976	720	1,341	1,656	1,695	1,321	1,061	1,251	1,931
East South Central:									
Kentucky.........................	3,723	277	575	642	633	472	349	337	438
Tennessee........................	4,717	329	694	793	800	627	468	440	566
Alabama..........................	3,990	296	619	685	663	496	385	370	476
Mississippi......................	2,598	221	440	461	414	302	232	221	306
West South Central:									
Arkansas.........................	2,349	177	363	379	364	291	218	220	336
Louisiana........................	4,462	405	725	805	782	543	395	373	435
Oklahoma.........................	3,298	281	495	541	555	412	312	301	401
Texas............................	15,989	1,440	2,524	2,776	2,888	2,057	1,460	1,328	1,514
Mountain:									
Montana..........................	824	70	128	131	146	106	76	72	96
Idaho............................	1,001	96	177	157	171	127	86	79	108
Wyoming..........................	511	52	85	80	103	66	45	38	42
Colorado.........................	3,178	264	452	553	639	453	287	249	280
New Mexico.......................	1,424	133	232	251	243	179	131	119	135
Arizona..........................	3,053	261	455	503	528	380	272	279	375
Utah.............................	1,652	206	340	283	284	182	122	107	128
Nevada...........................	911	70	123	150	168	129	97	87	87
Pacific:									
Washington.......................	4,349	345	620	708	813	607	391	372	492
Oregon...........................	2,674	205	387	404	490	374	237	234	344
California.......................	25,622	2,063	3,494	4,316	4,767	3,518	2,429	2,343	2,693
Alaska...........................	500	56	83	95	106	76	42	27	15
Hawaii...........................	1,039	90	152	186	192	140	91	95	94

[1]Formerly the North Central Region.

A4-3. States Ranked by Largest Numerical Increase in Population: 1980-84 and 1970-80

(Numbers in thousands)

State	Increase	Net migration	Rank	State	Increase	Net migration
1980-84				1970-80		
California........	1,955	+950	1	California........	3,697	+1,573
Texas.............	1,759	+1,009	2	Texas.............	3,031	+1,481
Florida...........	1,229	+1,092	3	Florida...........	2,955	+2,519
Georgia...........	373	+182	4	Arizona...........	943	+656
Arizona...........	335	+207	5	Georgia...........	875	+329
Virginia..........	289	+131	6	North Carolina....	797	+278
Colorado..........	288	+145	7	Washington........	719	+388
North Carolina....	283	+135	8	Virginia..........	695	+239
Oklahoma..........	273	+160	9	Colorado..........	680	+385
Louisiana.........	257	+58	10	Tennessee.........	665	+297

A4-4. Ten States with Highest Proportion 65 Years and Over: July 1, 1984

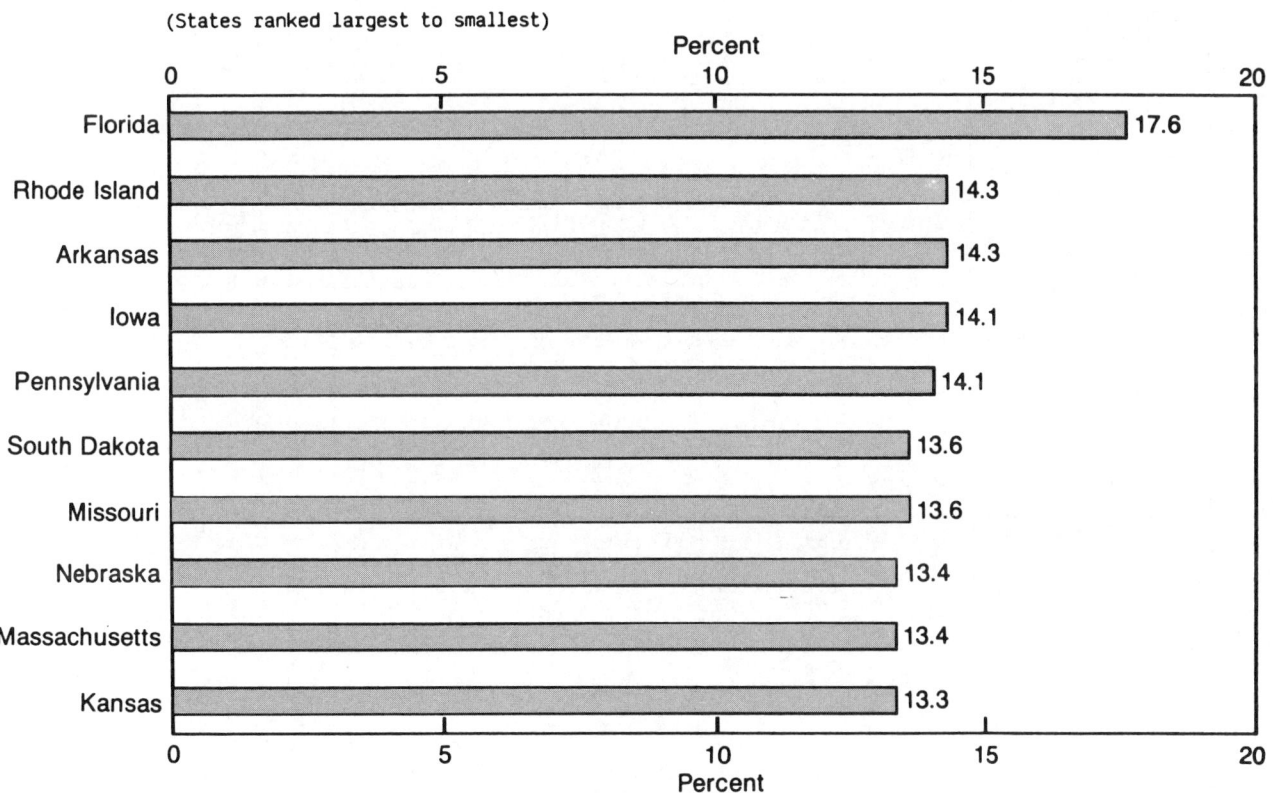

(States ranked largest to smallest)

A4–5. Distribution of Under-65 and 65+ Population by Metropolitan/Nonmetropolitan Residence, 1970 and 1980

Residential category	1970 Number (thousands)		1970 Percent distribution		1980 Number (thousands)		1980 Percent distribution		Index* 1970	Index* 1980	Ratio**
	Under 65	65+	Under 65	65+	Under 65	65+	Under 65	65+			
Total........................	180,584	19,235	100.0	100.0	194,357	23,743	100.0	100.0	100	100	100
Metropolitan areas...........	124,714	12,344	69.1	64.2	132,776	15,085	68.3	63.5	93	93	100
In central cities..........	56,236	6,640	31.1	34.5	53,496	7,162	27.5	30.2	111	110	99
Outside central cities.....	60,478	5,704	37.9	29.7	79,281	7,922	40.8	33.3	78	82	105
Metropolitan areas of: 1,000,000+											
In central cities........	30,506	3,816	16.9	19.8	27,610	3,760	14.2	15.8	117	111	95
Outside central cities...	41,682	3,484	23.1	18.1	47,792	4,680	24.6	19.7	78	80	103
Less than 1,000,000											
In central cities........	25,729	2,825	14.2	14.7	25,886	3,402	13.3	14.3	112	108	96
Outside central cities...	26,796	2,220	14.8	11.5	31,489	3,242	16.2	13.7	78	85	109
Nonmetropolitan areas.........	55,870	6,891	30.9	35.8	61,581	8,658	31.7	36.5	116	115	99
In counties:											
With no place of 2,500+....	6,289	902	3.5	4.7	7,343	1,150	3.8	4.8	134	126	94
With place of 2,500-24,999.	35,246	4,479	19.5	23.3	38,865	5,553	20.0	23.5	119	117	98
With place of 25,000+......	14,334	1,511	7.9	7.8	15,392	1,956	7.9	8.2	99	104	105
Designated metropolitan since 1970...............	7,520	843	4.2	4.4	9,587	1,181	4.9	5.1	105	102	97

* Index = proportion of 65+ divided by proportion under 65 x 100. Index of over 100 means that relatively more older people than younger people live in this residential category in percentage terms.

++ Ratio = Index for 1980 divided by Index for 1970 x 100. Ratio of over 100 means that proportionately this residential category has more older people in 1980 than in 1970.

A5. MOBILITY AND MIGRATION

A5-1. Percent Change Due to Net Migration, by State: 1980-84

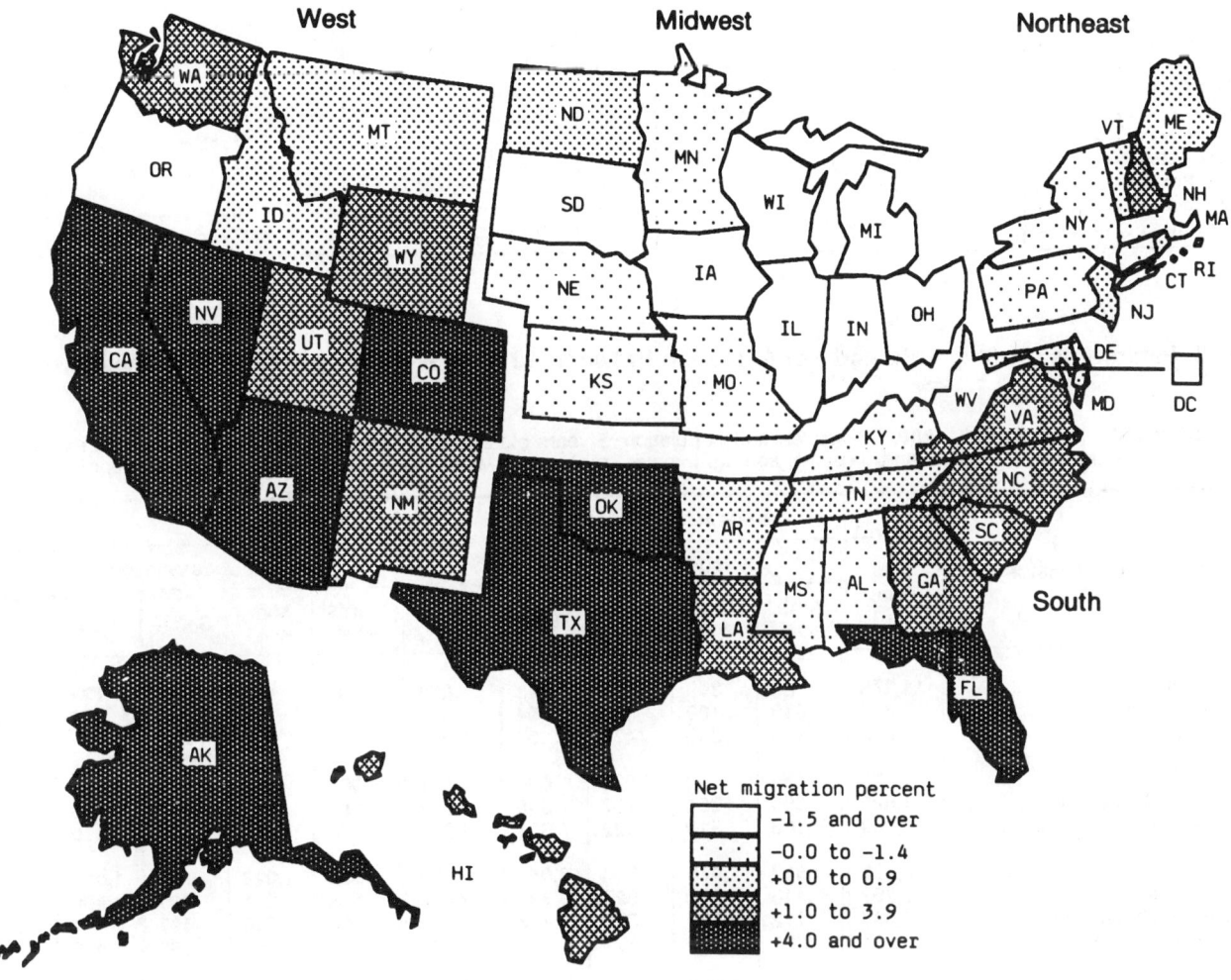

Net migration percent

	-1.5 and over
	-0.0 to -1.4
	+0.0 to 0.9
	+1.0 to 3.9
	+4.0 and over

A5-2. States Ranked by Largest Percent Increase in Population: 1980-84 and 1970-80

(Numbers in thousands)

State	Percent increase	Net migration percent	Rank	State	Percent increase	Net migration percent
1980-84				1970-80		
Alaska............	24.4	+14.8	1	Nevada...........	63.8	+49.7
Nevada............	13.8	+9.6	2	Arizona..........	53.1	+37.0
Utah..............	13.0	+3.6	3	Florida..........	43.5	+37.1
Florida...........	12.6	+11.2	4	Wyoming..........	41.3	+25.5
Texas.............	12.4	+7.1	5	Utah.............	37.9	+11.2
Arizona..........	12.3	+7.6	6	Alaska...........	32.8	+9.3
Colorado..........	10.0	+5.0	7	Idaho............	32.4	+15.4
New Mexico.......	9.3	+3.4	8	Colorado.........	30.8	+17.4
Oklahoma..........	9.0	+5.3	9	New Mexico.......	28.1	+11.4
Wyoming...........	8.9	+2.2	10	Texas............	27.1	+13.2

A5-3. Inmigrants, Outmigrants and Net Migration between 1975 and 1980, by Region and Division

[In thousands. As of April 1, 1980. Covers resident population, 5 years old and over. Based on a sample, see Appendix III. For composition of regions and divisions, see fig. I, inside front cover. Minus sign (−) indicates net outmigration]

REGION AND DIVISION	INMIGRANTS					OUTMIGRANTS					Net migration
	Total	By region of origin				Total	By region of destination				
		North-east	Mid-west	South	West		North-east	Mid-west	South	West	
Northeast [1]	1,275	(x)	360	654	261	3,059	(x)	465	1,817	777	−1,785
New England	699	313	109	183	94	897	193	111	381	212	−198
Middle Atlantic	1,082	193	250	471	167	2,668	313	354	1,436	565	−1,587
Midwest [1]	2,125	465	(x)	1,029	630	3,505	360	(x)	1,878	1,267	−1,380
East North Central	1,629	359	254	707	309	2,812	287	319	1,407	798	−1,182
West North Central	1,069	106	319	322	321	1,267	73	254	470	470	−198
South [1]	4,738	1,817	1,878	(x)	1,044	2,752	654	1,029	(x)	1,069	1,986
South Atlantic	3,262	1,443	902	527	390	2,240	519	501	721	499	1,022
East South Central	1,096	112	361	510	113	925	54	246	497	127	171
West South Central	1,954	261	615	537	541	1,161	81	282	355	443	794
West [1]	3,114	777	1,267	1,069	(x)	1,935	261	630	1,044	(x)	1,179
Mountain	1,814	260	575	390	589	1,137	74	247	349	468	677
Pacific	2,357	518	693	679	468	1,856	188	384	695	589	502

X Not applicable.   [1] Excludes intraregional migrants.

Source: U.S. Bureau of the Census, *1980 Census of Population, Supplementary Report*, PC80-S1-9.

A5-4. Changes in the Numbers of Persons and Interstate Migrants between 1960 and 1980 for the General Population and for the Population Age 60 Years and Over

	1960		1970		1980		% Change in Volume	
	n (000s)	Rate	n (000s)	Rate	n (000s)	Rate	1960-70	1970-80
Total U.S. Population	179,323		203,302		226,546		13.4	11.4
Age 60+ Population	22,820		27,538		35,637		20.7	29.4
Interstate Migrants:								
Age 5+	14,141	9.2	16,081	9.3	20,358	9.9	13.7	26.6
Age 60+	959	4.1	1,105	4.0	1,654	4.6	15.2	50.0

Sources: U.S. Census of Population, 1960, General Population Characteristics, Final Report; U.S. Census of Population, 1970, General Population Characteristics, Final Report; U.S. Bureau of the Census (1983). 1980 Public use microdata sample A [Machine-readable data file]. Washington, D.C.: U.S. Bureau of the Census (Producer and Distributor).

A5–5. Regional Patterns for Interstate Movers Aged 65+, 1975–1980

Residence in 1980	Residence in 1975				
	Total	North-east	North Central	South	West
Total number (000)...	1,000	257	285	269	191
Northeast...........	119	80	2	30	7
North Central......	119	5	50	35	29
South..............	475	113	143	159	60
West...............	287	59	90	43	95
Total percent (1975).	100.0	100.0	100.0	100.0	100.0
Northeast...........	11.9	31.1	0.7	11.2	3.7
North Central......	11.9	1.9	17.5	13.2	15.2
South..............	47.5	44.0	50.2	59.6	31.4
West...............	28.7	23.0	31.6	16.1	49.7
Total percent (1980).	100.0	25.7	28.5	26.7	19.1
Northeast...........	100.0	67.2	1.7	25.2	5.9
North Central......	100.0	4.2	42.0	29.4	24.4
South..............	100.0	25.1	30.1	33.5	12.6
West...............	100.0	20.6	31.4	15.0	33.1

A5-6. Detailed Mobility, Persons Aged 4–64 and 65+, 1975–1980

(Numbers in Thousands)

Residence in 1980 compared to residence in 1975*	4–64			65+		
	Number	Percent	Percent**	Number	Percent	Percent**
Total......................................	178,473	100.0	–	23,743	100.0	–
Same house (nonmovers)................	88,550	49.6	–	18,707	78.8	–
CC of SMSA*..........................	22,823	12.8	–	5,657	23.8	–
Balance of SMSA......................	37,211	20.8	–	6,175	26.0	–
Outside SMSA.........................	28,515	16.0	–	6,876	29.0	–
Different house within U.S. (movers).	86,198	48.3	100.0	4,948	20.8	100.0
Within same SMSA.....................	39,452	22.1	45.8	2,167	9.1	43.8
Within CC...........................	14,775	8.3	17.1	990	4.2	20.0
Within balance of SMSA.............	16,541	9.3	19.2	751	3.2	15.2
CC to balance of SMSA..............	5,749	3.2	6.7	320	1.3	6.5
Balance of SMSA to CC..............	2,385	1.3	2.8	108	0.5	2.2
Between SMSAs........................	13,798	7.7	16.0	753	3.2	15.2
Between CCs.........................	3,239	1.8	3.8	152	0.6	3.1
Between balance of SMSAs...........	4,948	2.8	5.7	247	1.0	5.0
CC to balance of SMSA..............	3,723	2.1	4.3	234	1.0	4.7
Balance of SMSA to CC..............	1,886	1.1	2.2	121	0.5	2.4
From outside SMSA to an SMSA.......	5,736	3.2	6.7	257	1.1	5.2
To CC...............................	2,300	1.3	2.7	91	0.4	1.8
To balance of SMSA.................	3,437	1.9	4.0	165	0.7	3.3
From SMSA to outside SMSA..........	6,856	3.8	8.0	481	2.0	9.7
From CC.............................	3,007	1.7	3.5	204	0.9	4.1
From balance of SMSA...............	3,850	2.2	4.5	277	1.2	5.6
Outside SMSA at both dates.........	20,358	11.4	23.6	1,289	5.4	26.1
Movers from abroad....................	3,725	2.1	–	88	0.4	–
To CC of SMSA......................	1,587	0.9	–	44	0.2	–
To balance of SMSA.................	1,509	0.8	–	32	0.1	–
To outside SMSA....................	629	0.4	–	12	–	–

* CC = Central city
SMSA = Standard Metropolitan Statistical Area
** Number of movers = 100.0%

A5-7. Ten States Receiving the Largest Share of Inmigrants Age 60+ in 1960, 1970, and 1980

Rank	1960			1970			1980[a]		
	State	n	%	State	n	%	State	n	%
1	FL	208,072	22.3	FL	269,141	24.6	FL	437,000	26.3
2	CA	126,883	13.6	CA	109,342	10.0	CA	145,000	8.7
3	NJ	36,019	3.9	AZ	46,451	4.2	AZ	95,000	5.7
4	NY	33,794	3.6	NJ	43,597	4.0	TX	78,000	4.7
5	IL	30,355	3.3	TX	38,682	3.5	NJ	49,000	2.9
6	AZ	29,571	3.2	PA	34,006	3.1	PA	40,000	2.4
7	OH	27,759	3.0	OH	30,492	2.8	NC	39,000	2.3
8	TX	26,770	2.9	NY	30,388	2.8	WA	36,000	2.2
9	PA	25,738	2.8	IL	29,434	2.7	IL	36,000	2.2
10	MI	20,308	2.2	MO	24,395	2.2	NY	35,000	2.1
Total Interstate Migrants	931,012			1,094,014			1,654,000		
% of Total in Top 10 States	60.8			59.9			59.5		

[a] Estimated numbers are rounded to the nearest thousand.
Sources: U.S. Census of Population, 1960, Detailed Population Characteristics, Table 100; U.S. Census of Population, 1970, Detailed Population Characteristics, Table 145; U.S. Bureau of the Census (1983). 1980 Public use microdata sample A [Machine-readable data file]. Washington, D.C.: U.S. Bureau of the Census (Producer and Distributor).

A5-8. Ten States Sending the Largest Share of Outmigrants Age 60+ in 1970 and 1980

	1970			1980a		
Rank	State	n	%	State	n	%
1	NY	154,300	14.3	NY	243,000	14.6
2	IL	86,900	8.1	CA	141,000	8.5
3	CA	74,400	6.9	IL	120,000	7.2
4	PA	53,000	5.0	FL	92,000	5.6
5	OH	53,400	5.0	NJ	87,000	5.2
6	MI	52,600	4.9	OH	86,000	5.2
7	NJ	50,100	4.6	PA	81,000	4.9
8	FL	46,000	4.0	MI	72,000	4.3
9	TX	30,300	2.8	MA	47,000	2.8
10	IN	29,200	2.7	IN	40,000	2.4

aNumbers estimated from the sample are rounded to the nearest thousand.

Sources: U.S. Bureau of the Census (1983). 1% 1970 and 1-in-40 1980 Census public use microdata samples [Machine-readable data file]. Washington, D.C.: U.S. Bureau of the Census (Producer and Distributor).

A5–9. Volume of Older Inmigrants in All States, and Rankings of Attractiveness and Impact, 1975–1980

State	Volume	Attractiveness[a]		Impact[b]	
		%	Rank	%	Rank
Alabama	17,200	1.03	29	2.82	35
Alaska	1,520	.09	49	7.74	9
Arizona	94,600	5.69	3	21.91	1
Arkansas	33,760	2.03	12	7.98	5
California	144,880	8.71	2	4.25	23
Colorado	27,160	1.63	18	7.76	7
Connecticut	18,320	1.10	27	3.43	28
Delaware	6,680	.40	42	7.76	8
District of Columbia	3,560	.21	46	3.43	31
Florida	437,040	26.29	1	19.40	2
Georgia	33,360	2.00	14	4.55	19
Hawaii	5,640	.34	43	4.94	14
Idaho	2,120	.55	37	6.91	10
Illinois	35,720	2.15	9	2.01	45
Indiana	23,120	1.39	23	8.82	34
Iowa	11,320	.68	36	2.17	42
Kansas	14,880	.90	31	3.60	27
Kentucky	17,880	1.07	28	3.17	32
Louisiana	12,120	.73	35	2.14	43
Maine	8,880	.53	38	4.63	17
Maryland	24,600	1.48	20	4.27	22
Massachusetts	21,920	1.32	22	2.18	41
Michigan	24,920	1.50	19	1.91	47
Minnesota	13,800	.83	32	2.12	44
Mississippi	13,800	.83	32	3.51	29
Missouri	30,400	1.83	17	3.48	30
Montana	5,360	.32	44	4.50	20

A5-9. Volume of Older Inmigrants in All States, and Rankings of Attractiveness and Impact, 1975-1980 (Continued)

Nebraska	7,960	.48	41	2.91	33
Nevada	24,160	1.45	21	2.40	39
New Hampshire	12,480	.75	34	8.75	4
New Jersey	49,400	2.97	5	4.02	26
New Mexico	17,160	1.03	30	10.42	3
New York	34,920	2.10	10	1.16	49
North Carolina	39,400	2.37	7	4.59	18
North Dakota	2,560	.15	48	2.36	40
Ohio	32,680	1.97	15	1.97	46
Oklahoma	22,600	1.36	24	4.46	21
Oregon	33,600	2.02	13	7.98	6
Pennsylvania	39,520	2.38	6	1.83	48
Rhode Island	4,360	.26	45	2.47	38
South Carolina	20,560	1.24	25	4.94	15
South Dakota	400	.02	51	.00	51
Tennessee	29,040	1.75	16	4.04	25
Texas	78,480	4.72	4	4.12	24
Utah	8,520	.51	40	5.48	18
Vermont	460	.03	50	.00	51
Virginia	34,280	2.06	11	4.81	16
Washington	35,880	2.34	8	5.88	11
West Virginia	8,600	.52	39	2.60	36
Wisconsin	19,640	1.18	26	2.55	37
Wyoming	2,920	.18	47	5.55	12

[a]Percentage of all U.S. interstate migrants age 60+.

[b]Percentage of the state's age 60+ population who moved there since 1975.

Source: U.S. Bureau of the Census (1983). 1-in-40 1980 Census public use microdata samples [Machine-readable data file]. Washington, D.C.: U.S. Bureau of the Census (Producer and Distributor).

A6. VETERANS

A6-1. The Aging Veteran Population, 1980-2020

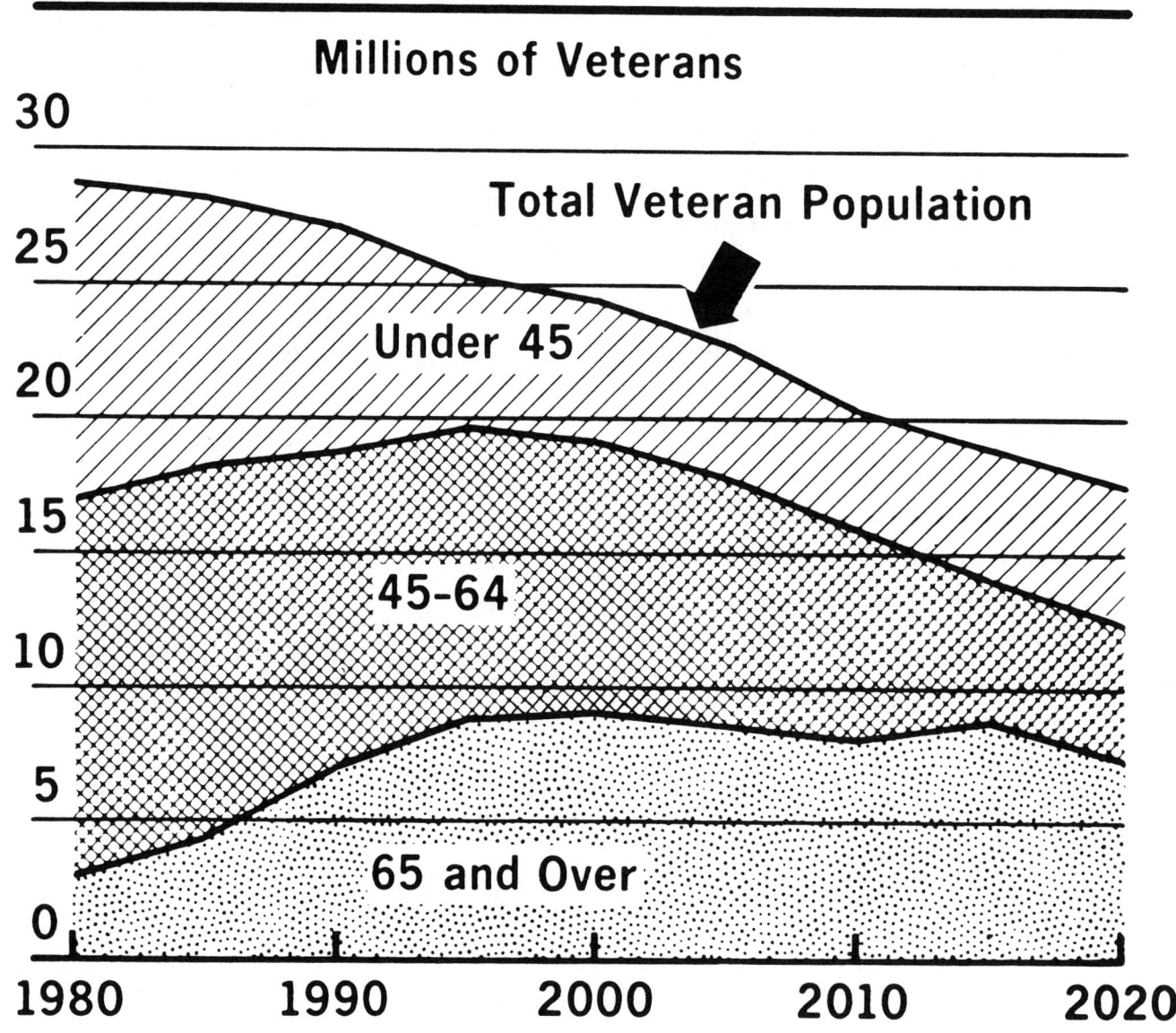

Millions of Veterans

Total Veteran Population

Under 45

45-64

65 and Over

A6–2. Actual and Projected Number of Veterans 65 Years and Older, 1971–2000

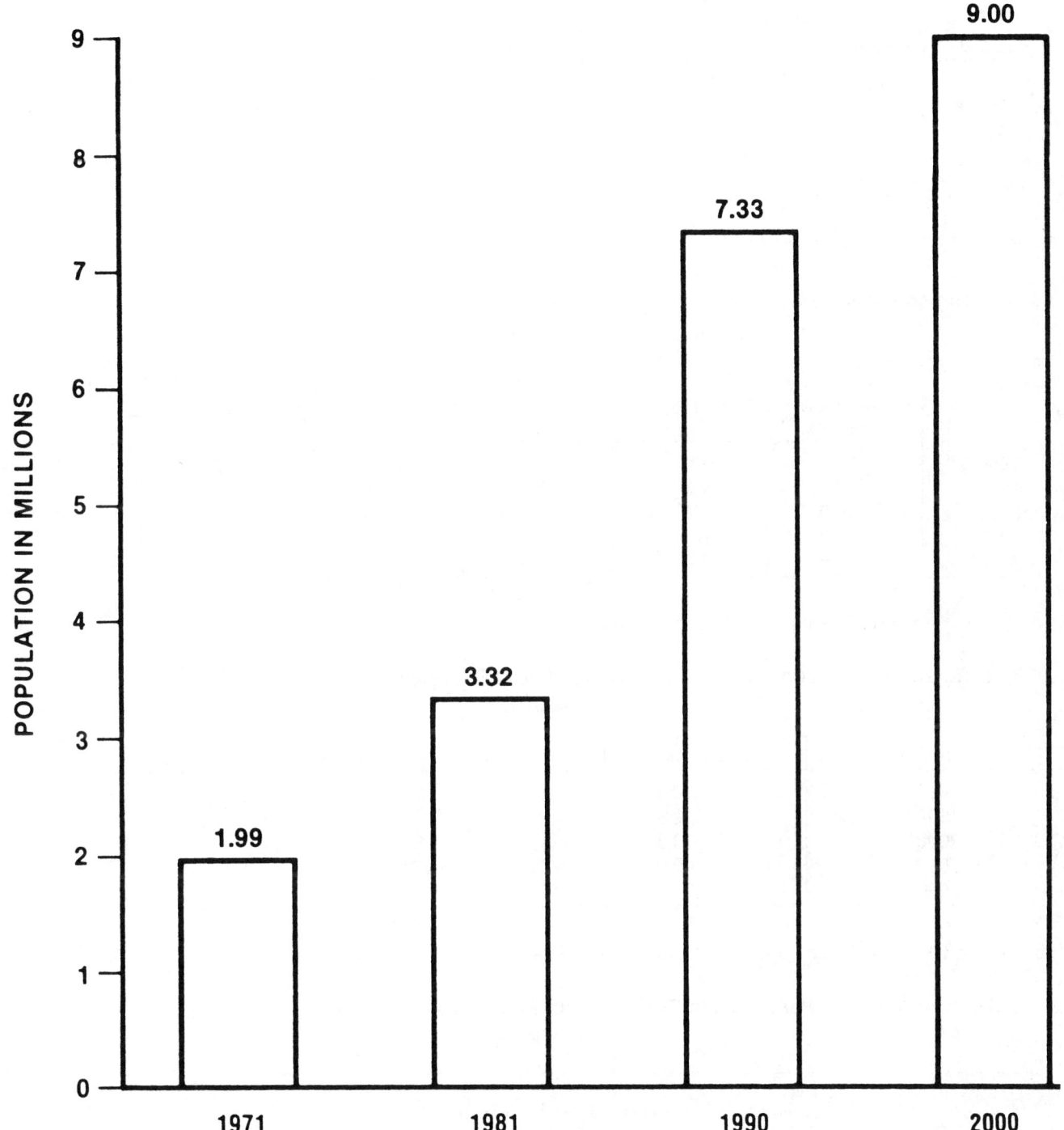

SOURCE: Veterans Administration, Research Division, Annual Report, 1982.

A6-3. Composition of Aged Veteran Population 1980-2020
(Millions)

Year	Total Veteran Population	Total Veteran Population 65+	65-74		75-84		85+	
			Number	Percent	Number	Percent	Number	Percent
1980	28.6	3.04	2.18	71.7	.64	21.1	.22	7.2
1990	27.1	7.16	5.62	78.5	1.33	18.6	.21	2.9
2000	24.3	8.97	5.01	55.8	3.45	38.4	.52	5.8
2010	20.7	8.13	3.72	45.8	3.02	37.2	1.38	17.0
2020	17.5	7.77	4.05	52.1	2.35	30.2	1.37	17.6

Source: VA Office of Reports and Statistics (March 1983)

A6-4. Proportion of Male and Female Veterans 65+ 1980-2020
(Millions)

Year	Total Vet. Population	Total Vet. Pop. 65+	MALE VETERANS		FEMALE VETERANS	
			Number 65+	Percent 65+	Number 65+	Percent 65+
1980	28.6	3.0	2.8	93.3	.20	6.7
1990	27.1	7.2	6.8	94.4	.40	5.6
2000	24.3	9.0	8.6	95.6	.40	4.4
2010	20.7	8.1	7.8	95.8	.34	4.2
2020	17.5	7.8	7.4	95.1	.38	4.9

Source: VA Office of Reports and Statistics (March 1983).

A6-5. Comparison of Male Veteran Population to Male U.S. Population 1980-2020
(Millions)

Year	Total U.S. Male Pop. 65+	Total Vet. Male Pop. 65+	Percent of Total
1980	10.4	2.8	27.4
1990	12.7	6.8	53.4
2000	13.7	8.6	62.5
2010	15.5	7.8	50.3
2020	21.0	7.4	35.2

Source: VA Office of Reports and Statistics (March 1983)

A6-6. Female Veterans: Proportion of Total Veteran Population 1980-2020
(Millions)

Year	Total Vet. Population	Total Male Vet.	Percent of Total	Total Female Vet.	Percent of Total
1980	28.6	27.49	96.1	1.11	3.9
1990	27.1	25.89	95.5	1.21	4.5
2000	24.3	23.03	94.8	1.27	5.2
2010	20.7	19.41	93.8	1.29	6.2
2020	17.5	16.19	92.5	1.31	7.5

Source: VA Office of Reports and Statistics (March 1983)

A6–7. Projected Change in Veteran Population 65 and Over, 2000–2020

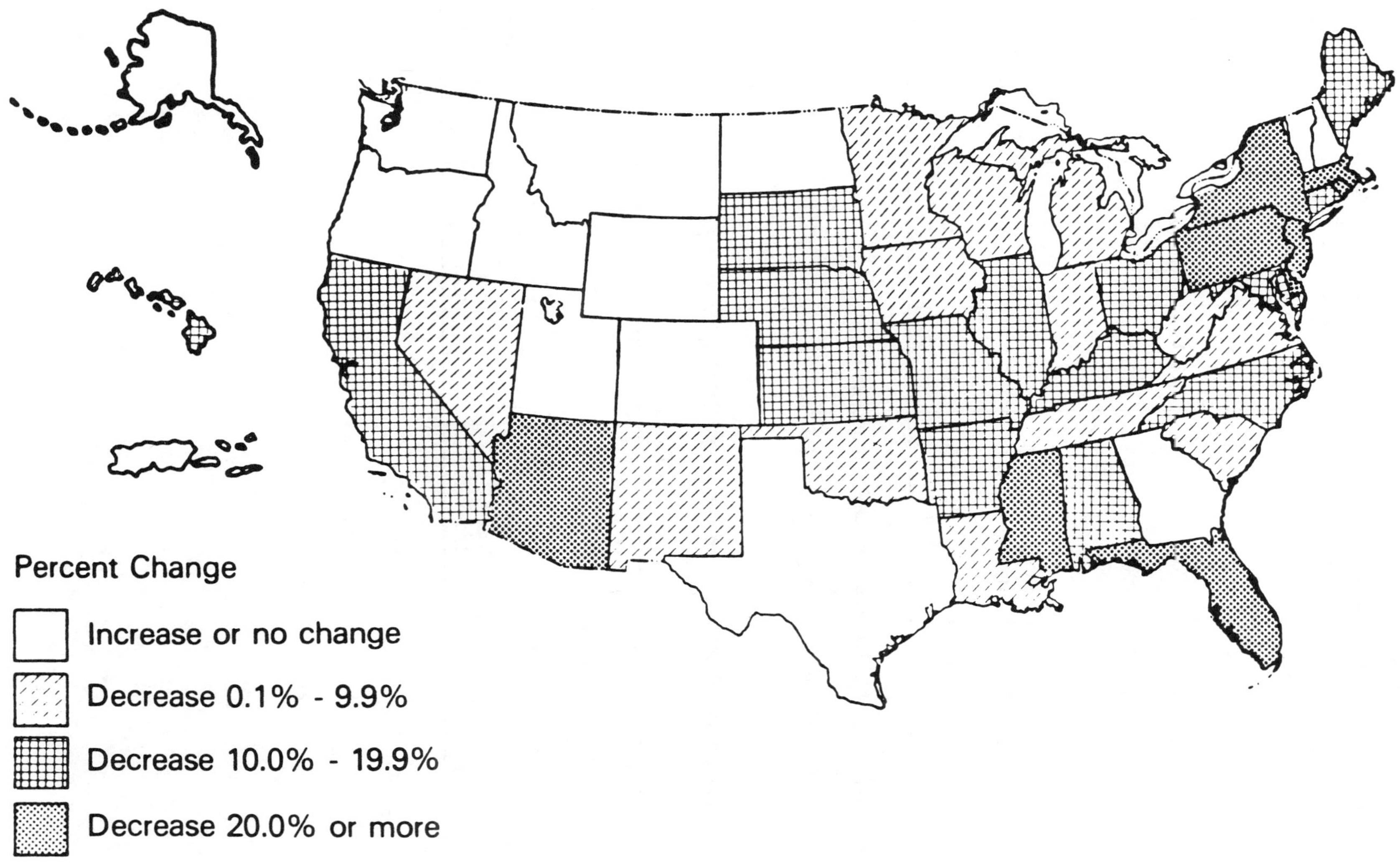

Percent Change

Increase or no change

Decrease 0.1% - 9.9%

Decrease 10.0% - 19.9%

Decrease 20.0% or more

A6–8. Distribution of Veterans by Race and Period of Service, 1979

Period of Service	Number (000's)	Total	Race				
			White	Black	Asian or Pacific Islands	American Indian	Other
Total	29,164	100.0	91.3	7.5	0.8	0.4	0.1
Vietnam Total	8,355	100.0	90.0	8.4	0.9	0.6	0.1
Vietnam Only	7,826	100.0	90.0	8.5	0.8	0.6	0.1
Korea, Total	5,724	100.0	91.2	7.4	1.0	0.4	0.0
Korea Only	4,216	100.0	90.9	8.0	0.9	0.2	0.0
WW II	12,415	100.0	92.1	6.9	0.8	0.3	0.0
Pre-WW II	795	100.0	93.9	6.2	0.0	0.0	0.0
Post-Vietnam	377	100.0	91.0	7.6	0.0	1.5	0.0
Between Korea and Vietnam	2,960	100.0	92.6	5.9	0.8	0.6	0.1
Between WW II and Korea	237	100.0	85.9	14.1	0.0	0.0	0.0

Note: Percentages may not add to 100.0 percent due to rounding.

Source: VA 1979 Survey of Veterans. p. 148.

A6–9. Projected Changes in Veterans 75 and Over 1980–2020

(Millions)

Year	Total 75+	Percent 75+	Percent Increase/ Decrease	Percent Increase From 1980
1980	.86	28.3	—	—
1990	1.54	21.5	79.1	79.1
2000	3.97	44.2	157.8	361.6
2010	4.40	54.2	10.8	411.6
2020	3.72	47.8	− 15.5	332.6

Source: VA Office of Reports and Statistics (March 1983)

A7. AGING IN OTHER COUNTRIES, USE OF OTHER LANGUAGES

A7-1. Estimated Population for 1975 and Projected Numbers for Year 2000 by Age Group and Major Area*

Area \ Age group	Year	(Thousands)				
		All ages	0-4	5-14	15-59	60+
World	1975	4,033,308	527,185	934,962	2,228,009	343,151
	2000	6,199,361	680,763	1,276,990	3,661,614	579,995
More developed regions a/	1975	1,093,181	86,668	184,525	656,101	165,885
	2000	1,272,316	91,440	182,364	767,455	231,057
Less developed regions b/	1975	2,940,126	440,522	750,443	1,571,904	177,258
	2000	4,927,045	589,325	1,094,631	2,894,158	348,930
Major geographical regions						
Africa	1975	405,845	73,202	108,292	204,594	19,758
	2000	828,050	129,885	220,577	434,910	42,681
Latin America	1975	322,592	50,476	84,244	168,164	19,709
	2000	608,122	81,581	144,418	340,610	41,513
Northern America	1975	236,379	17,645	42,010	142,233	34,493
	2000	289,546	19,730	43,138	180,301	46,375
East Asia	1975	1,063,449	121,442	239,688	612,817	89,502
	2000	1,406,063	115,428	226,443	904,392	159,800
South Asia	1975	1,255,320	204,648	334,213	655,349	61,109
	2000	2,205,880	270,354	517,321	1,288,203	130,000
Europe	1975	474,171	35,997	77,218	278,571	82,386
	2000	520,232	36,557	70,528	311,769	101,376
Oceania	1975	21,158	2,269	4,304	12,228	2,358
	2000	29,652	2,633	5,110	18,214	3,696
USSR	1975	254,393	21,523	45,003	154,034	33,833
	2000	311,817	24,615	49,483	183,181	54,536

a/ More developed regions include Northern America, Japan, Europe, Australia, New Zealand and USSR.

b/ Less developed regions include Africa, Latin America, China, other East Asia, South Asia, Melanesia, Micronesia and Polynesia.

*SOURCE: U.N. Bulletin on Aging, Vol. 5, No. 2, 1981.

A7-2. Percentage Increase of Population by Age Group and Area, 1975-2000*

Age group Area	All ages	0-4	5-14	15-59	60+
World	53.7	29.1	36.6	64.4	69.0
More developed regions a/	16.4	5.5	-1.2	17.0	39.3
Less developed regions b/	67.6	33.8	45.9	84.1	96.9
Major geographical regions					
Africa	104.0	77.4	103.7	112.6	116.0
Latin America	88.5	61.6	71.4	102.6	110.6
Northern America	22.5	11.8	2.7	26.8	34.5
East Asia	32.2	95.1	94.5	47.6	78.6
South Asia	75.7	32.1	54.8	96.6	112.7
Europe	9.7	1.6	-9.7	11.9	23.1
Oceania	40.2	16.1	18.7	49.0	56.8
USSR	22.6	14.4	10.0	18.9	61.2

a/ More developed regions include Northern America, Japan, Europe, Australia, New Zealand and USSR.

b/ Less developed regions include Africa, Latin America, China, other East Asia, South Asia, Melanesia, Micronesia and Polynesia.

*SOURCE: U.N. Bulletin on Aging, Vol. 5, No. 2, 1981.

A7-3. Life Expectancy Change 1950–1978 at Birth and Age 65

Country	At Birth				At Age 65			
	1950	1960	1970	1978	1950	1960	1970	1978
				Males				
Canada	66.23	68.14	69.25	70.54	13.35	13.34	13.67	14.23
U.S.	65.40	66.64	67.14	69.54	12.81	12.93	13.18	14.06
Japan	59.57[a]	66.32	70.31	72.97	11.08	11.75	12.66	14.63
Czechoslovakia	64.65	67.83	66.20	66.95[c]	12.01	12.79	11.41	11.69[c]
Denmark	69.46	70.51	70.93	71.35	13.72	13.68	13.84	13.76
France	63.96	67.55	60.09	70.23	12.18	12.60	13.36	14.09
West Germany	65.56	66.52	67.29	69.18	12.71	12.19	11.98	12.71
Hungary	64.96[b]	65.99	66.38	66.11	12.77[b]	12.37	12.01	11.71
Norway	70.87	71.33	71.02	72.40	15.10	14.42	13.81	14.29
Sweden	70.05	71.25	72.27	72.48	13.67	13.75	14.35	14.23
Great Britain	66.59	68.24	68.80	70.07	12.02	12.20	12.03	12.61
				Females				
Canada	70.46	73.86	76.09	78.13	14.91	15.80	17.29	18.60
U.S.	70.96	73.23	74.63	77.33	15.07	15.90	16.84	18.55
Japan	62.97[a]	70.19	74.66	78.33	13.15	14.24	15.50	17.66
Czechoslovakia	69.15	73.23	73.01	74.01[c]	13.48	14.74	14.38	14.85[c]
Denmark	72.23	74.02	76.04	77.56	14.51	15.11	16.71	17.73
France	69.65	74.08	76.62	78.44	14.64	15.67	17.29	18.45
West Germany	69.73	71.86	73.62	75.94	13.84	14.23	15.03	16.36
Hungary	68.83[b]	70.26	72.17	72.77	13.95[b]	13.88	14.43	14.50
Norway	74.39	75.79	77.39	78.74	16.05	15.97	16.83	17.84
Sweden	72.72	74.91	77.32	78.81	14.49	15.33	17.07	17.92
Great Britain	71.33	74.14	75.09	76.19	14.42	15.45	15.98	16.64

[a]Value for 1950–52
[b]Value for 1955
[c]Value for 1975

A7-4. Death Rates for the Population 60 Years and Over of Various Countries, by Sex and Age: Various Years from 1976 to 1978

(Deaths per 1,000 population in specified groups)

Country and year	Male						Female					
	60–64 years	65–69 years	70–74 years	75–79 years	80–84 years	85 years and over	60–64 years	65–69 years	70–74 years	75–79 years	80–84 years	85 years and over
Austria, 1977	22.9	37.3	61.6	98.0	146.2	232.0	11.4	19.0	34.1	62.6	112.0	206.3
Belgium, 1976	25.8	42.1	64.0	98.9	150.0	246.5	11.2	19.4	34.8	63.6	108.8	208.1
Czechoslovakia, 1977	28.2	44.9	71.8	107.5	163.9	269.4	13.7	22.7	40.7	72.7	127.0	226.1
Denmark, 1978	20.9	33.9	53.2	79.9	120.3	203.6	10.9	16.8	27.6	47.9	81.6	170.0
Finland, 1978	27.7	41.6	64.4	95.1	145.4	218.8	9.9	17.2	31.7	57.9	95.7	186.9
France, 1977	19.3	32.7	51.3	84.4	133.6	237.0	7.7	13.6	24.1	45.7	85.6	189.3
Germany, East, 1978	24.7	39.5	65.4	104.2	160.2	273.7	13.3	21.3	39.3	72.1	127.3	234.9
Germany, West, 1978	23.4	37.2	62.2	97.0	147.0	232.5	10.9	17.9	32.6	59.3	106.0	199.3
Hungary, 1978	29.4	43.8	71.0	112.5	169.1	265.0	15.2	24.8	43.4	77.6	133.3	233.4
Italy, 1977	21.0	33.9	53.3	85.5	135.2	230.2	9.5	16.6	29.4	55.5	104.4	199.4
Netherlands, 1978	20.6	33.8	53.7	81.3	121.1	206.1	8.6	14.3	25.7	46.1	82.9	169.7
Norway, 1978	18.7	29.7	49.0	76.9	117.8	208.4	8.5	14.6	25.5	49.3	84.4	176.0
Sweden, 1978	17.7	29.3	47.7	78.2	122.7	219.2	8.2	14.3	25.8	47.9	85.5	172.7
Switzerland, 1978	18.6	30.4	48.2	76.2	122.7	208.8	8.6	14.2	24.6	44.0	83.7	171.2
England and Wales, 1977	23.9	38.9	62.3	96.5	142.4	232.2	12.2	19.2	32.1	54.9	97.1	188.6
Australia, 1977	23.0	36.5	55.7	85.8	127.1	216.4	11.4	17.4	28.7	50.7	86.2	177.1
New Zealand, 1978	24.0	35.5	59.2	84.3	117.4	234.0	12.0	18.7	30.8	51.6	82.4	175.9
Japan, 1978	15.4	26.2	44.9	76.0	121.2	207.6	8.3	14.3	26.6	49.6	90.1	176.8
Israel, 1977	19.2	31.1	51.7	78.2	120.7	190.2	13.8	23.0	40.1	69.9	112.0	177.8
Yugoslavia, 1977	23.5	34.8	58.6	88.2	154.8	208.3	13.4	21.8	39.2	65.0	128.4	193.4
Canada, 1976	22.1	33.3	51.4	77.3	118.2	195.7	10.5	16.5	26.3	44.7	76.8	154.7
United States, 1978	24.1	34.4	52.4	80.7	116.0	172.6	12.1	16.9	27.2	47.1	75.1	135.4

Sources: United Nations, Demographic Yearbook, 1979, 1980; death rates for United States, 1978. "Final Mortality Statistics, 1978," Monthly Vital Statistics Report, Vol. 29, No. 6, Supplement (2), September 1980.

A7–5. Percent of the Foreign-Born Population in the Older Ages, for Specified Countries of Birth: 1970

(Numbers in thousands)

Country of birth	All ages		55 years and over	55 to 64 years	65 to 74 years	75 years and over	65 years and over
	Number	Percent					
All countries[1]	9,619	100.0	46.9	14.9	17.9	14.1	32.0
United Kingdom	686	100.0	49.5	15.2	19.4	14.9	34.3
Germany	833	100.0	45.2	15.1	17.7	12.4	30.1
Poland	548	100.0	69.3	20.4	24.4	24.5	48.9
U.S.S.R.	463	100.0	84.6	20.7	37.4	26.5	63.9
Italy	1,009	100.0	63.6	16.9	25.3	21.4	46.7
Canada	812	100.0	42.6	18.1	14.4	10.1	24.5
Latin America	1,804	100.0	20.2	9.9	7.0	3.2	10.3
All other countries	3,464	100.0	48.1	14.4	18.2	15.6	33.8

[1]Includes "not reported," not shown separately.

Source: U.S. Bureau of the Census, Census of Population: 1970, Subject Reports, Final Report PC(2)-1A, 1973, table 10.

A7–6. Ability to Speak English for Persons 65 Years and Over and for Persons of All Ages Who Speak a Language Other than English at Home: 1979

(Numbers in thousands)

Age and ability to speak English	Number	Percent
65 YEARS AND OVER		
Total persons	2,434	100.0
Speak English very well or well	1,722	70.8
Speak English not well	475	19.5
Speak English not at all	238	9.8
ALL AGES		
Total persons	17,985	100.0
Speak English very well or well	14,109	78.4
Speak English not well	2,739	15.2
Speak English not at all	1,137	6.3

Source: U.S. Bureau of the Census, Ancestry and Language, Current Population Reports, Series P-23, No. 116, March 1982.

A7-7. Social and Economic Characteristics of the Asian and Pacific Islander Population: 1980

[As of April 1. Based on a sample from the 1980 Census of Population and Housing, see text, p. 1; and Appendix III]

CHARACTERISTIC	NUMBER (1,000)		PERCENT DISTRIBUTION		CHARACTERISTIC	NUMBER (1,000)		PERCENT DISTRIBUTION	
	All races	Asian, Pacific Islander	All races	Asian, Pacific Islander		All races	Asian, Pacific Islander	All races	Asian, Pacific Islander
Total persons	226,546	3,726	100.0	100.0	FAMILY TYPE				
Under 5 years	16,296	320	7.2	8.6	Total families	59,190	818	100.0	100.0
5-14 years	34,940	625	15.4	16.8	With own children [3]	30,472	507	51.5	62.0
15-44 years	105,291	1,976	46.5	53.0	Married couple	48,990	691	82.8	84.4
45-64 years	44,518	584	19.7	15.7	With own children [3]	24,780	449	41.9	54.9
65 years and over	25,498	222	11.3	5.9	Female householder [3]	8,205	88	13.9	10.8
YEARS OF SCHOOL COMPLETED					With own children [3]	4,932	48	8.3	5.9
					Male householder [3]	1,995	39	3.4	4.8
Persons 25 yr. and over	132,836	2,137	100.0	100.0	With own children [3]	760	10	1.3	1.2
Elementary: 0-8 years	24,258	351	18.3	16.4	INCOME, 1979				
High school: 1-3 years	20,278	187	15.3	8.8	Total families	59,190	818	100.0	100.0
4 years	45,947	527	34.6	24.7	Less than $5,000	4,344	62	7.3	7.6
College: 1-3 years	20,795	368	15.7	17.2	$5,000-$9,999	7,746	86	13.1	10.5
4 years or more	21,558	704	16.2	32.9	$10,000-$14,999	8,709	98	14.7	11.9
LABOR FORCE STATUS					$15,000-$24,999	17,424	208	29.4	25.4
Persons 16 yr. and over	171,214	2,722	100.0	100.0	$25,000-$49,999	17,635	290	29.8	35.5
In labor force	106,085	1,813	62.0	66.6	$50,000 or more	3,332	74	5.6	9.1
Armed Forces	1,635	40	1.0	1.5	Median income (dol.) [4]	19,917	22,713	(x)	(x)
Civilian labor force	104,450	1,773	61.0	65.1	Persons below poverty level [5]	27,393	476	12.4	13.1
Employed	97,639	1,689	57.0	62.1					
Unemployed	6,810	84	4.0	3.1	HOUSING TENURE				
Unemployment rate [1]	6.5	4.7	(x)	(x)	Total occupied units	80,390	1,053	100.0	100.0
Not in labor force	65,130	909	38.0	33.4	Owner-occupied	51,796	542	64.4	51.4
					Renter-occupied	28,593	511	35.6	48.6

X Not applicable. [1] Total unemployment as percent of civilian labor force. [2] Children under 18 years old. [3] With no spouse present. [4] For definition of median, see *Guide to Tabular Presentation.* [5] For explanation of poverty level, see text, p. 429.

A7-8. Total Asian-American Population Increase April 1, 1980–Sept. 30, 1985

Asian Americans represent 2.1 percent of the total U.S. population of 239,447,000.

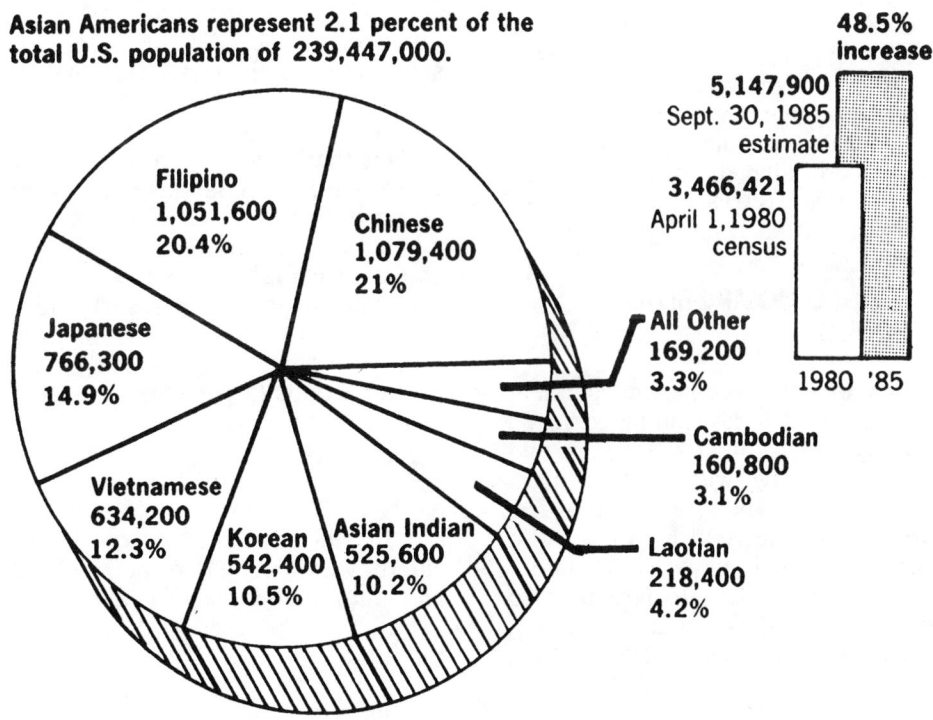

48.5% increase

5,147,900 Sept. 30, 1985 estimate

3,466,421 April 1, 1980 census

1980 '85

Filipino 1,051,600 20.4%

Chinese 1,079,400 21%

Japanese 766,300 14.9%

All Other 169,200 3.3%

Cambodian 160,800 3.1%

Vietnamese 634,200 12.3%

Korean 542,400 10.5%

Asian Indian 525,600 10.2%

Laotian 218,400 4.2%

SOURCE: Population Research Bureau.

THE WASHINGTON POST

B. Social Characteristics

LIVING ARRANGEMENTS AND MARITAL STATUS

In the last few decades, there has been an increase in the proportion of older people, especially women, who maintain their own households. In 1983, over 75 percent of men but less than 50 percent of women over 65 lived in a family setting. Sixty-seven percent of women in this age group were widowed, while about the same percentage of men were still married. Elderly widowed men remarry about seven times more often than women. The substantial difference in longevity between men and women and the age difference at the time of marriage account for these conditions.

EDUCATION

The educational attainment of the total population is steadily increasing. In 1979, about one-half of older Americans had less than a tenth-grade education, about nine percent were functionally illiterate, and about eight percent were college graduates. As a better educated population reaches the age of 65 and the less educated die off, the median level of education increases. By 1990, a majority of the elderly will have graduated from high school.

HOUSING, HOUSEHOLD COMPOSITION, INFORMAL SUPPORTS

For the majority of older people, independent living is the preferred mode today compared to 30 or 40 years ago. Only 6 percent of older men and 11 percent of older women live with their children. Contact of the elderly with their relatives is frequent because most of them have at least one child or other relatives living reasonably close. Older people living alone are more likely to rent than to live in their own homes; of those living in homes, 40 percent live in houses built before 1940, which are more likely to be in poorer condition than newer homes.

SOCIAL ACTIVITIES

Approximately 25 percent of the older population belong to religious organizations, which play an important role in their lives and serve many of their spiritual and social needs, including counseling, transportation, education, and recreation.

Older people maintain a strong interest in the election process and have a high voting record, possibly due to having more leisure time than younger people. During the 1980 presidential election when the 65+ population represented 15.4 percent of the potential voters, they cast 16.8 percent of the votes. Older men had proportionately better voting records than older women.

Older Americans not only take advantage of volunteer services but are also directly involved in such activities in civic, fraternal, and religious organizations.

A 1980 study of Louis Harris Associates indicates that over 50 percent of the older population listed travel as a favorite leisure activity, followed by needlepoint, weaving, and handicrafts (42 percent), photography (31 percent), singing in choirs or choral groups (19 percent), playing musical instruments (19 percent), painting or drawing (15 percent), writing stories or poems (12 percent), pottery or ceramics (8 percent), and work with local theater groups (5 percent).

SOCIAL PROBLEMS

In 1981, the most frequent offense against the elderly was larceny and theft, followed by burglaries and auto thefts. As offenders, the aged most frequently were accused of drunkenness, driving under the influence of alcohol, and disorderly conduct.

B1. LIVING ARRANGEMENTS AND MARITAL STATUS

B1-1. Social and Economic Characteristics of the White Population: 1983

CHARACTERISTIC	NUMBER (1,000)		PERCENT DISTRIBUTION		CHARACTERISTIC	NUMBER (1,000)		PERCENT DISTRIBUTION	
	Total	White	Total	White		Total	White	Total	White
Total persons	**229,587**	**196,036**	**100.0**	**100.0**	**FAMILY TYPE**				
Under 5 years	17,733	14,321	7.7	7.3	**Total families**	**61,393**	**53,407**	**100.0**	**100.0**
5–14 years	33,753	27,606	14.7	14.1	With own children [2]	30,818	26,006	50.2	48.7
15–44 years..........................	108,173	91,886	47.1	46.9	Married couple..............	49,908	45,252	81.3	84.7
45–64 years..........................	44,191	38,988	19.2	19.9	With own children [2]	24,363	21,701	39.7	40.6
65 years and over	25,737	23,234	11.2	11.9	Female householder [3]	9,469	6,507	15.4	12.2
					With own children [2]	5,718	3,707	9.3	6.9
YEARS OF SCHOOL COMPLETED					Male householder [3]	2,016	1,648	3.3	3.1
					With own children [2]	737	598	1.2	1.1
Persons 25 yr. and over	138,020	120,610	100.0	100.0	**FAMILY INCOME, 1982**				
Elementary: 0–8 years	20,833	17,035	15.1	14.1	**Total families**	**61,393**	**53,407**	**100.0**	**100.0**
High school:					Less than $5,000..................	3,684	2,482	6.0	4.6
1–3 years	17,681	14,593	12.8	12.1	$5,000–$9,999	6,521	4,962	10.6	9.3
4 years	52,060	46,370	37.7	38.4	$10,000–$14,999	7,653	6,461	12.5	12.1
College:					$15,000–$24,999	15,034	13,292	24.5	24.9
1–3 years	21,531	19,145	15.6	15.9	$25,000–$49,999	21,800	19,872	35.5	37.2
4 years or more	25,915	23,466	18.8	19.5	$50,000 or more	6,703	6,334	10.9	11.9
					Median income (dol.) [4]	23,433	24,603	(x)	(x)
LABOR FORCE STATUS									
					Persons below poverty level [5]	34,398	23,517	15.0	12.0
Civilians 16 yr. and over......	174,215	150,805	100.0	100.0					
Civilian labor force.............	111,550	97,021	64.0	64.3	**HOUSING TENURE**				
Employed.........................	100,834	88,893	57.9	58.9	**Total occupied units** ...	**83,918**	**73,182**	**100.0**	**100.0**
Unemployed.....................	10,717	8,128	6.2	5.4	Owner-occupied..................	54,494	49,484	64.9	67.6
Unemployment rate [1] ...	9.6	8.4	(x)	(x)	Renter-occupied..................	29,423	23,698	35.1	32.4
Not in labor force	62,665	53,784	36.0	35.7					

X Not applicable.   [1] Total unemployment as percent of civilian labor force.   [2] Children under 18 years old.   [3] With no spouse present.   [4] For definition of median, see Guide to Tabular Presentation.   [5] For explanation of poverty level, see text, p. 429.

B1-2. Social and Economic Characteristics of the Black Population: 1983

[As of March, except labor force status, annual average. Based on Current Population Survey, which covers civilian noninstitutional population and members of Armed Forces living off post or with their families on post, but excludes all other members of the Armed Forces. See text, pp. 1 and 2, and Appendix III]

CHARACTERISTIC	NUMBER (1,000)		PERCENT DISTRIBUTION		CHARACTERISTIC	NUMBER (1,000)		PERCENT DISTRIBUTION	
	Total	Black	Total	Black		Total	Black	Total	Black
Total persons..............	**229,587**	**27,263**	**100.0**	**100.0**	**FAMILY TYPE**				
Age:					**Total families**	**61,393**	**6,530**	**100.0**	**100.0**
Under 5 years	17,733	2,820	7.7	10.3	With own children [2]	30,818	3,890	50.2	59.6
5–14 years	33,753	5,000	14.7	18.3	Married couple..............	49,908	3,486	81.3	53.4
15–44 years..........................	108,173	13,100	47.1	48.1	With own children [2]	24,363	1,901	39.7	29.1
45–64 years..........................	44,191	4,220	19.2	15.5	Female householder [3]	9,469	2,734	15.4	41.9
65 years and over	25,737	2,123	11.2	7.8	With own children [2]	5,718	1,862	9.3	28.5
YEARS OF SCHOOL COMPLETED					Male householder [3]	2,016	309	3.3	4.7
					With own children [2]	737	127	1.2	1.9
Persons 25 yr. and over	138,020	13,940	100.0	100.0	**FAMILY INCOME, 1982**				
Elementary: 0–8 years	20,833	3,250	15.1	23.3	**Total families**	**61,393**	**6,530**	**100.0**	**100.0**
High school:					Less than $5,000..................	3,684	1,113	6.0	17.0
1–3 years	17,681	2,770	12.8	19.9	$5,000–$9,999....................	6,521	1,363	10.6	20.9
4 years	52,060	4,722	37.7	33.9	$10,000–$14,999	7,653	1,023	12.5	15.7
College:					$15,000–$24,999	15,034	1,431	24.5	21.9
1–3 years	21,531	1,868	15.6	13.4	$25,000–$49,999	21,800	1,428	35.5	21.9
4 years or more	25,915	1,330	18.8	9.5	$50,000 or more	6,703	173	10.9	2.6
					Median income (dol.) [4]	23,433	13,599	(x)	(x)
LABOR FORCE STATUS									
					Persons below poverty level [5]	34,398	9,697	15.0	35.6
Civilians 16 yr. and over........	174,215	18,925	100.0	100.0					
Civilian labor force..............	111,550	11,647	64.0	61.5	**HOUSING TENURE**				
Employed.........................	100,834	9,375	57.9	49.5	**Total occupied units** ...	**83,918**	**8,916**	**100.0**	**100.0**
Unemployed.....................	10,717	2,272	6.2	12.0	Owner-occupied..................	54,494	4,043	64.9	45.3
Unemployment rate [1] ...	9.6	19.5	(x)	(x)	Renter-occupied..................	29,423	4,873	35.1	54.7
Not in labor force	62,665	7,278	36.0	38.5					

X Not applicable.   [1] Total unemployment as percent of civilian labor force.   [2] Children under 18 years old.   [3] With no spouse present.   [4] For definition of median, see Guide to Tabular Presentation.   [5] For explanation of poverty level, see text, p. 429.

Source of tables 35 and 36: U.S. Bureau of the Census, *Current Population Reports*, series P-60, No. 142, and P-20, No. 388 and unpublished data. Labor force data are published by U.S. Bureau of Labor Statistics, *Employment and Earnings*, January 1984.

B1–3. Distribution of the Male and Female Populations 65 Years Old and Over by Living Arrangements: 1981

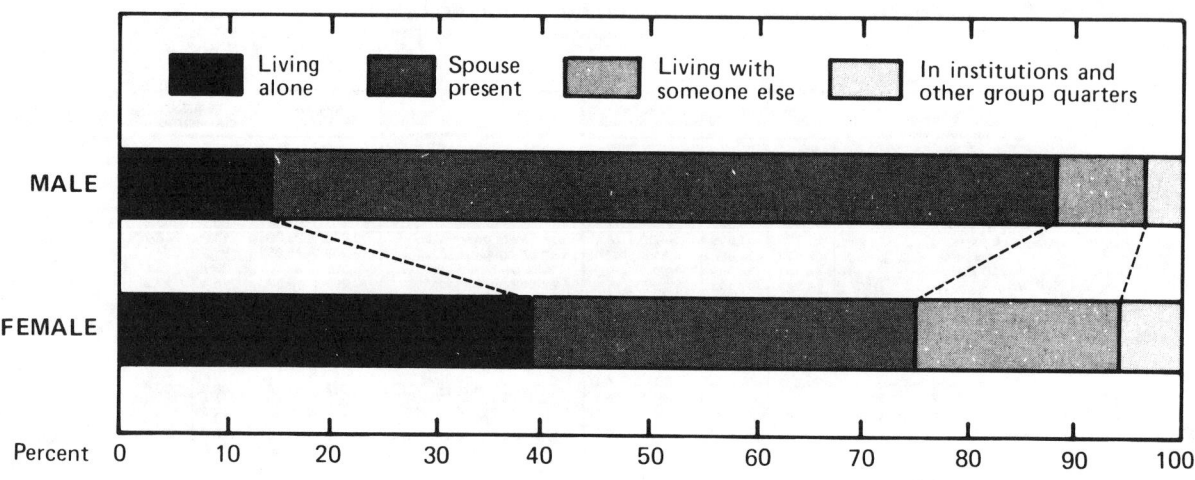

B1–4. Living Arrangements of Older Males and Females, 1983

	Age 55 to 64		Age 65 to 74		Age 75 plus	
	Males	Females	Males	Females	Males	Females
Percent in category:						
Not in household	1	1	2	1	8	13
Living alone	9	17	12	36	19	42
Living in household with someone (not spouse)	6	15	7	15	8	24
Living in household with spouse present	84	67	78	49	65	21

[1] Less than 0.5 percent

SOURCE: U. S. Bureau of the Census, Current Population Survey, March 1983, compiled by the Congressional Research Service.

B1–5. Percent Distribution of the Population 65 Years and Over by Family Status, by Sex: 1965 to 1981

(Total resident population excluding members of the Armed Forces in military barracks. Figures are for March of year indicated)

Family status	Both sexes				Male				Female			
	1981	1975	1970	1965	1981	1975	1970	1965	1981	1975	1970	1965
Total......................	100.0	100.0	100.0	100.0	100.0	100.0	100.0	100.0	100.0	100.0	100.0	100.0
In families.....................	64.1	65.8	67.1	70.4	80.3	79.8	79.1	80.2	53.2	56.1	58.5	62.9
Householder.....................	35.3	36.2	36.3	37.2	73.2	76.0	72.9	71.2	9.6	8.4	9.8	10.7
Married, spouse present........	29.4	30.0	28.9	29.2	70.3	73.1	69.0	66.8	1.6	(NA)	(NA)	(NA)
Other family householder.......	5.9	6.2	7.3	8.0	2.8	2.9	3.9	4.4	8.0	8.4	9.8	10.7
Spouse of householder...........	21.2	20.7	19.3	18.7	3.0	(NA)	(NA)	(NA)	33.5	35.0	33.3	33.3
Other relative..................	7.6	9.0	11.5	14.5	4.0	3.7	6.3	9.0	10.1	12.7	15.4	18.8
Not in families..................	35.9	34.2	32.9	29.6	19.7	20.2	20.9	19.8	46.8	43.9	41.5	37.1
Nonfamily householder...........	29.7	28.0	26.6	23.3	14.7	14.8	14.9	13.9	39.8	37.3	35.2	30.6
Secondary individuals...........	1.0	1.2	2.1	2.3	1.3	1.2	2.4	2.4	0.9	1.3	1.9	2.3
Inmates of institutions.........	5.2	4.9	4.1	4.0	3.8	4.2	3.6	3.5	6.2	5.3	4.4	4.3

NA Not applicable.

Source: U.S. Bureau of the Census, Current Population Reports, Series P-20, Nos. 144, 287, and 371, and unpublished data for March 1970 (revised).

B1–6. Percent Distribution of Households by Type, for Householders 65 Years and Over, by Age Group: 1970 to 1995

(Relates to the noninstitutional population excluding members of the Armed Forces in military barracks. Figures are for March of year indicated)

Type of household and age of householder	1970	1975	1981	1990[1]	1995[1]
HOUSEHOLDER 65 AND OVER					
All households...........................	100.0	100.0	100.0	100.0	100.0
Family households.........................	57.6	56.3	54.3	51.2	50.0
Married-couple family.....................	46.0	46.7	45.2	44.4	44.1
Other family, female householder..........	9.0	7.8	7.3	5.4	4.7
Other family, male householder............	2.6	1.9	1.8	1.3	1.2
Nonfamily households[2].....................	42.4	43.7	45.7	48.8	50.0
Male householder..........................	9.9	9.4	9.1	9.6	9.5
Female householder........................	32.5	34.2	36.6	39.2	40.5
HOUSEHOLDER 65 TO 74 YEARS					
All households...........................	100.0	100.0	100.0	100.0	100.0
Family households.........................	62.0	61.8	61.2	57.6	56.9
Married-couple family.....................	51.8	53.0	52.7	50.8	50.8
Other family, female householder..........	8.3	7.2	6.8	5.5	4.9
Other family, male householder............	1.9	1.6	1.7	1.3	1.2
Nonfamily households[2].....................	38.1	38.2	38.8	42.4	43.1
Male householder..........................	8.4	8.6	8.0	9.3	9.6
Female householder........................	29.7	29.7	30.8	33.1	33.5
HOUSEHOLDER 75 AND OVER					
All households...........................	100.0	100.0	100.0	100.0	100.0
Family households.........................	50.6	47.2	43.8	41.9	40.8
Married-couple family.....................	36.5	36.1	33.8	35.2	35.2
Other family, female householder..........	10.3	8.7	8.2	5.3	4.4
Other family, male householder............	3.7	2.4	1.9	1.4	1.2
Nonfamily households[2].....................	49.4	52.8	56.2	58.1	59.2
Male householder..........................	12.4	10.9	10.7	10.1	9.3
Female householder........................	37.0	41.9	45.5	48.0	49.9

[1]Base date of projections is March 1978.
[2]Corresponds to number of primary individuals.

B1-7. Living Arrangements of the Population 55 Years and Over, by Age and Sex: 1965 to 1981

(Numbers in thousands. Total resident population excluding members of the Armed Forces in military barracks. Figures are for March of year indicated)

Living arrangements and year	Male				Female			
	55 to 64 years	65 to 74 years	75 years and over	65 years and over	55 to 64 years	65 to 74 years	75 years and over	65 years and over
1981								
Number...................	10,256	6,874	3,632	10,506	11,671	8,981	6,555	15,536
In households...................	10,107	6,727	3,375	10,102	11,563	8,780	5,785	14,565
Living alone...................	928	761	689	1,450	2,051	3,075	2,959	6,034
Spouse present.............	8,275	5,429	2,354	7,783	7,762	4,247	1,263	5,510
Living with someone else.........	904	537	332	869	1,750	1,458	1,563	3,021
Not in households.............	149	147	257	404	108	201	770	971
Percent...................	100.0	100.0	100.0	100.0	100.0	100.0	100.0	100.0
In households...................	98.5	97.9	92.9	96.2	99.1	97.8	88.3	93.8
Living alone...................	9.0	11.1	19.0	13.8	17.6	34.2	45.1	38.8
Spouse present................	80.7	79.0	64.8	74.1	66.5	47.3	19.3	35.5
Living with someone else.........	8.8	7.8	9.1	8.3	15.0	16.2	23.8	19.4
Not in households.............	1.5	2.1	7.1	3.8	0.9	2.2	11.7	6.3
1975								
Percent...................	100.0	100.0	100.0	100.0	100.0	100.0	100.0	100.0
In households...................	98.1	97.1	92.7	95.6	98.8	97.5	90.0	94.4
Living alone...................	7.6	12.1	18.2	14.2	17.4	32.9	40.6	36.0
Spouse present................	80.7	79.6	63.3	74.0	66.1	46.2	20.1	35.6
Living with someone else.........	9.7	5.4	11.2	7.4	15.3	18.4	29.3	22.8
Not in households.............	1.9	2.9	7.3	4.4	1.2	2.5	10.0	5.6
1970								
Percent...................	100.0	100.0	100.0	100.0	100.0	100.0	100.0	100.0
In households...................	97.6	96.4	93.7	95.5	98.4	97.6	91.1	95.0
Living alone...................	7.2	11.3	19.1	14.1	17.1	31.6	37.0	33.8
Spouse present................	82.3	75.2	60.4	69.9	63.8	43.5	19.1	33.9
Living with someone else.........	8.1	9.9	14.2	11.5	17.5	22.4	35.0	27.4
Not in households.............	2.4	3.6	6.3	4.5	1.6	2.4	8.9	5.0
1965								
Percent...................	100.0	100.0	100.0	100.0	100.0	100.0	100.0	100.0
In households...................	97.5	97.5	93.6	96.2	98.4	97.4	92.0	95.3
Living alone...................	7.0	11.7	15.7	13.1	15.5	27.9	29.9	28.6
Spouse present................	80.3	75.3	54.0	67.9	63.8	43.3	19.0	34.1
Living with someone else.........	10.2	10.5	23.9	15.2	19.1	26.1	43.1	32.6
Not in households.............	2.5	2.5	6.4	3.8	1.6	2.6	8.0	4.7

Source: U.S. Bureau of the Census, Current Population Reports. Series P-20, Nos. 144, 287, and 372, and unpublished data for March 1970 (revised).

B1-8. Distribution of the Male and Female Populations 65 Years Old and Over by Marital Status: 1981

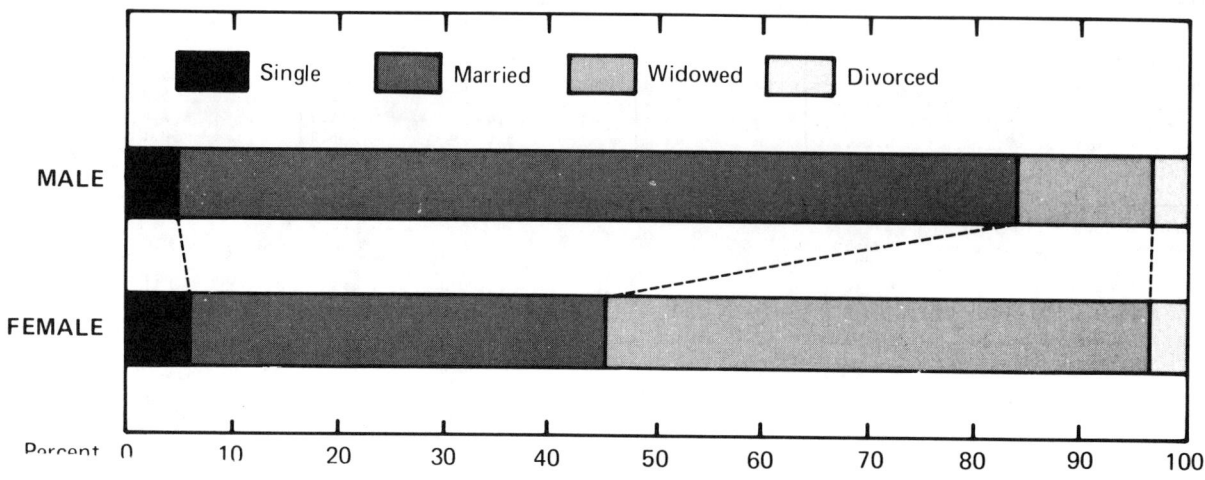

B1–9. Live Births, Deaths, Marriages, and Divorces: 1910 to 1983

[Prior to 1960, excludes Alaska and Hawaii. Figures for deaths and death rates for 1910–1930 are for death-registration States only. Beginning 1970, excludes births to, and deaths of, nonresidents of the U.S. See Appendix III. See also *Historical Statistics, Colonial Times to 1970,* series B 1–5, B 142, B 167, B 214, and B 216]

YEAR	NUMBER (1,000)					RATE PER 1,000 POPULATION				
	Births [1]	Deaths		Marriages [3]	Divorces [4]	Births [1]	Deaths		Marriages [3]	Divorces [4]
		Total	Infant [2]				Total	Infant [2]		
1910	2,777	697	(NA)	948	83	30.1	14.7	(NA)	10.3	.9
1915	2,965	916	78	1,008	104	29.5	13.2	99.9	10.0	1.0
1920	2,950	1,118	130	1,274	171	27.7	13.0	85.8	12.0	1.6
1925	2,909	1,192	135	1,188	175	25.1	11.7	71.7	10.3	1.5
1930	2,618	1,327	142	1,127	196	21.3	11.3	64.6	9.2	1.6
1935	2,377	1,393	120	1,327	218	18.7	10.0	55.7	10.4	1.7
1940	2,559	1,417	111	1,596	264	19.4	10.8	47.0	12.1	2.0
1945	2,858	1,402	105	1,613	485	20.4	10.6	38.3	12.2	3.5
1950	3,632	1,452	104	1,667	385	24.1	9.6	29.2	11.1	2.6
1955	4,097	1,529	107	1,531	377	25.0	9.3	26.4	9.3	2.3
1957	4,300	1,633	112	1,518	381	25.3	9.6	26.3	8.9	2.2
1960	4,258	1,712	111	1,523	393	23.7	9.5	26.0	8.5	2.2
1965	3,760	1,828	93	1,800	479	19.4	9.4	24.7	9.3	2.5
1966	3,606	1,863	86	1,857	499	18.4	9.5	23.7	9.5	2.5
1967	3,521	1,851	79	1,927	523	17.8	9.4	22.4	9.7	2.6
1968	3,502	1,930	76	2,069	584	17.5	9.7	21.8	10.4	2.9
1969	3,600	1,922	75	2,145	639	17.8	9.5	20.7	10.6	3.2
1970	3,731	1,921	75	2,159	708	18.4	9.5	20.0	10.6	3.5
1971	3,556	1,928	68	2,190	773	17.2	9.3	19.1	10.6	3.7
1972	3,258	1,964	60	2,282	845	15.6	9.4	18.5	10.9	4.0
1973	3,137	1,973	56	2,284	915	14.8	9.3	17.7	10.8	4.3
1974	3,160	1,934	53	2,230	977	14.8	9.1	16.7	10.5	4.6
1975	3,144	1,893	51	2,153	1,036	14.6	8.8	16.1	10.0	4.8
1976	3,168	1,909	48	2,155	1,083	14.6	8.8	15.2	9.9	5.0
1977	3,327	1,900	47	2,178	1,091	15.1	8.6	14.1	9.9	5.0
1978	3,333	1,928	46	2,282	1,130	15.0	8.7	13.8	10.3	5.1
1979	3,494	1,914	46	2,331	1,181	15.6	8.5	13.1	10.4	5.3
1980	3,612	1,990	46	2,390	1,189	15.9	8.8	12.6	10.6	5.2
1981	3,629	1,978	43	2,422	1,213	15.8	8.6	11.9	10.6	5.3
1982, prel	3,704	1,986	42	2,495	1,180	16.0	8.6	11.2	10.8	5.1
1983, prel	3,614	2,010	39	2,444	1,179	15.5	8.6	10.9	10.5	5.0

NA Not available.   [1] Through 1957, adjusted for underregistration.   [2] Infants under 1 year, excluding fetal deaths; rates per 1,000 registered live births.   [3] Includes estimates for some States through 1969 and also for 1976 and 1977 and marriage licenses for some States for all years except 1973 and 1975. Beginning 1978 includes nonlicensed marriages in California.   [4] Includes reported annulments and some estimated State figures for all years.

Source: U.S. National Center for Health Statistics, *Vital Statistics of the United States,* annual, and unpublished data.

B1–10. Headship Status of Older Women, 1950 to 1980

(Percentage Distribution)

Age and status	1950	1960	1970	1980
Total, 65 and over	100.0	100.0	100.0	100.0
Wives	34.8	36.5	36.2	38.0
Family heads	14.4	11.5	9.3	8.9
Nonfamily heads	19.1	26.8	35.7	41.8
Other	31.7	25.2	18.8	11.3

Note: Excludes the population in group quarters.

Source: U.S. Bureau of the Census, 1953: table 1; 1964:
table 2; 1973: table 2; 1981b: table 6.

B1–11. Marital Status, 45 and Over, by Sex: 1950 to 1980

(Percentage Distribution)

Age and status	FEMALE				MALE			
	1950	1960	1970	1980	1950	1960	1970	1980
45 to 54 years old	100.0	100.0	100.0	100.0	100.0	100.0	100.0	100.0
Never married	7.8	7.0	5.5	4.7	8.5	7.4	6.4	6.4
Married	77.6	79.9	81.1	79.1	85.7	87.7	88.1	85.3
Widowed	11.1	8.8	7.9	7.0	2.8	1.8	1.7	1.6
Divorced	3.5	4.2	5.5	9.2	3.0	3.1	3.8	6.7
55 to 64 years old	100.0	100.0	100.0	100.0	100.0	100.0	100.0	100.0
Never married	7.9	8.0	6.8	4.6	8.4	8.0	6.5	5.7
Married	65.0	66.0	68.0	69.9	81.4	83.9	85.6	85.3
Widowed	24.7	22.3	20.2	18.9	7.6	5.0	4.1	4.0
Divorced	2.4	3.6	5.0	6.7	2.6	3.1	3.8	5.0
65 and over	100.0	100.0	100.0	100.0	100.0	100.0	100.0	100.0
Never married	8.9	8.5	8.1	5.9	8.4	7.7	7.5	5.1
Married	35.7	37.4	36.5	39.7	65.7	70.8	72.4	77.6
Widowed	54.3	52.0	52.2	51.0	24.1	19.1	17.1	13.6
Divorced	1.1	2.0	3.2	3.4	1.9	2.3	3.0	3.7

Note: Married includes married, spouse absent.

Source: U.S. Bureau of the Census, 1975: Series A 160-171; 1981b: table 1.

B1–12. Marital Status of Older Males and Females, 1984

	Age 55 to 64		Age 65 to 74		Age 75 plus	
	Males	Females	Males	Females	Males	Females
Percent in category:						
Single	5	4	5	5	4	6
Married-spouse present	83	66	80	49	67	23
Married-spouse absent	2	3	2	2	3	1
Widowed	4	17	9	39	24	67
Divorced	6	9	4	5	2	3

Source: U.S. Bureau of the Census, Current Population Survey, March 1984, unpublished.

B1–13. Widowhood of Persons 55 and Over by Race and Sex, March, 1983

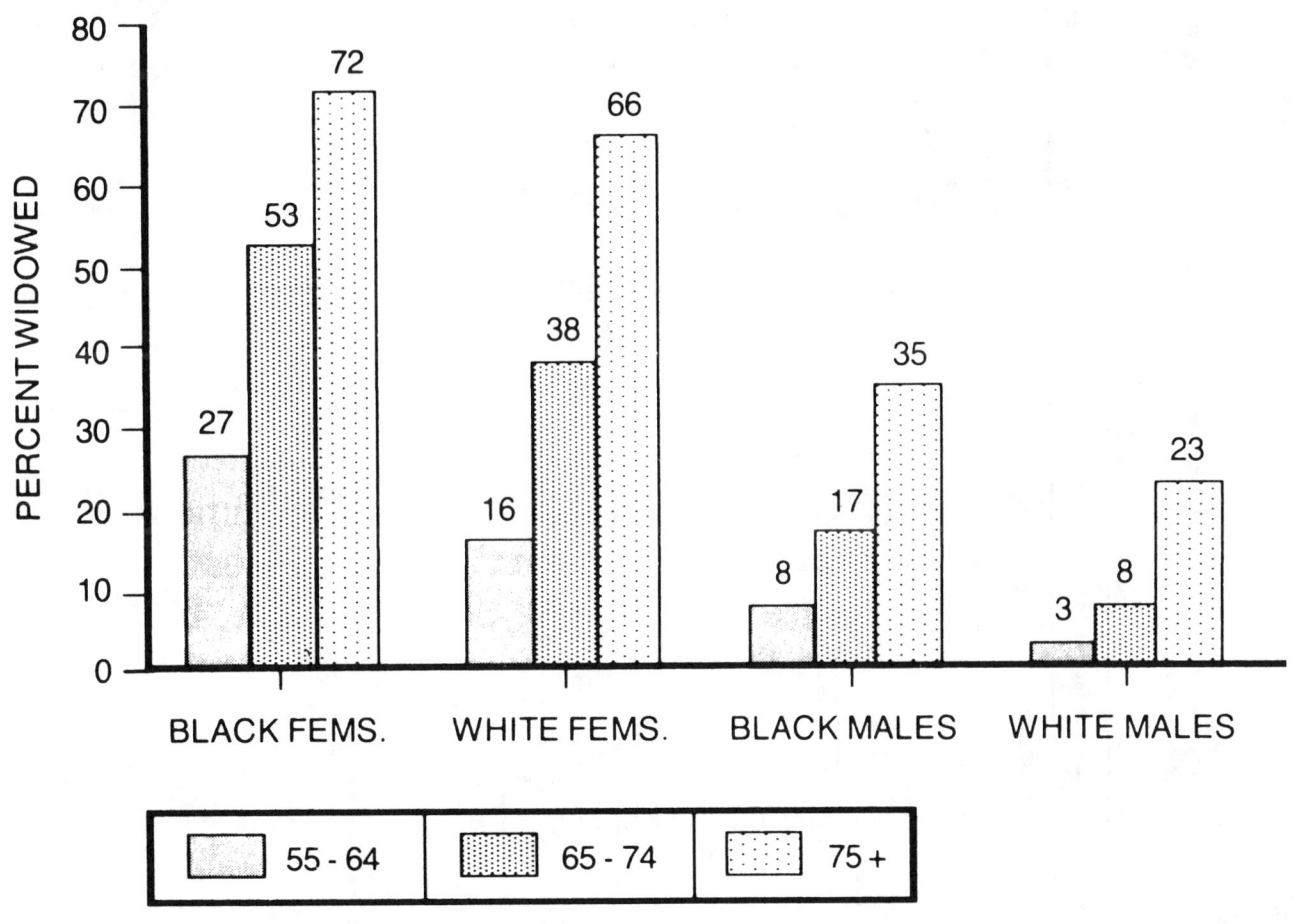

SOURCE: Bureau of the Census, CPS, Series P-20, No. 389.

B1–14. Marriage Rates by Previous Marital Status and Age of Bride and Groom: Marriage-Registration Area, 1981

[Based on sample data. Marriages of persons under 15 years of age are included in the total and in the youngest age group. Rates per 1,000 male and female population of specified age and previous marital status residing in area. Figures exclude data for Iowa. Figures for widowed and divorced, but not all previously married, exclude data for Michigan, Ohio, and South Carolina. Figures for all marriages include previous marital status not stated; previously married include widowed or divorced not stated.]

Previous marital status and age	Bride	Groom
ALL MARRIAGES		
15 years and over	54.3	66.8
15-17 years	19.1	2.9
18-19 years	83.8	36.9
20-24 years	121.7	96.0
25-44 years	99.9	118.3
25-29 years	129.2	129.4
30-34 years	98.2	119.8
35-44 years	65.9	98.7
45-64 years	17.8	51.4
65 years and over	2.2	14.8
SINGLE		
15 years and over	64.9	53.8
15-17 years	18.7	2.9
18-19 years	80.7	36.2
20-24 years	110.0	89.6
25-44 years	79.3	83.7
25-29 years	102.8	106.5
30-34 years	62.7	70.8
35-44 years	31.6	35.5
45-64 years	7.9	12.5
65 years and over	0.9	2.8

Previous marital status and age	Bride	Groom
PREVIOUSLY MARRIED		
15 years and over	39.9	112.5
15-24 years	280.0	323.0
25-44 years	119.7	198.1
25-29 years	193.5	257.5
30-34 years	128.3	216.3
35-44 years	79.8	159.8
45-64 years	19.9	74.2
65 years and over	2.3	18.5
Widowed, 15 years and over	8.5	30.8
15-44 years	48.4	116.7
45-64 years	12.0	53.9
65 years and over	2.0	16.9
Divorced, 15 years and over	96.3	150.8
15-24 years	282.2	319.7
25-44 years	129.1	197.9
25-29 years	202.6	256.6
30-34 years	133.8	217.2
35-44 years	88.2	158.7
45-64 years	30.2	82.6
65 years and over	5.7	23.0

B2. EDUCATION

B2-1. Educational Attainment by Age, 1981

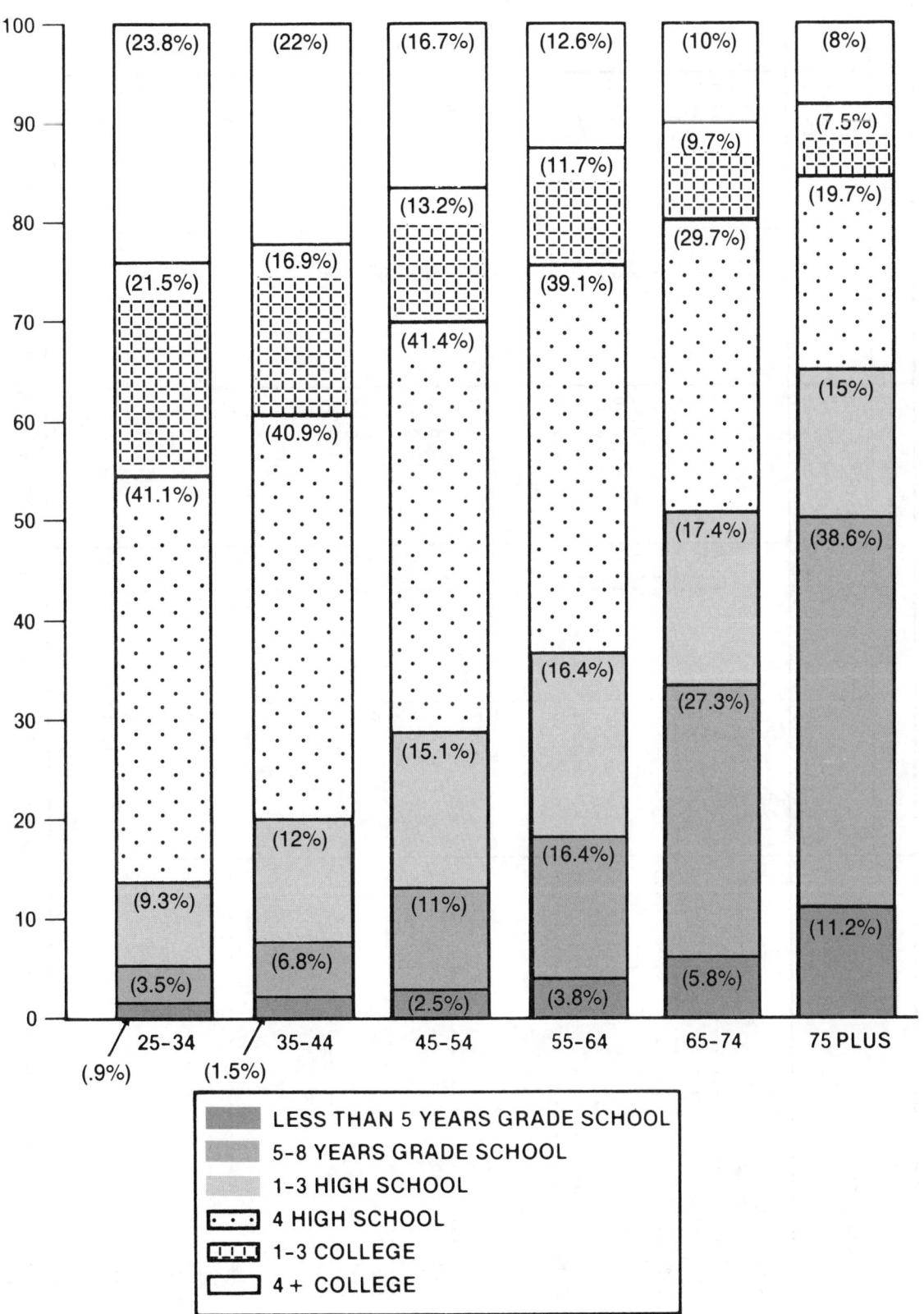

B2–2. Educational Attainment of the Population 65 Years and Over and 25 Years and Over, by Sex: 1959 to 2000

(Figures are for March of year indicated. Base date of projections is March 1979)

Sex and year	Median school years completed			Percent high school graduates		
	65 years and over	25 years and over	Ratio, 65 and over to 25 and over	65 years and over	25 years and over	Ratio, 65 and over to 25 and over
BOTH SEXES						
1959	8.3	11.0	0.75	19.4	42.9	0.45
1965	8.5	11.8	0.72	23.5	49.0	0.48
1970	8.7	12.2	0.71	28.3	55.2	0.51
1975	9.0	12.3	0.73	35.2	62.5	0.56
1981	10.3	12.5	0.82	41.8	69.7	0.60
1985	11.3	12.6	0.90	46.2	72.3	0.64
1990	12.1	12.7	0.95	53.3	75.6	0.71
1995	12.2	12.7	0.96	58.4	78.2	0.75
2000	12.4	12.8	0.97	63.7	80.4	0.79
MALE						
1959	8.2	10.7	0.77	18.1	41.3	0.44
1965	8.3	11.7	0.71	21.8	48.0	0.45
1970	8.6	12.2	0.70	25.9	55.0	0.47
1975	8.9	12.4	0.72	33.4	63.1	0.53
1981	10.1	12.6	0.80	40.8	70.3	0.58
1985	11.0	12.7	0.87	45.0	73.2	0.61
1990	12.1	12.8	0.95	52.7	76.7	0.69
1995	12.2	12.9	0.95	57.8	79.4	0.73
2000	12.4	12.9	0.96	62.4	81.4	0.77
FEMALE						
1959	8.4	11.2	0.75	20.4	44.4	0.46
1965	8.6	12.0	0.72	24.7	49.9	0.49
1970	8.8	12.1	0.73	30.1	55.4	0.54
1975	9.3	12.3	0.76	36.5	62.1	0.59
1981	10.4	12.5	0.83	42.5	69.1	0.62
1985	11.5	12.5	0.94	47.0	71.4	0.66
1990	12.1	12.6	0.96	53.7	74.6	0.72
1995	12.2	12.6	0.97	58.8	77.1	0.77
2000	12.4	12.7	0.98	64.6	79.4	0.81

Source: U.S. Bureau of the Census, Current Population Reports, Series P–20, Nos. 45, 99, 158, 207, 295, and 356, and unpublished data.

B2–3. Educational Attainment of Persons Aged 65 and Older, 1965–1990

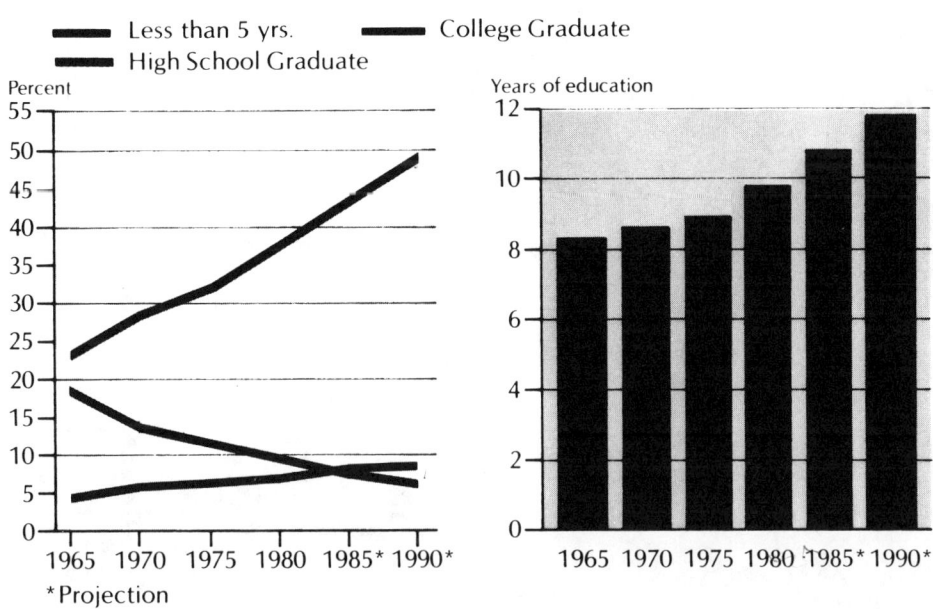

*Projection

B2-4. Educational Attainment by Age Group and Race, 1979

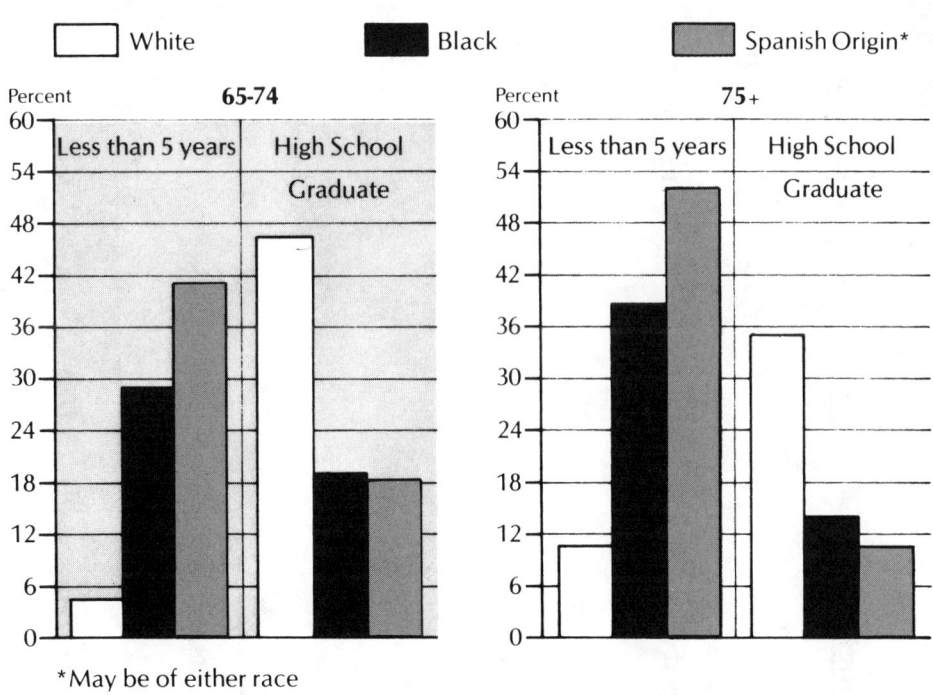

*May be of either race

Source: Bureau of the Census

B2-5. Years of School Completed by the Population 65 Years Old and Over, by Age, Sex, Race, and Spanish Origin: March 1980, and 1970

(Numbers in thousands. Noninstitutional population)

Age, Sex, Race and Spanish Origin	1980				1970			
	All persons	Percent completing . . .			All persons	Percent completing . . .		
		4 yrs. of high school or more	1 yr. of college or more	4 yrs. of college or more		4 yrs. of high school or more	1 yr. of college or more	4 yrs. of college or more
All Races 65 years old and over	23,743	40.7	16.7	8.5	19,713	28.3	12.6	6.3
Male 65 years old and over	9,783	39.1	17.7	10.2	8,364	25.9	13.4	7.9
Female 65 years old and over	13,960	41.8	15.9	7.3	11,349	30.1	11.9	5.2
White 65 years old and over	21,446	42.8	17.6	9.0	18,141	29.9	13.3	6.7
Black 65 years old and over	2,019	17.7	6.0	3.2	1,417	9.0	4.4	2.0
Spanish Origin[a] 65 years old and over	563	18.0	6.4	4.7	404	13.4	5.4	2.5

a. Persons of Spanish origin may be of any race.

Source: Adapted from Population Profile of the United States: 1980, Bureau of the Census, Series P-20, No. 363, Table 18, p. 25.

B2-6. Percent Literate for Persons 65 Years and Over and 14 Years and Over, by Race and by Nativity and Parentage: 1979

(Percentages are based on persons reporting on literacy and, hence, it is assumed that persons not reporting on literacy are distributed in the same proportion as persons who did report on literacy)

Age and literacy	Total[1]	Race		Nativity and parentage		
					Foreign birth or parentage	
		White	Black	Native of native parentage	Native of foreign parentage	Foreign born
65 years and over[2]...........	100.0	100.0	100.0	100.0	100.0	100.0
Reported able to read and write........	98.3	98.9	93.1	98.3	99.4	95.9
Reported unable to read and write.......	1.7	1.1	6.8	1.7	0.6	4.1
14 years old and over[2]...........	100.0	100.0	100.0	100.0	100.0	100.0
Reported able to read and write........	99.4	99.6	98.4	99.5	99.5	98.2
Reported unable to read and write.......	0.6	0.4	1.6	0.5	0.5	1.8

[1]Includes other races and persons not reporting nativity, not shown separately.
[2]About 4 percent of the population 65 years and over and about 3 1/2 percent of the population 14 years and over did not report on literacy.

Source: U.S. Bureau of the Census, Ancestry and Language, Current Population Reports, Series P-23, No. 116, table 8.

B2-7. Participation in Postsecondary Education, by Sex, Age Group, Race, Marital Status, and Labor Force Status: October 1982

(Numbers in thousands)

Item	Total population		Postsecondary participants		Percent of subgroup population in postsecondary education
	Number	Percent distribution	Number	Percent distribution	
Total population* ages 16+.........	172,882	100.0	18,206	100.0	10.5
Men	81,798	47.3	8,149	44.8	10.0
16-24	17,937	10.4	4,323	23.7	24.1
25-34	18,879	10.9	2,242	12.3	11.9
35-44	13,606	7.9	836	4.6	6.1
45-54	10,710	6.2	400	2.2	3.7
55-64	10,230	5.9	258	1.4	2.5
65+	10,431	6.0	91	0.5	1.0
Women	91,083	52.7	10,057	55.2	11.0
16-24	18,514	10.7	4,567	25.1	24.7
25-34	19,802	11.5	2,648	14.5	13.4
35-44	14,406	8.3	1,430	7.9	9.9
45-54	11,520	6.7	755	4.1	6.6
55-64	11,718	6.8	407	2.2	3.5
65+	15,123	8.7	249	1.4	1.6
White	149,834	86.7	15,863	87.1	10.6
Men	71,367	41.3	7,119	39.1	10.0
Women	78,465	45.4	8,744	48.0	11.1
Black	18,720	10.8	1,622	8.9	8.7
Men	8,333	4.8	640	3.5	7.7
Women	10,387	6.0	982	5.4	9.5
Other	4,322	2.5	720	4.0	16.7
Men	2,093	1.2	390	2.1	18.6
Women	2,230	1.3	330	1.8	14.8

B2-8. Distribution of Postsecondary Students, by Type of Education and by Sex, Race, Marital Status, Age Group, Labor Force Status, and Geographic Region: October 1982

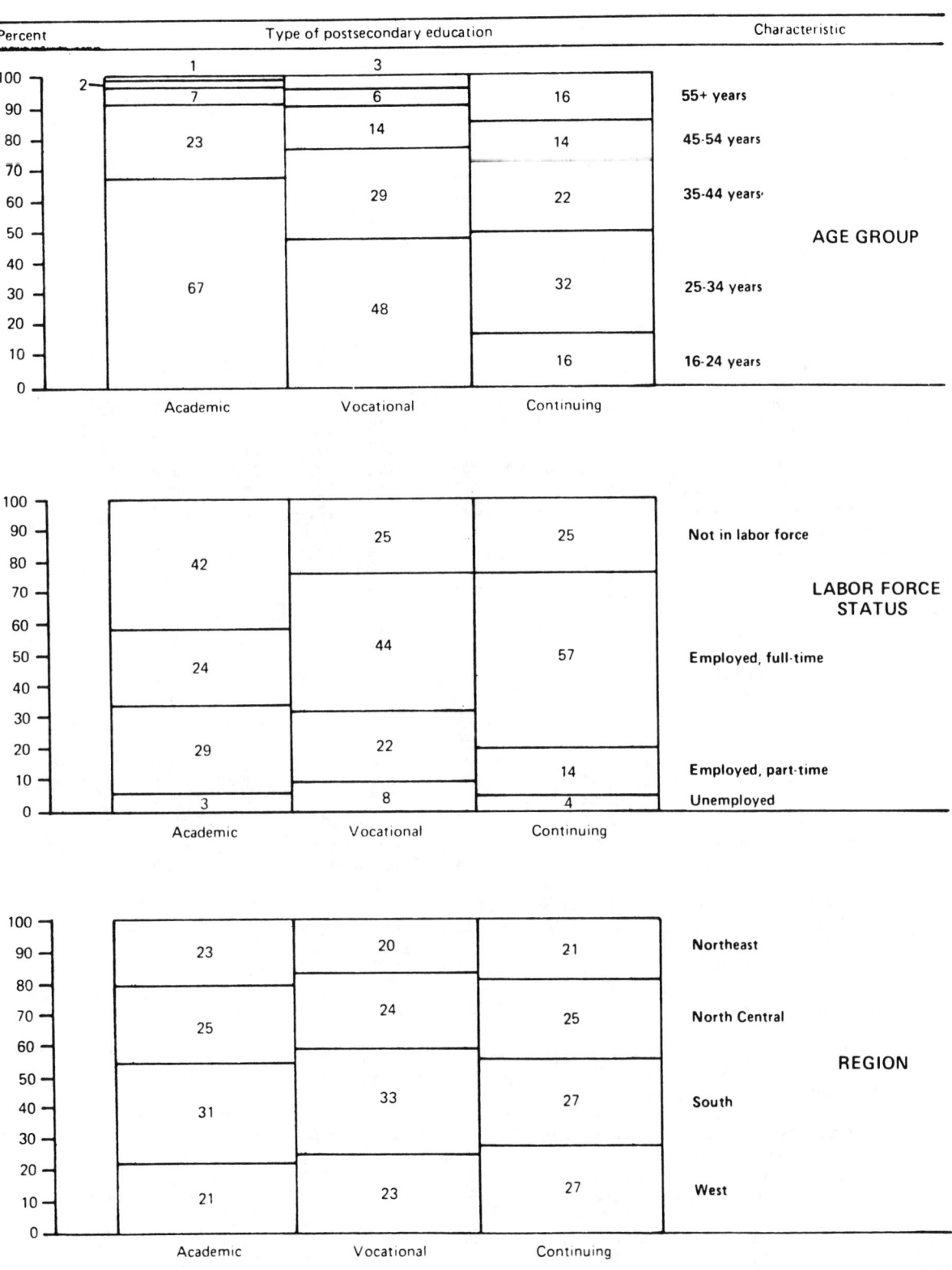

Note: Details may not add to total because of rounding.

B3. HOUSING, HOUSEHOLD COMPOSITION, INFORMAL SUPPORTS

B3-1. Characteristics of Households with Under-65 and 65+ Heads, 1980

Characteristics	Number (thousands)			Percent of total, all ages		Percent distribution	
	Heads all ages	Heads under 65	Heads 65+	Heads under 65	Heads 65+	Heads under 65	Heads 65+
Total households............	80,424	64,065	16,359	79.7	20.3	100.0	100.0
Tenure:							
Homeowner.................	52,803	40,965	11,838	77.6	22.4	63.9	72.4
Cash rent.................	25,927	21,870	4,057	84.4	15.6	34.1	24.8
No cash rent.............	1,695	1,230	465	72.6	27.4	1.9	2.8
Year structure built:							
After March 1970.........	18,399	16,333	2,066	88.8	11.2	25.5	12.6
1965-March 1970..........	8,944	7,418	1,526	82.9	17.1	11.6	9.3
1960-1964.................	7,855	6,508	1,347	82.8	17.2	10.2	8.2
1950-1959.................	13,483	10,743	2,740	79.7	20.3	16.8	16.7
1940-1949.................	7,457	5,372	2,085	72.0	28.0	8.4	12.7
Before 1940..............	24,287	17,692	6,594	72.8	27.2	27.6	40.3
Units in structure:							
1.........................	55,114	43,989	11,125	79.8	20.2	68.7	68.0
2-4.......................	9,707	7,727	1,981	79.6	20.4	12.1	12.1
5+.......................	11,723	9,307	2,417	79.4	20.6	14.5	14.8
In mobile home.............	3,879	3,043	836	78.4	21.6	4.7	5.1
In hotel or rooming house..	316	239	76	75.9	24.1	0.4	0.5
Number of bathrooms:							
None or shared...........	1,755	1,178	577	67.1	32.9	1.8	3.5
1 but separated..........	328	240	88	73.3	26.7	0.4	0.5
1	47,094	36,157	10,936	76.8	23.2	56.4	66.9
1.5	11,329	9,248	2,081	81.6	18.4	14.4	12.7
2	14,011	11,868	2,143	84.7	15.3	18.5	13.1
2.5+	5,907	5,372	535	90.9	9.1	8.4	3.3
Type of heating equipment:							
Central...................	43,790	36,086	7,704	82.4	17.6	56.3	47.1
Steam....................	13,629	10,533	3,096	77.3	22.7	16.4	18.9
Electric.................	5,876	4,756	1,120	80.9	19.1	7.4	6.8
Floor/Wall...............	6,300	4,885	1,416	77.5	22.5	7.6	8.7
Room heater..............	4,049	2,764	1,284	68.3	31.7	4.3	7.8
Other/Inadequate........	6,781	5,041	1,740	74.3	25.7	7.9	10.6
Air conditioned............	46,118	37,285	8,832	80.8	19.2	58.2	54.0
Water source:							
Public/Private system...	67,512	53,731	13,781	79.6	20.4	83.9	84.2
Individual well..........	11,832	9,509	2,323	80.4	19.6	14.8	14.2
Other....................	1,080	826	255	76.4	23.6	1.3	1.6
Electricity connected......	80,268	63,956	16,312	79.7	20.3	99.8	99.7
Type of sewage disposal:							
Public sewer.............	59,069	47,129	11,940	79.8	20.2	73.5	73.0
Septic tank/Cesspool....	20,641	16,494	4,147	79.9	20.1	25.7	25.3
Chemical toilet.........	16	10	6	60.5	39.5	0	0
Privy....................	589	368	220	62.6	37.4	0.6	1.3
Other....................	109	64	46	58.1	41.9	0.1	0.3

B3-2. United States—Age of Householder, Presence of Persons 65 Years Old and Over, and Location of Present Unit by Tenure of Present and Previous Unit: 1981

(NUMBERS IN THOUSANDS. DATA BASED ON SAMPLE, SEE TEXT. FOR MINIMUM BASE FOR DERIVED FIGURES (PERCENT, MEDIAN, ETC.) AND MEANING OF SYMBOLS, SEE TEXT)

PREVIOUS AND PRESENT UNIT: TENURE	PRESENT UNIT: AGE OF HOUSEHOLDER, PRESENCE OF PERSONS 65 YEARS OLD AND OVER, AND LOCATION									
	AGE OF HOUSEHOLDER							UNITS WITH PERSONS 65 YEARS OLD AND OVER		
	TOTAL	UNDER 25 YEARS	25 TO 29 YEARS	30 TO 34 YEARS	35 TO 44 YEARS	45 TO 64 YEARS	65 YEARS AND OVER	TOTAL	NONE	1 OR MORE
UNITED STATES										
UNITS OCCUPIED BY RECENT MOVERS	14 637	3 856	3 258	2 401	2 318	2 021	784	14 637	13 720	917
SAME HOUSEHOLDER IN PRESENT AND PREVIOUS UNIT	10 934	2 150	2 462	1 979	1 940	1 744	658	10 934	10 157	776
PREVIOUS UNIT OWNER OCCUPIED:										
PRESENT UNIT OWNER OCCUPIED	1 747	82	230	381	457	458	140	1 747	1 569	178
PRESENT UNIT RENTER OCCUPIED	1 567	226	293	298	313	315	122	1 567	1 428	139
PREVIOUS UNIT RENTER OCCUPIED:										
PRESENT UNIT OWNER OCCUPIED	1 467	207	423	309	270	204	53	1 467	1 397	71
PRESENT UNIT RENTER OCCUPIED	6 152	1 634	1 517	990	901	767	343	6 152	5 763	389
DIFFERENT HOUSEHOLDER IN PRESENT AND PREVIOUS UNIT	3 703	1 705	795	422	377	277	126	3 703	3 563	141
INSIDE STANDARD METROPOLITAN STATISTICAL AREAS										
UNITS OCCUPIED BY RECENT MOVERS	10 481	2 734	2 414	1 721	1 634	1 423	555	10 481	9 834	647
SAME HOUSEHOLDER IN PRESENT AND PREVIOUS UNIT	7 816	1 530	1 795	1 410	1 371	1 233	478	7 816	7 259	557
PREVIOUS UNIT OWNER OCCUPIED:										
PRESENT UNIT OWNER OCCUPIED	1 086	38	153	250	289	275	79	1 086	985	101
PRESENT UNIT RENTER OCCUPIED	1 062	162	198	201	207	204	89	1 062	966	96
PREVIOUS UNIT RENTER OCCUPIED:										
PRESENT UNIT OWNER OCCUPIED	992	121	281	220	190	151	29	992	946	46
PRESENT UNIT RENTER OCCUPIED	4 677	1 209	1 162	738	685	602	281	4 677	4 362	314
DIFFERENT HOUSEHOLDER IN PRESENT AND PREVIOUS UNIT	2 665	1 204	619	312	263	190	77	2 665	2 575	90
IN CENTRAL CITIES										
UNITS OCCUPIED BY RECENT MOVERS	5 060	1 374	1 105	831	732	728	289	5 060	4 724	336
SAME HOUSEHOLDER IN PRESENT AND PREVIOUS UNIT	3 722	792	818	664	590	608	249	3 722	3 437	285
PREVIOUS UNIT OWNER OCCUPIED:										
PRESENT UNIT OWNER OCCUPIED	278	8	34	79	62	69	26	278	246	31
PRESENT UNIT RENTER OCCUPIED	483	81	92	85	89	98	33	483	445	38
PREVIOUS UNIT RENTER OCCUPIED:										
PRESENT UNIT OWNER OCCUPIED	365	48	87	96	54	70	11	365	349	17
PRESENT UNIT RENTER OCCUPIED	2 596	655	606	403	385	372	175	2 596	2 397	199
DIFFERENT HOUSEHOLDER IN PRESENT AND PREVIOUS UNIT	1 338	582	287	168	142	120	40	1 338	1 287	51
NOT IN CENTRAL CITIES										
UNITS OCCUPIED BY RECENT MOVERS	5 421	1 360	1 309	890	902	694	266	5 421	5 110	312
SAME HOUSEHOLDER IN PRESENT AND PREVIOUS UNIT	4 095	738	977	746	781	624	228	4 095	3 822	272
PREVIOUS UNIT OWNER OCCUPIED:										
PRESENT UNIT OWNER OCCUPIED	808	30	120	171	227	207	53	808	738	70
PRESENT UNIT RENTER OCCUPIED	578	81	106	116	118	107	51	578	521	58
PREVIOUS UNIT RENTER OCCUPIED:										
PRESENT UNIT OWNER OCCUPIED	627	74	194	124	136	81	18	627	598	29
PRESENT UNIT RENTER OCCUPIED	2 081	553	557	335	300	230	106	2 081	1 965	116
DIFFERENT HOUSEHOLDER IN PRESENT AND PREVIOUS UNIT	1 327	622	332	144	121	70	37	1 327	1 287	39
OUTSIDE STANDARD METROPOLITAN STATISTICAL AREAS										
UNITS OCCUPIED BY RECENT MOVERS	4 156	1 122	843	680	683	598	229	4 156	3 886	270
SAME HOUSEHOLDER IN PRESENT AND PREVIOUS UNIT	3 117	620	667	569	569	512	180	3 117	2 898	219
PREVIOUS UNIT OWNER OCCUPIED:										
PRESENT UNIT OWNER OCCUPIED	662	44	76	131	167	183	60	662	585	77
PRESENT UNIT RENTER OCCUPIED	505	64	95	97	106	110	33	505	462	43
PREVIOUS UNIT RENTER OCCUPIED:										
PRESENT UNIT OWNER OCCUPIED	475	86	142	89	80	53	25	475	450	25
PRESENT UNIT RENTER OCCUPIED	1 475	426	354	252	216	165	62	1 475	1 401	74
DIFFERENT HOUSEHOLDER IN PRESENT AND PREVIOUS UNIT	1 039	502	176	110	115	87	49	1 039	988	51

B3–3. United States—Selected Characteristics of All Occupied Housing Units and of Units Occupied by Recent Movers: 1981

(NUMBERS IN THOUSANDS. DATA BASED ON SAMPLE, SEE TEXT. FOR MINIMUM BASE FOR DERIVED FIGURES (PERCENT, MEDIAN, ETC.) AND MEANING OF SYMBOLS, SEE TEXT)

CHARACTERISTICS	ALL OCCUPIED HOUSING UNITS					HOUSING UNITS OCCUPIED BY RECENT MOVERS				
		INSIDE SMSA'S					INSIDE SMSA'S			
	TOTAL	TOTAL	IN CENTRAL CITIES	NOT IN CENTRAL CITIES	OUTSIDE SMSA'S	TOTAL	TOTAL	IN CENTRAL CITIES	NOT IN CENTRAL CITIES	OUTSIDE SMSA'S
ALL OCCUPIED HOUSING UNITS										
PERSONS										
OWNER OCCUPIED	54 342	34 788	12 214	22 574	19 555	3 775	2 408	752	1 656	1 367
1 PERSON	8 515	5 358	2 322	3 035	3 158	527	342	121	221	185
2 PERSONS	17 783	11 211	4 103	7 108	6 572	1 226	847	269	578	379
3 PERSONS	9 856	6 377	2 051	4 327	3 479	789	470	145	325	319
4 PERSONS	10 294	6 722	2 053	4 669	3 572	736	447	114	334	289
5 PERSONS	4 944	3 169	941	2 228	1 775	330	192	56	136	138
6 PERSONS	1 845	1 226	441	785	620	105	65	22	43	40
7 PERSONS OR MORE	1 105	725	302	424	379	62	45	24	21	17
MEDIAN	2.6	2.6	2.4	2.8	2.5	2.7	2.5	2.4	2.6	2.9
RENTER OCCUPIED	28 833	21 893	12 464	9 429	6 940	10 862	8 073	4 308	3 765	2 789
1 PERSON	10 149	7 931	4 891	3 040	2 217	3 416	2 692	1 605	1 087	724
2 PERSONS	8 329	6 436	3 473	2 963	1 892	3 366	2 530	1 249	1 281	837
3 PERSONS	4 605	3 359	1 813	1 546	1 246	1 995	1 419	713	706	575
4 PERSONS	3 124	2 297	1 199	1 099	827	1 204	846	412	433	358
5 PERSONS	1 469	1 025	593	433	444	544	346	200	146	199
6 PERSONS	613	440	252	188	173	183	135	69	66	48
7 PERSONS OR MORE	546	404	245	159	142	154	106	60	46	48
MEDIAN	2.0	2.0	1.9	2.1	2.2	2.1	2.0	1.9	2.1	2.3
PERSONS PER ROOM										
OWNER OCCUPIED	54 342	34 788	12 214	22 574	19 555	3 775	2 408	752	1 656	1 367
0.50 OR LESS	34 538	22 279	8 075	14 204	12 259	2 267	1 529	474	1 055	738
0.51 TO 1.00	18 300	11 677	3 795	7 881	6 623	1 383	814	253	562	569
1.01 TO 1.50	1 143	646	268	378	497	86	44	13	31	42
1.51 OR MORE	362	187	76	110	175	39	20	11	9	19
RENTER OCCUPIED	28 833	21 893	12 464	9 429	6 940	10 862	8 073	4 308	3 765	2 789
0.50 OR LESS	16 293	12 324	6 888	5 436	3 969	5 771	4 321	2 209	2 112	1 450
0.51 TO 1.00	10 746	8 199	4 703	3 496	2 546	4 464	3 297	1 808	1 489	1 167
1.01 TO 1.50	1 258	961	583	378	297	430	305	187	119	125
1.51 OR MORE	537	409	290	119	128	198	150	105	45	48
HOUSEHOLD COMPOSITION BY AGE OF HOUSEHOLDER										
OWNER OCCUPIED	54 342	34 788	12 214	22 574	19 555	3 775	2 408	752	1 656	1 367
2-OR-MORE-PERSON HOUSEHOLDS	45 827	29 430	9 892	19 539	16 397	3 248	2 066	631	1 435	1 182
MARRIED-COUPLE FAMILIES, NO NONRELATIVES	36 137	24 892	7 975	16 916	14 246	2 711	1 697	507	1 190	1 014
UNDER 25 YEARS	887	431	137	294	456	314	166	46	120	148
25 TO 29 YEARS	3 127	1 885	630	1 255	1 242	576	364	105	259	211
30 TO 34 YEARS	4 747	3 090	961	2 129	1 657	606	408	147	261	198
35 TO 44 YEARS	8 538	5 603	1 541	4 061	2 936	595	377	88	269	217
45 TO 64 YEARS	15 330	10 119	3 349	6 770	5 211	504	318	94	224	186
65 YEARS AND OVER	6 508	3 764	1 356	2 408	2 744	116	63	27	36	53
OTHER MALE HOUSEHOLDER	2 257	1 555	607	948	703	265	180	58	122	85
UNDER 45 YEARS	1 086	753	278	475	333	210	139	42	98	70
45 TO 64 YEARS	771	556	222	334	214	44	33	15	18	11
65 YEARS AND OVER	400	246	107	138	155	11	8	2	6	4
OTHER FEMALE HOUSEHOLDER	4 433	2 984	1 309	1 674	1 449	272	189	66	123	83
UNDER 45 YEARS	1 752	1 183	493	690	569	205	142	45	97	63
45 TO 64 YEARS	1 673	1 183	505	678	490	45	31	13	19	14
65 YEARS AND OVER	1 008	618	311	306	390	23	16	8	8	6
1-PERSON HOUSEHOLDS	8 515	5 358	2 322	3 035	3 158	527	342	121	221	185
MALE HOUSEHOLDER	2 901	1 917	777	1 140	984	301	217	73	144	84
UNDER 45 YEARS	1 122	802	300	502	320	223	158	52	106	65
45 TO 64 YEARS	830	555	228	326	275	66	51	21	30	15
65 YEARS AND OVER	949	561	249	311	389	12	8	–	8	4
FEMALE HOUSEHOLDER	5 614	3 440	1 545	1 896	2 174	226	124	47	77	101
UNDER 45 YEARS	520	376	160	215	145	90	63	26	37	27
45 TO 64 YEARS	1 572	990	455	534	582	69	28	12	16	41
65 YEARS AND OVER	3 522	2 075	929	1 146	1 447	67	34	9	25	33
RENTER OCCUPIED	28 833	21 893	12 464	9 429	6 940	10 862	8 073	4 308	3 765	2 789
2-OR-MORE-PERSON HOUSEHOLDS	18 685	13 962	7 573	6 389	4 722	7 446	5 382	2 703	2 678	2 065
MARRIED-COUPLE FAMILIES, NO NONRELATIVES	10 822	7 709	3 801	3 908	3 113	4 108	2 837	1 261	1 575	1 271
UNDER 25 YEARS	1 822	1 251	547	704	571	1 173	824	351	463	349
25 TO 29 YEARS	2 380	1 667	759	908	713	1 091	748	320	428	343
30 TO 34 YEARS	1 701	1 174	571	603	527	654	443	194	248	211
35 TO 44 YEARS	1 741	1 273	646	627	468	591	396	182	215	195
45 TO 64 YEARS	2 115	1 528	836	692	587	466	320	157	163	146
65 YEARS AND OVER	1 063	816	442	374	247	132	105	48	58	26
OTHER MALE HOUSEHOLDER	2 418	1 903	1 046	856	516	1 238	931	495	436	307
UNDER 45 YEARS	1 967	1 553	811	742	415	1 134	857	446	411	277
45 TO 64 YEARS	330	263	181	82	68	89	64	46	19	25
65 YEARS AND OVER	121	87	55	32	34	15	10	3	6	5
OTHER FEMALE HOUSEHOLDER	5 444	4 350	2 726	1 625	1 094	2 101	1 614	947	667	487
UNDER 45 YEARS	4 046	3 254	2 008	1 246	791	1 846	1 414	811	603	432
45 TO 64 YEARS	988	802	520	282	185	213	169	112	57	44
65 YEARS AND OVER	411	294	198	97	116	41	30	23	7	11
1-PERSON HOUSEHOLDS	10 149	7 931	4 891	3 040	2 217	3 416	2 692	1 605	1 087	724
MALE HOUSEHOLDER	4 547	3 585	2 275	1 309	962	1 859	1 447	876	572	411
UNDER 45 YEARS	2 916	2 320	1 422	898	596	1 498	1 172	709	463	326
45 TO 64 YEARS	949	774	517	257	175	268	211	129	82	57
65 YEARS AND OVER	682	491	337	154	191	92	64	38	26	28
FEMALE HOUSEHOLDER	5 602	4 346	2 616	1 731	1 255	1 557	1 244	729	515	313
UNDER 45 YEARS	2 192	1 794	1 021	773	398	1 026	832	468	364	195
45 TO 64 YEARS	1 171	902	572	329	269	256	196	130	66	60
65 YEARS AND OVER	2 239	1 651	1 022	628	588	274	216	131	85	58

B3–4. Percentage of Women Heading Households: 1950 to 1980

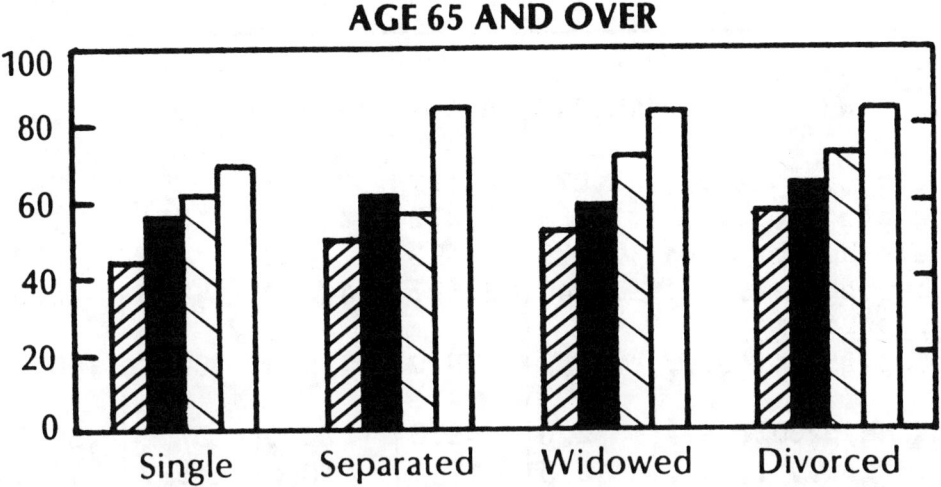

U.S. Bureau of the Census 1953: table 1; 1964; table 2; 1973; table 2; 1981b: table 6.

B3–5. Housing Costs as a Percentage of Household Income, by Age and Sex of Householder, 1984

	Median percentage by age							
	25 to 64	55 to 59	60 to 64	65 to 69	70 to 74	75 to 79	80 to 84	85 plus
Male:								
Rent	18.4	16.2	17.8	21.7	23.5	24.6	25.5	25.8
Own, with mortgage	18.1	13.9	15.6	20.5	24.0	27.6	30.5	33.4
Own, without mortgage	7.2	7.0	8.1	10.9	12.5	13.5	14.6	15.6
Female:								
Rent	27.2	25.9	27.2	29.8	30.8	31.4	31.7	31.8
Own, with mortgage	24.7	22.8	26.1	33.1	36.5	37.4	38.4	39.3
Own, without mortgage	13.1	12.8	14.6	17.5	19.1	20.5	21.4	22.3

SOURCE: U.S. Bureau of the Census, 1980 Census of Population and Housing, Public Use Microdata Sample, special tabulations.

B3–6. Housing Problems in Households Headed by Persons Aged 65+, 1978

Category	Total		Owners		Renters	
	All	Poor*	All	Poor*	All	Poor*
Number (thousands)						
Total occupied units...	15,844	8,607	11,283	5,372	4,561	3,235
With housing problems..	5,074	4,197	2,481	1,997	2,595	2,198
Inadequate..........	1,956	1,472	1,191	851	765	620
Adequate but crowded	79	28	50	13	30	15
Cost burdened**.....	3,040	2,697	1,240	1,133	1,800	1,563
Percent distribution						
Total occupied units...	100.0	100.0	100.0	100.0	100.0	100.0
With housing problems..	32.0	48.8	22.0	37.2	56.9	68.0
Inadequate..........	12.3	17.1	10.6	15.9	16.8	19.2
Adequate but crowded.	0.5	0.3	0.5	0.3	0.7	0.5
Cost burdened**......	19.2	31.3	11.0	21.1	39.5	48.3

* Family income is half or less of median family income adjusted for family size.

** Gross housing expenses greater than 30% of income (40% for owners with mortgages).

B3–7. Summary of HUD Elderly Housing Program Activities[1]

Sections and program	Status of program	Number of projects	Units	Mortgages	Elderly units	Percent of elderly units	Cum. fig. thru—
Unassisted programs:							
231—Mortgage insurance of housing for elderly	Active	495	65,900	$1,147,181,627	65,900	100.0	June 30, 1984.
221(d)(3), 221(d)(4)—Multifamily rental housing for low- and moderate-income families	do	3,611	364,398	6,030,755,185	25,798	7.0	Do.
207—Multifamily rental housing	do	6,696	722,182	19,042,503,043	101,713	14.0	Do.
		1,888	243,185	3,628,811,281	3,879	1.6	Do.
232—Nursing home and intermediate care facilities	do	1,453	174,126	2,347,559,517	174,126	100.0	Do.
Assisted programs:							
Title II—Low-income housing	do	14,994	469,008	NA	384,948	26.2	Do.
202—Direct loans for housing of elderly and handicapped	do	2,016	130,106	4,989,707,469	116,060	89.2	Do.
235*—Homeownership assistance for low- and moderate-income families	Inactive[3]	NA	473,033	8,456,660,790	66,224	14.0	Do.
	Active[3]	NA	117,089	4,409,450,088	3,981	3.4	Do.
236—Rental and co-op assistance for low- and moderate-income families	Inactive	4,058	435,669	7,557,569,585	56,128	12.8	Do.
202/236—202/236 conversion	do	182	28,591	487,075,452	28,591	100.0	Do.
8[4]—Low income rental assistance:							
Existing	Active	17,163	1,226,880	3,454,920,013	342,186	27.9	Do.
New construction	do	8,339	534,536	2,717,369,316	299,192	56.0	Do.
Substantial rehab	do	1,663	122,612	768,341,253	46,273	37.7	Do.
23—Low rent leased housing	Inactive	NA	163,267	NA	54,000+	35.0	December 1975.

[1] Figures obtained from Management Information Systems Division, Housing, Department of Housing and Urban Development.
[2] 235 figures are based on CY 1982 recertifications.
[3] Figures on inactive line are for original program; figures on active line are for revised program.
[4] Excludes 202/8 reservations.

B3–8. Contacts by Elderly with Surviving Children: United States, 1975

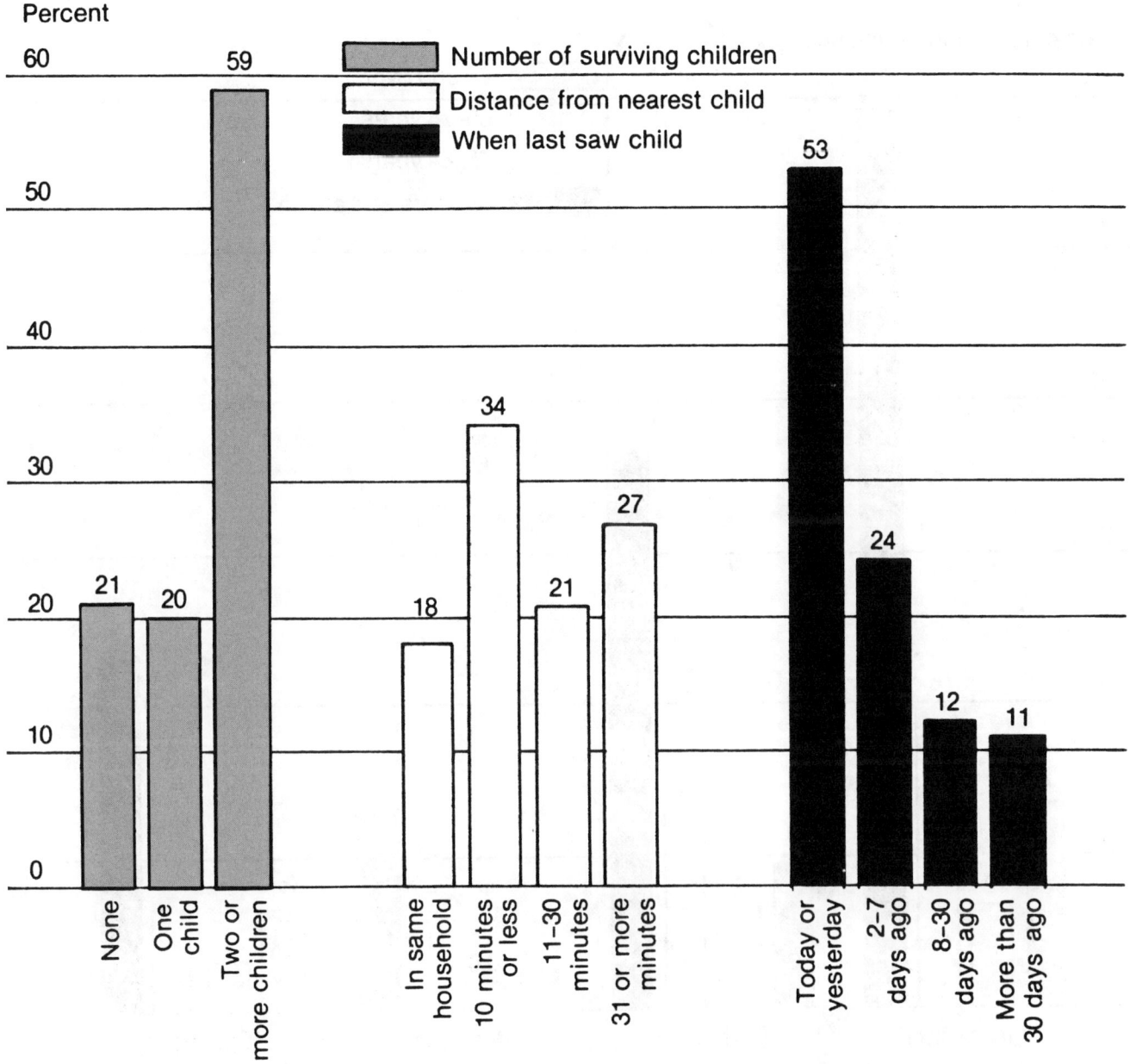

Percent

Note: Data on distance and frequency of contact exclude elderly persons with no surviving children.
Source: Administration on Aging.

B3-9. Percent of Elderly Needing Assistance in Four Activities of Daily Living by Age Groups: United States, 1978

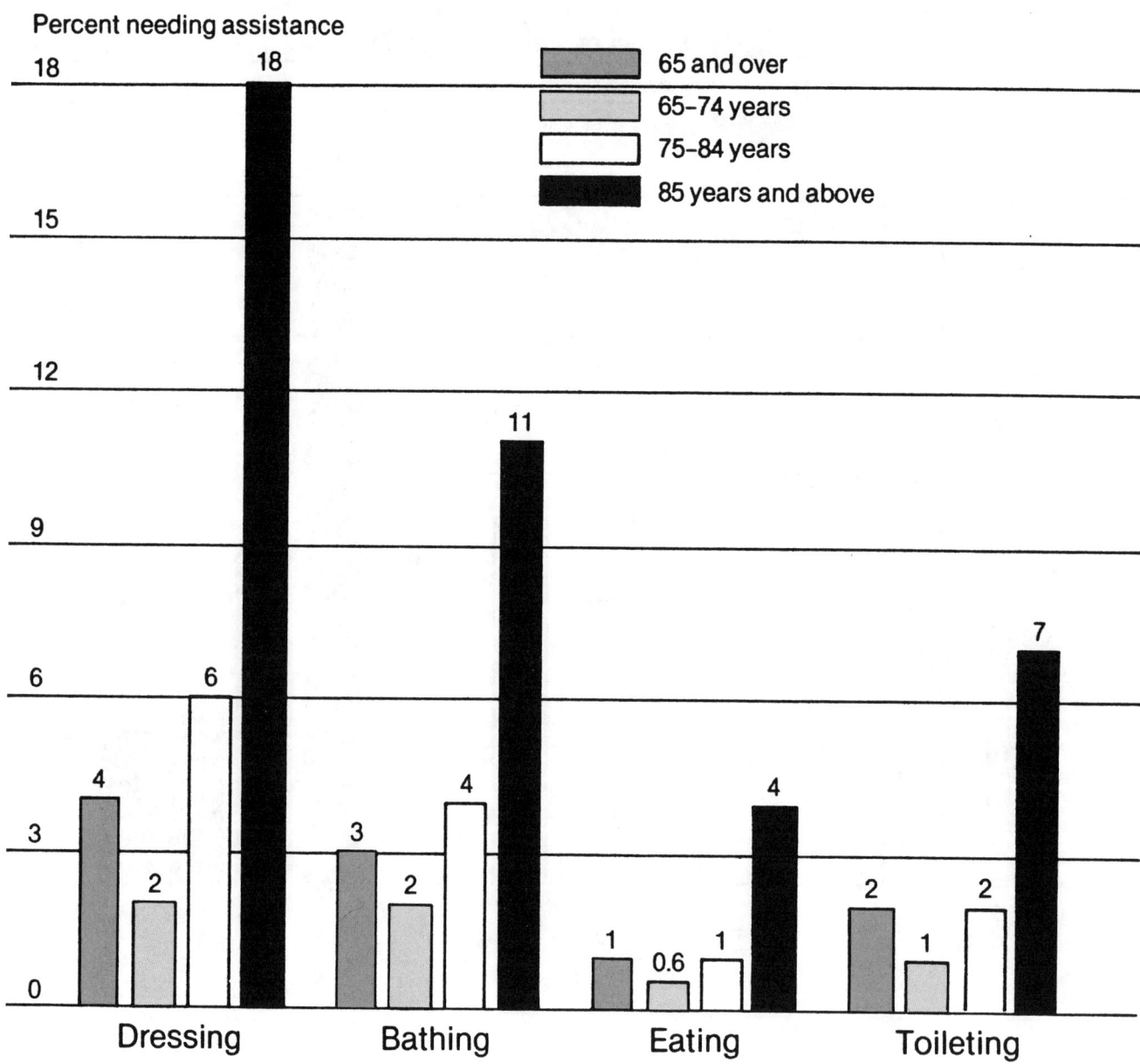

Note: Excludes elderly in institutions.
Source: National Center for Health Statistics.

B3-10. Persons 65 and Older Receiving Selected Home Services Provided by Family Members and Agencies, 1975

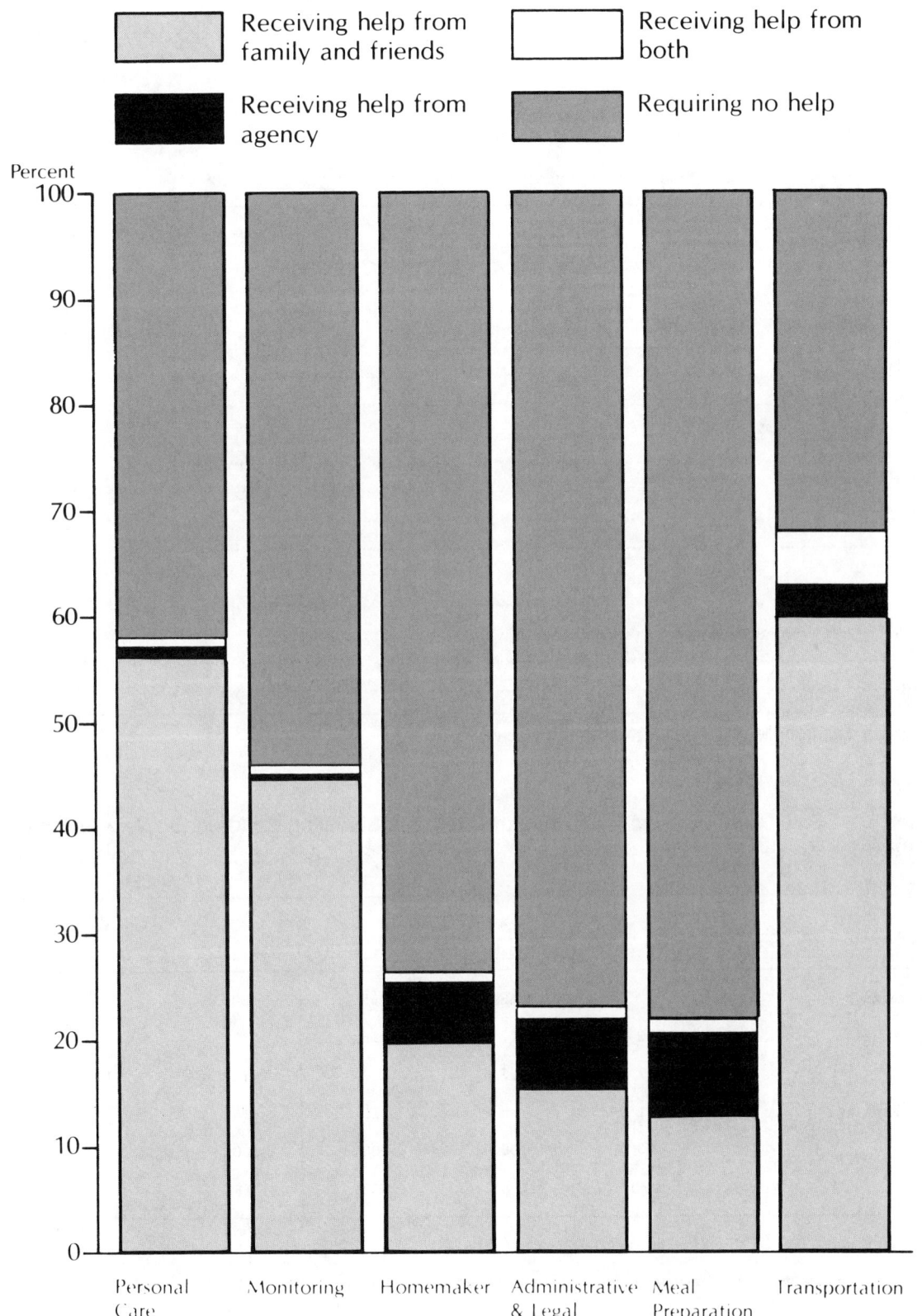

Source: General Accounting Office

B3-11. Percent Distributions of Caregivers by Relationship to 65 Plus Individual with Activity Limitations, 1982

	Care recipient	
	Male	Female
65 to 74:		
Spouse	45	18
Offspring	21	29
Other relative	21	33
Formal	13	20
75 to 84:		
Spouse	35	8
Offspring	23	35
Other relative	25	36
Formal	19	23
85+:		
Spouse	20	2
Offspring	34	39
Other relative	27	36
Formal	19	23
All 65+:		
Spouse	37	10
Offspring	24	34
Other relative	23	35
Formal	16	21

Source: Preliminary data from the 1982 National Long-Term Care Survey.

B3-12. When Last Saw Child, Persons Aged 65 and Over with Surviving Children, by Sex (Percentage Distribution), 1962 and 1975

When Last Saw Child	1962			1975		
	Men	Women	All	Men	Women	All
Today or yesterday[a]	62	68	65	50	54	53
2-7 days ago	20	17	18	23	25	24
8-30 days ago	7	7	7	13	12	12
More than 30 days ago	11	8	10	13	9	11
TOTAL	100	100	100	100	100	100
N =[b]	(896)	(1106)	(2002)	(1856)	(2696)	(4553)

[a]Includes persons who live in the same household with a child.

[b]The N (number) of cases for 1962 is unweighted; the number of cases for 1975 is weighted.

B3–13. Persons Aged 65 and Over Living with, Near, and at a Distance from their Children and Persons Aged 65 and Over with No Children Who Had Seen Their Doctor within Different Periods: 1975[a] (Percentage Distribution)

When Last Saw Doctor	Persons Sharing Household with Child		Living Within 10 Minutes Journey of Child		Living at a Distance of More Than 10 Minutes Journey		Persons with No Living Children	
	All	Ill in Bed During Past Year	All	Ill in Bed During Past Year	All	Ill in Bed During Past Year	All	Ill in Bed During Past Year
Within past month	36	44	36	52	32	48	28	52
Within past year[b]	48	50	44	42	50	44	50	45
More than 12 months ago or never	16	6	20	6	18	8	22	3
TOTAL	100	100	100	100	100	100	100	100
N (weighted) =	(781)	(265)	(1521)	(376)	(2138)	(569)	(1167)	(229)

[a]Excludes bedfast persons.

[b]Excludes within past month.

B3–14. Percentage of Persons Having Difficulty in Preparing Meals Who Receive Help from Different Sources[a]

Sources of Help[b]	Persons Having Difficulty with Meal Preparation[c]		
	Men	Women	All
Spouse	67	23	43
Child in household	12	33	23
Child outside household	3	6	5
Others in household	2	8	6
Others outside household[d]	6	14	11
Social services	0	0	0
None	8	15	12
TOTAL	100	100	100
N (weighted)=	(184)	(232)	(416)

[a]Excludes bedfast persons. Includes persons having difficulty and unable to do task.

[b]This is priority code. When more than one source of help was mentioned, the priority for coding used is the same as the order of the categories in the table; for example, when spouse was mentioned in combination with any other sources of help, the response was coded under spouse.

[c]The percentages of persons having difficulty with meal preparation are: total 8, men 8, and women 7.

[d]Includes private, domestic help as well as relatives, friends, neighbors, and others.

B4. SOCIAL ACTIVITIES: RELIGION, VOTING PATTERNS, VOLUNTEERISM, LEISURE ACTIVITIES

B4–1. Percent of Adults Who Are Church or Synagogue Members, by Age Group, 1979

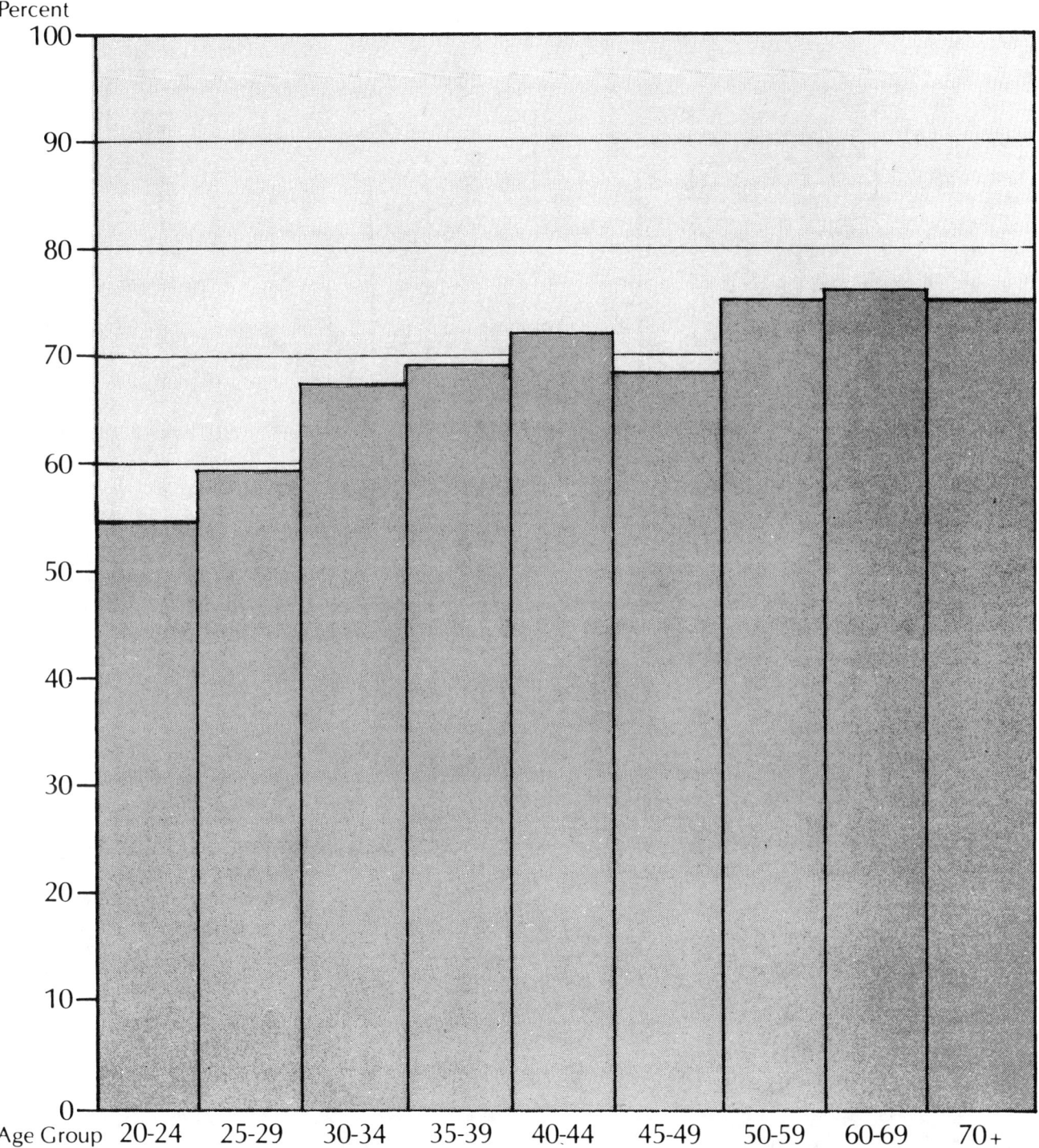

Source: Princeton Religion Research Center

B4–2. Spiritual Commitment of Older and Younger Persons, 1981

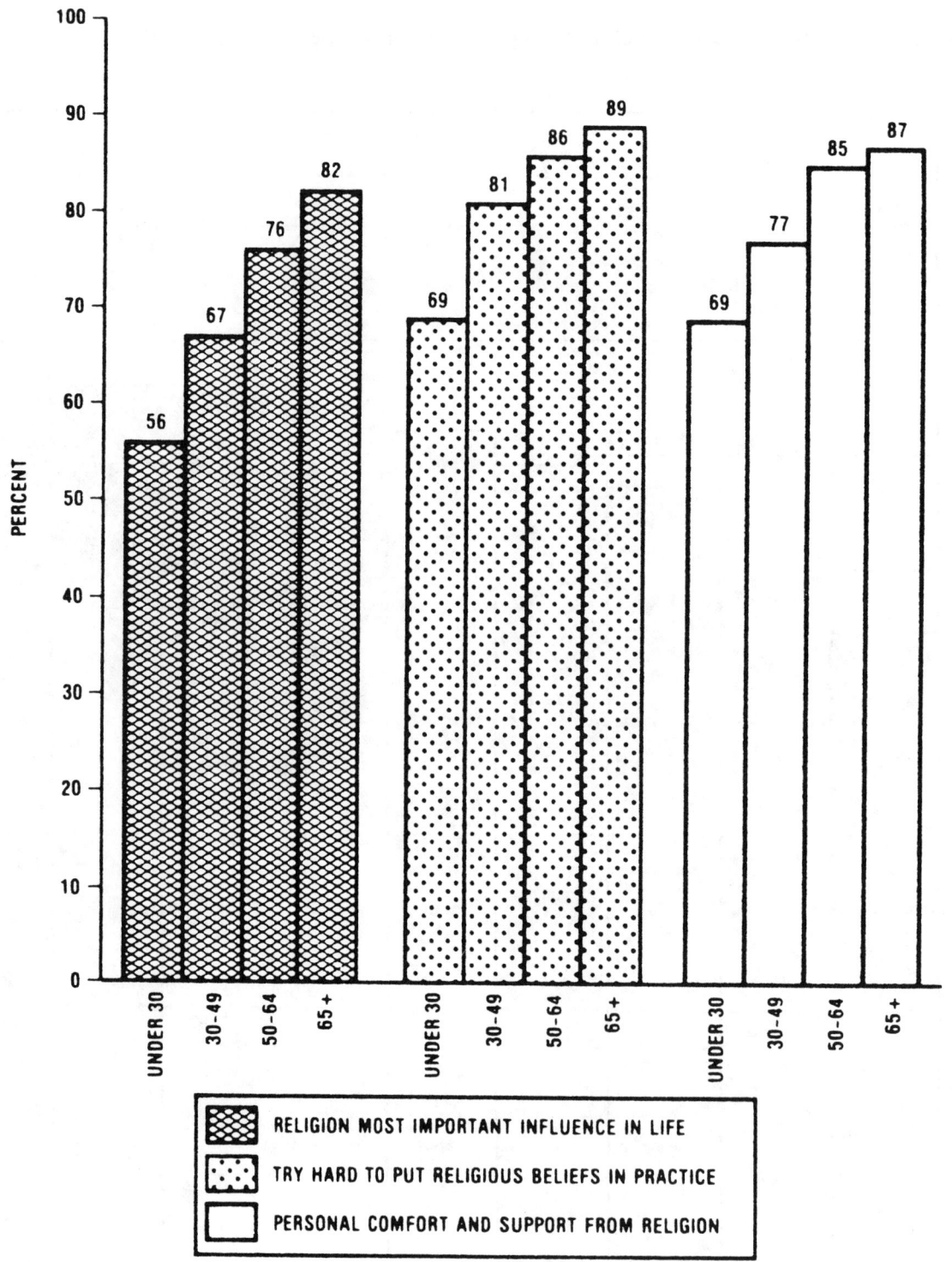

SOURCE: Religion in America 1982, The Gallup Report, Report Nos. 201-202, June-July,

B4-3. Religious Preference of the U.S. Population, by Age: 1977

Religion	Total	Under 20 years	20-24 years	25-34 years	35-44 years	45-64 years	65 years and over
Total, 18 years and over . . .	100.0	2.2	10.7	23.8	17.0	29.6	16.7
Protestant	100.0	1.9	9.5	21.4	16.9	31.4	18.9
Baptist.	100.0	2.4	11.4	23.2	17.5	29.3	16.3
Lutheran	100.0	1.1	8.9	21.0	17.7	33.6	17.8
Methodist.	100.0	1.7	6.8	19.1	15.0	34.7	22.8
Presbyterian	100.0	1.8	8.2	16.9	16.3	34.3	22.4
Episcopal-Anglican	100.0	1.7	6.6	21.3	15.4	34.8	20.1
Other Protestant	100.0	1.6	10.6	21.9	17.6	-29.4	19.0
Roman Catholic	100.0	2.6	11.6	25.9	17.5	29.0	13.5
Jewish	100.0	0.6	6.4	24.0	15.9	32.3	20.9
Other religion	100.0	2.9	18.2	29.2	17.7	23.0	9.1
No religion.	100.0	5.0	18.9	36.5	16.3	15.9	7.4

Source: The data for this table were tabulated from a dataset defined by the National Opinion Research Center. *General Social Surveys, 1972-83: Cumulative Codebook.* Chicago: National Opinion Research Center, University of Chicago, 1983.

B4-4. Percent Reported Voting in 1980 and 1982 Election by Age Group

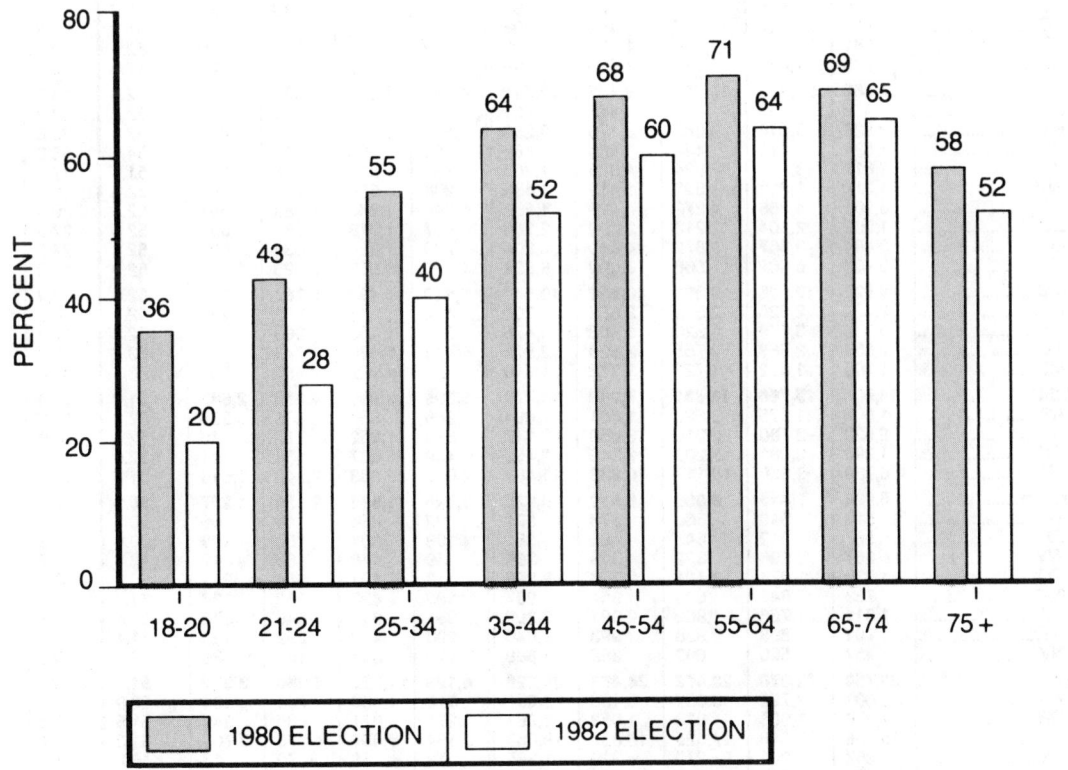

SOURCE: U.S. Bureau of the Census, Current Population Surveys, 1981 and 1983.

B4–5. Resident Population of Voting Age, 1976 to 1984, and by Selected Characteristics, 1980 and 1984—States

[In thousands, except percent. Estimated population, 18 years old and over, as of November, except as noted. Includes Armed Forces stationed in each State, aliens, and institutional population. For composition of regions see fig. 1 inside front cover]

REGION, DIVISION, AND STATE	1976	1978	1980	1982	1984 Total	18–24 years	25–44 years	45–64 years	65 yr. and over	Percent female of total	1980,[1] Black	Spanish origin[2]
U.S.	152,308	158,369	164,473	169,785	173,936	28,994	72,166	44,586	28,190	52.3	10.5	5.5
Region:												
Northeast	35,354	35,868	36,271	36,952	37,495	5,988	14,336	10,121	6,550	53.4	8.9	4.5
Midwest	40,248	41,373	42,177	42,735	43,035	7,231	17,626	10,917	7,261	52.4	8.1	1.8
South	49,113	51,645	54,504	57,079	59,153	10,053'	24,495	15,134	9,471	52.4	16.7	5.2
West	27,592	29,483	31,520	33,019	34,253	5,722	15,208	8,414	4,909	51.0	4.9	12.2
N.E	8,711	8,956	9,142	9,351	9,520	1,587	3,839	2,434	1,661	53.1	3.4	1.9
ME	759	791	810	830	848	138	338	220	153	52.4	.3	.4
NH	593	638	671	699	722	121	309	177	115	52.2	.4	.5
VT	337	353	370	381	391	68	169	91	63	52.3	.2	.6
MA	4,132	4,213	4,277	4,358	4,422	760	1,775	1,108	779	53.6	3.4	1.9
RI	689	707	709	723	733	124	280	191	139	53.5	2.5	1.8
CT	2,201	2,254	2,304	2,359	2,404	376	968	648	412	52.8	6.0	3.1
M.A.	26,643	26,912	27,130	27,601	27,974	4,401	10,997	7,686	4,889	53.4	10.7	5.4
NY	12,892	12,912	12,929	13,142	13,326	2,146	5,294	3,634	2,253	53.7	12.4	8.3
NJ	5,220	5,326	5,418	5,551	5,659	875	2,257	1,578	950	53.2	11.0	5.7
PA	8,531	8,673	8,783	8,909	8,989	1,381	3,446	2,475	1,686	53.3	8.1	1.0
E.N.C.	28,469	29,251	29,762	30,093	30,244	5,106	12,484	7,736	4,917	52.5	9.8	2.1
OH	7,461	7,638	7,738	7,818	7,846	1,290	3,201	2,068	1,287	52.8	9.2	.9
IN	3,692	3,812	3,890	3,942	3,969	681	1,633	1,015	640	52.5	6.8	1.3
IL	7,939	8,132	8,230	8,344	8,410	1,406	3,480	2,163	1,361	52.6	12.9	4.6
MI	6,214	6,406	6,529	6,543	6,530	1,129	2,755	1,632	1,014	52.2	11.7	1.4
WI	3,163	3,263	3,375	3,446	3,490	602	1,415	858	616	51.9	3.2	1.1
W.N.C	11,780	12,122	12,415	12,642	12,792	2,125	5,142	3,181	2,343	52.2	4.1	1.0
MN	2,726	2,823	2,931	3,001	3,044	525	1,279	720	520	51.8	1.1	.6
IA	2,026	2,075	2,097	2,113	2,119	335	838	534	412	52.4	1.2	.7
MO	3,408	3,499	3,576	3,636	3,682	608	1,446	942	686	53.0	9.3	.9
ND	442	455	466	480	491	83	201	119	88	50.0	.4	.5
SD	469	480	487	494	498	83	192	127	97	51.3	.3	.5
NE	1,081	1,108	1,130	1,151	1,163	192	467	288	216	52.1	2.6	1.4
KS	1,628	1,661	1,728	1,768	1,794	298	720	451	325	51.9	4.8	2.2
S.A	24,586	25,832	27,252	28,482	29,512	4,908	11,963	7,658	4,982	52.6	18.5	3.2
DE	412	426	431	445	457	85	186	118	68	52.8	14.2	1.3
MD	2,920	3,014	3,082	3,176	3,259	572	1,397	839	451	52.5	20.8	1.4
DC	525	515	494	489	482	85	208	115	74	54.8	65.8	2.8
VA	3,613	3,794	3,924	4,075	4,203	756	1,810	1,063	574	51.8	17.5	1.4
WV	1,314	1,363	1,398	1,419	1,433	208	580	387	257	52.6	3.2	.6
NC	3,907	4,088	4,272	4,429	4,559	794	1,888	1,183	694	52.5	20.3	.9
SC	1,993	2,104	2,213	2,309	2,386	437	1,018	597	335	52.4	27.3	1.0
GA	3,494	3,667	3,872	4,049	4,204	760	1,825	1,034	584	52.8	24.3	1.1
FL	6,408	6,862	7,566	8,090	8,529	1,210	3,052	2,323	1,945	52.9	11.3	8.5
E.S.C	9,624	10,048	10,392	10,658	10,861	1,840	4,433	2,787	1,802	52.8	17.4	.8
KY	2,434	2,528	2,594	2,654	2,700	462	1,115	683	440	52.1	6.6	.7
TN	3,033	3,179	3,320	3,408	3,476	567	1,436	903	570	52.8	14.2	.7
AL	2,554	2,669	2,755	2,823	2,875	485	1,160	749	482	53.2	12.9	.8
MS	1,603	1,672	1,722	1,772	1,810	325	722	452	309	53.1	31.0	.9
W.S.C	14,904	15,766	16,861	17,940	18,779	3,305	8,099	4,689	2,687	51.8	13.4	11.3
AR	1,502	1,575	1,626	1,661	1,694	266	657	435	336	52.8	14.1	.7
LA	2,623	2,760	2,916	3,050	3,147	583	1,352	777	436	52.4	26.6	2.3
OK	1,990	2,081	2,202	2,345	2,452	409	1,007	634	401	52.0	6.0	1.5
TX	8,789	9,350	10,117	10,883	11,487	2,047	5,083	2,843	1,514	51.5	11.1	17.7
Mt	6,834	7,413	8,058	8,537	8,928	1,529	3,984	2,158	1,257	50.9	2.2	10.9
MT	519	548	560	576	591	92	254	148	96	50.7	.2	1.0
ID	567	612	645	665	681	108	301	164	109	50.6	.3	3.2
WY	267	296	332	353	365	59	178	86	42	48.7	.7	4.4
CO	1,838	1,974	2,121	2,256	2,365	418	1,121	544	281	50.8	3.2	9.8
NM	783	841	899	951	997	182	428	250	136	51.4	1.7	33.1
AZ	1,611	1,766	1,962	2,091	2,200	361	914	548	376	51.4	2.5	13.3
UT	791	858	938	993	1,040	200	479	232	128	51.1	.7	3.6
NV	457	520	602	652	689	110	307	185	88	49.6	5.3	5.8
Pac	20,758	22,070	23,462	24,481	25,326	4,193	11,225	6,256	3,652	51.1	5.8	12.7
WA	2,601	2,792	3,037	3,136	3,202	510	1,438	760	494	50.9	2.4	2.3
OR	1,679	1,808	1,928	1,953	1,961	279	871	465	346	51.5	1.2	2.0
CA	15,598	16,546	17,525	18,357	19,063	3,194	8,391	4,775	2,703	51.3	7.1	16.1
AK	257	269	276	310	345	72	186	70	15	46.2	3.4	2.1
HI	624	657	696	725	755	135	336	187	94	48.7	1.9	6.0

[1] Based on enumerated population as of April 1.　　[2] Persons of Spanish origin may be of any race.

Source: U.S. Bureau of the Census, Current Population Reports, series P-25, Nos. 916 and 948.

B4–6. Reported Registration and Voting, by Age Group, November 1980
(Civilian noninstitutional population; numbers in thousands)

Status	18+ Number	18+ Per-cent	18–44 Number	18–44 Per-cent	45–64 Number	45–64 Per-cent	65+ Total Number	65+ Total Per-cent	65+ 65–74 Number	65+ 65–74 Per-cent	65+ 75+ Number	65+ 75+ Per-cent
All races												
Both sexes..........	157,085	100.0	89,423	100.0	43,569	100.0	24,094	100.0	15,324	100.0	8,770	100.0
Registered.........	105,035	66.9	54,039	60.4	33,029	75.8	17,960	74.6	11,835	77.2	6,133	69.9
Voted.............	93,066	59.2	47,183	52.8	30,205	69.3	15,677	65.1	10,622	69.3	5,055	57.6
Did not vote.....	11,969	7.6	6,856	7.7	2,824	6.5	2,290	9.5	1,213	7.9	1,077	12.3
Not registered*....	52,050	33.1	35,384	39.6	10,541	24.2	6,125	25.4	3,488	22.8	2,637	30.1
Not U.S. citizen.	6,343	4.0	4,420	4.9	1,345	3.1	580	2.4	340	2.2	240	2.7
Male.................	74,082	100.0	43,326	100.0	20,837	100.0	9,920	100.0	6,676	100.0	3,244	100.0
Registered.........	49,344	66.6	25,620	59.1	15,903	76.3	7,821	78.8	5,343	80.0	2,478	76.4
Voted.............	43,753	59.1	22,215	51.3	14,554	69.8	6,984	70.4	4,852	72.7	2,132	65.7
Did not vote.....	5,591	7.5	3,406	7.9	1,348	6.5	836	8.4	490	7.3	346	10.7
Not registered*....	24,738	33.4	17,705	40.9	4,934	23.7	2,098	21.1	1,333	20.0	765	23.6
Not U.S. citizen.	2,942	4.0	2,164	5.0	592	2.8	186	1.9	110	1.6	76	2.3
Female...............	83,003	100.0	46,097	100.0	22,732	100.0	14,174	100.0	8,648	100.0	5,526	100.0
Registered.........	55,691	67.1	28,418	61.6	17,126	75.3	10,147	71.6	6,493	75.1	3,654	66.1
Voted.............	49,312	59.4	24,967	54.2	15,651	68.9	8,694	61.3	5,770	66.7	2,924	52.9
Did not vote.....	6,378	7.7	3,449	7.5	1,475	6.5	1,454	10.3	723	8.4	731	13.2
Not registered*....	27,312	32.9	17,678	38.3	5,606	24.7	4,027	28.4	2,155	24.9	1,872	33.9
Not U.S. citizen.	3,402	4.1	2,255	4.9	752	3.3	394	2.8	230	2.7	164	3.0
White.................	137,676	100.0	77,225	100.0	38,703	100.0	21,748	100.0	13,789	100.0	7,959	100.0
Registered...........	94,112	68.4	47,898	62.0	29,808	77.0	16,406	75.4	10,755	78.0	5,651	71.0
Voted...............	83,855	60.9	42,143	54.6	27,365	70.7	14,347	66.0	9,669	70.1	4,678	58.8
Did not vote.......	10,257	7.5	5,756	7.5	2,443	6.3	2,058	9.5	1,085	7.9	973	12.2
Not registered*......	43,564	31.6	29,327	38.0	8,895	23.0	5,343	24.6	3,034	22.0	2,309	29.0
Not U.S. citizen...	4,762	3.5	3,260	4.2	1,038	2.7	463	2.1	263	1.9	200	2.5
Black.................	16,423	100.0	10,224	100.0	4,159	100.0	2,039	100.0	1,352	100.0	687	100.0
Registered...........	9,849	60.0	5,537	54.2	2,885	69.4	1,429	70.1	998	73.8	431	70.1
Voted...............	8,287	50.5	4,530	44.3	2,546	61.2	1,211	59.4	877	64.9	334	48.6
Did not vote.......	1,562	9.5	1,005	9.8	339	8.2	218	10.7	121	8.9	97	14.1
Not registered*......	6,574	40.0	4,688	45.9	1,275	30.7	610	29.9	354	30.7	256	37.3
Not U.S. citizen...	472	2.9	354	3.5	101	2.4	18	0.9	12	0.9	6	0.9
Spanish origin......**	8,210	100.0	5,074	100.0	1,798	100.0	538	100.0	349	100.0	189	100.0
Registered...........	2,984	36.3	1,837	31.3	910	50.6	237	44.1	160	45.8	77	40.7
Voted...............	2,453	29.9	1,408	25.3	768	42.7	198	36.8	141	40.4	57	30.2
Did not vote.......	531	6.5	348	5.9	143	8.0	40	7.4	20	5.7	20	10.6
Not registered*......	5,226	63.7	4,037	68.7	888	49.4	301	55.9	189	54.2	112	59.3
Not U.S. citizen...	2,645	32.2	1,987	33.8	489	27.2	168	31.2	115	33.0	53	28.0

* Includes "not known" and "unreported".

** May be of any race.

B4–7. Daily Adult Television and Newspaper Usage, 1979

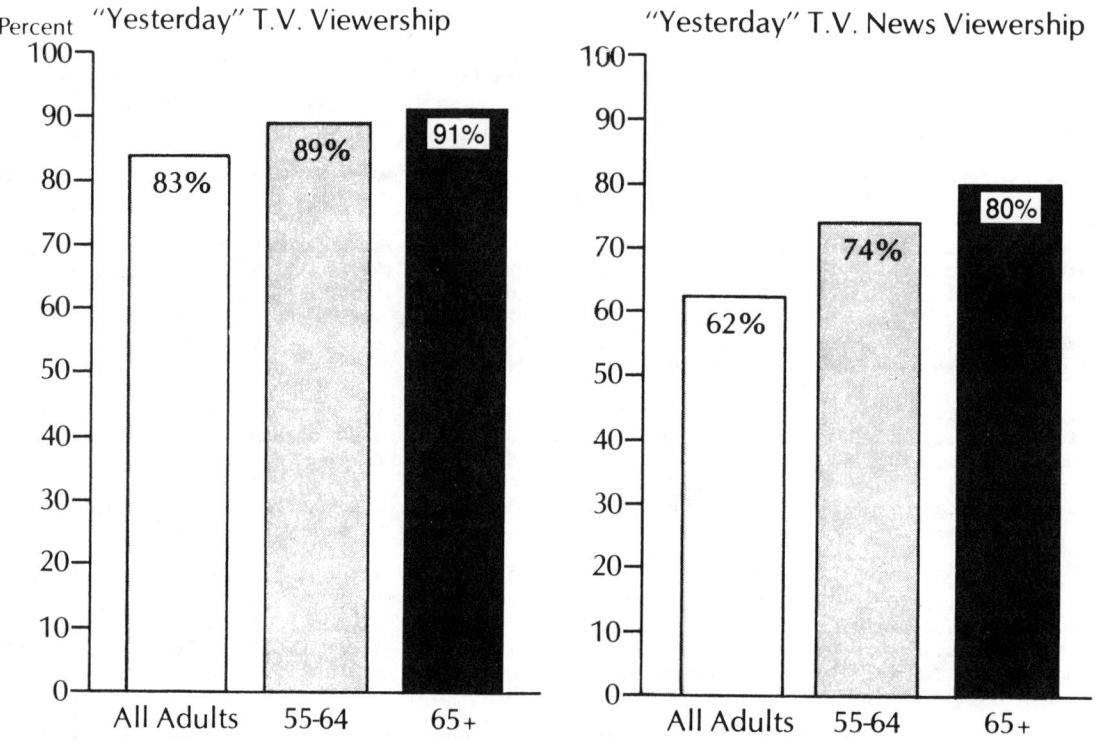

B4–8. Daily Adult Newspaper Readership

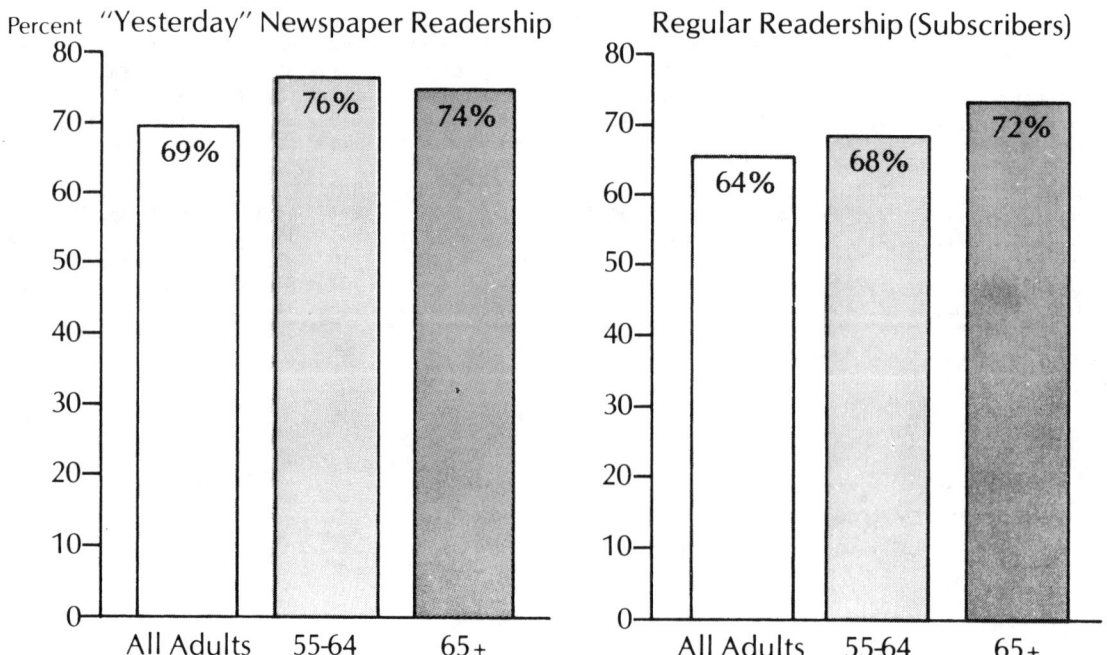

Source: Newspaper Advertising Bureau

B4–9. Percent of Persons 65 and Older Reporting Specific Leisure-Time Activities, 1980

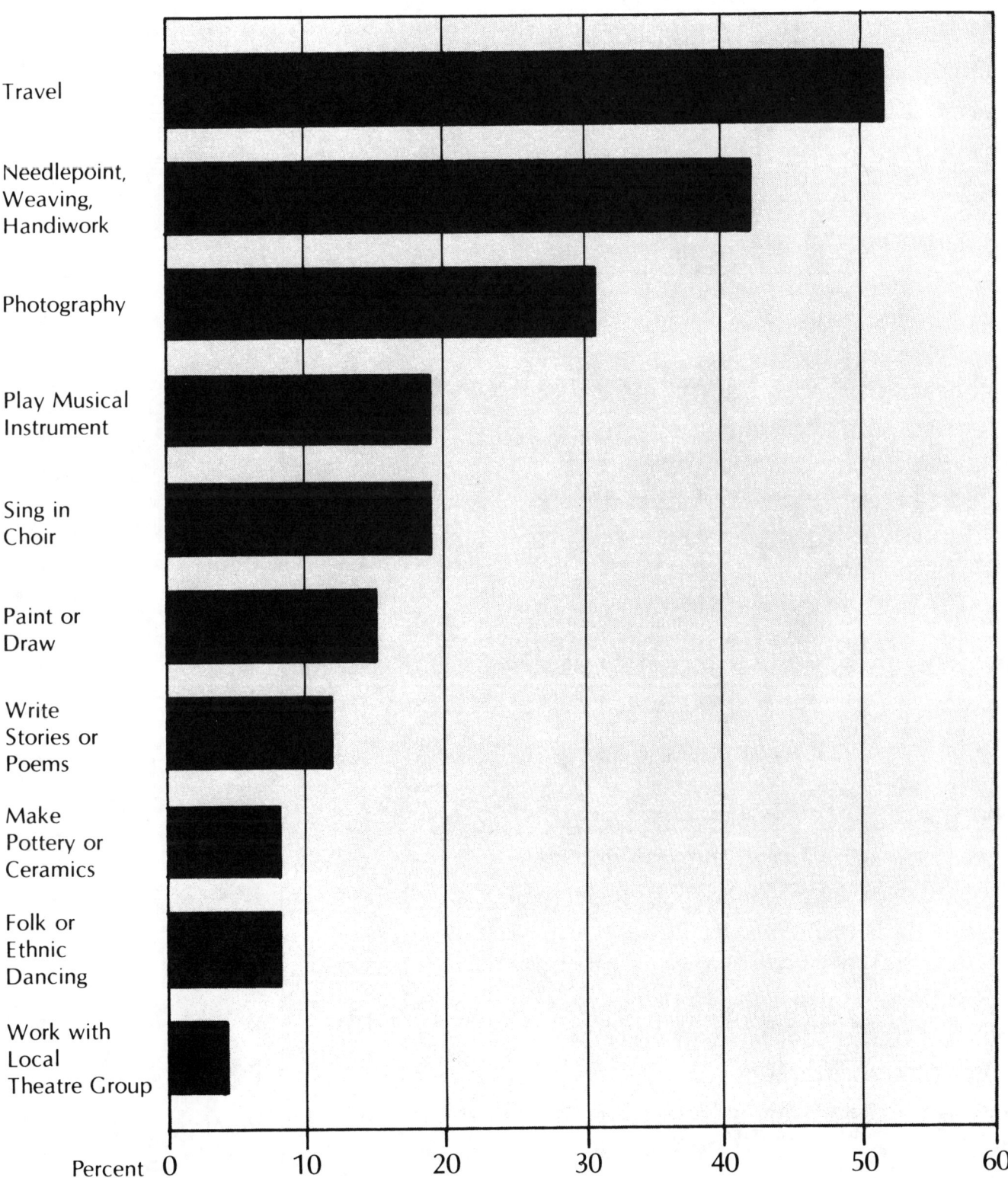

Source: National Council on Aging

B4–10. Life Satisfaction Statements, 1974 and 1981

Q: Here are some statements that people have made about life in general. For each statement, please tell me if you tend to agree or disagree with it. Let's begin with the first statement.

	65 AND OVER					
	1981			1974		
	AGREE	DIS-AGREE	NOT SURE	AGREE	DIS-AGREE	NOT SURE
	%	%	%	%	%	%
POSITIVE STATEMENTS						
AS I LOOK BACK ON MY LIFE, I AM FAIRLY WELL SATISFIED	87	11	2	87	10	3
COMPARED TO OTHER PEOPLE MY AGE, I MAKE A GOOD APPEARANCE	84	7	8	83	6	11
I'VE GOTTEN PRETTY MUCH WHAT I EXPECTED OUT OF LIFE	81	14	5	82	12	6
THE THINGS I DO ARE AS INTERESTING TO ME AS THEY EVER WERE	69	27	4	72	24	4
AS I GROW OLDER, THINGS SEEM BETTER THAN I THOUGHT THEY WOULD BE	53	38	9	64	26	10
I HAVE GOTTEN MORE OF THE BREAKS IN LIFE THAN MOST OF THE PEOPLE I KNOW	62	31	6	63	27	10
I WOULD NOT CHANGE MY PAST LIFE EVEN IF I COULD	64	29	6	62	29	9
I EXPECT SOME INTERESTING AND PLEASANT THINGS TO HAPPEN TO ME IN THE FUTURE	62	28	11	57	26	17
I AM JUST AS HAPPY AS WHEN I WAS YOUNGER	48	48	4	56	38	6
I HAVE MADE PLANS FOR THINGS I'LL BE DOING A MONTH OR A YEAR FROM NOW	49	47	4	53	43	6
THESE ARE THE BEST YEARS OF MY LIFE	33	60	7	32	58	10
NEGATIVE STATEMENTS						
I FEEL OLD AND SOMEWHAT TIRED	45	51	3	46	50	4
MY LIFE COULD BE HAPPIER THAN IT IS NOW	55	40	5	45	46	9
IN SPITE OF WHAT SOME PEOPLE SAY, THE LOT OF THE AVERAGE PERSON IS GETTING WORSE, NOT BETTER	48	39	13	34	45	21
WHEN I THINK BACK OVER MY LIFE, I DIDN'T GET MOST OF THE IMPORTANT THINGS I WANTED	36	59	4	32	61	7
THIS IS THE DREARIEST TIME OF MY LIFE	27	70	3	23	72	5
MOST OF THE THINGS I DO ARE BORING OR MONOTONOUS	21	76	3	14	82	4
COMPARED TO OTHER PEOPLE, I GET DOWN IN THE DUMPS TOO OFTEN	18	78	5	13	81	6

B4–11. When Last Attended Various Places, 1974 and 1981

Q.: When did you last attend (READ EACH ITEM) -- within the last day or two, within the last week or two, a month ago, two or three months ago, or longer ago than that?

	1981						1974*					
	WITHIN LAST DAY OR TWO %	WITHIN LAST WEEK OR TWO %	A MONTH AGO %	TWO OR THREE MONTHS AGO %	LONGER THAN THREE MONTHS AGO %	NEVER %	WITHIN LAST DAY OR TWO %	WITHIN LAST WEEK OR TWO %	A MONTH AGO %	TWO OR THREE MONTHS AGO %	LONGER THAN THREE MONTHS AGO %	NOT IN PAST YEAR %
A MOVIE												
18-64	7	21	14	13	42	2	3	21	21	14	10	30
65 AND OVER	1	3	3	5	72	14	*	3	5	4	8	78
PLACES TO SHOP												
18-64	56	32	4	1	3	4	53	35	3	1	1	3
65 AND OVER	42	37	6	4	8	3	34	40	6	2	1	10
A SENIOR CITIZENS CENTER OR GOLDEN AGE CLUB												
55-64	1	3	2	2	25	79	1	2	1	1	1	92
65 AND OVER	5	9	5	4	18	59	2	6	4	2	3	81
A RESTAURANT												
18-64	36	39	12	4	8	2	21	44	14	6	3	9
65 AND OVER	19	34	13	9	18	7	12	26	13	7	3	81
A COMMUNITY OR NEIGHBORHOOD CENTER OR RECREATION CENTER												
18-64	9	13	7	6	30	34	4	11	6	4	6	64
65 AND OVER	5	9	5	3	21	56	2	5	3	2	3	82
A CHURCH OR SYNAGOGUE												
18-64	16	27	12	8	31	5	17	34	10	5	7	26
65 AND OVER	18	35	8	6	25	8	17	40	7	3	5	23
A LIBRARY												
18-64	4	13	10	12	46	14	6	19	11	8	7	48
65 AND OVER	2	7	5	5	41	39	2	6	3	3	5	78
A DOCTOR OR CLINIC												
18-64	8	18	17	17	38	1	7	17	23	17	17	15
65 AND OVER	6	20	23	20	29	2	4	19	23	17	12	18
THE HOME OF A NEIGHBOR OR RELATIVE												
18-64	59	32	4	1	3	1	x	x	x	x	x	x
65 AND OVER	44	35	8	3	9	1	x	x	x	x	x	x

*IN 1974, ANYONE WHO HAD NOT ATTENDED WITHIN THE LAST YEAR WAS SCREENED OUT. THESE NUMBERS HAVE BEEN REPERCENTAGED ON TOTAL BASE FOR IMPROVED COMPARABILITY.
x = NOT ASKED.

B4–12. Interest in Attending a Senior Citizens Center or Golden Age Club among Public 55 and Over, 1974 and 1981

Q: Would you like to attend a senior citizens center or Golden Age Club, or not?

	1981*			1974**		
	WOULD LIKE TO ATTEND %	WOULD NOT LIKE TO ATTEND %	NOT SURE %	WOULD LIKE TO ATTEND %	WOULD NOT LIKE TO ATTEND %	NOT SURE %
TOTAL 55 AND OVER	27	65	9	22	65	13
55-64	35	60	5	24	61	15
65 AND OVER	22	74	4	21	68	11
MALE	23	68	9	18	71	11
FEMALE	31	62	7	25	60	15
UNDER $7,000 (1974)/$10,000 (1981)	30	61	9	24	60	16
$7,000-$14,999/$10,000-$19,999	30	63	6	21	69	10
$15,000 AND OVER/$20,000 AND OVER	25	64	9	20	68	12
SOME HIGH SCHOOL OR LESS	28	63	8	25	61	14
HIGH SCHOOL GRADUATE, SOME COLLEGE	30	62	9	20	67	13
COLLEGE GRADUATE	21	70	8	6	82	12
WHITE	25	67	8	21	68	11
BLACK	43	45	12	39	38	23
HISPANIC	29	56	15	x	x	x

*REPERCENTAGED TO EXCLUDE THOSE WHO VOLUNTEERED THEY WERE "ALREADY ATTENDING."
**BASED ON THOSE WHO HAD NOT ATTENDED A SENIOR CENTER IN THE PAST MONTH.

B4–13. Volunteerism among Public 65 and Over, 1974 and 1981

Q: Apart from any work you're paid for, do you do any volunteer work, or not?

Q: Would you like to do some volunteer work, or not? BASE: HAVEN'T DONE VOLUNTEER WORK

	1981			1974		
	DO VOLUNTEER WORK %	DO NOT DO VOLUNTEER WORK BUT WOULD LIKE TO %	POTENTIAL VOLUNTEER FORCE %	DO VOLUNTEER WORK %	DO NOT DO VOLUNTEER WORK BUT WOULD LIKE TO %	POTENTIAL VOLUNTEER FORCE %
TOTAL 65 AND OVER	23	10	33	22	10	32
65-69	28	13	41	28	11	39
70-79	23	9	32	20	10	30
80 AND OVER	12	9	21	12	10	22
MALE	24	11	35	20	8	28
FEMALE	22	10	32	23	12	35
UNDER $3,000/$5,000	12	9	21	12	12	24
$3,000-$6,999/$5,000-$9,999	21	14	35	19	10	29
$7,000-$14,999/$10,000-$19,999	31	12	43	35	8	43
$15,000 AND OVER/$20,000 AND OVER	36	14	50	36	6	42
SOME HIGH SCHOOL OR LESS	14	9	23	15	11	26
HIGH SCHOOL GRAD, SOME COLLEGE	28	13	41	31	8	39
COLLEGE GRADUATE	45	12	57	42	10	52
WHITE	24	10	34	23	10	33
BLACK	17	13	30	15	10	25
LABOR FORCE	25	18	43	33	11	44
RETIRED	24	10	34	20	10	30

B4–14. Activities at which "A Lot of Time" Is Spent, 1974 and 1981

Q: Now I'm going to read you some things that other people have said they do with their time. For each, would you tell me whether you personally spend a lot of time, some but not a lot, or hardly any time at all doing that?

	1981			1974		
	18-64 %	65 AND OVER %	NET DIFFERENCE	18-64 %	65 AND OVER %	NET DIFFERENCE
PARTICIPATING IN RECREATIONAL ACTIVITIES AND HOBBIES	36	26	-10	34	26	-8
SOCIALIZING WITH FRIENDS	45	38	-7	55	47	-8
SITTING AND THINKING	38	32	-6	37	31	-6
CARING FOR YOUNGER OR OLDER MEMBERS OF THE FAMILY	50	20	-30	53	27	-26
WATCHING TELEVISION	26	31	+5	23	36	+13
JUST DOING NOTHING	7	14	+7	9	15	+6
READING	33	39	+6	38	36	-2
TAKING WALKS, JOGGING, OR OTHER EXERCISE*	31	25	-6	22	25	+3
LISTENING TO THE RADIO	41	25	-16	x	x	x

*IN 1974, WAS WORDED: "GOING FOR WALKS."
x = NOT ASKED.

B5. SOCIAL PROBLEMS: VICTIMIZATION, OFFENSES, ALCOHOLISM, TRANSPORTATION

B5-1. The Greatest Problems Facing the Elderly

Q.: What do you personally feel are the <u>two or three</u> greatest problems facing the elderly in this country today? What else?

	TOTAL	AGE			SEX		RACE/ETHNICITY		
		18-54	55-64	65 AND OVER	MALE	FE-MALE	WHITE	BLACK	HIS-PANIC
BASE	3438	1095	490	1828	1574	1864	2487	495	389
	%	%	%	%	%	%	%	%	%
INFLATION, HIGH COST OF LIVING, HIGH PRICES	22	21	26	24	28	17	25	13	11
POOR/FAILING HEALTH, ILLNESS, SICKNESS	16	14	18	25	14	17	15	14	33
CRIME, BEING AFRAID TO GO OUT, LACK OF SAFETY/PROTECTION	13	15	11	7	13	13	13	16	12
MONEY, LACK OF MONEY	13	13	12	12	11	15	13	15	16
LOW/LACK OF INCOME, RETIREMENT INCOME	10	10	12	7	10	10	10	10	(2)
FINANCES, FINANCIAL PROBLEMS, ECONOMICS	10	10	9	9	9	10	11	5	7
NOT ENOUGH MONEY TO LIVE/ SURVIVE ON/TO SUPPORT THEM- SELVES, CAN'T MAKE ENDS MEET, HARD TO GET BY	9	9	12	11	8	11	9	10	10
SOCIAL SECURITY	9	10	8	6	9	10	10	7	6
LONELINESS	9	8	10	11	7	11	9	9	11
HIGH HEALTH/MEDICAL CARE COSTS/EXPENSES, CAN'T AFFORD TO MAINTAIN GOOD HEALTH	8	8	9	7	8	9	9	6	4
FIXED INCOMES	8	9	6	4	10	6	9	3	(1)
HIGH BILLS, CAN'T PAY BILLS	7	7	6	10	6	9	8	8	(2)
ABSENCE OF HUMAN CONTACT	6	7	6	7	6	7	6	7	9
LACK OF HOUSING, INADEQUATE HOUSING, FINDING A PLACE TO LIVE	6	7	4	4	5	6	6	4	3
NOT ENOUGH MONEY, POOR, DEPENDING ON/GETTING BY ON SOCIAL SECURITY	5	5	7	4	7	4	6	4	(4)
EMPLOYMENT, WORK, JOBS, WORK OPPORTUNITIES, NO ONE WILL HIRE THEM	5	6	2	3	5	5	4	11	12
TRANSPORTATION, LACK OF TRANSPORTATION	5	5	4	6	6	5	5	8	(5)
HEALTH/MEDICAL CARE	5	5	4	3	5	4	4	8	(6)

B5–2. Criminal Victimization Rates Persons 12 to 64 Years and 65 and Older 1973–80

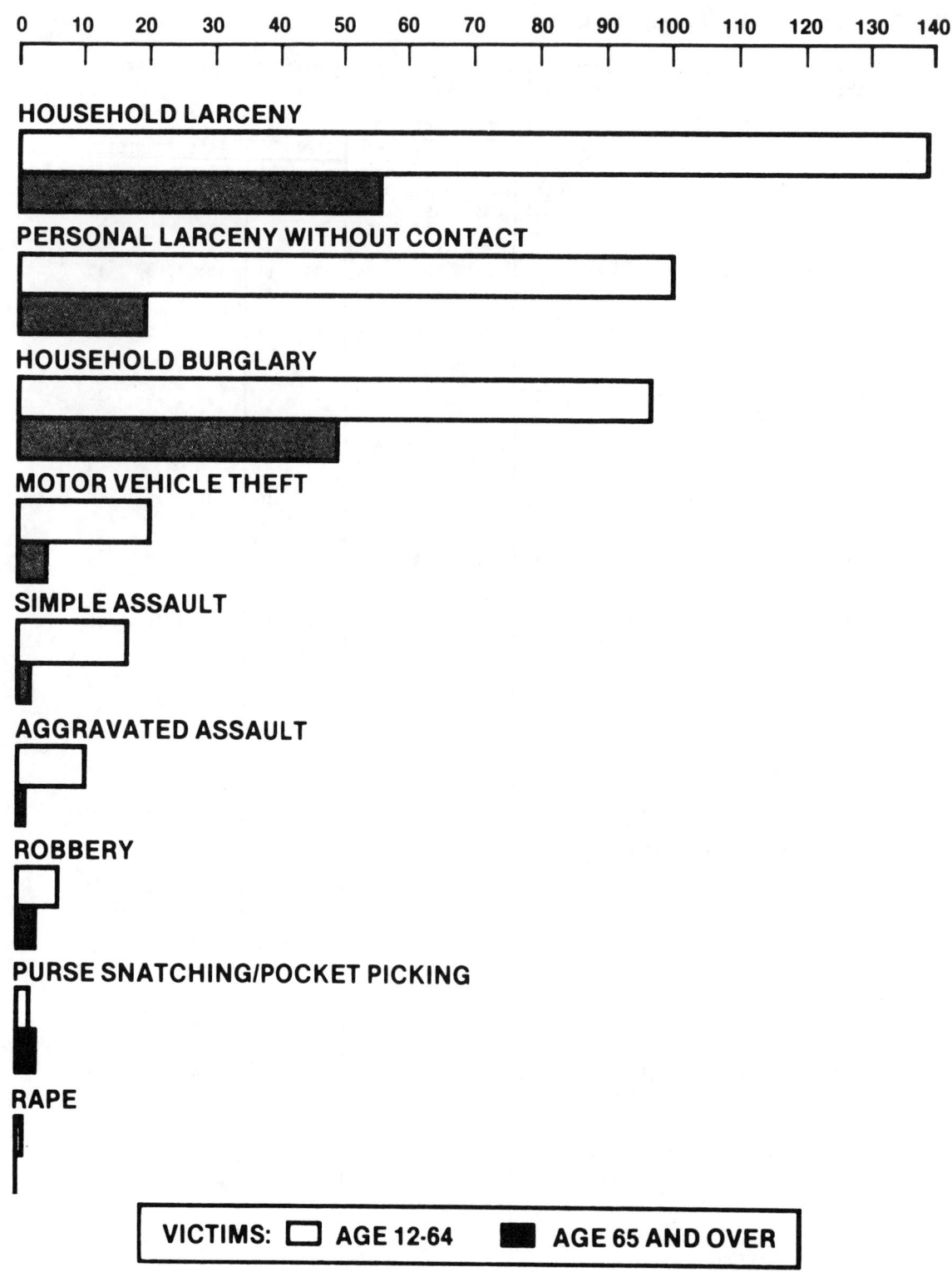

RATE PER 1,000 PERSONS OR HOUSEHOLDS

HOUSEHOLD LARCENY

PERSONAL LARCENY WITHOUT CONTACT

HOUSEHOLD BURGLARY

MOTOR VEHICLE THEFT

SIMPLE ASSAULT

AGGRAVATED ASSAULT

ROBBERY

PURSE SNATCHING/POCKET PICKING

RAPE

VICTIMS: ☐ AGE 12-64   ■ AGE 65 AND OVER

SOURCE: U.S. Department of Justice, Bureau of Justice Statistics, December 1981.

B5-3. Estimated Number of Personal Victimizations and Estimated Number Not Reported to Police, by Type of Victimization, and Sex and Age of Victim, United States, 1980[a]

	Age of victim (in years)									
	12 to 19				20 to 34				35 to 49	
	Total		Not reported to police		Total		Not reported to police		Total	
Type of victimization and sex of victim	Number	Percent	Number	Percent	Number	Percent	Number	Percent	Number	Percen
Rape and attempted rape										
Male	B	B	B	B	B	B	B	B	B	B
Female	46,820	100	B	B	76,432	100	44,588	58	14,318	100
Robbery:										
Male	221,909	100	123,857	56	305,464	100	131,961	43	91,345	100
Female	70,330	100	B	B	153,469	100	65,288	43	76,793	100
Robbery and attempted robbery with injury:										
Male	58,582	100	B	B	100,778	100	31,214	31	32,623	100
Female	14,755	100	B	B	63,886	100	B	B	37,519	100
Serious assault:										
Male	30,134	100	B	B	66,615	100	B	B	20,985	100
Female	B	B	B	B	B	B	B	B	B	B
Minor assault:										
Male	28,449	100	B	B	34,163	100	B	B	11,639	100
Female	7,215	100	B	B	41,620	100	B	B	23,972	100
Robbery without injury:										
Male	85,355	100	42,713	50	114,221	100	41,430	36	38,886	100
Female	33,595	100	B	B	67,614	100	B	B	21,871	100
Attempted robbery without injury:										
Male	77,971	100	59,191	76	90,465	100	59,318	66	19,836	100
Female	21,980	100	B	B	21,968	100	B	B	17,403	100
Assault:										
Male	911,079	100	590,228	65	1,382,387	100	706,350	51	339,516	100
Female	452,993	100	260,438	57	759,050	100	328,742	43	212,995	100
Aggravated assault:										
Male	359,205	100	196,350	55	590,333	100	246,849	42	128,195	100
Female	131,158	100	56,798	43	191,782	100	64,073	33	70,636	100
With injury:										
Male	135,379	100	67,642	50	196,787	100	63,163	32	41,935	100
Female	53,047	100	B	B	72,613	100	18,342	25	17,641	100
Attempted assault with weapon:										
Male	223,825	100	128,709	58	393,545	100	183,687	47	86,260	100
Female	78,111	100	35,290	45	119,169	100	45,731	38	52,995	100
Simple assault:										
Male	551,875	100	393,877	71	792,054	100	459,500	58	211,321	100
Female	321,835	100	203,640	63	567,269	100	264,669	47	142,359	100
With injury:										
Male	190,229	100	118,651	62	185,238	100	83,921	45	45,944	100
Female	96,334	100	66,271	69	179,560	100	74,877	42	45,763	100
Attempted assault without weapon:										
Male	361,646	100	275,226	76	606,816	100	375,579	62	165,378	100
Female	225,501	100	137,369	61	387,709	100	189,793	49	96,596	100
Personal larceny with contact:										
Male	47,345	100	B	B	53,949	100	B	B	19,896	100
Female	50,967	100	B	B	103,139	100	62,641	61	74,767	100
Purse snatching:										
Male	B	B	B	B	B	B	B	B	B	B
Female	19,076	100	B	B	38,622	100	B	B	32,849	100
Attempted purse snatching:										
Male	X	X	X	X	X	X	X	X	X	X
Female	B	B	B	B	B	B	B	B	B	B
Pocket picking:										
Male	45,993	100	B	B	53,949	100	B	B	19,896	100
Female	24,703	100	B	B	54,748	100	B	B	27,529	100
Personal larceny without contact:										
Male	1,745,803	100	1,430,847	82	3,143,039	100	2,151,788	68	1,153,880	100
Female	1,569,814	100	1,341,245	85	2,689,878	100	1,800,532	67	1,282,984	100

[a] Subcategories may not sum to total because of rounding

Source: Table constructed by SOURCEBOOK staff from data provided by the U.S. Department of Justice, Bureau of Justice Statistics.

B5-3. Estimated Number of Personal Victimizations and Estimated Number Not Reported to Police, by Type of Victimization, and Sex and Age of Victim, United States, 1980 (Continued)

Age of victim (in years)													
50 to 64				65 or older				Total					
Not reported to police		Total		Not reported to police		Total		Not reported to police		Total		Not reported to police	
Number	Percent	Number	Percent	Number	Percent	Number	Percent	Number	Percent	Number	Percent	Number	Percent
B	B	B	B	B	B	B	B	B	B	20,011	100	B	B
B	B	0	X	X	X	2,644	100	B	B	140,214	100	74,436	53
40,570	44	84,702	100	20,680	24	49,964	100	B	B	753,384	100	339,144	45
19,753	26	54,208	100	B	B	29,841	100	B	B	384,641	100	132,537	34
B	B	38,430	100	B	B	13,064	100	B	B	243,478	100	72,115	30
B	B	20,845	100	·B	B	17,287	100	B	B	154,292	100	40,762	26
B	B	21,603	100	B	B	7,723	100	B	B	147,059	100	34,462	23
B	B	B	B	B	B	B	B	B	B	51,555	100	B	B
B	B	16,827	100	B	B	5,341	100	B	B	96,419	100	37,653	39
B	B	19,390	100	B	B	10,540	100	B	B	102,738	100	29,697	29
B	B	27,158	100	B	B	21,511	100	B	B	287,131	100	119,750	42
B	B	24,944	100	B	B	7,330	100	B	B	155,354	100	49,081	32
B	B	19,114	100	B	B	15,390	100	B	B	222,776	100	147,280	66
B	B	8,420	100	B	B	5,224	100	B	B	74,995	100	42,694	57
133,936	39	150,054	100	71,569	48	57,401	100	B	B	2,840,438	100	1,532,227	54
81,645	38	86,653	100	35,465	41	18,913	100	B	B	1,530,605	100	711,918	47
45,019	35	61,075	100	B	B	23,395	100	B	B	1,162,202	100	517,173	44
24,354	34	34,505	100	B	B	6,498	100	B	B	434,578	100	155,864	36
B	B	11,875	100	B	B	3,849	100	B	B	389,825	100	146,129	37
B	B	14,832	100	B	B	1,321	100	B	B	159,454	100	51,580	32
33,490	39	49,200	100	B	B	19,546	100	B	B	772,377	100	371,044	48
B	B	19,672	100	B	B	5,177	100	B	B	275,124	100	104,285	38
88,916	42	88,979	100	54,981	62	34,007	100	B	B	1,678,236	100	1,015,055	60
57,291	40	52,148	100	B	B	12,415	100	B	B	1,096,027	100	556,054	51
B	B	11,382	100	B	B	8,590	100	B	B	441,383	100	224,026	51
B	B	13,902	100	B	B	2,629	100	B	B	338,187	100	157,623	47
77,567	47	77,597	100	47,764	62	25,416	100	B	B	1,236,853	100	791,028	64
46,375	48	38,247	100	B	B	9,787	100	B	B	757,839	100	398,431	53
B	B	31,797	100	B	B	21,280	100	B	B	174,267	100	113,265	65
B	B	50,338	100	B	B	64,270	100	B	B	343,481	100	208,179	61
B	B	B	B	B	B	B	B	B	B	3,091	100	B	B
B	B	22,179	100	B	B	18,587	100	B	B	131,313	100	50,837	39
X	X	X	X	X	X	X	X	X	X	0	X	X	X
B	B	B	B	B	B	B	B	B	B	48,865	100	B	B
B	B	31,797	100	B	B	19,542	100	B	B	171,177	100	110,174	64
B	B	20,075	100	B	B	36,247	100	B	B	163,303	100	116,976	72
727,392	63	699,340	100	477,424	68	263,734	100	161,146	61	7,005,796	100	4,948,597	71
836,754	65	731,997	100	494,229	68	224,491	100	130,074	58	6,499,165	100	4,602,833	71

B5–4. Percentage Distribution of Arrests for Index Offenses against Property among the 55 and Over Age Group, 1971, 1976, and 1981

	1971	1976	1981	% Increase
Burglary	7.7	3.5	1.5	44
Larceny-Theft	89.0	95.0	92.0	61
Auto theft	3.3	1.5	5.5	30
N	18,318	38,758	45,861	

Source: Federal Bureau of Investigation. Uniform Crime Reports. 1971, 1976, 1981.

B5–5. Percentage Distribution of Arrests for Misdemeanor Offenses among the 55 and Over Age Group, 1971, 1976, and 1981

	1971	1976	1981	% Increase
Sex offenses	.8	1.4	1.6	33
Drug abuse violations	.4	.6	1.9	67
Gambling	4.2	3.5	2.5	−33
Drunkenness	71.1	57.8	43.3	−55
Driving under influence	15.0	29.5	39.0	41
Disorderly conduct	8.5	7.2	11.7	−1
N	341,001	255,916	246,190	

Source: Federal Bureau of Investigation. Uniform Crime Reports. 1971, 1976, 1981.

B5–6. Distribution of Victims by Type of Crime within Age Categories

	12-16	17-20	21-26	27-32	33-39	40-49	50-64	65 and over
Type of Crime								
Assault	74.8	73.3	70.8	72.2	71.4	65.6	50.2	28.1
Robbery	17.4	15.7	16.9	16.3	19.2	22.3	27.0	39.1
Personal larceny	5.0	7.2	7.3	9.2	7.1	10.9	21.9	31.3
Rape	2.8	3.8	5.0	2.3	2.3	1.2	.9	1.5
Violent crime (Rape and assault combined)	77.6	77.1	75.8	74.5	73.7	66.8	51.1	29.6
Predatory crime (Robbery and personal larceny combined)	22.4	22.9	24.2	25.5	26.3	33.2	48.9	70.4
(N)	(1,155)	(973)	(1,075)	(567)	(369)	(463)	(473)	(236)

Source: G. E. Antunes et al., "Patterns of Personal Crime against the Elderly," *Gerontologist,* 1977, 17, 323 (Secondary Analysis, LEAA Surveys–1973, 1974).

B5-7. Approximate Income of Household in which Elder Abuse Was Cited

Household income	Number	Percent of total citings (n=183)
Less than $5,200	49	27
$5,200-9,000	42	23
$9,001-14,000	14	8
$14,001-19,000	7	4
More than $19,000	3	2
NA	68	37
TOTAL	183	101

Source: Data derived from a survey conducted by the House Select Committee on Aging, cited in U.S. House of Representatives, House Select Committee on Aging, Elder Abuse: A Hidden Problem (Washington, D.C., 1980), p. 61.

B5-8. Sex of Abused Persons across Age Distribution

	Males				Females			
	Abuse citings		National population		Abuse citings		National population	
Age	No.	%	No. x 1,000	%	No.	%	No. x 1,000	%
Under 65	4	29	4,381	47	10	71	4,981	53
65 to 69	8	24	3,739	44	25	76	4,708	56
70 to 74	4	9	2,597	42	29	91	3,540	58
75 to 79	5	16	1,589	39	27	84	2,479	61
80 and over	8	15	1,644	34	55	85	2,198	66
TOTAL	29	17	13,950	42	146	83	18,906	58

Source: Data derived from a survey conducted by the House Select Committee on Aging, cited in U.S. House of Representatives, House Select Committee on Aging, Elder Abuse: A Hidden Problem (Washington, D.C., 1980), p. 59.

B5-9. Drinking by Age and Sex: Quantity, Frequency, and Variability (Men)

Age by Sex	N	Percent Abstainers	Percent Moderate 1–60/Month	Percent Heavy 60+/Month	Percent of all Drinkers Who Are Heavy Drinkers
Men					
18–20	(37)	5	79	17	18
21–25	(82)	10	54	38	40
26–30	(87)	20	50	29	36
31–40	(154)	25	55	19	25
41–50	(107)	27	52	21	29
51–60	(130)	32	51	17	25
61–70	(91)	38	53	8	13
70+	(72)	41	45	13	22
Total	(762)	25	54	21	28

B5-10. Drinking by Age and Sex: Quantity, Frequency, and Variability (Women)

Age by Sex	N	Percent Abstainers	Percent Moderate 1–60/Month	Percent Heavy 60+/Month	Percent of all Drinkers Who Are Heavy Drinkers
Women					
18–20	(52)	31	64	5	7
21–25	(130)	15	78	6	7
26–30	(125)	30	65	5	7
31–40	(208)	27	65	9	12
41–50	(137)	43	46	10	18
51–60	(143)	50	46	4	8
61–70	(102)	61	38	1	3
70+	(103)	61	39	0	0
Total	(1,010)	40	54	5	8
Sample Total		(1,772)	33	54	13	19

B5–11. Cigarette Smoking Status of Persons 20 Years of Age and Over, According to Sex, Race, and Age: United States, 1965, 1976, 1980, and 1983

(Data are based on household interviews of a sample of the civilian noninstitutionalized population)

Sex, race,[1] and age	Smoking status							
	Current smoker[2]				Former smoker			
	1965	1976	1980[3]	1983[4]	1965	1976	1980[3]	1983[4]
MALE								
Total[5,6]			Percent of persons					
All ages, 20 years and over[7].....	52.1	41.6	37.9	34.8	20.3	29.6	30.5	31.8
20-24 years...........................	59.2	45.9	39.7	37.5	9.0	12.2	12.1	10.8
25-34 years...........................	60.7	48.5	43.1	38.0	14.7	18.3	20.6	20.0
35-44 years...........................	58.2	47.6	42.6	40.1	20.6	27.3	27.6	29.3
45-64 years...........................	51.9	41.3	40.8	35.6	24.1	37.1	36.9	39.5
65 years and over.....................	28.5	23.0	17.9	20.8	28.1	44.4	47.4	49.7
White								
All ages, 20 years and over[7].......	51.3	41.0	37.1	---	21.2	30.7	31.9	---
20-24 years...........................	58.1	45.3	39.0	---	9.6	13.3	12.2	---
25-34 years...........................	60.1	47.7	42.0	---	15.5	18.9	21.9	---
35-44 years...........................	57.3	46.8	42.4	---	21.5	28.9	28.8	---
45-64 years...........................	51.3	40.6	40.0	---	25.1	38.1	38.4	---
65 years and over.....................	27.7	22.8	16.6	---	28.7	45.6	50.1	---
Black								
All ages, 20 years and over[7].......	59.6	50.1	44.9	---	12.6	20.2	20.6	---
20-24 years...........................	67.4	52.8	45.5	---	3.8	4.1	*10.6	---
25-34 years...........................	68.4	59.4	52.0	---	6.7	11.8	11.9	---
35-44 years...........................	67.3	58.8	44.2	---	12.3	13.8	21.2	---
45-64 years...........................	57.9	49.7	48.8	---	15.3	28.6	26.3	---
65 years and over.....................	36.4	26.4	27.9	---	21.5	33.0	26.6	---
FEMALE								
Total[5,6]								
All ages, 20 years and over[7].......	34.2	32.5	29.8	29.5	8.2	13.9	15.7	16.1
20-24 years...........................	41.9	34.2	32.7	36.1	7.3	10.4	11.0	11.5
25-34 years...........................	43.7	37.5	31.6	32.3	9.9	12.9	14.4	13.1
35-44 years...........................	43.7	38.2	34.9	33.6	9.6	15.8	18.9	17.0
45-64 years...........................	32.0	34.8	30.8	30.5	8.6	15.9	17.1	18.1
65 years and over.....................	9.6	12.8	16.8	13.5	4.5	11.7	14.2	18.0
White								
All ages, 20 years and over[7].......	34.5	32.4	30.0	---	8.5	14.6	16.3	---
20-24 years...........................	41.9	34.4	33.3	---	8.0	11.4	12.5	---
25-34 years...........................	43.4	37.1	31.6	---	10.3	13.7	14.7	---
35-44 years...........................	43.9	38.1	35.6	---	9.9	17.0	20.2	---
45-64 years...........................	32.7	34.7	30.6	---	8.8	16.4	17.4	---
65 years and over.....................	9.8	13.2	17.4	---	4.5	11.5	14.3	---

See footnotes at end of table.

B5-11. Cigarette Smoking Status of Persons 20 Years of Age and Over, According to Sex, Race, and Age: United States, 1965, 1976, 1980, and 1983 (Continued)

(Data are based on household interviews of a sample of the civilian noninstitutionalized population)

Sex, race,[1] and age	Smoking status							
	Current smoker[2]				Former smoker			
	1965	1976	1980[3]	1983[4]	1965	1976	1980[3]	1983[4]
FEMALE--Continued	Percent of persons							
Black								
All ages, 20 years and over[7].......	32.7	34.7	30.6	---	5.9	10.2	11.8	---
20-24 years...........................	44.2	34.9	32.3	---	2.5	5.0	*2.2	---
25-34 years...........................	47.8	42.5	34.2	---	6.7	8.9	11.6	---
35-44 years...........................	42.8	41.3	36.5	---	7.0	9.6	12.5	---
45-64 years...........................	25.7	38.1	34.3	---	6.6	11.9	14.1	---
65 years and over.....................	7.1	9.2	*9.4	---	4.5	13.3	14.1	---

[1]In 1965 and 1976, the racial classification of persons in the National Health Interview Survey was determined by interviewer observation. In 1980 and 1983, race was determined by asking the household respondent.
[2]A current smoker is a person who has smoked at least 100 cigarettes and who now smokes; includes occasional smokers.
[3]Final estimates. Based on data for the last 6 months of 1980.
[4]Provisional estimates based on data from the first 6 months of 1983. Computed by the Division of Epidemiology and Health Promotion.
[5]Base of percent excludes persons with unknown smoking status.
[6]Includes all other races not shown separately.
[7]Age adjusted by the direct method to the 1970 civilian noninstitutionalized population, using 5 age groups.

NOTE: Data in this table should not be compared with data in Health, United States, 1981 or Health, United States, 1982. The 1980 data in the 1981 edition were preliminary estimates, and the data in the 1982 edition were final estimates but did not include age-adjusted data.

SOURCE: Division of Health Interview Statistics, National Center for Health Statistics: Data from the National Health Interview Survey.

B5–12. Age of Drivers: Total Number and Number in Accidents, 1976

Age Group	Number (millions)	Percent	Fatal Number	Fatal Percent	All Accidents Number (millions)	All Accidents Percent	Per Number of Drivers Fatal [a]	Per Number of Drivers All [b]
All ages	133.8	100.0	59,000	100.0	24.8	100.0	44	21
60–64	6.8	5.1	2,100	3.5	1.0	3.5	31	15
65–69	5.7	4.3	1,600	2.7	0.9	3.2	28	16
70–74	3.7	2.8	1,200	2.0	0.3	1.0	32	8
75 +	2.6	1.9	1,800	3.1	0.6	2.1	69	23

[a] Drivers in fatal accidents per 100,000 drivers in age group.
[b] Drivers in in all accidents per 100 drivers in age group.

Source: *Accident Facts, 1977 Edition* (National Safety Council, Chicago, Illinois, 1977).

B5–13. Number and Percent of Trips Taken by Mode of Travel and Purpose, 1979

Purpose	Friend or Relative's Vehicle Number	Friend or Relative's Vehicle Percent	Own Vehicle Number	Own Vehicle Percent	Walk Number	Walk Percent	Bus Number	Bus Percent	Taxi Number	Taxi Percent	Other Number	Other Percent	Total Number	Total Percent
Recreation	179	28.3	96	18.2	81	26.1	14	38.1	1	7.7	9	23.7	380	24.3
Grocery Shopping	124	19.6	105	19.9	65	21.0	4	9.8	3	23.1	3	7.9	304	19.4
Nongrocery Shopping	109	17.2	84	15.9	45	14.5	5	12.2	2	15.3	2	15.2	247	15.8
Personal & Government Business	60	9.5	48	9.1	53	17.1	2	4.9	1	7.7	5	13.2	169	10.8
Work	19	3.0	84	15.9	18	5.8	14	34.1	—	—	3	7.9	138	8.8
Medical	63	10.0	36	6.8	17	5.5	2	4.9	6	46.2	6	15.8	130	8.3
Religious & Related	69	10.9	29	5.5	19	6.1	—	—	—	—	9	23.7	126	8.1
Other	10	1.5	46	8.7	12	3.8	—	—	—	—	1	2.6	69	4.4
Total	633	100.0	528	100.0	310	100.0	41	100.0	13	100.0	38	100.0	1563	100.0

C. Health Aspects

SELF-ASSESSMENT AND CHRONIC HEALTH PROBLEMS

During the twentieth century, the health status of the population in general and the elderly in particular has significantly improved due to the great advances in public health, medical research, and medical care. At the turn of the century, acute and infectious diseases were the main health problems; in the 1980s, the main health problems are chronic diseases and disabilities. In spite of the fact that 20 percent of the elderly suffer from at least a mild degree of disability, and 80 percent have at least one chronic condition, four out of five assess their health as good or excellent. The most prevalent chronic conditions affecting the elderly are arthritis, hypertension, hearing impairments, and heart conditions.

MENTAL HEALTH PROBLEMS

Psychiatric problems are less common among the older than the younger population, but cognitive impairments are common problems of the aged. About 55 percent of the elderly who are confined in nursing homes suffer from chronic mental conditions or senility. Among those living in the community, 15 to 25 percent have at least mild symptoms of mental illness ranging from depression to senile dementia.

CAUSES OF DEATH, DEATH RATES

About 75 percent of all deaths are due to three causes: heart disease, cancer, and stroke. Overall death rates have been declining significantly during the past 30 years. Due to new medical advances and modifications in eating, smoking, and exercise habits, death rates from heart disease declined during the last 20 years while death rates from cancer increased.

HEALTH SERVICES UTILIZATION, PHYSICIAN CARE

While the average person visits a physician five times a year, persons between 65 and 74 make 7.4 visits, and those over 75 make 8.2 visits. About five million of the elderly were sufficiently disabled in 1985 to require long-term care; many others require assistance to maintain an independent lifestyle. Just as contact with physicians increases, the need for support services, nursing homes, hospitals, and medications increases greatly with age, particularly after age 85; only dentists are seen less frequently.

HOSPITALS AND NURSING HOMES

Hospitalization of the older population occurs twice as often and they stay twice as long as younger people. In 1983, the elderly made up 12 percent of the population but accounted for 29 percent of all hospital discharges and one-third of all personal health care expenditures. Their average hospital stay was 10 days, and they required twice as many prescription drugs. In 1985, about 1.5 million or 5 percent of the elderly lived in nursing homes, but at least 20 percent spent some time in such homes. The very old require more support services and nursing home care. Projections indicate that the nursing home population will increase by 50 percent by the year 2000.

C1. SELF-ASSESSMENT

C1-1. Self-Assessment of Health by Sex and Age, 1981

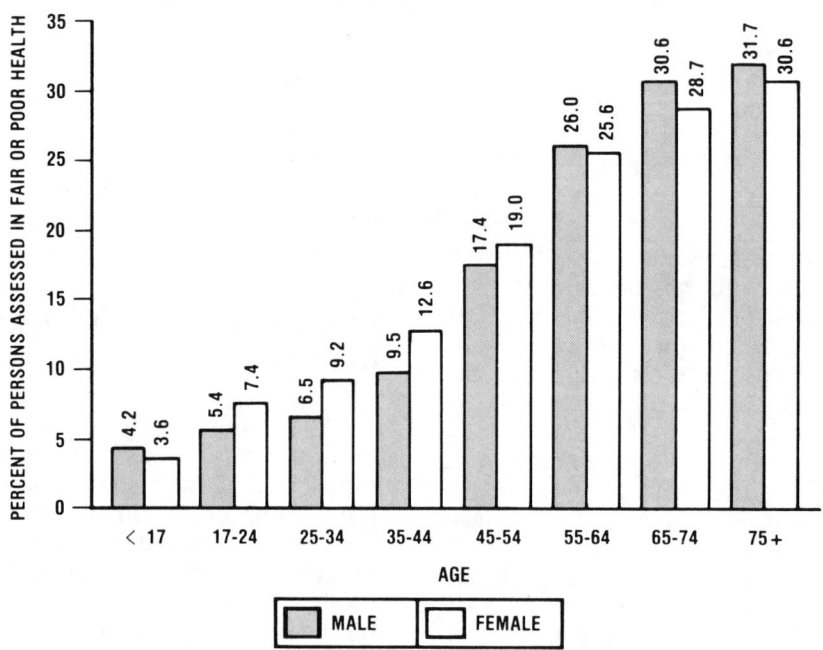

C1-2. Self-Assessment of Health by Income Range, Persons 65 Years and Older, 1981

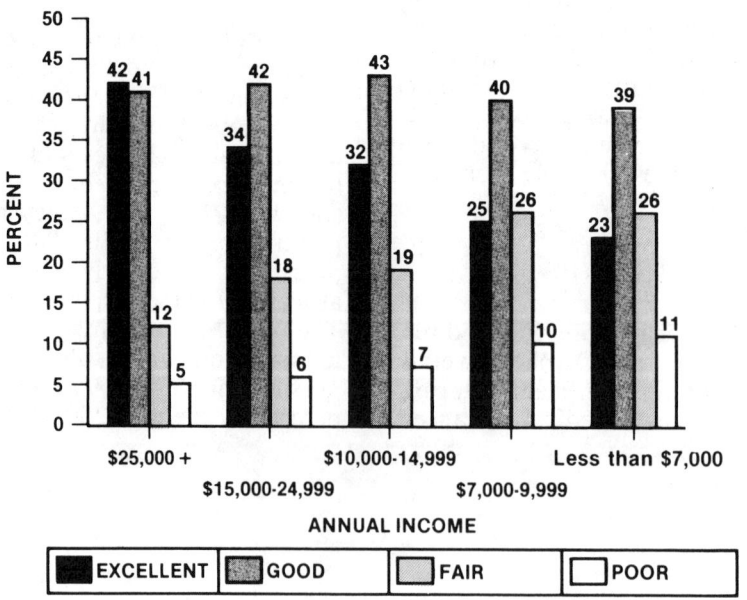

SOURCE: National Center for Health Statistics, 1981 Health Interview Survey, unpublished.

C1–3. Self-Assessment of Health Status, Persons 65 and Over, by Sex, Race and Income, 1979

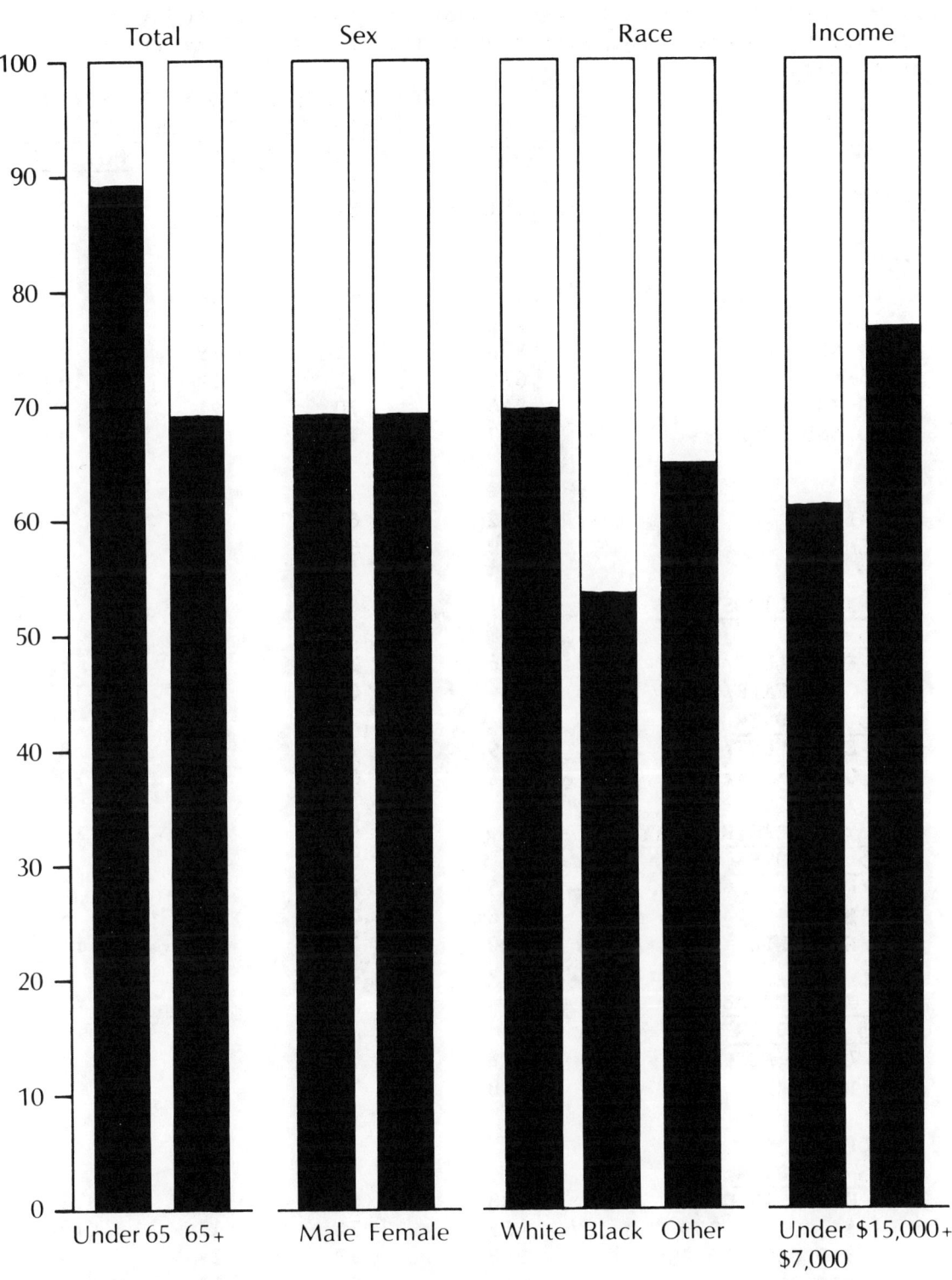

C1–4. Health Status of the Elderly Now vs. Ten or Twenty Years Ago

Q.: Let me read you some statements about people over 65 today compared with ten or twenty years ago. For each statement, please tell me if you tend to agree or disagree.

	BASE	OLDER PEOPLE TODAY ARE HEALTHIER THAN OLDER PEOPLE WERE THEN		
		AGREE %	DISAGREE %	NOT SURE %
TOTAL	3451	64	28	8
AGE				
18-54	1098	62	30	8
55-64	492	67	26	7
65 AND OVER	1836	71	19	9
65-69	675	71	19	10
70-79	844	70	21	9
80 AND OVER	317	75	17	9
SEX				
MALE	1582	67	25	8
FEMALE	1869	62	30	8
AGE X HEALTH STATUS				
55-64				
EXCELLENT/GOOD	306	78	17	5
ONLY FAIR/POOR	184	46	43	10
65 AND OVER				
EXCELLENT/GOOD	989	78	14	8
ONLY FAIR/POOR	841	63	27	10
AGE X RACE/ETHNICITY				
65 AND OVER				
WHITE	1345	75	16	9
BLACK	274	45	49	6
HISPANIC	190	39	51	11
AGE X EMPLOYMENT				
65 AND OVER				
LABOR FORCE	126	77	15	7
RETIRED	1438	72	20	9
INCOME				
65 AND OVER				
UNDER $5,000	428	60	28	12
$5,000-$9,999	465	74	17	10
$10,000-$19,999	348	73	19	8
$20,000 AND OVER	212	84	11	5
AGE X PENSION COVERAGE				
65 AND OVER				
COVERED	701	79	14	7
NOT COVERED	1104	66	24	11

C1-5. Two or Three Greatest Problems Facing the Elderly in Health and Medical Care

Q.: When it comes to health and medical care, what do you personally feel are the two or three greatest problems facing elderly people 65 and over? What else?

	TOTAL	AGE 18-54	AGE 55-64	AGE 65 AND OVER	18-54 MALE	18-54 FE-MALE	55-64 MALE	55-64 FE-MALE	65 AND OVER MALE	65 AND OVER FE-MALE
BASE	3443 %	1095 %	489 %	1834 %	542 %	553 %	244 %	245 %	784 %	1050 %
COSTS, EXPENSE, HIGH MEDICAL/HEALTH CARE BILLS, COST OF MEDICAL BILLS	28	31	23	19	32	29	28	18	20	18
LACK OF MONEY/FINANCES, INFLATION	22	24	22	14	23	25	25	20	15	13
TRANSPORTATION TO AND FROM DOCTOR/MEDICAL, FACILITIES/CLINICS	22	23	19	18	23	24	19	19	15	20
LACK OF PERSONAL/QUALITY/PROPER MEDICAL CARE/ATTENTION	12	14	10	6	16	12	10	10	6	5
POOR/FAILING HEALTH, ILLNESS	12	11	11	14	13	10	14	9	15	14
HIGH DOCTOR BILLS, COST OF DOCTORS' VISITS	12	10	14	18	9	10	15	14	21	17
HIGH COSTS/EXPENSE/PRICE OF MEDICATION/PRESCRIPTIONS	11	10	11	15	8	12	11	11	14	17
HIGH COSTS OF HOSPITALIZATION/HOSPITAL STAYS	11	9	14	14	9	10	14	15	14	14
AVAILABILITY OF HOME CARE	8	8	9	11	6	9	5	13	6	14
MEDICARE IS INSUFFICIENT/PAYS TOO LITTLE (NOT 100%), NEED SUPPLEMENTAL INSURANCE FOR MEDICARE	7	7	7	10	7	7	9	6	9	10
NOT ENOUGH HEALTH INSURANCE/COVERAGE, LACK HEALTH INSURANCE	6	7	6	5	6	7	6	6	7	4
LACK OF CARING/INTERESTED/PROPER/GOOD/THOROUGH DOCTORS	6	6	6	5	6	7	5	7	5	6
INSURANCE DOESN'T PROVIDE FULL COVERAGE/EWNOUGH FINANCIAL ASSISTANCE	5	6	5	5	6	5	6	5	6	4
LACK OF/INADEQUATE FACILITIES TO CARE FOR THEM/FOR THEM TO GO TO, NO/OVERCROWDED HOSPITALS	5	6	3	2	7	4	3	3	2	2

C1-6. The Age at which the Average Man and Woman Becomes Old

Q: I'd like to start by asking you at what age do you think the average man becomes old? Just think about men, not women.

Q: At what age do you think the average woman becomes old?

	THE AVERAGE MAN						THE AVERAGE WOMAN					
	1981			1974			1981			1974		
	TOTAL	18-64	65 AND OVER	TOTAL	18-64	65 AND OVER	TOTAL	18-64	65 AND OVER	TOTAL	18-64	65 AND OVER
	%	%	%	%	%	%	%	%	%	%	%	%
UNDER 40 YEARS	1	2	*	1	1	*	2	3	*	1	1	1
40-49 YEARS	4	4	1	4	5	2	5	6	2	5	5	3
50-59 YEARS	13	15	4	11	11	8	14	16	7	11	11	8
60-64 YEARS	19	20	12	12	12	11	19	21	12	10	11	8
65-69 YEARS	17	17	18	11	10	11	16	16	15	8	8	8
70-74 YEARS	18	19	16	10	10	8	14	14	14	9	10	7
75-79 YEARS	6	5	9	3	3	3	6	5	10	3	3	4
80 YEARS AND OVER	5	5	6	1	1	4	5	5	8	2	1	2
NEVER	1	1	2	2	2	3	2	2	3	2	2	5
IT DEPENDS	10	9	20	22	23	23	10	9	19	23	24	23
WHEN HE/SHE STOPS WORKING	1	*	1	4	4	4	*	*	1	2	2	2
WHEN HIS/HER HEALTH FAILS	3	2	5	11	11	13	2	1	5	13	12	16
WHEN SHE CAN'T HAVE BABIES ANYMORE, MENOPAUSE	x	x	x	x	x	x	*	*	*	2	2	1
OTHER	*	*	*	3	3	2	-	12	-	3	3	2
NOT SURE	2	2	4	5	4	8	2	2	5	6	5	10
CHRONOLOGICAL CONCEPT OF OLD AGE (ALL NUMERICAL RESPONSES)	83	86	66	53	53	46	81	85	68	49	50	41
NONCHRONOLOGICAL CRITERIA FOR OLD AGE (ALL NON-AGE RESPONSES)	15	13	28	42	43	45	14	13	28	45	45	49
MEDIAN CHRONOLOGICAL AGE	66 years			63 years			65 years			62 years		

*LESS THAN 0.5%.
x = NOT ASKED.

C2. CHRONIC HEALTH PROBLEMS, DISABILITIES, ACTIVITY LIMITATIONS

C2-1. Selected Health Characteristics by Age, 1981

Characteristic	Age: 45-54	55-64	65-74	65 PLUS	75 PLUS
Persons injured per 100 persons per year	22	20	14	18	26
Restricted activity days per person per year	24	31	35	40	48
Bed disability days per person per year	8.5	9.5	11.5	14	18
Incidence of acute conditions per 100 persons per year	143	113	111	107	101
Dental visits per person per year	1.8	1.9	1.6	1.5	1.3
Percent seeing dentist in last year	51.6%	47.6%	38.6%	34.6%	27.9%
Doctor visits per person per year	4.7	5.5	6.3	6.3	6.4
Percent seeing doctor in last year	71.8%	75.2%	78.3%	80.2%	83.3%
Percent with short-stay hospital episodes in the last year	10.9%	12.9%	16.6%	18.0%	20.4%
Average number of days spent in short-stay hospitals	8.9	9.0	9.3	10.0	11.0
Discharges per 100 persons per year	16.0	19.1	25.9	28.4	32.5

SOURCE: National Center for Health Statistics, 1981 Health Interview Survey, unpublished.

C2-2. Prevalence of Top Chronic Conditions, Persons 65 Years and Older, 1981

Condition	Total Conditions For all Persons	Total for Persons 65 Years and Older	Rate per 1000 Persons Age 17-44	45-64	65 Plus
Arthritis	27,238,293	11,547,889	47.7	246.5	464.7
Hypertensive Disease	25,523,526	9,406,958	54.2	243.7	378.6
Hearing Impairments	18,665,650	7,051,238	43.8	142.9	283.8
Heart Conditions	17,186,106	6,883,416	37.9	122.7	277.0
Chronic Sinusitis	31,036,480	4,562,037	158.4	177.5	183.6
Visual Impairments	9,083,717	3,395,397	27.4	55.2	136.6
Orthopedic Impairments	18,416,051	3,185,565	90.5	117.5	128.2
Arteriosclerosis	3,398,230	2,410,125	.5	21.3	97.0
Diabetes	5,499,737	2,073,037	8.6	56.9	83.4
Varicose Veins	6,129,874	2,067,311	19.0	50.1	83.2
Hemorrhoids	8,848,365	1,637,487	43.7	66.6	65.9
Frequent Constipation	3,599,159	1,471,915	9.2	22.4	59.2
Disease of Urinary System	5,689,273	1,395,187	25.8	31.7	56.1
Hay Fever	17,873,906	1,290,449	100.2	77.5	51.9
Corns and Callosities	4,289,880	1,289,933	14.0	35.8	51.9
Hernia of Abdominal Cavity	3,697,855	1,220,156	8.9	33.1	49.1

SOURCE: National Center for Health Statistics, Division of Health Interview Statistics, unpublished.

C2-3. Limitation of Activity Due to Chronic Conditions by Type of Limitations and Age, 1981

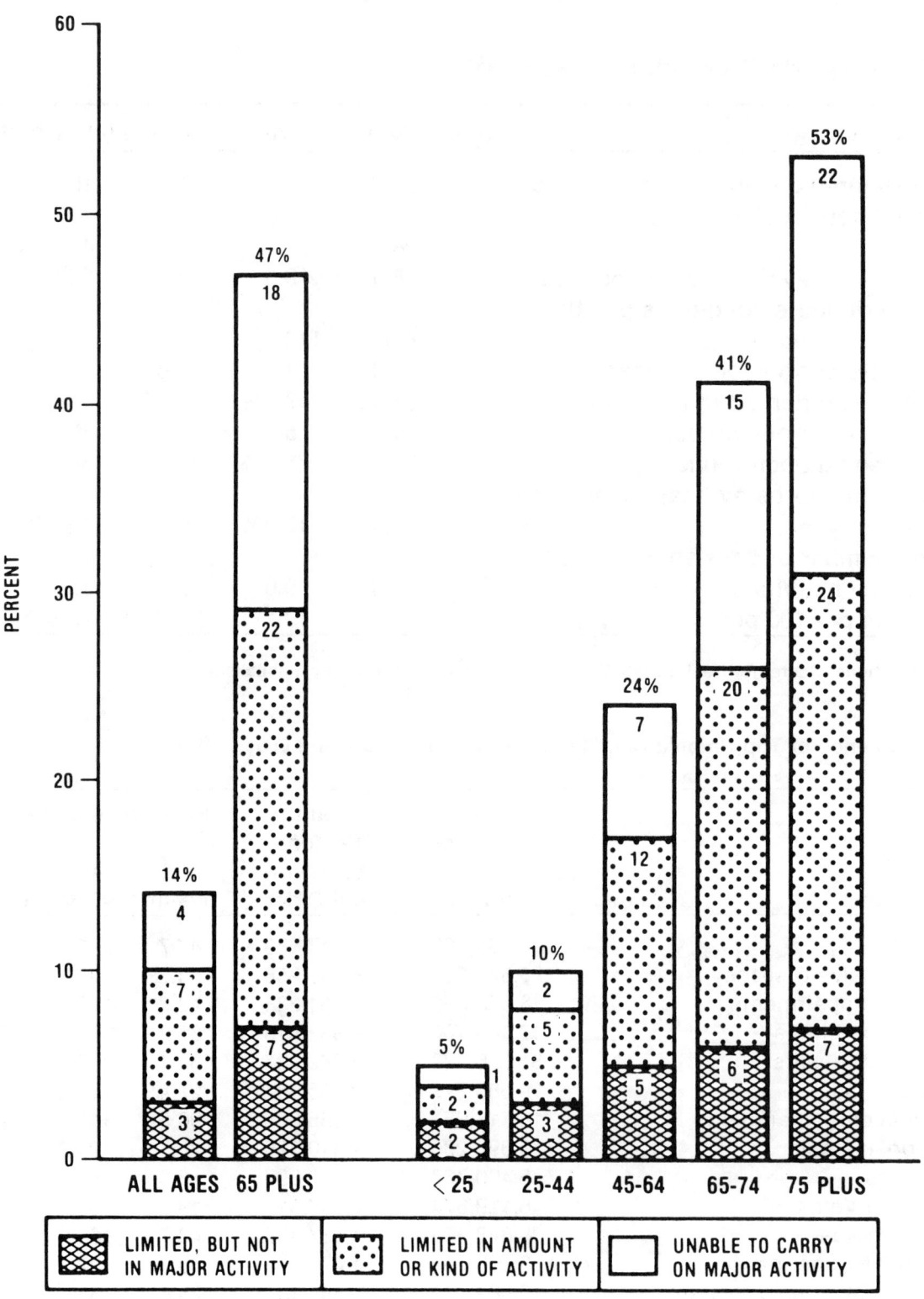

SOURCE: National Center for Health Statistics, 1981 Health Interview Survey, unpublished.

C2–4. Limitation in Activity Due to Chronic Conditions Actual and Projected, 1980–2060

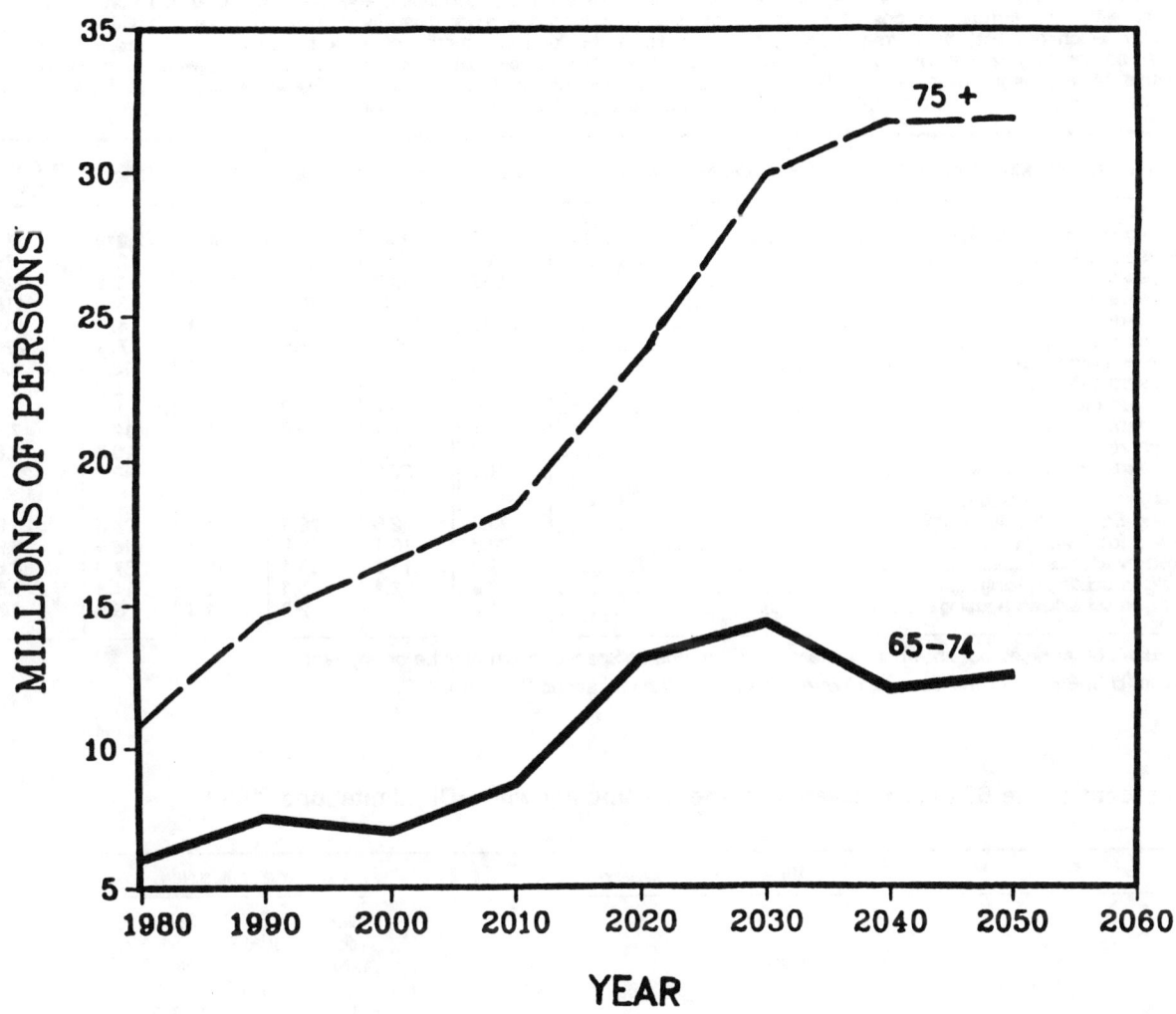

Source: Based on 1980 Health Interview Surveys National
          Center for Health Statistics; and US Bureau of
          the Census, "Projections of the US: 1982-2050,"
          Current Population Reports, Series P-25, No. 922
          (Washington, D.C.: USGPO, 1982)

C2–5. Persons with Work Disability by Selected Characteristics: 1982

[In thousands, except percent. As of March. Covers civilian noninstitutional population and members of Armed Forces living off post or with their families on post. Persons are classified as having a work disability if they (1) have a health problem or disability which prevents them from working or which limits the kind or amount of work they can do; (2) have a service-connected disability or ever retired or left a job for health reasons; (3) did not work in survey reference week or previous year because of long-term illness or disability; or (4) are under age 65, and are covered by Medicare or receive Supplemental Security Income. Based on Current Population Survey; see text, pp. 1 and 2 and Appendix III]

AGE AND PARTICIPATION STATUS IN ASSISTANCE PROGRAMS	Total [1]	Male	Female	White	Black	Spanish origin [2]
Persons with work disability	**13,102**	**6,697**	**6,405**	**10,657**	**2,214**	**696**
16–24 years old	1,205	618	587	932	251	78
25–34 years old	1,947	1,035	912	1,541	372	126
35–44 years old	1,942	992	950	1,553	348	116
45–54 years old	2,735	1,378	1,357	2,211	472	151
55–64 years old	5,273	2,674	2,599	4,420	771	226
Percent work disabled of total population	**8.9**	**9.3**	**8.5**	**8.4**	**13.4**	**8.0**
16–24 years old	3.3	3.4	3.1	3.0	5.0	3.0
25–34 years old	5.0	5.4	4.7	4.7	8.4	4.8
35–44 years old	7.1	7.4	6.8	6.5	12.1	7.4
45–54 years old	12.3	12.8	11.7	11.3	20.8	13.8
55–64 years old	24.1	26.2	22.3	22.6	40.0	28.4
Percent of work disabled—						
Receiving Social Security income	30.4	32.6	28.1	31.3	26.8	26.9
Receiving food stamps	20.8	16.1	25.8	15.3	46.9	36.9
Covered by Medicaid	19.8	13.8	26.1	16.1	37.0	34.6
Residing in public housing	3.9	2.4	5.3	2.2	11.5	7.5
Residing in subsidized housing	1.7	1.2	2.2	1.4	3.2	2.7

[1] Includes other races not shown separately.   [2] Persons of Spanish origin may be of any race.

Source: U.S. Bureau of the Census, *Current Population Reports*, series P-23, No. 127.

C2–6. Percent of the 65 Plus Population in the Community with ADL Limitations, 1982

IADL	ADL score			
Age/sex	Mildly disabled [1]	Disabled [2]	Severely disabled [3]	Total
	1–2	3–4	5–6	
65 to 74:	4.2	1.8	2.1	12.6
Male	3.4	1.7	2.4	11.7
Female	4.7	1.9	1.9	13.3
75 to 84:	9.0	3.6	4.5	25.0
Male	6.5	2.5	4.6	20.9
Female	10.3	4.3	4.4	27.6
85 +	17.4	7.8	10.4	45.8
Male	15.7	7.7	7.5	40.8
Female	18.2	7.9	11.8	48.2
All 65 +	6.6	2.8	3.5	18.9
Male	5.1	2.3	3.3	16.0
Female	7.7	3.2	3.6	20.9

[1] Limited, but not in a major activity such as eating, dressing, cooking or toileting.
[2] Limited in amount or kind of major activity.
[3] Unable to carry on major activities.

Source: Preliminary data from the 1982 National Long-Term Care Survey.

C2-7. Activity Limitation of Noninstitutional Elderly Medicare Beneficiaries, by Selected Characteristics: United States, 1980

Characteristic	Elderly Population in millions	With some activity limitation	With no limitation
		percent of persons	
Total	23.7	40	60
Age			
65–69 years..	9.1	31	69
70–74 years..	6.8	39	61
75–79 years..	4.3	47	53
80 years and over...	3.5	52	48
Sex			
Male	9.8	52	48
Female..	13.9	31	69

Several indices are used to measure the extent that activity limitations actually interfere with or impose some reduction on a person's life. These indices include:

• Bed disability days—days on which illness or injury keep a person in bed all or most of the day;

C2-8. Top Ten Chronic Conditions for Elderly—Rates Per 1,000 Persons, 1982

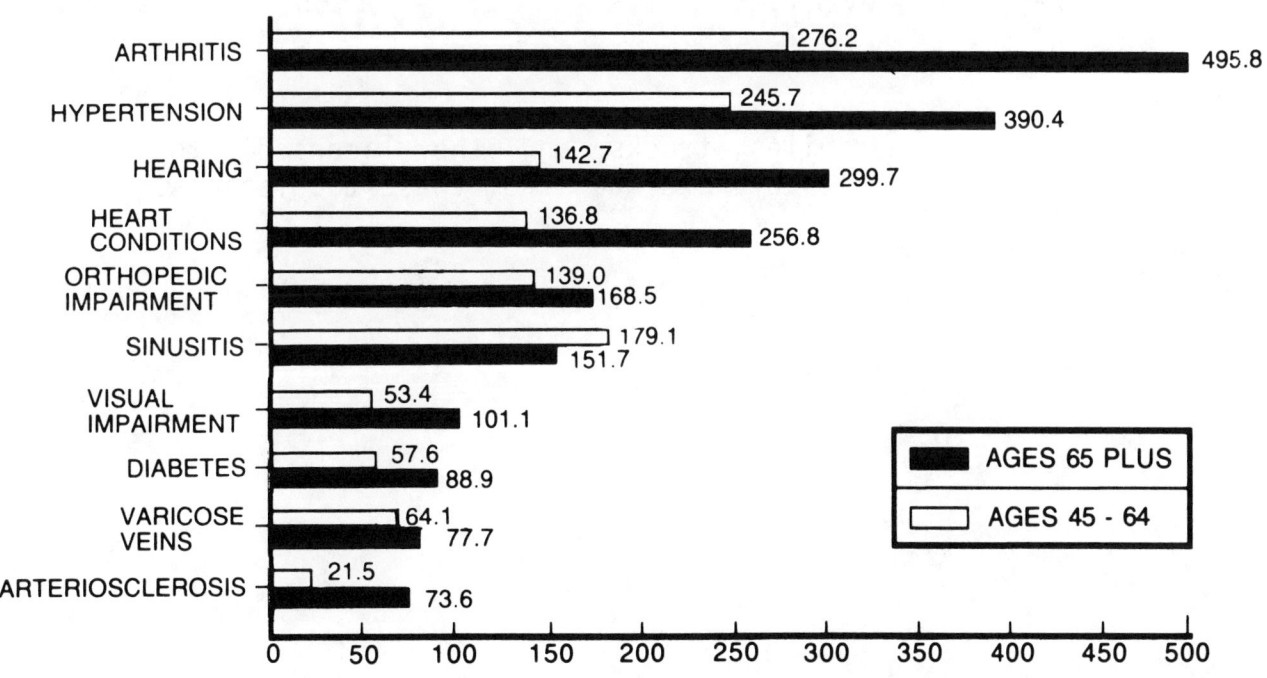

SOURCE: National Center for Health Statistics, 1982 HIS Survey.

C2-9. Tabulation of Products with Highest Frequencies of Deaths to Persons 65 Years of Age and Older*

Product	Number of Fatalities
General Home Fire Involvement	952
Stairs	623
Beds	261
Clothing	188
Farm Tractors	157
Bathtubs and Showers	140
Ladders	118
Chairs	114
Heating Equipment	105
Cigarettes, Tobacco	92
Swimming	74
Mobile Homes	69
Wheelchairs, Canes and Walkers	67
Ranges and Ovens	65
Bicycles	51

*Note: Automobiles, trucks, and other licensed motor vehicles are excluded from these tabulations.

C2–10. Tabulation of Products with High Injury Frequencies to Persons 65 Years of Age and Older, and High Proportions of Injuries to This Age Group

Product	Number of Injuries	Percent
Orthopedic Beds	2,200	51%
Wheelchairs, Canes and Walkers	12,200	49%
Floors	94,200	22%
Rugs and Carpets	11,900	22%
Eyeglasses	3,500	21%
Sinks and Toilets	6,700	21%
Bathtubs and Showers	14,600	16%
Chairs	27,300	15%
Power Lawn Mowers	3,500	14%
Power Saws	7,800	14%
Wringer Washers	1,000	14%
Ladders	13,200	14%
Beds	25,900	13%
Vacuum Cleaners	1,200	12%
Porches and Balconies	9,600	12%
Stairs	91,300	12%

C3. MENTAL HEALTH PROBLEMS

C3–1. Use of Mental Health Services by the Elderly. United States, 1971 and 1975

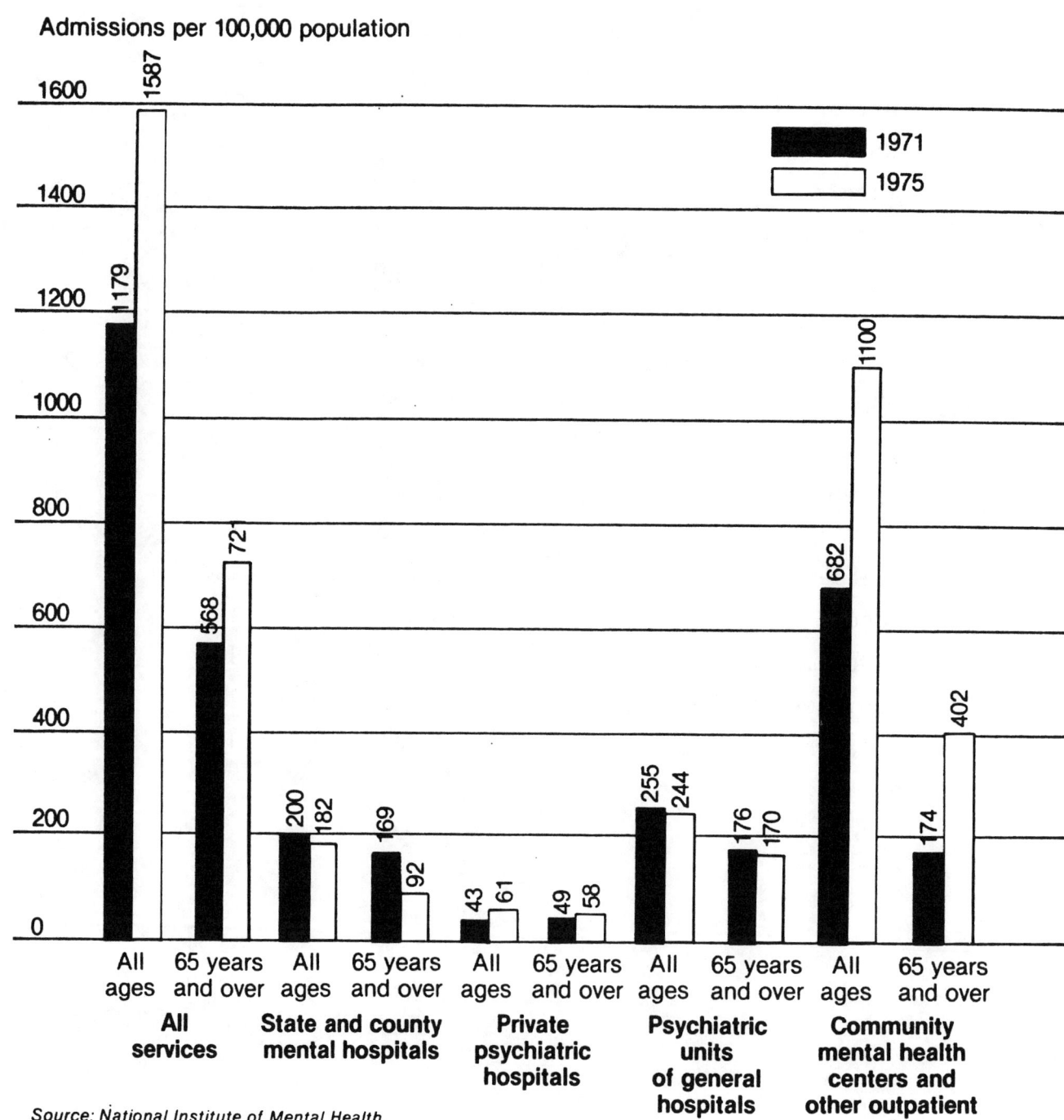

Admissions per 100,000 population

Source: National Institute of Mental Health.

C3–2. Selected Mental Health Measures for the Elderly by Place of Residence: United States

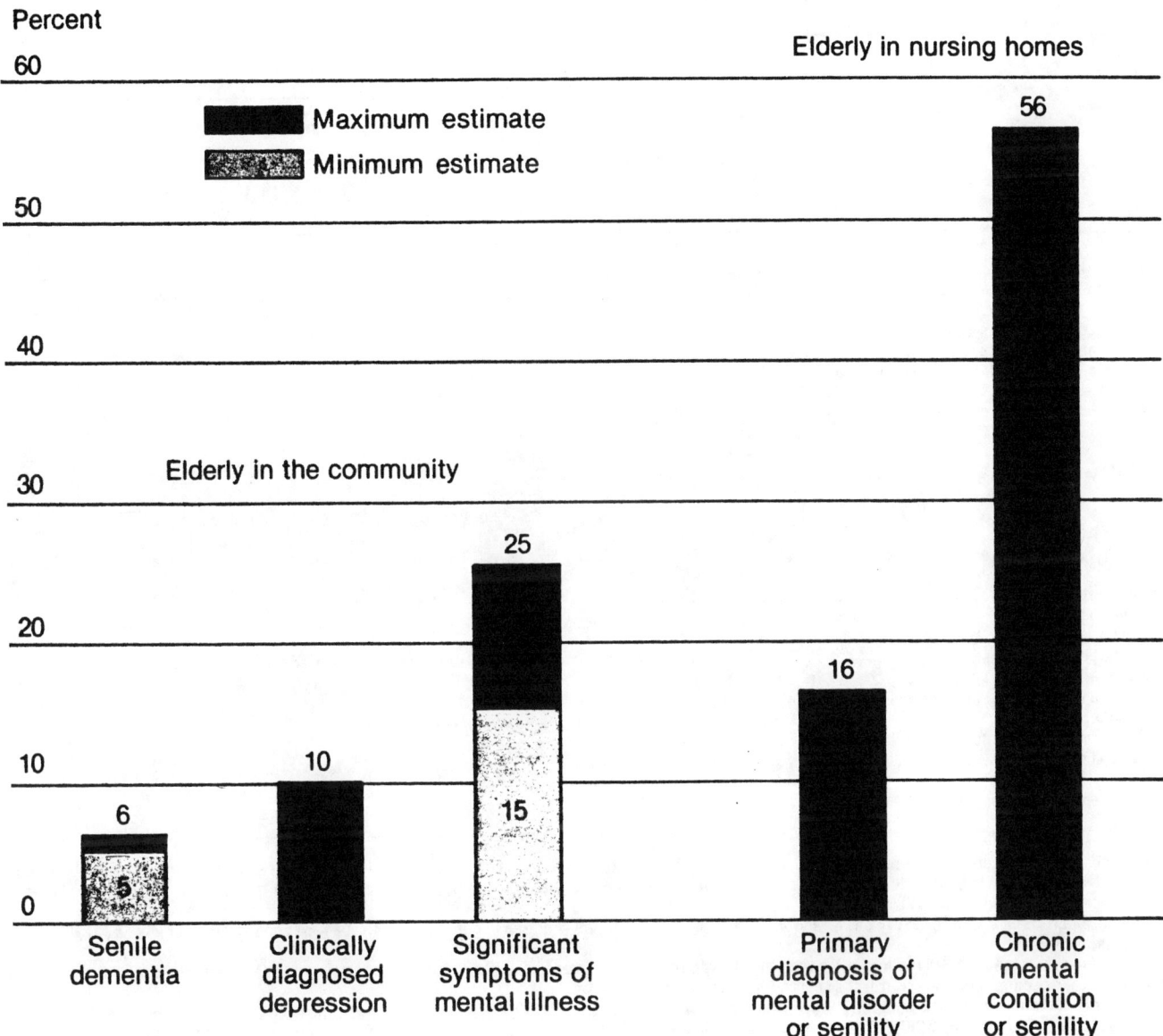

Note: Data cover the period 1976–1979.

Source: 1977 Report of the Secretary's Committee on Mental Health and Illness of the Elderly, National Institute of Mental Health, National Center for Health Statistics.

C3-3. Inpatient and Outpatient Care Episodes in Selected Mental Health Facilities and Number per 1,000 Civilian Population, According to Type of Facility: United States, Selected Years 1955–81

(Data are based on reporting by facilities)

Type of facility	Year				
	1955	1965	1975	1979[1]	1981[2]
	Number of episodes in thousands				
All facilities..............................	1,675	2,637	6,435	6,360	5,863
Inpatient services.................................	1,296	1,566	1,817	1,758	1,606
General hospital psychiatric service..............	266	519	566	562	562
State and county hospitals........................	819	805	599	527	499
Private hospitals[3]..............................	123	125	165	184	211
Veterans Administration psychiatric service[4]......	88	116	214	206	206
Federally funded community mental health centers[5]..	---	---	247	254	---
Other multiservice mental health facilities[5].......................................	---	---	26	25	128
Outpatient services[6]..............................	379	1,071	4,618	4,602	4,257
	Number per 1,000 civilian population				
All facilities..............................	10.3	13.8	30.3	28.6	25.8
Inpatient services.................................	8.0	8.2	8.5	7.7	7.1
General hospital psychiatric service..............	1.6	2.7	2.7	2.5	2.5
State and county hospitals........................	5.0	4.2	2.8	2.4	2.2
Private hospitals[3]..............................	0.8	0.7	0.8	0.8	0.9
Veterans Administration psychiatric service[4]......	0.5	0.6	1.0	0.9	0.9
Federally funded community mental health centers[5]..	---	---	1.2	1.1	---
Other multiservice mental health facilities[5].......................................	---	---	0.0	0.0	0.6
Outpatient services[6]..............................	2.3	5.6	21.9	20.6	18.7

[1]Revised data. Since 1979 data are not available for Veterans Administration medical centers and clinics, non-Federal general hospital psychiatric services, and inpatient and outpatient services, or federally funded community mental health centers (CMHC's); 1980 data are used.
[2]Provisional data. Since 1981 data are not available for non-Federal general hospital psychiatric services; 1980 data are used.
[3]Includes estimates of episodes of care in residential treatment centers for emotionally disturbed children.
[4]Includes Veterans Administration medical centers and clinics.
[5]With the advent of block grants, the changes in definition of CMHC's, and the discontinuation of CMHC monitoring by the National Institute of Mental Health, facilities formerly classified as CMHC's have been reclassified as other facility types, primarily "multiservice mental health facilities, not elsewhere classified" and "freestanding psychiatric outpatient clinics."
[6]Excludes outpatient episodes of Veterans Administration hospitals and clinics.

SOURCE: National Institute of Mental Health: Trends in patient care episodes in mental health facilities, 1955-1977. Statistical Note 154. Public Health Service, Rockville, Md., Sept. 1980; Mental Health, United States, 1983, Public Health Service, Rockville, Md., 1983; Unpublished data from the Survey and Reports Branch, Division of Biometry and Epidemiology.

C3–4. Inpatient Days of Care in Mental Health Facilities and Average Annual Percentage Change, According to Type of Facility: United States, 1971, 1975, and 1979

(Data are based on reporting by facilities)

Type of facility	Year			Average annual percent change 1971-79
	1971	1975	1979[1]	
	Number of inpatient days in thousands			
All facilities[2]	153,104	104,677	84,866	-7.1
Non-Federal psychiatric hospitals	123,420	74,985	55,663	-9.5
State and county hospitals	119,200	70,584	50,589	-10.2
Private hospitals	4,220	4,401	5,074	2.3
Veterans Administration psychiatric services[3]	14,277	11,725	10,628	-4.8
Non-Federal general hospital psychiatric units	6,826	8,349	8,435	3.6
Residential treatment centers for emotionally disturbed children	6,356	5,900	6,531	0.3
Federally funded community mental health centers	2,225	3,718	3,609	5.5

[1]Revised data. 1979 data are not available for Veterans Administration neuropsychiatric hospitals and general hospital inpatient psychiatric units (Veterans Administration and non-Federal), 1980 data are used for federally funded community mental health centers, and 1977 data are used for Veterans Administration psychiatric services and non-Federal general hospital psychiatric inpatient units.
[2]Excludes inpatient days for multiservice mental health facilities not elsewhere classified, which represent less than 1 percent of all inpatient days in each year.
[3]Includes Veterans Administration neuropsychiatric hospitals and Veterans Administration general hospitals with separate psychiatric inpatient settings.

NOTE: Comparable data for years later than 1979 are not available because of reclassification of facility types by the National Institute of Mental Health in 1981.

SOURCE: Division of Biometry and Epidemiology, National Institute of Mental Health: Unpublished data.

C3–5. VA Inpatients with Mental Disorders, 1983

(Percent)

Diagnosis	GMS Hospital	Psych Hospital	VA Domiciliary	VA Nursing Home	Total
Psychiatric	26.7	77.0	54.2	30.4	39.3
Non-psychiatric	73.3	23.0	45.8	69.6	60.7
Total	60.9	19.5	8.6	11.0	100.0

Source: VA, Annual Patient Census (1983).

C4. CAUSES OF DEATH, DEATH RATES

C4–1. Fifteen Leading Causes of Death by Age Group, 1980

	65-74	75-84	85 PLUS
1.	Heart Disease (40.6%)	Heart Disease (44.7%)	Heart Disease (48.6%)
2.	Cancer (Malignant Neoplasms) (27.3%)	Cancer (Malignant Neoplasms) (18.4%)	Cerebrovascular Disease (14.3%)
3.	Cerebrovascular Disease (7.3%)	Cerebrovascular Disease (11.8%)	Cancer (Malignant Neoplasms) (10%)
4.	Chronic Obstructive Pulmonary Disease and Related Conditions (4.3%)	Chronic Obstructive Pulmonary Disease and Related Conditions (3.4%)	Pneumonia and Influenza (5.5%)
5.	Diabetes (2.2%)	Pneumonia and Influenza (3.3%)	Atherosclerosis (4.1%)
6.	Accidents (1.9%)	Diabetes (2%)	Accidents (1.8%)
7.	Pneumonia and Influenza (1.9%)	Atherosclerosis (1.9%)	Chronic Obstructive Pulmonary Disease and Related Conditions (1.7%)
8.	Chronic Liver Disease and Cirrhosis (1.4%)	Accidents (1.8%)	Diabetes (1.4%)
9.	Nephritis, Nephrotic Syndrome and Nephrosis (.8%)	Nephritis, Nephrotic Syndrome and Nephrosis (1%)	Nephritis, Nephrotic Syndrome and Nephrosis (1%)
10.	Atherosclerosis (.8%)	Flu (Septicemia) (.5%)	Hypertension (.6%)
11.	Suicide (.6%)	Hypertension (.5%)	Flu (Septicemia) (.5%)
12.	Flu (Septicemia) (.5%)	Chronic Liver Disease and Cirrhosis (.5%)	Hernias and Intestinal Obstructions (.4%)
13.	Hypertension (.4%)	Ulcers (Stomach and Duodenum) (.4%)	Ulcers (.3%)
14.	Benign Neoplasms (.3%)	Hernia and Intestinal Obstructions (.3%)	Nutritional Deficiencies (.3%)
15.	Ulcers (Stomach and Duodenum) (.3%)	Benign Neoplasms (.3%)	Gallbladder Disorders (.3%)
	All other causes (9.3%)	All other causes (9.4%)	All other causes (8.9%)

SOURCE: National Center for Health Statistics: Advance report, final mortality statistics, 1980. *Monthly Vital Statistics Report*, Vol. 32, No. 4, Supplement DHHS Pub. No. (PHS) 83-1120. Public Health Service, Hyattsville, Md., August 1983.

C4-2. Death Rates for All Causes, According to Race, Sex, and Age: United States, Selected Years 1950-83

(Data are based on the National Vital Statistics System)

Race, sex, and age	Year							
	1950[1]	1960[1]	1970	1979	1980	1981	1982[1,2]	1983[1,2]
Total[3]	Number of deaths per 100,000 resident population							
All ages, age adjusted[4]...	841.5	760.9	714.3	577.0	585.8	568.2	556.4	549.6
All ages, crude..........	963.8	954.7	945.3	852.2	878.3	862.4	857.6	858.9
Under 1 year.................	3,299.2	2,696.4	2,142.4	1,332.9	1,288.3	1,207.3	1,143.7	1,076.8
1-4 years..................	139.4	109.1	84.5	64.2	63.9	60.2	55.5	51.7
5-14 years.................	60.1	46.6	41.3	31.5	30.6	29.4	27.8	27.3
15-24 years................	128.1	106.3	127.7	114.8	115.4	107.1	104.7	95.8
25-34 years................	178.7	146.4	157.4	133.0	135.5	132.1	126.9	121.6
35-44 years................	358.7	299.4	314.5	229.8	227.9	221.3	207.9	203.3
45-54 years................	853.9	756.0	730.0	589.7	584.0	573.5	556.4	541.9
55-64 years................	1,911.7	1,735.1	1,658.8	1,338.0	1,346.3	1,322.1	1,292.4	1,298.8
65-74 years................	4,067.7	3,822.1	3,582.7	2,929.0	2,994.9	2,922.3	2,904.5	2,883.4
75-84 years................	9,331.1	8,745.2	8,004.4	6,496.6	6,692.6	6,429.9	6,350.3	6,309.7
85 years and over..............	20,196.9	19,857.5	17,539.4	14,962.4	15,980.3	15,379.7	15,228.6	15,422.3
White male								
All ages, age adjusted[4].....	963.1	917.7	893.4	738.4	745.3	724.4	709.7	701.8
All ages, crude............	1,089.5	1,098.5	1,086.7	963.3	983.3	965.1	957.6	958.6
Under 1 year.................	3,400.5	2,694.1	2,113.2	1,276.0	1,230.3	1,182.0	1,129.2	1,078.0
1-4 years..................	135.5	104.9	83.6	64.2	66.1	60.5	55.5	54.3
5-14 years.................	67.2	52.7	48.0	36.6	35.0	34.2	32.1	31.5
15-24 years................	152.4	143.7	170.8	167.0	167.0	154.5	148.2	137.9
25-34 years................	185.3	163.2	176.6	166.7	171.3	167.3	156.7	155.5
35-44 years................	380.9	332.6	343.5	257.5	257.4	252.4	237.7	236.4
45-54 years................	984.5	932.2	882.9	711.3	698.9	686.5	671.0	649.4
55-64 years................	2,304.4	2,225.2	2,202.6	1,734.5	1,728.5	1,692.0	1,648.6	1,636.5
65-74 years................	4,864.9	4,848.4	4,810.1	3,991.5	4,035.7	3,926.9	3,893.2	3,849.6
75-84 years................	10,526.3	10,299.6	10,098.8	8,624.0	8,829.8	8,565.2	8,506.5	8,482.4
85 years and over..............	22,116.3	21,750.0	20,392.6	17,924.0	19,097.3	18,454.0	18,333.3	18,797.3
White female								
All ages, age adjusted[4].....	645.0	555.0	501.7	402.5	411.1	401.4	395.1	391.5
All ages, crude............	803.3	800.9	812.6	771.8	806.1	799.6	802.3	810.4
Under 1 year.................	2,566.8	2,007.7	1,614.6	986.7	962.5	935.4	906.2	789.6
1-4 years..................	112.2	85.2	66.1	50.4	49.3	47.7	44.3	42.0
5-14 years.................	45.1	34.7	29.9	23.2	22.9	21.6	20.2	20.9
15-24 years................	71.5	54.9	61.6	55.2	55.5	53.2	52.3	50.1
25-34 years................	112.8	85.0	84.1	64.7	65.4	64.7	62.8	62.4
35-44 years................	235.8	191.1	193.3	140.9	138.2	133.6	129.7	122.3
45-54 years................	546.4	458.8	462.9	374.5	372.7	370.9	357.6	356.2
55-64 years................	1,293.8	1,078.9	1,014.9	862.8	876.2	869.4	860.9	867.0
65-74 years................	3,242.8	2,779.3	2,470.7	1,997.9	2,066.6	2,032.8	2,029.0	2,018.0
75-84 years................	8,481.5	7,696.6	6,698.7	5,258.6	5,401.7	5,176.3	5,090.1	5,067.7
85 years and over..............	19,679.5	19,477.7	16,729.5	14,027.9	14,979.6	14,438.2	14,278.0	14,390.5

See footnotes at end of table.

C4-2. Death Rates for All Causes, According to Race, Sex, and Age: United States, Selected Years 1950-83 (Continued)

(Data are based on the National Vital Statistics System)

Race, sex, and age	Year							
	1950[1]	1960[1]	1970	1979	1980	1981	1982[1,2]	1983[1,2]
Black male	Number of deaths per 100,000 resident population							
All ages, age adjusted[4].....	1,373.1	1,246.1	1,318.6	1,073.3	1,112.8	1,067.7	1,045.5	1,024.7
All ages, crude............	1,260.3	1,181.7	1,186.6	999.6	1,034.1	991.6	974.3	950.2
Under 1 year.................. }	1,412.6	5,306.8	4,298.9	2,666.5	2,586.7	2,164.8	2,049.5	2,098.7
1-4 years.................... }		208.5	150.5	108.1	110.5	105.3	97.6	71.6
5-14 years...................	95.1	75.1	67.1	49.3	47.4	45.2	48.1	43.9
15-24 years..................	289.7	212.0	320.6	197.8	209.1	186.7	197.2	153.7
25-34 years..................	503.5	402.5	559.5	404.4	407.3	387.1	381.0	330.9
35-44 years..................	878.1	762.0	956.6	699.7	689.8	667.9	611.1	604.4
45-54 years..................	1,905.0	1,624.8	1,777.5	1,479.3	1,479.9	1,432.5	1,331.0	1,300.5
55-64 years..................	3,773.2	3,316.4	3,256.9	2,794.6	2,873.0	2,804.1	2,708.9	2,813.7
65-74 years..................	5,310.3	5,798.7	5,803.2	4,916.8	5,131.1	5,046.3	5,159.9	5,057.9
75-84 years.................. }	10,101.9	8,605.1	9,454.9	8,165.5	9,231.6	8,635.1	8,620.4	8,552.9
85 years and over............ }		14,844.8	14,415.4	14,465.4	16,098.8	15,396.4	15,732.1	15,386.0
Black female								
All ages, age adjusted[4].....	1,106.7	916.9	814.4	605.0	631.1	599.1	570.9	571.5
All ages, crude............	1,002.0	905.0	829.2	695.3	733.3	707.3	680.3	687.8
Under 1 year.................. }	1,139.3	4,162.2	3,368.8	2,208.2	2,123.7	1,823.4	1,582.5	1,581.1
1-4 years.................... }		173.3	129.4	91.9	84.4	81.6	65.7	66.5
5-14 years...................	72.8	53.8	43.8	30.8	30.5	30.0	25.6	25.7
15-24 years..................	213.1	107.5	111.9	71.8	70.5	64.0	62.0	56.8
25-34 years..................	393.3	273.2	231.0	146.0	150.0	141.1	142.2	119.0
35-44 years..................	758.1	568.5	533.0	321.2	323.9	306.1	287.3	275.9
45-54 years..................	1,576.4	1,177.0	1,043.9	759.2	768.2	723.9	705.1	664.3
55-64 years..................	3,089.4	2,510.9	1,986.2	1,502.7	1,561.0	1,527.9	1,449.2	1,530.4
65-74 years..................	4,000.2	4,064.2	3,860.9	2,914.6	3,057.4	2,929.7	2,796.7	2,934.4
75-84 years.................. }	8,347.0	6,730.0	6,691.5	5,594.4	6,212.1	5,822.3	5,578.6	5,392.9
85 years and over............ }		13,052.6	12,131.7	10,982.7	12,367.2	11,933.0	11,660.9	12,273.5

[1] Includes deaths of nonresidents of the United States.
[2] Provisional data.
[3] Includes all races and both sexes.
[4] Age adjusted by the direct method to the total population of the United States as enumerated in 1940, using 11 age groups

SOURCES: National Center for Health Statistics: Vital Statistics of the United States, Vol. II, Mortality, Part A, 1950-81. Public Health Service. Washington. U.S. Government Printing Office; Annual summary of births, deaths, marriages, and divorces, United States, 1983. Monthly Vital Statistics Report. Vol. 32-No. 13. DHHS Pub. No. (PHS) 84-1120. Public Health Service. Hyattsville, Md., Sept. 21, 1984; Data computed by the Division of Analysis from data compiled by the Division of Vital Statistics; U.S. Bureau of the Census: Population estimates and projections. Current Population Reports. Series P-25, No. 310. Washington. U.S. Government Printing Office, June 1965; 1950 Nonwhite Population by Race, Special report P-E No. 3B. Washington. U.S. Government Printing Office, 1951; General population characteristics, United States summary, 1960 and 1970. U.S. Census of Population. Final reports PC(1)-1B and PC(1)-B1. Washington. U.S. Government Printing Office, 1961 and 1972.

C4-3. Age-Adjusted Death Rates for Selected Causes of Death, According to Race and Sex: United States, Selected Years 1950-83

(Data are based on the National Vital Statistics System)

Race, sex, and cause of death	Year							
	1950[1]	1960[1]	1970	1979	1980	1981	1982[1,2]	1983[1,2]
Total[3]	Deaths per 100,000 resident population							
All causes.........................	841.5	760.9	714.3	577.0	585.8	568.2	556.4	549.6
Diseases of heart......................	307.6	286.2	253.6	199.5	202.0	195.0	191.0	188.5
Cerebrovascular diseases................	88.8	79.7	66.3	41.6	40.8	38.1	36.2	34.3
Malignant neoplasms.....................	125.4	125.8	129.9	130.8	132.8	131.6	133.4	132.3
Respiratory system...................	12.8	19.2	28.4	35.2	36.4	36.6	37.7	38.1
Digestive system....................	47.7	41.1	35.2	33.1	33.0	32.5	32.1	31.8
Breast[4]...........................	22.2	22.3	23.1	22.3	22.7	22.7	22.7	22.8
Pneumonia and influenza.................	26.2	28.0	22.1	11.2	12.9	12.3	11.1	11.2
Chronic liver disease and cirrhosis.....	8.5	10.5	14.7	12.0	12.2	11.4	10.4	10.4
Diabetes mellitus.......................	14.3	13.6	14.1	9.8	10.1	9.8	9.2	9.8
Accidents and adverse effects...........	57.5	49.9	53.7	42.9	42.3	39.8	37.2	34.9
Motor vehicle accidents..............	23.3	22.5	27.4	23.2	22.9	21.8	19.6	18.1
Suicide.................................	11.0	10.6	11.8	11.7	11.4	11.5	11.6	11.7
Homicide and legal intervention.........	5.4	5.2	9.1	10.2	10.8	10.4	9.7	8.2
White male								
All causes.........................	963.1	917.7	893.4	738.4	745.3	724.4	709.7	701.8
Diseases of heart......................	381.1	375.4	347.6	276.8	277.5	268.8	---	---
Cerebrovascular diseases................	87.0	80.3	68.8	42.9	41.9	38.9	---	---
Malignant neoplasms.....................	130.9	141.6	154.3	158.7	160.5	158.3	---	---
Respiratory system...................	21.6	34.6	49.9	57.0	58.0	57.8	---	---
Digestive system....................	54.0	47.5	41.9	40.0	39.8	39.3	---	---
Pneumonia and influenza.................	27.1	31.0	26.0	14.4	16.2	15.6	---	---
Chronic liver disease and cirrhosis.....	11.6	14.4	18.8	15.6	15.7	14.8	---	---
Diabetes mellitus.......................	11.3	11.6	12.7	9.3	9.5	9.3	---	---
Accidents and adverse effects...........	80.9	70.5	76.2	63.3	62.3	59.1	---	---
Motor vehicle accidents..............	35.9	34.0	40.1	35.5	34.8	33.4	---	---
Suicide.................................	18.1	17.5	18.2	18.6	18.9	18.9	---	---
Homicide and legal intervention.........	3.9	3.9	7.3	9.9	10.9	10.3	---	---
White female								
All causes.........................	645.0	555.0	501.7	402.5	411.1	401.4	395.1	391.5
Diseases of heart......................	223.6	197.1	167.8	131.3	134.6	129.8	---	---
Cerebrovascular diseases................	79.7	68.7	56.2	35.9	35.2	33.1	---	---
Malignant neoplasms.....................	119.4	109.5	107.6	105.7	107.7	107.2	---	---
Respiratory system...................	4.6	5.1	10.1	17.0	18.2	18.8	---	---
Digestive system....................	41.1	33.9	28.1	25.5	25.4	24.7	---	---
Breast[4]...........................	22.5	22.4	23.4	22.4	22.8	22.8	---	---
Pneumonia and influenza.................	18.9	19.0	15.0	7.8	9.4	9.0	---	---
Chronic liver disease and cirrhosis.....	5.8	6.6	8.7	7.0	7.0	6.7	---	---
Diabetes mellitus.......................	16.4	13.7	12.8	8.3	8.7	8.4	---	---
Accidents and adverse effects...........	30.6	25.5	27.2	21.6	21.4	20.2	---	---
Motor vehicle accidents..............	10.6	11.1	14.4	12.3	12.3	11.7	---	---
Suicide.................................	5.3	5.3	7.2	6.3	5.7	6.0	---	---
Homicide and legal intervention.........	1.4	1.5	2.2	2.9	3.2	3.1	---	---

See footnotes at end of table.

C4–3. Age-Adjusted Death Rates for Selected Causes of Death, According to Race and Sex: United States, Selected Years 1950–83 (Continued)

(Data are based on the National Vital Statistics System)

Race, sex, and cause of death	Year							
	1950[1]	1960[1]	1970	1979	1980	1981	1982[1,2]	1983[1,2]
Black male	Deaths per 100,000 resident population							
All causes..........................	1,373.1	1,246.1	1,318.6	1,073.3	1,112.8	1,067.7	1,045.5	1,024.7
Diseases of heart......................	415.5	381.2	375.9	314.1	327.3	316.7	---	---
Cerebrovascular diseases................	146.2	141.2	124.2	77.9	77.5	72.7	---	---
Malignant neoplasms....................	126.1	158.5	198.0	221.8	229.9	232.0	---	---
Respiratory system..................	16.9	36.6	60.8	78.7	82.0	84.1	---	---
Digestive system...................	59.4	60.4	58.9	60.7	62.1	62.1	---	---
Pneumonia and influenza................	63.8	70.2	53.8	24.2	28.0	26.4	---	---
Chronic liver disease and cirrhosis.....	8.8	14.8	33.1	30.3	30.6	27.3	---	---
Diabetes mellitus......................	11.5	16.2	21.2	17.0	17.7	16.8	---	---
Accidents and adverse effects...........	105.7	100.0	119.5	81.3	82.0	74.7	---	---
Motor vehicle accidents..............	39.8	38.2	50.1	33.7	32.9	30.7	---	---
Suicide................................	7.0	7.8	9.9	12.5	11.1	11.0	---	---
Homicide and legal intervention........	51.1	44.9	82.1	70.1	71.9	69.2	---	---
Black female								
All causes..........................	1,106.7	916.9	814.4	605.0	631.1	599.1	570.9	571.5
Diseases of heart......................	349.5	292.6	251.7	190.9	201.1	191.2	---	---
Cerebrovascular diseases................	155.6	139.5	107.9	60.9	61.7	58.1	---	---
Malignant neoplasms....................	131.9	127.8	123.5	125.1	129.7	127.1	---	---
Respiratory system..................	4.1	5.5	10.9	17.4	19.5	20.1	---	---
Digestive system...................	40.2	37.5	34.1	35.0	35.4	34.5	---	---
Breast[4]..........................	19.3	21.3	21.5	22.7	23.3	23.7	---	---
Pneumonia and influenza................	50.4	43.9	29.2	10.9	12.7	11.3	---	---
Chronic liver disease and cirrhosis.....	5.7	8.9	17.8	13.3	14.4	12.7	---	---
Diabetes mellitus......................	22.7	27.3	30.9	20.8	22.1	21.3	---	---
Accidents and adverse effects...........	38.5	35.9	35.3	23.9	25.1	21.6	---	---
Motor vehicle accidents..............	10.3	10.0	13.8	8.7	8.4	7.7	---	---
Suicide................................	1.7	1.9	2.9	2.9	2.4	2.5	---	---
Homicide and legal intervention........	11.7	11.8	15.0	13.9	13.7	12.9	---	---

[1] Includes deaths of nonresidents of the United States.
[2] Provisional data.
[3] Includes all other races not shown separately.
[4] Female only.

NOTES: Age-adjusted rates are computed by the direct method to the total population of the United States as enumerated in 1940, using 11 age groups. For data years shown, the code numbers for cause of death are based on the then current International Classification of Diseases, which are described in Appendix II, tables IV and V.

SOURCES: National Center for Health Statistics: Vital Statistics Rates in the United States, 1940-1960, by R. D. Grove and A. M. Hetzel. DHEW Pub. No. (PHS) 1677. Public Health Service. Washington. U.S. Government Printing Office, 1968; Unpublished data from the Division of Vital Statistics; Vital Statistics of the United States, Vol. II, Mortality, Part A, 1950-81. Public Health Service. Washington. U.S. Government Printing Office; Annual summary of births, deaths, marriages, and divorces, United States, 1983. Monthly Vital Statistics Report. Vol. 32-No. 13. DHHS Pub. No. (PHS) 84-1120. Public Health Service. Hyattsville, Md., Sept. 21, 1984; Data computed by the Division of Analysis from data compiled by the Division of Vital Statistics; U.S. Bureau of the Census: Population estimates and projections. Current Population Reports. Series P-25, No. 310. Washington. U.S. Government Printing Office, June 1965; General population characteristics, United States summary, 1960 and 1970. U.S. Census of Population. Final reports PC(1)-1B and PC(1)-B1. Washington. U.S. Government Printing Office, 1961 and 1972.

C4-4. Death Rates for Diseases of Heart, According to Race, Sex, and Age: United States, Selected Years 1950-83

(Data are based on the National Vital Statistics System)

Race, sex, and age	Year							
	1950[1]	1960[1]	1970	1979	1980	1981	1982[1,2]	1983[1,2]
Total[3]	Number of deaths per 100,000 resident population							
All ages, age adjusted[4]...	307.6	286.2	253.6	199.5	202.0	195.0	191.0	188.5
All ages, crude..........	355.5	369.0	362.0	326.5	336.0	328.7	328.3	327.6
Under 1 year...............	3.5	6.6	13.1	20.2	22.8	21.3	19.5	20.5
1-4 years.................	1.3	1.3	1.7	2.1	2.6	2.5 ⎫	1.2	1.4
5-14 years................	2.1	1.3	0.8	0.8	0.9	0.9 ⎭		
15-24 years...............	6.8	4.0	3.0	2.6	2.9	2.6	2.9	2.4
25-34 years...............	19.4	15.6	11.4	8.4	8.3	8.4	7.7	7.5
35-44 years...............	86.4	74.6	66.7	45.3	44.6	43.2	41.8	40.2
45-54 years...............	308.6	271.8	238.4	184.6	180.2	177.7	169.7	166.1
55-64 years...............	808.1	737.9	652.3	499.0	494.1	481.5	464.0	467.1
65-74 years...............	1,839.8	1,740.5	1,558.2	1,199.8	1,218.6	1,175.8	1,161.4	1,144.1
75-84 years...............	4,310.1	4,089.4	3,683.8	2,925.2	2,993.1	2,850.3	2,811.7	2,737.1
85 years and over..........	9,150.6	9,317.8	8,468.0	7,310.9	7,777.1	7,458.8	7,481.0	7,502.6
White male								
All ages, age adjusted[4].....	381.1	375.4	347.6	276.8	277.5	268.8	---	---
All ages, crude............	433.0	454.6	438.3	378.2	384.0	375.8	---	---
Under 1 year...............	4.1	6.9	12.0	19.2	22.5	20.0	---	---
1-4 years.................	1.1	1.0	1.5	1.7	2.1	2.2	---	---
5-14 years................	1.7	1.1	0.8	0.8	0.9	0.9	---	---
15-24 years...............	5.8	3.6	3.0	2.8	2.9	2.6	---	---
25-34 years...............	20.1	17.6	12.3	9.8	9.1	9.4	---	---
35-44 years...............	110.6	107.5	94.6	63.2	61.8	60.6	---	---
45-54 years...............	423.6	413.2	365.7	279.5	269.8	265.6	---	---
55-64 years...............	1,081.7	1,056.0	979.3	746.1	730.6	708.7	---	---
65-74 years...............	2,308.3	2,297.0	2,177.2	1,718.0	1,729.7	1,669.9	---	---
75-84 years...............	4,907.3	4,839.9	4,617.6	3,808.9	3,883.2	3,751.5	---	---
85 years and over..........	9,950.5	10,135.8	9,693.0	8,458.5	8,958.0	8,596.0	---	---
White female								
All ages, age adjusted[4].....	223.6	197.1	167.8	131.3	134.6	129.8	---	---
All ages, crude............	289.4	306.5	313.8	305.1	319.2	314.6	---	---
Under 1 year...............	2.7	4.3	7.0	13.2	15.7	18.0	---	---
1-4 years.................	1.1	0.9	1.2	1.7	2.1	2.2	---	---
5-14 years................	1.9	0.9	0.7	0.7	0.8	0.8	---	---
15-24 years...............	5.3	2.8	1.7	1.6	1.7	1.6	---	---
25-34 years...............	12.2	8.2	5.5	3.9	3.9	4.2	---	---
35-44 years...............	40.5	28.6	23.9	17.1	16.4	16.2	---	---
45-54 years...............	141.9	103.4	91.4	71.5	71.2	71.2	---	---
55-64 years...............	460.2	383.0	317.7	246.1	248.1	243.7	---	---
65-74 years...............	1,400.9	1,229.8	1,044.0	775.0	796.7	769.4	---	---
75-84 years...............	3,925.2	3,629.7	3,143.5	2,447.1	2,493.6	2,359.0	---	---
85 years and over..........	9,084.7	9,280.8	8,207.5	7,053.7	7,501.6	7,215.1	---	---

See footnotes at end of table.

C4-4. Death Rates for Diseases of Heart, According to Race, Sex, and Age: United States, Selected Years 1950-83 (Continued)

(Data are based on the National Vital Statistics System)

Race, sex, and age	Year							
	1950[1]	1960[1]	1970	1979	1980	1981	1982[1,2]	1983[1,2]
Black male	Number of deaths per 100,000 resident population							
All ages, age adjusted[4].....	415.5	381.2	375.9	314.1	327.3	316.7	---	---
All ages, crude............	348.4	330.6	330.3	290.2	301.0	289.7	---	---
Under 1 year................... }	4.8	13.9	33.5	42.7	42.8	35.6	---	---
1-4 years...................... }		3.8	3.9	4.3	6.3	4.4	---	---
5-14 years.....................	6.4	3.0	1.4	1.0	1.3	1.7	---	---
15-24 years....................	18.0	8.7	8.3	6.1	8.3	6.7	---	---
25-34 years....................	51.9	43.1	41.6	26.8	30.3	29.3	---	---
35-44 years....................	198.1	168.1	189.2	132.5	136.6	129.3	---	---
45-54 years....................	624.1	514.0	512.8	438.4	433.4	426.1	---	---
55-64 years....................	1,434.0	1,236.8	1,135.4	969.3	987.2	981.5	---	---
65-74 years....................	2,140.1	2,281.4	2,237.8	1,805.7	1,847.2	1,812.7	---	---
75-84 years.................... }	4,107.9	3,533.6	3,783.4	3,193.7	3,578.8	3,302.5	---	---
85 years and over.............. }		6,037.9	6,330.8	6,094.2	6,819.5	6,394.5	---	---
Black female								
All ages, age adjusted[4].....	349.5	292.6	251.7	190.9	201.1	191.2	---	---
All ages, crude............	289.9	268.5	261.0	234.1	249.7	241.1	---	---
Under 1 year................... }	3.9	12.0	31.3	37.9	43.6	29.2	---	---
1-4 years...................... }		2.8	4.2	4.0	4.4	4.0	---	---
5-14 years.....................	8.8	3.0	1.8	1.3	1.7	1.4	---	---
15-24 years....................	19.8	10.0	6.0	4.3	4.6	4.2	---	---
25-34 years....................	52.0	35.9	24.7	15.5	15.7	13.7	---	---
35-44 years....................	185.0	125.3	99.8	61.1	61.7	56.0	---	---
45-54 years....................	526.8	360.7	290.9	204.1	202.4	197.8	---	---
55-64 years....................	1,210.7	952.3	710.5	513.5	530.1	517.2	---	---
65-74 years....................	1,659.4	1,680.5	1,553.2	1,158.9	1,210.3	1,152.3	---	---
75-84 years.................... }	3,499.3	2,926.9	2,964.1	2,461.4	2,707.2	2,509.4	---	---
85 years and over.............. }		5,650.0	5,669.8	5,060.6	5,796.5	5,583.9	---	---

[1]Includes deaths of nonresidents of the United States.
[2]Provisional data.
[3]Includes all races and both sexes.
[4]Age adjusted by the direct method to the total population of the United States as enumerated in 1940, using 11 age groups.

NOTE: For data years shown, the code numbers for cause of death are based on the then current International Classification of Diseases, which are described in Appendix II, tables IV and V.

SOURCES: National Center for Health Statistics: Vital Statistics of the United States, Vol. II, Mortality, Part A, 1950-81. Public Health Service. Washington. U.S. Government Printing Office; Annual summary of births, deaths, marriages, and divorces, United States, 1983. Monthly Vital Statistics Report. Vol. 32-No. 13. DHHS Pub. No. (PHS) 84-1120. Public Health Service. Hyattsville, Md., Sept. 21, 1984; Data computed by the Division of Analysis from data compiled by the Division of Vital Statistics; U.S. Bureau of the Census: Population estimates and projections. Current Population Reports. Series P-25, No. 310. Washington. U.S. Government Printing Office, June 1965; 1950 Nonwhite Population by Race, Special report P-E No. 3B. Washington. U.S. Government Printing Office, 1951; General population characteristics, United States summary, 1960 and 1970. U.S. Census of Population. Final reports PC(1)-1B and PC(1)-B1. Washington. U.S. Government Printing Office, 1961 and 1972.

C4-5. Death Rates for Suicide, According to Race, Sex, and Age: United States, Selected Years 1950-83

(Data are based on the National Vital Statistics System)

Race, sex, and age	1950[1]	1960[1]	1970	1979	1980	1981	1982[1,2]	1983[1,2]
Total[3]	Number of deaths per 100,000 resident population							
All ages, age adjusted[4]	11.0	10.6	11.8	11.7	11.4	11.5	11.6	11.7
All ages, crude	11.4	10.6	11.6	12.1	11.9	12.0	12.2	12.4
Under 1 year	-	...	...	...	...	...	...	...
1-4 years	-	...	...	...	...	...	0.3	0.4
5-14 years	0.2	0.3	0.3	0.4	0.4	0.5		
15-24 years	4.5	5.2	8.8	12.4	12.3	12.3	12.6	11.7
25-34 years	9.1	10.0	14.1	16.3	16.0	16.3	15.6	16.2
35-44 years	14.3	14.2	16.9	15.4	15.4	15.9	16.6	15.1
45-54 years	20.9	20.7	20.0	16.5	15.9	16.1	16.0	16.9
55-64 years	27.0	23.7	21.4	16.6	15.9	16.4	16.1	17.2
65-74 years	29.3	23.0	20.8	17.8	16.9	16.2	16.9	17.3
75-84 years	31.1	27.9	21.2	20.8	19.1	18.6	19.9	25.0
85 years and over	28.8	26.0	20.4	17.9	19.2	17.7	17.6	22.0
White male								
All ages, age adjusted[4]	18.1	17.5	18.2	18.6	18.9	18.9	---	---
All ages, crude	19.0	17.6	18.0	19.6	19.9	20.0	---	---
Under 1 year	-	...	...	...	...	...	---	---
1-4 years	-	...	...	...	...	...	---	---
5-14 years	0.3	0.5	0.5	0.6	0.7	0.8	---	---
15-24 years	6.6	8.6	13.9	20.5	21.4	21.1	---	---
25-34 years	13.8	14.9	19.9	25.4	25.6	26.2	---	---
35-44 years	22.4	21.9	23.3	22.4	23.5	24.3	---	---
45-54 years	34.1	33.7	29.5	24.0	24.2	23.9	---	---
55-64 years	45.9	40.2	35.0	26.3	25.8	26.3	---	---
65-74 years	53.2	42.0	38.7	33.4	32.5	30.3	---	---
75-84 years	61.9	55.7	45.5	48.0	45.5	43.8	---	---
85 years and over	61.9	61.3	50.3	50.2	52.8	53.6	---	---
White female								
All ages, age adjusted[4]	5.3	5.3	7.2	6.3	5.7	6.0	---	---
All ages, crude	5.5	5.3	7.1	6.5	5.9	6.2	---	---
Under 1 year	-	...	...	...	...	...	---	---
1-4 years	-	...	...	...	...	...	---	---
5-14 years	0.1	*0.1	0.1	0.3	0.2	0.3	---	---
15-24 years	2.7	2.3	4.2	4.9	4.6	4.9	---	---
25-34 years	5.2	5.8	9.0	7.8	7.5	7.7	---	---
35-44 years	8.2	8.1	13.0	10.1	9.1	9.5	---	---
45-54 years	10.5	10.9	13.5	11.6	10.2	11.1	---	---
55-64 years	10.7	10.9	12.3	9.9	9.1	9.4	---	---
65-74 years	10.6	8.8	9.6	7.8	7.0	7.3	---	---
75-84 years	8.4	9.2	7.2	6.7	5.7	5.5	---	---
85 years and over	8.9	6.1	6.1	5.0	5.8	3.7	---	---

See footnotes at end of table.

C4–5. Death Rates for Suicide, According to Race, Sex, and Age: United States, Selected Years 1950–83 (Continued)

(Data are based on the National Vital Statistics System)

Race, sex, and age	Year							
	1950[1]	1960[1]	1970	1979	1980	1981	1982[1,2]	1983[1,2]
Black male	Number of deaths per 100,000 resident population							
All ages, age adjusted[4].........	7.0	7.8	9.9	12.5	11.1	11.0	---	---
All ages, crude..................	6.3	6.4	8.0	11.5	10.3	10.2	---	---
Under 1 year.........................	-	...	...	...	...	...	---	---
1-4 years...........................		...	...	...	...	...	---	---
5-14 years..........................	-	*0.1	*0.1	0.2	0.3	0.2	---	---
15-24 years.........................	4.9	4.1	10.5	14.0	12.3	11.1	---	---
25-34 years.........................	9.3	12.4	19.2	24.9	21.8	21.8	---	---
35-44 years.........................	10.4	12.8	12.6	16.9	15.6	15.5	---	---
45-54 years.........................	10.4	10.8	13.8	13.8	12.0	12.3	---	---
55-64 years.........................	16.5	16.2	10.6	12.8	11.7	12.5	---	---
65-74 years.........................	10.0	11.3	8.7	13.5	11.1	9.7	---	---
75-84 years.........................	6.2	*6.6	*8.9	10.5	10.5	18.0	---	---
85 years and over...................		*6.9	10.3	15.4	18.9	12.7	---	---
Black female								
All ages, age adjusted[4].........	1.7	1.9	2.9	2.9	2.4	2.5	---	---
All ages, crude..................	1.5	1.6	2.6	2.8	2.2	2.4	---	---
Under 1 year.........................	-	...	...	...	...	...	---	---
1-4 years...........................		...	...	...	...	...	---	---
5-14 years..........................	-	*0.0	*0.2	0.1	0.1	0.1	---	---
15-24 years.........................	1.8	1.3	3.8	3.3	2.3	2.4	---	---
25-34 years.........................	2.6	3.0	5.7	5.4	4.1	4.6	---	---
35-44 years.........................	2.0	3.0	3.7	4.1	4.6	4.2	---	---
45-54 years.........................	3.5	3.1	3.7	2.9	2.8	2.5	---	---
55-64 years.........................	1.1	*3.0	*2.0	3.8	2.3	2.9	---	---
65-74 years.........................	1.9	*2.3	*2.9	2.6	1.7	3.0	---	---
75-84 years.........................	2.4	*1.3	*1.7	2.5	1.4	1.0	---	---
85 years and over...................		-	3.2	1.0	-	1.8	---	---

[1] Includes deaths of nonresidents of the United States.
[2] Provisional data.
[3] Includes all races and both sexes.
[4] Age adjusted by the direct method to the total population of the United States as enumerated in 1940, using 11 age groups.

NOTE: For data years shown, the code numbers for cause of death are based on the then current <u>International Classification of Diseases</u>, which are described in Appendix II, tables IV and V.

SOURCES: National Center for Health Statistics: <u>Vital Statistics of the United States</u>, Vol. II, Mortality, Part A, 1950-81. Public Health Service. Washington. U.S. Government Printing Office; Annual summary of births, deaths, marriages, and divorces, United States, 1983. <u>Monthly Vital Statistics Report</u>. Vol. 32-No. 13. DHHS Pub. No. (PHS) 84-1120. Public Health Service. Hyattsville, Md., Sept. 21, 1984; Data computed by the Division of Analysis from data compiled by the Division of Vital Statistics; U.S. Bureau of the Census: Population estimates and projections. <u>Current Population Reports</u>. Series P-25, No. 310. Washington. U.S. Government Printing Office, June 1965; <u>1950 Nonwhite Population by Race</u>, Special Report P-E, No. 3B. Washington. U.S. Government Printing Office, 1951; General population characteristics, United States summary, 1960 and 1970. <u>U.S. Census of Population</u>. Final reports PC(1)-1B and PC(1)-B1. Washington. U.S. Government Printing Office, 1961 and 1972.

C4–6. Age-Specific Death Rates per 100,000 Adult Whites, United States, 1982, Presented by Sex*

Age in years	Males	Females	Male/Female Ratio (%)
55–59	1,304	679	192
60–64	2,028	1,053	193
65–69	3,231	1,640	197
70–74	4,771	2,489	192
75–79	7,232	3,992	181
80–84	10,810	6,751	160
≥85	18,333	14,278	128
All ages†	958	802	119

* Death rates are provisional based on a 10 per cent sample of 1982 death certificates.[4]

† Includes persons under 55 years of age.

C4–7. Ratios of Black and Other Races to White Death Rates for the Population 55 Years and Over, by Age and Sex: 1900–02 to 1980

Sex and year	55 to 64 years	65 to 74 years	75 to 84 years	85 years and over	65 years and over
BOTH SEXES					
1980 (prov.)	1.61	1.23	1.15	0.57	1.00
1978	1.55	1.22	1.06	0.60	0.97
1968	1.64	1.32	0.94	0.70	1.00
1954[1]	1.70	1.33	0.82	0.53	0.98
1940[1]	1.79	1.08	0.85	0.73	1.01
1930[2]	1.79	1.26	0.92	0.89	1.15
1900–02[3]	1.56	1.23	0.98	0.82	1.13
MALE					
1980 (prov.)	1.57	1.11	1.05	0.57	1.02
1968	1.45	1.17	0.89	0.69	0.96
1954[1]	1.49	1.08	0.80	0.56	0.95
1940[1]	1.47	1.16	0.89	0.79	1.02
1930[2]	1.58	1.22	0.99	0.96	1.16
1900–02[3]	1.48	1.21	1.02	0.93	1.13
FEMALE					
1980 (prov.)	1.72	1.40	1.20	0.56	0.97
1968	2.01	1.52	0.97	0.69	1.02
1954[1]	2.13	1.27	0.81	0.60	1.00
1940[1]	1.97	1.26	0.80	0.68	1.00
1930[2]	2.08	1.30	0.85	0.83	1.14
1900–02[3]	1.65	1.24	0.95	0.76	1.13

[1]Excludes Alaska and Hawaii.
[2]Texas excluded from Death Registration States.
[3]For the original Death Registration States; Black population only.

Source: Based on U.S. Bureau of the Census, United States Life Tables, 1930. 1936; U.S. Public Health Service, National Center for Health Statistics, annual volume of Vital Statistics of the United States, 1940, 1954, and 1968; and U.S. Public Health Service, National Center for Health Statistics, Monthly Vital Statistics Report, Final Mortality Statistics, 1978, Vol. 29, No. 6, Supplement (2), September 1980, and Monthly Vital Statistics Report. Provisional Data, Vol. 29, No. 13, September 1981.

C5. HEALTH SERVICES UTILIZATION, PHYSICIAN CARE

C5–1. Interval since Last Physician Visit, According to Selected Patient Characteristics: United States, 1964, 1977, and 1982

(Data are based on household interviews of a sample of the civilian noninstitutionalized population)

Selected characteristic	Interval since last physician visit								
	Less than 1 year			1 year-less than 2 years			2 years or more		
	1964	1977	1982	1964	1977	1982	1964	1977	1982
	Percent of population								
Total[1,2,3]...........	66.0	75.1	74.5	13.8	11.3	10.9	17.6	12.6	12.9
Age									
Under 17 years............	67.0	74.8	77.0	14.8	14.0	12.0	14.7	10.0	8.8
Under 6 years............	79.1	88.7	89.2	11.4	7.2	6.4	6.4	2.7	2.3
6-16 years..............	59.6	68.7	70.5	16.9	17.0	15.1	19.7	13.3	12.4
17-44 years................	65.9	74.5	71.1	14.7	11.4	12.1	17.2	13.0	15.1
45-64 years...............	63.5	74.4	73.3	12.8	9.0	9.2	21.8	15.7	15.9
65 years and over..........	68.8	79.6	81.3	9.2	6.5	5.7	20.3	13.3	11.8
Sex[1]									
Male......................	62.4	71.1	70.0	14.7	12.4	11.9	19.7	15.3	16.2
Female....................	69.3	78.7	78.6	13.0	10.3	9.9	15.8	10.2	9.9
Race[1,4]									
White.....................	67.3	75.3	74.9	13.7	11.1	10.6	17.0	12.6	12.8
Black[5]....................	57.0	74.5	73.3	14.6	12.1	12.2	21.8	12.0	12.3
Family income[1,6]									
Less than $7,000..........	57.5	76.2	76.1	12.9	10.1	10.1	23.3	12.8	12.1
$7,000-$9,999..............	61.6	72.9	73.8	14.0	11.6	11.0	20.8	14.4	13.4
$10,000-$14,999............	66.3	74.5	72.7	14.3	11.3	11.5	17.6	13.4	14.4
$15,000-$24,999............	69.7	75.3	73.8	13.9	11.2	11.1	15.2	12.9	13.4
$25,000 or more...........	73.0	76.8	76.9	12.8	11.1	10.2	13.2	11.4	11.6
Geographic region[1]									
Northeast.................	67.5	75.6	77.2	14.0	11.5	9.8	17.3	12.1	11.4
North Central.............	65.9	75.2	74.4	14.0	11.1	10.9	18.4	12.9	13.0
South.....................	64.0	74.3	73.0	13.6	11.9	11.8	17.9	12.7	13.3
West......................	68.4	75.9	74.1	13.5	10.2	10.4	16.2	12.8	13.7
Location of residence[1]									
Within SMSA...............	67.5	75.9	75.6	13.7	11.1	10.5	16.9	12.1	12.1
Outside SMSA..............	63.5	73.5	72.1	14.0	11.8	11.6	18.9	13.8	14.5

[1]Age adjusted by the direct method to the 1970 civilian noninstitutionalized population, using 4 age groups.
[2]Includes all other races not shown separately.
[3]Includes unknown family income.
[4]In 1964 and 1977, the racial classification of persons in the National Health Interview Survey was determined by interviewer observation. In 1982, race was determined by asking the household respondent.
[5]1964 data are for all other races.
[6]Family income categories for 1982. Adjusting for inflation, corresponding income categories in 1964 were: less than $2,000; $2,000-$3,999; $4,000-$6,999; $7,000-$9,999; and $10,000 or more; and, in 1977 were: less than $5,000; $5,000-$6,999; $7,000-$9,999; $10,000-$14,999; and $15,000 or more.

SOURCE: Division of Health Interview Statistics, National Center for Health Statistics: Data from the National Health Interview Survey.

C5-2. Physician Visits, According to Source or Place of Care and Selected Patient Characteristics: United States, 1964, 1976, and 1981

(Data are based on household interviews of a sample of the civilian noninstitutionalized population)

Selected characteristic	All sources or places[1]			Physician visits								
				Doctor's office or clinic or group practice			Hospital outpatient department[2]			Telephone		
	1964	1976	1981	1964	1976	1981	1964	1976	1981	1964	1976	1981
	Number per person			Percent of visits								
Total[3,4,5]	4.6	4.9	4.6	69.7	67.3	68.6	12.2	13.2	13.3	11.0	12.6	12.2
Age												
Under 17 years	3.7	4.0	4.1	62.2	64.5	64.4	13.7	13.3	13.3	18.3	17.0	16.8
Under 6 years	5.3	6.3	6.4	59.4	61.0	61.6	14.1	12.8	12.5	20.9	20.5	20.0
6-16 years	2.7	3.0	3.0	65.6	67.7	67.5	13.2	13.7	14.2	15.2	13.8	13.2
17-44 years	4.6	4.7	4.2	73.8	67.7	69.5	13.0	13.1	13.6	8.1	11.0	10.7
45-64 years	5.0	5.7	5.1	76.8	68.5	71.3	10.0	15.0	14.1	6.1	9.9	8.9
65 years and over	6.7	6.9	6.3	64.2	72.9	73.8	8.5	9.5	10.6	8.2	9.9	9.6
Sex[3]												
Male	4.0	4.3	4.1	69.9	66.4	67.5	13.2	15.2	15.7	9.3	10.6	10.3
Female	5.1	5.4	5.1	69.5	67.8	69.3	11.4	11.9	11.7	12.2	13.9	13.4
Race[3,6]												
White	4.7	4.9	4.6	71.0	68.6	70.2	10.2	11.3	11.1	11.7	13.6	13.3
Black[7]	3.6	4.8	4.7	56.2	56.7	57.3	32.7	27.9	27.6	4.2	5.8	5.4
Family income[3,8]												
Less than $7,000	3.9	5.6	5.6	62.0	58.5	59.1	25.9	20.1	21.7	4.8	10.3	10.9
$7,000-$9,999	4.2	4.8	4.9	65.2	62.4	66.0	22.3	19.3	15.6	6.6	8.4	12.1
$10,000-$14,999	4.7	4.8	4.5	69.5	67.6	67.2	11.1	14.9	14.4	11.7	10.8	12.5
$15,000-$24,999	4.8	4.9	4.5	71.5	68.4	69.5	7.4	13.4	10.8	13.8	13.1	13.9
$25,000 or more	5.2	4.9	4.4	72.9	70.4	73.0	6.7	8.9	10.3	12.9	14.6	12.2
Geographic region[3]												
Northeast	4.5	4.9	4.6	67.2	62.5	65.7	10.1	15.8	14.7	11.5	13.0	12.7
North Central	4.4	4.7	4.5	72.2	69.5	70.2	10.6	11.4	12.2	11.7	14.3	13.5
South	4.3	4.7	4.5	68.9	68.1	67.4	14.0	13.3	13.1	11.0	10.9	11.9
West	5.5	5.4	4.8	70.9	68.7	71.6	14.3	12.7	13.8	9.5	12.7	10.4
Location of residence[3]												
Within SMSA	4.8	5.1	4.7	68.2	65.8	67.5	12.3	13.8	13.6	12.1	13.4	12.8
Outside SMSA	4.1	4.5	4.4	72.9	70.9	71.0	11.9	11.8	12.7	8.8	10.8	10.8

[1] Includes all other sources or places of care not shown separately.
[2] Includes hospital outpatient clinic or emergency room.
[3] Age adjusted by the direct method to the 1970 civilian noninstitutionalized population, using 4 age groups.
[4] Includes all other races not shown separately.
[5] Includes unknown family income.
[6] In 1964 and 1976, the racial classification of persons in the National Health Interview Survey was determined by interviewer observation. In 1981, race was determined by asking the household respondent.
[7] 1964 data are for all other races.
[8] Family income categories for 1981. Adjusting for inflation, corresponding income categories in 1964 were: less than $2,000; $2,000-$3,999; $4,000-$6,999; $7,000-$9,999; and $10,000 or more; and, in 1976 were: less than $5,000; $5,000-$6,999; $7,000-$9,999; $10,000-$14,999; and $15,000 or more.

NOTE: Data for 1982 are not included because the effect of major questionnaire changes in the 1982 National Health Interview Survey is currently being evaluated.

SOURCE: Division of Health Interview Statistics, National Center for Health Statistics: Data from the National Health Interview Survey.

C5-3. Measures and Correlates of Health Services Utilization* 1981/82

Per Cent† Utilization According to

Health service use	Age 60-64 (n=229)	Age 65-69 (n=150)	Age 70-74 (n=162)	Age 75+ (n=160)	Male (n=299)	Female (n=404)	Spanish-speaking only (n=397)	Spanish and English‡ (n=294)	Income <$3999 (n=160)	Income $4000-5999 (n=200)	Income $6000-7999 (n=164)	Income $8000+ (n=125)	Insurance (n=454)	No Insurance (n=239)
Physician care														
Did not see doctor last year	24.1	25.7	13.0	18.5¶	24.2	18.0	21.3	19.2	25.2	15.0	19.0	23.4	16.2	28.9¶
Saw a general practitioner§	86.6	73.6	83.6	87.4¶	81.7	84.7	87.6	78.4¶	87.1	83.5	81.8	77.9	66.3	82.9¶
Saw a specialist	30.4	30.0	34.3	35.9	34.8	31.4	27.7	39.6¶	31.6	32.7	26.5	41.1	33.8	30.4
Source of care														
local private doctor	46.6	50.7	50.6	53.8	51.9	48.5	49.1	50.2	34.6	47.5	66.9	56.5¶	54.3	41.2¶
Neighborhood clinic	22.4	21.8	16.9	12.3	18.1	19.1	20.1	16.9	20.9	20.4	15.5	15.2	19.2	17.6
Hospital	23.6	23.6	28.0	31.4	27.4	26.0	24.3	29.8	37.0	28.9	18.4	22.8¶	26.3	27.5
Hospital care														
In hospital or nursing home last year	9.0	6.7	11.8	12.2	11.0	9.3	(9.0)	11.3	11.4	11.6	9.3	7.4	11.3	7.6

* For each correlate χ² tests were performed for each measure; statistically significant results are indicated by¶.
† Per cents do not add to 100 because cases in the category of "other" have been excluded.
‡ Indicates respondents who are bilingual or English-speaking only.
§ Per cents are computed by use of respondents who saw a doctor in the past year.
¶ Statistically significant: $P/\chi^2 < 0.05$.

C5-4. Protection Against Short-Term Sickness Income Loss: 1970 to 1981

[In millions of dollars, except percent. "Short-term sickness" refers to short-term or temporary nonwork-connected disability (lasting not more than 6 months) and the first 6 months of long-term disability. See also *Historical Statistics, Colonial Times to 1970*, series H 115-124]

ITEM	1970	1974	1975	1976	1977	1978	1979	1980	1981
Short-term sickness: Income loss	16,757	21,804	23,595	26,447	28,225	32,811	36,072	38,529	41,278
Total protection provided [1]	5,888	8,232	9,002	9,819	10,559	11,751	13,371	15,058	15,638
Protection as percent of loss	35.1	37.8	38.2	37.1	37.4	35.8	37.1	39.1	37.9
Benefits provided by protection:									
Individual insurance	694	851	973	881	940	1,210	1,322	1,280	1,291
Group benefits to workers in private employment	2,952	4,144	4,328	4,900	5,284	5,782	6,987	8,265	8,536
Private cash insurance [2]	1,476	2,024	2,011	2,267	2,344	2,403	3,216	3,903	3,484
Publicly operated cash sickness funds [3]	411	485	538	581	582	609	699	770	953
Sick leave	1,066	1,634	1,779	2,052	2,359	2,770	3,072	3,593	4,099
Sick leave for government employees	2,242	3,107	3,542	3,868	4,144	4,579	4,892	5,338	5,640

[1] Provided by individual insurance, group benefits to workers in private employment, and sick leave for government employees. Beginning 1974, includes benefits for the sixth month of disability payable under old-age, survivors, disability, and health insurance program, not shown separately. [2] Group accident and sickness insurance and self-insurance privately written either on a voluntary basis or in compliance with State temporary disability insurance laws in CA, NJ, and NY. Includes a small but undetermined amount of group disability insurance benefits paid to government workers and to self-employed persons through farm, trade, or professional associations. [3] Includes State-operated plans in RI, CA, and NJ; State Insurance Fund and special fund for disabled unemployed in New York; and provisions of Railroad Unemployment Insurance Act.

Source: U.S. Social Security Administration, *Social Security Bulletin*, August 1984.

C5-5. Volume of Physician Visits for 1983

All ages	1,172,640
25 to 44	319,109
45 to 64	269,617
65 to 74	116,520
75 plus	79,889
65 plus	196,418

65 plus as percent of total equals 16.8 percent.

[17] National Center for Health Statistics. Hospital Discharge Survey. Unpublished tabulations. 1983.

[18] U.S. Senate Special Committee on Aging, 1984.

C5-6. Interval since Last Visit

[Number in thousands]

	Less than 1 year	1 to 2 years	2 to 5 years	5 plus years
All ages	168,514	24,499	22,181	8,246
25 to 44	46,836	7,844	7,840	2,578
45 to 64	32,385	4,070	4,624	2,421
65 to 74	12,568	1,011	1,206	895
75 plus	8,070	449	558	367
Percent:				
All ages	75.4	11.0	9.9	3.7
25 to 44	71.9	12.0	12.0	4.0
45 to 64	74.4	9.4	10.6	4.0
65 to 74	80.2	6.4	7.7	5.7
75 plus	85.4	4.8	5.9	3.9

Average number of visits per person per year

	Percent
All ages	5.2
25 to 44	4.8
45 to 64	6.1
65 to 74	7.4
75 plus	8.4

C5–7. Annual Number of Physician Visits per Adult Presented by Age, Sex, and Functional Status, All Races Combined, United States, 1980

	No Limitations		Limited in Minor Activities		Limited in Major Activities		Cannot Perform Major Activities	
	Male	Female	Male	Female	Male	Female	Male	Female
Age in years								
35–44	2.8	4.0	7.7	11.1	5.9	11.3	15.2	28.6
45–54	3.0	3.9	4.6	8.3	5.9	11.5	12.2	23.1
55–64	3.1	4.2	6.3	8.3	7.6	10.7	10.3	19.5
65–74	3.6	5.2	6.5	6.9	7.4	10.3	8.3	13.4
≥75	5.0	4.9	—*	5.7	7.1	6.9	9.3	9.8
All ages†	3.3	4.5	6.0	8.7	7.6	10.7	10.4	15.4

* Numerator too small to form a useful figure.
† Includes persons under 35 years.

C5–8. Discharge Rates from Short-Term Hospitals per 1,000 Individuals, Presented by Age and Sex, All Races Combined, United States, 1981

	Discharge Rates		Male/Female Ratio (%)
	Male	Female	
Age in years			
<15	80	65	123
15–44	90	206	44
47–54	166	187	89
55–64	224	206	109
65–74	364	304	120
≥75	545	473	115
All ages	140	197	71

C5–9. Projected Expenditures for Physicians' Services, Hospital Care, and Nursing Home Care, and Percent Distribution by Age: United States, 1978 and 2003

	Physicians' Services			Hospital Care			Nursing Home Care		
	1978	2003 constant mortality	2003 declining mortality	1978	2003 constant mortality	2003 declining mortality	1978	2003 constant mortality	2003 declining mortality
Expenditures in billions of dollars	36.3	47.2	49.6	73.9	97.5	105.8	14.5	22.6	30.3

Percent Distribution									
Under 20 years	15.4	12.7	12.3	9.6	7.8	7.3	—	—	—
20-64 years	62.5	64.2	61.9	62.7	62.4	59.2	—	—	—
Under 65 years	—	—	—	—	—	—	16.6	13.3	9.9
65 years and over	22.3	23.1	25.8	27.7	29.8	33.6	83.4	86.7	90.1

SOURCE: U.S. Department of Health and Human Services, *Changing Mortality Patterns, Health Services Utilization, and Health Care Expenditures: United States 1978-2003.*

C5–10. Regional Variations in Median Physician Fees, 1984

Region* and type of visit	General practitioners	Family practitioners	All surgical specialists	All nonsurgical specialists
East				
Initial visit	$25	$25	$42	$40
Revisit	20	21	26	26
South				
Initial visit	23	25	36	36
Revisit	20	20	24	24
Midwest				
Initial visit	21	21	35	33
Revisit	18	18	21	21
West				
Initial visit	31	27	46	45
Revisit	25	22	26	29

*East includes New England and Mid-eastern states; South, South Atlantic, Mid-southern and Southwestern states; Midwest, Great Lakes and Plains states; and West, Rocky Mountain and Far Western states.

SOURCE: *Medical Economics Continuing Survey.* Copyright (c) 1984. Published by Medical Economics Company, at Oradell, N.J. 07649. Reprinted by permission.

C6. HOSPITALS AND NURSING HOMES

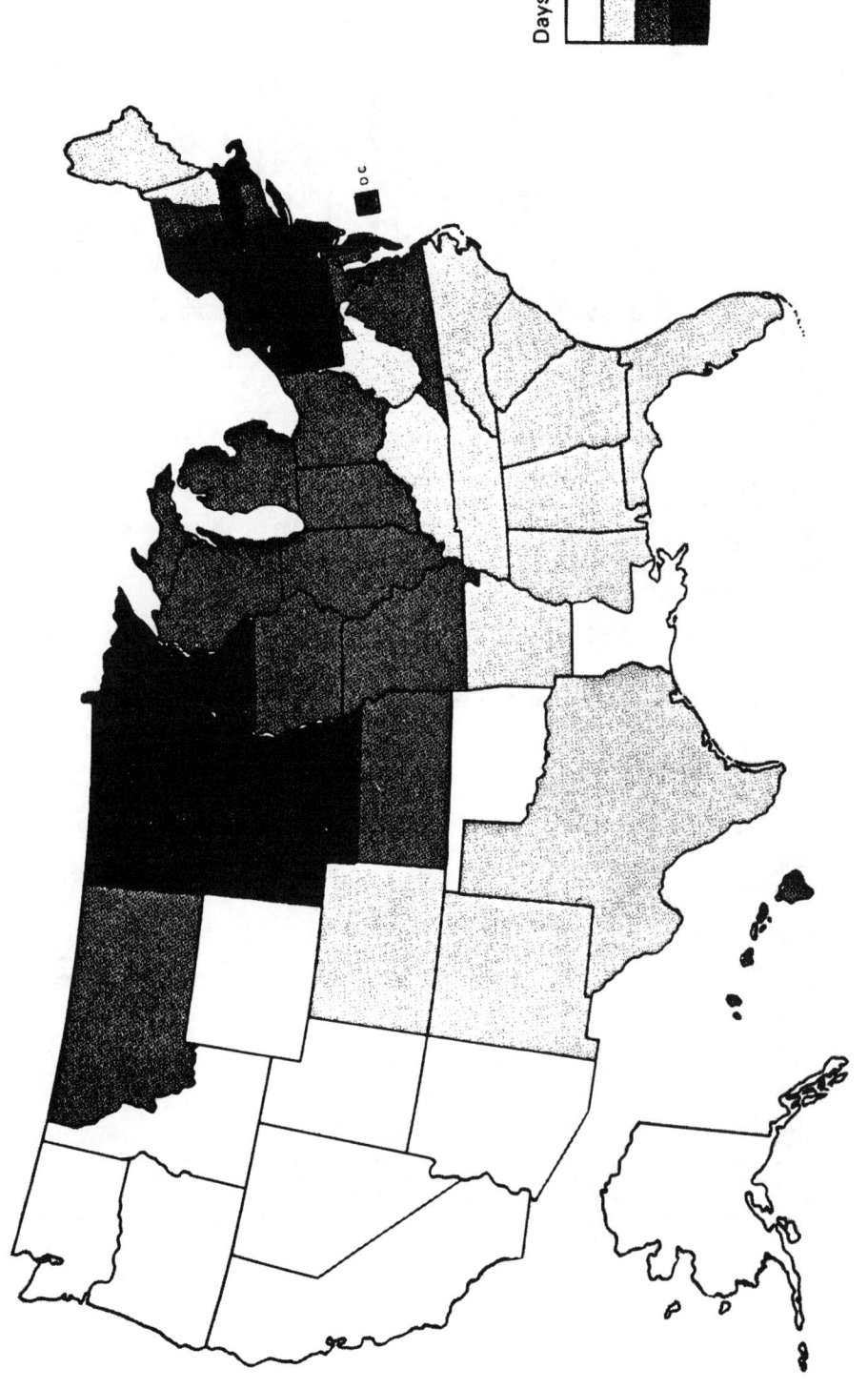

C6–1. Average Length of Stay in Community Hospitals: 1982

Days per stay

Under 6.6

6.6–7.7

7.8–8.3

8.4 and over

NOTE: Data refer to non-Federal short-term general and other specialty hospitals.

SOURCE: American Hospital Association.

C6-2. Admissions, Average Length of Stay, and Outpatient Visits in Short-Stay Hospitals, According to Type of Ownership: United States, Selected Years 1960-82

(Data are based on reporting by a census of hospitals)

Type of ownership	Year								
	1960	1970	1975	1977	1978	1979	1980	1981	1982
Admissions				Number in thousands					
All ownerships.............	24,324	30,706	35,270	36,227	36,433	37,034	38,140	38,417	38,332
Federal....................	1,354	1,454	1,751	1,874	1,858	1,874	1,942	1,923	1,903
Non-Federal................	22,970	29,252	33,519	34,353	34,575	35,160	36,198	36,494	36,429
Nonprofit..................	16,788	20,948	23,735	24,284	24,443	24,885	25,576	25,955	25,908
Proprietary...............	1,550	2,031	2,646	2,849	2,880	2,963	3,165	3,239	3,316
State-local government.....	4,632	6,273	7,138	7,220	7,253	7,312	7,458	7,299	7,205
Average length of stay				Number of days					
All ownerships.............	8.4	8.7	8.0	7.9	7.9	7.8	7.8	7.9	7.9
Federal....................	21.4	17.0	14.4	12.9	13.2	12.8	12.9	12.5	12.6
Non-Federal................	7.6	8.2	7.7	7.6	7.6	7.6	7.6	7.6	7.6
Nonprofit..................	7.4	8.2	7.8	7.8	7.8	7.7	7.7	7.8	7.8
Proprietary...............	5.7	6.8	6.6	6.6	6.5	6.6	6.5	6.6	6.6
State-local government.....	8.8	8.7	7.6	7.4	7.4	7.4	7.4	7.6	7.5
Outpatient visits[1]				Number in thousands					
All ownerships.............	---	173,058	245,938	254,483	253,896	252,461	255,320	257,254	304,089
Federal....................	---	39,514	49,627	50,245	47,434	48,587	48,568	50,524	53,200
Non-Federal................	---	133,545	196,311	204,238	206,461	203,873	206,752	206,729	250,888
Nonprofit..................	---	90,992	132,368	139,045	142,617	140,525	142,864	143,953	176,838
Proprietary...............	---	4,698	7,713	8,355	8,911	9,289	9,696	9,961	13,193
State-local government.....	---	37,854	56,230	56,838	54,933	54,060	54,192	52,816	60,857

[1]Because of modifications in the collection of outpatient data for 1977 and 1982, there are discontinuities in the trends for this item.

NOTE: Excludes psychiatric and tuberculosis and other respiratory disease hospitals.

SOURCES: American Hospital Association: Hospitals. JAHA 35(15):396-401 and 45(15):463-467, Aug. 1961 and Aug. 1971; Hospital Statistics, 1976-83 Editions. Chicago, 1976-83. (Copyrights 1961, 1971, 1976-83: Used with the permission of the American Hospital Association.)

C6–3. Duration of Stay in Short-Stay Non-Federal Hospitals by Average Number of Days Persons Age 65 Years and Older, 1983

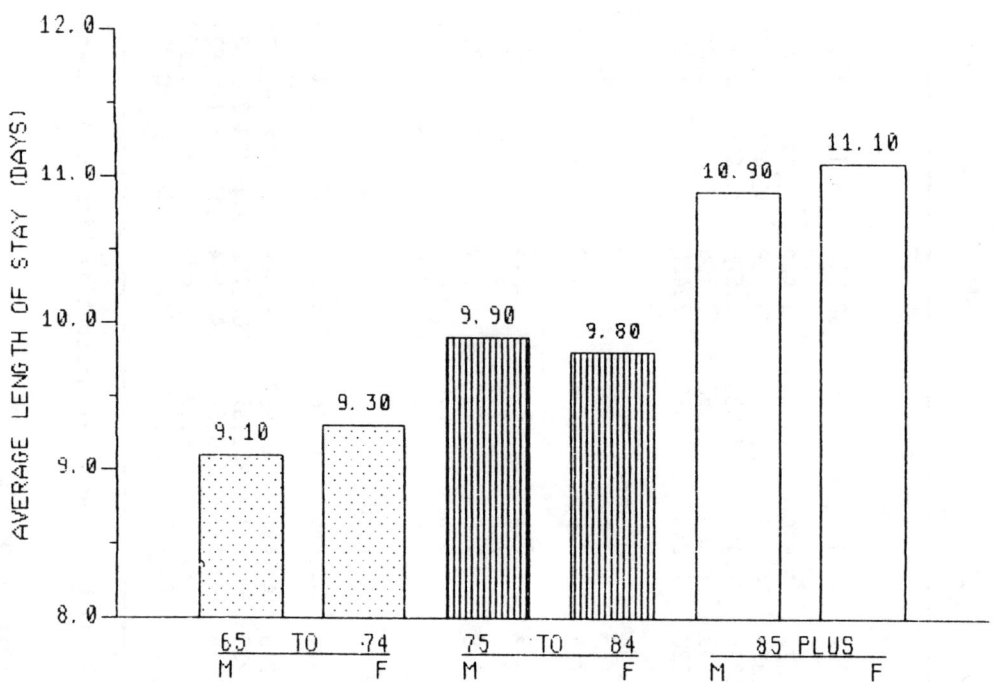

Source: National Center for Health Statistics, 1981 National Hospital Discharge Survey, 1983

C6–4. Average Cost to Patient per Day for Semiprivate Hospital Room by Region, 1984–1985

	Northeast		North Central		South		West	
	July 1984	Jan. 1985	July 1984	Jan. 1985	July 1984	Jan. 1985	July 1984	Jan. 1985
Dollars	222.29	225.08	213.67	216.14	165.61	169.83	245.66	250.03

NOTE: Northeast includes New England and Middle Atlantic states; North Central, East North Central and West North Central states; South, South Atlantic, East South Central and West South Central states; and West, Mountain and Pacific states. Data exclude Puerto Rico.

SOURCE: Health Insurance Association of America, *Survey of Hospital Semiprivate Room Charges,* Jan. 1985.

C6–5. Population 65 Years and Over in Nursing Homes, by Age

(Numbers in thousands)

Age (years)	1963	1973	1977	1982[1]
65 and over	448	961	1,126	1,316
65 to 74	93	159	211	232
75 to 84	207	394	465	527
85 and over	148	408	450	557

[1] Based on 1982 estimate and proportion of the population for each age group in nursing homes in 1977: 65 and over, 0.049; 65 to 74, 0.0144; 75 to 84, 0.064; 85 and over, 0.2259.

C6–6. Older Americans in Need of Long-Term Care, 1980–2040

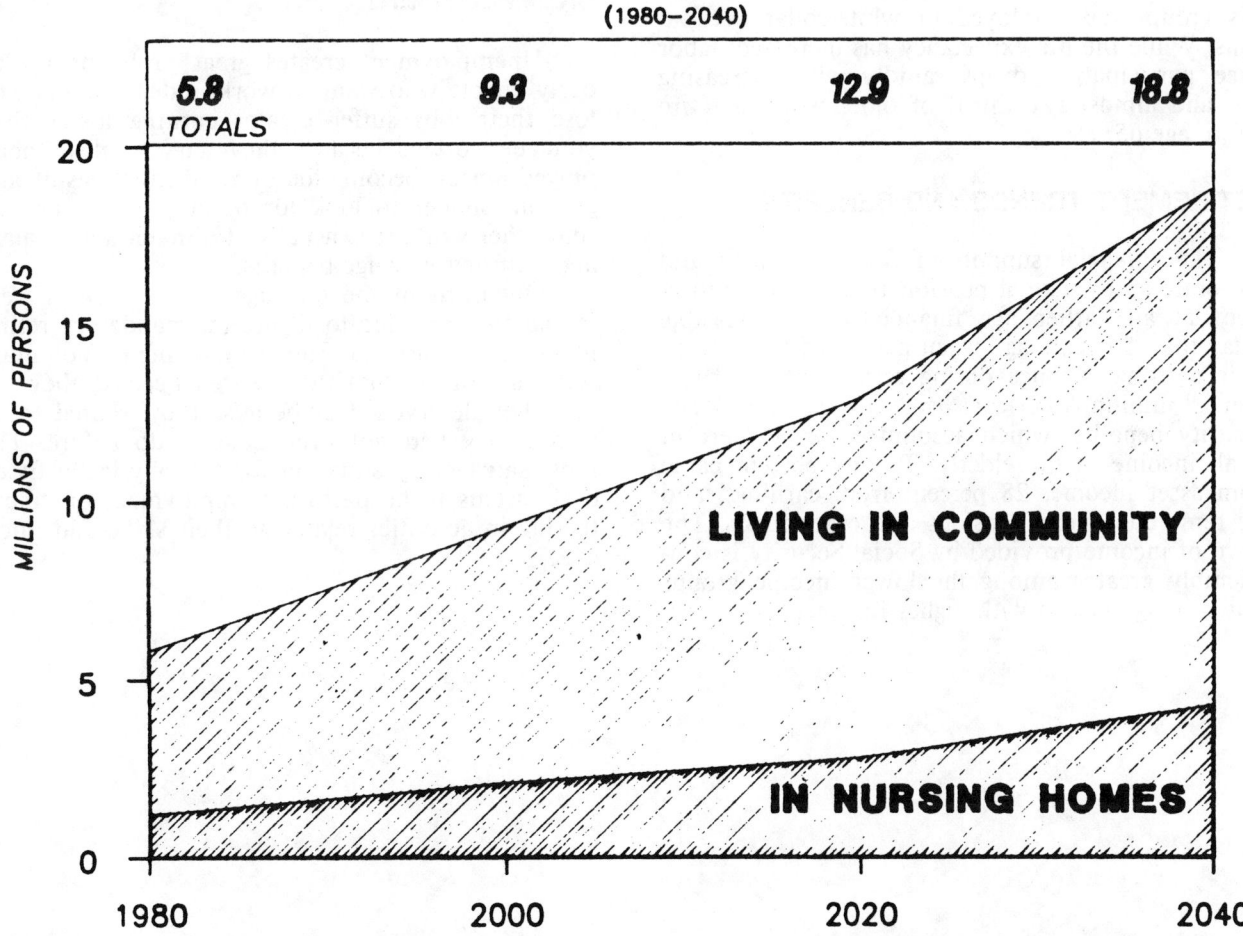

SOURCE: 1982 National Long-Term Care Survey and 1977 National Nursing Home Survey and Social Security Administration Projections.

D. Employment Conditions

LABOR FORCE PARTICIPATION

The dramatic change in the population's age distribution since the turn of the century is reflected by the change in the labor force participation of the 65+ population. At the turn of the century, the average man basically worked until he died; he spent only 3 percent of his lifetime in retirement. Today, he is spending one-fifth of his life in retirement. In 1984, the 65+ population made up only 3 percent of the total labor force; three-quarters of this group was employed in white-collar occupations. While the life expectancy has increased, labor force participation drops rapidly with increasing age, and almost two-thirds of older workers retire before age 65.

RETIREMENT TRENDS AND BENEFITS

The financial support of Social Security and corporate and personal pension funds makes retirement at an earlier age financially more feasible today than 50 years ago when people had to rely on their personal savings during retirement. In 1982, over 29 million Americans aged 60+ received Social Security benefits, which accounted for 34 percent of all income of the elderly. Twenty percent came from asset income, 28 percent from earnings, and the remainder from pensions and other funds. The share of income provided by Social Security is considerably greater among the lower income groups than among persons with higher incomes.

PART-TIME WORK

Regardless of age, most retirees would prefer to continue part-time work after retirement. Sixty percent of retired women have part-time employment, compared to 45 percent of men. The proportion of older people working part-time is considerably greater now than it was 25 years ago.

UNEMPLOYMENT

Unemployment creates great problems for elderly people who want to work; older workers who lose their jobs suffer greater earning losses than younger workers because they tend to stay unemployed longer, become discouraged more easily, and give up sooner to look for other jobs. If they do find other work, it is usually at a much lower salary and with fewer fringe benefits.

One-third of the 65+ age group workers were forced to retire due to ill health, mandatory retirement, or failure to find employment. Voluntary retirees indicate that they retired because they felt that they deserved it or because they wanted to do things they had not been able to do before. The most satisfactory situation for the physically fit elderly seems to be part-time employment or volunteering in activities related to their skills and interests.

D1. LABOR FORCE PARTICIPATION

D1-1. Employment Status of the Civilian Noninstitutional Population 16 Years and Over, 1951 to 1985

(Numbers in thousands)

Year and month	Civilian noninsti- tutional population	Civilian labor force				Unemployment rates		
		Total	Percent of population	Employed	Unemployed	Total	Men	Women
Annual averages								
1951	104,621	62,017	59.2	59,961	2,055	3.3	2.8	4.4
1952	105,231	62,138	59.0	60,250	1,883	3.0	2.8	3.6
1953[1]	107,056	63,015	58.9	61,179	1,834	2.9	2.8	3.3
1954	108,321	63,643	58.8	60,109	3,532	5.5	5.3	6.0
1955	109,683	65,023	59.3	62,170	2,852	4.4	4.2	4.9
1956	110,954	66,552	60.0	63,799	2,750	4.1	3.8	4.8
1957	112,265	66,929	59.6	64,071	2,859	4.3	4.1	4.7
1958	113,727	67,639	59.5	63,036	4,602	6.8	6.8	6.8
1959	115,329	68,369	59.3	64,630	3,740	5.5	5.2	5.9
1960[1]	117,245	69,628	59.4	65,778	3,852	5.5	5.4	5.9
1961	118,771	70,459	59.3	65,746	4,714	6.7	6.4	7.2
1962[1]	120,153	70,614	58.8	66,702	3,911	5.5	5.2	6.2
1963	122,416	71,833	58.7	67,762	4,070	5.7	5.2	6.5
1964	124,485	73,091	58.7	69,305	3,786	5.2	4.6	6.2
1965	126,513	74,455	58.9	71,088	3,366	4.5	4.0	5.5
1966	128,058	75,770	59.2	72,895	2,875	3.8	3.2	4.8
1967	129,874	77,347	59.6	74,372	2,975	3.8	3.1	5.2
1968	132,028	78,737	59.6	75,920	2,817	3.6	2.9	4.8
1969	134,335	80,734	60.1	77,902	2,832	3.5	2.8	4.7
1970	137,085	82,771	60.4	78,678	4,093	4.9	4.4	5.9
1971	140,216	84,382	60.2	79,367	5,016	5.9	5.3	6.9
1972[1]	144,126	87,034	60.4	82,153	4,882	5.6	5.0	6.6
1973[1]	147,096	89,429	60.8	85,064	4,365	4.9	4.2	6.0
1974	150,120	91,949	61.3	86,794	5,156	5.6	4.9	6.7
1975	153,153	93,775	61.2	85,846	7,929	8.5	7.9	9.3
1976	156,150	96,158	61.6	88,752	7,406	7.7	7.1	8.6
1977	159,033	99,009	62.3	92,017	6,991	7.1	6.3	8.2
1978[1]	161,910	102,251	63.2	96,048	6,202	6.1	5.3	7.2
1979	164,863	104,962	63.7	98,824	6,137	5.8	5.1	6.8
1980	167,745	106,940	63.8	99,303	7,637	7.1	6.9	7.4
1981	170,130	108,670	63.9	100,397	8,273	7.6	7.4	7.9
1982	172,271	110,204	64.0	99,526	10,678	9.7	9.9	9.4
1983	174,215	111,550	64.0	100,834	10,717	9.6	9.9	9.2
1984	176,383	113,544	64.4	105,005	8,539	7.5	7.4	7.6
Monthly data, seasonally adjusted[2]								
1984:								
August	176,583	113,629	64.3	105,148	8,481	7.5	7.2	7.8
September	176,763	113,764	64.4	105,394	8,370	7.4	7.2	7.5
October	176,956	114,016	64.4	105,649	8,367	7.3	7.1	7.7
November	177,135	114,074	64.4	105,932	8,142	7.1	7.0	7.3
December	177,306	114,464	64.6	106,273	8,191	7.2	7.1	7.2
1985:								
January	177,384	114,875	64.8	106,391	8,484	7.4	7.2	7.7
February	177,516	115,084	64.8	106,685	8,399	7.3	7.1	7.5
March	177,667	115,514	65.0	107,119	8,396	7.3	7.0	7.6
April	177,799	115,371	64.9	106,945	8,426	7.3	7.1	7.5
May	177,944	115,373	64.8	106,960	8,413	7.3	6.9	7.7
June	178,096	114,783	64.5	106,370	8,413	7.3	7.3	7.4
July	178,263	115,314	64.7	106,862	8,451	7.3	7.2	7.5
August	178,405	115,299	64.6	107,172	8,127	7.0	6.8	7.3

[1] Not strictly comparable with prior years. For an explanation, see "Historical Comparability" under the Household Data section of the Explanatory Notes.

[2] The population figures are not adjusted for seasonal variation.

D1–2. Employment Status of the Civilian Noninstitutional Population by Age, Sex, and Race, 1985

(Numbers in thousands)

Age, sex, and race	Civilian noninstitutional population	August 1985								
		Civilian labor force					Not in labor force			
		Total	Percent of population	Employed	Unemployed		Total	Keeping house	Going to school	Unable to work	Other reasons
					Number	Percent of labor force					
TOTAL											
16 years and over	178,405	116,679	65.4	108,628	8,051	6.9	61,726	30,629	1,539	2,494	27,065
16 to 19 years	14,448	8,940	61.9	7,590	1,350	15.1	5,508	732	527	21	4,227
16 to 17 years	7,235	3,793	52.4	3,196	596	15.7	3,443	303	226	3	2,911
18 to 19 years	7,212	5,147	71.4	4,394	753	14.6	2,065	429	301	18	1,316
20 to 24 years	20,045	16,186	80.7	14,487	1,699	10.5	3,859	1,765	540	58	1,497
25 to 54 years	94,712	76,746	81.0	72,341	4,403	5.7	17,967	13,021	465	865	3,616
25 to 34 years	40,818	33,544	82.2	31,222	2,322	6.9	7,274	5,355	332	183	1,403
25 to 29 years	20,997	17,254	82.2	15,948	1,306	7.6	3,743	2,681	213	99	748
30 to 34 years	19,821	16,289	82.2	15,273	1,016	6.2	3,532	2,674	118	84	655
35 to 44 years	31,471	25,963	82.5	24,634	1,330	5.1	5,507	4,017	103	285	1,102
35 to 39 years	17,345	14,301	82.5	13,520	781	5.5	3,044	2,261	70	133	583
40 to 44 years	14,126	11,663	82.6	11,113	550	4.7	2,463	1,759	34	151	520
45 to 54 years	22,423	17,238	76.9	16,486	752	4.4	5,186	3,649	29	397	1,111
45 to 49 years	11,583	9,219	79.6	8,786	432	4.7	2,364	1,725	16	161	463
50 to 54 years	10,841	8,019	74.0	7,699	319	4.0	2,822	1,924	13	237	648
55 to 64 years	22,144	11,977	54.1	11,469	508	4.2	10,167	5,323	6	602	4,237
55 to 59 years	11,272	7,233	64.2	6,913	321	4.4	4,038	2,424	4	292	1,319
60 to 64 years	10,872	4,744	43.6	4,556	188	4.0	6,129	2,899	2	310	2,918
65 years and over	27,057	2,831	10.5	2,741	90	3.2	24,226	9,788	1	948	13,488
65 to 69 years	9,348	1,714	18.3	1,668	46	2.7	7,633	3,136	2	219	4,277
70 years and over	17,709	1,117	6.3	1,073	45	4.0	16,592	6,653	–	730	9,210
Men											
16 years and over	84,558	65,501	77.5	61,403	4,098	6.3	19,057	453	744	1,420	16,439
16 to 19 years	7,252	4,742	65.4	3,987	754	15.9	2,510	43	243	17	2,207
16 to 17 years	3,689	2,056	55.8	1,698	359	17.4	1,632	30	116	–	1,486
18 to 19 years	3,563	2,685	75.4	2,290	396	14.7	878	14	127	16	721
20 to 24 years	9,720	8,596	88.4	7,744	851	9.9	1,125	28	274	33	790
25 to 54 years	46,075	43,348	94.1	41,164	2,183	5.0	2,727	141	226	607	1,754
25 to 34 years	19,919	18,915	95.0	17,757	1,157	6.1	1,004	42	161	138	663
25 to 29 years	10,250	9,681	94.5	9,026	655	6.8	569	18	114	84	352
30 to 34 years	9,669	9,233	95.5	8,731	502	5.4	436	24	47	54	311
35 to 44 years	15,318	14,574	95.1	13,957	617	4.2	744	44	44	201	455
35 to 39 years	8,449	8,074	95.6	7,709	365	4.5	375	21	30	93	231
40 to 44 years	6,869	6,500	94.6	6,247	253	3.9	369	23	14	107	225
45 to 54 years	10,838	9,860	91.0	9,451	409	4.1	979	54	20	268	636
45 to 49 years	5,617	5,242	93.3	5,018	223	4.3	375	21	12	105	237
50 to 54 years	5,222	4,618	88.4	4,432	185	4.0	604	33	8	164	399
55 to 64 years	10,397	7,076	68.1	6,805	270	3.8	3,322	77	2	404	2,838
55 to 59 years	5,339	4,269	80.0	4,103	167	3.9	1,070	39	–	199	831
60 to 64 years	5,058	2,806	55.5	2,703	104	3.7	2,252	38	2	205	2,007
65 years and over	11,113	1,740	15.7	1,701	39	2.2	9,373	164	–	359	8,849
65 to 69 years	4,190	1,054	25.1	1,028	25	2.4	3,136	45	–	126	2,965
70 years and over	6,923	687	9.9	673	14	2.0	6,237	119	–	234	5,884
Women											
16 years and over	93,847	51,178	54.5	47,225	3,953	7.7	42,669	30,175	795	1,074	10,626
16 to 19 years	7,196	4,198	58.3	3,603	595	14.2	2,997	689	284	4	2,020
16 to 17 years	3,547	1,736	49.0	1,499	238	13.7	1,810	273	110	2	1,425
18 to 19 years	3,649	2,462	67.5	2,104	358	14.5	1,187	416	174	2	595
20 to 24 years	10,325	7,590	73.5	6,742	848	11.2	2,734	1,737	266	25	706
25 to 54 years	48,637	33,397	68.7	31,177	2,220	6.6	15,240	12,880	239	258	1,862
25 to 34 years	20,899	14,630	70.0	13,465	1,165	8.0	6,270	5,313	171	45	740
25 to 29 years	10,747	7,573	70.5	6,922	651	8.6	3,174	2,663	99	15	396
30 to 34 years	10,152	7,056	69.5	6,542	514	7.3	3,096	2,650	71	30	344
35 to 44 years	16,153	11,390	70.5	10,677	713	6.3	4,763	3,973	60	84	647
35 to 39 years	8,896	6,227	70.0	5,811	416	6.7	2,669	2,237	40	40	352
40 to 44 years	7,257	5,163	71.1	4,866	297	5.7	2,094	1,736	20	44	295
45 to 54 years	11,585	7,378	63.7	7,035	343	4.6	4,207	3,595	9	129	475
45 to 49 years	5,966	3,977	66.7	3,768	209	5.3	1,989	1,704	4	56	226
50 to 54 years	5,619	3,401	60.5	3,267	134	3.9	2,218	1,891	5	73	249
55 to 64 years	11,747	4,902	41.7	4,664	238	4.9	6,845	5,245	4	197	1,399
55 to 59 years	5,932	2,964	50.0	2,810	154	5.2	2,968	2,385	3	93	488
60 to 64 years	5,814	1,937	33.3	1,853	84	4.3	3,877	2,861	1	105	911
65 years and over	15,943	1,091	6.8	1,039	51	4.7	14,853	9,624	1	589	4,638
65 to 69 years	5,158	660	12.8	640	21	3.1	4,497	3,091	2	93	1,312
70 years and over	10,786	430	4.0	400	31	7.1	10,355	6,534	–	496	3,326

D1–2. Employment Status of the Civilian Noninstitutional Population by Age, Sex, and Race, 1985 (Continued)

(Numbers in thousands)

Age, sex, and race	Civilian noninstitutional population	August 1985									
		Civilian labor force					Not in labor force				
		Total	Percent of population	Employed	Unemployed		Total	Keeping house	Going to school	Unable to work	Other reasons
					Number	Percent of labor force					
WHITE											
16 years and over	153,819	100,866	65.6	94,864	6,002	6.0	52,953	26,836	1,087	1,971	23,058
16 to 19 years	11,862	7,688	64.8	6,718	971	12.6	4,174	522	368	17	3,267
16 to 17 years	5,918	3,284	55.5	2,841	443	13.5	2,633	220	167	2	2,244
18 to 19 years	5,945	4,404	74.1	3,877	527	12.0	1,540	302	201	14	1,023
20 to 24 years	16,814	13,897	82.7	12,690	1,208	8.7	2,916	1,406	401	46	1,063
25 to 54 years	81,123	66,089	81.5	62,744	3,345	5.1	15,035	11,224	312	643	2,854
25 to 34 years	34,503	28,591	82.9	26,894	1,697	5.9	5,912	4,519	224	128	1,041
25 to 29 years	17,678	14,648	82.9	13,727	920	6.3	3,031	2,270	138	69	555
30 to 34 years	16,824	13,943	82.9	13,166	776	5.6	2,881	2,249	86	60	487
35 to 44 years	27,217	22,480	82.6	21,441	1,038	4.6	4,737	3,522	69	221	925
35 to 39 years	14,963	12,315	82.3	11,715	599	7.5	2,648	2,035	44	109	491
40 to 44 years	12,254	10,165	83.0	9,726	438	4.3	2,089	1,531	25	113	433
45 to 54 years	19,405	15,019	77.4	14,409	610	4.1	4,385	3,185	20	293	888
45 to 49 years	9,996	7,995	80.0	7,650	345	4.3	2,001	1,512	13	123	365
50 to 54 years	9,410	7,025	74.7	6,759	265	4.9	2,385	1,723	6	170	524
55 to 64 years	19,617	10,649	54.3	10,243	407	3.8	8,967	4,741	5	494	3,728
55 to 59 years	9,908	6,403	64.6	6,154	249	3.9	3,505	2,142	4	231	1,127
60 to 64 years	9,709	4,246	43.7	4,089	157	3.7	5,463	2,599	1	263	2,600
65 years and over	24,403	2,541	10.4	2,470	72	2.8	21,861	8,942	1	772	12,146
65 to 69 years	8,360	1,537	18.4	1,499	39	2.5	6,823	2,833	2	164	3,824
70 years and over	16,042	1,004	6.3	971	33	3.3	15,038	6,109	–	607	8,322
Men											
16 years and over	73,436	57,369	78.1	54,246	3,123	5.4	16,067	331	513	1,135	14,088
16 to 19 years	5,971	4,061	68.0	3,510	551	13.6	1,910	28	170	12	1,700
16 to 17 years	3,024	1,786	59.0	1,508	278	15.6	1,238	19	81	–	1,138
18 to 19 years	2,947	2,275	77.2	2,002	273	12.0	672	9	89	12	562
20 to 24 years	8,225	7,411	90.1	6,781	629	8.5	815	20	210	26	559
25 to 54 years	39,945	37,940	95.0	36,245	1,695	4.5	2,006	90	131	456	1,328
25 to 34 years	17,064	16,380	96.0	15,503	877	5.4	684	23	97	96	468
25 to 29 years	8,733	8,351	95.6	7,868	482	5.8	383	8	69	60	246
30 to 34 years	8,331	8,029	96.4	7,634	395	4.9	302	15	28	36	223
35 to 44 years	13,394	12,832	95.8	12,342	490	3.8	563	27	23	154	358
35 to 39 years	7,369	7,087	96.2	6,799	288	4.1	282	12	14	74	182
40 to 44 years	6,025	5,745	95.3	5,543	201	3.5	281	15	9	81	176
45 to 54 years	9,487	8,729	92.0	8,401	328	3.8	759	40	11	206	501
45 to 49 years	4,906	4,622	94.2	4,446	176	3.8	284	16	9	79	180
50 to 54 years	4,582	4,107	89.6	3,955	152	3.7	475	24	2	127	322
55 to 64 years	9,263	6,376	68.8	6,160	216	3.4	2,887	57	2	334	2,494
55 to 59 years	4,722	3,833	81.2	3,703	130	3.4	889	33	1	155	701
60 to 64 years	4,541	2,543	56.0	2,457	86	3.4	1,998	25	1	179	1,794
65 years and over	10,030	1,581	15.8	1,550	32	2.0	8,449	135	–	308	8,006
65 to 69 years	3,771	956	25.4	936	21	2.2	2,815	38	–	102	2,675
70 years and over	6,259	625	10.0	614	11	1.8	5,634	97	–	205	5,332
Women											
16 years and over	80,384	43,498	54.1	40,619	2,879	6.6	36,886	26,505	574	836	8,971
16 to 19 years	5,891	3,628	61.6	3,208	419	11.6	2,263	494	198	4	1,567
16 to 17 years	2,893	1,498	51.8	1,333	165	11.0	1,395	200	86	2	1,106
18 to 19 years	2,998	2,129	71.0	1,875	254	11.9	868	293	112	2	461
20 to 24 years	8,588	6,487	75.5	5,908	578	8.9	2,102	1,386	191	21	504
25 to 54 years	41,178	28,149	68.4	26,499	1,650	5.9	13,029	11,134	181	187	1,526
25 to 34 years	17,439	12,211	70.0	11,391	820	6.7	5,228	4,496	127	33	573
25 to 29 years	8,945	6,297	70.4	5,859	438	7.0	2,648	2,262	69	9	309
30 to 34 years	8,493	5,914	69.6	5,532	381	6.4	2,579	2,234	58	24	264
35 to 44 years	13,822	9,648	69.8	9,099	549	5.7	4,174	3,494	46	67	567
35 to 39 years	7,594	5,228	68.8	4,916	311	6.0	2,366	1,991	30	35	309
40 to 44 years	6,229	4,420	71.0	4,183	237	5.4	1,808	1,503	16	32	257
45 to 54 years	9,917	6,291	63.4	6,009	282	4.5	3,627	3,144	8	87	387
45 to 49 years	5,090	3,373	66.3	3,204	169	5.0	1,717	1,483	4	44	185
50 to 54 years	4,828	2,918	60.4	2,804	113	3.9	1,910	1,661	4	43	202
55 to 64 years	10,354	4,274	41.3	4,083	191	4.5	6,080	4,684	3	160	1,234
55 to 59 years	5,186	2,571	49.6	2,451	120	4.7	2,615	2,110	3	75	427
60 to 64 years	5,168	1,703	33.0	1,632	71	4.2	3,465	2,574	–	85	807
65 years and over	14,372	960	6.7	920	40	4.2	13,412	8,807	1	464	4,140
65 to 69 years	4,589	581	12.7	563	18	3.1	4,008	2,795	2	62	1,149
70 years and over	9,783	379	3.9	357	22	5.8	9,404	6,012	–	402	2,990

D1-2. Employment Status of the Civilian Noninstitutional Population by Age, Sex, and Race, 1985 (Continued)

(Numbers in thousands)

Age, sex, and race	Civilian noninstitutional population	August 1985									
		Civilian labor force					Not in labor force				
		Total	Percent of population	Employed	Unemployed		Total	Keeping house	Going to school	Unable to work	Other reasons
					Number	Percent of labor force					
BLACK											
16 years and over	19,700	12,593	63.9	10,788	1,805	14.3	7,107	3,048	291	481	3,287
16 to 19 years	2,154	1,053	48.9	712	341	32.4	1,100	187	119	4	790
16 to 17 years	1,083	424	39.2	294	130	30.7	658	71	41	–	546
18 to 19 years	1,071	629	58.7	418	211	33.5	442	116	78	4	244
20 to 24 years	2,649	1,879	70.9	1,441	438	23.3	770	303	112	12	343
25 to 54 years	10,569	8,340	78.9	7,421	919	11.0	2,229	1,364	59	205	601
25 to 34 years	4,887	3,865	79.1	3,324	541	14.0	1,022	637	47	52	286
25 to 29 years	2,586	2,040	78.9	1,708	333	16.3	546	323	41	30	153
30 to 34 years	2,300	1,825	79.3	1,615	208	11.4	476	315	7	21	134
35 to 44 years	3,306	2,726	82.4	2,463	263	9.7	580	378	11	55	136
35 to 39 years	1,823	1,542	84.6	1,381	161	10.4	280	187	5	21	68
40 to 44 years	1,483	1,184	79.8	1,082	102	8.6	300	192	5	34	68
45 to 54 years	2,376	1,749	73.6	1,635	115	6.6	626	349	1	98	179
45 to 49 years	1,233	958	77.7	894	65	6.8	276	167	1	34	74
50 to 54 years	1,143	791	69.2	741	51	6.4	351	182	–	64	105
55 to 64 years	2,063	1,066	51.6	976	90	8.4	998	477	1	94	426
55 to 59 years	1,095	660	60.3	596	64	9.8	435	223	–	50	162
60 to 64 years	968	406	41.9	380	26	6.3	562	254	1	43	264
65 years and over	2,265	254	11.2	238	17	6.5	2,010	717	–	166	1,127
65 to 69 years	819	147	17.9	142	5	3.4	671	242	–	52	378
70 years and over	1,446	107	7.4	96	11	10.3	1,339	476	–	115	749
Men											
16 years and over	8,806	6,392	72.6	5,542	850	13.3	2,413	110	131	259	1,912
16 to 19 years	1,057	580	54.9	398	182	31.4	477	12	56	4	404
16 to 17 years	543	227	41.9	160	67	29.5	315	8	26	–	280
18 to 19 years	514	353	68.6	238	115	32.6	161	4	29	4	124
20 to 24 years	1,203	958	79.6	763	196	20.4	245	8	49	7	181
25 to 54 years	4,718	4,163	88.2	3,743	421	10.1	554	45	26	140	343
25 to 34 years	2,187	1,955	89.4	1,716	239	12.2	231	17	20	42	152
25 to 29 years	1,159	1,026	88.6	881	146	14.2	133	10	18	24	82
30 to 34 years	1,027	929	90.4	835	93	10.0	99	8	3	18	70
35 to 44 years	1,469	1,334	90.8	1,219	115	8.6	135	15	5	38	77
35 to 39 years	807	745	92.3	679	66	8.8	62	7	1	16	39
40 to 44 years	661	589	89.0	540	49	8.3	73	9	4	22	38
45 to 54 years	1,062	874	82.4	808	66	7.6	187	13	1	60	114
45 to 49 years	551	473	85.9	441	33	6.9	78	4	1	24	49
50 to 54 years	511	401	78.5	367	34	8.5	110	9	–	36	65
55 to 64 years	925	557	60.2	510	47	8.5	368	18	–	60	290
55 to 59 years	496	343	69.2	312	32	9.2	153	5	–	36	112
60 to 64 years	429	214	49.8	198	16	7.3	215	13	–	24	178
65 years and over	904	134	14.8	129	5	3.8	770	27	–	48	694
65 to 69 years	348	77	22.2	75	2	3.2	270	5	–	22	244
70 years and over	556	57	10.2	54	3	(¹)	499	23	–	27	450
Women											
16 years and over	10,894	6,201	56.9	5,246	955	15.4	4,694	2,937	160	221	1,375
16 to 19 years	1,097	473	43.1	314	159	33.6	624	175	63	–	386
16 to 17 years	540	197	36.4	134	63	32.1	343	63	15	–	266
18 to 19 years	557	277	49.6	181	96	34.7	281	112	49	–	120
20 to 24 years	1,446	921	63.7	679	243	26.3	525	295	63	5	162
25 to 54 years	5,851	4,177	71.4	3,678	498	11.9	1,675	1,319	33	65	258
25 to 34 years	2,700	1,910	70.7	1,608	302	15.8	790	620	27	10	134
25 to 29 years	1,427	1,014	71.1	827	187	18.4	413	313	23	6	71
30 to 34 years	1,273	896	70.4	780	115	12.9	377	307	4	3	64
35 to 44 years	1,837	1,392	75.8	1,244	149	10.7	445	363	6	17	59
35 to 39 years	1,016	797	78.5	702	95	12.0	218	180	4	5	29
40 to 44 years	822	595	72.4	542	53	8.9	227	183	1	12	30
45 to 54 years	1,314	875	66.6	827	48	5.5	439	336	–	38	65
45 to 49 years	682	485	71.0	453	32	6.5	198	163	–	10	25
50 to 54 years	632	390	61.8	374	17	4.3	241	173	–	28	40
55 to 64 years	1,138	508	44.7	466	43	8.4	629	459	1	34	136
55 to 59 years	599	317	52.9	284	33	10.3	282	218	–	14	50
60 to 64 years	539	192	35.6	182	10	5.3	347	241	1	19	86
65 years and over	1,361	120	8.8	109	11	9.5	1,241	690	–	118	433
65 to 69 years	471	70	14.9	67	3	(¹)	401	237	–	30	134
70 years and over	890	50	5.6	42	8	(¹)	840	453	–	88	299

¹ Data not shown where base is less than 75,000.

D1–3. Civilian Labor Force Participation Rates by Age, 1948–83

(Percent)

Year, sex, and race	16 years and over	16 to 19 years			20 years and over						
		Total	16 to 17 years	18 to 19 years	Total	20 to 24 years	25 to 34 years	35 to 44 years	45 to 54 years	55 to 64 years	65 years and over
TOTAL											
1948	58.8	52.5	41.7	63.4	59.4	64.1	63.1	66.7	65.1	56.9	27.0
1949	58.9	52.2	41.2	63.3	59.5	64.9	63.2	67.2	65.3	56.2	27.3
1050	59.2	51.8	40.7	62.9	59.9	65.9	63.5	67.5	66.4	56.7	26.7
1951	59.2	52.2	42.6	62.6	59.8	64.8	64.2	67.6	67.2	56.9	25.8
1952	59.0	51.3	42.7	61.2	59.7	62.2	64.7	68.0	67.5	57.5	24.8
1953	58.9	50.2	40.7	60.9	59.6	61.2	64.0	68.9	68.1	58.0	24.8
1954	58.8	48.3	37.9	59.1	59.6	61.6	64.3	68.8	68.4	58.7	23.9
1955	59.3	48.9	38.5	60.7	60.1	62.7	64.8	68.9	69.7	59.5	24.1
1956	60.0	50.9	41.9	61.2	60.7	64.1	64.8	69.5	70.5	60.8	24.3
1957	59.6	49.6	40.2	60.4	60.4	64.0	64.9	69.5	70.9	60.1	22.9
1958	59.5	47.4	37.3	59.4	60.5	64.4	65.0	69.6	71.5	60.5	21.8
1959	59.3	46.7	36.9	58.9	60.4	64.3	65.0	69.5	71.9	61.0	21.1
1960	59.4	47.5	37.6	59.5	60.5	65.2	65.4	69.4	72.2	60.9	20.8
1961	59.3	46.9	36.3	58.4	60.5	65.7	65.6	69.5	72.1	61.5	20.1
1962	58.8	46.1	34.9	58.2	60.0	65.3	65.2	69.7	72.2	61.5	19.1
1963	58.7	45.2	34.5	58.5	60.1	65.1	65.6	70.1	72.5	62.0	17.9
1964	58.7	44.5	35.1	57.2	60.2	66.3	65.8	70.0	72.9	61.9	18.0
1965	58.9	45.7	35.8	57.1	60.3	66.4	66.4	70.7	72.5	61.9	17.8
1966	59.2	48.2	38.5	58.3	60.5	66.5	67.1	71.0	72.7	62.2	17.2
1967	59.6	48.4	39.0	58.4	60.9	67.1	68.2	71.6	72.7	62.3	17.2
1968	59.6	48.3	39.1	58.5	60.9	67.0	68.6	72.0	72.8	62.2	17.2
1969	60.1	49.4	40.5	59.3	61.3	68.2	69.1	72.5	73.4	62.1	17.3
1970	60.4	49.9	41.0	59.8	61.6	69.2	69.7	73.1	73.5	61.8	17.0
1971	60.2	49.7	40.7	59.6	61.4	69.3	69.9	73.2	73.2	61.3	16.2
1972	60.4	51.9	42.3	62.3	61.4	70.8	70.9	73.3	72.7	60.0	15.6
1973	60.8	53.7	44.5	63.6	61.7	72.6	72.3	74.0	72.5	58.4	14.6
1974	61.3	54.8	45.5	64.8	62.0	74.0	73.6	74.6	72.7	57.8	14.0
1975	61.2	54.0	44.4	64.1	62.1	73.9	74.4	75.0	72.6	57.2	13.7
1976	61.6	54.5	44.6	64.7	62.4	74.7	75.7	76.0	72.5	56.6	13.1
1977	62.3	56.0	46.2	66.2	63.0	75.7	77.0	77.0	72.8	56.3	13.0
1978	63.2	57.8	48.6	67.3	63.8	76.8	78.3	78.1	73.5	56.3	13.3
1979	63.7	57.9	48.6	67.2	64.3	77.5	79.2	79.2	74.3	56.2	13.1
1980	63.8	56.7	46.9	66.5	64.5	77.2	79.9	80.0	74.9	55.7	12.5
1981	63.9	55.4	45.2	65.6	64.8	77.3	80.5	80.7	75.7	55.0	12.2
1982	64.0	54.1	43.2	64.5	65.0	77.1	81.0	81.2	75.9	55.1	11.9
1983	64.0	53.5	41.6	64.6	65.0	77.2	81.3	81.6	76.0	54.5	11.7

D1–4. Civilian Population and Labor Force, 1940–85

[Numbers in thousands]

Period	Resident population, total [1]	Civilian population [1]			Civilian labor force aged 16 or older [2]			Unemployment as percent of civilian labor force [3]	
		Total	Under age 18	Aged 65 or older	Total	Employed	Unemployed	Unadjusted	Seasonally adjusted
1940	132,457	132,129	...	...	55,640	47,520	8,120	14.6	...
1945	133,434	128,112	...	...	53,860	52,820	1,040	1.9	...
1950	151,868	150,790	...	...	62,208	58,920	3,288	5.3	...
1955	165,069	162,967	...	...	65,023	62,171	2,852	4.4	...
1960	179,979	178,140	64,463	16,675	69,628	65,778	3,852	5.5	...
1961	182,992	181,143	65,750	17,089	17,459	65,746	4,714	6.7	...
1962	185,771	183,677	67,087	17,457	70,614	66,702	3,911	5.5	...
1963	188,483	186,493	68,383	17,778	71,833	67,762	4,070	5.7	...
1964	191,141	189,141	69,644	18,127	73,091	69,305	3,786	5.2	...
1965	193,526	191,605	69,688	18,451	74,455	71,088	3,366	4.5	...
1966	195,576	193,420	69,857	18,755	75,770	72,895	2,875	3.8	...
1967	197,457	195,264	69,903	19,071	77,347	74,372	2,975	3.8	...
1968	199,399	197,113	69,865	19,365	78,737	75,920	2,817	3.6	...
1969	201,385	199,145	69,728	19,680	80,734	77,902	2,832	3.5	...
1970	203,984	201,895	66,222	20,107	82,771	78,678	4,093	4.9	...
1971	206,827	204,866	66,173	20,561	84,382	79,367	5,016	5.9	...
1972	209,824	207,511	66,075	21,020	87,034	82,153	4,882	5.6	...
1973	211,357	209,600	65,597	21,525	89,429	85,064	4,365	4.9	...
1974	213,342	211,636	64,877	22,061	91,949	86,794	5,156	5.6	...
1975	215,465	213,788	63,980	22,696	93,775	85,846	7,929	8.5	...
1976	217,563	215,894	63,102	23,278	96,158	88,752	7,406	7.7	...
1977	219,760	218,106	62,150	23,892	99,009	92,017	6,991	7.1	...
1978	222,095	220,467	61,427	24,502	102,251	96,048	6,202	6.1	...
1979	224,567	222,969	60,661	25,134	104,962	98,824	6,137	5.8	...
1980	227,236	225,632	60,087	25,708	106,940	99,303	7,637	7.1	...
1981	229,518	227,870	59,551	26,253	108,670	100,397	8,273	7.6	...
1982	231,786	230,117	62,810	26,826	110,238	99,541	10,696	9.7	...
1983	233,981	232,286	62,575	27,384	111,501	100,817	10,684	9.6	...
1984	236,108	234,395	63,756	20,040	113,544	105,005	8,539	7.5	...
1984									
May	235,753	234,065	...	...	113,722	105,162	8,560	7.2	7.5
June	235,925	234,232	...	...	113,619	105,391	8,228	7.4	7.2
July	236,108	234,395	...	...	113,868	105,377	8,491	7.5	7.5
August	236,328	234,609	...	...	113,629	105,148	8,481	7.3	7.5
September	236,530	234,820	...	...	113,754	105,394	8,370	7.4	7.4
October	236,748	235,049	...	...	114,016	105,649	8,367	7.4	7.3
November	236,937	235,239	...	...	114,074	105,932	8,142	6.9	7.1
December	237,102	235,403	...	...	114,464	106,273	8,191	7.0	7.2
1985									
January	237,318	235,621	...	...	114,875	106,391	8,484	8.0	7.4
February	237,483	235,783	...	...	115,084	106,685	8,399	7.8	7.3
March	237,605	235,904	...	...	115,514	107,119	8,396	7.5	7.3
April	237,758	236,054	...	...	115,371	106,945	8,426	7.1	7.3
May	237,921	236,219	...	...	115,373	106,960	8,413	7.0	7.3

[1] Includes Alaska and Hawaii for all years. Annual data are estimated as of July 1. Data not adjusted for Census undercounts and of age misreporting. Comparability of estimates for data in the 1970's in tables published earlier affected by recomputations based on data from the 1980 Census of the population. Source for data is Bureau of the Census, **Current Population Reports** (Population Estimates and Projections, Series P-25).

[2] Annual data are averages of monthly figures. Beginning 1960, includes Alaska and Hawaii. Data for 1950 and 1955 adjusted to reflect definitions adopted January 1957; two groups (those on temporary layoff and those wait-ing to start new wage and salary jobs within 30 days) formerly classified as employed—with a job, not at work—were assigned to other classifications, chiefly to the unemployed. Beginning 1962, comparability with previous years affected somewhat by the introduction of material from the 1960 census (level of labor force and employment lowered by about 150,000). Before January 1967, series show aged 14 or older. Source for data is the Bureau of Labor Statistics, **Employment and Earnings**.

[3] Rate computed from data in Department of Commerce, **Survey of Current Business.**

D1-5. Labor Force Participation by Age and Sex, Third Quarter 1984

[In thousands]

Labor force status[1]	60 to 64			65 plus		
	Total	Male	Female	Total	Male	Female
Civilian labor force	4,712	2,787	1,925	2,938	1,783	1,155
Labor force participation rate (percent)	43.7	56.0	33.1	11.1	16.5	7.4
Number employed	4,504	2,654	1,850	2,847	1,735	1,122

[1] Not seasonally adjusted.

Note: The U.S. Labor Force includes workers who are employed and actively seeking employment. The participation rate is the percentage of individuals in a given group (e.g. age group) who are in the labor force.

Source: U.S. Department of Labor, Bureau of Labor Statistics. Current Population Survey, unpublished.

(NOTE: This data presents a picture of specific age groups at one point in time and does not necessarily imply a trend that follows the aging process specifically.)

D1-6. Employment by Industry by Age, Third Quarter 1984

[Not seasonally adjusted]

	Age		
	55 to 59	60 to 64	65 plus
Distribution (in percent):			
Mining	1	0.1	0.1
Construction	7	7	5
Manufacturing—durables	14	14	6
Manufacturing—nondurables	10	9	6
Transportation/Public utilities	8	7	3
Trade—wholesale and retail	17	20	24
Finance, insurance real estate	6	7	9
Services	30	31	42
Public administration	6	5	5

Source: U.S. Department of Labor, Bureau of Labor Statistics, Current Population Survey, unpublished.

D1-7. Employment by Occupation by Age, Third Quarter 1984

[Not seasonally adjusted]

Occupation	Age		
	55 to 59	60 to 64	65 plus
Distribution (in percent):			
Managerial and professional	25	23	23
Technical, sales, administration support	28	31	29
Service	12	14	20
Precision production, craft repair	14	12	8
Operators, fabricators, laborers	16	15	9
Farming, forestry, fishing	4	6	11
Armed Forces	0	0	0

Source: U.S. Department of Labor, Bureau of Labor Statistics, Current Population Survey, unpublished.

D1-8. Labor Force Participation Rates for Pension Income Recipients, by Type of Pension and Age: Monthly Average, Third Quarter 1984

(Percentages)

Type of pension	Total	Age		
		Under 55 years	55 to 64 years	65 years and over
Total with pensions	14.6	38.8	22.1	9.7
Social Security	10.7	18.7	13.6	9.5
Private pensions	13.3	31.1	25.0	8.0
State or local pensions	13.1	(B)	19.1	7.4
Federal pensions	17.5	(B)	31.6	7.5
U.S. military pensions	63.4	86.0	62.8	15.8
Federal railroad retirement pensions	3.9	(B)	(B)	3.7

B   Base less than 200,000.

D2. RETIREMENT TRENDS AND BENEFITS

D2-1. Retirement Ages Equivalent to Age 65 Retirement in 1940, by Selected Measures

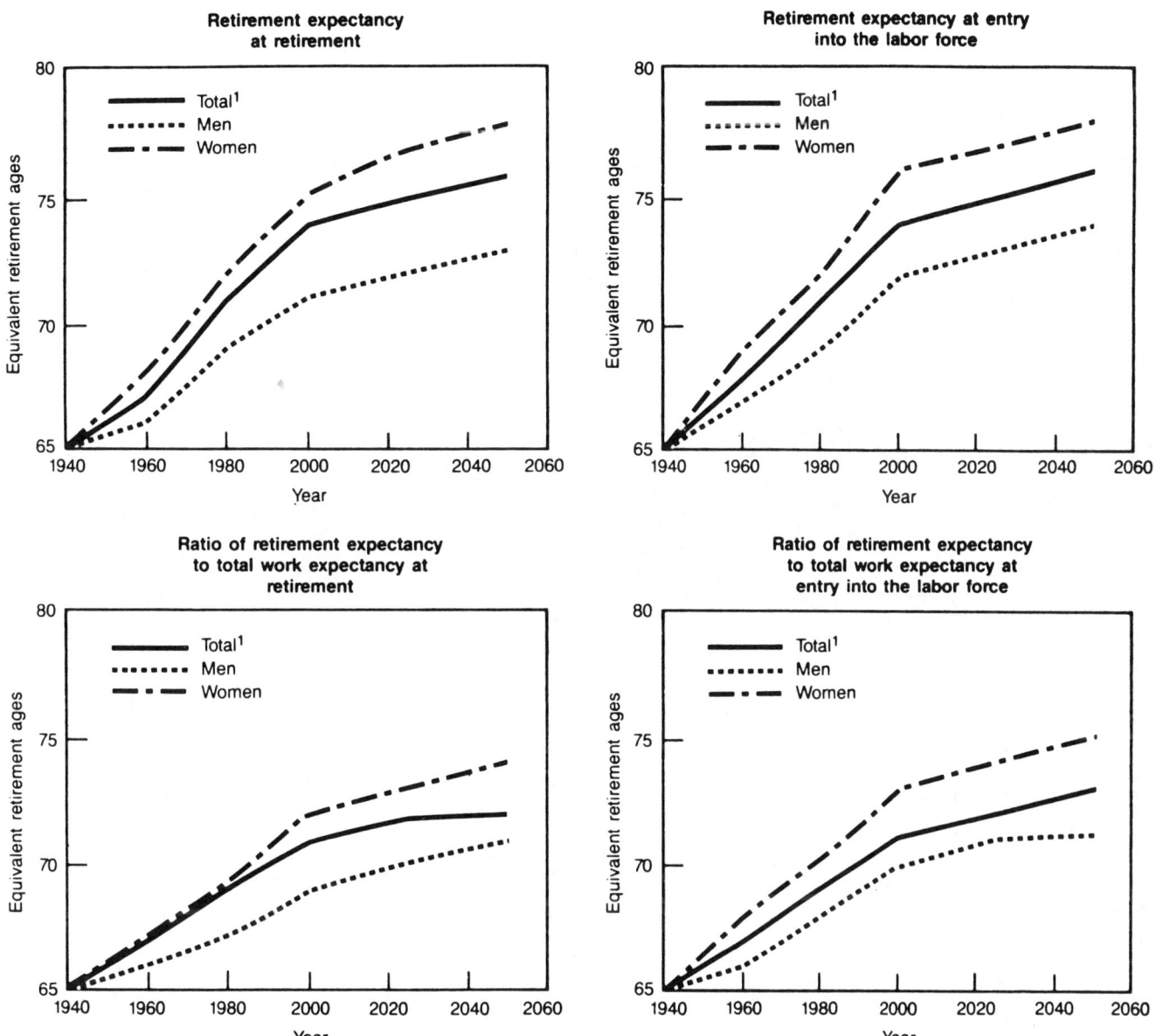

[1]Weighted average from Actuarial Note No. 105. See Francisco R. Bayo and Joseph F. Faber, **Equivalent Retirement Ages: 1940-2050**, Office of the Actuary, Social Security Administration, June 1981.

D2-2. Percent of Income of the Working Age Population that May Have to Be Transferred to Retirees to Keep Relative Incomes the Same

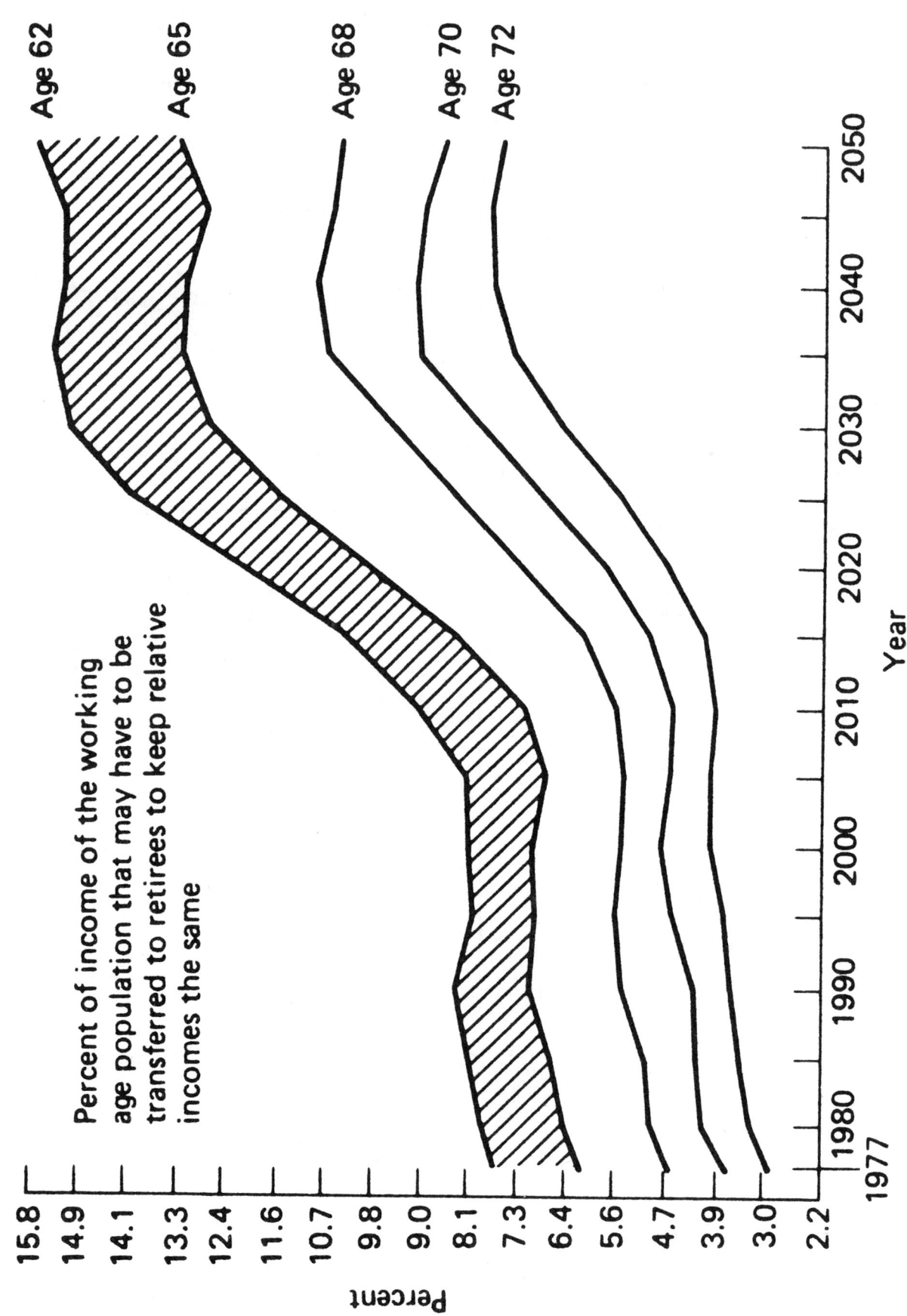

Percent of income of the working age population that may have to be transferred to retirees to keep relative incomes the same

Age 62

Age 65

Age 68

Age 70

Age 72

Year

Percent

15.8
14.9
14.1
13.3
12.4
11.6
10.7
9.8
9.0
8.1
7.3
6.4
5.6
4.7
3.9
3.0
2.2

1977 1980 1990 2000 2010 2020 2030 2040 2050

Source: Derived from Richard Lancaster, *Retirement Income Adequacy.* Staff Technical Paper, U.S. Office of Management and Budget, August 1979.

D2-3. Retirement Expectancy at Entry into the Labor Force:[1] Retirement Ages Equivalent to Age 65 Retirement for Selected Base Years

[In years:months]

Calendar year	Base year of age 65 retirement								
	1940			1960			1980		
	Total [2]	Men	Women	Total [2]	Men	Women	Total [2]	Men	Women
1940.............	65:00	65:00	65:00	...	...	...	...	...	...
1945.............	66:04	65:11	66:08	...	...	...	...	...	...
1950.............	67.06	66:10	68:00	...	...	...	...	...	...
1955.............	68:05	67:06	69:02	...	...	...	...	...	...
1960.............	68:05	67:02	69:05	65:00	65:00	65:00	...	...	...
1965.............	68:08	67:02	70:00	65:03	65:00	65:06	...	...	...
1970.............	69:02	67:05	70:09	65:09	65:02	66:03	...	...	...
1975.............	70:05	68:06	72:00	67:00	66:04	67:06	...	...	...
1980 [3]	71:04	69:06	72:10	67:11	67:04	68:04	65:00	65:00	65:00
1985 [3]	72:04	70:05	74:00	68:11	68:03	69:06	65:00	65:11	66:01
1990 [3]	73:03	71:03	75:00	69:10	69:01	70:06	66:11	66:09	67:01
1995 [3]	73:11	71:09	75:09	70:06	69:08	71:03	67:07	67:04	67:10
2000 [3]	74:03	72:01	76:01	70:10	69:11	71:07	67:11	67:08	68:02
2025 [3]	75:06	73:02	77:05	70:00	71:01	72:10	69:01	68:09	69:05
2050 [3]	76:08	74:03	78:08	73:02	72:01	74:01	70:03	69:09	70:08

[1] Assumed to be age 20.
[2] Weighted average from Actuarial Note No. 105. See Francisco R. Bayo and Joseph F. Faber, **Equivalent Retirement Ages: 1940-2050**, Office of the Actuary, Social Security Administration, June 1981.
[3] Based on intermediate mortality assumptions described in the 1981 Report of the Board of Trustees of the OASDI Trust Funds.

D2-4. Ratio of Retirement Expectancy to Total Past Work Expectancy at Retirement: Retirement Ages Equivalent to Age 65 Retirement for Selected Base Years

[In year:months]

Calendar year	Base year of age 65 retirement								
	1940			1960			1980		
	Total [1]	Men	Women	Total [1]	Men	Women	Total [1]	Men	Women
1940.............	65:00	65:00	65:00	...	...	...	...	...	...
1945.............	66:00	65:08	66:00	...	...	...	...	...	...
1950.............	66:06	66:01	66:08	...	...	...	...	...	...
1955.............	66:11	66:06	67:03	...	...	...	...	...	...
1960.............	67:00	66:03	67:05	65:00	65:00	65:00	...	...	...
1965.............	67:03	66:03	67:10	65:03	65:00	65:08	...	...	...
1970.............	67:08	66:06	68:05	65:08	65:03	66:00	...	...	...
1975.............	68:06	67:01	69:03	66:05	65:11	66:10	...	...	...
1980 [2]	69:01	67:09	69:10	67:00	66:06	67:04	65:00	65:00	65:00
1985 [2]	69:09	68:02	70:08	67:08	67:01	68:01	65:08	65:07	65:09
1990 [2]	70:05	68:09	71:05	68:03	67:07	68:10	66:03	66:01	66:05
1995 [2]	70:10	69:01	72:00	68:09	67:11	69:04	66:08	66:05	66:11
2000 [2]	71:01	69:05	72:03	69:00	68:01	69:07	66:11	66:07	67:02
2025 [2]	72:00	70:03	73:03	69:10	68:11	70:06	67:09	67:05	68:00
2050 [2]	72:11	71:00	74:03	70:08	69:09	71:05	68:07	68:02	68:11

[1] Weighted average from Actuarial Note No. 105. See Francisco R. Bayo and Joseph F. Faber, **Equivalent Retirement Ages: 1940-2050**, Office of the Actuary, Social Security Administration, June 1981.
[2] Based on intermediate mortality assumptions described in the 1981 Report of the Board of Trustees of the OASDI Trust Funds.

D2-5. Number of Beneficiaries Aged 60 or Older, by Age, Race, and Sex, at End of 1982

[In thousands]

Age [1]	Total [2]	Men	Women	Age [1]	Total [2]	Men	Women
	Total				**Black**		
Total	29,382	11,744	17,638	Total	2,233	919	1,314
60-61	601	238	363	60-61	72	29	43
62-64	3,823	1,548	2,275	62-64	305	129	176
65-69	7,982	3,476	4,506	65-69	622	271	351
70-74	6,776	2,848	3,928	70-74	524	222	302
75 or older	10,200	3,635	6,565	75 or older	710	268	442
75-79	4,884	1,901	2,983	75-79	363	144	219
80-84	2,985	1,044	1,941	80-84	205	76	129
85-89	1,603	492	1,111	85-89	98	33	65
90-94	593	164	429	90-94	34	11	23
95 or older.	135	34	101	95 or older.	10	4	6
	White				**Other**		
Total	26,767	10,636	16,131	Total	382	189	193
60-61	521	205	315	60-61	10	4	6
62-64	3,464	1,396	2,068	62-64	54	23	31
65-69	7,235	3,148	4,087	65-69	125	57	68
70-74	6,164	2,578	3,586	70-74	88	48	40
75 or older	9,384	3,309	6,075	75 or older	105	57	48
75-79	4,464	1,724	2,740	75-79	57	33	24
80-84	2,749	950	1,799	80-84	31	17	14
85-89	1,494	455	1,039	85-89	12	5	7
90-94	554	151	403	90-94	4	2	2
95 or older.	123	29	94	95 or older.	1	(3)	1

[1] Age on birthday in 1982.
[2] The sum of the individual categories may not equal total because of independent rounding.
[3] Less than 500.

D2-6. Monthly Cash Benefits in Current-Payment Status before and after the December 1983 Benefit Increase, by Type of Beneficiary and Reduction Status

Type of beneficiary and reduction status	Total number	Total benefit amount [1] (in thousands)		Average benefit			
				Amount		Increase	
		Before increase	After increase	Before increase	After increase	Amount	Percent
All beneficiaries	36,056,449	$13,672,127	$14,148,846	. . .	. . .	. . .	3.5
Retired workers, spouses, and children	24,910,713	9,842,785	10,186,157	. . .	. . .	. . .	3.5
Retired workers.	21,361,524	9,094,012	9,411,423	$425.72	$440.58	$14.86	3.5
Men	11,330,325	5,415,982	5,604,903	478.01	494.68	16.67	3.5
Benefits actuarially reduced	6,683,880	2,878,592	2,979,002	430.68	445.70	15.02	3.5
Benefits not actuarially reduced	4,646,445	2,537,390	2,625,901	546.09	565.14	19.05	3.5
Women	10,031,199	3,678,030	3,806,520	366.66	379.47	12.81	3.5
Benefits actuarially reduced	7,110,154	2,382,015	2,465,246	335.02	346.72	11.70	3.5
Benefits not actuarially reduced	2,921,045	1,296,015	1,341,275	443.68	459.18	15.50	3.5
Spouses	3,033,537	661,084	684,147	217.93	225.53	7.60	3.5
Children	515,652	87,689	90,587	170.05	175.68	5.63	3.3
Disabled workers, spouses, and children	3,830,944	1,298,024	1,343,667	. . .	. . .	. . .	3.5
Disabled workers.	2,577,399	1,135,969	1,175,884	440.74	456.23	15.49	3.5
Men	1,735,946	843,104	872,743	485.67	502.75	17.08	3.5
Women	841,453	292,865	303,141	348.05	360.26	12.21	3.5
Spouses	310,118	38,672	40,073	124.70	129.22	4.52	3.6
Children	943,427	123,383	127,710	130.78	135.37	4.59	3.5
Survivors.	7,263,440	2,524,894	2,612,378	. . .	. . .	. . .	3.5
Widows and widowers.	4,688,501	1,779,686	1,841,814	379.59	392.84	13.25	3.5
Widowed mothers and fathers	401,417	119,495	123,665	297.68	308.07	10.39	3.5
Children	2,162,052	621,837	642,888	287.61	297.35	9.74	3.4
Parents	11,470	3,876	4,011	337.89	349.68	11.79	3.5
Special age-72 beneficiaries [2].	51,352	6,425	6,643	. . .	. . .	. . .	3.4

[1] Totals may not add due to rounding.
[2] Authorized by 1966 legislation for persons aged 72 or older not insured under the regular or transitional provisions of the Social Security Act.

D2-7. Examples of Monthly Cash Benefit Awards for Selected Beneficiary Families with First Eligibility in 1983, by Average Indexed Monthly Earnings, Effective December 1983

Beneficiary family	Average indexed monthly earnings of insured worker									
	$100	$254	$600	$1,000	$1,300	$1,528	$1,900	$2,200	$2,587	$2,837
Primary insurance amount	93.10	236.60	351.10	483.60	583.00	658.40	716.20	762.70	822.90	861.70
Maximum family benefit	139.70	354.90	546.00	906.30	1,040.40	1,152.70	1,253.70	1,335.30	1,440.50	1,508.50
Disability maximum family benefit [1]	93.10	236.60	526.70	725.40	874.40	987.70	1,074.30	1,144.10	1,234.30	...
Disabled worker:										
Worker alone	93.00	236.00	351.00	483.00	583.00	658.00	716.00	762.00	822.00	...
Worker, spouse, and 1 child	93.00	236.00	325.00	723.00	873.00	986.00	1,074.00	1,142.00	1,232.00	...
Retired worker claiming benefits at age 62 [2]:										
Worker alone	74.00	189.00	280.00	386.00	466.00	526.00	...	...	...	...
Worker with spouse claiming benefits at—										
Age 65 or older	120.00	307.00	455.00	627.00	757.00	855.00	...	...	...	...
Age 62 [2]	108.00	277.00	411.00	567.00	684.00	772.00	...	...	...	...
Widow or widower claiming benefits at—										
Age 65 or older [3]	93.00	236.00	351.00	483.00	583.00	658.00	716.00	762.00	822.00	861.00
Age 60	66.00	169.00	251.00	345.00	416.00	470.00	512.00	545.00	588.00	616.00
Disabled widow or widower claiming benefits at age 50 [4]	46.00	118.00	175.00	241.00	291.00	329.00	358.00	381.00	411.00	430.00
1 surviving child	69.00	177.00	263.00	362.00	437.00	493.00	537.00	572.00	617.00	646.00
Widow or widower aged 65 or older and 1 child	138.00	354.00	546.00	845.00	1,020.00	1,151.00	1,253.00	1,334.00	1,439.00	1,507.00
Widowed mother or father and 1 child	138.00	354.00	526.00	724.00	874.00	986.00	1,074.00	1,144.00	1,234.00	1,292.00
Widowed mother or father and 2 children	138.00	354.00	546.00	906.00	1,038.00	1,152.00	1,251.00	1,335.00	1,440.00	1,506.00

[1] The 1980 Amendments to the Social Security Act provide for different family maximum amounts for disability cases. For disabled workers entitled after June 1980, the maximum is the smaller of (1) 85 percent of the worker's AIME (or 100 percent of the PIA, if larger), or (2) 150 percent of the PIA.
[2] Assumes maximum reduction.
[3] A widow(er)'s benefit amount is limited to the amount the spouse would have been receiving if still living but not less than 82½ percent of the PIA.
[4] Effective January 1984 disabled widow(er)'s will receive the same percentage of the PIA as widows aged 60 (71½ percent).

D2-8. Minimum and Maximum Monthly Retired-Worker Benefits Payable to Individuals Who Retired at Age 65, 1940-83

Year of attainment of age 65 [1]	Minimum benefit		Maximum benefit [3]				Year of attainment of age 65 [1]	Minimum benefit		Maximum benefit [3]			
	Payable at the time of retirement	Payable effective December 1983 [2]	Payable at the time of retirement		Payable effective December 1983 [2]			Payable at the time of retirement	Payable effective December 1983 [2]	Payable at the time of retirement		Payable effective December 1983 [2]	
			Men	Women	Men	Women				Men	Women	Men	Women
1940	$10.00	$189.30	$41.20	...	$365.90	...	1962	40.00	189.30	121.00	$123.00	497.30	$505.70
1941	10.00	189.30	41.60	...	365.90	...	1963	40.00	189.30	122.00	125.00	501.40	513.30
1942	10.00	189.30	42.00	...	370.40	...	1964	40.00	189.30	123.00	127.00	505.70	521.80
1943	10.00	189.30	42.40	...	370.40	...							
1944	10.00	189.30	42.80	...	374.40	...	1965	44.00	189.30	131.70	135.90	505.70	521.80
							1966	44.00	189.30	132.70	135.90	509.40	521.80
1945	10.00	189.30	43.20	...	370.40	...	1967	44.00	189.30	135.90	140.00	521.80	548.60
1946	10.00	189.30	43.60	...	379.00	...	1968	[4] 55.00	189.30	[4] 156.00	[4] 161.60	529.80	548.60
1947	10.00	189.30	44.00	...	382.50	...	1969	55.00	189.30	160.50	167.30	545.30	568.30
1948	10.00	189.30	44.40	...	382.50	...							
1949	10.00	189.30	44.80	...	386.20	...	1970	64.00	189.30	189.80	196.40	560.40	580.10
							1971	70.40	189.30	213.10	220.40	571.90	591.10
1950	10.00	189.30	45.20	...	391.10	...	1972	70.40	189.30	216.10	224.70	580.10	602.90
1951	20.00	189.30	68.50	...	391.10	...	1973	84.50	189.30	266.10	276.40	595.10	618.20
1952	20.00	189.30	68.50	...	391.10	...	1974	84.50	189.30	274.60	284.90	613.90	637.10
1953	25.00	189.30	85.00	...	432.00	...							
1954	25.00	189.30	85.00	...	432.00	...	1975	93.80	189.30	316.30	333.70	637.10	672.00
							1976	101.40	189.30	364.00	378.80	678.40	706.10
1955	30.00	189.30	98.50	...	432.00	...	1977	107.90	189.30	412.70	422.40	723.00	739.90
1956	30.00	189.30	103.50	...	456.20	...	1978	114.30	189.30	459.80	...	760.50	...
1957	30.00	189.30	106.50	...	477.00	...	1979	121.80	189.30	503.40	...	781.80	...
1958	30.00	189.30	106.50	...	477.00	...							
1959	33.00	189.30	116.00	...	477.00	...	1980	133.90	189.30	572.00	...	808.20	...
							1981	153.10	189.30	677.00	...	836.90	...
1960	33.00	189.30	119.00	...	489.00	...	1982	[5] 170.30	189.30	[5] 679.30	...	755.00	...
1961	33.00	189.30	120.00	...	492.80	...	1983	[5] 166.40	172.20	709.50	...	734.30	...

[1] Assumes retirement at beginning of year.
[2] The final benefit amount payable after SMI premium or any other deductions is rounded to next lower $1.
[3] Benefit for both men and women shown in men's columns except where women's benefit appears separately. Assumes no prior period of disability.
[4] Effective for February 1968.
[5] Derived from transitional guarantee computation based on 1978 PIA table.

D2–9. Public Employee Retirement Systems—Beneficiaries and Benefits: 1970 to 1981

[Number of beneficiaries as of June 30]

YEAR	Unit	Total	LEVEL OF GOVERNMENT				TYPE OF BENEFIT			
			Federal			State and local	Age and service	Dis-ability	Survivor	
			Total [1]	Civil service	Armed Forces				Month-ly	Lump-sum
Beneficiaries:										
1970	1,000	3,050	1,759	959	773	1,291	2,204	419	427	(x)
1975	1,000	4,428	2,480	1,372	1,073	1,948	3,243	549	636	(x)
1977	1,000	5,006	2,735	1,488	1,208	2,271	3,660	611	735	(x)
1978	1,000	5,275	2,857	1,564	1,252	2,418	3,863	650	763	(x)
1979	1,000	5,535	2,946	1,617	1,286	2,589	4,063	672	801	(x)
1980	1,000	5,873	3,083	1,707	1,330	2,790	4,385	643	845	(x)
1981	1,000	6,208	3,200	1,805	1,364	3,008	4,573	732	902	(x)
Benefits:										
1970	Mil. dol	9,355	6,075	2,820	3,133	3,280	7,210	1,312	645	189
1975	Mil. dol	21,617	14,592	7,532	6,808	7,025	17,200	2,707	1,439	271
1977	Mil. dol	27,429	18,429	9,626	8,479	9,000	21,795	3,500	1,842	292
1978	Mil. dol	30,869	20,709	10,925	9,420	10,160	24,520	3,904	2,111	334
1979	Mil. dol	35,068	23,578	12,519	10,642	11,490	27,891	4,376	2,434	368
1980	Mil. dol	41,088	28,042	15,065	12,478	13,046	32,582	5,204	2,884	418
1981	Mil. dol	46,595	31,813	17,523	13,939	14,782	37,020	5,718	3,376	480

X Not applicable.   [1] Includes other Federal systems, not shown separately.

D2–10. Public Employee Retirement Systems—Average Annual Benefits per Annuitant: 1970 to 1981

LEVEL OF GOVERNMENT AND TYPE OF BENEFIT	CURRENT DOLLARS					CONSTANT (1981) DOLLARS [1]				
	1970	1975	1979	1980	1981	1970	1975	1979	1980	1981
All recipients, all gov'ts	$3,005	$4,821	$6,269	$6,925	$7,428	$6,300	$7,474	$7,490	$7,511	$7,428
Age and service	3,271	5,304	6,865	7,430	8,095	6,857	8,223	8,202	8,059	8,095
Disability	3,136	4,931	6,511	8,093	7,811	6,574	7,645	7,779	8,778	7,811
Survivor	1,512	2,263	3,039	3,413	3,742	3,170	3,509	3,631	3,702	3,742
Federal recipients, total	3,440	5,875	7,994	9,087	9,930	7,212	9,108	9,551	9,856	9,930
Age and service	4,065	6,873	9,221	10,114	11,444	8,522	10,656	11,017	10,970	11,444
Disability	3,174	5,254	7,273	9,578	8,990	6,654	8,146	8,689	10,388	8,990
Survivor	1,446	2,558	3,795	4,376	4,874	3,031	3,966	4,534	4,746	4,874
State and local recipients, total	2,413	3,478	4,305	4,535	4,767	5,059	5,392	5,143	4,919	4,767
Age and service	2,452	3,690	4,657	4,907	5,158	5,140	5,721	5,564	5,322	5,158
Disability	2,965	3,867	4,442	4,682	4,929	6,216	5,995	5,307	5,078	4,929
Survivor	1,667	1,719	1,849	1,946	2,047	3,495	2,665	2,209	2,111	2,047

[1] Constant dollar figures are based on implicit price deflators for personal consumption expenditures published by U.S. Bureau of Economic Analysis; see table 779.

Source of tables 617 and 618: U.S. Social Security Administration, *Social Security Bulletin*, December 1982; and unpublished data.

D2–11. Retirement Chosen or Forced? 1974 and 1981 Base: Retired

Q: Did you retire by choice, or were you forced to retire?

| | 65 AND OVER | | | | | |
| | 1981 | | | 1974 | | |
	RETIRED BY CHOICE %	FORCED TO RETIRE %	NOT SURE %	RETIRED BY CHOICE %	FORCED TO RETIRE %	NOT SURE %
TOTAL 65 AND OVER	62	37	1	61	37	2
MALE	60	39	*	58	41	1
FEMALE	64	35	1	66	32	2
UNDER $3,000 (1974)/$5,000 (1981)	53	45	1	53	46	1
$3,000–$6,999 (1974)/$5,000–$9,999 (1981)	62	37	1	62	36	2
$7,000–$14,999 (1974)/$10,000–$19,999 (1981)	62	38	*	68	30	2
$15,000 AND OVER (1974)/$20,000 AND OVER (1981)	69	31	–	65	35	–
WHITE	64	35	1	63	36	1
BLACK	49	51	1	47	49	4
SOME HIGH SCHOOL OR LESS	58	41	1	58	41	1
HIGH SCHOOL GRADUATE, SOME COLLEGE	69	30	1	67	30	3
COLLEGE GRADUATE	66	34	–	70	30	–

*LESS THAN 0.5%.

D3. PART-TIME WORK

D3-1. Full-Time/Part-Time Status of the Civilian Noninstitutional Population, by Age Group and Sex, Monthly Average 1981

(Numbers in thousands)

Status	45-54	55-64	65+
Male			
Full-time labor force............	9,685	6,779	1,044
Employed........................	9,306	6,551	1,020
Full time....................	9,047	6,354	949
Part time (economic reasons)	249	197	71
Unemployed......................	379	228	24
Rate........................	3.9	3.4	2.3
Part-time labor force...........	183	391	822
Percent of total labor force	1.9	5.4	44.1
Employed part time.............	171	358	791
Percent of total employed...	1.8	5.2	43.7
Unemployed......................	11	32	31
Rate........................	6.2	8.3	3.8
Percent of total unemployed.	2.9	12.4	56.8
Female			
Full-time labor force...........	5,687	3,706	525
Employed........................	5,422	3,562	506
Full time....................	5,087	3,329	455
Part time (economic reasons).	335	233	51
Unemployed......................	265	144	20
Rate........................	4.7	3.9	3.8
Part-time labor force...........	1,415	1,093	651
Percent of total labor force.	19.9	22.8	56.3
Employed part time.............	1,355	1,054	628
Percent of total employed....	20.0	22.8	55.4
Unemployed......................	60	40	23
Rate........................	4.2	3.6	3.5
Percent of total unemployed..	18.4	21.6	53.9

D3-2. Persons 45 Years and Over on Part- and Full-Time Work Schedules, 1960, 1970, 1982, 1984

(Percent distribution)

Sex and age	1960 Full time	1960 Part time	1970 Full time	1970 Part time	1982 Full time	1982 Part time	1984 Full time	1984 Part time
Males:								
45 to 64	94	6	96	4	93	7	94	6
65 plus	70	30	62	38	52	48	54	46
Females:								
45 to 64	78	22	77	23	76	27	75	25
65 plus	57	43	51	49	40	60	39	61

SOURCE: U.S. Department of Labor, Bureau of Labor Statistics, Current Population Survey.

*Figures may not total 100 percent due to rounding.

D3-3. Persons on Part-Time Schedules for Economic Reasons by Type of Industry, Sex, and Age, 1957-83

(In thousands)

Year	Total	Agriculture	Nonagricultural industries Total	Men Total	Men 16 to 17 years	Men 18 to 24 years	Men 25 to 44 years	Men 45 to 64 years	Men 65 years and over	Women Total	Women 16 to 17 years	Women 18 to 24 years	Women 25 to 44 years	Women 45 to 64 years	Women 65 years and over
1957	2,469	300	2,169	1,263	99	181	488	418	76	906	58	117	383	315	32
1958	3,280	327	2,953	1,793	114	257	727	607	88	1,161	57	166	482	413	42
1959	2,640	304	2,336	1,320	115	223	494	419	67	1,016	62	140	405	367	41
1960	2,860	300	2,560	1,476	114	251	552	489	70	1,083	75	167	420	385	36
1961	3,142	329	2,813	1,625	127	305	598	527	66	1,188	65	178	460	443	40
1962	2,661	325	2,337	1,308	113	243	476	422	55	1,029	65	171	386	372	34
1963	2,620	332	2,291	1,263	106	255	436	407	59	1,025	65	183	384	355	38
1964	2,455	318	2,137	1,154	106	235	398	368	49	982	60	177	350	359	37
1965	2,209	281	1,928	1,005	108	226	322	310	40	923	55	205	308	325	30
1966[1]	1,894	230	1,664	863	75	195	277	273	43	801	47	164	286	279	27
1967	2,163	250	1,913	987	81	214	331	310	51	925	52	199	312	331	33
1968	1,970	255	1,715	830	90	194	250	250	47	886	55	201	286	314	30
1969	2,056	246	1,810	888	98	210	284	252	45	921	64	212	311	308	27
1970	2,446	247	2,198	1,106	98	285	374	303	46	1,091	70	269	355	362	35
1971	2,688	237	2,451	1,209	104	338	404	317	46	1,241	79	322	410	391	40
1972	2,648	218	2,430	1,180	136	370	364	268	42	1,249	94	340	412	361	41
1973	2,554	211	2,343	1,118	126	355	358	241	38	1,224	96	361	397	331	38
1974	2,988	238	2,751	1,332	129	405	458	295	46	1,419	103	402	472	405	41
1975	3,804	262	3,542	1,763	135	537	635	410	48	1,778	112	540	613	477	37
1976	3,607	273	3,334	1,616	129	548	555	343	44	1,717	112	540	597	432	35
1977	3,608	239	3,369	1,574	140	545	540	302	47	1,794	114	577	641	421	41
1978	3,516	219	3,298	1,473	143	520	516	246	49	1,824	127	561	660	428	49
1979	3,577	204	3,373	1,494	134	503	523	278	53	1,879	113	582	714	428	47
1980	4,321	258	4,064	1,909	132	606	754	364	51	2,155	122	669	821	496	48
1981	4,768	268	4,499	2,079	133	678	809	407	51	2,421	122	723	976	551	49
1982	6,170	318	5,852	2,779	133	857	1,155	573	61	3,073	124	892	1,311	686	61
1983	6,266	269	5,997	2,758	125	929	1,136	508	59	3,240	119	1,001	1,386	675	59

[1] Data for 1966 forward refer to persons 16 years and over; 14 years and over for prior years.

NOTE: Data refer to persons who worked less than 35 hours during the survey week because of slack work, job changing during the week, material shortages, inability to find full-time work, etc.

D3-4. Helpfulness of Various Flexible Work Arrangements for Working Americans 55 and Over, Base: Labor Force 55 and Over

Q: How much help would each of the following be to you personally if you wanted to work after retirement -- a great deal, some, hardly any, or no help at all?

	TOTAL 55+	55-64	65 AND OVER
BASE	392	266	126
	%	%	%
GREATER AVAILABILITY OF PART-TIME WORK			
OF HELP	80	84	56
NOT OF HELP	16	14	31
A JOB SHARED WITH SOMEONE ELSE SO THAT EACH PERSON CAN TAKE MORE TIME AWAY FROM WORK BUT THE JOB STILL GETS DONE			
OF HELP	71	73	56
NOT OF HELP	25	24	36
A JOB THAT ALLOWS A DAY OR TWO A WEEK TO WORK AT HOME			
OF HELP	74	77	57
NOT OF HELP	22	20	34
FREEDOM TO SET A WORK SCHEDULE AS LONG AS YOU WORK 70 HOURS EVERY TWO WEEKS			
OF HELP	57	58	50
NOT OF HELP	38	37	42
GREATER AVAILABILITY OF REGULAR FULL-TIME JOBS			
OF HELP	44	44	41
NOT OF HELP	54	54	53
FOUR-DAY WORK WEEKS WITH LONGER HOURS EACH DAY BUT WITH A THREE-DAY BREAK			
OF HELP	39	40	28
NOT OF HELP	57	57	68

NOTE: "OF HELP" = OF "A GREAT DEAL" AND "SOME" HELP;
       "NOT OF HELP" = OF "HARDLY ANY" AND "NO HELP AT ALL."

D4. UNEMPLOYMENT

D4–1. Rate and Duration of Unemployment, by Age and Sex, 1980

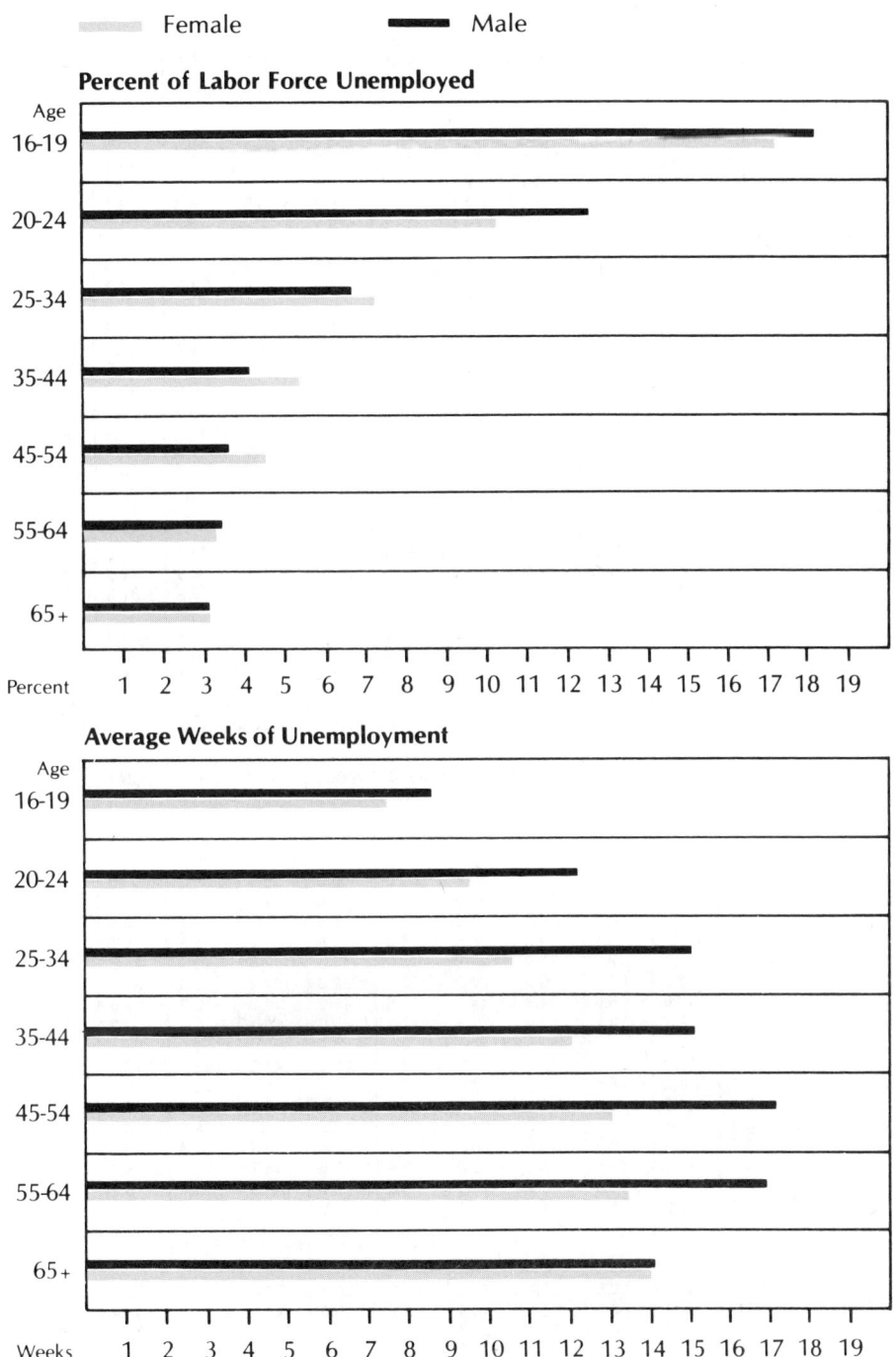

Source: Department of Labor

D4-2. Percent Distribution of Total and Long-Term Unemployment by Sex, Age, and Race, 1970–83

(Numbers in thousands)

Sex, age, and race	1970	1971	1972	1973	1974	1975	1976	1977	1978	1979	1980	1981	1982	1983
	Total unemployed													
Total:														
Number (thousands)	4,093	5,016	4,882	4,365	5,156	7,929	7,406	6,991	6,202	6,137	7,637	8,273	10,678	10,717
Percent	100.0	100.0	100.0	100.0	100.0	100.0	100.0	100.0	100.0	100.0	100.0	100.0	100.0	100.0
SEX AND AGE														
Men	54.7	55.6	54.5	52.0	52.6	56.0	54.4	52.3	50.4	50.6	55.8	55.3	57.9	58.4
16 to 19 years	14.7	13.8	14.6	15.0	14.8	12.2	12.7	12.6	13.2	13.3	12.0	11.6	10.2	9.4
16 to 17 years	7.5	6.9	7.3	8.1	7.7	5.6	6.0	6.0	6.9	6.4	5.6	5.2	4.4	3.8
18 to 19 years	7.2	6.9	7.3	6.9	7.1	6.6	6.7	6.5	6.3	6.9	6.4	6.4	5.8	5.6
20 to 24 years	11.7	12.7	12.8	11.9	12.4	13.5	12.7	12.3	12.1	11.8	13.9	13.8	13.2	12.8
25 to 44 years	15.7	16.6	15.2	14.7	15.6	18.7	18.0	17.6	15.9	16.5	21.1	21.3	25.0	25.8
45 to 64 years	10.9	11.1	10.3	9.0	8.6	10.2	9.7	8.4	7.9	7.9	8.1	7.9	8.8	9.8
65 years and over	1.7	1.4	1.5	1.3	1.2	1.3	1.3	1.4	1.3	1.2	.8	.7	.6	.7
Women	45.3	44.4	45.5	48.0	47.4	44.0	45.6	47.7	49.5	49.4	44.2	44.7	42.1	41.6
16 to 19 years	12.4	11.3	12.3	13.4	13.0	10.2	10.6	11.4	12.6	12.3	10.0	9.7	8.3	7.7
16 to 17 years	5.7	5.0	5.7	6.5	5.9	4.5	4.8	5.2	6.0	5.7	4.6	4.2	3.4	3.2
18 to 19 years	6.7	6.4	6.6	7.0	7.1	5.7	5.8	6.2	6.6	6.6	5.4	5.4	4.9	4.5
20 to 24 years	9.4	9.7	10.3	10.9	10.9	9.8	10.2	10.7	11.4	11.3	9.8	10.1	9.2	9.0
25 to 44 years	14.4	14.5	14.4	15.2	15.3	15.6	16.4	17.1	17.9	18.3	17.6	18.3	18.0	18.3
45 to 64 years	8.3	8.0	7.8	7.6	7.5	7.8	7.6	7.8	6.9	6.9	6.3	6.7	6.3	6.3
65 years and over	.8	.8	.8	.7	.7	.7	.7	.7	.7	6.4	.5	.5	.4	.4
RACE AND SEX														
White	81.6	81.6	80.2	79.2	79.9	81.4	80.3	78.4	76.4	76.8	77.7	76.7	77.2	75.8
Men	45.4	46.1	44.6	42.2	42.3	45.9	44.2	41.5	39.1	39.5	44.2	43.3	45.4	45.3
Women	36.2	35.5	35.6	37.0	37.6	35.4	36.1	36.9	37.3	37.3	33.6	33.4	31.8	30.5
Black	(¹)	(¹)	18.5	19.3	18.6	17.1	17.9	19.8	21.3	21.3	19.6	20.9	20.1	21.2
Men	(¹)	(¹)	9.1	9.0	9.5	9.3	9.3	9.9	10.2	10.2	10.3	10.8	10.9	11.3
Women	(¹)	(¹)	9.3	10.3	9.0	7.9	8.5	9.9	11.1	11.1	9.3	10.2	9.1	9.9
	Unemployed 15 weeks and over													
Total:														
Number (thousands)	663	1,187	1,167	826	955	2,505	2,366	1,942	1,414	1,241	1,871	2,285	3,485	4,210
Percent	100.0	100.0	100.0	100.0	100.0	100.0	100.0	100.0	100.0	100.0	100.0	100.0	100.0	100.0
SEX AND AGE														
Men	60.1	62.1	61.7	59.2	60.4	61.5	60.5	58.8	58.0	57.8	63.8	62.8	64.4	66.3
16 to 19 years	9.2	9.3	9.1	9.0	11.0	7.7	7.4	7.6	8.2	8.2	7.7	8.0	6.9	5.7
16 to 17 years	4.5	4.1	4.0	4.2	4.5	2.7	2.6	2.9	3.1	3.1	3.1	2.7	2.2	1.6
18 to 19 years	4.7	5.2	5.1	4.8	6.5	5.0	4.8	4.7	5.1	5.2	4.6	5.3	4.6	4.1
20 to 24 years	10.0	12.1	12.6	11.9	12.2	14.9	13.3	12.8	12.7	11.5	14.6	15.4	13.9	12.8
25 to 44 years	18.9	21.2	20.5	20.9	20.0	23.1	22.6	22.8	21.5	22.7	28.7	27.5	31.1	33.3
45 to 64 years	17.8	16.8	16.6	14.9	14.7	13.6	15.2	11.8	13.3	13.6	11.9	11.1	11.8	13.8
65 years and over	4.2	2.7	2.9	2.5	2.6	2.1	2.0	2.1	2.4	1.9	.8	.8	.7	.7
Women	39.9	37.9	38.4	40.8	39.6	38.5	39.5	41.2	42.0	42.3	36.2	37.2	35.6	33.7
16 to 19 years	7.1	5.8	6.6	7.8	7.4	5.1	5.4	5.8	6.7	6.1	4.6	5.2	4.5	3.5
16 to 17 years	3.2	1.9	2.5	3.0	3.0	2.0	1.9	2.3	2.5	2.2	1.6	1.8	1.3	1.1
18 to 19 years	3.9	3.8	4.1	4.8	4.4	3.1	3.5	3.6	4.1	3.9	3.0	3.3	3.3	2.4
20 to 24 years	6.9	7.1	6.8	8.0	8.2	7.7	7.8	8.3	8.8	9.4	7.1	7.3	7.2	6.1
25 to 44 years	14.0	14.2	13.4	13.8	12.9	15.4	15.5	16.3	16.8	18.0	16.8	17.3	16.7	16.9
45 to 64 years	10.6	9.8	10.3	10.2	10.0	9.2	9.7	9.8	8.7	8.2	7.1	7.1	6.8	6.8
65 years and over	1.2	1.0	1.4	1.0	1.2	1.0	1.2	1.2	.9	.6	.5	.4	.4	.4
RACE AND SEX														
White	81.3	80.9	80.6	77.1	77.6	80.3	80.2	77.4	72.2	72.9	75.5	73.2	74.9	74.6
Men	50.0	51.1	50.5	46.9	46.9	49.7	48.6	45.3	42.1	42.9	49.2	47.3	49.3	50.5
Women	31.3	30.0	30.1	30.2	30.7	30.7	31.6	32.1	30.0	30.0	26.2	25.9	25.6	24.2
Black	(¹)	(¹)	17.9	21.9	21.2	18.1	18.2	21.0	25.5	25.4	22.1	24.3	22.8	22.9
Men	(¹)	(¹)	10.0	11.7	12.7	11.0	10.9	12.5	14.4	13.9	13.0	14.0	13.6	14.2
Women	(¹)	(¹)	7.7	10.1	8.5	7.1	7.2	8.6	11.0	11.5	9.1	10.4	9.2	8.7

See footnote at end of table.

D4–2. Percent Distribution of Total and Long-Term Unemployment by Sex, Age, and Race, 1970–83 (Continued)

(Numbers in thousands)

Sex, age, and race	1970	1971	1972	1973	1974	1975	1976	1977	1978	1979	1980	1981	1982	1983
						Unemployed 27 weeks and over								
Total:														
Number (thousands)	235	519	566	343	381	1,203	1,348	1,028	648	535	820	1,162	1,176	2,559
Percent	100.0	100.0	100.0	100.0	100.0	100.0	100.0	100.0	100.0	100.0	100.0	100.0	100.0	100.0
SEX AND AGE														
Men	62.4	62.3	62.3	61.4	63.0	62.9	61.5	60.9	59.4	59.7	64.8	66.3	66.6	68.9
16 to 19 years	5.5	7.2	6.9	7.2	8.0	5.5	5.1	5.9	6.2	7.1	5.2	6.5	5.8	4.5
16 to 17 years	3.4	2.7	3.0	3.0	2.9	1.6	1.7	2.1	2.4	2.5	2.1	2.1	1.7	1.0
18 to 19 years	2.1	4.4	3.9	4.2	5.1	3.9	3.4	3.9	3.9	4.8	3.1	4.5	4.1	3.5
20 to 24 years	9.3	1.0	10.9	10.9	10.2	13.8	12.6	12.2	11.1	9.1	14.3	15.1	13.2	12.5
25 to 44 years	20.3	21.3	21.9	21.9	23.1	24.6	24.2	23.9	22.3	24.7	30.0	30.6	33.2	36.9
45 to 64 years	21.5	19.3	18.9	18.9	18.0	16.3	17.7	15.9	16.6	16.4	14.1	13.0	13.8	15.3
65 years and over	5.9	3.5	3.7	3.3	3.5	2.7	1.9	2.9	3.5	2.3	1.1	.9	.7	.8
Women	37.6	37.9	37.7	38.6	37.0	37.1	38.5	39.0	40.6	40.3	35.0	33.8	33.4	31.0
16 to 19 years	4.2	5.0	4.3	6.6	5.4	3.7	4.0	4.4	5.5	5.0	3.9	3.8	3.2	2.3
16 to 17 years	1.3	1.5	1.8	1.8	2.1	1.5	1.3	1.7	1.7	1.7	1.2	1.1	.7	.6
18 to 19 years	3.0	3.5	2.5	4.8	3.2	2.2	2.8	2.8	3.9	3.3	2.6	2.7	2.4	1.6
20 to 24 years	5.9	6.0	6.0	6.9	7.0	6.6	7.0	7.2	7.7	8.7	6.9	6.1	6.5	5.2
25 to 44 years	13.9	14.1	14.1	12.3	11.3	14.8	15.1	15.8	16.7	16.4	15.8	15.9	16.2	15.9
45 to 64 years	11.8	11.4	11.7	11.7	11.8	10.6	11.1	10.3	9.3	10.0	7.9	7.5	7.1	7.2
65 years and over	1.7	1.4	1.6	1.2	1.3	1.5	1.3	1.5	1.1	.6	.6	.5	.3	.4
RACE AND SEX														
White	80.0	81.4	81.5	77.2	77.2	80.3	79.6	76.7	69.8	69.3	73.1	71.0	72.7	73.1
Men	52.3	51.8	51.3	49.1	49.3	50.5	49.1	47.1	42.2	42.1	48.6	48.0	49.2	51.5
Women	27.7	29.8	30.1	28.1	27.9	29.8	30.4	29.7	27.6	27.2	24.3	23.0	23.5	21.5
Black	(¹)	(¹)	17.1	22.0	22.0	18.4	18.9	21.9	28.0	29.2	24.5	26.6	38.1	24.3
Men	(¹)	(¹)	10.1	11.9	13.1	11.7	11.5	13.0	15.6	16.6	14.6	16.4	24.1	15.6
Women	(¹)	(¹)	6.9	10.1	8.8	6.7	7.4	9.0	12.2	12.4	9.8	10.1	13.9	8.7

¹ Not available.

D4–3. Unemployed Jobseekers by Sex, Age, Race, and Jobsearch Methods Used, 1982–83

Year, sex, age, and race	Thousands of persons		Methods used as a percent of total jobseekers						Average number of methods used
	Total unemployed	Total jobseekers	Public employment agency	Private employment agency	Employer directly	Placed or answered ads	Friends or relatives	Other	
1982									
Total, 16 years and over	10,678	8,429	24.2	5.8	77.8	34.7	16.3	4.7	1.63
16 to 19 years	1,977	1,847	15.5	3.1	82.5	27.1	14.3	3.2	1.46
20 to 24 years	2,392	1,954	26.7	5.8	79.1	35.5	15.5	3.6	1.66
25 to 34 years	3,037	2,263	27.7	7.0	76.0	38.8	17.5	4.7	1.72
35 to 44 years	1,552	1,137	27.8	6.9	75.8	37.1	17.1	5.9	1.71
45 to 54 years	966	689	26.0	7.3	75.3	35.7	17.1	6.7	1.68
55 to 64 years	647	458	21.0	6.3	71.8	34.9	17.7	10.0	1.62
65 years and over	107	80	16.2	3.7	70.0	26.2	17.5	5.0	1.39
Men, 16 years and over	6,179	4,635	26.9	5.8	78.8	32.6	18.3	5.8	1.68
16 to 19 years	1,090	1,000	17.0	3.1	83.2	26.1	16.2	2.9	1.48
20 to 24 years	1,407	1,106	29.7	5.8	80.0	33.1	17.6	3.9	1.70
25 to 34 years	1,791	1,234	31.0	6.8	77.1	37.4	19.9	5.8	1.78
35 to 44 years	879	596	31.9	7.4	76.5	33.9	20.0	8.2	1.78
45 to 54 years	550	374	28.9	7.8	77.5	33.2	17.9	10.2	1.75
55 to 64 years	393	272	21.0	5.9	72.8	30.9	18.8	14.0	1.63
65 years and over	69	53	17.0	3.8	77.4	20.8	17.0	3.8	1.40
Women, 16 years and over	4,499	3,793	20.9	5.8	76.5	37.3	13.8	3.4	1.58
16 to 19 years	886	847	13.7	3.2	81.7	28.3	12.2	3.5	1.43
20 to 24 years	985	848	22.6	6.0	77.9	38.6	12.7	3.3	1.61
25 to 34 years	1,246	1,029	23.6	7.2	74.7	40.5	14.6	3.3	1.64
35 to 44 years	673	541	23.3	6.5	74.9	40.9	14.0	3.1	1.63
45 to 54 years	416	315	22.5	6.3	72.7	39.0	16.5	2.9	1.60
55 to 64 years	254	186	21.0	7.0	70.4	40.9	16.7	4.8	1.61
65 years and over	38	27	(¹)	(¹)	(¹)	(¹)	(¹)	(¹)	(¹)
White, 16 years and over	8,241	6,339	22.4	5.9	78.1	37.0	16.5	4.7	1.65
Men	4,846	3,526	25.4	5.9	79.1	34.7	18.4	6.1	1.70
Women	3,395	2,813	18.8	5.8	76.8	39.8	14.0	3.0	1.58
Black, 16 years and over	2,142	1,839	29.9	5.8	77.5	27.1	15.2	4.4	1.60
Men	1,167	972	32.2	5.8	78.5	25.1	17.8	4.4	1.64
Women	975	867	27.5	5.8	76.4	29.3	12.2	4.3	1.55
1983									
Total, 16 years and over	10,717	8,800	24.4	5.2	79.3	33.8	16.7	4.9	1.64
16 to 19 years	1,829	1,722	14.6	2.5	84.4	25.1	14.1	4.2	1.45
20 to 24 years	2,330	1,983	25.3	5.0	80.2	34.8	15.9	3.8	1.65
25 to 34 years	3,078	2,443	28.6	5.9	78.2	37.4	16.6	4.5	1.71
35 to 44 years	1,650	1,276	27.9	6.4	78.1	36.7	19.3	5.6	1.74
45 to 54 years	1,039	772	26.8	6.2	76.0	35.0	18.7	6.7	1.69
55 to 64 years	677	511	24.3	7.0	73.6	34.2	19.0	8.8	1.67
65 years and over	114	93	12.9	3.2	69.9	28.0	24.7	7.5	1.46
Men, 16 years and over	6,260	4,949	27.0	5.2	80.2	32.0	19.2	5.9	1.70
16 to 19 years	1,003	941	15.3	2.6	84.7	23.5	17.1	3.7	1.47
20 to 24 years	1,369	1,125	28.3	5.0	82.0	31.6	18.2	3.9	1.69
25 to 34 years	1,822	1,368	31.5	5.7	79.5	36.3	19.1	5.6	1.78
35 to 44 years	947	699	32.5	6.3	79.1	35.5	21.7	7.9	1.83
45 to 54 years	613	440	29.5	6.6	76.1	33.4	20.9	9.1	1.76
55 to 64 years	433	316	25.6	7.3	73.4	31.6	19.9	11.4	1.69
65 years and over	73	61	9.8	3.3	72.1	27.9	26.2	6.6	1.46
Women, 16 years and over	4,457	3,850	21.1	5.1	78.1	36.1	13.6	3.7	1.58
16 to 19 years	825	781	13.8	2.4	83.9	27.0	10.4	4.9	1.42
20 to 24 years	961	858	21.3	4.9	77.9	38.9	12.8	3.5	1.59
25 to 34 years	1,255	1,076	24.8	6.0	76.6	38.8	13.5	3.2	1.63
35 to 44 years	703	577	22.2	6.4	76.9	38.0	16.3	2.8	1.63
45 to 54 years	427	332	23.5	5.4	75.9	37.3	16.0	3.6	1.62
55 to 64 years	244	195	22.1	6.7	73.8	38.5	16.9	4.6	1.63
65 years and over	41	32	(¹)	(¹)	(¹)	(¹)	(¹)	(¹)	(¹)
White, 16 years and over	8,128	6,494	23.3	5.4	79.5	35.5	17.0	5.1	1.66
Men	4,859	3,728	26.1	5.6	80.5	33.5	19.3	6.3	1.71
Women	3,270	2,765	19.6	5.1	78.2	38.2	13.8	3.6	1.58
Black, 16 years and over	2,272	2,027	27.7	4.6	79.0	28.2	15.5	4.0	1.59
Men	1,213	1,059	29.8	4.2	79.9	26.5	18.1	4.2	1.63
Women	1,059	969	25.4	5.1	78.1	30.0	12.7	3.9	1.55

¹ Data not shown where base is less than 35,000.

NOTE: The jobseekers total is less than the total unemployed because it does not include persons on layoff or waiting to begin a new job within 30 days; groups for whom jobseeking is not collected. The percent using each method will always total more than 100 because many jobseekers use more than one method.

E. Economic Status

SOURCES OF INCOME

The elderly rely heavily on Social Security benefits and asset income. Between 1968 and 1983, the share of income for elderly families provided by Social Security grew from 23.9 percent to 34.3 percent. During this period, the share provided by asset income increased from 14.6 to 20.9 percent. At the same time, the share contributed by earnings fell from 48.2 to 28 percent. Asset income is unevenly divided: one-third of the elderly have none, and of the remainder, the lower income group derive a much smaller proportion of their income from this source than the more affluent group. In 1982, Social Security provided 80 percent of the income of persons receiving less than $5,000 per year, but only 19 percent for people with incomes of $20,000 or more. While older persons generally have substantially less cash income than those under 65, several noncash factors favor the elderly: tax treatment, reduced family size, paid-up mortgages, and in-kind benefits such as Medicare, Medicaid, group health insurance, and food stamps. One-fourth of the elderly have money left for luxuries after paying their expenses for a comfortable level of everyday living. Among the assets of the elderly are savings accounts, personal property, home and other real estate equity, and annuities. Income from pensions is on the increase and will in the future provide a substantial portion due to the legislation providing strong incentives to invest in IRA, Keogh, and profit-sharing plans.

INDIVIDUAL/FAMILY/HOUSEHOLD INCOME BY AGE, SEX, AND RACE

Persons who are 85 years or older have significantly lower cash incomes than those in the 65 to 74 and 75 to 84 age groups. In 1983, the median cash income of couples aged 85 and over ($11,988) was less than three-quarters of the median cash income of couples aged 65 to 74 ($17,798). Women over 65 account for over half of the elderly population, but account for over three-quarters of the poor. The nonwhite elderly have substantially lower incomes than their white counterparts. The median income of elderly white men is almost twice as much as that of black and Hispanic men. In 1983, the median family income headed by an individual of 65 or over was $16,862, compared to $6,904 for single persons in the group. Social Security income accounts for a larger proportion of single persons' incomes than that of families. The median income of single elderly men is substantially higher than that of single women.

LIVING EXPENSES, TAXES, COST INDEXES

The Consumer Price Index is presented in cost index tables at 100 in June 1967; by June 1985, it had risen to 322.3. Because many elderly are primarily on fixed incomes, price increases are of great concern to them. The rises in medical costs (391 percent), housing (342 percent), and transportation (314 percent) contribute to their financial problems.

POVERTY STATUS

Poverty can be defined in a number of ways, depending on whether only cash income is counted. If third-party payments (e.g., Medicare and Medicaid), noncash benefits (e.g., food stamps, subsidized housing), or other services are included, the situation is changed. In general, however, the elderly tend to be poorer than other adults, and the poverty rate increases among them as they grow older. In 1983, 3.7 million or 14.1 percent of the 65+ population had incomes below the poverty level, as compared to 12 percent of the younger population. Poverty is highest among black women, generally higher among women than among men, and higher among the black and Hispanic population. Poverty rates in general have declined over the last 20 years; this decline is projected to be somewhat greater among the elderly than among the general population.

E1. SOURCES OF INCOME

E1–1. Shares of Income for the Older Noninstitutionalized Population, 1982[1]

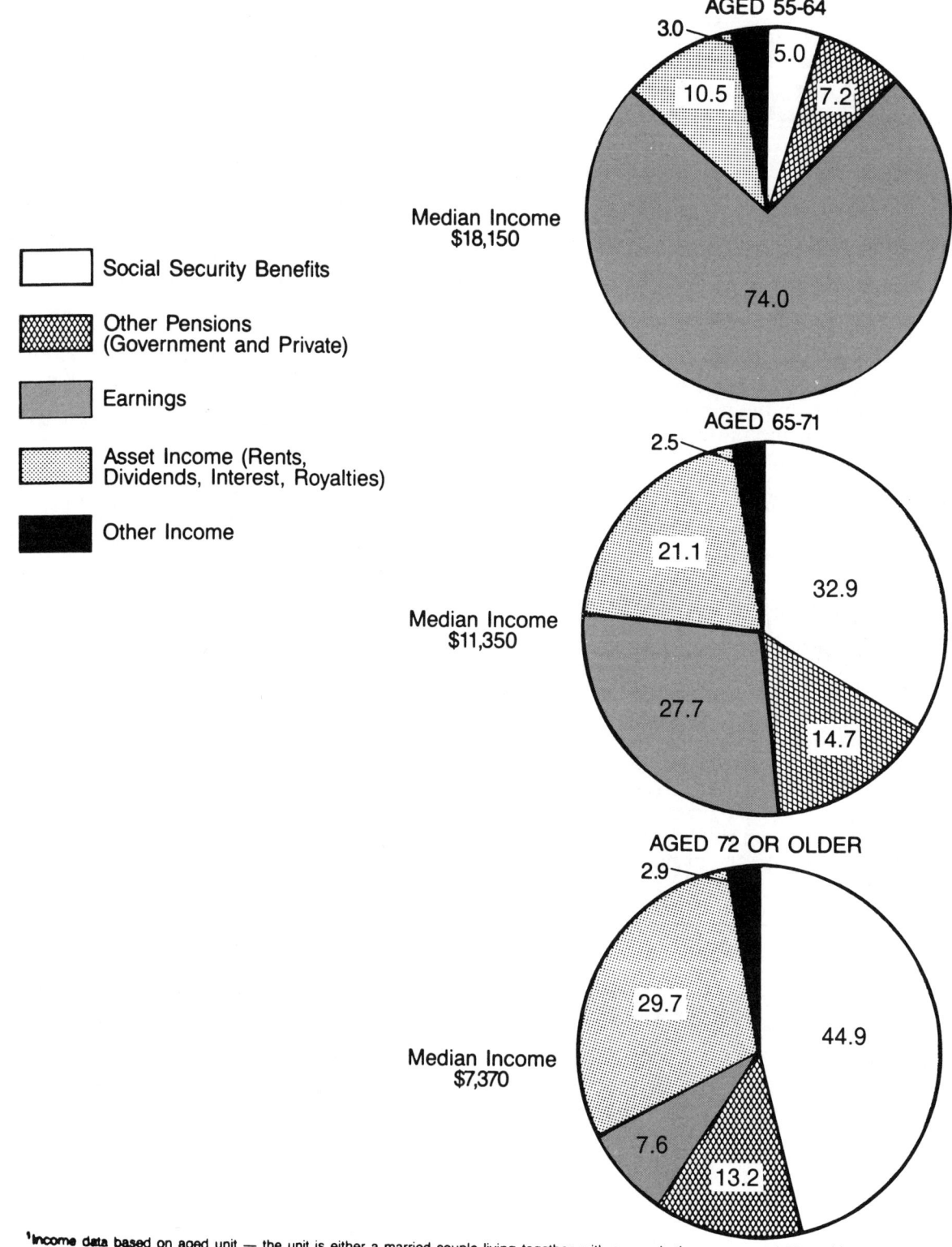

Social Security Benefits

Other Pensions (Government and Private)

Earnings

Asset Income (Rents, Dividends, Interest, Royalties)

Other Income

AGED 55-64

3.0
5.0
10.5
7.2
74.0

Median Income $18,150

AGED 65-71

2.5
21.1
32.9
27.7
14.7

Median Income $11,350

AGED 72 OR OLDER

2.9
29.7
44.9
7.6
13.2

Median Income $7,370

[1] Income data based on aged unit — the unit is either a married couple living together, with one or both persons aged 55 or older, or a person aged 55 or older who does not live with a spouse.

E1-2. Income Sources by Age, Sex, and Marital Status: Percent of Aged Persons with Money Income from Specified Sources, 1982[1]

Source of income	All persons			Married persons			Nonmarried persons		
	55-61	62-64	65 and older	55-61	62-64	65 and older	55-61	62-64	65 and older
Men									
Number(in thousands)............	7,795	2,868	10,544	6,715	2,413	8,097	1,079	455	2,448
Percent of units with---									
Earnings....................	82	60	24	84	61	26	70	52	18
Retirement benefits..........	21	56	92	21	55	93	23	59	91
Social Security2/.............	8	46	88	8	45	89	10	51	87
Benefits other than Social Security.	16	32	42	17	33	44	15	28	36
Other public pensions.........	9	12	14	9	13	14	8	8	13
Railroad retirement........	0	1	2	0	1	2	0	1	2
Government employee pensions....	8	11	12	8	11	12	8	7	10
Private pensions or annuities.....	8	21	29	8	21	31	7	20	24
Income from assets.............	69	69	72	72	72	75	51	52	60
Veterans' benefits............	6	9	5	5	9	4	11	11	7
Public assistance............	4	6	10	4	6	9	9	9	14
Women									
Number(in thousands)............	8,410	3,321	15,222	5,949	1,988	5,887	2,462	1,334	9,335
Percent of units with---									
Earnings....................	50	36	10	45	31	10	61	45	10
Retirement benefits..........	14	59	93	9	54	93	27	66	92
Social Security2/.............	9	55	91	6	52	92	18	59	90
Benefits other than Social Security.	7	14	21	5	9	15	13	22	24
Other public pensions.........	4	7	10	2	5	8	6	9	12
Railroad retirement........	0	1	2	0	1	1	0	2	2
Government employee pensions....	2	4	7	2	4	7	2	3	7
Private pensions or annuities.....	4	8	10	3	4	7	7	14	13
Income from assets.............	65	68	66	71	72	74	52	61	61
Veterans' benefits............	2	1	2	0	0	0	6	3	4
Public assistance............	6	7	15	3	4	8	14	11	19

1/ Receipt of sources is ascertained by response to a yes/no question which is imputed by CPS. A married couple receives a source if one or both persons are recipients of that source.
2/ Recipients of Social Security may be receiving retired-worker benefits, dependents' or survivors' benefits, disability benefits, transitionally insured, or special age-72 benefits.

E1-3. Income Sources by Age, Sex, and Race: Percent of Aged Persons with Money Income from Specified Sources, 1982[1]

Source of income	White			Black		
	55-61	62-64	65 and older	55-61	62-64	65 and older
Men						
Number (in thousands).............	7,007	2,576	9,508	660	234	846
Percent of units with---						
Earnings....................	83	60	25	69	51	17
Retirement benefits..........	22	57	93	19	50	91
Social Security2/.............	8	47	89	12	42	88
Benefits other than Social Security.	17	34	44	9	24	25
Other public pensions.........	9	12	14	5	9	11
Railroad retirement........	0	1	2	0	1	2
Government employee pensions....	9	11	12	5	8	9
Private pensions or annuities.....	8	22	31	4	15	14
Income from assets.............	73	72	76	31	34	32
Veterans' benefits............	6	9	5	8	9	6
Public assistance............	4	6	10	8	12	16
Women						
Number (in thousands).............	7,429	2,970	13,759	810	299	1,277
Percent of units with---						
Earnings....................	50	36	10	52	43	10
Retirement benefits..........	14	60	93	16	55	88
Social Security2/.............	9	55	92	13	51	86
Benefits other than Social Security.	8	15	22	5	9	11
Other public pensions.........	4	7	11	3	4	8
Railroad retirement........	0	1	2	0	0	2
Government employee pensions....	2	4	7	2	3	4
Private pensions or annuities.....	4	9	11	2	5	3
Income from assets.............	70	72	70	28	30	27
Veterans' benefits............	2	1	2	1	2	2
Public assistance............	5	6	13	18	17	31

1/ Receipt of sources is ascertained by response to a yes/no question which is imputed by CPS. A married couple receives a source if one or both persons are recipients of that source.
2/ Recipients of Social Security may be receiving retired-worker benefits, dependents' or survivors' benefits, disability benefits, transitionally insured, or special age-72 benefits.

E1-4. Income Sources by Age, Race, and Social Security Beneficiary Status: Percent of Aged Units with Money Income from Specified Sources: 1982[1]

Source of income	Beneficiaries[2]			Nonbeneficiaries		
	55-61	62-64	65 and older	55-61	62-64	65 and older
	White					
Number(in thousands).............	1,165	2,012	16,229	7,820	1,699	1,575
Percent of units with---						
Earnings.............................	47	44	20	88	85	41
Retirement benefits..................	100	100	100	16	21	32
Social Security[2]................	100	100	100	--	--	--
Benefits other than Social Security.	34	43	38	16	21	32
Other public pensions............	12	13	14	9	13	25
Railroad retirement.............	0	1	1	0	2	10
Government employee pensions....	11	12	13	9	11	15
Private pensions or annuities.....	23	33	26	7	8	8
Income from assets..................	57	70	73	73	74	59
Veterans' benefits..................	14	9	4	5	5	4
Public assistance...................	12	9	14	6	6	21
	Black					
Number(in thousands).............	163	196	1,550	921	214	229
Percent of units with---						
Earnings.............................	36	40	18	74	68	27
Retirement benefits..................	100	100	100	7	15	21
Social Security[2]................	100	100	100	--	--	--
Benefits other than Social Security.	16	26	18	7	15	21
Other public pensions............	5	6	9	4	11	17
Railroad retirement.............	0	0	1	0	1	7
Government employee pensions....	5	6	8	4	10	11
Private pensions or annuities.....	10	19	9	3	4	3
Income from assets..................	22	21	28	30	44	28
Veterans' benefits..................	13	8	5	4	6	2
Public assistance...................	21	13	26	17	19	46

1/ Receipt of sources is ascertained by response to a yes/no question which is imputed by CPS. A married couple receives a source if one or both persons are recipients of that source.
2/ Recipients of Social Security may be receiving retired-worker benefits, dependents' or survivors' benefits, disability benefits, transitionally insured, or special age-72 benefits.

E1-5. Income from Social Security Benefits by Age, Sex, and Marital Status: Percentage Distribution of Aged Units, 1982

Income (recipients only)1/	Married couples			Nonmarried persons								
				Total			Men			Women		
	55-61	62-64	65 and older	55-61	62-64	65 and older	55-61	62-64	65 and older	55-61	62-64	65 and older
Number(in thousands)	792	1,199	7,326	549	1,017	10,394	103	229	2,099	445	788	8,295
Total percent.......	100	100	100	100	100	100	100	100	100	100	100	100
$1-$499..............	2	1	0	3	2	0	5	1	0	2	2	0
$500-$999............	3	2	1	2	3	0	0	4	0	2	3	0
$1,000-$1,499........	2	4	1	2	3	1	0	5	1	3	2	1
$1,500-$1,999........	7	3	1	7	7	5	1	4	4	9	8	5
$2,000-$2,499........	5	4	2	11	8	7	8	10	6	12	7	8
$2,500-$2,999........	5	6	2	10	6	6	9	4	6	10	7	6
$3,000-$3,499........	6	7	2	14	9	9	15	6	7	14	10	9
$3,500-$3,999........	9	5	3	11	13	12	10	8	10	12	15	12
$4,000-$4,499........	8	4	4	11	10	11	10	8	8	12	11	12
$4,500-$4,999........	8	5	5	11	13	14	7	10	10	12	14	15
$5,000-$5,999........	13	17	10	6	15	20	12	19	23	5	14	19
$6,000-$6,999........	12	15	12	6	8	9	15	14	13	4	6	8
$7,000-$7,999........	8	9	15	2	3	3	6	7	6	1	2	2
$8,000-$8,999........	6	7	14	0	0	2	2	0	3	0	0	2
$9,000-$9,999........	2	3	10	1	0	1	0	0	2	1	0	1
$10,000 or more........	3	5	20	0	0	0	0	1	0	1	0	0
Median income2/........	$4,580	$5,540	$7,560	$3,490	$3,940	$4,450	$4,070	$4,460	$4,880	$3,400	$3,870	$4,350

1/ Recipients of Social Security may be receiving retired-worker benefits, dependents' or survivors' benefits, disability benefits, transitionally insured, or special age-72 benefits. Units with a person reporting receipt of both Social Security benefits and railroad retirement are excluded. This is less than 1 percent of beneficiaries aged 55-61, 1 percent aged 62-64, and 1 percent aged 65 and older.
2/ Rounded to the nearest $10. Medians for 1982 are calculated more precisely than those for previous years in this data series. See technical appendix for further detail.

E1-6. Income from Social Security Benefits by Sex, Race, and Marital Status: Percentage Distribution of Aged Units, 65 and Older, 1982

Income (recipients only)1/	White					Black				
	All units	Married couples	Nonmarried persons			All units	Married couples	Nonmarried persons		
			Total	Men	Women			Total	Men	Women
Number(in thousands)..	15,986	6,734	9,252	1,801	7,451	1,527	477	1,049	267	783
Total percent.....	100	100	100	100	100	100	100	100	100	100
$1-$499........	0	0	0	0	0	1	1	0	0	1
$500-$999......	1	1	0	0	0	0	0	1	0	1
$1,000-$1,499..	1	1	1	1	1	2	1	2	2	2
$1,500-$1,999..	3	1	4	3	4	9	2	12	12	12
$2,000-$2,499..	4	2	6	6	7	12	2	16	11	18
$2,500-$2,999..	4	2	5	6	5	10	4	13	8	15
$3,000-$3,499..	6	2	8	6	9	10	5	12	10	12
$3,500-$3,999..	8	3	11	9	12	10	3	13	13	12
$4,000-$4,499..	8	4	11	7	12	8	5	9	12	9
$4,500-$4,999..	10	5	15	10	16	8	10	7	10	6
$5,000-$5,999..	16	9	21	25	20	12	17	10	15	8
$6,000-$6,999..	11	11	10	14	9	7	15	4	6	3
$7,000-$7,999..	8	15	3	7	3	4	10	1	1	1
$8,000-$8,999..	7	14	2	4	2	3	9	0	0	0
$9,000-$9,999..	5	10	1	2	1	2	6	0	1	0
$10,000 or more	9	21	0	0	0	3	9	0	0	0
Median income2/	$5,310	$7,670	$4,600	$5,080	$4,490	$3,820	$5,980	$3,210	$3,710	$3,050

1/ Recipients of Social Security may be receiving retired-worker benefits, dependents' or survivors' benefits, transitionally insured, or special age-72 benefits. Units with a person reporting receipt of both Social Security benefits and railroad retirement are excluded. This is less than 1 percent of beneficiaries aged 55-61, 1 percent aged 62-64, and 1 percent aged 65 and older.

2/ Rounded to the nearest $10. Medians for 1982 are calculated more precisely than those for previous years in this data series. See technical appendix for further detail.

E1-7. Source of Income as a Percentage of Income, 1968-83

Year	Social Security/ railroad retirement	Asset income	SSI/Public assistance	Pensions	Earnings
Families with a head 65 and older:					
1968	22.9	14.6	1.3	12.3	48.2
1970	25.0	14.5	1.4	12.5	46.6
1972	28.1	14.0	1.1	12.5	44.2
1974	31.1	15.4	1.3	13.5	38.8
1976	32.3	15.6	1.4	14.5	36.1
1978	32.2	15.7	1.2	13.8	37.1
1980	32.4	19.4	1.1	15.6	31.4
1981	33.0	21.7	1.0	14.9	29.5
1982	33.1	21.4	0.8	14.8	29.9
1983	34.3	20.9	0.8	16.0	28.0
Unrelated individuals 65 and older:					
1968	34.2	26.5	4.1	14.4	20.8
1970	37.3	24.1	4.1	15.4	19.1
1972	41.7	24.2	3.2	14.3	16.6
1974	44.9	21.7	3.7	16.2	13.6
1976	46.9	20.9	3.0	15.7	13.4
1978	45.9	22.7	2.7	16.9	11.8
1980	47.4	24.4	2.5	14.6	11.2
1981	45.9	26.6	1.9	14.1	11.5
1982	45.3	28.7	1.8	14.1	10.1
1983	44.0	28.7	1.9	15.5	9.8

Source: U.S. Bureau of the Census, Current Population Reports Series P-60, 1965-83.

E1–8. Mean Total Money Income of the Aged and Nonaged and the Ratio of Income of the Aged to that of the Nonaged for Various Economic Units at 2-year Intervals, 1950–82[1]

[In 1967 dollars]

| Year | Aged | | | | Nonaged | | | | Ratio | | | |
| | Families | Unrelated individuals | Persons | | Families | Unrelated individuals | Persons | | Families | Unrelated individuals | Persons | |
			Men	Women			Men	Women			Men	Women
1950	$3,960	$1,390	$2,630	$1,120	$5,590	$2,670	$4,760	$2,060	0.71	0.52	0.55	0.54
1952	4,200	1,720	2,780	1,240	5,990	2,940	4,910	2,200	.70	.59	.57	.56
1954	4,310	1,520	2,670	1,280	6,200	2,860	5,100	2,250	.70	.53	.52	.57
1956	4,560	1,620	2,890	1,260	7,040	3,260	5,790	2,420	.65	.50	.50	.52
1958	4,260	1,650	2,640	1,260	7,060	3,430	5,760	2,410	.60	.48	.46	.52
1960	4,960	1,850	3,130	1,410	7,750	3,650	6,350	2,550	.64	.51	.49	.55
1962	5,110	2,030	3,250	1,450	8,120	4,000	6,720	2,700	.63	.51	.48	.54
1964	5,670	2,260	3,800	1,670	8,620	4,280	7,060	2,890	.66	.53	.54	.58
1966	(2)	(2)	(2)	(2)	(2)	(2)	(2)	(2)	(2)	(2)	(2)	(2)
1968	5,960	2,540	3,830	1,910	10,120	5,020	8,070	3,210	.59	.51	.47	.60
1970	6,140	2,480	3,870	1,960	10,450	5,320	8,410	3,330	.59	.47	.46	.59
1972	6,680	2,750	4,300	2,190	11,070	5,420	8,800	3,640	.60	.51	.49	.60
1974	6,620	2,860	4,400	2,200	10,840	5,310	8,450	3,470	.61	.54	.52	.63
1976	6,820	2,860	4,380	2,270	10,800	5,510	8,360	3,500	.63	.52	.52	.65
1978	7,050	3,070	4,380	2,390	11,230	5,880	8,580	3,400	.63	.52	.51	.70
1980	6,850	2,920	4,130	2,350	10,580	5,630	7,810	3,170	.65	.52	.53	.74
1982	7,270	3,250	4,500	2,580	10,250	5,560	7,450	3,260	.71	.58	.60	.79

[1] Rounded to the nearest $10.   [2] Not available.

E1–9. Median Total Money Income of the Aged and Nonaged and the Ratio of Income of the Aged to that of the Nonaged for Various Economic Units at 2-year Intervals, 1950–82[1]

[In 1967 dollars]

| Year | Aged | | | | Nonaged | | | | Ratio | | | |
| | Families | Unrelated individuals | Persons | | Families | Unrelated individuals | Persons | | Families | Unrelated individuals | Persons | |
			Men	Women			Men	Women			Men	Women
1950	$2,660	$910	$1,460	$780	$4,910	$2,270	$4,150	$1,760	0.54	0.40	0.35	0.49
1952	2,870	1,020	1,590	830	5,240	2,530	4,380	1,910	.55	.40	.36	.44
1954	2,860	1,000	1,590	870	5,570	2,280	4,620	1,910	.51	.44	.34	.46
1956	3,160	1,140	1,790	910	6,130	2,690	5,200	2,020	.52	.42	.34	.45
1958	3,100	1,110	1,780	900	6,340	2,790	5,210	2,000	.48	.40	.34	.45
1960	3,290	1,230	1,950	930	6,850	3,110	5,670	2,120	.50	.40	.34	.44
1962	3,560	1,390	2,120	1,030	7,190	3,220	6,040	2,200	.50	.43	.35	.47
1964	3,630	1,400	2,190	1,020	7,730	3,550	6,380	2,370	.47	.39	.34	.43
1966	3,750	1,480	2,220	1,120	8,380	3,810	6,890	2,540	.45	.39	.32	.44
1968	4,410	1,660	2,540	1,260	9,120	4,290	7,290	2,800	.48	.39	.35	.45
1970	4,350	1,680	2,640	1,310	9,400	4,530	7,480	3,040	.46	.37	.35	.43
1972	4,770	1,920	3,000	1,520	9,920	4,580	7,800	3,010	.52	.42	.38	.50
1974	4,960	2,010	3,080	1,620	9,780	4,530	7,760	2,980	.51	.44	.40	.54
1976	5,110	2,050	3,100	1,650	9,740	4,720	7,500	2,960	.52	.43	.41	.56
1978	5,200	2,200	3,060	1,720	9,670	5,020	7,730	2,820	.54	.44	.40	.61
1980	5,220	2,080	2,970	1,710	8,560	4,380	6,990	2,540	.61	.48	.42	.67
1982	5,580	2,230	3,180	1,860	9,030	4,910	6,540	2,570	.62	.45	.49	.72

[1] Rounded to the nearest $10.

E1-10. OASDI Cash Benefits: Amount of Monthly Benefits in Current-Payment Status for Retired Workers and Their Spouses and Children and for Survivors, 1940–84

[In thousands]

At end of selected month	Total	Retired workers [1]	Wives and husbands [1][2]	Children [3]	Widowed mothers [4]	Widows and widowers [1][5]	Parents [1]	Persons with special age-72 benefits [6]
December:								
1940	$4,070	$2,539	$361	$668	$402	$90	$11	...
1945	23,801	12,538	2,040	4,858	2,391	1,893	81	...
1950	126,856	77,678	11,995	19,366	5,801	11,481	535	...
1955	411,613	276,942	39,416	46,444	13,403	34,152	1,256	...
1960	888,320	596,849	87,867	88,578	23,795	89,054	2,178	...
1961	1,003,937	675,154	94,366	96,347	25,425	110,179	2,466	...
1962	1,099,227	741,961	100,305	105,108	26,838	122,475	2,541	...
1963	1,166,587	789,064	103,059	110,071	27,438	134,403	2,552	...
1964	1,224,240	827,548	104,769	114,947	27,954	146,476	2,547	...
1965	1,395,817	931,523	114,035	141,802	30,882	174,883	2,683	...
1966	1,502,863	983,338	115,686	154,618	31,983	192,821	2,642	$21,777
1967	1,575,646	1,026,047	117,016	164,706	32,686	207,692	2,587	24,913
1968	1,880,601	1,227,875	135,479	196,216	37,833	253,923	2,787	26,488
1969	1,964,275	1,287,300	137,176	205,260	38,406	269,799	2,687	23,647
1970	2,385,926	1,576,551	163,263	245,515	45,258	328,245	2,965	24,128
1971	2,763,022	1,840,748	184,420	280,203	51,163	380,963	3,103	22,423
1972	3,514,741	2,363,098	229,973	348,964	62,457	483,161	3,620	23,468
1973	3,821,165	2,556,956	238,072	362,931	67,578	571,654	3,488	20,485
1974	4,445,170	3,003,601	270,609	409,101	76,980	663,569	3,627	17,684
1975	5,047,656	3,436,752	301,623	456,662	85,678	747,903	3,685	15,354
1976	5,624,858	3,859,827	330,560	497,056	92,475	827,479	3,686	13,774
1977	6,270,000	4,333,016	364,805	540,541	101,116	914,469	3,665	12,388
1978	6,933,292	4,831,614	395,645	575,607	109,717	1,005,939	3,675	11,095
1979	7,950,300	5,582,292	443,799	634,904	121,957	1,153,289	3,829	10,229
1980	9,432,299	6,685,732	518,961	715,078	138,558	1,360,201	4,085	9,684
1981	10,901,677	7,794,868	590,266	791,834	151,509	1,560,102	4,230	8,868
1982	11,997,917	8,705,289	645,823	754,501	155,887	1,724,420	4,186	7,811
1983	12,834,854	9,440,715	685,827	729,376	123,559	1,844,802	3,996	6,579
1983								
January	12,084,770	8,779,456	650,464	757,007	155,831	1,730,187	4,149	7,677
February	12,131,904	8,815,421	652,418	762,475	155,409	1,734,516	4,120	7,545
March	12,153,202	8,830,541	652,831	766,997	153,837	1,737,503	4,091	7,402
April	12,175,167	8,846,880	653,288	771,853	151,219	1,740,617	4,059	7,252
May	12,126,987	8,859,864	653,834	707,427	150,651	1,744,055	4,031	7,124
June	12,155,272	8,893,861	655,746	695,520	150,196	1,748,939	4,015	6,996
July	12,178,461	8,933,719	657,696	670,644	150,674	1,754,865	3,985	6,877
August	12,221,289	8,968,778	659,344	671,382	150,383	1,760,688	3,955	6,758
September	12,258,407	9,003,980	655,355	701,319	120,101	1,767,066	3,934	6,651
October	12,320,522	9,052,516	658,597	706,276	119,352	1,773,308	3,914	6,559
November	12,374,519	9,098,027	661,843	706,507	119,345	1,778,451	3,883	6,462
December	12,834,854	9,440,715	685,827	729,376	123,559	1,844,802	3,996	6,579
1984								
January	12,891,120	9,486,716	686,851	733,115	123,522	1,850,503	3,965	6,449

[1] Persons aged 65 and older (and aged 62-64, beginning 1956 for women and 1961 for men).

[2] Includes, beginning 1950, wife beneficiaries under age 65 with entitled children in their care and, beginning September 1965, entitled divorced wives.

[3] Includes, beginning 1957, disabled persons aged 18 and older whose disability began before age 22 (age 18 before January 1973) and, beginning September 1965, entitled full-time students aged 18-21. Beginning January 1973, students who attain age 22 before end of semester may continue to receive benefits until end of semester.

[4] Includes, beginning 1950, surviving divorced mothers with entitled children in their care and, beginning June 1975, widowed fathers with entitled children in their care.

[5] Includes, beginning September 1965, widows aged 60-61 and entitled surviving divorced wives aged 60 and older; beginning March 1968, disabled widows aged 50-59 and disabled widowers aged 50-61; and, beginning January 1973, nondisabled widowers aged 60-61.

[6] Authorized by 1966 legislation for persons aged 72 and older not insured under the regular or transitional provisions of the Social Security Act.

E1-11. Shares of Income for the Older Noninstitutionalized Population, 1984[1]

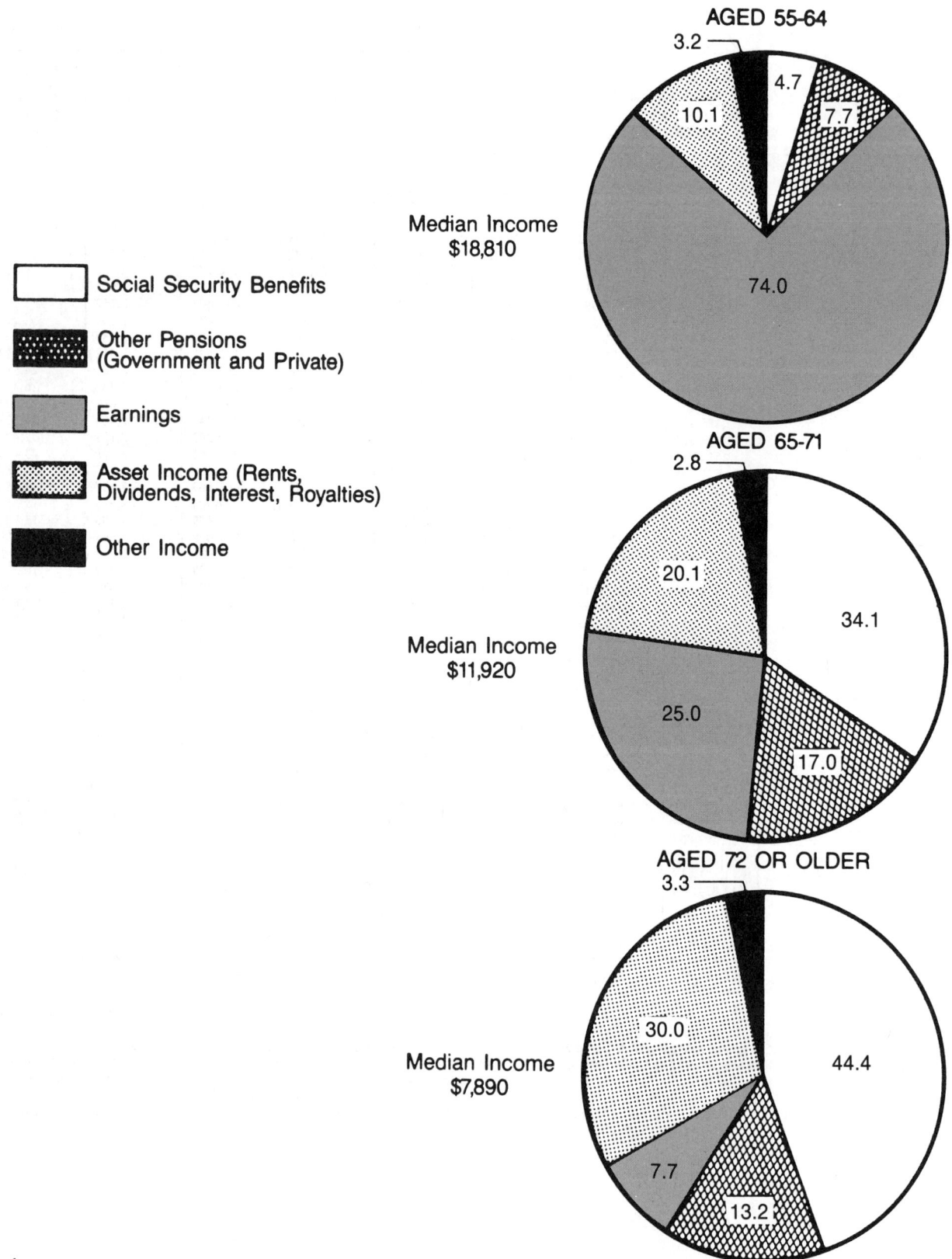

Legend:
- Social Security Benefits
- Other Pensions (Government and Private)
- Earnings
- Asset Income (Rents, Dividends, Interest, Royalties)
- Other Income

AGED 55-64 — Median Income $18,810: 3.2, 4.7, 7.7, 74.0, 10.1

AGED 65-71 — Median Income $11,920: 2.8, 34.1, 17.0, 25.0, 20.1

AGED 72 OR OLDER — Median Income $7,890: 3.3, 44.4, 13.2, 7.7, 30.0

[1]Income data based on aged unit — the unit is either a married couple living together, with one or both persons aged 55 or older, or a person aged 55 or older who does not live with a spouse.

E1–12. Labor Force and Estimated Workers Covered under Social Insurance Programs, 1939–82

[In millions]

Employment and coverage status	1939 [1]	1949 [1]	1960	1965	1970	1975	1977	1978	1979	1980	1981	1982
Total labor force	55.6	63.7	73.1	78.5	86.2	94.9	100.6	103.7	106.0	106.9	110.7	112.7
Paid civilian population	43.6	56.7	64.6	71.6	77.6	84.8	92.0	95.2	97.5	97.0	96.9	98.4
Wage and salary workers	33.2	45.9	55.3	63.6	70.8	77.6	84.3	87.2	89.2	88.4	88.5	89.5
Self-employed	10.4	10.8	9.3	8.0	6.9	7.2	7.7	8.0	8.3	8.6	8.4	8.9
Unpaid family workers	2.1	2.0	1.4	1.1	.8	.7	.7	.7	.6	.6	.5	.5
Unemployed	9.5	3.4	4.5	2.9	2.6	7.2	5.9	5.7	5.7	7.2	9.0	11.6
Armed Forces	.4	1.6	2.5	2.8	3.4	·2.2	2.1	2.1	1.6	1.6	1.7	2.2
Civilian population covered by public retirement programs	27.2	40.1	60.9	68.4	75.3	82.2	88.8	89.8	94.5	93.5	[4] 93.6	94.8
OASDHI [2]	24.0	34.3	55.4	62.7	69.2	75.7	82.1	83.2	87.6	86.5	86.6	87.9
Wage and salary workers	24.0	34.3	48.0	56.1	63.4	69.3	75.6	76.4	80.6	79.3	[4] 79.5	80.5
Self-employed	. . . .	. . . .	7.4	6.6	5.8	6.4	6.5	6.8	7.0	7.2	[4] 7.1	7.4
Railroad Retirement system	1.2	1.4	.9	.8	.6	.5	.5	.5	.5	.5	.5	.4
Government employees retirement systems [3] .	2.0	4.4	4.6	4.9	5.5	6.0	6.2	6.4	6.4	6.5	6.5	6.5
Civilian population covered by other social insurance programs:												
Unemployment insurance	22.6	33.1	43.7	50.3	55.8	69.7	75.8	85.8	87.9	87.2	89.9	87.9
Workers' compensation	22.0	35.3	44.6	52.3	59.0	68.6	74.2	74.5	77.4	79.1	79.8	77.8
Temporary disability insurance	. . . .	5.3	11.3	13.0	14.6	15.7	16.7	18.0	18.1	18.4	18.4	18.1

[1] Monthly averages; for all other years, data as of December.
[2] Excludes members of the Armed Forces and railroad employees, shown separately.
[3] Excludes State and local government employees covered by both OASDHI and their own retirement program. Data represents yearly average.

[4] Data not available.

Source: Labor force data from the Bureau of the Census, current population survey reported in **Employment and Earnings**. Social insurance coverage estimates prepared by the Social Security Administration.

E1–13. Social Security—Average Monthly Benefit Payments to Retired Workers: 1970–1984

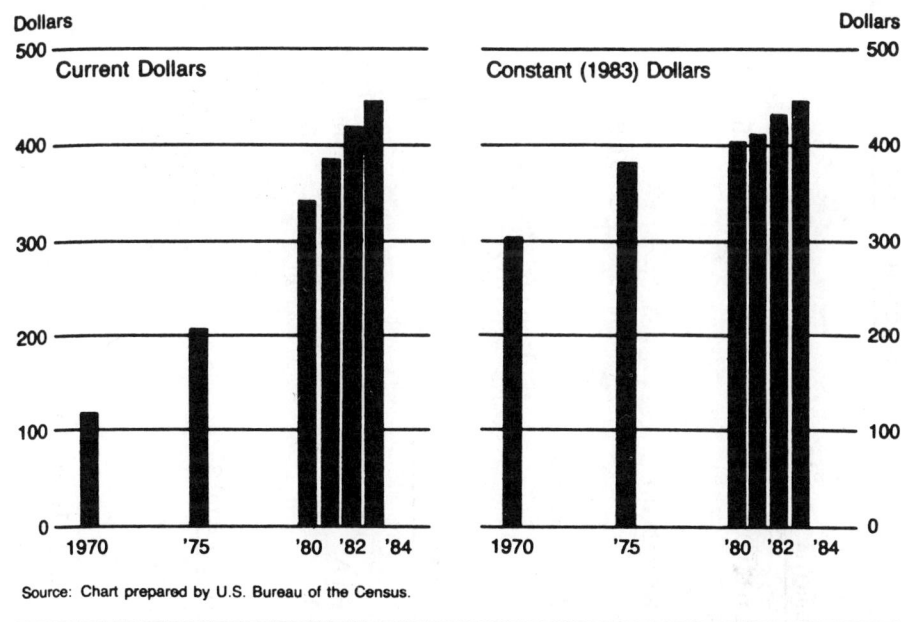

Source: Chart prepared by U.S. Bureau of the Census.

E1–14. Relation between Preretirement Earnings and Postretirement Social Security Benefits, 65-Year-Old Workers at Different Earnings Levels, 1982

	Maximum earner[1]		Average earner		Full-Time minimum wage		Part-time minimum wage	
	+spouse	single	+spouse	single	+spouse	single	+spouse	single
Preretirement 1981								
Gross monthly earnings	$2,475	$2,475	$1,129	$1,129	$581	$581	$290	$290
Less: taxes and expenses	859	1,048	276	339	96	133	37	39
Disposable earned income	1,616	1,427	853	790	485	448	253	251
Postretirement 1982								
AIME	1,258	1,258	847	847	459	459	229	229
January PIA	606	606	476	476	319	319	226	226
Plus: SSI	0	0	0	0	0	0	41	34
Replacement rates								
OASI benefit/gross earnings	38%	25%	65%	44%	85%	57%	121%	81%
OASI and SSI benefit/ net earnings	58%	44%	87%	62%	102%	74%	155%	107%

1. With dependent spouse.

Source: *Retirement Income Opportunities in an Aging America: Coverage and Benefit Entitlement*, Employee Benefit Research Institute (Washington, D.C., 1981), p. 42

E. Economic Status   169

E2. INDIVIDUAL/FAMILY/HOUSEHOLD INCOME BY AGE, SEX, AND RACE

E2-1. SSI: Number of Persons Receiving Federally Administered Payments and Total Amount, by Reason for Eligibility, July 1985

Reason for eligibility	Number	Amount of payments (in thousands)		
		Total	Federal SSI	State supplementation [1]
Total........	4,084,635	$918,755	$750,733	$168,022
Aged............	1,509,493	247,634	188,509	59,124
Blind	[2] 81,316	22,192	16,626	5,566
Disabled	[3] 2,493,826	648,929	545,598	103,331

[1] Excludes payments for State supplementation under State-administered programs.
[2] Includes approximately 23,000 persons aged 65 or older.
[3] Includes approximately 497,000 persons aged 65 or older.

E2-2. SSI: Number of Persons Awarded Federally Administered Payments, by Reason for Eligibility, 1974-85

Period	Total	Aged	Blind	Disabled
1974 [1]	890,768	498,555	5,206	387,007
1975.............	702,147	259,823	5,834	436,490
1976.............	542,355	171,798	4,735	365,822
1977.............	557,570	189,750	5,753	362,067
1978.............	532,447	177,224	6,375	348,848
1979.............	483,993	159,927	6,476	317,590
1980.............	496,137	169,862	7,576	318,699
1981 [2]	315,429	89,414	5,429	220,586
1982 [3]	280,798	76,119	5,059	199,620
1983.............	419,648	135,240	6,879	277,529
1984.............	554,251	201,432	7,221	345,598
1984				
June.............	58,623	26,446	675	31,502
July	50,460	23,638	553	26,269
August............	44,553	16,421	572	27,560
September	51,527	16,410	714	34,403
October	41,017	12,364	551	28,102
November	43,978	12,866	601	30,511
December	42,344	11,413	647	30,284
1985				
January	35,632	9,794	475	25,363
February	40,309	11,809	571	27,929
March	38,818	10,767	545	27,506
April	48,985	13,650	776	34,559
May.............	43,055	12,054	559	30,442
June.............	46,188	12,270	644	33,274

[1] Reflects data for May-December.
[2] Excludes data for January and September.
[3] Excludes data for August.

E2–3. OASDI Cash Benefits: Estimated Number of Beneficiaries with Monthly Benefits in Current-Payment Status, by Age Group and Type of Benefit, 1940–85

[In thousands. Adjusted to exclude duplication arising from dual entitlement; see the **1983 Annual Statistical Supplement**, p. 260]

At end of selected month	Total, all ages [1]	Under age 62	Total, aged 62 or older	Aged 62 or older							
				Aged 62–64				Aged 65 or older			
				Total	Retired workers	Disabled workers	Spouses and children and survivors [2]	Total	Retired workers	Spouses and children and survivors [2]	Persons with special age-72 benefits [3]
December:											
1940	222	75	147	(4)	...	...	(4)	147	112	35	...
1945	1,287	510	777	(4)	...	...	(4)	776	518	258	...
1950	3,462	877	2,586	1	...	...	1	2,585	1,771	814	...
1955	7,912	1,622	6,291	3	...	...	3	6,287	4,474	1,812	...
1956	9,070	1,701	7,369	338	113	...	225	7,031	4,999	2,032	...
1957	11,081	2,009	9,072	729	266	46	417	8,343	5,931	2,411	...
1958 [5]	12,390	2,231	10,159	837	299	77	461	9,322	6,621	2,701	...
1959	13,667	2,560	11,107	968	334	105	529	10,139	7,191	2,948	...
1960	14,811	2,883	11,928	1,041	357	127	557	10,887	7,704	3,183	...
1961	16,471	3,406	13,065	1,375	648	141	586	11,690	8,277	3,413	...
1962	18,032	3,858	14,174	1,659	873	156	630	12,515	8,865	3,650	...
1963	19,016	4,109	14,907	1,748	946	163	639	13,159	9,318	3,841	...
1964	19,783	4,274	15,509	1,848	998	183	667	13,661	9,671	3,990	...
1965	20,867	4,735	16,132	1,854	992	197	665	14,278	10,108	4,169	...
1966	22,767	5,199	17,568	1,954	1,028	230	696	15,614	10,631	4,349	634
1967	23,705	5,491	18,214	2,013	1,040	258	714	16,202	10,979	4,494	729
1968	24,560	5,829	18,733	2,096	1,084	283	729	16,635	11,337	4,622	676
1969	25,314	6,088	19,226	2,195	1,141	304	751	17,031	11,682	4,746	603
1970	26,229	6,380	19,849	2,332	1,225	322	785	17,517	12,122	4,861	534
1971	27,292	6,744	20,548	2,479	1,333	352	794	18,069	12,594	5,003	472
1972	28,476	7,160	21,316	2,665	1,440	390	835	18,651	13,115	5,126	410
1973	29,868	7,577	22,291	2,835	1,560	420	856	19,456	13,805	5,294	358
1974	30,853	7,859	22,994	2,973	1,631	462	880	20,021	14,328	5,415	278
1975	32,085	8,309	23,777	3,134	1,723	512	899	20,643	14,865	5,554	224
1976	33,024	8,512	24,511	3,264	1,781	563	920	21,247	15,384	5,675	188
1977	34,083	8,711	25,372	3,410	1,868	598	945	21,961	15,965	5,837	159
1978	34,587	8,587	26,000	3,412	1,861	609	942	22,588	16,497	5,958	134
1979	35,125	8,422	26,702	3,447	1,906	601	941	23,255	17,064	6,078	112
1980	35,619	8,199	27,419	3,576	2,017	603	956	23,843	17,565	6,185	93
1981	36,006	7,894	28,112	3,674	2,115	595	965	24,438	18,081	6,281	76
1982	35,840	7,061	28,779	3,803	2,213	589	1,001	24,976	18,551	6,363	63
1983	36,085	6,527	29,557	3,938	2,321	580	1,036	25,620	19,098	6,471	51
1984	36,479	6,352	30,127	4,040	2,407	573	1,060	26,087	19,499	6,547	40
1984											
July	36,051	6,242	29,809	4,055	2,421	578	1,057	25,754	19,223	6,487	44
August	36,137	6,243	29,894	4,073	2,429	581	1,063	25,822	19,278	6,499	44
September	36,299	6,339	29,959	4,078	2,433	578	1,067	25,881	19,330	6,509	43
October	36,378	6,368	30,010	4,065	2,422	577	1,066	25,946	19,382	6,521	42
November	36,418	6,364	30,055	4,055	2,415	575	1,064	26,000	19,429	6,530	41
December	36,479	6,352	30,127	4,040	2,407	573	1,060	26,087	19,499	6,547	40
1985											
January	36,598	6,367	30,231	4,086	2,452	571	1,063	26,146	19,550	6,557	39
February	36,654	6,389	30,265	4,079	2,452	568	1,059	26,186	19,583	6,564	39
March	36,677	6,421	30,256	4,074	2,453	567	1,054	26,182	19,582	6,562	38
April	36,699	6,431	30,268	4,078	2,459	565	1,053	26,190	19,590	6,564	37
May	36,686	6,384	30,302	4,074	2,458	564	1,052	26,227	19,619	6,573	36
June	36,685	6,347	30,338	4,073	2,458	563	1,052	26,265	19,650	6,580	35
July	[6] 36,629	(7)	(7)	(7)	[6] 2,486	(7)	(7)	(7)	[6] 19,695	(7)	[6] 36

[1] At the end of 1984 an estimated 47,000 railroad retirement beneficiaries would have been eligible for social security benefits had they applied. These persons receive their social security benefits as part of their railroad retirement annuity and are not included in the above tabulations. Of these 47,000 beneficiaries, 24,000 were retired workers, 5,000 were disabled workers, and 18,000 were spouses and children.

[2] Includes spouses and children of disabled workers.

[3] Authorized by 1966 legislation for persons aged 72 or older not insured under the regular or transitional provisions of the Social Security Act.

[4] Fewer than 500.

[5] November data; December data not available.

[6] Based on sample data.

[7] Data not available.

E2-4. Total Money Income by Age, Race, and Social Security Beneficiary Status: Percentage Distribution of Aged Units, 1982

Income	White						Black					
	Beneficiaries[1]			Nonbeneficiaries			Beneficiaries[1]			Nonbeneficiaries		
	55-61	62-64	65 and older	55-61	62-64	65 and older	55-61	62-64	65 and older	55-61	62-64	65 and older
Number(in thousands)	1,165	2,012	16,229	7,820	1,699	1,575	163	196	1,550	921	214	229
Total percent	100	100	100	100	100	100	100	100	100	100	100	100
Less than $1,000	1	1	0	3	4	17	1	1	0	9	12	18
$1,000-$1,999	1	1	1	1	1	4	3	3	4	5	2	5
$2,000-$2,999	3	2	2	1	1	4	7	9	9	4	2	7
$3,000-$3,999	6	5	7	2	3	9	20	16	24	8	9	27
$4,000-$4,999	9	7	9	2	1	3	13	11	13	5	4	9
$5,000-$5,999	7	5	10	2	3	5	11	7	13	5	3	2
$6,000-$6,999	6	6	7	2	2	4	7	9	7	5	3	4
$7,000-$7,999	3	5	6	2	2	2	6	2	5	3	6	3
$8,000-$8,999	5	5	5	2	2	2	5	2	4	4	3	1
$9,000-$9,999	5	4	5	2	2	3	2	3	3	4	2	4
$10,000-$10,999	4	5	5	2	3	3	5	11	4	4	3	0
$11,000-$11,999	2	5	4	2	2	1	0	1	1	5	5	3
$12,000-$12,999	3	4	4	3	2	2	0	7	2	4	5	2
$13,000-$13,999	3	3	3	2	2	2	4	1	1	3	2	3
$14,000-$14,999	3	3	3	2	3	1	1	2	1	1	4	2
$15,000-$19,999	11	14	11	11	14	7	10	8	4	10	9	4
$20,000-$24,999	8	9	7	12	12	7	3	2	2	8	9	3
$25,000-$29,999	7	4	4	10	11	6	2	4	1	5	6	0
$30,000 or more	12	11	8	36	31	18	2	1	1	8	12	3
Median income[2]	$10,880	$11,870	$9,490	$23,270	$21,110	$8,770	$5,520	$6,610	$4,970	$9,220	$10,920	$3,470

1/ Beneficiaries may be receiving retired-worker benefits, dependents' or survivors' benefits, disability benefits, transitionally insured, or special age-72 benefits.
2/ Rounded to the nearest $10. Medians for 1982 are calculated more precisely than those for previous years in this data series. See technical appendix for further detail.

E2-5. Median Income of Persons Age 65 and Older by Marital Status, 1983

Marital status	Both sexes	Male	Female
Married	$7,616	$10,415	$4,560
Single	7,450	7,103	7,727
Widowed	6,336	8,206	6,047
Divorced	6,697	6,919	6,605
Total	6,974	9,766	5,599

Source: U.S. Bureau of the Census, unpublished data from the March 1983 Current Population Survey.

E2-6. Mean Household Income in Constant 1983 Dollars, 1980-1983

Household type	1980		1981		1982		1983	
	Income	Percent change	Income	Percent change	Income	Percent change	Income	Percent change
	Dollars		Dollars		Dollars		Dollars	
All households:								
Before tax	25,461	-5.4	24,958	-2.0	25,087	+0.5	25,401	+1.3
After tax	19,670	NA	19,162	-2.6	19,511	+1.8	NA	NA
White:								
Before tax	26,489	-5.3	26,004	-1.8	26,121	+0.4	26,455	+1.3
After tax	20,371	NA	19,875	-2.4	20,234	+1.8	NA	NA
Black:								
Before tax	16,887	-6.0	16,271	-3.6	16,251	-0.1	16,531	+1.7
After tax	13,841	NA	13,234	-4.4	13,370	+1.0	NA	NA
Spanish:								
Before tax	20,156	-9.1	20,123	-0.2	19,352	-3.8	19,369	+0.1
After tax	16,380	NA	16,228	-0.9	15,787	-2.7	NA	NA
Age 65 and over:								
Before tax	15,265	-0.2	15,603	+2.2	16,377	+5.0	16,386	+0.1
After tax	13,274	NA	13,498	+1.7	14,208	+5.3	NA	NA
Female head, no husband present, with related children:								
Before tax	13,841	NA	13,483	-2.6	12,974	-3.8	NA	NA
After tax	11,956	NA	11,577	-3.2	11,216	-3.1	NA	NA

Note: NA = Not available.

Sources: U.S. Department of Commerce, Bureau of the Census, 1983, Estimating after-tax money income distribution using data from the March Current Population Survey, Current Population Reports, Series P-23, No. 126. U.S. Department of Commerce, Bureau of the Census, 1984, After-tax money income estimates of households, 1981, Current Population Reports, Series P-23, No. 132. U.S. Department of Commerce, Bureau of the Census, 1984, After-tax money income estimates of households, 1982, Current Population Reports, Special Studies, Series P-23, No. 137.

E2-7. Median Income of Women and Men 25 to 64 Years Old and 65 Years and Over, by Type of Income Received in 1981[1]

Type of income	25 to 64 years		65 and over	
	Women	Men	Women	Men
Total	$ 5,827	$18,220	$ 4,706	$ 8,138
Wage or salary	10,029	20,111	8,911	13,726
Nonfarm self-employment	5,310	16,786	7,197	15,154
Farm self-employment	3,519	12,204	10,272	8,216
Property (interest, dividends, rent, trusts)	7,520	21,932	5,880	9,998
Social Security and Railroad Retirement	4,673	7,817	4,798	7,902
Supplemental Security	3,554	3,600	3,507	3,606
Public assistance or welfare	4,160	3,969	3,730	(²)
Veterans, unemployment and workers' compensation	7,705	14,393	4,846	7,618
Unemployment compensation only	7,644	13,921	(²)	(²)
Retirement, total	9,689	17,487	8,934	11,307
Private pensions or annuities	9,151	12,857	8,279	10,683
Military retirement pensions only	(²)	26,383	(²)	14,692
Federal employee pensions only	10,828	17,556	9,675	14,879
State or local employee pensions only	10,320	18,078	9,944	10,791
Other combinations	(²)	21,434	(²)	19,542
Other	10,301	15,400	6,126	10,092
Combinations of income types				
Earnings	9,760	19,680	8,734	13,186
Earnings and property	11,053	22,607	9,880	14,897
Government transfer payments	5,249	12,361	4,743	7,954
Government transfer payments only	3,333	4,222	3,409	4,275
Government transfer payments and other income	6,917	14,653	5,872	9,385
Public assistance or supplemental security or both	3,821	3,693	3,502	3,593
Social Security or retirement income or both	5,213	11,788	4,824	8,042
Social Security or supplemental security or both	4,348	7,201	4,736	7,839

[1] Includes persons who worked less than year round full time.
[2] Base less than 75,000.
Source: Unpublished data. U.S. Department of Commerce, Bureau of the Census.

E2-8. Total Money Income of Nonmarried Persons: Percentage Distribution of Aged Persons 65 and Older, 1982

Income	Nonmarried men				Nonmarried women			
	Total1/	Widowed	Never married	Divorced	Total1/	Widowed	Never married	Divorced
Number(in thousands).	2,448	1,399	501	347	9,335	7,655	829	625
Total percent........	100	100	100	100	100	100	100	100
Less than $1,000.........	2	2	4	1	3	2	8	3
$1,000-$1,999............	1	1	2	2	2	2	4	2
$2,000-$2,999............	4	4	4	2	5	5	5	4
$3,000-$3,999............	10	8	12	10	16	16	10	17
$4,000-$4,999............	10	11	8	8	14	14	11	17
$5,000-$5,999............	12	10	12	13	14	15	7	11
$6,000-$6,999............	10	11	7	10	8	9	7	6
$7,000-$7,999............	7	6	9	8	6	7	5	3
$8,000-$8,999............	5	5	5	5	5	5	5	6
$9,000-$9,999............	5	5	4	5	4	4	5	5
$10,000-$10,999..........	4	4	2	4	3	3	4	3
$11,000-$11,999..........	3	4	2	4	3	3	4	3
$12,000-$12,999..........	3	3	1	4	2	2	3	3
$13,000-$13,999..........	3	2	5	3	2	2	2	1
$14,000-$14,999..........	1	2	0	2	1	1	2	3
$15,000-$19,999..........	6	7	8	4	5	5	8	6
$20,000-$24,999..........	5	6	3	4	3	3	6	3
$25,000-$29,999..........	2	2	4	1	1	1	2	3
$30,000 or more..........	6	6	7	9	2	2	3	0
Median income2/..........	$7,190	$7,450	$7,180	$7,230	$5,620	$5,620	$6,820	$5,540

1/ Includes those who are separated or married but living apart from the spouse.
2/ Rounded to the nearest $10. Medians for 1982 are calculated more precisely than those for previous years in this data series. See technical appendix for further detail.

E2-9. Family Total Money Income by Age, Sex, and Marital Status: Percentage Distribution of Aged Units, 1982

Income	Age 55-61	Age 62-64	Age 65 and older				
			Total	65-67	68-72	73-79	80 and older
	All units						
Number(in thousands).	10,256	4,201	19,880	3,784	5,840	5,829	4,427
Total percent........	100	100	100	100	100	100	100
Less than $1,000.........	2	1	1	1	1	1	2
$1,000-$1,999............	1	1	1	1	1	1	1
$2,000-$2,999............	1	1	2	1	1	2	2
$3,000-$3,999............	2	4	6	4	5	7	8
$4,000-$4,999............	3	4	7	4	5	8	9
$5,000-$5,999............	2	3	8	5	7	9	9
$6,000-$6,999............	2	3	6	4	6	6	7
$7,000-$7,999............	2	3	5	4	5	6	5
$8,000-$8,999............	2	3	5	3	5	4	6
$9,000-$9,999............	2	3	5	4	4	5	5
$10,000-$10,999..........	3	5	4	4	4	5	4
$11,000-$11,999..........	2	4	4	3	4	3	3
$12,000-$12,999..........	2	3	4	4	4	3	3
$13,000-$13,999..........	2	2	3	4	3	3	2
$14,000-$14,999..........	2	3	3	3	3	3	2
$15,000-$19,999..........	11	14	11	14	13	10	9
$20,000-$24,999..........	11	10	8	10	10	7	6
$25,000-$29,999..........	10	9	5	7	7	5	4
$30,000 or more..........	37	25	14	19	14	12	11
Median income1/..........	$23,400	$17,650	$11,470	$15,000	$12,640	$10,270	$9,140
	Married couples						
Number(in thousands).	6,715	2,413	8,097	2,000	2,791	2,220	1,086
Total percent........	100	100	100	100	100	100	100
Less than $1,000.........	1	1	1	1	1	1	2
$1,000-$1,999............	0	0	0	0	1	0	0

E2–10. Mean Real Money Income before Tax (in 1983 Dollars) of Families and Unrelated Individuals, Selected Years, 1950–83

[Dollars]

Economic group and year	Age (years)				
	25–34	35–44	45–54	55–64	65 and over
Families [1]					
1950	14,910	17,510	18,140	16,900	11,780
1960	20,480	24,130	24,810	22,160	14,740
1970	26,570	31,850	34,810	30,730	18,260
1980	25,760	32,420	36,460	32,890	20,370
1983	24,730	32,460	36,530	32,060	21,420
Unrelated individuals					
1950	8,920	9,280	8,270	6,670	4,150
1960	11,880	13,730	11,230	8,710	5,510
1970	18,640	17,940	15,740	13,070	7,380
1980	16,890	19,730	16,530	13,150	8,640
1983	16,420	20,120	18,200	14,070	10,040

[1] Age determined by age of head of household.

Note.—Money income converted to 1983 dollars using the consumer price index for urban wage earners and clerical workers (CPI-W) and rounded to the nearest $10.

Source: Council of Economic Advisers, based on data from Department of Commerce (Bureau of the Census).

E2–11. Mean Real Money Income before Tax of the Elderly and Nonelderly, 1970 and 1983

Economic group	1970	1983
Elderly (65 years and over)		
Family income	$18,260	$21,420
Family income per capita [1]	7,630	9,080
Income of unrelated individuals	7,380	10,040
Non-elderly (25–64 years)		
Family income	$31,050	$30,940
Family income per capita [1]	8,110	8,960
Income of unrelated individuals	15,820	16,900
Income ratios (elderly to non-elderly)		
Family	.59	.69
Family per capita	.94	1.01
Unrelated individuals	.47	.59

[1] Bureau of the Census publications do not include a measure of average family size prior to 1976. The 1970 measures of mean per capita income are estimated from information on the income of families of varying sizes.

Note.—Money income converted to 1983 dollars using CPI-W and rounded to the nearest $10.
Age of family determined by age of head of household.

Source: Council of Economic Advisers, based on data from Department of Commerce (Bureau of the Census) and Department of Health and Human Services *(Social Security Bulletin)*.

E2-12. Median Family Income, by Age of Family Members, 1983

Family type and age of head or spouse	Median family income
Families:	
Member 65 to 74	$17,798
Member 75 to 84	14,155
Member 85 and over	11,988
Unrelated individuals:	
65 to 74	7,651
75 to 84	6,509
85 and over	5,912

Source: Special Tabulation of March 1984 Current Population Survey.

E2-13. Median Family Income, Older and Younger Families and Unrelated Individuals, 1984

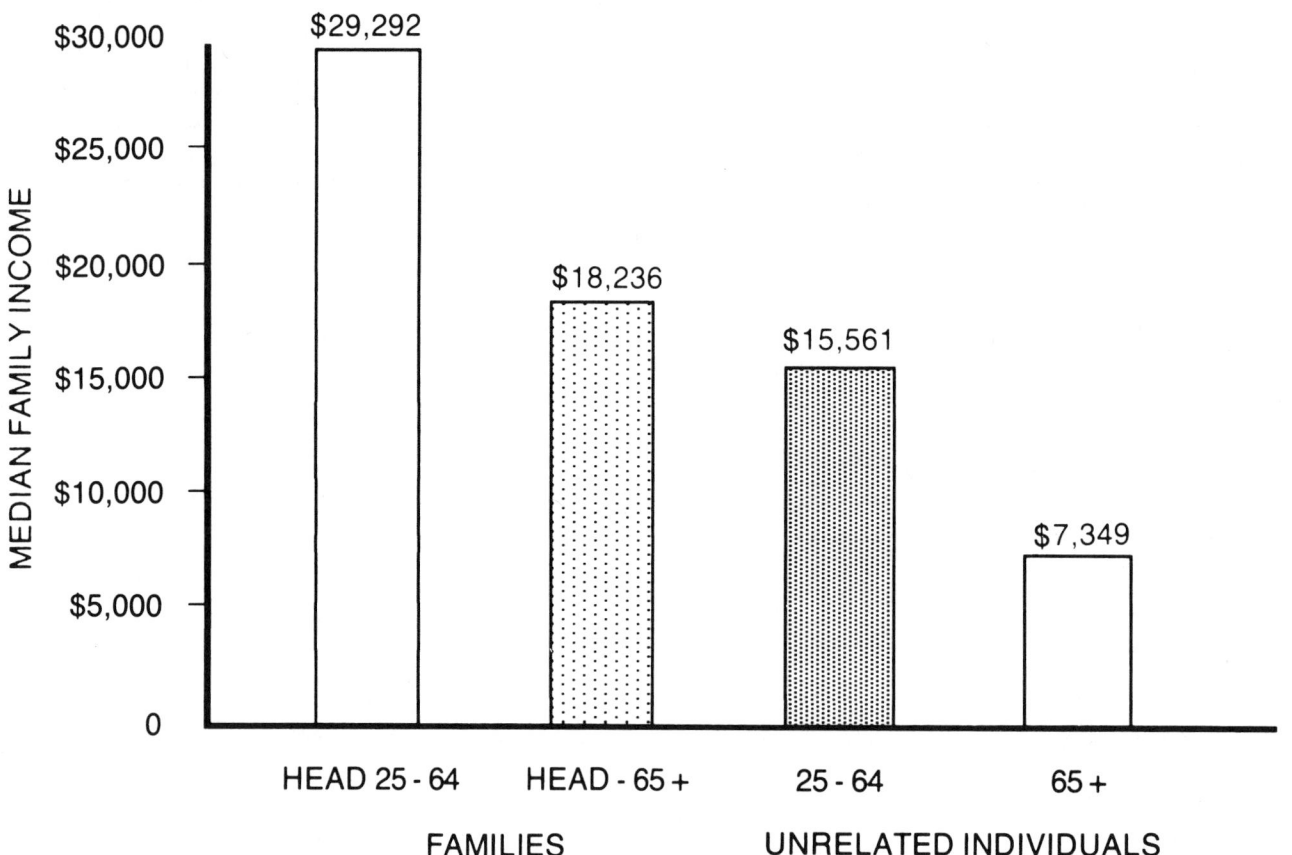

SOURCE: Unpublished data provided by the U.S. Bureau of the Census, September 1985.

E2–14. Income from Earnings by Age, Sex, and Marital Status: Percentage Distribution of Aged Units, 1982

Income (recipients only)	Married couples			Nonmarried persons								
				Total			Men			Women		
	55-61	62-64	65 and older	55-61	62-64	65 and older	55-61	62-64	65 and older	55-61	62-64	65 and older
Number (in thousands)	6,076	1,752	2,922	2,265	833	1,402	757	238	444	1,507	596	959
Total percent	100	100	100	100	100	100	100	100	100	100	100	100
Less than $1,000	2	5	13	5	10	20	4	12	14	5	9	23
$1,000-$1,999	1	3	6	4	3	10	2	2	5	5	3	13
$2,000-$2,999	1	2	6	3	5	11	4	4	10	3	5	12
$3,000-$3,999	1	3	6	5	7	7	3	3	11	6	9	6
$4,000-$4,999	1	3	7	4	10	8	4	8	7	4	11	8
$5,000-$5,999	1	2	7	4	5	10	5	4	9	4	6	10
$6,000-$6,999	1	3	4	4	5	5	3	3	7	4	5	5
$7,000-$7,999	1	2	4	4	6	3	3	4	5	5	6	3
$8,000-$8,999	2	3	3	5	4	2	4	4	2	5	4	2
$9,000-$9,999	2	2	3	4	3	2	3	4	3	5	2	1
$10,000-$10,999	2	3	3	5	4	2	4	7	3	6	3	1
$11,000-$11,999	2	1	3	4	3	2	3	3	1	5	4	2
$12,000-$12,999	2	3	3	4	3	2	4	2	3	3	4	1
$13,000-$13,999	2	3	1	4	3	2	3	3	3	4	3	2
$14,000-$14,999	2	3	2	3	3	1	3	3	1	4	3	1
$15,000-$19,999	11	13	9	16	12	5	14	8	6	16	14	5
$20,000-$24,999	14	13	6	10	5	4	13	10	4	8	4	4
$25,000 or more	49	34	15	13	10	6	24	20	11	8	6	3
Median income 1/	$24,270	$17,890	$7,270	$11,400	$7,810	$4,060	$14,600	$10,400	$5,110	$10,330	$7,050	$3,350

1/ Rounded to the nearest $10. Medians for 1982 are calculated more precisely than those for previous years in this data series.

E2–15. Income from Earnings by Race and Marital Status: Percentage Distribution of Aged Units 65 and Older, 1982

Income (recipients only)	White			Black		
	All units	Married couples	Nonmarried persons	All units	Married couples	Nonmarried persons
Number (in thousands)	3,886	2,643	1,242	342	195	146
Total percent	100	100	100	100	100	100
Less than $1,000	16	14	20	18	15	22
$1,000-$1,999	7	6	10	13	11	15
$2,000-$2,999	8	6	11	8	6	11
$3,000-$3,999	6	5	7	9	8	10
$4,000-$4,999	7	7	7	8	5	12
$5,000-$5,999	8	7	10	4	5	4
$6,000-$6,999	4	4	6	6	8	5
$7,000-$7,999	4	4	3	5	4	7
$8,000-$8,999	3	3	2	3	4	1
$9,000-$9,999	2	3	2	3	2	3
$10,000-$10,999	3	3	2	4	6	1
$11,000-$11,999	2	2	2	4	5	3
$12,000-$12,999	3	3	2	2	3	0
$13,000-$13,999	1	1	2	1	1	1
$14,000-$14,999	2	2	1	3	3	1
$15,000-$19,999	8	9	5	7	9	4
$20,000-$24,999	6	6	4	2	3	1
$25,000 or more	12	16	6	3	3	3
Median income 1/	$5,720	$7,330	$4,170	$4,250	$6,240	$3,040

1/ Rounded to the nearest $10. Medians for 1982 are calculated more precisely than those for previous years in this data series.

E2–16. Selected Characteristics of Households, by Mean Monthly Income and Program Participation Status: Monthly Average, Third Quarter 1984

Characteristic	Number (thous.)	Mean monthly income	Percent of households in which one or more persons received means-tested benefits		
			Total	Cash	Noncash
All households......................	84,609	$2,306	15.6	8.3	14.7
RACE AND SPANISH ORIGIN OF HOUSEHOLDER					
White..	73,338	2,406	12.3	6.2	11.4
Black..	9,358	1,476	40.2	23.9	39.5
Spanish origin[1]...........................	4,078	1,814	31.9	18.0	31.3
TYPE OF HOUSEHOLD					
Householders under 65 years................	67,137	2,526	14.6	7.7	13.9
Family households..........................	51,931	2,780	15.8	8.2	15.1
Married-couple families.................	41,664	3,075	9.4	3.9	8.7
Female householder, no husband present, with own children under 18 years......	6,037	1,164	53.4	34.6	53.0
All other family households............	4,230	2,181	24.3	13.3	23.5
Nonfamily households....................	15,207	1,659	10.5	5.9	9.9
Single person household.................	12,724	1,465	10.1	5.4	9.5
Male.....................................	6,590	1,730	6.9	3.7	6.4
Female...................................	6,134	1,181	13.5	7.3	12.8
Multiple-person household...............	2,483	2,652	12.6	8.0	12.3
Householders 65 years and over.............	17,472	1,462	19.4	10.7	17.7
Family households..........................	9,181	1,962	14.5	8.9	12.8
Married-couple families.................	7,585	2,010	10.7	6.3	9.4
All other family households............	1,597	1,735	32.2	21.4	29.0
Nonfamily households......................	8,290	908	25.0	12.6	23.1
Single person household.................	8,054	891	24.7	12.2	22.9
Male.....................................	1,640	1,120	19.4	9.7	17.0
Female...................................	6,414	833	26.0	12.8	24.3
Multiple-person household...............	236	1,469	34.0	27.7	31.9

[1] Persons of Spanish origin may be of any race.

E2–17. Mean Household Income for Pension Income Recipients, by Type of Pension and Sex of Recipient: Monthly Average, Third Quarter 1984

Type of pension	Total	Male	Female
Total with pensions...	$1,835	$2,038	$1,673
Social Security..	1,715	1,829	1,635
Social Security only....................................	1,598	1,606	1,595
Private pensions..	1,955	2,082	1,737
State or local pensions..............................	2,301	2,521	2,131
Federal pensions...	2,253	2,488	1,929
U.S. military pensions.................................	3,558	3,619	2,561
Federal railroad retirement pensions............	1,667	1,919	1,452

E2–18. Households Receiving Medicare or Medicaid, by Income Level: 1982

[Households as of **March 1983**. See headnote, table 595. Persons of Spanish origin may be of any race. For definitions of household types, see text, p. 4. Hhlds.=households]

RACE, SPANISH ORIGIN, AND HOUSEHOLD TYPE	RECIPIENT HOUSEHOLDS (1,000)							RECIPIENT HHLDS. AS PERCENT OF TOTAL		
	Total	Total money income				Below poverty level	Above poverty level	Total	Below poverty level	Above poverty level
		Under $5,000	$5,000–$9,999	$10,000–$14,999	$15,000 and over					
MEDICARE										
Total households[1]	20,823	3,249	5,738	3,572	8,264	3,605	17,218	24.8	29.6	24.0
White	18,589	2,595	5,028	3,285	7,681	2,712	15,877	25.4	30.9	24.6
Black	1,936	612	817	259	447	822	1,114	21.7	26.7	19.1
Spanish origin	561	127	170	84	180	180	381	13.7	15.7	13.0
Married-couple families	9,974	384	1,827	1,999	5,765	833	9,141	20.0	22.0	19.8
Female family householder[2]	1,897	181	448	365	904	369	1,528	20.0	10.7	25.3
Nonfamily households	8,428	2,658	3,364	1,121	1,284	2,333	6.095	37.4	50.2	34.1
MEDICAID										
Total households[1]	8,068	2,984	2,461	999	1,624	4,766	3,302	9.6	39.2	4.6
White	5,476	1,886	1,657	698	1,234	2,946	2,530	7.5	33.6	3.9
Black	2,324	1,050	697	263	313	1,689	635	26.1	54.8	10.9
Spanish origin	830	295	321	92	122	568	262	20.3	49.7	8.9
Married-couple families	2,639	314	801	502	1,022	1,023	1,616	5.3	27.0	3.5
Female family householder[2]	3,024	1,317	1,063	322	322	2,265	759	31.9	66.0	12.6
Nonfamily households	2,113	1,300	516	127	170	1,358	755	9.4	29.2	4.2

[1] Includes items not shown separately.   [2] No spouse present.

Source: U.S. Bureau of the Census, *Current Population Reports*, series P–60, No. 143.

E3. LIVING EXPENSES, TAXES, COST INDEXES

E3–1. Average Out-Of-Pocket Expenditures for All Elderly Households in 1986

	Out-of-Pocket	Insurance Premiums	Total
Non-Institutionalized	$1,110	$690	$1,800
Institutionalized	$11,430	$620	$12,050
All Elderly	$1,980	$690	$2,670

SOURCE: ICF estimates.

E3–2. CPI-U: All Items, Food and Beverages, 1974–85

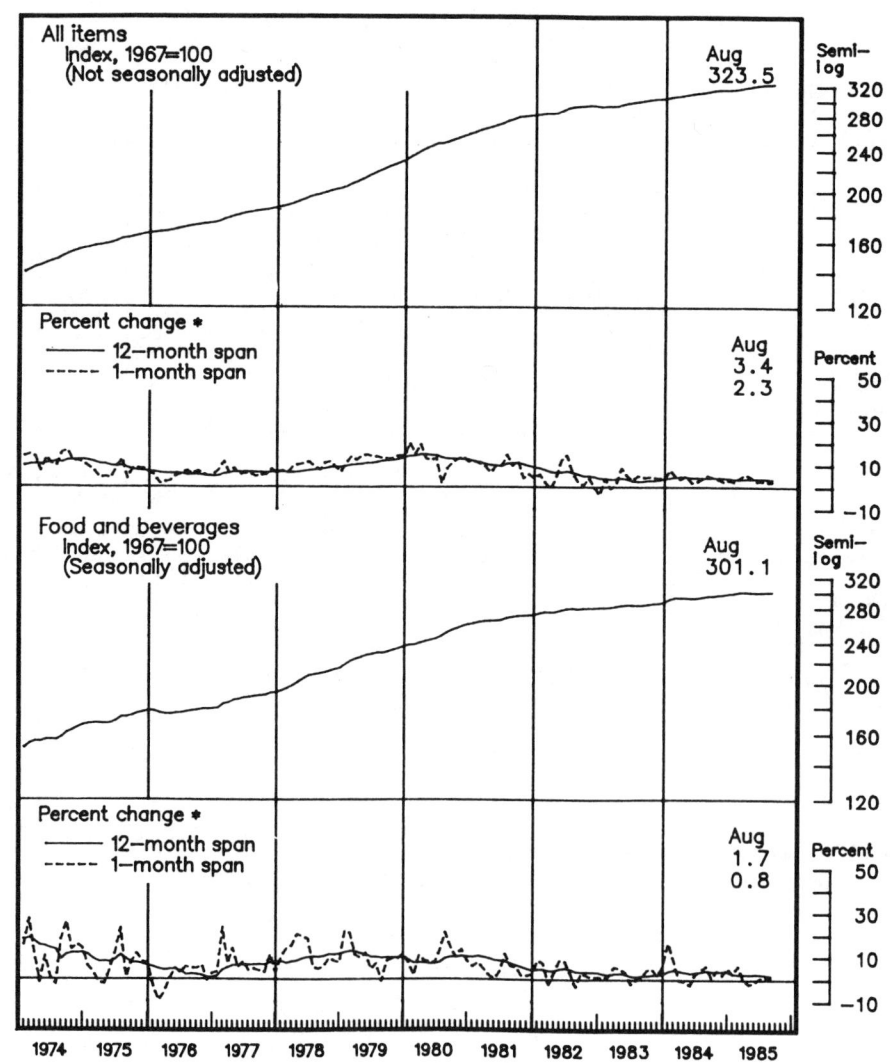

* Percent changes over 12–month spans are calculated from unadjusted data. Percent changes over 1–month spans are annual rates calculated from seasonally adjusted data.

E3-3. CPI-U: Housing, Apparel and Upkeep, 1974-85

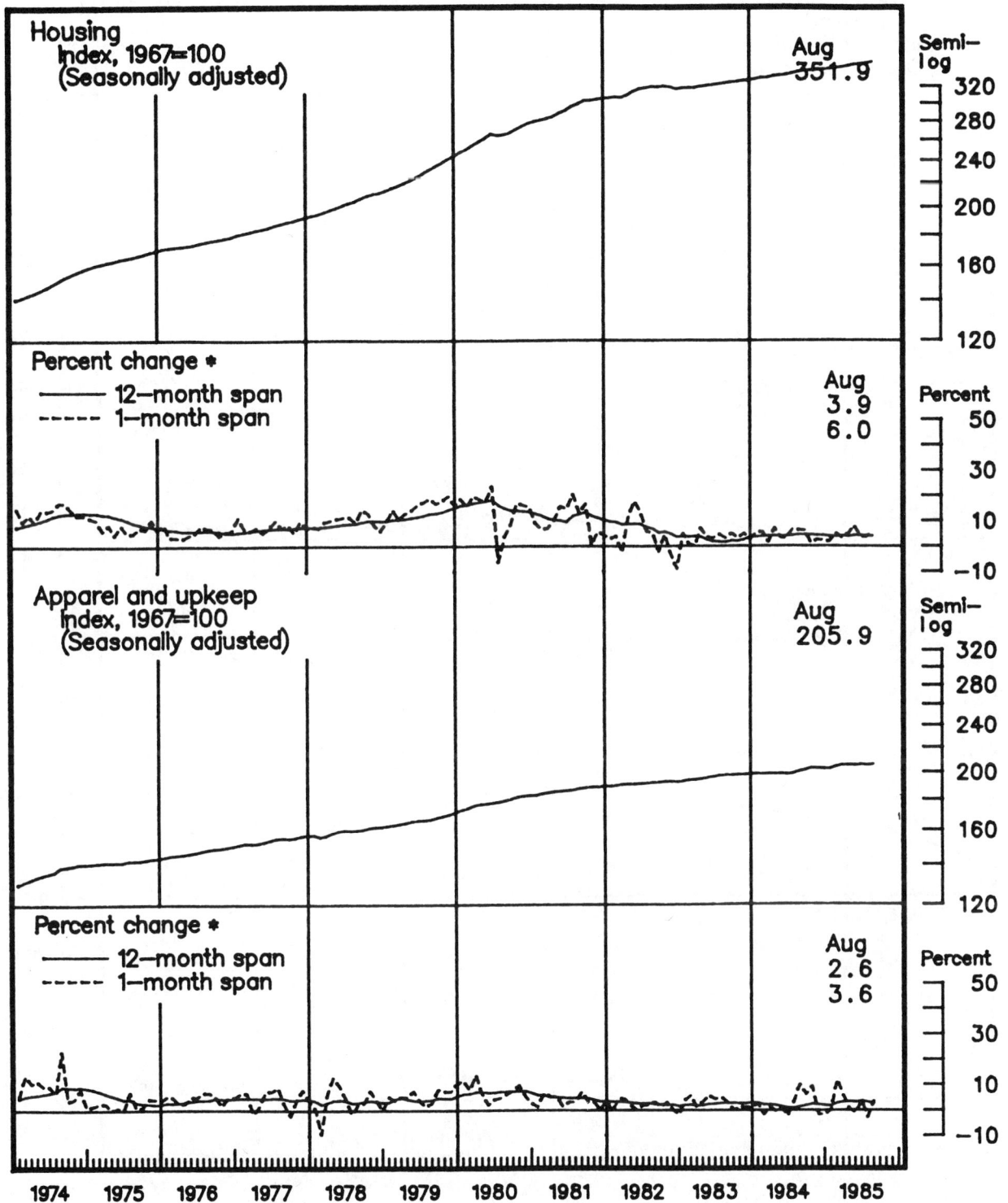

* Percent changes over 12—month spans are calculated from unadjusted data. Percent changes over 1—month spans are annual rates calculated from seasonally adjusted data.

E3–4. CPI-U: Entertainment, Other Goods and Services, 1974–85

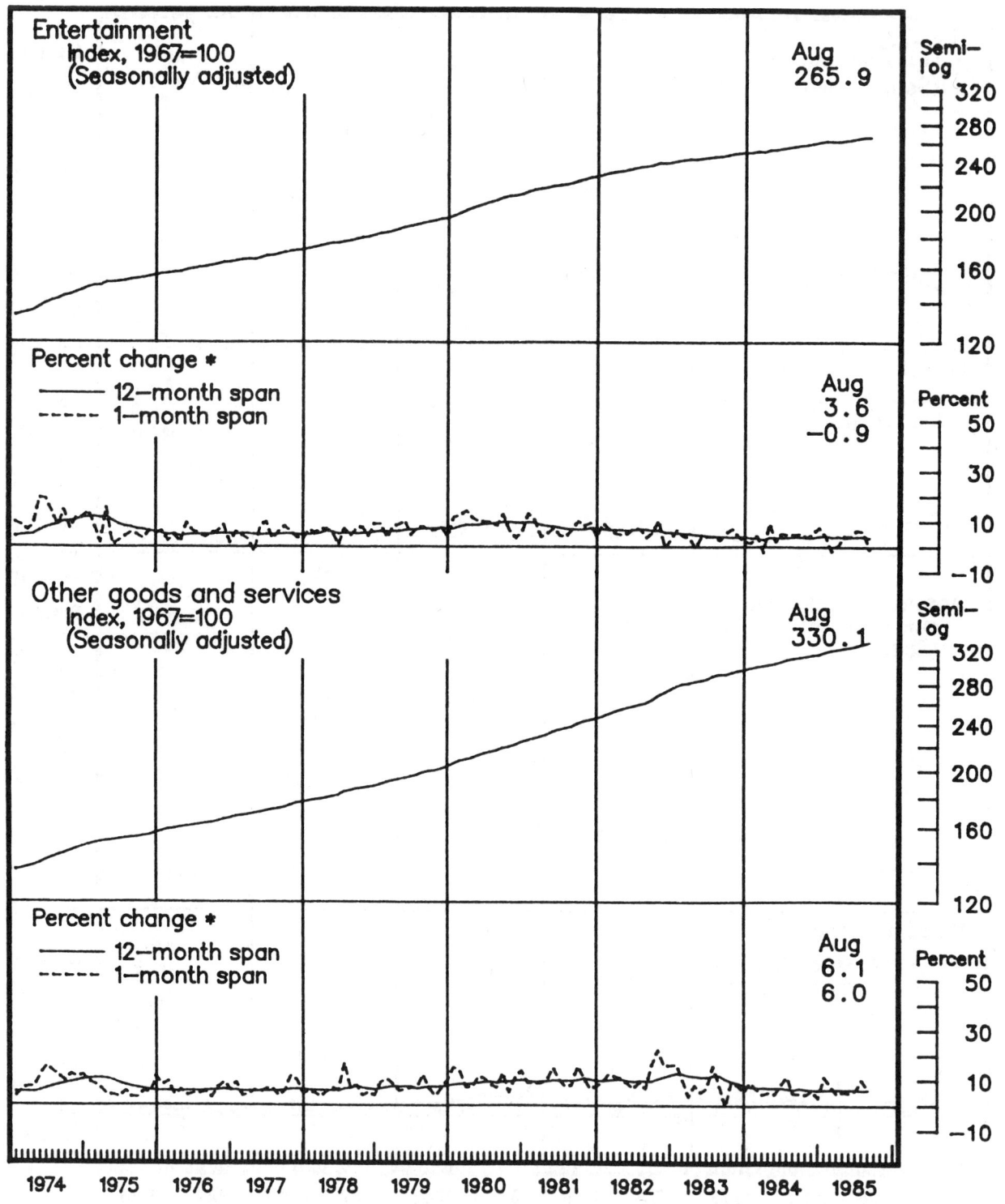

* Percent changes over 12–month spans are calculated from unadjusted data. Percent changes over 1–month spans are annual rates calculated from seasonally adjusted data.

E3–5. CPI-U: Transportation and Medical Care, 1974–85

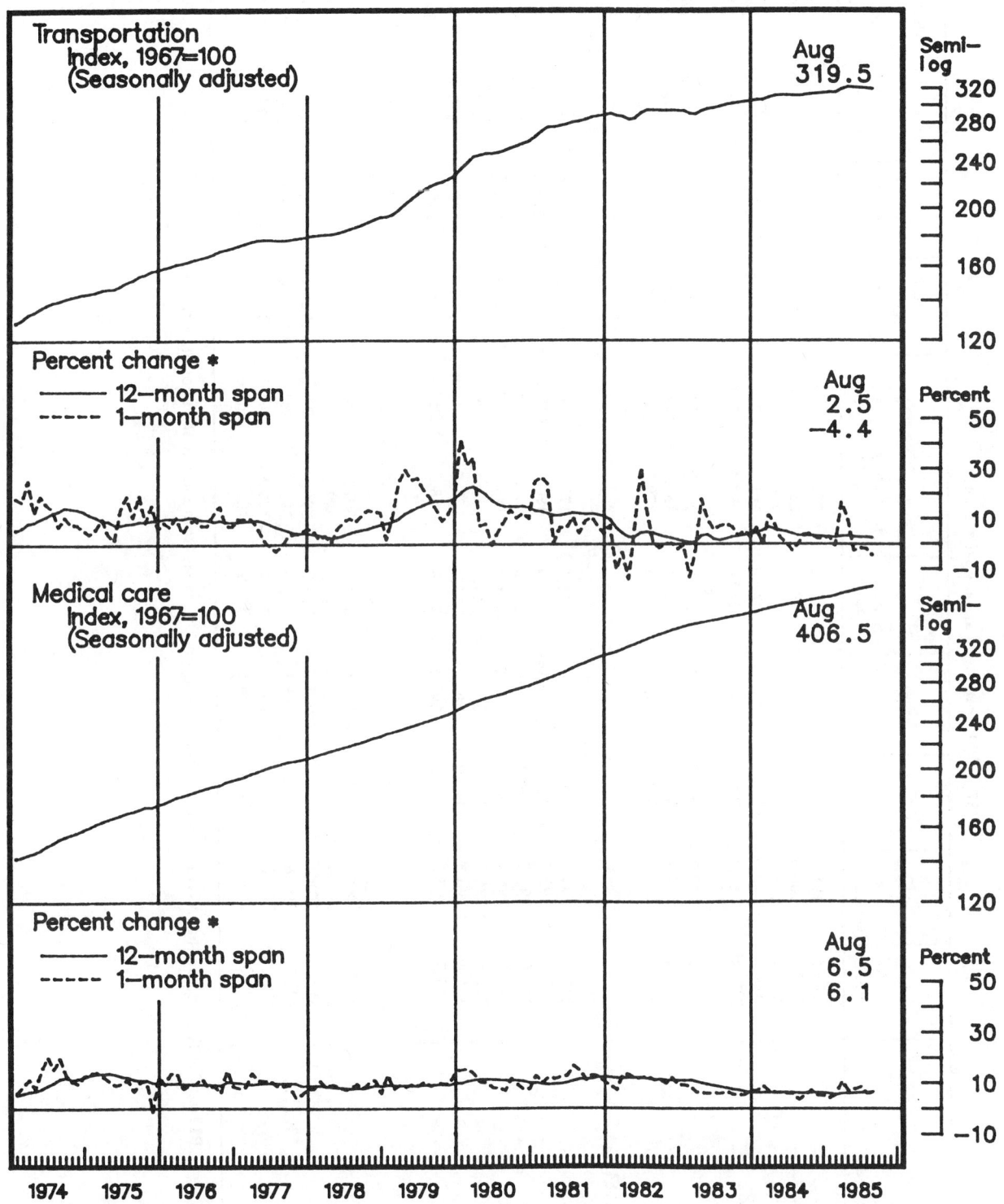

* Percent changes over 12–month spans are calculated from unadjusted data. Percent changes over 1–month spans are annual rates calculated from seasonally adjusted data.

E3–6. Consumer Price Index for All Urban Consumers, 1977–85

[1967 = 100; yearly data are annual averages]

Period [1]	All items	Food and beverages	Housing	Apparel and upkeep	Transportation	Medical care	Entertainment	Other goods and services	Personal care	All services	All items less medical care
1977	181.5	188.0	186.5	154.2	177.2	202.4	167.7	172.2	170.9	194.3	180.3
1978	195.4	206.3	202.8	159.6	185.5	219.4	176.6	183.3	182.0	210.9	194.0
1979	217.4	228.5	227.6	166.6	212.0	239.7	188.5	196.7	195.8	234.2	216.1
1980	246.8	248.0	263.3	178.4	249.7	265.9	205.3	214.5	213.1	270.3	245.5
1981	272.4	267.3	293.5	186.9	280.0	294.5	221.4	235.7	232.0	305.7	270.9
1982	289.1	278.2	314.6	191.8	291.5	328.7	235.5	260.0	248.1	333.3	286.8
1983	298.4	284.4	323.1	196.5	298.4	357.3	246.0	288.3	261.1	344.9	295.1
1984	311.1	295.1	336.5	200.2	311.7	379.5	255.1	307.7	271.4	363.0	307.3
1984											
June	310.7	294.3	336.2	197.4	313.1	378.0	254.5	304.4	270.6	361.9	306.9
July	311.7	295.3	338.1	196.6	312.9	380.3	255.3	306.5	271.8	364.5	307.9
August	313.0	296.9	339.5	200.1	312.9	381.9	256.4	307.2	272.6	366.5	309.2
September	314.5	296.4	341.4	204.2	313.7	383.1	257.3	314.6	273.6	368.9	310.7
October	315.3	296.6	341.2	205.7	315.5	385.5	258.3	315.8	274.7	369.7	311.4
November	315.3	296.3	340.9	205.2	316.1	387.5	259.0	316.5	276.3	369.9	311.3
December	315.5	297.2	341.2	203.2	315.8	388.5	260.1	316.7	276.6	370.6	311.5
1985											
January	316.1	299.3	342.0	199.8	314.7	391.1	261.0	319.1	277.2	372.1	311.9
February	317.4	301.4	343.6	201.8	314.3	393.8	261.3	320.5	278.2	373.5	313.1
March	318.8	301.6	344.7	205.3	316.7	396.5	262.2	321.1	278.7	375.0	314.5
April	320.1	301.6	345.9	205.9	320.0	398.0	263.3	321.8	279.8	376.2	315.8
May	321.3	301.0	348.5	205.3	321.4	399.5	263.6	322.3	280.9	378.9	317.0
June	322.3	301.4	350.4	204.6	321.8	401.7	264.8	323.0	281.7	381.3	317.9

[1] Annual data from **CPI Detailed Report**, Annual Averages Section, table 1A. Monthly data is from Bureau of Labor Statistics **News**.

E3-7. Consumer Price Index and Average Annual Percent Change for All Items and Selected Items: United States, Selected Years 1950-83

(Data are based on reporting by samples of providers and other retail outlets)

Year	All items	Medical care	Food	Apparel and upkeep	Housing	Energy	Personal care
			Consumer Price Index				
1950	72.1	53.7	74.5	79.0	72.8	---	68.3
1955	80.2	64.8	81.6	84.1	82.3	---	77.9
1960	88.7	79.1	88.0	89.6	90.2	94.2	90.1
1965	94.5	89.5	94.4	93.7	94.9	96.3	95.2
1970	116.3	120.6	114.9	116.1	118.2	107.0	113.2
1975	161.2	168.6	175.4	142.3	164.5	176.6	150.7
1976	170.5	184.7	180.8	147.6	174.6	189.3	160.5
1977	181.5	202.4	192.2	154.2	186.5	207.3	170.9
1978	195.4	219.4	211.4	159.6	202.8	220.4	182.0
1979	217.4	239.7	234.5	166.6	227.6	275.9	195.8
1980	246.8	265.9	254.6	178.4	263.3	361.1	213.1
1981	272.4	294.5	274.6	186.9	293.5	410.0	232.0
1982	289.1	328.7	285.7	191.8	314.7	416.1	248.3
1983	298.4	357.3	291.7	196.5	323.1	1419.3	261.1
			Average annual percent change				
1950-55	2.2	3.8	1.8	1.3	2.5	---	2.7
1955-60	2.0	4.1	1.5	1.3	1.9	---	3.0
1960-65	1.3	2.5	1.4	0.9	1.0	0.4	1.1
1965-70	4.2	6.1	4.0	4.4	4.5	2.1	3.5
1970-75	6.7	6.9	8.8	4.2	6.8	10.5	5.9
1975-76	5.8	9.5	3.1	3.7	6.1	7.2	6.5
1976-77	6.5	9.6	6.3	4.5	6.8	9.5	6.5
1977-78	7.7	8.4	10.0	3.5	8.7	6.3	6.5
1978-79	11.3	9.3	10.9	4.4	12.2	25.2	7.6
1979-80	13.5	10.9	8.6	7.1	15.7	30.9	8.8
1980-81	10.4	10.8	7.9	4.8	11.5	13.5	8.9
1981-82	6.1	11.6	4.0	2.6	7.2	1.5	7.0
1982-83	3.2	8.7	2.1	2.5	2.7	10.8	5.2

[1] Excludes motor oil, coolant, and other products as of January 1983.

NOTE: 1967=100.

SOURCE: Bureau of Labor Statistics, U.S. Department of Labor: Consumer Price Index. Various releases.

E3-8. Consumer Price Index for All Items and Medical Care Components: United States, Selected Years 1950-83

(Data are based on reporting by samples of providers and other retail outlets)

Item and medical care component	Year								
	1950	1960	1965	1970	1975	1980	1981	1982	1983
	Consumer Price Index								
CPI, all items................	72.1	88.7	94.5	116.3	161.2	246.8	272.4	289.1	298.4
Less medical care.............	---	89.4	94.9	116.1	160.9	245.5	270.9	286.8	295.1
CPI, all services.............	58.7	83.5	92.2	121.6	166.6	270.3	305.7	333.3	344.9
All medical care.............	53.7	79.1	89.5	120.6	168.6	265.9	294.5	328.7	357.3
Medical care services........	49.2	74.9	87.3	124.2	179.1	287.4	318.2	356.0	387.0
Professional services........	---	---	---	119.7	164.5	252.0	277.9	301.5	323.0
Physician services..........	55.2	77.0	88.3	121.4	169.4	269.3	299.0	327.1	352.3
Dental services.............	63.9	82.1	92.2	119.4	161.9	240.2	263.3	283.6	302.7
Other professional services[1]..........	---	---	---	---	---	123.6	135.2	144.3	153.0
Other medical care services..	---	---	---	129.7	196.9	330.1	366.9	421.9	464.4
Hospital and other medical services[1]...........									
Hospital room..............	30.3	57.3	75.9	145.4	236.1	418.9	481.1	556.7	619.7
Other hospital and medical care services[1]....	---	---	---	---	---	132.8	151.2	170.5	190.0
Medical care commodities.....	88.5	104.5	100.2	103.6	118.8	168.1	186.5	205.7	223.3
Prescription drugs...........	92.6	115.3	102.0	101.2	109.3	154.8	172.5	192.7	213.8
Nonprescription drugs and medical supplies[1]......	---	---	---	---	---	120.9	133.6	145.8	155.2
Eyeglasses[1]...............	---	---	---	---	---	117.5	125.6	131.1	135.9
Internal and respiratory over-the-counter drugs......	---	---	98.0	106.2	130.1	188.1	211.4	234.2	251.7
Nonprescription medical equipment and supplies[1]......	---	---	---	---	---	118.2	129.1	141.1	149.9

[1]Dec. 1977=100.

NOTE: 1967=100, except where noted.

SOURCE: Bureau of Labor Statistics, U.S. Department of Labor: *Consumer Price Index*. Various releases.

E3–9. Consumer Price Index Average Annual Percent Change for All Items and Medical Care Components: United States, Selected Years 1950–83

(Data are based on reporting by samples of providers and other retail outlets)

Item and medical care component	Period						
	1950-60	1960-65	1965-70	1970-80	1980-81	1981-82	1982-83
	Average annual percent change						
CPI, all items..............	2.1	1.3	4.2	7.8	10.2	6.1	3.2
Less medical care..........	---	1.2	4.1	7.8	10.3	5.9	2.9
CPI, all services..........	3.6	2.0	5.7	8.3	13.0	9.0	3.5
All medical care...........	4.0	2.5	6.1	8.2	10.4	11.6	8.7
Medical care services......	4.3	3.1	7.3	8.8	10.3	11.9	8.7
Professional services......	---	---	---	7.7	9.8	8.5	7.1
Physician services........	3.4	2.8	6.6	8.3	10.6	9.4	7.7
Dental services...........	2.5	2.3	5.3	7.2	9.1	7.7	6.7
Other professional services[1]...............	---	---	---	---	8.4	6.7	6.0
Other medical care services.....	---	---	---	9.8	10.7	15.0	10.1
Hospital and other medical services[1].............	---	---	---	---	14.1	14.2	11.4
Hospital room.............	6.6	5.8	13.9	11.2	14.5	15.7	11.3
Other hospital and medical care services[1]...	---	---	---	---	13.7	12.8	11.4
Medical care commodities.............	1.7	-0.8	0.7	5.0	11.1	10.3	8.6
Prescription drugs........	2.2	-2.4	-0.2	4.3	11.3	11.7	10.9
Nonprescription drugs and medical supplies[1]...........	---	---	---	---	10.9	9.1	6.4
Eyeglasses[1]...............	---	---	---	---	6.5	4.4	3.7
Internal and respiratory over-the-counter drugs......	---	---	1.6	5.9	12.8	10.8	7.5
Nonprescription medical equipment and supplies[1].....	---	---	---	---	9.9	9.3	6.2

[1]Dec. 1977=100.

NOTE: 1967=100, except where noted.

SOURCE: Bureau of Labor Statistics, U.S. Department of Labor: Consumer Price Index. Various releases.

E3–10. Increases in Wages, Prices, and Social Security Benefits, 1950–83

Item	Percent change				
	1950 to 1960	1960 to 1970	1970 to 1980	1970 to 1983	1950 to 1983
Median annual wages and salaries [1]	46	58	104	138	451
Consumer price index [2]	23	31	112	156	312
Average monthly social security benefit for retired workers	69	60	189	273	905

[1] Data are for persons 14 years of age and over through 1977 and for persons 15 years of age and over beginning 1978.
[2] CPI–W.

Sources: Department of Commerce (Bureau of the Census), Department of Health and Human Services (Social Security Administration), and Council of Economic Advisers.

E3–11. Returns of Taxpayers Age 65 or Over: Selected Income and Tax Items, by Size of Adjusted Gross Income, 1982

(All figures are estimates based on samples — money amounts are in thousands of dollars)

Size of adjusted gross income	Number of returns	Adjusted gross income less deficit	Exemptions		Salaries and wages		Total net profit less loss from business activities		Sales of capital assets net gain less loss	
			Total number of exemptions	Number of exemptions for age 65 or over	Number of returns	Amount	Number of returns	Amount	Number of returns	Amount
	(1)	(2)	(3)	(4)	(5)	(6)	(7)	(8)	(9)	(10)
All returns, total	10,654,559	210,850,555	31,427,058	13,955,570	3,898,662	49,035,824	1,763,576	4,305,294	2,417,557	9,651,259
No adjusted gross income	97,165	−1,934,462	288,428	125,196	20,543	189,045	76,077	−1,804,103	23,287	191,325
$1 under $5,000	1,158,994	3,715,731	3,045,084	1,366,575	430,010	1,233,942	216,714	45,909	94,021	90,198
$5,000 under $10,000	3,029,646	22,706,351	8,333,746	3,749,214	987,965	5,051,166	300,320	157,722	365,418	219,938
$10,000 under $15,000	2,068,543	25,593,765	6,253,011	2,791,242	664,185	5,024,614	263,252	119,625	339,065	250,416
$15,000 under $20,000	1,309,617	22,663,272	4,057,530	1,791,407	488,972	4,907,496	170,269	287,449	326,994	170,986
$20,000 under $25,000	793,446	17,600,744	2,393,608	1,068,846	278,816	3,296,852	126,882	168,484	197,526	182,784
$25,000 under $30,000	545,431	14,921,535	1,741,318	767,826	237,499	4,112,241	88,520	205,472	192,819	330,697
$30,000 under $40,000	633,208	21,730,121	1,997,489	844,184	327,649	7,188,737	136,106	497,778	235,964	436,054
$40,000 under $50,000	398,061	17,603,299	1,275,704	549,608	192,495	4,613,367	108,389	579,417	203,274	440,207
$50,000 under $75,000	345,943	20,786,687	1,124,206	501,883	135,160	3,991,116	123,815	991,549	230,266	933,432
$75,000 under $100,000	116,590	9,864,413	382,388	165,485	46,659	1,913,609	61,171	843,247	78,972	600,137
$100,000 under $200,000	113,413	15,008,505	383,493	168,051	61,545	3,865,389	61,965	861,599	90,788	1,264,481
$200,000 under $500,000	35,795	10,317,709	121,168	53,083	**27,164	**3,648,251	23,433	698,708	31,058	1,441,956
$500,000 under $1,000,000	**8,707	**10,272,887	**29,885	**12,970	**	**	**6,663	**652,439	**8,105	**3,098,648
$1,000,000 or more	**		**	**	**	**			**	**
Taxable returns, total	8,703,931	202,409,564	25,372,058	11,382,102	3,147,668	45,900,860	1,277,539	5,725,469	2,186,580	9,340,763
No adjusted gross income	982	−160,504	3,593	1,684	429	23,810	971	−347,902	780	65,918
$1 under $5,000	184,665	849,095	374,327	184,665	41,235	124,422	9,601	−5,635	*11,195	*16,314
$5,000 under $10,000	2,256,477	17,381,225	5,571,625	2,624,340	667,525	3,461,531	146,122	68,818	268,627	201,513
$10,000 under $15,000	2,000,821	24,780,234	6,022,386	2,697,459	651,516	4,924,556	235,468	190,429	325,683	232,279
$15,000 under $20,000	1,299,130	22,487,005	4,027,926	1,779,311	486,615	4,821,738	160,502	321,077	325,373	169,844
$20,000 under $25,000	783,814	17,387,159	2,363,403	1,054,545	273,559	3,266,693	120,610	159,008	192,221	182,411
$25,000 under $30,000	541,733	14,816,868	1,733,246	763,790	237,161	4,110,472	84,822	198,645	192,818	330,671
$30,000 under $40,000	628,008	21,553,657	1,979,554	835,616	326,843	7,165,057	135,253	548,070	235,476	428,297
$40,000 under $50,000	391,322	17,330,279	1,262,222	542,867	192,494	4,613,361	108,370	581,237	196,536	402,195
$50,000 under $75,000	343,859	20,657,705	1,119,815	499,688	135,048	3,984,810	123,703	996,527	229,280	921,432
$75,000 under $100,000	115,550	9,783,565	380,254	164,445	46,605	1,901,956	60,131	799,744	78,972	600,137
$100,000 under $200,000	113,103	14,973,046	382,763	167,686	61,489	3,857,439	61,909	867,748	90,479	1,254,430
$200,000 under $500,000	35,766	10,309,243	121,076	53,044	**27,149	**3,645,014	23,417	698,296	31,038	1,440,008
$500,000 under $1,000,000	**8,701	**10,260,987	**29,868	**12,962	**	**	**6,660	**649,409	**8,102	**3,095,316
$1,000,000 or more	**		**	**	**	**			**	**
Nontaxable returns, total	1,950,628	8,440,992	6,055,000	2,573,468	750,994	3,134,965	486,037	−1,420,175	230,977	310,496

E3–12. Households by Before- and After-Tax Income in 1980

Taxes skew the income distribution downwards.

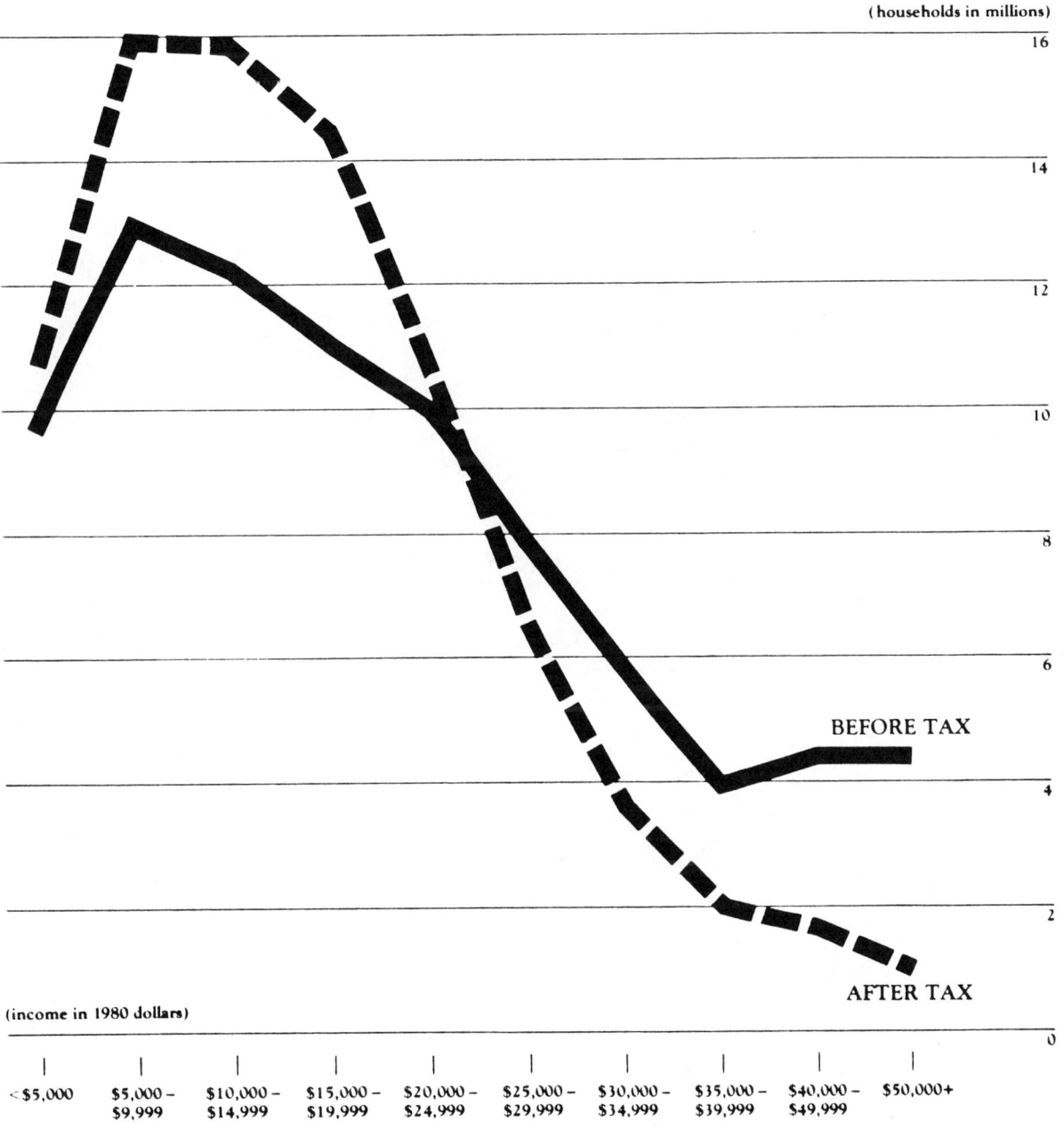

(households in millions)

16

14

12

10

8

6

BEFORE TAX

4

2

AFTER TAX

(income in 1980 dollars)

0

| <$5,000 | $5,000 – $9,999 | $10,000 – $14,999 | $15,000 – $19,999 | $20,000 – $24,999 | $25,000 – $29,999 | $30,000 – $34,999 | $35,000 – $39,999 | $40,000 – $49,999 | $50,000+ |

E3–13. Percent of Mean Household Income Paid in Taxes,[1] 1980–1982

[Calculated using current dollars]

Household type	1980	1981	1982
All households	22.7	23.2	22.2
White	23.1	23.6	22.5
Black	18.0	18.7	17.7
Spanish	18.7	19.4	18.3
Elderly	13.0	13.5	13.2
Female headed..............................	13.6	14.1	13.6

[1] These taxes include Federal individual income taxes, State individual income taxes, FICA (Social Security) taxes and Federal retirement payroll taxes, and property taxes on owner-occupied housing.

Sources: U.S. Department of Commerce, Bureau of the Census, 1981, Money income of households in the United States, 1979, Current Population Reports, Consumer Income, Series P-60, No. 126. U.S. Department of Commerce, Bureau of the Census, 1983, Estimating after-tax money income distribution using data from the March Current Population Survey, Current Population Reports, Series P-23, No. 126. U.S. Department of Commerce, Bureau of the Census, 1984, After-tax money income estimates of households, 1981, Current Population Reports, Series P-23, No. 132. U.S. Department of Commerce, Bureau of the Census, 1984, After-tax money income estimates of households, 1982, Current Population Reports, Special Studies, Series P-23, No. 137. U.S. Department of Commerce, Bureau of the Census, 1984, Money income and poverty status of families and persons in the United States, 1983, Current Population Reports, Consumer Income, Series P-60, No. 145.

E3–14. Where Your Tax Dollars Go

The Census Bureau reported last week that the typical American paid $267.04 more in federal, state and local taxes last year than the year before.

According to "Governmental Finances in 1983-84," released Nov. 14, Americans paid an average of $3,112.42 in fiscal 1984 taxes. That was up 9.4 percent from the prior year. The biggest chunk of revenue came from individual income taxes, with the three levels of government collecting $1,526.85 per American in this tax. That was up from $1,470.49 in 1983.

Sales, receipts and customs taxes were second at $692.57 per capita, up from $618.50, followed by property taxes at $408.44, up from $381.46.

Corporate income taxes, which are actually also paid by individuals indirectly, cost Americans $313.09 apiece, up from $219.16.

Total government revenue at all levels was $5,536.47 per person including taxes, charges, fees, utility income, insurance and other sources. That was an increase from $5,049.21 in 1983.

Spending per American, totaling all three levels of government, is shown below.

	FY 1983	FY 1984
National defense and international relations	$977.70	$1,050.31
Old age, survivors, disability and health benefits	946.61	993.05
Education	754.97	798.63
Interest on general debt	537.57	583.95
Miscellaneous	461.04	465.05
Public welfare	356.80	374.43
Natural resources	234.02	276.50
Utilities	225.71	233.16
Employee retirement	172.04	187.91
Hospitals	167.11	174.66
Highways	159.05	170.68
Postal Service	100.70	112.72
Police protection	86.57	90.42
Health	74.34	76.80
Housing and urban renewal	79.16	74.56
General government	62.98	66.88
Unemployment compensation	105.16	60.46
Government financial administration	56.45	60.38
Corrections	43.86	49.83
Space research and technology	29.13	30.50
Air transportation	23.01	28.22
Social insurance administration	25.20	25.93
Water transport and terminals	15.10	13.30

SOURCE: ASSOCIATED PRESS

E3–15. Taxing Incomes

The proportion of before-tax income paid to federal and state governments rises with income, but falls for social security and property taxes.

(Average taxes paid in 1980 and average taxes as a percent of before-tax income)

Before-Tax Income	Average Before-Tax Income	Households Paying One or More Taxes		Federal Income Taxes		State Income Taxes		FICA Payroll Taxes		Federal Retirement Taxes		Property Taxes	
		Avg. Tax	Percent	Avg. Tax	Percent	Avg. Tax	Percent	Avg. Tax	Percent	Avg. Tax	Percent	Avg. Tax	Percent
Total	$21,063	$ 5,180	24.6%	$ 4,011	19.0%	$ 859	4.1%	$1,114	5.3%	$1,251	5.9%	$ 575	2.7%
Under $2,500 [1]	732	288	39.3	[2]	[2]	31	4.2	104	14.2	[2]	[2]	361	49.3
$2,500 to $4,999	3,777	303	8.0	128	3.4	44	1.2	166	4.4	[2]	[2]	312	8.3
$5,000 to $7,499	6,204	502	8.1	329	5.3	75	1.2	287	4.6	216	3.5	365	5.9
$7,500 to $9,999	8,734	835	9.6	519	5.9	121	1.4	422	4.8	355	4.1	372	4.3
$10,000 to $12,499	11,182	1,397	12.5	801	7.2	186	1.7	572	5.1	527	4.7	401	3.6
$12,500 to $14,999	13,682	1,898	13.9	1,085	7.9	244	1.8	692	5.1	584	4.3	405	3.0
$15,000 to $17,499	16,144	2,648	16.4	1,464	9.1	327	2.0	848	5.3	771	4.8	457	2.8
$17,500 to $19,999	18,694	3,405	18.2	1,903	10.2	427	2.3	989	5.3	925	4.9	468	2.5
$20,000 to $22,499	21,126	4,213	19.9	2,389	11.3	538	2.5	1,125	5.3	1,072	5.1	532	2.5
$22,500 to $24,999	23,690	4,906	20.7	2,847	12.0	652	2.8	1,232	5.2	1,151	4.9	524	2.2
$25,000 to $27,499	26,115	5,760	22.1	3,369	12.9	785	3.0	1,345	5.2	1,232	4.7	592	2.3
$27,500 to $29,999	28,679	6,418	22.4	3,830	13.4	884	3.1	1,424	5.0	1,334	4.7	601	2.1
$30,000 to $32,499	31,106	7,357	23.7	4,454	14.3	1,037	3.3	1,530	4.9	1,367	4.4	659	2.1
$32,500 to $34,999	33,667	8,230	24.4	5,048	15.0	1,166	3.5	1,591	4.7	1,473	4.4	690	2.0
$35,000 to $37,499	36,116	9,079	25.1	5,650	15.6	1,314	3.6	1,697	4.7	1,456	4.0	751	2.1
$37,500 to $39,999	38,643	9,934	25.7	6,294	16.3	1,450	3.8	1,764	4.6	1,626	4.2	748	1.9
$40,000 to $44,999	42,184	11,313	26.8	7,259	17.2	1,671	4.0	1,850	4.4	1,669	4.0	839	2.0
$45,000 to $49,999	47,227	13,302	28.2	8,829	18.7	1,930	4.1	1,962	4.2	2,044	4.3	904	1.9
$50,000 to $59,999	54,102	16,205	30.0	11,158	20.6	2,411	4.5	2,031	3.8	1,993	3.7	1,035	1.9
$60,000 to $74,999	65,840	21,610	32.8	15,767	23.9	3,210	4.9	2,086	3.2	2,427	3.7	1,038	1.6
$75,000 and over	99,704	41,172	41.3	33,041	33.1	5,711	5.7	2,083	2.1	[2]	[2]	1,416	1.4

[1]Includes households with losses. [2]Less than 75,000.

E3-16. Cost of Food at Home Estimated for Food Plans at 4 Cost Levels, April 1985, U.S. Average[1]

Sex-age group	Cost for 1 week				Cost for 1 month			
	Thrifty plan	Low-cost plan	Moderate-cost plan	Liberal plan	Thrifty plan	Low-cost plan	Moderate-cost plan	Liberal plan
FAMILIES								
Family of 2:[2]								
20-50 years	$37.40	$47.10	$57.90	$71.60	$161.80	$203.90	$251.10	$310.20
51 years and over	35.30	45.10	55.40	66.00	153.10	195.40	240.00	286.00
Family of 4:								
Couple, 20-50 years and children--								
1-2 and 3-5 years	54.40	67.60	82.50	100.80	235.40	293.10	357.60	436.90
6-8 and 9-11 years	62.40	79.60	99.20	119.20	270.40	344.90	430.30	516.60
INDIVIDUALS[3]								
Child:								
1-2 years	9.80	11.80	13.80	16.50	42.40	51.30	59.70	71.70
3-5 years	10.60	13.00	16.10	19.20	45.90	56.40	69.60	83.20
6-8 years	13.00	17.20	21.50	25.10	56.40	74.60	93.20	108.80
9-11 years	15.40	19.60	25.10	29.00	66.90	84.90	108.80	125.80
Male:								
12-14 years	16.20	22.20	27.60	32.40	70.10	96.30	119.70	140.40
15-19 years	16.80	23.10	28.50	33.00	72.80	99.90	123.30	142.90
20-50 years	17.90	22.80	28.40	34.20	77.40	98.70	123.30	148.20
51 years and over ...	16.20	21.60	26.50	31.60	70.30	93.60	114.70	137.10
Female:								
12-19 years	16.10	19.20	23.20	28.00	69.60	83.40	100.70	121.40
20-50 years	16.10	20.00	24.20	30.90	69.70	86.70	105.00	133.80
51 years and over ...	15.90	19.40	23.90	28.40	68.90	84.00	103.50	122.90

[1]Assumes that food for all meals and snacks is purchased at the store and prepared at home. Estimates for the thrifty food plan were computed from quantities of foods published in Family Economics Review, 1984 No. 1. Estimates for the other plans were computed from quantities of foods published in Family Economics Review, 1983 No. 2. The costs of the food plans are estimated by updating prices paid by households surveyed in 1977-78 in USDA's Nationwide Food Consumption Survey. USDA updates these survey prices using information from the Bureau of Labor Statistics (CPI Detailed Report, table 3) to estimate the costs for the food plans.

[2]10 percent added for family size adjustment. See footnote 3.

[3]The costs given are for individuals in 4-person families. For individuals in other size families, the following adjustments are suggested: 1-person--add 20 percent; 2-person--add 10 percent; 3-person--add 5 percent; 5- or 6-person--subtract 5 percent; 7- or more-person--subtract 10 percent.

E3–17. Average Health Expenditures for Older Woman Households with Health Expenses in 1986

Type of Household	Average Expenses for Households with Expenses	Average Expenses and Insurance Premiums for Households with Expenses
Single Woman	$6,740	$7,240
Married Couple	$8,500	$9,400

SOURCE: ICF estimates.

E3–18. Percent of Older Woman Households with Expenditures by Type of Expenditure in 1986

Type of Expenditure	Married Couple Households	Single Woman Households	All Older Woman Households
Hospital Inpatient Care	37%	22%	29%
Physicians Services	91%	81%	86%
Dental Services	53%	37%	44%
Other Professional Services	39%	32%	35%
Prescription Drugs	92%	85%	88%
Eyeglasses and Appliances	44%	33%	38%
Other Health Services	19%	12%	15%
Nursing Home Care	4%	12%	8%
Total	98%	95%	97%

a/   This table excludes payments made for SMI premiums and other health insurance premiums.

SOURCE: ICF estimates.

E3–19. Percentage of Income Spent on Household Energy, by Income Class—1981

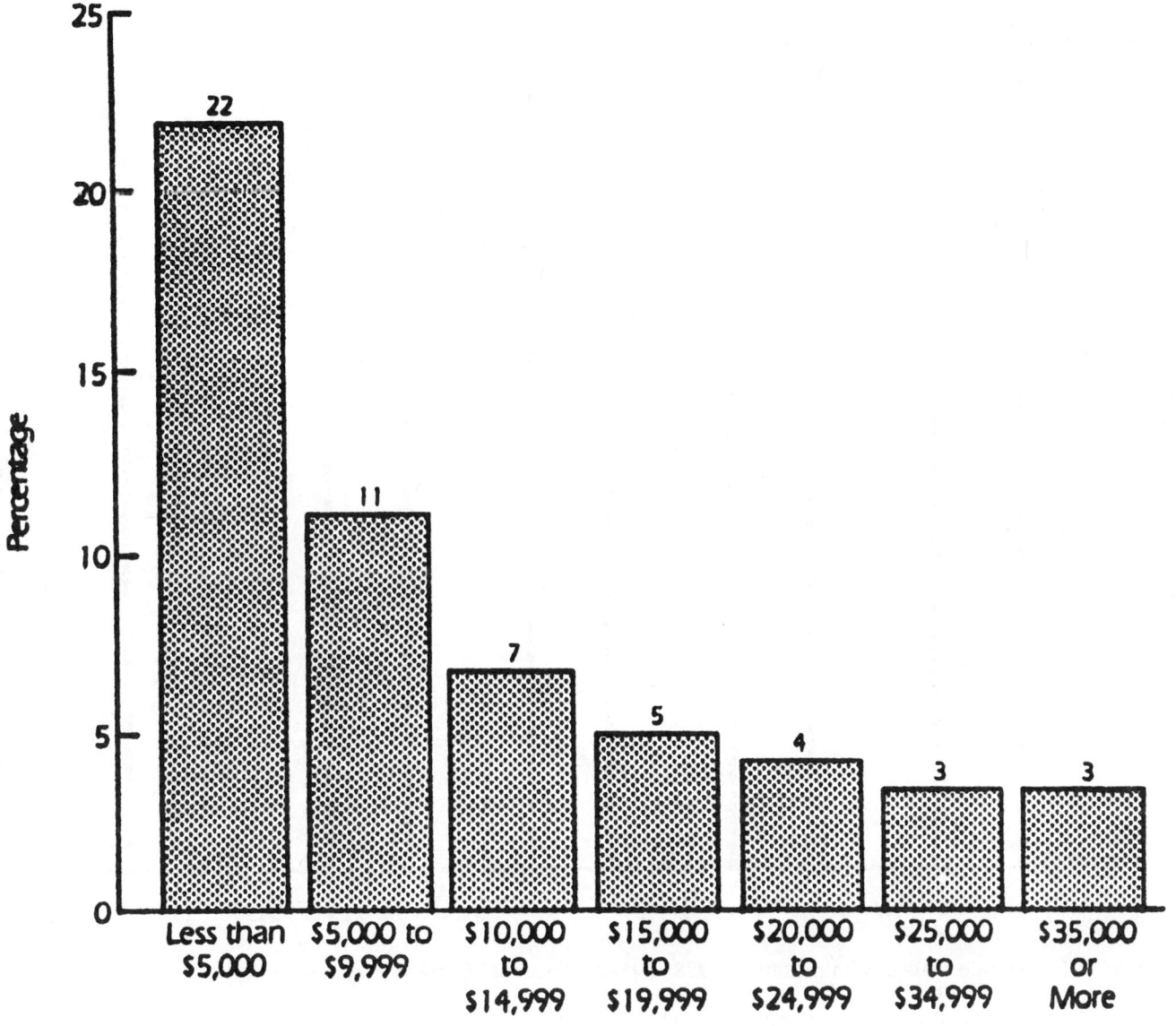

1980 Family Income

Note: Household energy includes all uses of natural gas, electricity, fuel oil or kerosene, and LPG. It does not include motor gasoline.

Source: Energy Information Administration, 1981 Residential Energy Consumption Survey.

E3–20. Average Household Expenditures for All Major Household Fuels—1978 to 1982

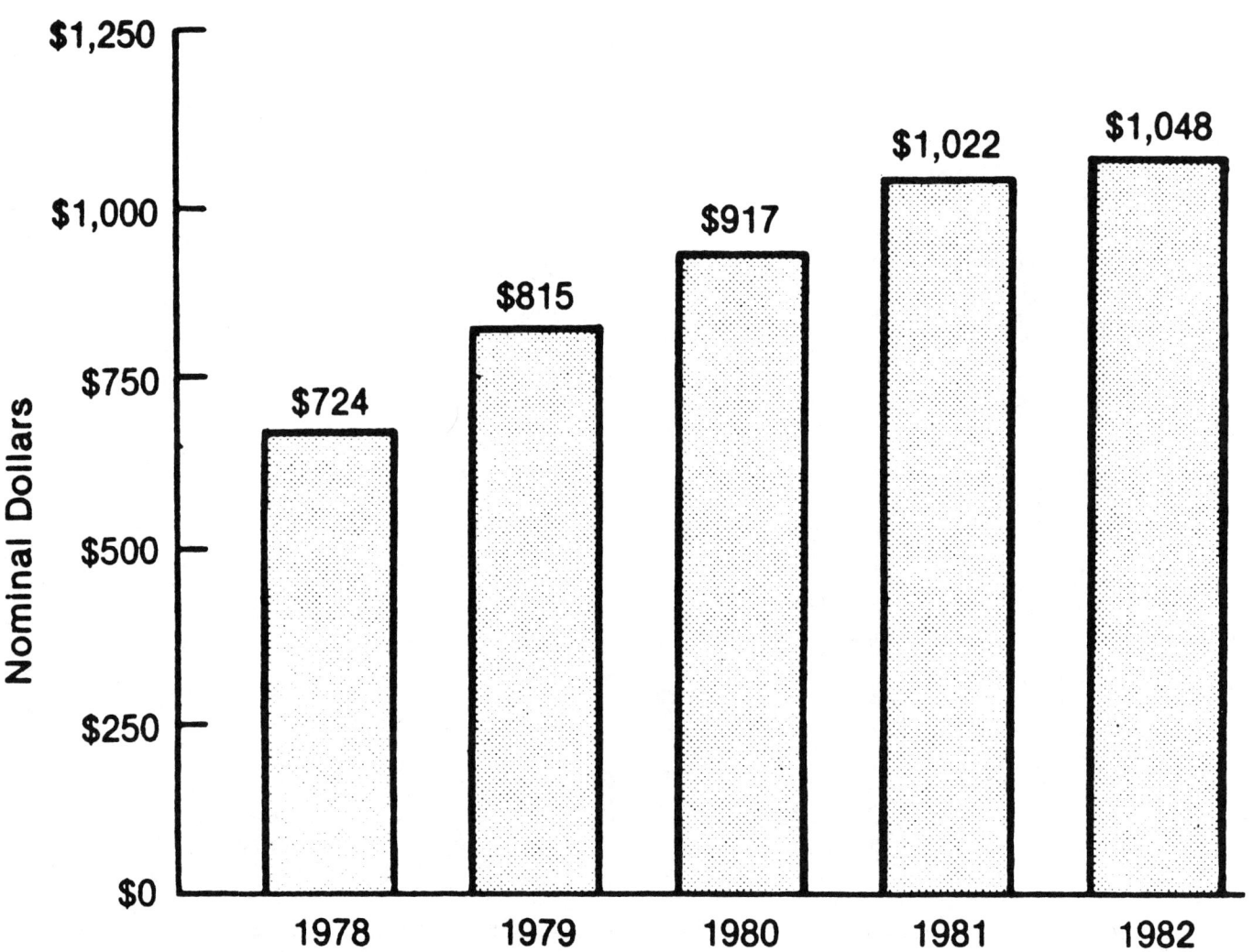

SOURCE: Energy Information Administration, 1978 to 1982 Residential Energy Consumption Surveys.

RECS: Consumption and Expenditures, April 1982 Through March 1983: National Data Energy Information Administration.

E4. POVERTY STATUS

E4–1. Poverty Remains High for Some Groups

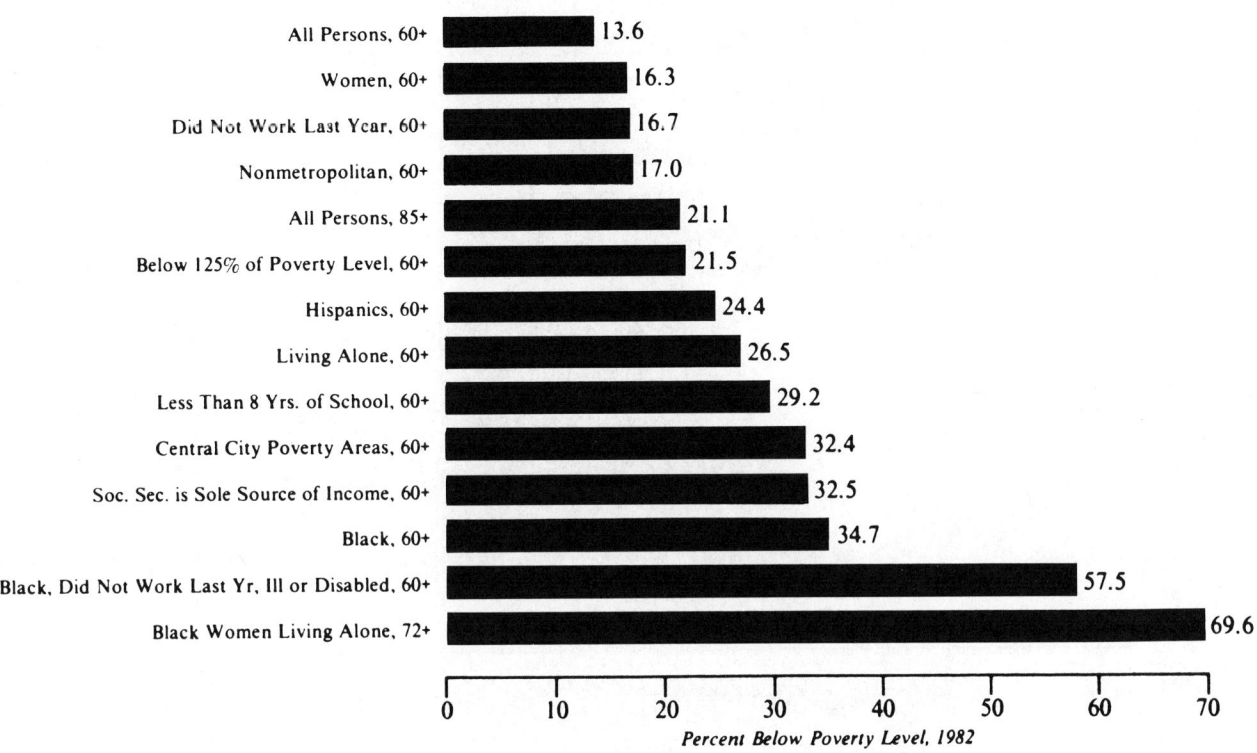

Source: U.S. Bureau of the Census

E4–2. Persons below the Poverty Level; Persons below 125 Percent of the Poverty Level, 1982

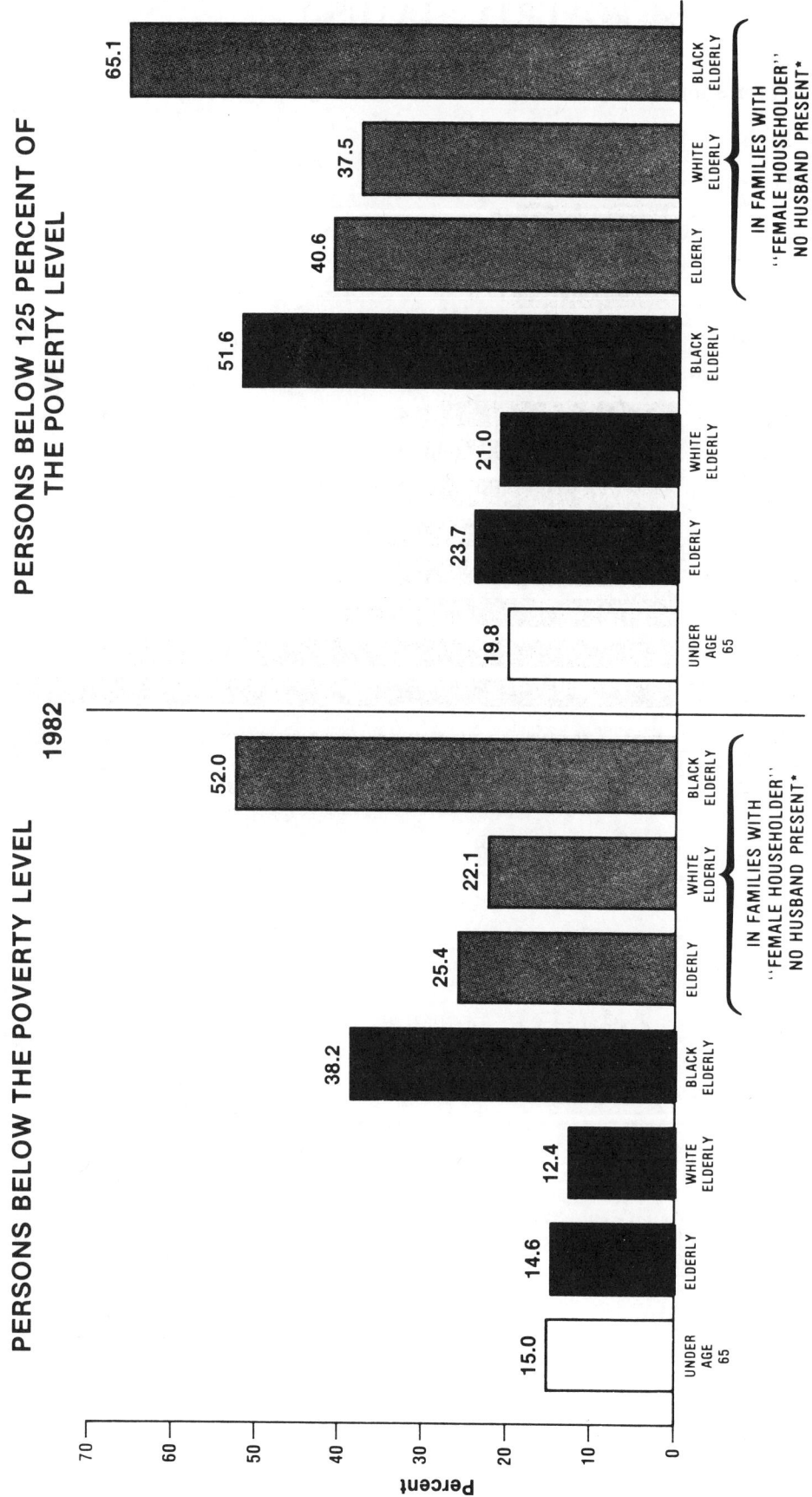

*includes female "unrelated individuals"

SOURCE: U.S. Bureau of the Census. Money Income and Poverty Status of Families and Persons in the United States: 1982, Current Population Reports, Series P-60, No. 140.

E4-3. Percent of the Aged and Nonaged Populations with Incomes below the Poverty Line for Various Economic Units in 1960, 1970, 1980, and 1982

Economic unit and sex	Aged				Nonaged			
	1960	1970	1980	1982	1960	1970	1980	1982
Families and unrelated individuals								
Families	27	16	9	9	16	8	10	12
Headed by men	26	16	8	8	(1)	6	6	7
Headed by women	31	20	15	16	32	32	32	31
Unrelated individuals	66	47	31	27	(1)	20	17	19
Men	60	39	24	21	(1)	14	14	15
Women	68	50	32	29	(1)	26	21	22
Persons								
Total [2]	35	24	16	15	(1)	9	10	12
Men	(1)	19	11	10	(1)	7	8	9
Women	(1)	28	19	18	(1)	10	12	14

[1] Not available.

[2] Nonaged persons are those aged 22–64.

E4–4. Number and Percent of Elderly Living in Poverty by Race, Sex, and Living Arrangement 1983

Race and sex	Number (thousands)			Percent		
	In families	Unrelated individuals	Total number	In families	Unrelated individuals	Total percent
White:						
Male	496	298	794	6.1	18.5	8.2
Female	552	1,507	2,059	7.0	24.5	14.7
Total	1,048	1,805	2,853	6.6	23.3	12.0
Black:						
Male	142	105	247	21.9	45.0	28.3
Female	204	340	544	26.4	63.4	41.7
Total	346	445	791	24.3	58.4	36.3
Hispanic origin:						
Male	38	22	60	17.7	(1)	22.4
Female	35	53	88	13.7	45.7	23.7
Total	73	75	148	15.5	43.7	23.1
All races:						
Male	656	412	1,072	7.4	22.1	10.0
Female	771	1,861	2,640	8.8	27.7	17.0
Total	1,427	2,273	3,711	8.1	26.5	14.1

[1]Base is smaller than 75,000.

SOURCE: Bureau of the Census. Characteristics of the Population Below the Poverty Level: 1983. Current Population Reports, Series P-60, No. 147, Table 3.

E4–5. Income Distribution of the Elderly by Age, 1986

Relative to the Poverty Line	65-69	70-74	75-84	85+	Total
Less than 125% of Poverty Line	8%	15%	23%	31%	17%
125-200% of Poverty Line	15%	18%	19%	14%	17%
200-400% of Poverty Line	36%	37%	36%	37%	36%
More than 400% of Poverty Line	42%	31%	22%	17%	30%
Total	100%	100%	100%	100%	100%

SOURCE: ICF estimates.

E4–6. Selected Characteristics of the Aged—Poverty Status in 1983 of Persons 60 Years and Over, by Age and Sex

[NUMBERS IN THOUSANDS. PERSONS AS OF MARCH 1984.]

CHARACTERISTIC	ALL INCOME LEVELS						BELOW POVERTY LEVEL					
				65 YEARS OLD AND OVER						65 YEARS OLD AND OVER		
	TOTAL	60 AND 61 YEARS	62 TO 64 YEARS	TOTAL	65 TO 71 YEARS	72 YEARS AND OVER	TOTAL	60 AND 61 YEARS	62 TO 64 YEARS	TOTAL	65 TO 71 YEARS	72 YEARS AND OVER
BOTH SEXES												
FAMILY STATUS AND COMPOSITION												
TOTAL	37 014	4 441	6 282	26 291	12 180	14 111	4 945	526	708	3 711	1 325	2 386
IN FAMILIES	26 411	3 691	5 043	17 677	9 130	8 547	2 109	311	371	1 427	588	839
HOUSEHOLDER	14 348	2 015	2 651	9 682	5 013	4 669	1 247	190	216	841	356	485
WITH RELATED CHILDREN UNDER 18 YEARS	1 165	290	293	583	385	198	304	63	70	172	112	59
MEAN NUMBER OF CHILDREN	1.57	1.47	1.56	1.62	1.65	1.57	2.02	(B)	(B)	1.98	2.15	(B)
MEAN SIZE OF FAMILY	2.45	2.68	2.61	2.36	2.45	2.27	2.82	3.03	3.22	2.67	3.07	2.37
SPOUSE OF HOUSEHOLDER	9 630	1 544	2 142	5 944	3 515	2 429	668	113	134	421	187	234
OTHER FAMILY MEMBERS	2 433	132	250	2 051	602	1 449	194	7	22	165	45	120
IN RELATED SUBFAMILIES	244	31	37	176	95	81	52	6	9	36	20	16
MARRIED, SPOUSE PRESENT	239	31	35	174	93	81	49	6	7	36	20	16
OTHER	4	-	2	2	2	-	2	-	2	-	-	-
IN UNRELATED SUBFAMILIES	37	2	12	23	9	14	14	-	3	11	6	6
UNRELATED INDIVIDUALS	10 566	748	1 227	8 591	3 042	5 549	2 822	215	334	2 273	732	1 541
LIVING ALONE	9 717	670	1 081	7 966	2 812	5 154	2 540	198	291	2 051	645	1 406
LIVING WITH NONRELATIVES	849	77	146	625	230	395	282	17	44	222	86	135
IN HOUSEHOLDS	715	72	114	528	202	327	244	17	35	192	82	110
IN GROUP QUARTERS	134	5	32	97	29	68	39	-	9	29	4	25
TYPE OF RESIDENCE												
TOTAL	37 014	4 441	6 282	26 291	12 180	14 111	4 945	526	708	3 711	1 325	2 386
METROPOLITAN AREAS	24 021	2 975	4 220	16 826	7 905	8 921	2 729	286	413	2 030	757	1 273
INSIDE POVERTY AREAS	2 529	292	424	1 812	827	985	712	88	109	515	216	299
OUTSIDE POVERTY AREAS	21 492	2 683	3 796	15 014	7 078	7 936	2 018	198	304	1 515	541	974
INSIDE CENTRAL CITIES	10 592	1 210	1 782	7 600	3 422	4 178	1 488	167	237	1 083	430	654
INSIDE POVERTY AREAS	1 840	221	316	1 304	597	706	552	68	90	394	182	212
OUTSIDE POVERTY AREAS	8 752	989	1 466	6 296	2 825	3 471	935	99	147	689	248	442
OUTSIDE CENTRAL CITIES	13 429	1 765	2 438	9 226	4 483	4 743	1 241	120	175	947	327	619
INSIDE POVERTY AREAS	688	71	108	509	230	279	159	20	18	121	34	87
OUTSIDE POVERTY AREAS	12 740	1 693	2 329	8 718	4 253	4 465	1 082	100	157	826	294	532
NONMETROPOLITAN AREAS	12 993	1 466	2 062	9 465	4 275	5 190	2 216	240	296	1 681	568	1 113
INSIDE POVERTY AREAS	4 603	544	670	3 389	1 470	1 919	1 157	150	154	853	296	556
OUTSIDE POVERTY AREAS	8 390	923	1 392	6 076	2 806	3 270	1 059	89	141	829	272	557
MARITAL STATUS												
TOTAL	37 014	4 441	6 282	26 291	12 180	14 111	4 945	526	708	3 711	1 325	2 386
SINGLE	1 948	219	325	1 404	603	801	382	48	71	264	102	162
MARRIED, SPOUSE PRESENT	21 840	3 291	4 482	14 067	7 902	6 165	1 526	245	286	996	434	562
MARRIED, SPOUSE ABSENT	739	114	145	480	251	229	254	43	38	173	73	100
SEPARATED	461	79	108	275	175	100	167	36	29	102	54	49
OTHER	277	35	37	205	76	129	87	7	9	70	19	51
WIDOWED	10 805	513	935	9 357	2 876	6 481	2 383	132	208	2 043	584	1 459
DIVORCED	1 682	304	395	984	549	435	400	58	106	236	133	103
WORK EXPERIENCE												
PERSONS	37 014	4 441	6 282	26 291	12 180	14 111	4 945	526	708	3 711	1 325	2 386
WORKED LAST YEAR	9 524	2 617	2 913	3 994	2 821	1 173	565	175	162	229	141	88
50 TO 52 WEEKS	6 056	1 898	1 965	2 193	1 523	670	241	79	77	85	46	39
FULL-TIME	4 421	1 631	1 611	1 179	903	276	114	42	38	33	23	10
49 WEEKS OR LESS	3 468	719	948	1 801	1 298	503	324	96	85	143	94	49
FULL-TIME	1 675	470	591	613	484	129	116	42	37	37	28	9
MAIN REASON FOR WORKING PART YEAR:												
ILL OR DISABLED	431	101	119	210	131	80	65	17	10	38	27	11
KEEPING HOUSE	446	103	119	224	177	46	41	9	13	19	16	3
UNABLE TO FIND WORK	573	268	188	117	88	29	76	39	28	9	5	4
RETIRED	1 520	131	382	1 007	731	276	102	10	22	70	40	30
OTHER	498	117	139	243	171	72	40	21	11	8	8	-
MEAN NUMBER OF WEEKS WORKED	42.2	45.5	43.5	39.2	39.0	39.6	32.0	33.9	33.6	29.4	28.6	30.7
DID NOT WORK LAST YEAR	27 490	1 824	3 369	22 297	9 360	12 937	4 380	351	547	3 483	1 184	2 298
MAIN REASON FOR NOT WORKING:												
ILL OR DISABLED	4 886	533	700	3 653	1 355	2 298	1 480	184	173	1 122	380	742
KEEPING HOUSE	6 775	765	1 177	4 833	2 304	2 529	938	99	181	657	269	388
UNABLE TO FIND WORK	175	58	57	59	46	13	51	20	19	12	9	4
RETIRED	15 450	449	1 407	13 594	5 595	7 999	1 875	46	166	1 663	515	1 148
OTHER	204	18	28	158	60	98	37	2	8	28	12	16
FAMILY HOUSEHOLDERS	14 348	2 015	2 651	9 682	5 013	4 669	1 247	190	216	841	356	485
WORKED LAST YEAR	5 098	1 438	1 564	2 095	1 484	612	229	85	70	74	47	27
50 TO 52 WEEKS	3 350	1 083	1 087	1 180	827	353	111	44	31	36	21	15
FULL-TIME	2 674	1 004	973	697	542	155	71	32	22	17	12	5
49 WEEKS OR LESS	1 747	356	477	915	656	259	118	41	38	38	26	12
FULL-TIME	922	266	339	317	257	60	46	20	15	12	12	-
MAIN REASON FOR WORKING PART YEAR:												
ILL OR DISABLED	207	58	55	94	60	34	18	6	3	10	10	-
KEEPING HOUSE	48	11	14	23	17	6	9	3	2	4	3	1
UNABLE TO FIND WORK	328	158	115	55	39	16	44	23	20	1	-	1
RETIRED	954	83	237	633	458	175	35	2	9	23	14	9
OTHER	211	46	55	109	82	28	11	7	5	-	-	-
MEAN NUMBER OF WEEKS WORKED	42.5	46.4	44.0	38.9	38.6	39.4	33.4	35.3	(B)	(B)	(B)	(B)
DID NOT WORK LAST YEAR	9 250	576	1 087	7 587	3 529	4 057	1 018	105	146	767	309	458
MAIN REASON FOR NOT WORKING:												
ILL OR DISABLED	1 723	243	309	1 171	509	661	369	62	61	246	90	156
KEEPING HOUSE	635	66	88	481	228	253	118	14	24	79	34	45
UNABLE TO FIND WORK	70	29	25	15	13	2	23	13	7	2	2	-
RETIRED	6 793	234	664	5 895	2 769	3 127	505	15	53	436	180	256
OTHER	28	4	1	24	10	14	3	-	-	3	3	-

SEE FOOTNOTE(S) AT END OF TABLE.

E4–6. Selected Characteristics of the Aged—Poverty Status in 1983 of Persons 60 Years and Over, by Age and Sex (Continued)

[NUMBERS IN THOUSANDS. PERSONS AS OF MARCH 1984.]

CHARACTERISTIC	ALL INCOME LEVELS						BELOW POVERTY LEVEL					
	TOTAL	60 AND 61 YEARS	62 TO 64 YEARS	65 YEARS OLD AND OVER TOTAL	65 TO 71 YEARS	72 YEARS AND OVER	TOTAL	60 AND 61 YEARS	62 TO 64 YEARS	65 YEARS OLD AND OVER TOTAL	65 TO 71 YEARS	72 YEARS AND OVER
BOTH SEXES--CONTINUED												
WORK EXPERIENCE--CONTINUED												
UNRELATED INDIVIDUALS[1]	10 566	748	1 227	8 591	3 042	5 549	2 822	215	334	2 273	732	1 541
WORKED LAST YEAR	2 164	438	587	1 139	732	407	256	64	61	131	77	54
50 TO 52 WEEKS	1 339	314	389	636	407	229	98	26	31	40	21	20
FULL-TIME	862	271	275	316	231	84	32	9	8	15	10	5
49 WEEKS OR LESS	826	124	198	504	325	178	158	38	30	90	56	34
FULL-TIME	355	72	117	166	110	57	53	14	16	23	14	9
MAIN REASON FOR WORKING PART YEAR:												
ILL OR DISABLED	146	18	36	91	50	41	37	7	5	24	14	10
KEEPING HOUSE	104	9	21	74	50	24	17	3	4	10	9	1
UNABLE TO FIND WORK	137	57	43	37	28	9	24	10	9	5	3	2
RETIRED	312	18	68	226	155	72	61	6	11	45	26	19
OTHER	126	22	30	75	42	33	19	11	2	7	5	2
MEAN NUMBER OF WEEKS WORKED	41.7	45.0	42.9	39.8	40.0	39.4	30.0	(B)	(B)	26.4	25.6	(B)
DID NOT WORK LAST YEAR	8 402	310	640	7 452	2 309	5 142	2 567	151	274	2 142	655	1 487
MAIN REASON FOR NOT WORKING:												
ILL OR DISABLED	1 789	168	187	1 433	468	965	910	107	92	711	236	475
KEEPING HOUSE	1 493	42	134	1 318	376	942	449	20	73	356	120	236
UNABLE TO FIND WORK	58	8	24	27	17	9	22	2	12	7	5	2
RETIRED	4 963	82	281	4 601	1 423	3 177	1 159	20	91	1 047	285	762
OTHER	98	10	15	73	25	48	27	2	5	20	9	11
SOURCE OF INCOME												
PERSONS	37 014	4 441	6 282	26 291	12 180	14 111	4 945	526	708	3 711	1 325	2 386
EARNINGS ONLY	1 126	514	453	159	127	32	170	96	47	28	22	6
WAGE OR SALARY INCOME ONLY	994	444	408	143	113	29	130	74	33	23	18	6
SELF-EMPLOYMENT INCOME ONLY	132	71	45	16	13	3	40	21	14	4	4	-
WAGE OR SALARY AND SELF-EMPLOYMENT INCOME	-	-	-	-	-	-	-	-	-	-	-	-
EARNINGS AND INCOME OTHER THAN EARNINGS	8 365	2 092	2 454	3 819	2 683	1 137	384	77	110	197	119	78
EARNINGS AND SOCIAL SECURITY INCOME ONLY	675	25	162	487	331	156	111	5	45	61	41	20
EARNINGS AND SUPPLEMENTAL SECURITY INCOME ONLY	11	2	8	1	1	-	5	2	2	1	1	-
EARNINGS, SOCIAL SECURITY, AND SUPPLEMENTAL SECURITY INCOME ONLY	15	1	-	14	5	8	9	-	-	9	3	6
EARNINGS AND OTHER INCOME ONLY	7 640	2 062	2 283	3 295	2 333	962	251	69	64	119	70	49
OTHER COMBINATIONS	25	2	-	22	12	11	8	2	-	6	3	3
INCOME OTHER THAN EARNINGS ONLY	26 669	1 540	3 170	21 960	9 212	12 748	4 095	269	487	3 340	1 134	2 206
SOCIAL SECURITY INCOME ONLY	4 449	101	520	3 828	1 562	2 266	1 384	38	183	1 163	424	738
SUPPLEMENTAL SECURITY INCOME ONLY	465	59	53	353	117	236	251	42	35	173	62	111
OTHER INCOME ONLY	1 143	480	313	349	160	189	242	82	44	116	41	75
OTHER TRANSFER PAYMENTS ONLY[1]	129	60	33	36	13	24	61	36	12	13	4	9
SOCIAL SECURITY AND SUPPLEMENTAL SECURITY INCOME ONLY	1 087	38	60	989	335	654	629	25	40	564	184	381
SOCIAL SECURITY AND OTHER INCOME ONLY	18 173	343	1 919	15 910	6 799	9 111	1 447	41	156	1 249	405	845
SOCIAL SECURITY INCOME AND OTHER TRANSFER PAYMENTS ONLY[1]	532	22	79	431	183	248	105	3	19	83	21	62
SOCIAL SECURITY AND ''ALL OTHER'' INCOME ONLY[1]	17 641	322	1 840	15 479	6 616	8 863	1 342	38	137	1 166	384	783
OTHER COMBINATIONS	1 353	518	305	530	239	291	143	40	29	74	18	56
NO INCOME	853	295	206	353	159	194	296	85	65	147	51	96
FAMILY HOUSEHOLDERS	14 348	2 015	2 651	9 682	5 013	4 669	1 247	190	216	841	356	485
EARNINGS ONLY	520	236	220	64	56	8	64	41	18	6	6	-
WAGE OR SALARY INCOME ONLY	440	196	190	54	48	5	43	31	10	3	3	-
SELF-EMPLOYMENT INCOME ONLY	80	40	30	10	8	2	21	10	8	3	3	-
WAGE OR SALARY AND SELF-EMPLOYMENT INCOME	-	-	-	-	-	-	-	-	-	-	-	-
EARNINGS AND INCOME OTHER THAN EARNINGS	4 575	1 202	1 344	2 029	1 427	603	165	44	52	68	41	27
EARNINGS AND SOCIAL SECURITY INCOME ONLY	307	11	74	222	160	62	51	2	22	27	16	11
EARNINGS AND SUPPLEMENTAL SECURITY INCOME ONLY	6	2	3	1	1	-	3	2	-	1	1	-
EARNINGS, SOCIAL SECURITY, AND SUPPLEMENTAL SECURITY INCOME ONLY	3	-	-	3	1	2	2	-	-	2	-	2
EARNINGS AND OTHER INCOME ONLY	4 252	1 189	1 267	1 795	1 260	536	107	40	31	36	22	15
OTHER COMBINATIONS	7	-	-	7	4	3	2	-	-	2	2	-
INCOME OTHER THAN EARNINGS ONLY	9 148	536	1 075	7 537	3 502	4 035	956	89	137	729	286	444
SOCIAL SECURITY INCOME ONLY	1 326	36	145	1 145	526	619	361	15	44	302	127	175
SUPPLEMENTAL SECURITY INCOME ONLY	103	19	15	68	18	50	51	13	14	24	8	15
OTHER INCOME ONLY	215	80	58	77	35	42	72	23	16	34	12	21
OTHER TRANSFER PAYMENTS ONLY[1]	54	19	18	18	8	10	22	7	7	8	3	5
SOCIAL SECURITY AND SUPPLEMENTAL SECURITY INCOME ONLY	276	.	16	246	88	157	128	8	9	111	43	68
SOCIAL SECURITY AND OTHER INCOME ONLY	6 717	180	730	5 806	2 734	3 072	306	13	48	245	92	153
SOCIAL SECURITY INCOME AND OTHER TRANSFER PAYMENTS ONLY[1]	217	17	50	149	83	66	30	3	13	14	8	6
SOCIAL SECURITY AND ''ALL OTHER'' INCOME ONLY[1]	6 500	163	680	5 657	2 651	3 006	276	10	35	231	83	148
OTHER COMBINATIONS	512	206	111	195	101	94	38	17	7	14	4	10
NO INCOME	105	41	12	52	29	24	63	16	9	37	23	14
UNRELATED INDIVIDUALS	10 566	748	1 227	8 591	3 042	5 549	2 822	215	334	2 273	732	1 541
EARNINGS ONLY	297	116	113	68	47	22	79	40	20	19	13	6
WAGE OR SALARY INCOME ONLY	271	102	105	64	42	22	62	29	15	18	12	6
SELF-EMPLOYMENT INCOME ONLY	26	14	8	4	4	-	17	11	5	1	1	-
WAGE OR SALARY AND SELF-EMPLOYMENT INCOME	-	-	-	-	-	-	-	-	-	-	-	-
EARNINGS AND INCOME OTHER THAN EARNINGS	1 868	322	474	1 072	686	386	176	24	40	112	64	48
EARNINGS AND SOCIAL SECURITY INCOME ONLY	210	3	41	167	98	69	48	2	18	29	20	9
EARNINGS AND SUPPLEMENTAL SECURITY INCOME ONLY	2	1	2	-	-	-	2	-	2	-	-	-
EARNINGS, SOCIAL SECURITY, AND SUPPLEMENTAL SECURITY INCOME ONLY	12	1	-	11	4	7	8	-	-	7	3	5
EARNINGS AND OTHER INCOME ONLY	1 632	315	432	885	579	307	114	20	21	72	40	33
OTHER COMBINATIONS	11	2	-	9	5	4	5	2	-	4	1	2

SEE FOOTNOTE(S) AT END OF TABLE.

E4–6. Selected Characteristics of the Aged—Poverty Status in 1983 of Persons 60 Years and Over, by Age and Sex (Continued)

[NUMBERS IN THOUSANDS. PERSONS AS OF MARCH 1984.

CHARACTERISTIC	ALL INCOME LEVELS						BELOW POVERTY LEVEL					
	TOTAL	60 AND 61 YEARS	62 TO 64 YEARS	65 YEARS OLD AND OVER			TOTAL	60 AND 61 YEARS	62 TO 64 YEARS	65 YEARS OLD AND OVER		
				TOTAL	65 TO 71 YEARS	72 YEARS AND OVER				TOTAL	65 TO 71 YEARS	72 YEARS AND OVER
BOTH SEXES--CONTINUED												
SOURCE OF INCOME--CONTINUED												
UNRELATED INDIVIDUALS--CONTINUED												
INCOME OTHER THAN EARNINGS ONLY.	8 318	292	629	7 397	2 299	5 096	2 484	134	262	2 088	645	1 444
SOCIAL SECURITY INCOME ONLY.	1 311	28	111	1 172	350	822	742	18	96	629	204	425
SUPPLEMENTAL SECURITY INCOME ONLY.	199	25	22	153	58	95	164	22	17	125	51	74
OTHER INCOME ONLY.	192	64	36	92	31	62	117	40	20	57	18	39
OTHER TRANSFER PAYMENTS ONLY[1]	56	38	11	7	3	4	34	27	5	3	1	2
SOCIAL SECURITY AND SUPPLEMENTAL SECURITY INCOME ONLY	558	19	29	510	157	353	441	17	29	395	114	281
SOCIAL SECURITY AND OTHER INCOME ONLY. . .	5 753	80	389	5 284	1 648	3 636	939	25	82	832	245	587
SOCIAL SECURITY INCOME AND OTHER TRANSFER PAYMENTS ONLY[1]	257	4	18	235	82	153	68	-	2	66	12	54
SOCIAL SECURITY AND ''ALL OTHER'' INCOME ONLY[2]	5 496	76	371	5 049	1 566	3 483	871	25	80	766	233	532
OTHER COMBINATIONS	306	78	42	185	55	131	81	13	18	50	12	38
NO INCOME.	83	18	12	54	10	43	83	18	12	54	10	43
TYPE OF INCOME												
PERSONS[3]	37 014	4 441	6 282	26 291	12 180	14 111	4 945	526	708	3 711	1 325	2 386
EARNINGS[3].	9 491	2 607	2 906	3 978	2 810	1 169	554	173	157	225	141	84
WAGE AND SALARY INCOME	8 057	2 318	2 591	3 148	2 299	849	393	129	104	160	103	57
NONFARM SELF-EMPLOYMENT INCOME	1 333	289	335	710	444	266	112	30	46	36	20	16
FARM SELF-EMPLOYMENT INCOME.	446	93	96	257	165	92	68	22	13	32	19	13
INCOME OTHER THAN EARNINGS[3].	35 033	3 632	5 622	25 779	11 894	13 885	4 480	346	597	3 537	1 253	2 284
SOCIAL SECURITY INCOME	27 917	583	3 348	23 985	10 868	13 118	3 709	113	440	3 156	1 117	2 039
SUPPLEMENTAL SECURITY INCOME	2 085	147	159	1 780	609	1 170	1 130	93	94	943	316	628
OTHER TRANSFER PAYMENTS[1]	2 627	619	649	1 359	691	668	433	111	82	241	79	161
DIVIDENDS, INTEREST, AND RENT.	25 654	3 010	4 328	18 316	8 654	9 662	1 608	121	193	1 294	425	870
PRIVATE PENSIONS, GOVERNMENT EMPLOYEE PENSIONS, ALIMONY, ANNUITIES, ETC	10 395	839	1 566	7 991	4 051	3 940	352	38	72	242	111	131
NO INCOME.	853	295	206	353	159	194	296	85	65	147	51	96
FAMILY HOUSEHOLDERS[3]	14 348	2 015	2 651	9 682	5 013	4 669	1 247	190	216	841	356	485
EARNINGS[3].	5 095	1 438	1 564	2 093	1 483	610	229	85	70	74	47	27
WAGE AND SALARY INCOME	4 112	1 244	1 338	1 529	1 128	402	132	59	36	37	27	10
NONFARM SELF-EMPLOYMENT INCOME	869	180	231	459	294	164	57	17	27	14	6	8
FARM SELF-EMPLOYMENT INCOME.	356	76	75	205	134	71	53	15	12	26	14	12
INCOME OTHER THAN EARNINGS[3].	13 721	1 738	2 417	9 566	4 928	4 638	1 120	133	189	798	327	471
SOCIAL SECURITY INCOME	10 449	274	1 292	8 884	4 454	4 430	886	38	129	719	297	422
SUPPLEMENTAL SECURITY INCOME	529	62	53	414	154	260	232	33	28	170	63	107
OTHER TRANSFER PAYMENTS[1]	1 360	376	387	597	380	218	132	45	42	45	24	21
DIVIDENDS, INTEREST, AND RENT.	10 441	1 456	1 910	7 075	3 680	3 395	388	56	64	269	98	171
PRIVATE PENSIONS, GOVERNMENT EMPLOYEE PENSIONS, ALIMONY, ANNUITIES, ETC	5 476	510	887	4 079	2 283	1 796	84	12	19	59	39	20
NO INCOME.	105	41	12	52	29	24	63	16	9	37	23	14
UNRELATED INDIVIDUALS[3]	10 566	748	1 227	8 591	3 042	5 549	2 822	215	334	2 273	732	1 541
EARNINGS[3].	2 165	438	587	1 141	732	408	256	64	61	131	77	54
WAGE AND SALARY INCOME	1 932	398	555	979	647	332	208	47	52	109	65	45
NONFARM SELF-EMPLOYMENT INCOME	228	38	43	146	79	68	38	12	9	17	8	8
FARM SELF-EMPLOYMENT INCOME.	48	10	6	32	19	13	12	7	-	5	4	1
INCOME OTHER THAN EARNINGS[3].	10 186	614	1 103	8 469	2 985	5 484	2 660	157	302	2 200	708	1 492
SOCIAL SECURITY INCOME	8 827	156	755	7 916	2 737	5 179	2 250	64	228	1 958	618	1 340
SUPPLEMENTAL SECURITY INCOME	1 049	61	69	918	302	616	787	52	60	676	221	455
OTHER TRANSFER PAYMENTS[1]	882	146	162	574	231	343	266	56	31	180	51	129
DIVIDENDS, INTEREST, AND RENT.	6 962	405	754	5 803	2 035	3 768	952	34	90	828	248	580
PRIVATE PENSIONS, GOVERNMENT EMPLOYEE PENSIONS, ALIMONY, ANNUITIES, ETC	3 186	171	375	2 640	1 070	1 571	227	22	45	160	60	100
NO INCOME.	83	18	12	54	10	43	83	18	12	54	10	43
TENURE AND LIVING ARRANGEMENTS												
ALL PERSONS.	37 014	4 441	6 282	26 291	12 180	14 111	4 945	526	708	3 711	1 325	2 386
LIVING WITH RELATIVES.	26 411	3 691	5 043	17 677	9 130	8 547	2 109	311	371	1 427	588	839
OWNER-OCCUPIED UNITS	22 743	3 196	4 439	15 108	7 841	7 268	1 540	213	282	1 045	423	622
RENTER-OCCUPIED UNITS.	3 668	495	604	2 569	1 289	1 280	569	98	89	382	164	218
PUBLIC	275	35	42	198	99	99	86	15	19	52	26	26
PRIVATE.	3 393	460	562	2 371	1 190	1 181	483	82	71	330	139	192
SUBSIDIZED	138	6	14	118	58	60	35	-	3	32	10	22
FAMILY HOUSEHOLDERS.	14 348	2 015	2 651	9 682	5 013	4 669	1 247	190	216	841	356	485
OWNER-OCCUPIED UNITS	12 348	1 732	2 323	8 294	4 329	3 965	912	129	160	623	261	361
RENTER-OCCUPIED UNITS.	1 999	283	328	1 388	684	704	335	61	56	218	94	124
PUBLIC	159	20	29	110	55	55	54	12	12	30	17	13
PRIVATE.	1 840	262	300	1 278	629	650	281	49	44	188	77	111
SUBSIDIZED	73	3	5	66	27	38	17	-	2	15	6	9
LIVING WITH NONRELATIVES ONLY.	886	79	158	648	239	409	297	17	46	233	92	141
OWNER-OCCUPIED UNITS	533	46	92	395	142	253	164	5	29	129	53	76
RENTER-OCCUPIED UNITS.	353	34	66	253	97	156	133	12	17	104	39	65
PUBLIC	15	7	-	8	1	7	8	3	-	6	-	5
PRIVATE.	338	27	66	245	96	149	125	10	17	98	38	60
SUBSIDIZED	9	-	-	9	6	3	7	-	-	6	6	1
LIVING ALONE	9 717	670	1 081	7 966	2 812	5 154	2 540	198	291	2 051	645	1 406
OWNER-OCCUPIED UNITS	6 058	402	658	4 998	1 787	3 211	1 345	91	138	1 116	358	758
RENTER-OCCUPIED UNITS.	3 660	269	423	2 968	1 025	1 944	1 195	107	153	935	288	648
PUBLIC	575	32	54	489	174	315	277	19	29	229	72	157
PRIVATE.	3 085	237	368	2 480	851	1 629	918	88	124	706	216	490
SUBSIDIZED	388	21	21	346	91	255	146	16	17	113	31	81

SEE FOOTNOTE(S) AT END OF TABLE.

E4–6. Selected Characteristics of the Aged—Poverty Status in 1983 of Persons 60 Years and Over, by Age and Sex (Continued)

[NUMBERS IN THOUSANDS. PERSONS AS OF MARCH 1984.

CHARACTERISTIC	ALL INCOME LEVELS						BELOW POVERTY LEVEL					
	TOTAL	60 AND 61 YEARS	62 TO 64 YEARS	65 YEARS OLD AND OVER			TOTAL	60 AND 61 YEARS	62 TO 64 YEARS	65 YEARS OLD AND OVER		
				TOTAL	65 TO 71 YEARS	72 YEARS AND OVER				TOTAL	65 TO 71 YEARS	72 YEARS AND OVER
FEMALE												
FAMILY STATUS AND COMPOSITION												
TOTAL	21 321	2 373	3 406	15 542	6 809	8 733	3 400	319	442	2 640	921	1 719
IN FAMILIES	13 209	1 856	2 555	8 799	4 483	4 315	1 155	171	213	771	317	454
HOUSEHOLDER	2 345	303	352	1 690	745	944	392	61	70	261	112	150
WITH RELATED CHILDREN UNDER 18 YEARS	382	76	72	234	138	96	160	29	29	102	63	40
MEAN NUMBER OF CHILDREN	1.74	1.67	(B)	1.76	1.94	1.50	2.14	(B)	(B)	2.15	(B)	(B)
MEAN SIZE OF FAMILY	2.70	2.80	2.78	2.66	2.79	2.56	3.18	(B)	(B)	3.12	3.76	2.65
SPOUSE OF HOUSEHOLDER	9 098	1 449	2 048	5 602	3 339	2 262	619	104	128	387	171	216
OTHER FAMILY MEMBERS	1 766	104	155	1 507	399	1 108	145	7	15	123	34	88
IN RELATED SUBFAMILIES	110	14	22	74	49	26	26	4	6	16	12	4
MARRIED, SPOUSE PRESENT	106	14	20	72	47	26	24	4	4	16	12	4
OTHER	4	-	2	2	2	-	2	-	2	-	-	-
IN UNRELATED SUBFAMILIES	28	2	9	17	7	11	10	-	2	8	6	2
UNRELATED INDIVIDUALS	8 084	515	842	6 727	2 319	4 406	2 235	148	227	1 861	598	1 262
LIVING ALONE	7 619	472	777	6 370	2 197	4 174	2 063	141	205	1 717	550	1 167
LIVING WITH NONRELATIVES	464	44	65	356	122	234	172	7	21	143	49	95
IN HOUSEHOLDS	374	39	48	286	113	173	141	7	19	116	46	69
IN GROUP QUARTERS	91	4	17	70	9	61	30	-	3	27	2	25
TYPE OF RESIDENCE												
TOTAL	21 321	2 373	3 406	15 542	6 809	8 733	3 400	319	442	2 640	921	1 719
METROPOLITAN AREAS	13 905	1 577	2 261	10 068	4 432	5 636	1 952	179	272	1 501	533	968
INSIDE POVERTY AREAS	1 497	156	228	1 113	476	637	481	50	62	368	148	221
OUTSIDE POVERTY AREAS	12 408	1 420	2 033	8 955	3 955	4 999	1 471	129	209	1 133	385	748
INSIDE CENTRAL CITIES	6 308	650	989	4 669	1 992	2 677	1 086	111	155	819	308	511
INSIDE POVERTY AREAS	1 115	120	178	817	355	462	372	38	54	280	125	155
OUTSIDE POVERTY AREAS	5 193	531	811	3 852	1 637	2 215	714	74	101	538	183	356
OUTSIDE CENTRAL CITIES	7 597	926	1 272	5 399	2 440	2 959	866	67	116	682	225	458
INSIDE POVERTY AREAS	383	37	49	297	121	175	109	13	9	88	22	65
OUTSIDE POVERTY AREAS	7 214	890	1 222	5 102	2 318	2 784	757	55	108	595	202	392
NONMETROPOLITAN AREAS	7 416	796	1 146	5 475	2 377	3 098	1 449	140	170	1 138	388	750
INSIDE POVERTY AREAS	2 593	288	383	1 923	820	1 103	715	87	89	539	195	344
OUTSIDE POVERTY AREAS	4 823	508	763	3 552	1 557	1 995	733	53	81	599	193	406
MARITAL STATUS												
TOTAL	21 321	2 373	3 406	15 542	6 809	8 733	3 400	319	442	2 640	921	1 719
SINGLE	1 142	124	148	870	309	561	207	23	23	160	52	108
MARRIED, SPOUSE PRESENT	9 608	1 531	2 141	5 935	3 545	2 390	662	110	142	410	187	223
MARRIED, SPOUSE ABSENT	395	68	84	243	136	107	167	25	27	115	54	60
SEPARATED	257	50	69	138	94	44	112	23	23	66	39	26
OTHER	138	17	15	105	42	63	55	1	4	49	15	34
WIDOWED	9 076	444	785	7 847	2 441	5 406	2 082	117	179	1 786	528	1 258
DIVORCED	1 100	205	248	647	379	269	283	45	70	168	99	69
WORK EXPERIENCE												
PERSONS	21 321	2 373	3 406	15 542	6 809	8 733	3 400	319	442	2 640	921	1 719
WORKED LAST YEAR	3 904	1 123	1 180	1 600	1 182	417	262	87	64	110	67	42
50 TO 52 WEEKS	2 417	774	790	853	626	225	106	33	36	38	19	19
FULL-TIME	1 503	578	547	378	303	75	23	8	6	9	7	2
49 WEEKS OR LESS	1 486	349	390	747	554	192	156	55	29	72	48	24
FULL-TIME	586	171	196	218	171	47	39	17	7	15	9	6
MAIN REASON FOR WORKING PART YEAR:												
ILL OR DISABLED	177	44	45	87	58	29	23	7	4	13	6	7
KEEPING HOUSE	401	99	101	201	157	44	37	8	11	18	15	3
UNABLE TO FIND WORK	189	91	57	42	33	9	28	19	7	3	3	-
RETIRED	442	46	107	289	221	68	44	6	4	34	22	12
OTHER	277	69	81	126	84	42	23	15	3	5	3	2
MEAN NUMBER OF WEEKS WORKED	42.3	44.5	43.7	39.7	39.7	39.6	31.9	31.2	(B)	30.0	(B)	(B)
DID NOT WORK LAST YEAR	17 418	1 249	2 226	13 943	5 627	8 316	3 139	232	377	2 530	853	1 676
MAIN REASON FOR NOT WORKING:												
ILL OR DISABLED	3 118	272	357	2 489	809	1 680	1 066	105	105	856	296	560
KEEPING HOUSE	6 717	763	1 164	4 789	2 286	2 503	928	98	178	652	268	384
UNABLE TO FIND WORK	92	23	29	40	33	7	18	5	8	6	6	-
RETIRED	7 326	185	655	6 485	2 447	4 038	1 098	23	83	992	274	718
OTHER	166	7	20	139	52	87	28	-	4	24	10	14
FAMILY HOUSEHOLDERS	2 345	303	352	1 690	745	944	392	61	70	261	112	150
WORKED LAST YEAR	485	158	148	179	132	47	44	21	13	10	8	1
50 TO 52 WEEKS	329	110	109	110	83	27	19	9	7	4	4	-
FULL-TIME	215	89	76	50	42	8	6	3	-	3	3	-
49 WEEKS OR LESS	156	48	39	69	49	20	24	12	6	6	5	1
FULL-TIME	49	15	19	14	12	3	4	1	-	3	3	-
MAIN REASON FOR WORKING PART YEAR:												
ILL OR DISABLED	20	8	6	6	6	-	2	-	2	-	-	-
KEEPING HOUSE	30	8	9	14	10	4	8	2	2	3	2	1
UNABLE TO FIND WORK	37	20	13	3	2	1	8	6	2	-	-	-
RETIRED	44	4	6	35	24	10	3	-	-	3	3	-
OTHER	24	8	5	11	7	5	5	4	-	1	1	-
MEAN NUMBER OF WEEKS WORKED	43.6	45.2	45.7	40.4	40.0	(B)	(B)	(B)	(B)	(B)	(B)	(B)
DID NOT WORK LAST YEAR	1 860	145	204	1 511	613	898	349	40	57	252	103	148
MAIN REASON FOR NOT WORKING:												
ILL OR DISABLED	486	52	59	375	113	262	149	20	19	110	40	70
KEEPING HOUSE	596	65	77	454	215	238	110	13	22	75	32	43
UNABLE TO FIND WORK	19	3	7	9	9	-	9	3	3	2	2	-
RETIRED	743	23	61	660	271	389	80	3	14	63	28	35
OTHER	15	2	-	14	5	9	1	-	-	1	1	-

E4–6. Selected Characteristics of the Aged—Poverty Status in 1983 of Persons 60 Years and Over, by Age and Sex (Continued)

[NUMBERS IN THOUSANDS. PERSONS AS OF MARCH 1984.

CHARACTERISTIC	ALL INCOME LEVELS						BELOW POVERTY LEVEL					
	TOTAL	60 AND 61 YEARS	62 TO 64 YEARS	65 YEARS OLD AND OVER TOTAL	65 TO 71 YEARS	72 YEARS AND OVER	TOTAL	60 AND 61 YEARS	62 TO 64 YEARS	65 YEARS OLD AND OVER TOTAL	65 TO 71 YEARS	72 YEARS AND OVER
FEMALE--CONTINUED												
WORK EXPERIENCE--CONTINUED												
UNRELATED INDIVIDUALS	8 084	515	842	6 727	2 319	4 408	2 235	148	227	1 861	598	1 262
WORKED LAST YEAR	1 470	304	377	788	523	265	156	40	31	84	47	36
50 TO 52 WEEKS	928	221	274	433	293	139	60	15	20	25	10	15
FULL-TIME	576	186	186	204	156	49	13	4	3	6	3	2
49 WEEKS OR LESS	542	83	103	355	230	125	96	26	11	59	37	22
FULL-TIME	210	42	60	107	70	37	25	9	4	12	6	6
MAIN REASON FOR WORKING PART YEAR:												
ILL OR DISABLED	89	12	14	63	39	24	16	3	2	11	5	6
KEEPING HOUSE	79	9	8	61	37	24	15	3	2	10	9	1
UNABLE TO FIND WORK	77	32	19	25	21	4	14	7	5	3	3	-
RETIRED	194	14	35	145	100	45	39	4	3	32	19	12
OTHER	103	16	27	61	33	28	12	8	-	4	1	2
MEAN NUMBER OF WEEKS WORKED	42.3	45.2	15.3	39.7	40.3	38.5	30.9	(B)	(B)	27.2	(B)	(B)
DID NOT WORK LAST YEAR	6 614	211	465	5 939	1 795	4 143	2 079	108	195	1 777	551	1 226
MAIN REASON FOR NOT WORKING:												
ILL OR DISABLED	1 435	111	129	1 196	365	830	753	73	67	613	204	409
KEEPING HOUSE	1 485	42	134	1 310	374	936	448	20	73	355	120	234
UNABLE TO FIND WORK	41	4	14	23	16	7	8	-	5	4	4	-
RETIRED	3 570	51	178	3 341	1 016	2 325	850	14	48	787	214	573
OTHER	82	3	9	70	25	45	20	-	2	19	9	10
SOURCE OF INCOME												
PERSONS	21 321	2 373	3 406	15 542	6 809	8 733	3 400	319	442	2 640	921	1 719
EARNINGS ONLY	525	269	187	68	44	25	81	48	20	14	8	6
WAGE OR SALARY INCOME ONLY	492	245	183	64	39	25	74	42	18	14	8	6
SELF-EMPLOYMENT INCOME ONLY	32	24	4	4	4	-	7	6	1	-	-	-
WAGE OR SALARY AND SELF-EMPLOYMENT INCOME	-	-	-	-	-	-	-	-	-	-	-	-
EARNINGS AND INCOME OTHER THAN EARNINGS	3 349	844	986	1 519	1 129	390	170	37	40	93	60	33
EARNINGS AND SOCIAL SECURITY INCOME ONLY	336	21	92	223	151	71	45	5	18	22	16	6
EARNINGS AND SUPPLEMENTAL SECURITY INCOME ONLY	7	2	5	-	-	-	3	2	2	-	-	-
EARNINGS, SOCIAL SECURITY, AND SUPPLEMENTAL SECURITY INCOME ONLY	8	-	-	8	4	3	4	-	-	4	3	1
EARNINGS AND OTHER INCOME ONLY	2 985	820	889	1 277	967	310	114	29	20	65	41	25
OTHER COMBINATIONS	14	2	-	12	7	5	3	2	-	1	-	1
INCOME OTHER THAN EARNINGS ONLY	16 740	1 010	2 052	13 678	5 511	8 168	2 923	171	329	2 423	814	1 609
SOCIAL SECURITY INCOME ONLY	3 096	61	391	2 645	1 046	1 598	976	26	138	812	296	516
SUPPLEMENTAL SECURITY INCOME ONLY	356	45	35	275	87	188	184	29	22	133	46	87
OTHER INCOME ONLY	876	385	236	254	118	137	143	46	15	81	29	52
OTHER TRANSFER PAYMENTS ONLY[1]	52	23	13	16	3	13	29	17	5	6	2	5
SOCIAL SECURITY AND SUPPLEMENTAL SECURITY INCOME ONLY	764	29	41	694	240	454	450	19	32	399	129	270
SOCIAL SECURITY AND OTHER INCOME ONLY	10 851	185	1 162	9 503	3 890	5 613	1 080	30	102	948	303	645
SOCIAL SECURITY INCOME AND OTHER TRANSFER PAYMENTS ONLY[1]	273	7	40	227	75	152	70	2	9	59	12	48
SOCIAL SECURITY AND ''ALL OTHER'' INCOME ONLY[2]	10 577	178	1 123	9 276	3 815	5 462	1 010	28	93	889	291	598
OTHER COMBINATIONS	797	304	186	307	129	177	91	21	19	51	12	39
NO INCOME	708	250	181	277	126	151	227	63	54	110	39	71
FAMILY HOUSEHOLDERS	2 345	303	352	1 690	745	944	392	61	70	261	112	150
EARNINGS ONLY	87	47	29	11	8	3	12	10	2	-	-	-
WAGE OR SALARY INCOME ONLY	83	43	29	11	8	3	10	8	2	-	-	-
SELF-EMPLOYMENT INCOME ONLY	4	4	-	-	-	-	2	2	-	-	-	-
WAGE OR SALARY AND SELF-EMPLOYMENT INCOME	-	-	-	-	-	-	-	-	-	-	-	-
EARNINGS AND INCOME OTHER THAN EARNINGS	399	111	119	168	124	44	32	11	11	10	8	1
EARNINGS AND SOCIAL SECURITY INCOME ONLY	65	9	15	41	27	14	12	2	4	5	4	1
EARNINGS AND SUPPLEMENTAL SECURITY INCOME ONLY	2	2	-	-	-	-	2	2	-	-	-	-
EARNINGS, SOCIAL SECURITY, AND SUPPLEMENTAL SECURITY INCOME ONLY	-	-	-	-	-	-	-	-	-	-	-	-
EARNINGS AND OTHER INCOME ONLY	332	101	104	127	97	30	18	7	6	4	4	-
OTHER COMBINATIONS	-	-	-	-	-	-	-	-	-	-	-	-
INCOME OTHER THAN EARNINGS ONLY	1 809	132	200	1 477	592	885	317	34	54	230	88	142
SOCIAL SECURITY INCOME ONLY	465	11	58	396	159	237	138	9	19	110	45	64
SUPPLEMENTAL SECURITY INCOME ONLY	63	12	10	42	8	33	28	6	10	12	2	10
OTHER INCOME ONLY	49	23	11	15	4	11	17	4	5	8	2	6
OTHER TRANSFER PAYMENTS ONLY[1]	15	5	5	5	1	4	7	1	3	3	1	3
SOCIAL SECURITY AND SUPPLEMENTAL SECURITY INCOME ONLY	115	8	9	97	37	61	46	6	6	35	14	21
SOCIAL SECURITY AND OTHER INCOME ONLY	1 032	40	98	894	370	525	73	4	9	60	22	38
SOCIAL SECURITY INCOME AND OTHER TRANSFER PAYMENTS ONLY[1]	61	6	18	38	15	23	14	2	4	8	4	4
SOCIAL SECURITY AND ''ALL OTHER'' INCOME ONLY[2]	971	34	80	856	355	501	59	2	5	52	18	34
OTHER COMBINATIONS	85	38	15	33	14	18	14	5	5	4	1	3
NO INCOME	51	13	4	34	21	13	32	6	4	22	15	6
UNRELATED INDIVIDUALS	8 084	515	842	6 727	2 319	4 408	2 235	148	227	1 861	598	1 262
EARNINGS ONLY	176	72	62	42	20	22	48	24	11	13	8	6
WAGE OR SALARY INCOME ONLY	169	68	62	39	17	22	44	20	11	13	8	6
SELF-EMPLOYMENT INCOME ONLY	7	4	-	3	3	-	4	4	-	-	-	-
WAGE OR SALARY AND SELF-EMPLOYMENT INCOME	-	-	-	-	-	-	-	-	-	-	-	-
EARNINGS AND INCOME OTHER THAN EARNINGS	1 294	232	315	747	503	244	108	17	21	71	40	31
EARNINGS AND SOCIAL SECURITY INCOME ONLY	133	2	30	101	60	41	25	2	10	14	9	5
EARNINGS AND SUPPLEMENTAL SECURITY INCOME ONLY	2	-	2	-	-	-	2	-	2	-	-	-
EARNINGS, SOCIAL SECURITY, AND SUPPLEMENTAL SECURITY INCOME ONLY	8	-	-	8	4	3	4	-	-	4	3	1
EARNINGS AND OTHER INCOME ONLY	1 144	229	283	632	435	197	75	13	9	53	28	25
OTHER COMBINATIONS	8	2	-	6	4	2	2	2	-	-	-	-

SEE FOOTNOTE(S) AT END OF TABLE.

E4–6. Selected Characteristics of the Aged—Poverty Status in 1983 of Persons 60 Years and Over, by Age and Sex (Continued)

[NUMBERS IN THOUSANDS. PERSONS AS OF MARCH 1984.

CHARACTERISTIC	ALL INCOME LEVELS						BELOW POVERTY LEVEL					
	TOTAL	60 AND 61 YEARS	62 TO 64 YEARS	65 YEARS OLD AND OVER			TOTAL	60 AND 61 YEARS	62 TO 64 YEARS	65 YEARS OLD AND OVER		
				TOTAL	65 TO 71 YEARS	72 YEARS AND OVER				TOTAL	65 TO 71 YEARS	72 YEARS AND OVER

FEMALE--CONTINUED

SOURCE OF INCOME--CONTINUED

UNRELATED INDIVIDUALS--CONTINUED

INCOME OTHER THAN EARNINGS ONLY.	6 551	199	458	5 893	1 789	4 104	2 017	96	189	1 733	545	1 188
SOCIAL SECURITY INCOME ONLY.	1 041	16	86	940	289	651	590	12	74	504	172	331
SUPPLEMENTAL SECURITY INCOME ONLY.	160	18	13	129	48	81	127	16	9	103	41	62
OTHER INCOME ONLY.	118	33	12	74	21	52	80	25	4	51	15	36
OTHER TRANSFER PAYMENTS ONLY¹.	26	15	6	5	1	4	20	15	3	3	1	2
SOCIAL SECURITY AND SUPPLEMENTAL SECURITY INCOME ONLY	431	15	24	393	120	273	347	13	24	310	89	222
SOCIAL SECURITY AND OTHER INCOME ONLY.	4 578	69	298	4 211	1 268	2 944	816	22	68	726	217	509
SOCIAL SECURITY INCOME AND OTHER TRANSFER PAYMENTS ONLY	175	1	12	161	51	110	53	-	2	51	7	44
SOCIAL SECURITY AND ''ALL OTHER'' INCOME ONLY²	4 403	67	285	4 050	1 216	2 834	763	22	66	675	209	465
OTHER COMBINATIONS	222	49	27	147	44	103	57	8	10	39	10	29
NO INCOME.	62	12	6	44	6	38	62	12	6	44	6	38

TYPE OF INCOME

PERSONS³	21 321	2 373	3 406	15 542	6 809	8 733	3 400	319	442	2 640	921	1 719
EARNINGS³.	3 874	1 113	1 174	1 587	1 172	415	251	85	59	106	67	39
WAGE AND SALARY INCOME	3 552	1 038	1 123	1 391	1 056	335	216	76	52	89	59	30
NONFARM SELF-EMPLOYMENT INCOME	343	84	65	194	119	75	30	7	7	16	7	8
FARM SELF-EMPLOYMENT INCOME.	52	14	10	28	18	10	7	4	-	3	3	-
INCOME OTHER THAN EARNINGS³.	20 089	1 853	3 039	15 197	6 639	8 558	3 093	208	369	2 516	874	1 642
SOCIAL SECURITY INCOME	16 529	354	1 999	14 176	6 139	8 037	2 621	84	294	2 244	781	1 463
SUPPLEMENTAL SECURITY INCOME	1 487	101	104	1 282	437	846	824	63	68	693	232	462
OTHER TRANSFER PAYMENTS¹	999	206	198	595	223	373	252	54	29	170	45	125
DIVIDENDS, INTEREST, AND RENT.	14 381	1 530	2 296	10 555	4 760	5 795	1 125	63	116	947	315	632
PRIVATE PENSIONS, GOVERNMENT EMPLOYEE PENSIONS, ALIMONY, ANNUITIES, ETC	4 230	323	579	3 328	1 576	1 752	232	26	44	162	65	98
NO INCOME.	708	250	181	277	126	151	227	63	54	110	39	71

FAMILY HOUSEHOLDERS³	2 345	303	352	1 690	745	944	392	61	70	261	112	150
EARNINGS³.	485	158	148	179	132	47	44	21	13	10	8	1
WAGE AND SALARY INCOME	447	147	143	157	124	33	38	19	10	9	8	1
NONFARM SELF-EMPLOYMENT INCOME	38	9	7	22	8	13	5	2	3	-	-	-
FARM SELF-EMPLOYMENT INCOME.	5	2	-	2	-	2	-	-	-	-	-	-
INCOME OTHER THAN EARNINGS³.	2 208	243	320	1 645	716	929	349	-	-	239	96	143
SOCIAL SECURITY INCOME	1 831	86	211	1 534	668	866	276	45	64	213	89	124
SUPPLEMENTAL SECURITY INCOME	232	36	26	169	59	110	99	21	43	60	21	38
OTHER TRANSFER PAYMENTS¹	193	42	48	103	43	60	43	19	21	24	9	15
DIVIDENDS, INTEREST, AND RENT.	1 275	159	193	923	417	506	76	8	11	50	19	30
PRIVATE PENSIONS, GOVERNMENT EMPLOYEE PENSIONS, ALIMONY, ANNUITIES, ETC	515	67	65	382	204	178	22	5	6	11	6	5
NO INCOME.	51	13	4	34	21	13	32	6	4	22	15	6

UNRELATED INDIVIDUALS³	8 084	515	842	6 727	2 319	4 408	2 235	148	227	1 861	598	1 262
EARNINGS³.	1 471	304	377	789	523	266	156	40	31	84	47	36
WAGE AND SALARY INCOME	1 361	291	370	700	476	224	135	34	31	70	42	28
NONFARM SELF-EMPLOYMENT INCOME	114	12	13	88	51	38	17	4	-	13	5	8
FARM SELF-EMPLOYMENT INCOME.	19	4	3	12	7	5	5	4	-	1	1	-
INCOME OTHER THAN EARNINGS³.	7 845	431	773	6 640	2 292	4 348	2 125	112	209	1 803	584	1 219
SOCIAL SECURITY INCOME	6 892	127	559	6 206	2 102	4 103	1 833	52	177	1 604	513	1 092
SUPPLEMENTAL SECURITY INCOME	821	42	49	731	242	489	627	37	41	549	180	369
OTHER TRANSFER PAYMENTS¹	540	83	78	378	135	244	188	36	12	139	31	108
DIVIDENDS, INTEREST, AND RENT.	5 499	304	541	4 654	1 598	3 055	803	25	68	710	221	489
PRIVATE PENSIONS, GOVERNMENT EMPLOYEE PENSIONS, ALIMONY, ANNUITIES, ETC	2 277	125	244	1 908	775	1 133	179	18	30	131	49	82
NO INCOME.	62	12	6	44	6	38	62	12	6	44	6	38

TENURE AND LIVING ARRANGEMENTS

ALL PERSONS.	21 321	2 373	3 406	15 542	6 809	8 733	3 400	319	442	2 640	921	1 719
LIVING WITH RELATIVES	13 209	1 856	2 555	8 799	4 483	4 315	1 155	171	213	771	317	454
OWNER-OCCUPIED UNITS	11 204	1 574	2 225	7 406	3 790	3 615	805	113	148	544	217	328
RENTER-OCCUPIED UNITS.	2 006	282	330	1 393	693	700	350	58	65	227	100	127
PUBLIC	160	22	27	111	57	54	51	7	15	28	15	14
PRIVATE.	1 845	261	303	1 282	636	645	299	51	50	198	85	113
SUBSIDIZED	77	5	10	61	36	25	21	-	2	19	8	11
FAMILY HOUSEHOLDERS.	2 345	303	352	1 690	745	944	392	61	70	261	112	150
OWNER-OCCUPIED UNITS	1 777	209	269	1 299	570	728	242	33	39	170	76	95
RENTER-OCCUPIED UNITS.	568	94	83	391	175	216	150	27	32	91	36	55
PUBLIC	57	10	15	32	19	13	23	5	9	10	6	3
PRIVATE.	511	84	67	359	156	203	127	23	23	81	30	52
SUBSIDIZED	23	2	-	21	9	12	7	-	-	7	3	4
LIVING WITH NONRELATIVES ONLY.	493	45	74	373	129	245	182	7	23	151	54	97
OWNER-OCCUPIED UNITS	307	30	49	228	82	146	103	4	15	84	31	53
RENTER-OCCUPIED UNITS.	186	16	25	145	46	99	79	3	8	67	23	44
PUBLIC	10	4	-	6	-	5	5	1	-	4	-	4
PRIVATE.	175	11	25	139	46	93	74	3	8	63	22	41
SUBSIDIZED	3	-	-	3	2	1	3	-	-	3	2	1
LIVING ALONE	7 619	472	777	6 370	2 197	4 174	2 063	141	205	1 717	550	1 167
OWNER-OCCUPIED UNITS	4 881	304	528	4 049	1 445	2 603	1 132	70	115	946	317	630
RENTER-OCCUPIED UNITS.	2 738	167	250	2 322	751	1 570	932	71	90	771	233	538
PUBLIC	446	19	36	390	132	259	232	13	16	203	63	139
PRIVATE.	2 293	148	213	1 931	620	1 312	700	58	74	568	170	398
SUBSIDIZED	333	17	16	301	76	224	123	10	3	97	26	71

¹OTHER TRANSFER PAYMENTS INCLUDE PUBLIC ASSISTANCE, UNEMPLOYMENT COMPENSATION, WORKMEN'S COMPENSATION, AND VETERANS' PAYMENTS.
²''ALL OTHER'' INCOME INCLUDES DIVIDENDS, INTEREST, RENT, PRIVATE PENSIONS, GOVERNMENT EMPLOYEE PENSIONS, ALIMONY, AND ANNUITY INCOME.
³DETAIL DOES NOT ADD TO TOTAL BECAUSE SOME PERSONS RECEIVE MORE THAN ONE OF THE SPECIFIED TYPES OF INCOME.

E4–7. Age, Type of Residence, Region, and Work Experience—Poverty Status of Persons, by Race and Spanish Origin, 1983

(Numbers in thousands. Persons as of March 1984.

| Characteristic | Total | | | White | | | Black | | | Spanish origin[1] | | |
| | | Below poverty level | | | Below poverty level | | | Below poverty level | | | Below poverty level | |
	Total	Number	Percent of total	Total	Number	Percent of total	Total	Number	Percent of total	Total	Number	Percent of total
AGE												
Both Sexes												
Total	231 612	35 266	15.2	197 671	23 974	12.1	27 668	9 885	35.7	14 938	4 249	28.4
Under 3 years	10 838	2 720	25.1	8 726	1 747	20.0	1 745	849	48.7	1 011	412	40.7
3 to 5 years	10 368	2 582	24.9	8 414	1 655	19.7	1 584	797	50.3	998	428	42.9
6 to 13 years	26 437	5 780	21.9	21 565	3 692	17.1	3 938	1 819	46.2	2 469	925	37.5
14 and 15 years	7 268	1 399	19.3	5 978	870	14.6	1 050	463	44.1	590	199	33.8
16 to 21 years	23 021	4 132	17.9	19 037	2 611	13.7	3 301	1 343	40.7	1 726	516	29.9
22 to 44 years	83 118	10 511	12.6	71 070	7 318	10.3	9 621	2 735	28.4	5 426	1 267	23.4
45 to 54 years	22 240	2 023	9.1	19 408	1 420	7.3	2 286	536	23.5	1 235	192	15.6
55 to 59 years	11 310	1 173	10.4	10 066	859	8.5	1 033	290	28.1	478	83	17.2
60 to 64 years	10 723	1 234	11.5	9 634	941	9.8	920	257	27.9	359	78	21.7
65 years and over	26 291	3 711	14.1	23 771	2 860	12.0	2 191	796	36.3	645	149	23.1
Total, under 18 years	62 140	13 807	22.2	50 628	8 778	17.3	9 380	4 384	46.7	5 651	2 160	38.2
Related children under 18 years	61 943	13 668	22.1	50 469	8 674	17.2	9 350	4 354	46.6	5 622	2 138	38.0
Total, 5 to 17 years	44 243	9 334	21.1	36 188	5 909	16.3	6 543	2 999	45.8	3 955	1 457	36.8
Related children 5 to 17 years	44 046	9 194	20.9	36 029	5 805	16.1	6 513	2 969	45.6	3 926	1 434	36.5
Male												
Total	112 280	15 182	13.5	96 300	10 294	10.7	12 902	4 180	32.4	7 217	1 914	26.5
Under 16 years	28 063	6 253	22.3	22 855	3 928	17.2	4 190	1 994	47.6	2 616	1 006	38.5
16 to 21 years	11 487	1 834	16.0	9 553	1 125	11.8	1 594	621	39.0	801	222	27.8
22 to 44 years	40 969	4 273	10.4	35 440	3 114	8.8	4 388	949	21.6	2 551	490	19.2
45 to 54 years	10 747	822	7.7	9 475	614	6.5	1 014	182	17.9	607	76	12.6
55 to 59 years	5 322	456	8.6	4 809	342	7.1	441	107	24.2	207	31	14.8
60 to 64 years	4 944	473	9.6	4 458	375	8.4	395	79	19.9	164	27	16.7
65 years and over	10 748	1 072	10.0	9 709	796	8.2	879	249	28.3	272	61	22.3
Total, under 18 years	31 734	6 885	21.7	25 900	4 308	16.6	4 718	2 221	47.1	2 905	1 106	38.1
Related children under 18 years	31 694	6 851	21.6	25 869	4 282	16.6	4 712	2 214	47.0	2 898	1 100	37.9
Female												
Total	119 332	20 084	16.8	101 371	13 680	13.5	14 766	5 704	38.6	7 721	2 335	30.2
Under 16 years	26 847	6 229	23.2	21 828	4 037	18.5	4 125	1 934	46.9	2 453	958	39.1
16 to 21 years	11 533	2 298	19.9	9 484	1 486	15.7	1 707	722	42.3	926	293	31.7
22 to 44 years	42 149	6 239	14.8	35 630	4 205	11.8	5 233	1 785	34.1	2 875	777	27.0
45 to 54 years	11 493	1 201	10.4	9 933	806	8.1	1 272	355	27.9	629	116	18.4
55 to 59 years	5 988	717	12.0	5 258	516	9.8	592	184	31.0	271	52	19.1
60 to 64 years	5 779	761	13.2	5 176	565	10.9	525	178	34.0	195	51	25.9
65 years and over	15 542	2 640	17.0	14 062	2 064	14.7	1 312	547	41.7	372	88	23.7
Total, under 18 years	30 406	6 922	22.8	24 728	4 470	18.1	4 661	2 163	46.4	2 746	1 054	38.4
Related children under 18 years	30 250	6 817	22.5	24 600	4 392	17.9	4 638	2 140	46.1	2 723	1 038	38.1
TYPE OF RESIDENCE												
Total	231 612	35 266	15.2	197 671	23 974	12.1	27 668	9 885	35.7	14 938	4 249	28.4
Nonfarm	226 047	33 948	15.0	192 248	22 733	11.8	27 567	9 828	35.7	14 761	4 174	28.3
Farm	5 565	1 317	23.7	5 423	1 241	22.9	101	56	55.7	177	75	42.4
Inside metropolitan areas	157 615	21 750	13.8	131 577	13 770	10.5	21 039	7 017	33.4	12 817	3 567	27.8
Inside central cities	64 907	12 872	19.8	47 384	6 661	14.1	14 905	5 514	37.0	7 511	2 394	31.9
In poverty areas	11 513	5 044	43.8	4 959	1 794	36.2	6 222	3 090	49.7	2 248	1 086	48.3
Outside central cities	92 709	8 878	9.6	84 193	7 110	8.4	6 135	1 503	24.5	5 306	1 173	22.1
In poverty areas	4 361	1 288	29.5	3 076	708	23.0	1 225	554	45.2	764	297	38.8
Outside metropolitan areas	73 997	13 516	18.3	66 094	10 204	15.4	6 628	2 867	43.3	2 121	682	32.1
In poverty areas	25 154	6 393	25.4	20 240	4 089	20.2	4 350	2 043	47.0	937	384	41.0
REGION												
Total	231 612	35 266	15.2	197 671	23 974	12.1	27 668	9 885	35.7	14 938	4 249	28.4
Northeast	49 132	6 561	13.4	43 133	4 745	11.0	5 198	1 688	32.5	2 627	1 028	39.
North Central	58 295	8 536	14.6	52 395	6 353	12.1	5 206	2 039	39.2	1 093	286	26.2
South	78 570	13 484	17.2	62 861	7 729	12.3	14 641	5 485	37.5	4 880	1 259	25.8
West	45 616	6 684	14.7	39 282	5 148	13.1	2 622	672	25.6	6 339	1 675	26.4

E4–7. Age, Type of Residence, Region, and Work Experience—Poverty Status of Persons, by Race and Spanish Origin, 1983 (Continued)

(Numbers in thousands. Persons as of March 1984.

Characteristic	Total			White			Black			Spanish origin[1]		
		Below poverty level			Below poverty level			Below poverty level			Below poverty level	
	Total	Number	Percent of total	Total	Number	Percent of total	Total	Number	Percent of total	Total	Number	Percent of total
WORK EXPERIENCE IN 1983												
Total, 15 years and over	180 303	23 465	13.0	155 967	16 439	10.5	19 877	6 178	31.1	10 145	2 380	23.5
Worked..................	118 629	9 440	8.0	104 325	7 165	6.9	11 477	1 966	17.1	6 395	933	14.6
50 to 52 weeks	77 286	3 072	4.0	68 195	2 440	3.6	7 210	533	7.4	3 962	301	7.6
Full time.......................	66 838	2 066	3.1	58 866	1 668	2.8	6 305	315	5.0	3 504	224	6.4
49 weeks or less[2]	41 343	6 368	15.4	36 130	4 726	13.1	4 266	1 433	33.6	2 432	632	26.0
Duration of unemployment:												
1 to 4 weeks.....................	3 388	458	13.5	2 991	343	11.5	319	95	29.7	213	53	25.0
5 to 14 weeks..................	6 173	866	14.0	5 371	653	12.1	687	194	28.2	388	81	20.9
15 to 26 weeks	4 985	940	18.9	4 167	688	16.5	699	223	31.9	368	114	30.9
27 weeks or more	4 472	1 406	31.5	3 631	1 007	27.7	729	363	49.8	363	140	38.5
Did not work	60 795	13 993	23.0	50 898	9 250	18.2	8 297	4 206	50.7	3 692	1 446	39.2
Main reason did not work:												
Ill or disabled	8 707	2 909	33.4	6 764	1 870	27.6	1 790	975	54.5	451	185	41.0
Keeping house	21 141	4 472	21.2	18 728	3 217	17.2	1 864	1 083	58.1	1 657	685	41.4
Going to school	10 061	2 364	23.5	7 435	1 287	17.3	2 094	898	42.9	882	308	34.9
Unable to find work..............	3 713	1 849	49.8	2 352	1 002	42.6	1 264	788	62.4	225	130	57.6
Retired	16 215	2 001	12.3	14 907	1 628	10.9	1 083	342	31.6	376	81	21.5
All other reasons	959	398	41.5	713	246	34.4	202	120	59.6	100	57	56.9
In Armed Forces	879	32	3.6	743	23	3.1	104	6	5.8	59	2	(B)

[1]Persons of Spanish orgin may be of any race.
[2]Includes 'no weeks' unemployed, not shown separately.

F. Expenditures for the Elderly

FEDERAL OUTLAYS FOR THE ELDERLY, SOCIAL SECURITY, VETERANS

In 1985, the federal government spent $263.5 billion, or 27.5 percent of the total federal budget, on expenses benefitting the elderly. Of this amount, over half (55 percent) is for Social Security and over one-fourth (26.5 percent) for Medicare and Medicaid. The remainder goes for the support of older veterans, for retirement pay of military and civil service employees and their survivors, supplemental social insurance (SSI), and miscellaneous other programs. Social Security and all but a portion of Medicare are financed through dedicated taxes collected expressly and exclusively for that purpose. About five percent of the elderly receive SSI benefits.

Veterans represent an increasing proportion of the elderly male population. While more than three million veterans received compensation, pensions, or retirement in 1983, the largest expenditure of the Veterans Administration is for health care of older veterans.

HEALTH CARE EXPENDITURES

The elderly population is a major user of health care services. Health care costs are highest during the last two years of a person's life. Medicare was created in 1965 to help pay the health costs of older Americans and the disabled; Medicaid is a federal and state program which helps low-income individuals of all ages to get health care. Due to inflation and the high price of advanced medical technology and drugs, expenditures for health care for all age groups have been rising faster than any other category of the Consumer Price Index, requiring ever larger funding from public and private sources. In 1970, about 9 percent of the total federal budget went for health care; in 1985, about 11 percent were used for this purpose. As the average age of the population has increased, not only federal but personal out-of-pocket expenditures of older individuals for health care have risen. These expenditures averaged over $1,500 or about 15 percent of total income in 1984; this is a higher proportion than personal health care expenditures amounted to before Medicare and Medicaid were enacted, and it is expected to increase in the future.

PUBLIC AND PRIVATE PENSIONS

In 1985, federal pension programs other than Social Security amounted to about 10 percent of all federal outlays for the elderly. State and local government pension plans paid approximately 18 billion dollars to retired or disabled employees and their dependents. In 1983, about one-half of all employees in the private sector were covered by pension plans.

F1. OVERVIEW OF FEDERAL OUTLAYS

F1-1. Budget Outlays by Superfunction as a Percent of GNP, 1940–1990

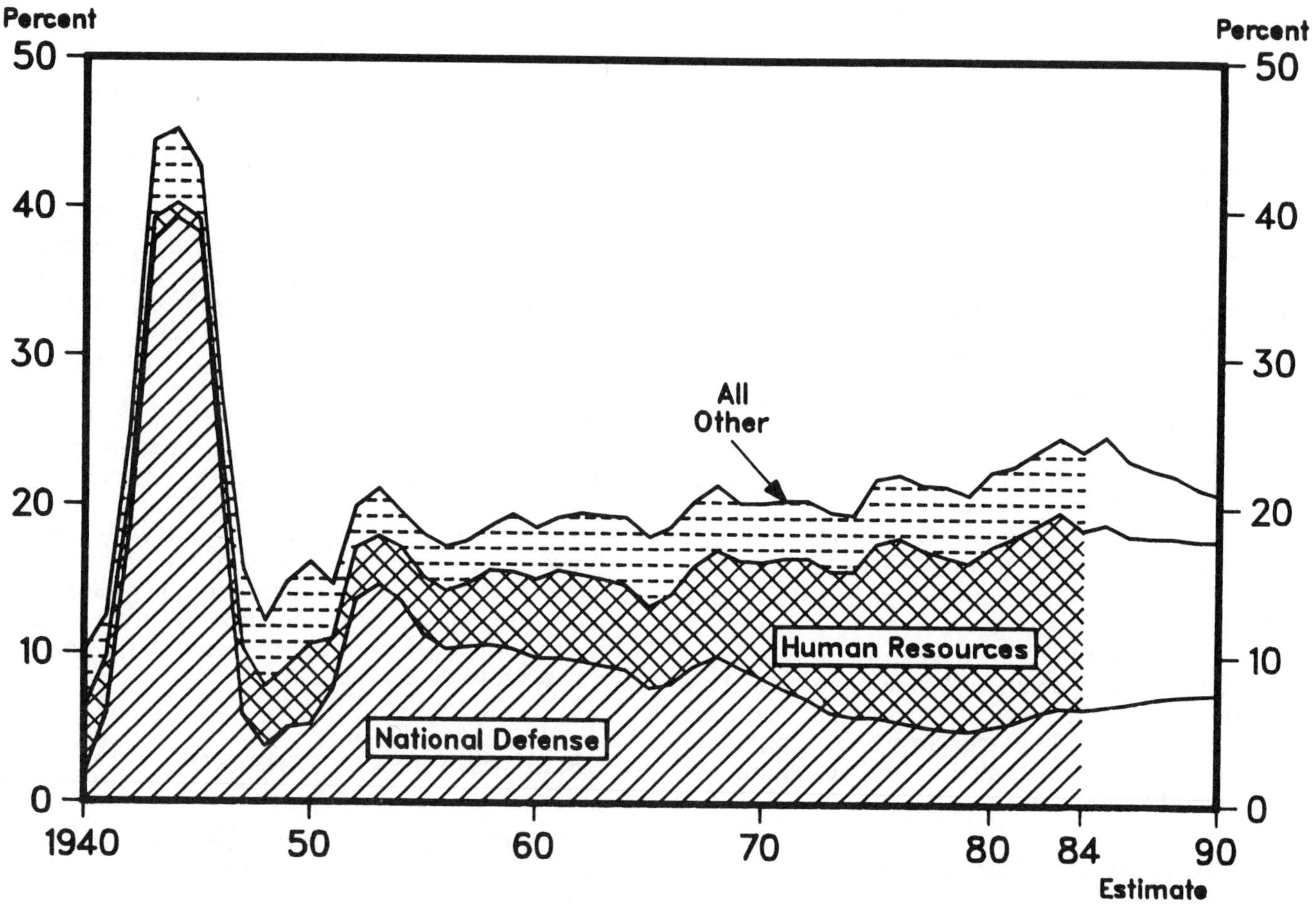

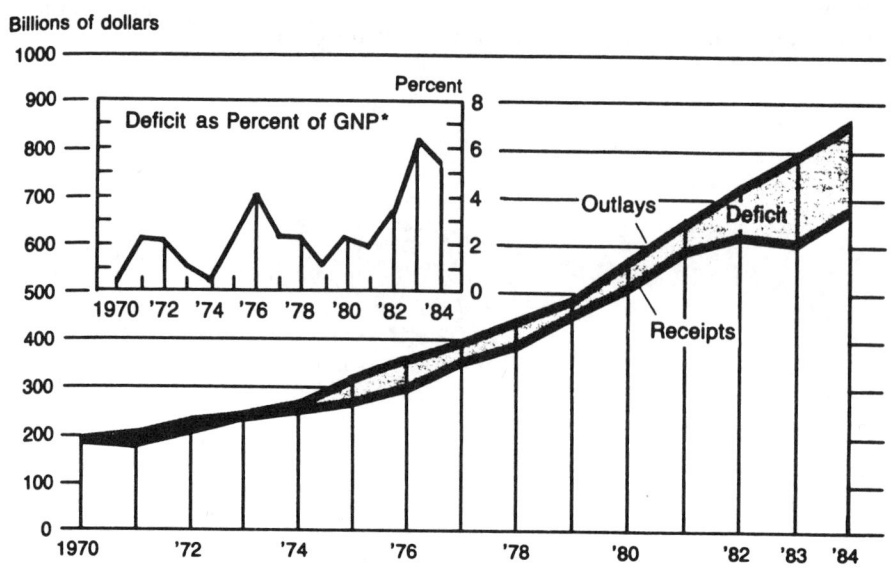

F1-2. Federal Budget Receipts and Outlays: 1970 to 1984

F1–3. Federal Budget Receipts and Outlays as a Percent of GNP: 1970 to 1984

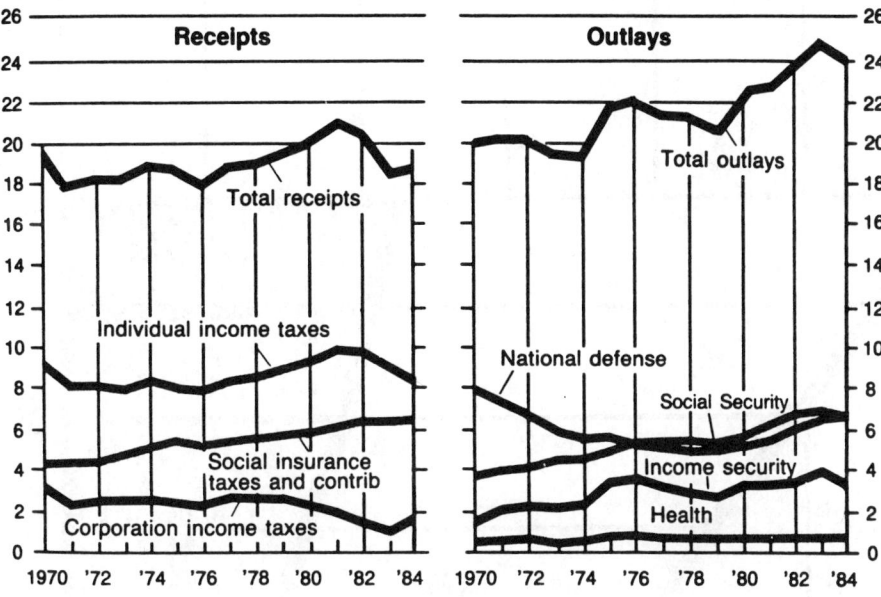

F1–4. Federal Outlays Benefiting the Elderly,[1] 1984–1985

(In millions of dollars)

	Fiscal year—	
	1984 actual	1985 estimate
Medicare[2]	53,307.0	61,391.0
Medicaid	7,435.0	8,508.0
Other federal health[2]	4,064.6	4,361.0
Health subtotal	64,806.6	74,260.0
Social Security	129,284.0	140,381.0
Supplemental Security Income (SSI)[3]	2,832.0	3,169.0
Veterans compensation-pensions	5,031.0	5,425.0
Other retired, disabled, and survivors benefits	24,645.7	26,018.8
Retirement/disability subtotal	161,792.7	174,993.8
National Institute on Aging	100.0	125.0
Older American volunteer programs	91.0	103.0
Senior community service employment	321.3	318.9
Administration on Aging	824.4	805.9
Subsidized housing[4] [5]	4,382.6	9,549.5
Section 202 elderly housing loans[6]	595.0	514.4
Food stamps[7]	610.0	615.3
Social services (Title XX)	366.2	369.0
Low income home energy assistance[8]	622.0	630.0
Other miscellaneous[9]	1,323.0	1,279.7
Other subtotal	1,598.2	1,614.3
Total elderly outlays	235,835.0	263,564.5
Percent of total federal outlays[10]	27.7	27.5

[1] Most estimates are based on federal agency information, are for recipients aged 65 and over, and include the effects of proposed legislation such as COLA freeze. Some federal programs (e.g., consumer activities, USDA extension services, national park services) have been excluded due to lack of data.

[2] Rough estimates due to limited data.

[3] Fiscal year 1983 and fiscal year 1988 outlays represent 13-month benefit periods. Fiscal year 1984 and fiscal year 1990 outlays reflect an 11-month benefit period.

[4] HUD defines "elderly" beneficiaries as households with head of household age 62 and over.

[5] Financing changed from loan guarantees to direct loans results in one time fiscal year 1985 outlay increase in Public Housing.

[6] Reflects net disbursements for new direct loans.

[7] Includes Nutrition Assistance to Puerto Rico.

[8] Based on 30 percent of total program obligations.

[9] Drop in unemployment rates and associated reduction in outlays causes the decrease between fiscal years 1983–1985.

[10] Total federal outlays includes items categorized as off-budget before fiscal year 1985.

SOURCE: Office of Management and Budget.

F1–5. Social Welfare Expenditures under Public Programs: 1970 to 1982

Billions of dollars

Source Chart prepared by U S Bureau of the Census

F1-6. Federal Benefits for the Aged, by Type of Benefit: 1971 to 1984

[For years ending **June 30** except, beginning **1979**, ending **Sept. 30**. Reflects outlays, including effects of proposed legislation, for recipients aged 65 and over in most cases. Estimates based on Federal agency information—which may be administrative counts, samples, or less accurate estimates from Federal, State and program staff. Other Federal programs that assist the elderly (e.g. consumer activities, USDA extension service, National Park Service) have been excluded due to data limitations]

TYPE OF BENEFIT	BENEFITS (bil. dol.)								PERCENT		
	1971	1975	1979	1980	1981	1982	1983	1984	1971	1980	1984
Total outlays	44.0	81.3	116.4	144.2	173.3	196.0	218.4	238.0	100.0	100.0	100.0
Cash benefits	34.2	64.7	85.2	101.3	122.3	137.2	150.0	161.1	77.7	70.2	67.7
Social security	27.1	51.8	69.0	81.2	97.1	111.2	122.5	132.2	61.6	56.3	55.5
Railroad employees	1.7	2.8	3.2	3.6	4.1	4.0	3.8	4.1	3.9	2.5	1.7
Federal civilian employees	2.3	5.5	6.2	7.8	11.6	11.1	11.8	12.4	5.2	5.4	5.2
Uniformed services members	.7	1.1	.8	1.8	2.0	3.0	3.3	4.0	1.6	1.2	1.7
Coal miners [1]	.1	.2	1.1	1.3	1.2	1.3	1.3	1.3	.2	.9	.5
Supplemental security income	[2] 1.4	1.8	1.7	2.3	2.6	2.7	2.9	2.5	[2] 3.2	1.6	1.1
Veterans pensions [3]	.9	1.5	3.2	3.3	3.7	3.9	4.4	4.6	2.0	2.3	1.9
In-kind benefits	9.8	16.6	31.2	36.8	45.0	52.8	59.5	68.1	22.3	25.5	28.6
Medicare	7.5	12.8	24.6	29.3	35.8	42.6	48.4	56.4	17.0	20.3	23.7
Medicaid	1.9	2.6	4.3	4.7	6.0	6.0	6.5	6.9	4.3	3.3	2.9
Food stamps	.2	1.0	.5	.5	.9	.9	.6	.6	.5	.3	.3
Subsidized public housing	.2	.4	1.6	2.3	2.3	3.3	4.0	4.2	.5	1.6	1.8
Other [4]	(NA)	(NA)	.1	6.1	6.0	6.0	8.9	8.8	(NA)	4.2	3.7

NA Not available. [1] Prior to 1979, represents benefit for coal miners' widows only. [2] Represents Federal grants to States for aid to the aged, blind, and disabled. [3] Includes other veterans' compensation for aged beginning 1979. [4] Includes Administration on Aging, National Institute on Aging, ACTION, White House Conference on Aging, other Federal health programs, other Social Security benefits, Farmers Home Administration and Elderly Housing Loans programs, social services, energy assistance, unemployment, and other miscellaneous discretionary program outlays.

Source: U.S. Office of Management and Budget, *The Budget of the United States Government*, annual; and unpublished data.

F1-7. Public Aid Payments: 1970 to 1983

[**In millions of dollars.** Supplemental Security Income data cover federally- and State-administered payments.

PROGRAM	1970	1975	1976	1977	1978	1979	1980	1981	1982	1983
Payments, total	8,443	16,313	17,499	18,222	18,577	19,477	21,994	(NA)	(NA)	(NA)
Supplemental Security Income	(X)	5,878	6,066	6,306	6,552	7,075	7,941	8,593	8,981	9,404
Aged	(X)	2,605	2,508	2,448	2,433	2,526	2,734	2,818	2,824	2,814
Blind	(X)	131	138	146	152	166	190	206	217	229
Disabled	(X)	3,142	3,422	3,709	3,966	4,381	5,014	5,566	5,909	6,357
Public assistance	8,443	10,435	11,433	11,916	12,025	12,402	14,048	(NA)	(NA)	(NA)
Old-age assistance	1,862	5	5	5	5	9	9	9	8	(NA)
Blind	98	(Z)	(Z)	(Z)	(Z)	(Z)	(Z)	(Z)	(Z)	(NA)
Permanently, totally disabled	1,000	3	3	3	4	9	9	10	10	(NA)
Families with dependent children	4,853	9,211	10,141	10,604	10,730	11,069	12,475	12,981	12,878	(NA)
Emergency assistance	11	78	56	66	81	84	113	124	102	(NA)
General assistance	618	1,138	1,228	1,238	1,205	1,231	1,442	(NA)	(NA)	(NA)

NA Not available. X Not applicable. Z Less than $500,000.

Source: U.S. Social Security Administration, *Social Security Bulletin*, monthly; and *Public Assistance Statistics*, monthly.

F1–8. Public Income-Maintenance Programs: Cash Benefit Payments, 1940–85

[In millions; includes payments outside the United States and benefits to spouses and children where applicable]

Period	Total [1][2]	Retirement, disability, and survivor benefits							Unemployment benefits		Temporary disability benefits		Workers' compensation benefits [14]	Public assistance payments [2][15]	Supplemental security income payments [16]
		Monthly				Lump sum [9]									
		OASDI [3]	Railroad retirement [4]	Public employee retirement [5]		Veterans' pension and compensation [8]	OASDI	Other [10]	State laws [11]	Railroad [12]	State laws [12]	Railroad [13]			
				Federal civil service [6]	Other [7]										
1940	$2,171.4	$23.5	$115.6	$62.0	$183.1	$423.5	$11.8	$24.9	$518.7	$16.0	...	...	$161.0	$631.3	...
1945	3,507.5	247.8	138.9	83.9	253.7	952.1	26.1	39.2	572.5	2.4	$4.7	...	283.0	902.8	...
1950	8,395.4	928.4	298.1	184.2	600.4	2,223.8	32.7	54.0	1,407.8	59.8	89.3	$28.1	415.0	2,073.9	...
1955	14,478.1	4,855.3	560.8	370.4	1,043.0	2,745.9	112.9	82.8	1,466.9	93.3	192.7	51.9	591.0	2,311.3	...
1960	25,564.0	11,080.5	942.4	804.5	1,793.3	3,436.9	164.3	135.2	2,867.1	157.7	311.3	56.9	860.0	2,953.9	...
1965	36,335.2	18,093.7	1,133.2	1,366.0	3,229.8	4,196.0	216.9	203.6	2,283.4	60.5	425.9	40.8	1,214.0	3,763.7	...
1970	60,473.8	31,569.8	1,756.2	2,796.6	6,369.4	5,480.1	293.6	288.6	4,183.7	38.7	664.6	56.2	1,981.0	4,864.4	...
1975	138,597.7	66,585.7	3,282.7	7,511.2	13,834.7	7,668.2	337.0	420.8	18,188.1	89.5	902.4	47.6	4,568.0	9,288.5	5,878.2
1976	151,467.9	75,332.1	3,570.1	8,563.2	15,679.9	8,409.2	332.5	441.5	16,537.2	134.7	930.8	84.4	5,204.0	10,196.3	6,065.8
1977	162,326.7	84,263.8	3,823.8	9,605.1	17,531.9	9,078.7	312.0	441.6	13,337.8	99.8	954.9	74.2	5,950.0	10,669.1	6,306.0
1978	172,822.2	92,530.7	4,021.4	10,898.6	19,638.9	9,595.6	344.5	485.5	9,890.8	124.5	1,045.2	68.5	6,813.0	10,705.6	6,551.7
1979	192,772.7	103,973.7	4,377.5	12,498.4	22,549.4	10,570.7	298.6	531.9	10,212.0	82.5	1,177.8	60.9	8,507.0	10,742.6	7,206.5
1980	227,597.4	120,271.7	4,866.6	15,042.5	25,558.8	11,358.4	250.2	606.0	18,756.5	176.1	1,299.8	63.2	9,632.0	12,144.4	7,857.5
1981	241,037.4	128,740.6	5,371.1	17,523.1	28,884.0	12,476.7	226.0	587.8	13,538.5	207.2	1,525.0	58.4	10,596.0	13,188.2	8,529.4
1982	282,976.9	155,699.0	5,843.2	19,283.9	32,090.4	13,315.4	135.2	567.0	20,735.3	338.7	1,567.9	55.6	11,403.0	13,030.4	8,989.9
1983	(17)	166,902.1	6,043.2	20,592.4	(17)	13,680.5	130.6	(17)	18,903.8	339.1	1,580.2	50.1	12,183.0	13,891.8	9,524.1
1984	(17)	175,499.9	6,131.2	21,471.5	(17)	13,832.4	167.9	(17)	13,495.5	152.9	1,800.0	42.0	13,650.0	14,581.9	10,432.7
1984															
May	...	14,519.6	515.5	1,776.2	...	1,142.0	11.0	16.2	1,119.8	10.1	...	6.0	87.2	1,205.4	861.4
June	...	14,626.8	500.4	1,785.5	...	1,155.8	14.0	11.4	957.8	7.1	...	5.7	87.0	1,184.0	872.4
July	...	14,499.7	507.2	1,791.8	...	1,156.9	10.4	16.0	983.7	6.1	...	6.0	87.0	1,195.7	862.3
Aug	...	14,485.4	505.6	1,789.7	...	1,181.5	10.1	13.9	1,028.5	7.3	...	6.8	87.8	1,230.2	867.2
Sept	...	14,484.7	513.6	1,803.1	...	1,156.1	10.8	12.9	865.3	6.6	...	6.2	87.8	1,198.4	887.1
Oct	...	14,586.1	506.6	1,800.6	...	1,154.2	12.2	17.5	951.4	8.9	...	7.0	85.8	1,219.8	871.0
Nov	...	14,630.2	516.5	1,798.5	...	1,150.6	9.5	11.5	951.4	10.4	...	6.7	85.5	1,230.8	881.8
Dec	...	15,401.2	529.1	1,801.4	...	1,179.9	8.1	12.5	1,136.8	12.5	...	5.6	85.2	1,237.4	882.5
1985															
Jan	...	15,282.6	515.8	1,858.6	...	1,160.5	12.0	16.8	1,518.9	19.4	...	6.4	84.7	1,250.7	908.3
Feb	...	15,411.8	519.2	1,883.3	...	1,177.4	11.2	12.0	1,461.7	15.4	...	5.8	85.8	1,255.9	916.4
Mar	...	15,543.2	527.6	1,887.1	...	1,185.4	14.9	14.2	1,453.2	15.7	...	6.1	87.0	1,275.9	916.5
Apr	...	15,400.6	520.8	1,912.8	...	1,179.2	14.0	16.3	1,359.5	12.8	...	6.4	86.8	1,275.6	933.5
May	...	15,365.7	523.7	1,897.8	...	1,166.5	11.9	14.6	(17)	8.1	...	5.8	86.1	1,248.9	932.3

[1] Emergency relief funds of $1,630.3 million in 1940 total, not included elsewhere. Includes training allowances to unemployed workers under Area Redevelopment Act and Manpower Development and Training Act for 1961-75, not shown separately.

[2] Beginning December 1980, includes public assistance revisions for 1940-79.

[3] Retirement and survivor benefits beginning 1940; disability benefits beginning 1957. Beginning October 1966, includes special benefits authorized by 1966 legislation for persons aged 72 or older not insured under the regular or transitional provisions of the Social Security Act.

[4] Includes annuities to widows under joint-and-survivor election before 1947. Beginning February 1967, includes supplemental annuities for career railroad employees.

[5] Excludes refunds of contributions to employees who leave service.

[6] Includes survivor annuities under joint-and-survivor elections before 1948.

[7] Represents Federal contributory systems other than civil service, Federal noncontributory systems for civilian employees and career military personnel, and systems for State and local employees. Monthly data not available.

[8] Payments to veterans and survivors of deceased veterans, including special allowances for survivors of veterans who did not qualify under OASDHI (Servicemen's and Veterans' Survivor Benefit Act of 1956) and through June 1973, subsistence payments to disabled veterans undergoing training.

[9] Death payments.

[10] Includes annual and monthly data for railroad retirement, veterans' programs, and Federal civil service retirement. For "other" public employee systems, annual data only.

[11] Annual and monthly totals include regular State unemployment insurance program and payments made by States as agents of the Federal Government under the Federal employees' unemployment compensation program and under the Ex-Servicemen's Compensation Act of 1958. Annual data only for payments under Servicemen's Readjustment Act of 1944, Veterans' Readjustment Act of 1952, Trade Expansion Act of 1962, Disaster Relief Act of 1970, and the temporary and permanent extended unemployment insurance programs. Beginning 1961, includes program in Puerto Rico. Beginning 1981, State unemployment insurance and Ex-Servicemen's Compensation Act only.

[12] Benefits in Rhode Island (from 1943), in California (from 1947), in New Jersey (from 1949), in New York (from 1950), in Puerto Rico (from 1970), in Hawaii (from 1972), including payments under private plans where applicable. Monthly data not available.

[13] Benefits began 1947.

[14] Under Federal workers' compensation laws and under State laws paid by private insurance carriers, State funds, and self-insurers. Beginning 1959, includes data for Alaska and Hawaii. Monthly data refer only to Federal black lung benefits administered by Social Security Administration (starting 1970).

[15] Includes aid to families with dependent children and general assistance. Through 1973 includes old-age assistance, aid to the blind, and aid to the permanently and totally disabled. Includes payments to intermediate-care facilities (July 1968-December 1971), and payments for emergency assistance, beginning July 1969. Includes money payments under medical assistance for the aged (1960-69). Excludes medical vendor payments. Starting 1974, includes money payments to the aged, blind, and disabled in Guam, Puerto Rico, and the Virgin Islands under federally aided public assistance programs.

[16] Supersedes the public assistance programs of old-age assistance, aid to the blind, and aid to the permanently and totally disabled in the 50 States and the District of Columbia, beginning 1974; beginning 1978, in the Northern Mariana Islands. Annual, but not monthly, totals include payments under State-administered supplementation programs.

[17] Data not available.

Source: Based on reports of administrative agencies on a checks-issued basis (including retroactive payments) where available. Data for public assistance and State unemployment insurance programs adjusted monthly, other data adjusted annually.

F1–9. Public Assistance: Total Money Payments, by Program, and Emergency Assistance Payments, 1945–83

[In thousands. Data subject to revision.]

Year	Total [1]	Money payments						Emergency assistance payments [4]
		Total [2]	Old-age assistance [3]	Aid to the blind [3]	Aid to the permanently and totally disabled [3]	Aid to families with dependent children	General assistance	
1945	$990,704	$990,704	$726,550	$26,557	...	$149,667	$87,930	...
1950	2,372,204	2,372,204	1,461,624	52,698	$7,967	551,653	298,262	...
1955	2,525,585	2,525,585	1,490,352	67,958	135,168	617,841	214,266	...
1960	3,276,707	3,276,707	1,629,541	86,231	237,366	1,000,784	322,465	...
1961	3,426,895	3,426,895	1,571,309	84,739	256,910	1,156,769	355,991	...
1962	3,531,067	3,531,067	1,571,162	84,039	282,711	1,298,774	292,709	...
1963	3,666,628	3,666,628	1,615,023	85,335	318,948	1,365,851	279,623	...
1964	3,842,754	3,842,754	1,612,983	86,558	357,856	1,510,352	272,737	...
1965	4,025,903	4,025,903	1,600,708	85,121	417,720	1,660,186	259,225	...
1966	4,336,075	4,336,075	1,633,675	85,615	487,301	1,863,925	263,866	...
1967	4,956,901	4,956,901	1,702,091	87,711	574,574	2,266,400	325,847	...
1968	5,706,592	5,694,890	1,676,632	88,885	658,589	2,849,298	421,211	$2,445
1969	6,893,920	6,668,986	1,752,730	92,204	788,079	3,563,427	472,360	11,030
1970	8,864,428	8,431,848	1,862,412	98,292	999,861	4,852,964	618,319	11,396
1971	10,814,361	10,143,441	1,888,878	100,840	1,189,636	6,203,528	760,559	19,843
1972	11,066,718	11,022,538	1,876,755	105,515	1,390,509	6,909,260	740,499	44,180
1973	11,397,212	11,357,947	1,743,465	104,373	1,609,572	7,212,035	688,502	39,265
1974	8,813,762	8,749,731	4,725	88	2,947	7,916,563	825,408	64,031
1975	10,434,353	10,356,837	4,599	79	2,953	9,210,995	1,138,211	77,516
1976	11,431,072	11,375,923	4,783	75	3,066	10,140,134	1,227,865	55,779
1977	11,915,076	11,848,824	4,938	76	3,426	10,602,775	1,237,609	66,252
1978	12,024,019	11,942,961	5,076	82	3,754	10,728,668	1,205,381	81,058
1979	12,402,333	12,318,290	9,448	170	9,064	11,068,864	1,230,744	84,043
1980	14,048,471	13,935,233	8,873	135	8,702	12,475,245	1,442,278	113,238
1981	13,124,505	13,001,038	9,400	159	10,364	12,981,509	...	123,897
1982	12,977,019	12,880,063	8,039	139	9,869	12,862,016	...	96,956
1983	13,982,588	13,857,342	7,889	136	9,846	13,839,471	...	125,246

[1] Includes money payments for institutional services in intermediate-care facilities for 1968–71.

[2] Includes money payments for medical assistance for the aged for 1960–69.

[3] Superseded by supplemental security income program in the 50 States and the District of Columbia beginning 1974. Data for 1974 and thereafter are for only Guam, Puerto Rico, and the Virgin Islands.

[4] Money payments to families and medical vendor payments to needy families with children, authorized under title IV of the Social Security Act.

F1–10. Number and Percentage Distribution of Persons Receiving Federally Administered Payments, by Reason for Eligibility, Race, and Sex, December 1983

Race and sex	Total	Aged	Blind	Disabled
Total number.............	3,901,497	1,515,400	78,960	2,307,137
Total percent.............	100.0	100.0	100.0	100.0
White......................	58.3	55.2	59.1	60.3
Black......................	26.3	23.0	27.2	28.5
Other......................	4.1	5.1	4.3	3.4
Not reported..............	11.3	16.7	9.4	7.8
Men........................	34.5	26.0	42.2	39.8
White......................	20.3	13.7	26.0	24.5
Black......................	8.6	5.5	10.8	10.5
Other......................	1.7	1.9	1.9	1.5
Not reported..............	3.9	4.9	3.6	3.3
Women......................	65.4	73.9	57.5	60.2
White......................	37.9	41.5	33.0	35.7
Black......................	17.7	17.4	16.4	18.0
Other......................	2.4	3.2	2.3	1.9
Not reported..............	7.4	11.8	5.8	4.6

F1–11. Number and Percentage Distribution of Adults Receiving Federally Administered Payments, by Reason for Eligibility and Age, December 1983

Age	Total	Aged	Blind	Disabled
Total number.............	3,665,117	1,515,400	71,448	2,078,269
Total percent.............	100.0	100.0	100.0	100.0
18-21......................	2.5	---	4.7	4.2
22-29......................	7.9	---	13.6	13.4
30-39......................	7.7	---	13.3	13.1
40-49......................	7.0	---	10.3	12.1
50-59......................	11.9	---	15.5	20.5
60-64......................	8.3	---	10.0	14.3
65-69......................	12.5	12.9	9.2	12.4
70-74......................	14.0	21.0	8.3	9.0
75-79......................	12.0	27.7	5.2	.9
80 and over...............	16.1	38.3	9.9	.1

F1-12. Number of Persons in Concurrent Receipt of Federally Administered Payments and Unearned Income Other than Social Security Benefits and Average Monthly Unearned Income, by Reason for Eligibility and Type of Income, December 1983

Type of income	Total	Aged	Blind	Disabled
	Number with unearned income other than Social Security benefits			
Total......................	412,858	201,233	8,874	202,751
Veterans' benefits..............	96,263	47,908	1,507	46,848
Compensation..................	8,368	2,015	99	6,254
Pension......................	87,895	45,893	1,408	40,594
Railroad retirement.............	5,561	3,321	142	2,098
Black lung benefits.............	1,283	360	21	902
Employment pensions.............	25,977	19,720	417	5,840
Workers' compensation...........	1,409	331	24	1,054
Support and maintenance in kind.	138,237	66,454	2,826	68,957
Support from absent parents.....	12,526	--	455	12,071
Asset income 1/..................	78,989	44,196	2,327	32,466
Assistance based on need........	6,713	355	195	6,163
Other...........................	45,900	18,588	960	26,352
	Average monthly amount of unearned income			
Total......................	$82.41	$73.10	$80.89	$91.71
Veterans' benefits..............	122.79	107.05	109.84	139.29
Compensation..................	110.21	109.75	109.68	110.37
Pension......................	123.99	106.94	109.86	143.75
Railroad retirement.............	238.50	224.91	281.46	257.10
Black lung benefits.............	183.07	252.42	211.76	154.73
Employment pensions.............	93.76	88.85	106.70	109.44
Workers' compensation...........	165.19	112.35	201.42	180.95
Support and maintenance in kind.	68.35	66.46	80.18	69.69
Support from absent parents.....	99.83	--	99.57	99.84
Asset income 1/..................	13.38	14.13	10.91	12.53
Assistance based on needed......	86.20	107.08	89.41	84.90
Other...........................	122.82	100.86	149.79	137.33

1/ Rents, interest, and dividends.

F1–13. Number of Persons Receiving Federally Administered Payments, by Reason for Eligibility, December 1983; and Total Federal and State Payments, by Type of Payment, 1983

Number of persons (December 1983)		Total payments (1983)	
Reason for eligibility	Number	Type of payment	Amount (in thousands)
Total 1/..................	3,901,497	Total.....................	$9,404,227
Aged........................	1,515,400	Federal SSI.....................	7,422,524
Blind........................	78,960	State supplementation..........	1,981,703
Disabled.....................	2,307,137	Federally administered.......	1,711,319
		State-administered..........	• 270,384

1/ Excludes 54,270 persons receiving State-administered State supplementation only.

F1–14. All Persons, Adult Units, and Children Receiving Federally Administered Payments and Average Monthly Amount, by Reason for Eligibility and Type of Payment, December 1983

Type of payment	All persons	Adult units						Blind and disabled children
		Aged		Blind		Disabled		
		Individual	Couple	Individual	Couple	Individual	Couple	
					Number			
Total...................	3,901,497	1,249,174	132,159	64,313	3,717	1,911,399	65,595	236,380
Federal SSI payments..........	3,589,521	1,116,078	109,491	57,720	3,113	1,809,350	55,895	235,301
Federal SSI payments only...	2,343,783	766,628	82,875	33,910	2,099	1,112,660	39,540	155,733
Federal SSI and State supplementation..........	1,245,738	349,450	26,616	23,810	1,014	696,690	16,355	79,568
State supplementation.........	1,557,714	482,546	49,284	30,403	1,618	798,739	26,055	80,647
State supplementation only..	311,976	133,096	22,668	6,593	604	102,049	9,700	1,079
					Average monthly amount			
Total...................	$211.68	$163.12	$263.89	$257.38	$382.15	$247.68	$314.21	$280.96
Federal SSI payments..........	188.94	143.77	218.33	217.38	296.81	219.33	252.05	262.33
State supplementation.........	94.81	89.75	222.60	131.75	306.83	95.86	228.88	58.12

F1–15. Senior Community Service Employment Program (SCSEP): Funding, Enrollment, and Participant Characteristics Program Year July 1, 1983, to June 30, 1984

Funding	$319,450,000
Enrollment:	
Authorized positions established	62,500
Unsubsidized placements	12,458
Characteristics (percent):	
Sex:	
Male	34
Female	66
Educational status:	
8th grade and less	31
9th through 11th grade	21
High school graduate or equivalent	32
1–3 years of college	12
4 years of college or more	5
Veteran	14
Ethnic group:	
White	65
Black	23
Hispanic	8
American Indian/Alaskan Native	2
Asian/Pacific Islands	3
Economically disadvantaged	100
Poverty level or less	83
Age:	
55–59	24
60–64	29
65–69	22
70–74	16
75 and over	9

Source: U.S. Department of Labor, Employment and Training Administration.

F1–16. JTPA Enrollment, Oct. 1, 1983-June 30, 1984 (Title II-A Grants)

Item	Number served	Percent
Total participants	585,800	100
45 to 54 years	29,300	5.0
55 years and over	11,700	2.0

Source: U.S. Department of Labor, Employment and Training Administration.

F2. SOCIAL SECURITY

F2-1. Outlays for Social Security and Medicare

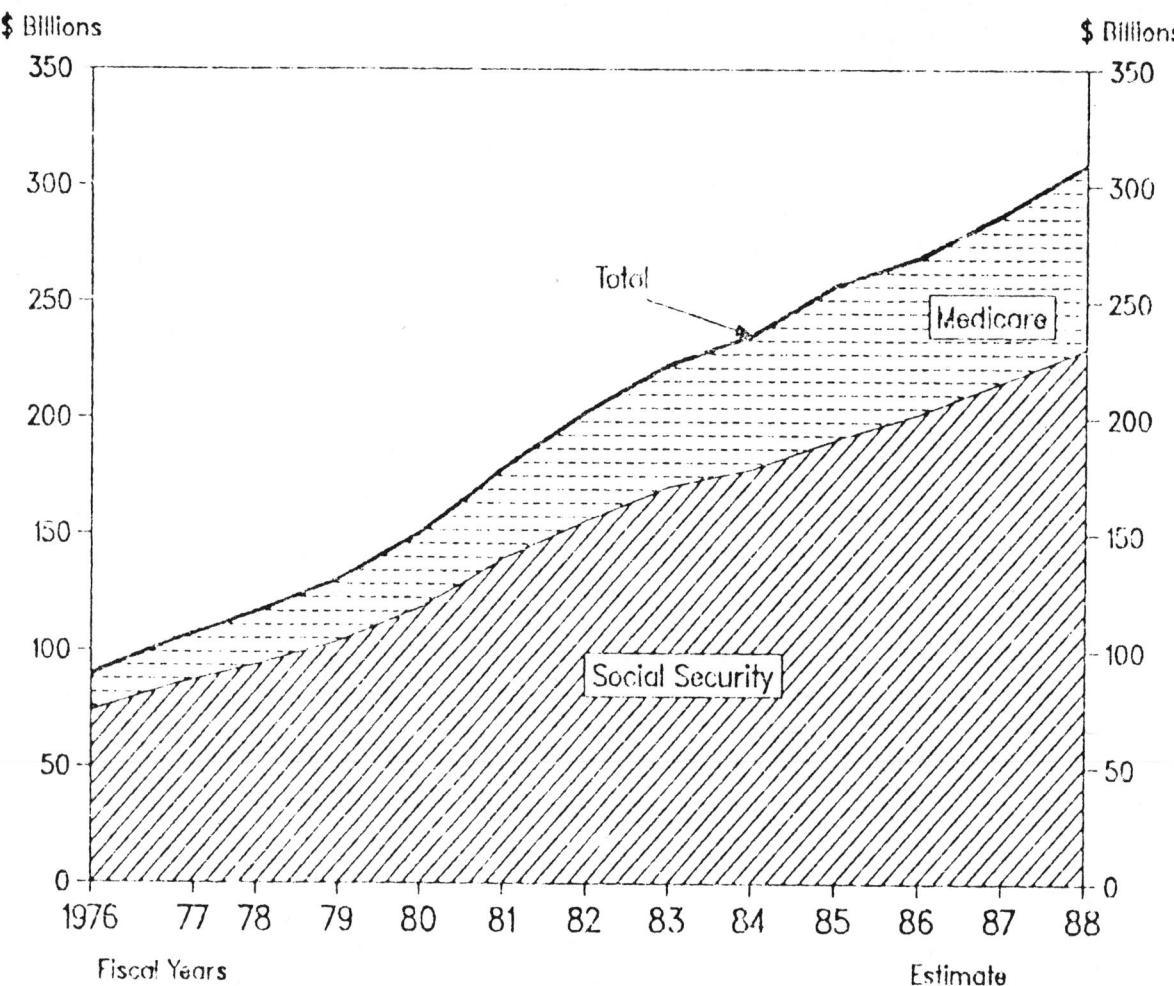

F2–2. Fully Insured Population as Percent of Population in Social Security Area,[1] as of January 1, 1945–85

Percent

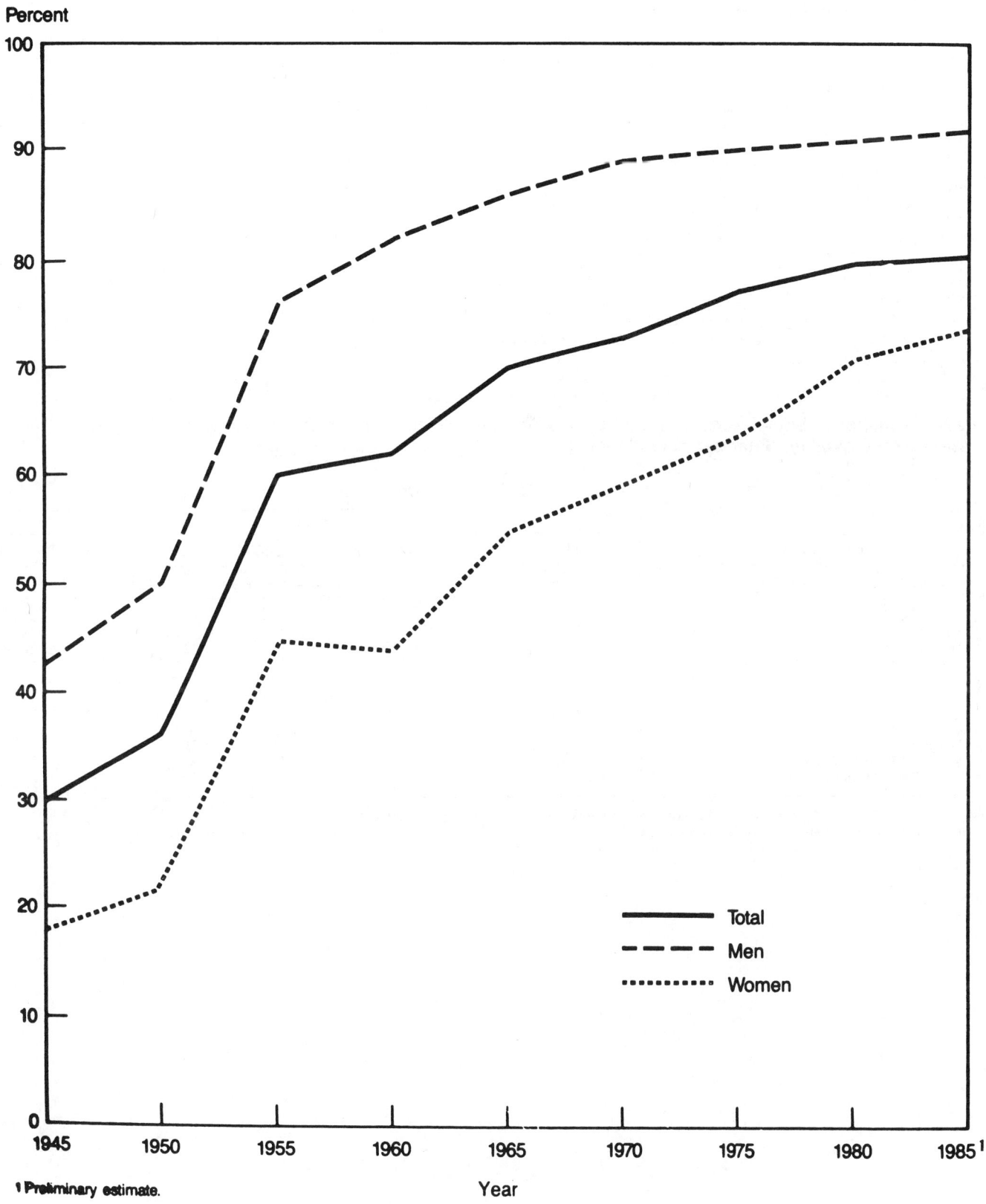

1 Preliminary estimate.

Year

F2–3. Percent of Aged Population Receiving Social Security Benefits and Adult Assistance Payments, Selected Years, 1940–84

End of year	Percent receiving—		Persons receiving both social security and adult assistance [1] as percent of—	
	Social security	adult assistance [1]	Social security beneficiaries	adult assistance recipients
1940	0.7	21.7	14.3	0.5
1945	6.2	19.4	8.1	2.6
1950	16.4	22.4	12.6	9.8
1955	39.4	17.9	8.6	19.2
1960	61.6	14.1	6.6	28.5
1965	75.2	11.7	7.0	44.7
1970	85.5	10.4	7.4	60.4
1972	85.6	9.6	7.1	63.3
1975	90.4	11.1	8.6	69.5
1980	91.4	8.7	6.7	70.2
1984	91.3	7.3	5.6	71.0

[1] For 1940–73, data refer to old-age assistance; data for 1975–84 refer to supplemental security income.

F2–4. Number of Social Security Beneficiaries Aged 65 or Older and Number Receiving Benefits Based on Disability, Selected Years, 1940–84

[In thousands]

Type of beneficiary	End of year						
	1940	1950	1960	1970	1972	1980	1984
	Beneficiaries aged 65 or older						
Total	147	2,598	10,887	17,517	18,651	23,843	26,086
Retired workers	112	1,771	7,704	12,122	13,115	17,565	19,499
Dependents and survivors	35	827	3,183	4,861	5,126	6,185	6,547
Persons with special age-72 benefits [1]	...	...	...	534	410	93	40
	Beneficiaries with benefits based on disability						
Total	...	...	559	1,813	2,202	3,436	3,210
Disabled workers	...	...	[2] 455	1,493	1,833	2,859	2,597
Disabled children aged 18 or older	...	...	[2] 104	271	305	450	506
Disabled widows and widowers	...	...	...	[3] 49	64	128	107

[1] Authorized by 1966 legislation for persons aged 72 or older not insured under the regular or transitional provisions of the Social Security Act.
[2] Benefits to disabled workers and disabled children aged 18 or older were first payable in 1957.
[3] Benefits to disabled widows and widowers were first payable in 1968.

F2–5. Selected Social Insurance Programs—Source of Funds from Contributions and Transfers: 1970 to 1983

[In millions of dollars. OASDHI = Old-age, survivors, disability and health insurance]

PROGRAM AND SOURCE OF FUNDS	1970	1975	1976	1977	1978	1979	1980	1981	1982	1983
Social Security (OASDHI) trust funds:										
Old-age and survivors insurance (OASI)	30,705	57,241	63,976	70,185	76,086	88,476	103,996	123,301	124,353	143,878
Employer	14,489	27,184	30,430	33,344	36,253	42,288	49,731	58,972	59,105	63,935
Employee	14,204	26,947	30,164	33,093	35,921	41,898	49,436	58,656	58,918	63,731
Self-employed	1,564	2,684	2,768	3,135	3,297	3,733	4,289	4,999	5,649	5,049
Government [1] [2]	449	425	614	613	615	557	540	675	680	[3] 11,162
Disability insurance	4,497	7,534	8,336	9,266	13,554	15,232	13,385	16,906	22,169	19,112
Employer	2,154	3,562	3,951	4,379	6,492	7,257	6,307	8,074	10,597	8,379
Employee	2,117	3,530	3,916	4,346	6,450	7,186	6,254	8,035	10,574	8,339
Self-employed	210	352	365	413	471	671	694	629	824	830
Government [1]	16	90	103	128	142	118	130	168	174	[3] 1,565
Hospital insurance (HI) [4]	5,820	12,316	13,020	15,072	18,408	21,883	24,982	34,157	35,976	41,283
Employer	2,412	5,647	6,260	6,855	8,556	10,211	11,713	16,226	16,966	18,366
Employee	2,365	5,598	6,206	6,803	8,489	10,119	11,640	16,153	16,910	18,307
Self-employed	169	395	403	456	493	629	739	856	1,061	943
Government [1] [2] [5]	874	670	141	946	858	908	871	900	1,015	[3] 3,639
Voluntarily insured [6]	(x)	7	9	12	13	16	18	22	24	27
Supplementary medical insurance [7]	2,189	4,566	5,870	7,633	8,757	9,364	10,466	15,013	15,981	19,097
Aged	1,096	1,759	1,878	2,030	2,221	2,452	2,707	3,356	3,341	3,845
Disabled	(x)	158	183	217	249	267	304	366	356	391
Government	1,093	2,648	3,810	5,386	6,287	6,645	7,455	11,291	12,284	14,861
Railroad retirement [8]	968	1,506	2,298	1,810	2,450	2,508	2,630	2,627	3,304	(NA)
Employer	510	1,146	1,333	1,386	1,437	1,659	1,722	1,817	2,036	(NA)
Employee	439	356	465	424	450	536	594	684	858	(NA)
Government [1]	19	4	500	–	563	313	313	126	410	(NA)
Federal civil service	3,870	9,507	10,770	13,802	14,306	16,328	19,986	22,554	(NA)	(NA)
Employer (Federal and DC gov't.)	2,001	6,905	7,965	10,816	11,118	12,916	16,220	18,506	(NA)	(NA)
Employee [9]	1,869	2,600	2,805	2,986	3,188	3,412	3,766	4,048	(NA)	(NA)
State and local government [10]	7,895	14,560	16,560	18,470	20,380	22,702	25,654	(NA)	(NA)	(NA)
Employer (government)	4,920	9,880	11,510	13,010	14,500	16,434	18,776	(NA)	(NA)	(NA)
Employee	2,975	4,680	5,050	5,460	5,880	6,268	6,878	(NA)	(NA)	(NA)

– Represents zero.   NA Not available.   X Not applicable.   [1] Represents cost of gratuitous wage credits for military service.   [2] Includes Federal payments for special age-72 benefits.   [3] See footnotes 2 and 4, table 605.   [4] Includes transfers from railroad retirement account for HI coverage of railroad workers.   [5] Includes transfers of appropriations for HI benefits for persons not insured for cash benefits under OASI, DI or railroad retirement. For 1978–1981, includes reimbursements for Professional Standards Review Organization.   [6] Beginning July 1973, aged ineligibles may voluntarily enroll for HI.   [7] Includes premiums paid on behalf of eligibles by State governments under "buy-in" arrangements.   [8] Excludes HI contributions (included with HI above) and includes employer contributions to supplemental benefit account.   [9] Includes voluntary contributions to purchase additional annuity.   [10] Estimated.

Source: U.S. Social Security Administration, *Annual Statistical Supplement* to the *Social Security Bulletin*.

F2-6. Old-Age and Survivors Insurance Trust Fund: Status, 1940–85

[In thousands. Calendar and fiscal year data appear in alternate months of the **Bulletin**.
Data for interim years appear in table 14 of the **Bulletin's 1983 Annual Statistical Supplement**.]

Period	Receipts			Expenditures				Assets at end of period [1]		
	Net contribution income [2]	Payments from general fund of the Treasury [3]	Net interest [4]	Benefit payments [5]	Rehabilitation services for disabled [6]	Transfers to railroad retirement account [7]	Net administrative expenses [8]	Invested in U.S. Government securities [9]	Cash balances	Total assets [10]
Fiscal year:										
1940	$550,000	...	$42,489	$15,805	...	...	$12,288	$1,738,100	$6,598	$1,744,698
1945	1,309,919	...	123,854	239,834	...	...	26,950	6,546,281	67,100	6,613,381
1950	2,106,388	$3,604	256,778	727,266	...	...	56,841	12,644,823	247,789	12,892,612
1955	5,087,154	...	438,029	4,333,147	...	-$9,551	103,202	20,580,491	560,511	21,141,001
1960	9,842,685	...	517,130	10,269,709	...	600,437	202,369	19,748,848	1,079,877	20,828,725
1965	15,857,212	...	586,237	15,225,894	...	435,638	300,283	18,765,724	1,414,761	20,180,485
1970	29,954,673	442,151	1,349,613	26,266,928	$1,239	578,818	474,035	30,106,913	2,509,443	32,616,355
1975	56,017,343	447,323	2,292,182	54,838,818	7,731	981,785	847,723	39,879,154	68,659	39,947,814
1976	59,554,690	425,317	2,347,000	62,140,449	7,480	1,212,303	934,746	37,955,347	24,529	37,979,876
July-Sept.1976 (transition quarter)	16,105,848	...	80,432	16,875,545	1,714	...	233,703	37,042,171	13,031	37,055,202
1977	68,894,809	613,902	2,286,888	71,270,519	7,502	1,207,841	992,737	35,397,620	-25,407	35,372,213
1978	74,046,779	612,927	2,151,741	78,524,092	6,461	1,588,664	1,086,186	30,955,085	23,179	30,978,264
1979	84,357,910	614,918	1,920,140	87,591,968	16,980	1,447,532	1,072,006	27,317,094	425,752	27,742,846
1980	97,607,645	557,037	1,886,219	100,615,304	11,090	1,441,988	1,159,659	23,565,572	1,000,185	24,565,757
1981	119,016,091	539,936	2,016,252	119,413,467	[12]7,542	1,584,932	1,298,107	23,244,031	589,989	23,834,020
1982	124,246,412	674,715	1,708,114	134,654,629	6,158	1,793,280	1,474,003	11,921,518	613,706	12,535,224
1983	136,127,311	6,096,177	6,210,157	148,024,189	668	2,250,821	1,551,227	25,502,697	1,157,977	26,660,674
1984	158,685,629	124,514	1,918,513	155,824,605	6,054	2,404,002	1,585,237	27,223,772	345,817	27,569,589
1984										
June	14,886,185	...	2,158,572	13,137,936	109	2,404,002	118,327	26,148,999	164,446	26,313,445
July	14,468,921	...	-144,062	13,006,860	...	...	183,803	26,882,389	565,397	27,447,786
August	12,824,718	...	46,512	[13]26,122,576	...	...	110,101	21,110,061	-7,023,720	14,086,341
September	13,778,086	...	-129,260	[13]31,227	...	...	134,351	27,223,772	345,817	27,569,589
October	13,402,535	...	67,035	13,115,726	...	...	127,032	26,646,992	1,149,412	27,796,404
November	12,667,071	...	-93,951	13,152,720	...	...	120,590	26,362,274	733,976	27,096,250
December	13,163,420	104,978	755,303	13,855,102	...	...	147,931	26,320,805	796,121	27,116,926
1985										
January	16,229,206	...	-82,393	13,746,321	...	...	137,819	24,122,088	893,547	25,015,635
February	14,877,997	...	-35,524	13,866,621	...	...	130,958	24,665,511	1,195,032	25,860,543
March	14,138,236	...	-40,142	13,956,378	...	...	124,147	25,643,329	234,793	25,878,122
April	19,330,183	...	-18,696	13,836,912	...	...	150,930	30,288,509	913,264	31,201,773
May	14,506,538	...	-94,222	13,817,578	...	...	122,071	31,245,061	429,382	31,674,443
June	14,829,589	...	926,738	13,853,128	...	2,310,169	119,767	30,856,517	291,197	31,147,714

[1] Includes gifts.

[2] Fiscal year 1983 includes, in addition to the annual contributions on 1983 wage credits of $233 million, a net amount of $5,388 million representing (a) retroactive contributions on deemed wage credits for military service in 1957-82, less (b) all reimbursements received prior to 1983 for the costs of such credits. Fiscal year 1984 and June 1984 include $466 million representing an adjustment for the retroactive contributions on deemed wage credits for military service in 1957-83. Fiscal year 1984 and July 1984 include $316 million in annual contributions on 1984 wage credits. Beginning in January 1984, includes payments from the general fund of the Treasury for tax credits on wages paid in 1984 to employees and on net earnings from self-employment in 1984-89. Beginning in January 1984, reflects taxation of benefits.

[3] Appropriations from general fund to meet cost of benefits arising from deemed military wage credits and special age-72 benefits. Includes reimbursements (a) in 1947-52 and in 1967 and later, for costs of noncontributory wage credits for military service performed before 1957; (b) in 1972-83, for costs of deemed wage credits for military service performed after 1956; and (c) in 1969 and later, for costs of benefits to certain uninsured persons who attained age 72 before 1968. The amount shown for 1978 also includes $2,724,000 as a single reimbursement for the estimated total costs of granting noncontributory wage credits to U.S. citizens who were interned during World War II at places within the United States operated by the Federal Government for the internment of persons of Japanese ancestry. Fiscal year 1983 reflects $5,416 million, under the provisions of Public Law 98-21, for noncontributory wage credits for military service performed before 1957.

[4] Interest and profit on investments after adjustment for interest on reimbursed administrative expenses. Net interest includes net profits or losses on marketable investments. Beginning in 1967, administrative expenses are charged currently to the trust fund on an estimated basis, with a final adjustment, including interest, made in the following fiscal year. The amounts of these interest adjustments are included in net interest. Fiscal year 1983 reflects $6,493 million, fiscal year 1984 and June 1984 reflect $1,732 million in interest on deemed wage credits for military service performed after 1956. Beginning in fiscal year 1983, net interest reflects interest on interfund borrowing, interest on advance tax transfers, and interest on reimbursement for unnegotiated checks.

[5] Beginning in fiscal year 1983, benefit payments reflect deductions for unnegotiated checks.

[6] Beginning in 1967, includes payments for vocational rehabilitation services furnished to disabled-child beneficiaries and disabled-widow and -widower beneficiaries.

[7] The purpose of the financial interchange provided by the Railroad Retirement Act, as amended, is to place the trust funds in the same position in which they would have been if railroad employment had always been covered under OASDI-HI. Transfers include (a) interest from railroad retirement account to OASI trust fund on amount held to the credit of the trust fund, 1954-57; (b) principal and interest from OASI trust fund, beginning 1958, and from DI trust fund, beginning 1961, to railroad retirement account; (c) principal and interest from railroad retirement account to DI trust fund in 1959 and 1960 and to the HI trust fund, beginning 1966. Payments to the trust fund from the railroad retirement account, indicated by negative expenditure figures, increase income and total assets; payments from the trust fund to the account, indicated by positive figures, increase expenditures and reduce total assets.

[8] Under the 1956 amendments, all HHS administrative expenses were paid initially from the OASI trust fund with subsequent reimbursements, from the DI trust fund for the allocated cost of DI operations. For 1958-65, all OASI reimbursements for administration came from the DI trust fund. Beginning 1966, the DI, HI, and SMI trust funds are charged currently with the expenses of their respective operations (including construction); all other costs (data processing, research, etc.) are paid initially from the OASI trust fund and included in subsequent allocation of total administration amount for all four trust funds. Includes income from sales of supplies, materials, etc. as an offsetting expense.

[9] Book value: includes net unamortized premium and discount, accrued interest purchased, and repayment of interest accrued on bonds at time of purchase.

[10] Total assets include amounts owed to the DI and HI trust funds as a result of interfund borrowing. The amounts owed totaled $17,518,523 thousand as of December 31, 1982, and remained at that level until the repayment of $4,364,000 thousand on January 31, 1985. The balance owed was thereby reduced to $13,154,523 thousand.

F2–7. Concurrent Receipt of OASDI and SSI Benefits, December 1983

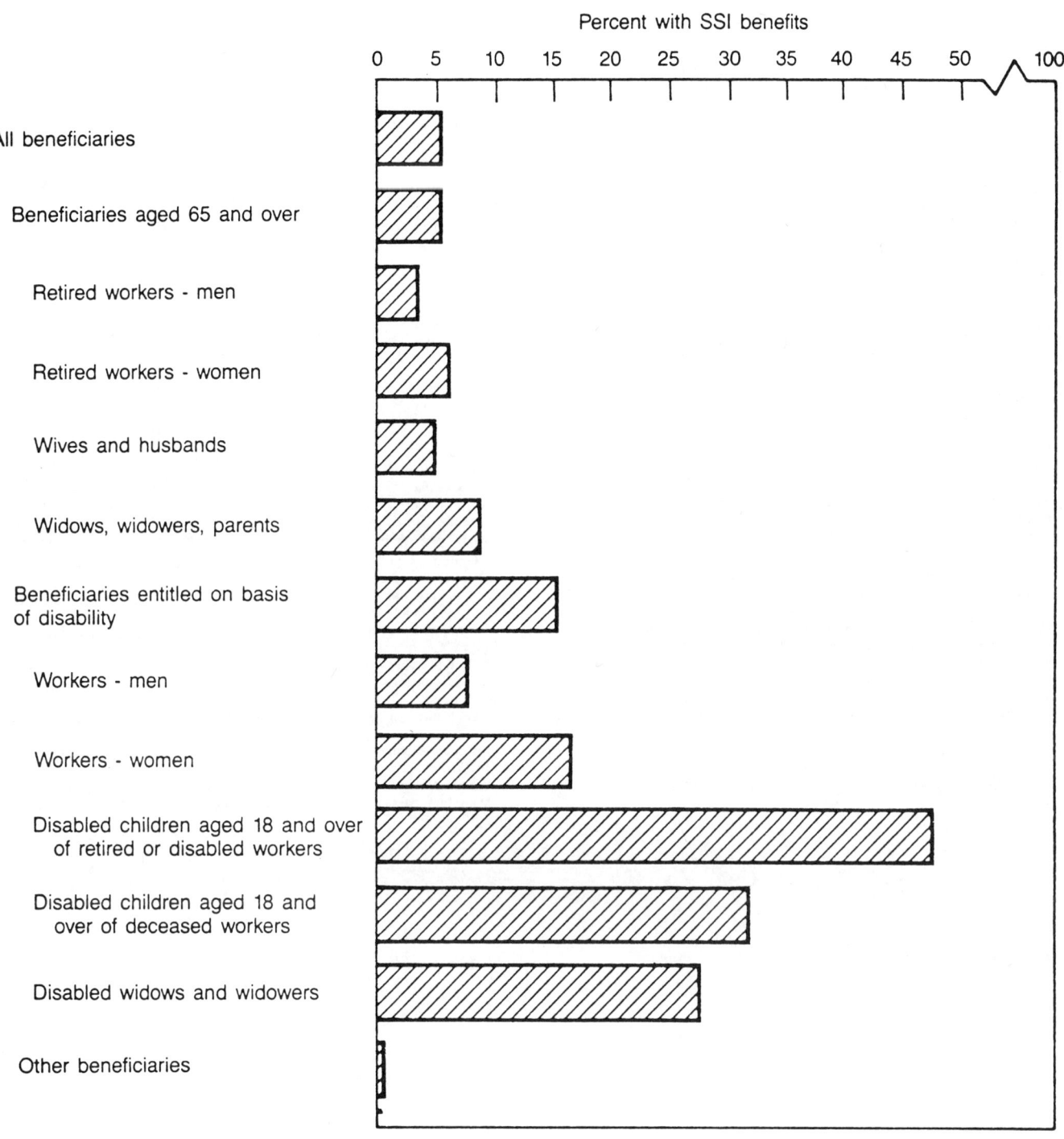

F2-8. Monthly SSI Payment Levels of Aged Individuals and Couples Living Independently, Based on Combined Federal Payment and Optional Supplement, January 1985[1]

State	Individual [2][3]	Couple [2][3]	State	Individual [2][3]	Couple [2][3]
Alabama	$325.00	$488.00	Missouri	325.00	488.00
Alaska	586.00	859.00	Montana	325.00	488.00
Arizona	325.00	488.00	Nebraska	[8] 386.00	[8] 580.00
Arkansas	325.00	488.00	Nevada	361.40	562.46
California	504.00	936.00	New Hampshire	[9] 339.00	[9] 489.00
Colorado	383.00	766.00	New Jersey	356.25	513.36
Connecticut	[4] 465.70	[4] 574.20	New Mexico	325.00	488.00
Delaware	325.00	488.00	New York	385.91	564.03
District of Columbia	340.00	518.00	North Carolina	325.00	488.00
Florida	325.00	488.00	North Dakota	325.00	488.00
Georgia	325.00	488.00	Ohio	325.00	488.00
Hawaii	329.90	496.80	Oklahoma	385.00	608.00
Idaho	[5] 383.00	[5] 514.00	Oregon	326.70	488.00
Illinois	(6)	(6)	Pennsylvania	357.40	536.70
Indiana	325.00	488.00	Rhode Island	378.80	589.74
Iowa	325.00	488.00	South Carolina	325.00	488.00
Kansas	325.00	488.00	South Dakota	340.00	503.00
Kentucky	325.00	488.00	Tennessee	325.00	488.00
Louisiana	325.00	488.00	Texas	325.00	488.00
Maine	335.00	503.00	Utah	335.00	508.00
Maryland	325.00	488.00	Vermont	378.00	[10] 584.50
Massachusetts	453.82	689.72	Virginia	325.00	488.00
Michigan	351.70	528.00	Washington	[11] 363.30	[11] 525.40
Minnesota	[7] 360.00	[7] 554.00	West Virginia	325.00	488.00
Mississippi	325.00	488.00	Wisconsin	424.70	649.00
			Wyoming	345.00	528.00

[1] For those without countable income. These payments are reduced by the amount of countable income of the individual or couple.

[2] Effective January 1985, the Federal SSI payment level for an individual living in his or her own household and having no countable income is $325. An eligible couple living in their own household receives a monthly payment of $488. Payment levels of these amounts indicate that an optional State supplement is not payable.

[3] For recipients who live in another person's household and receive support and maintenance there, the Federal SSI payment rate is reduced by one-third.

[4] Budget process used to establish payment amounts. The amounts shown assume eligibility for the highest rental allowance in the maximum budget amount.

[5] State provides an additional income disregard of $20 per month of any income including SSI. The combined Federal and State amount excludes the disregard.

[6] Optional supplement amount is equal to the difference between monthly Federal SSI payments plus other income and the income maintenance needs based on State standards. The income maintenance needs of each case are determined individually regardless of living arrangement.

[7] Payment level for Hennepin County. State has 10 geographic payment levels.

[8] State provides an additional income disregard of $7.50 per month of unearned income including SSI. The combined Federal and State amount excludes the disregard.

[9] The combined Federal and State amount excludes the additional monthly income disregards provided by the State. The State's monthly income disregards of any income including SSI are $13 for an individual living independently and $20 for a couple.

[10] State has two geographic payment levels; higher level shown in table.

[11] Amount paid in King, Kitsap, Pierce, Snohomish, and Thurston counties.

F2–9. Number and Percentage Distribution of Individuals and Children Receiving Federal SSI Payments, by Reason for Eligibility and Monthly Amount, December 1983

Monthly amount	Individuals 1/			Blind and disabled children
	Aged	Blind	Disabled	
Total number.........	1,116,078	57,720	1,809,350	235,301
Total percent........	100.0	100.0	100.0	100.0
Less than $10..............	2.0	1.2	1.1	.3
$10-$19.....................	2.9	1.7	1.6	.5
$20-$39.....................	13.3	7.7	9.5	10.1
$40-$59.....................	8.5	3.9	4.2	.6
$60-$79.....................	7.5	3.5	3.8	.7
$80-$99.....................	6.4	3.2	3.5	.8
$100-$119.................	5.8	3.2	3.4	.9
$120-$139.................	5.3	3.2	3.1	1.1
$140-$179.................	20.0	9.6	8.3	2.7
$180-$219.................	5.2	9.4	8.8	8.9
$220-$259.................	1.1	3.2	2.4	5.7
$260-$299.................	1.3	3.7	3.7	7.6
$300 and over 2/..........	20.6	46.4	46.6	60.2

1/ Excludes couples.
2/ Individuals living in their own household with no countable income were eligible for a Federal SSI payment of $304.30.

F2–10. Number and Percentage Distribution of Couples Receiving Federal SSI Payments, by Reason for Eligibility and Monthly Amount, December 1983

Monthly amount	Couples		
	Aged	Blind	Disabled
Total number............	109,491	3,113	55,895
Total percent...........	100.0	100.0	100.0
Less than $10.................	1.2	.7	1.1
$10-$19......................	1.5	1.2	1.1
$20-$39......................	5.3	2.3	3.4
$40-$59......................	6.7	3.3	4.8
$60-$79......................	6.5	3.1	5.0
$80-$99......................	6.3	4.2	5.0
$100-$119...................	6.2	3.9	5.3
$120-$139...................	5.7	3.8	5.0
$140-$179...................	8.7	6.9	9.3
$180-$219...................	11.2	8.8	9.0
$220-$259...................	11.3	8.4	8.6
$260-$299...................	1.9	5.4	5.1
$300 and over 1/.............	27.4	47.9	37.2

1/ Couples living in their own household with no countable income were eligible for a Federal SSI payment of $456.40.

F2-11. Number of Persons Receiving Federally Administered SSI Payments, by Reason for Eligibility and Age, 1974-84

[In thousands]

Month and year	Total	Aged 65 or older				Under age 65		
		Total	Aged	Blind	Disabled	Total	Blind	Disabled
January 1974	3,216	1,952	1,865	23	64	1,264	49	1,214
December 1974	3,996	(1)	2,286	(1)	(1)	(1)	(1)	(1)
December 1975	4,314	2,508	2,307	22	179	1,806	52	1,754
December 1976	4,236	2,397	2,148	22	227	1,839	54	1,785
December 1977	4,238	2,353	2,051	25	277	1,885	52	1,832
December 1978	4,217	2,312	1,968	25	319	1,905	52	1,853
December 1979	4,150	2,258	1,872	25	361	1,892	52	1,840
December 1980	4,142	2,226	1,807	25	394	1,916	53	1,862
December 1981	4,019	2,121	1,687	24	419	1,898	55	1,843
December 1982	3,857	2,011	1,549	23	439	1,847	54	1,792
December 1983	3,901	2,003	1,515	23	465	1,898	56	1,842
December 1984	4,029	2,037	1,530	23	484	1,992	58	1,935

[1] Data on age distribution not available for December 1974.

F2-12. Projected Beneficiaries and Benefit Payments of the Supplemental Security Income System, 1980-2055

Year	Beneficiaries (Millions)				Benefit Payments (Billions of 1972 Dollars)			
	Aged	Blind	Disabled	Total	Aged	Blind	Disabled	Total
1980	2.15	0.08	2.19	4.42	$1.82	$0.11	$2.75	$4.68
1990	1.88	0.09	2.39	4.36	1.59	0.13	3.01	4.73
2000	1.33	0.10	2.60	4.03	1.13	0.14	3.27	4.54
2010	1.57	0.11	3.03	4.71	1.33	0.16	3.81	5.30
2020	2.02	0.12	3.29	5.43	1.72	0.18	4.14	6.03
2030	1.44	0.13	3.26	4.83	1.22	0.19	4.09	5.50
2040	1.02	0.14	3.26	4.42	0.86	0.20	4.10	5.17
2050	0.75	0.14	3.45	4.34	0.63	0.21	4.34	5.18
2055	0.57	0.15	3.50	4.22	0.48	0.22	4.39	5.09
Rate of Growth								
1980-2010	−1.04%	1.07%	1.09%	0.21%	−1.04%	1.26%	1.09%	0.42%
2010-2055	−2.22	0.69	0.32	−0.24	−2.24	0.71	0.32	−0.09
1980-2055	−1.75	0.84	0.63	−0.06	−1.76	0.93	0.63	0.11

Source: Projections of the Macroeconomic-Demographic Model

F3. EXPENDITURES FOR VETERANS

F3-1. Outlays for Veterans Benefits and Services

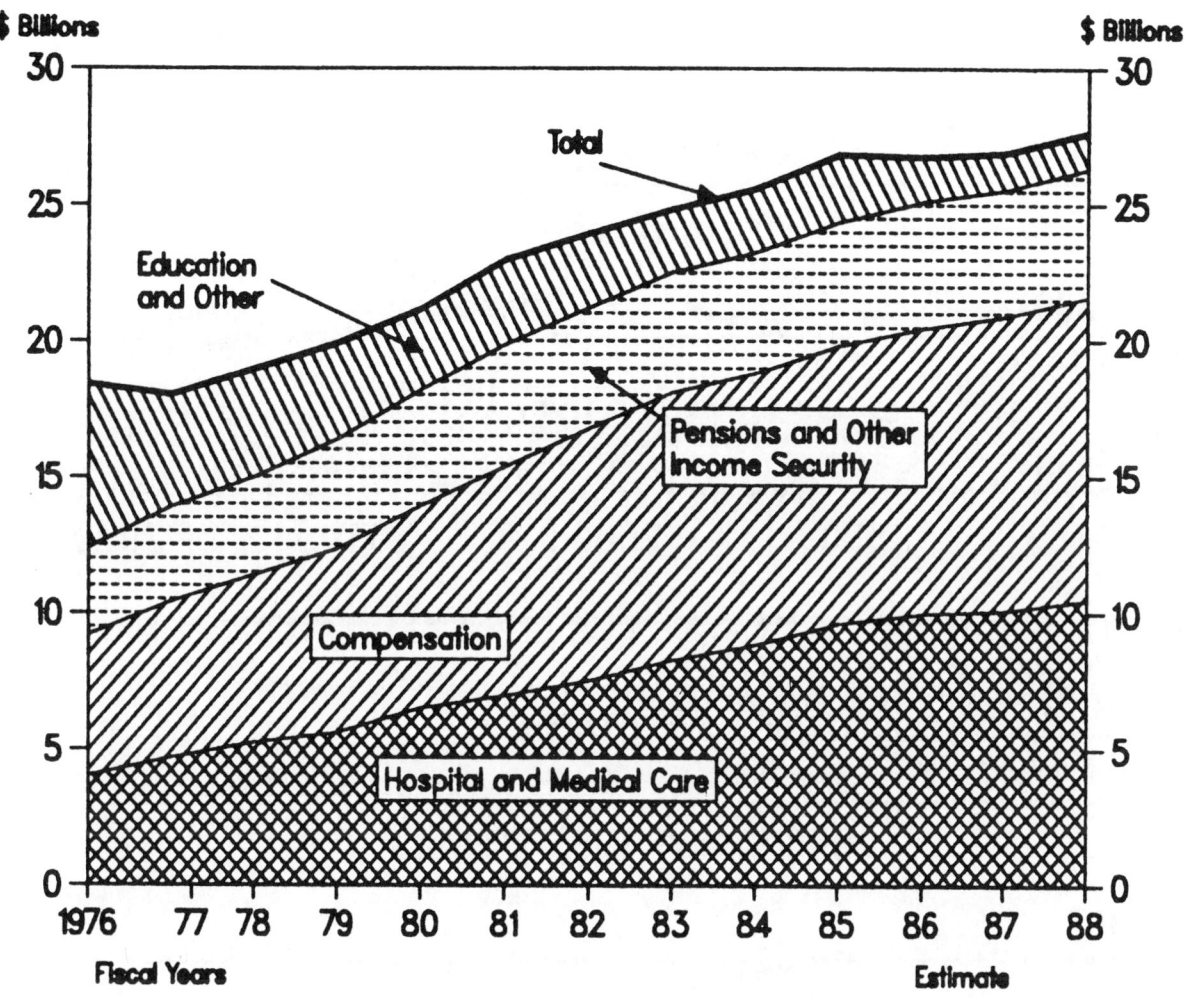

F3–2. Projected Need for VA Pensions, 1990–2020

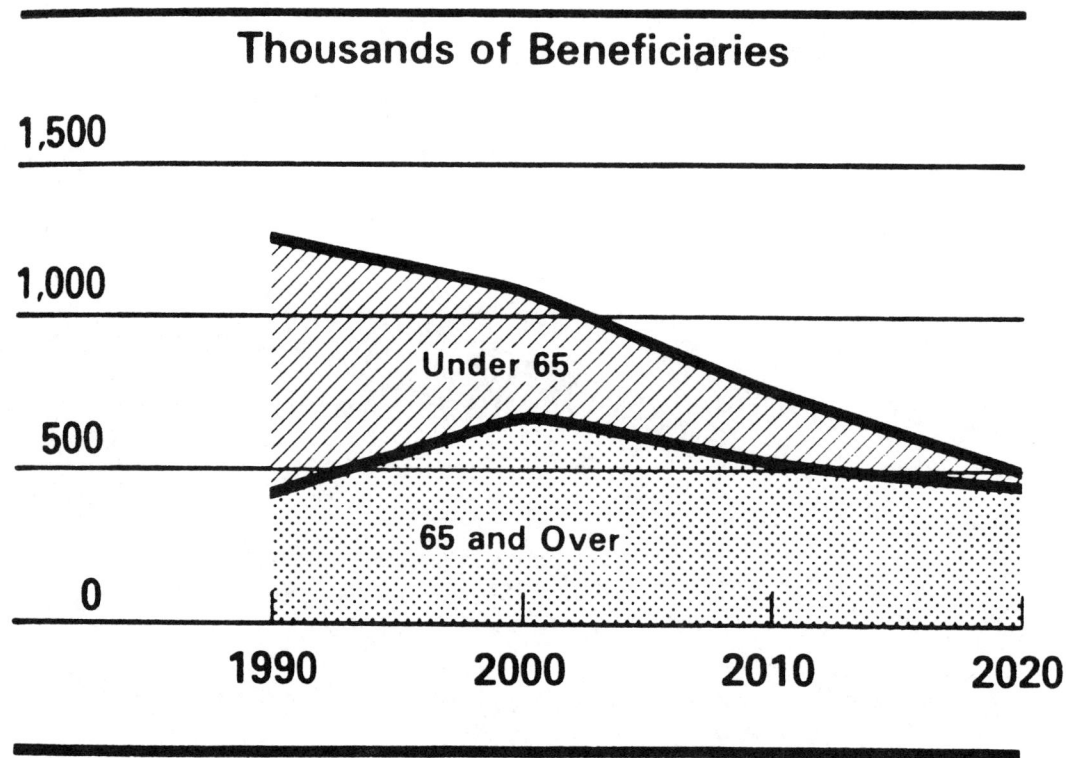

Thousands of Beneficiaries

F3–3. Projected Appropriations Needed for DVB, 1990–2020

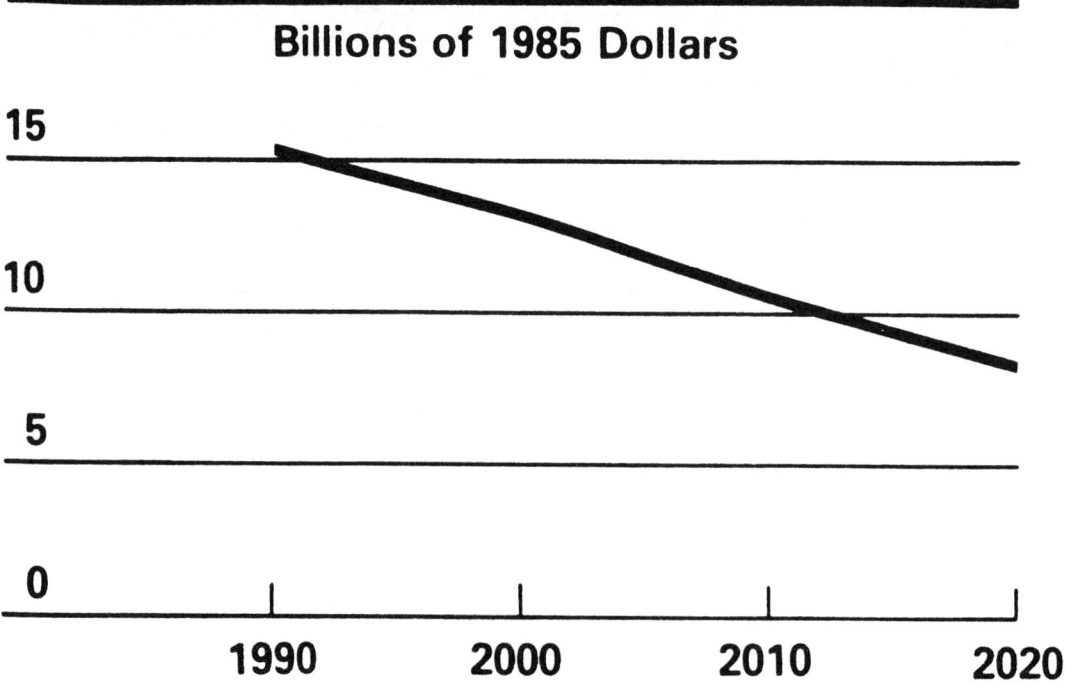

Billions of 1985 Dollars

F3–4. Veterans Receiving Compensation or Pension Compared with Estimated Veteran Population by Period of Service, 1983

	Number Receiving Compensation/ Pension or Retirement	Percent Receiving Compensation/ Pension by Period of Service	Percent Receiving Compensation Pension or Retirement	Number Receiving Compensation Only	Percent Receiving Compensation Only by Period of Service	Percent Receiving Compensation	Number Receiving Pension	Percent Receiving Pension by Period of Service	Percent Receiving Pension
Total	3,154,029	100.0	10.5	2,279,070	100.0	7.6	874,783	100.0	2.9
World War I	166,497	5.3	37.1	25,417	1.1	5.7	140,919	16.1	31.4
World War II	1,800,760	57.1	14.8	1,167,481	51.2	9.6	633,279	72.4	5.2
Korean Conflict	316,758	10.0	6.8	233,820	10.3	5.0	82,938	9.5	1.8
Vietnam Era	585,645	18.6	6.9	568,234	25.0	6.7	17,411	2.0	.2
Peacetime	284,127	9.0	6.6	284,127	12.5	6.6	NA	0.0	—
Old Wars	242	0.0	—	6	0.0	—	236	0.0	—

Source: VA Office of Reports and Statistics.

F3–5. Marital Status of Veterans Using VA Institutional Care, 1983

Marital Status	**(Percent)**			
	Hospital	Domiciliary	Nursing Home	All Types Total
Divorced	19.3	37.4	17.2	20.7
Married	43.8	8.9	35.8	37.9
Single	22.2	31.9	23.8	23.7
Separated	5.1	8.8	4.1	5.3
Widowed	7.8	10.7	17.2	10.5
Unknown	1.8	2.4	2.1	1.9
Total	63.4	11.1	25.5	100.0

Source: VA, Annual Patient Census (1983).

F3-6. Type of Health Insurance Coverage for Veterans Aged 55 and Over by Selected Socio-Demographic Characteristics

	Estimated Number of Veterans (in Thousands)	Private Only	Private & Medicare Only	Private & Medicaid Only	Private, Medicare, & Medicaid	Medicare Only	Medicaid Only	Medicare & Medicaid Only	No Insurance	Total
				Percent Distribution						
Total	11,650	53	23	*	3	9	1	2	9	100
Age										
55-59	3,850	80	3	*	1	3	*	1	12	100
60-64	3,690	76	6	*	1	4	*	1	12	100
65-69	2,170	8	61	1	9	15	*	4	2	100
70-74	1,000	6	59	*	9	21	1	3	1	100
75+	940	2	49	*	7	26	1	9	6	100
Income										
Less than $10,000	2,040	17	23	1	5	26	1	5	22	100
$10,000-$19,999	2,880	39	35	*	5	9	*	3	9	100
$20,000-$39,999	3,690	72	18	*	2	3	*	1	4	100
$40,000 or more	1,710	82	14	*	*	1	*	1	2	100
Sex										
Male	11,330	53	23	*	4	9	*	2	9	100
Female	320	55	27	*	1	7	1	*	9	100
Race										
White	10,370	54	25	*	4	8	*	2	7	100
Other	1,180	41	15	*	1	17	1	4	21	100

F4. HEALTH CARE EXPENDITURES

F4–1. National Health Expenditures: 1970 to 1983

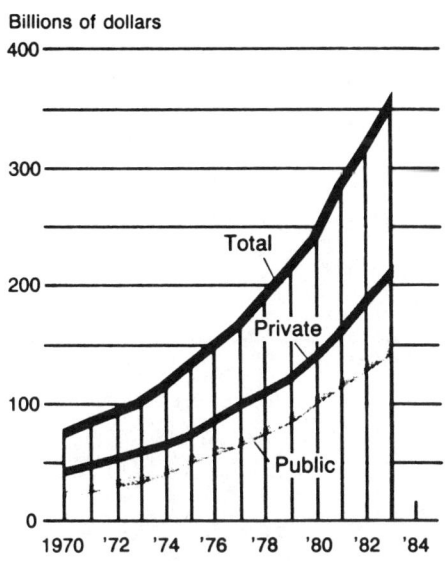

¹ Gross national product.
Source: Chart prepared by U.S. Bureau of the Census. For data, see table 142.

F4–2. National Health Expenditures and Percent of Gross National Product, 1960–1984

	1960	1965	1970	1975	1980	1981	1982	1983	1984
Expenditures in billions of dollars	26.9	41.9	75.0	132.7	248.0	285.8	322.3	355.4	390.9
Percent of GNP	5.8	6.1	7.6	8.6	9.4	9.7	10.5	10.8	10.7

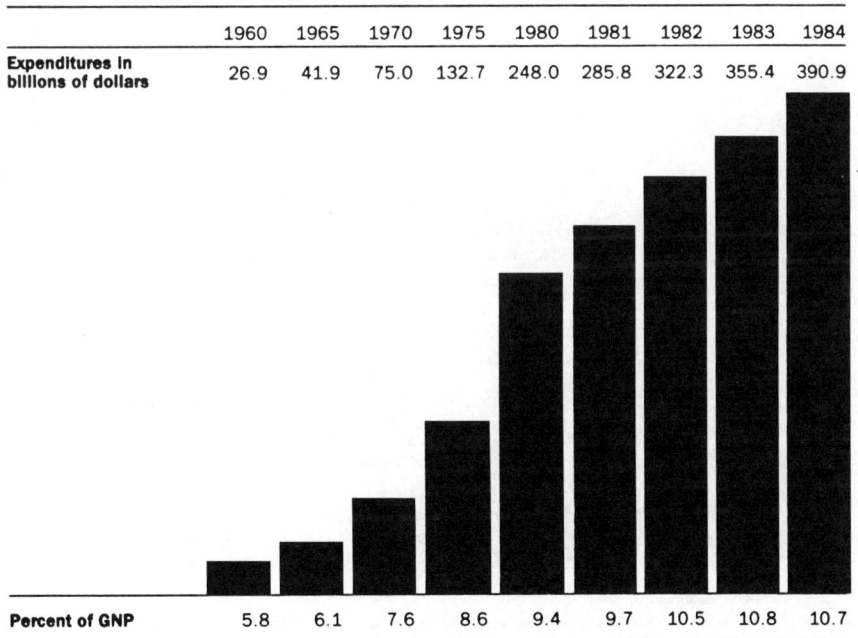

F4–3. Out-of-Pocket Health Care Expenditures for Persons Age 65 and Over: Per Capita 1966–1984*

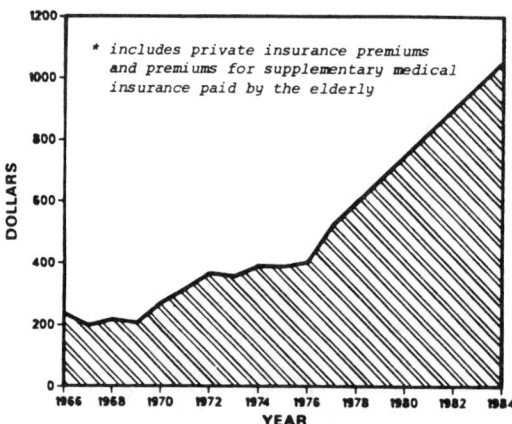

Source: Health Care Financing Administration, Bureau of
Data Management and Strategy, Health Care Spend-
ing Bulletin, July 1984; and Robert Gibson and
Marjorie Mueller, "Differences by Age Group in
Health Care Spending," Social Security Bulletin,
June 1976; and Office of Financial and Actuarial
Analysis, Bureau of Data Management and Strategy,
Health Care Financing Administration, July 1984.

F4–4. Outlays for Health, 1976–1988

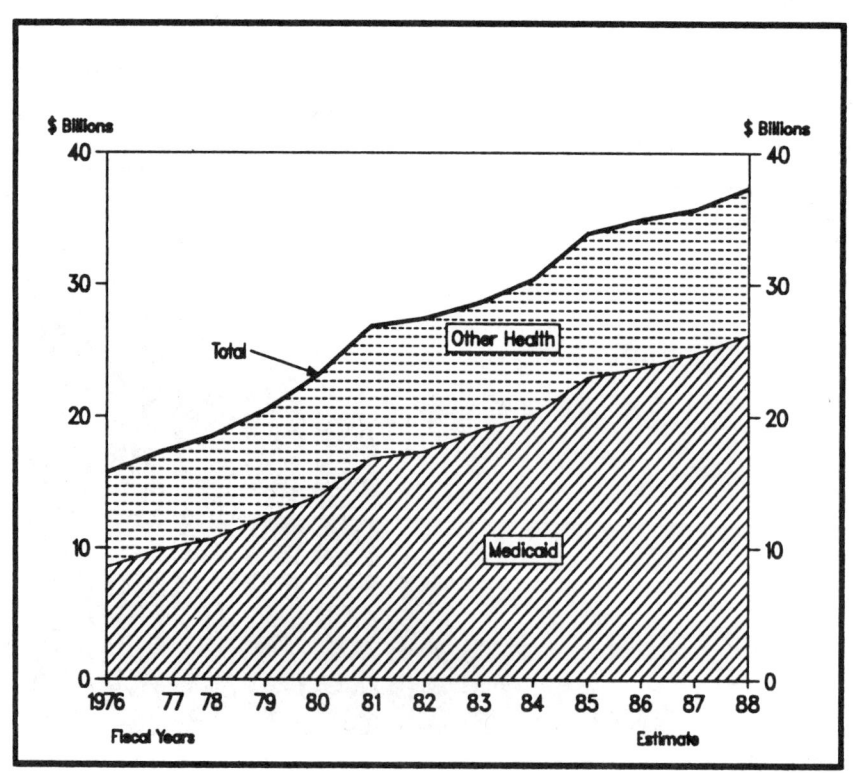

F4–5. National Health Expenditures, by Type: 1970 to 1983

[In millions of dollars, except percent. See also *Historical Statistics, Colonial Times to 1970*, series B 248–261]

TYPE OF EXPENDITURE	1970	1975	1977	1978	1979	1980	1981	1982	1983
Total	**74,984**	**132,673**	**170,173**	**190,004**	**215,052**	**248,013**	**285,828**	**322,329**	**355,400**
Average annual percent change [1]	[2] 12.3	12.1	13.3	11.7	13.2	15.3	15.2	12.8	10.3
Private expenditures	**47,222**	**76,310**	**100,069**	**110,063**	**124,192**	**142,170**	**164,161**	**186,485**	**206,617**
Health services and supplies	44,662	72,975	96,603	106,531	120,433	137,890	159,004	180,362	199,789
Direct patient payments	26,498	38,036	46,400	50,642	55,836	62,477	70,785	77,233	85,203
Insurance premiums [3]	16,871	33,178	48,016	53,577	62,011	72,468	84,798	99,332	110,482
Other	1,293	1,761	2,187	2,312	2,586	2,944	3,421	3,798	4,105
Medical research	215	264	273	282	299	313	325	339	354
Medical facilities construction	2,345	3,072	3,193	3,250	3,460	3,967	4,832	5,784	6,474
Public expenditures	**27,762**	**56,363**	**70,104**	**79,941**	**90,860**	**105,843**	**121,667**	**135,844**	**148,783**
Percent Federal of public	63.6	65.8	67.6	67.3	67.2	67.1	68.7	68.7	69.0
Health services and supplies	24,922	51,297	64,402	73,710	84,189	98,200	113,662	127,762	140,349
Medicare [4]	7,496	16,317	22,525	25,932	30,336	36,819	44,754	52,371	58,828
Temporary disability insurance [5]	66	73	74	80	58	52	52	55	58
Workers' compensation (medical) [5]	1,409	2,432	3,191	3,663	4,493	5,162	5,674	5,998	6,423
Public assistance medical payments [6]	6,321	15,098	18,858	21,118	24,340	28,111	32,279	34,861	37,187
Defense Dept. hospital, medical	1,782	2,830	3,062	3,442	3,779	4,207	4,917	5,689	6,589
Maternal, child health programs	429	589	683	726	765	810	893	912	1,016
Public health activities	1,420	3,157	4,327	5,340	6,358	7,711	8,636	10,045	11,226
Veterans' hospital, medical care	1,764	3,495	4,400	4,984	5,313	5,941	6,624	7,125	7,660
Medical vocational rehabilitation	149	224	250	259	279	281	294	322	382
State and local hospitals [7]	3,320	5,230	4,871	5,660	5,829	6,093	6,420	7,230	7,923
Other [8]	767	1,851	2,163	2,505	2,639	3,012	3,119	3,155	3,057
Medical research	1,754	3,071	3,631	4,137	4,416	5,110	5,277	5,539	5,809
Medical facilities construction	1,086	1,995	2,071	2,093	2,255	2,532	2,728	2,543	2,625

[1] Change from prior year shown, except as noted. For explanation of average annual percent change, see Guide to Tabular Presentation.   [2] Change from 1965.   [3] Covers insurance benefits and amount retained by insurance companies for expenses, additions to reserves, and profits (net cost of insurance).   [4] Represents expenditures for benefits and administrative cost from Federal hospital and medical insurance trust funds under old-age, survivors, disability, and health insurance programs; see text, p. 351.   [5] Includes medical benefits paid under public law by private insurance carriers and self-insurers.   [6] Payments made directly to suppliers of medical care. (Primarily Medicaid.)   [7] Expenditures not offset by other revenues.   [8] Covers expenditures for Alcohol, Drug Abuse, and Mental Health Administration; Indian Health Service; school health and other programs.

Source: U.S. Health Care Financing Administration, *Health Care Financing Review*, Winter 1984.

F4–6. National Health Expenditures, by Object: 1970 to 1983

[See also *Historical Statistics, Colonial Times to 1970*, series B 221–235]

OBJECT OF EXPENDITURE	EXPENDITURE (bil. dol.)								PERCENT		
	1970	1975	1978	1979	1980	1981	1982	1983	1970	1980	1983
Total	**75.0**	**132.7**	**190.0**	**215.1**	**248.0**	**285.8**	**322.3**	**355.4**	**100.0**	**100.0**	**100.0**
Spent by—											
Consumers	43.4	71.2	104.2	117.8	134.9	155.6	176.6	195.7	57.8	54.4	55.1
Government	27.8	56.4	79.9	90.9	105.8	121.7	135.8	148.8	37.0	42.7	41.9
Philanthropy and industry	3.9	5.1	5.8	6.3	7.2	8.6	9.9	10.9	5.1	2.9	3.1
Spent for—											
Health services and supplies	69.6	124.3	180.2	204.6	236.1	272.7	308.1	340.1	92.8	95.2	95.7
Personal health care expenses	65.4	117.1	167.4	189.6	219.1	253.4	284.7	313.3	87.2	88.4	88.2
Hospital care	28.0	52.4	76.2	87.0	101.3	117.9	134.9	147.2	37.3	40.8	41.4
Physicians' services	14.3	24.9	35.8	40.2	46.8	54.8	61.8	69.0	19.1	18.9	19.4
Dentists' services	4.7	8.2	11.8	13.3	15.4	17.3	19.5	21.8	6.3	6.2	6.1
Other professional services [1]	1.6	2.6	4.1	4.7	5.6	6.4	7.1	8.0	2.1	2.3	2.3
Drugs and sundries	8.0	11.9	15.1	17.1	18.5	20.5	21.8	23.7	10.7	7.5	6.7
Eyeglasses and appliances [2]	1.9	3.2	4.1	4.7	5.1	5.6	5.5	6.2	2.6	2.1	1.8
Nursing home care	4.7	10.1	15.2	17.4	20.4	23.9	26.5	28.8	6.3	8.2	8.1
Other health services	2.1	3.8	4.8	5.1	5.9	7.0	7.6	8.5	2.8	2.4	2.4
Net cost of insurance and administration [3]	2.8	4.0	7.5	8.6	9.2	10.6	13.4	15.6	3.8	3.7	4.4
Government public health activities	1.4	3.2	5.3	6.4	7.7	8.6	10.0	11.2	1.9	3.1	3.2
Medical research	2.0	3.3	4.4	4.7	5.4	5.6	5.9	6.2	2.6	2.2	1.7
Medical facilities construction	3.4	5.1	5.3	5.7	6.5	7.6	8.3	9.1	4.8	2.6	2.6

[1] Includes services of registered and practical nurses in private duty, visiting nurses, podiatrists, physical therapists, clinical psychologists, chiropractors, naturopaths, and Christian Science practitioners.   [2] Includes fees of optometrists and expenditures for hearing aids, orthopedic appliances, artifical limbs, crutches, wheelchairs, etc.   [3] Administrative expenses of federally financed health programs.

Source: U.S. Health Care Financing Administration, *Health Care Financing Review*, Winter 1984.

F4-7. National Health Expenditures, and Percent Distribution, According to Type of Expenditure: United States, Selected Years 1950-83

(Data are compiled by the Health Care Financing Administration)

Type of expenditure	1950	1960	1965	1970	1975	1980	1981	1982	1983
					Amount in billions				
Total...................	$12.7	$26.9	$41.9	$75.0	$132.7	$248.0	$285.8	$322.3	$355.4
					Percent distribution				
All expenditures.........	100.0	100.0	100.0	100.0	100.0	100.0	100.0	100.0	100.0
Health services and supplies......	92.4	93.6	91.6	92.8	93.7	95.2	95.4	95.6	95.7
Personal health care......	86.0	88.0	85.5	87.2	88.3	88.4	88.7	88.3	88.2
Hospital care.........	30.4	33.8	33.3	37.3	39.5	40.8	41.3	41.9	41.4
Physician services......	21.7	21.1	20.2	19.1	18.8	18.9	19.2	19.2	19.4
Dentist services......	7.6	7.4	6.7	6.3	6.2	6.2	6.1	6.0	6.1
Nursing home care......	1.5	2.0	4.9	6.3	7.6	8.2	8.4	8.2	8.1
Other professional services......	3.1	3.2	2.5	2.1	2.0	2.3	2.2	2.2	2.3
Drugs and drug sundries......	13.6	13.6	12.4	10.7	9.0	7.5	7.2	6.8	6.7
Eyeglasses and appliances......	3.9	2.9	2.8	2.6	2.4	2.1	2.0	1.7	1.8
Other health services......	4.2	4.0	2.7	2.8	2.8	2.4	2.4	2.4	2.4
Expenses for prepayment......	3.6	4.1	4.2	3.8	3.0	3.7	3.7	4.1	4.4
Government public health activities...	2.9	1.5	1.9	1.9	2.4	3.1	3.0	3.1	3.2
Research and construction......	7.6	6.4	8.4	7.2	6.3	4.8	4.6	4.4	4.3
Research......	0.9	2.5	3.6	2.6	2.5	2.2	2.0	1.8	1.7
Construction......	6.7	3.9	4.8	4.6	3.8	2.6	2.6	2.6	2.6

NOTE: The Health Care Financing Administration has made revisions in their health expenditure estimates. Data in this table may differ from that appearing in earlier volumes of Health, United States.

SOURCE: Bureau of Data Management and Strategy: National health expenditures, 1983, by R. M. Gibson, K. R. Levit, H. Lazenby, and D. R. Waldo. Health Care Financing Review. HCFA Pub. No. 03177. Health Care Financing Administration. Washington. U.S. Government Printing Office, winter 1984.

F4–8. Where the Medicare Dollar for the Elderly Goes: 1984

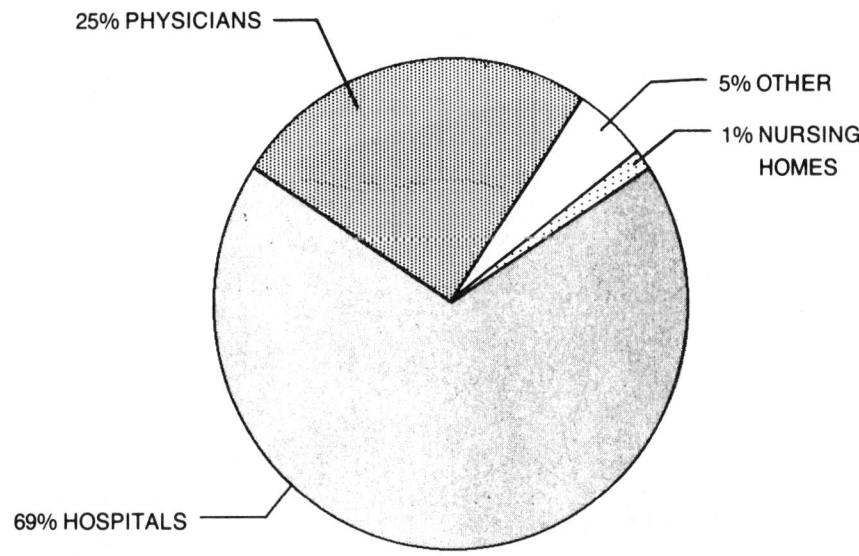

SOURCE: Health Care Financing Administration, Office of Financial and Actuarial Analysis.

F4–9. Where the Out-of-Pocket Dollar for the Elderly Goes: 1984

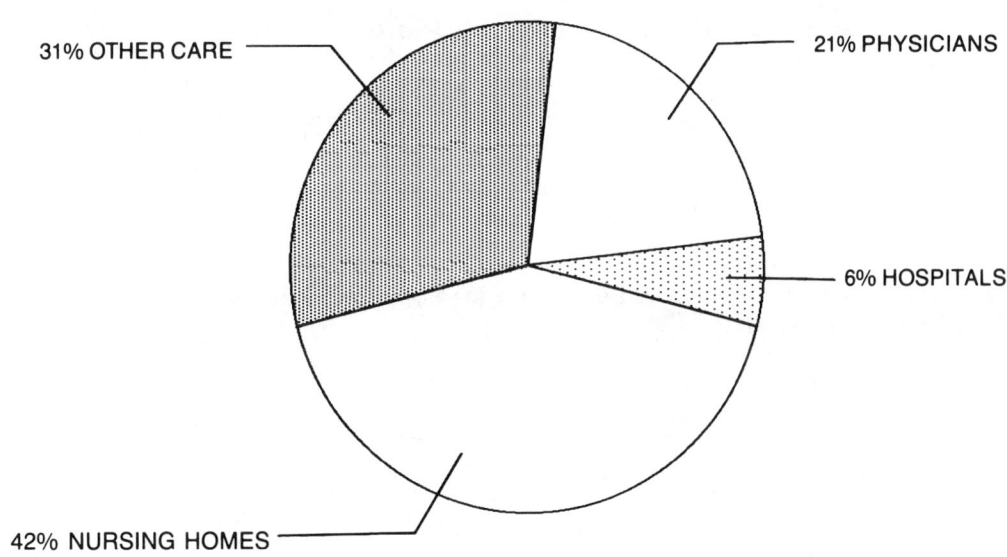

SOURCE: Health Care Financing Administration, Office of Financial and Actuarial Analysis.

F4-10. Distribution of Per Capita Personal Health Care Expenditures for People 65 Years of Age and Over, by Type of Service and Source of Funds: United States, 1984

Year and source of funds	Total per capita	Type of service				
		Total	Hospital	Physician	Nursing home	Other care
1984:						
Total per capita	$4,202	100.0	45.2	20.7	20.9	13.2
Private	1,379	100.0	15.7	25.0	33.1	26.2
Consumer	1,363	100.0	15.3	25.3	33.1	26.3
Out-of-pocket	1,059	100.0	5.6	21.4	41.6	31.3
Insurance	304	100.0	49.2	38.6	3.3	8.9
Other private	16	100.0	42.1	1.9	39.1	17.0
Government	2,823	100.0	59.7	18.6	15.0	6.8
Medicare	2,051	100.0	69.2	24.5	0.9	5.4
Medicaid	536	100.0	17.0	3.1	68.1	11.8
Other government	236	100.0	73.2	2.4	16.5	7.9

F4-11. Personal Health Care Expenditures in Millions for People 65 Years of Age or Over, by Source of Funds and Type of Service: United States, 1984

Year and source of funds	Type of service				
	Total care	Hospital	Physician	Nursing home	Other care
1984:					
Total	$119,872	$54,200	$24,770	$25,105	$15,798
Private	39,341	6,160	9,827	13,038	10,316
Consumer	38,875	5,964	9,818	12,856	10,237
Out-of-pocket	30,198	1,694	6,468	12,569	9,467
Insurance	8,677	4,270	3,350	287	770
Other private	466	196	9	182	79
Government	80,531	48,040	14,943	12,067	5,482
Medicare	58,519	40,524	14,314	539	3,142
Medicaid	15,288	2,595	467	10,418	1,808
Other government	6,724	4,920	162	1,110	532
Exhibit: Population (in millions)	28.5				

F4-12. Personal Health Care Expenditures Per Capita for People 65 Years of Age or Over, by Source of Funds and Type of Service: United States, 1984

Year and source of funds	Type of service				
	Total care	Hospital	Physician	Nursing home	Other care
1984:					
Total	$4,202	$1,900	$868	$880	$554
Private	1,379	216	344	457	362
Consumer	1,363	209	344	451	359
Out-of-pocket	1,059	59	227	441	332
Insurance	304	150	117	10	27
Other private	16	7	1	6	3
Government	2,823	1,684	524	423	192
Medicare	2,051	1,420	502	19	110
Medicaid	536	91	16	365	63
Other government	236	172	6	39	19

Source: Waldo, Daniel R., and Lazenby, Helen C.; *Demographic Characteristics and Health Care Use and Expenditures by the Aged in the United States: 1977-1984;* "Health Care Financing Review," vol. 6, No. 1, fall, 1984.

F4–13. Medicare—Persons Served and Reimbursements: 1971 to 1981

[Persons served are enrollees who use covered services, incurred expenses greater than the applicable deductible amounts and for whom Medicare paid benefits. Reimbursements are amounts paid to providers for covered services; excludes deductibles, coinsurance amounts, and charges for noncovered services.

TYPE OF COVERAGE AND SERVICE	Unit	PERSONS 65 YEARS OLD AND OVER					DISABLED			
		1971	1975	1979	1980	1981	1975	1979	1980	1981
Persons served, total [1]	1,000	9,425	12,032	15,221	16,271	17,036	975	1,654	1,760	1,845
Hospital insurance [1]	1,000	4,416	4,963	5,698	6,024	6,229	475	700	728	754
Inpatient hospital	1,000	4,386	4,913	5,633	5,951	6,072	472	694	721	739
Skilled-nursing services	1,000	239	260	247	248	243	8	9	9	8
Home health services	1,000	167	329	601	675	881	22	46	51	67
Supplementary medical insurance [1]	1,000	9,075	11,762	15,041	16,099	16,858	924	1,614	1,723	1,810
Physicians' and other medical services	1,000	8,801	11,396	14,582	15,627	16,380	865	1,523	1,631	1,717
Outpatient services	1,000	2,171	3,768	5,928	6,629	7,096	399	823	909	975
Home health services	1,000	83	161	269	302	187	13	23	25	14
Persons served per 1,000 enrollees, total [1]	Rate	451	528	610	638	655	450	568	594	615
Hospital insurance [1]	Rate	213	221	232	240	243	219	240	246	251
Inpatient hospital	Rate	212	219	230	237	237	218	238	243	246
Skilled-nursing services	Rate	12	12	10	10	10	4	3	3	3
Home health services	Rate	8	15	25	27	34	10	16	17	22
Supplementary medical insurance [1]	Rate	454	536	624	652	670	471	607	634	656
Physicians' and other medical services	Rate	441	519	605	633	651	442	573	600	622
Outpatient services	Rate	109	172	246	269	282	204	310	334	353
Home health services	Rate	4	7	11	12	7	7	9	9	5
Reimbursements, total	Mil. dol	7,349	12,689	24,310	29,134	34,490	1,509	3,747	4,478	5,315
Hospital insurance	Mil. dol	5,364	9,209	17,137	20,353	24,153	987	2,341	2,765	3,317
Inpatient hospital	Mil. dol	5,156	8,840	16,477	19,583	23,111	968	2,297	2,714	3,243
Skilled-nursing services	Mil. dol	166	233	306	331	361	9	13	13	14
Home health services	Mil. dol	42	136	353	440	682	10	31	38	60
Supplementary medical insurance	Mil. dol	1,986	3,481	7,173	8,781	10,336	522	1,406	1,713	1,998
Physicians' and other medical services	Mil. dol	1,848	3,050	6,045	7,361	8,688	295	810	997	1,199
Outpatient services	Mil. dol	125	374	997	1,261	1,557	221	583	701	791
Home health services	Mil. dol	13	56	131	159	91	5	13	16	8
Reimbursements, per person served, total	Dollars	780	1,055	1,597	1,791	2,024	1,548	2,265	2,544	2,881
Hospital insurance	Dollars	1,215	1,855	3,007	3,379	3,877	2,077	3,345	3,798	4,400
Inpatient hospital	Dollars	1,176	1,799	2,925	3,291	3,806	2,051	3,312	3,765	4,389
Skilled-nursing services	Dollars	694	896	1,239	1,336	1,486	1,049	1,452	1,571	1,693
Home health services	Dollars	251	413	588	652	774	478	671	733	900
Supplementary medical insurance	Dollars	219	296	477	545	613	565	871	994	1,104
Physicians' and other medical services	Dollars	210	268	415	471	530	341	532	611	698
Outpatient services	Dollars	57	99	168	190	219	554	708	771	811
Home health services	Dollars	161	347	488	526	488	420	569	619	541

[1] Persons are counted once for each type of covered service used, but are not double counted in totals.

Source: U.S. Health Care Financing Administration, *Health Care Financing Program Statistics*, and unpublished data.

F4-14. Medicare—Hospital Utilization and Hospital and Physician Charges: 1970 to 1982

[Data reflect date claims approved for payment and cover only claims approved and recorded in Health Care Financing Administration central records before December 31, 1983. Includes Puerto Rico, outlying areas and enrollees in foreign countries]

ITEM	Unit	PERSONS 65 YEARS OLD AND OVER					DISABLED [1]			
		1970	1975	1980	1981	1982	1975	1980	1981	1982
Hospital inpatient care:										
Admissions	1,000	6,141	7,404	9,258	9,648	10,084	850	1,317	1,350	1,394
Per 1,000 enrollees [2]	Rate	304	332	369	377	386	394	445	450	472
Covered days of care	Millions	80	84	97	98	101	9	13	14	14
Per 1,000 enrollees [2]	Rate	3,949	3,786	3,861	3,847	3,852	4,136	4,483	4,536	4,638
Per admission	Days	13.0	11.4	10.5	10.2	10.0	10.5	10.1	10.1	9.8
Hospital charges	Mil. dol	5,946	12,021	26,119	33,829	40,987	1,320	3,976	4,777	5,668
Per day	Dollars	74	142	290	344	407	148	299	351	414
Percent of charges reimbursed	Percent	77.1	75.2	69.6	68.7	67.2	73.1	68.5	67.9	66.7
Physician charges	Mil. dol	[3] 2,157	3,907	8,802	10,483	12,383	344	1,079	1,294	1,495
Percent reimbursed	Percent	[3] 72.9	74.1	77.8	78.2	77.9	75.6	78.6	78.8	78.5

[1] Coverage not limited with respect to age.   [2] Hospital insurance enrollment as of July 1.
[3] Data reflect date paid claims were recorded in Health Care Financing Administration records.
Source: U.S. Health Care Financing Administration, *Health Care Financing Review*, quarterly, and unpublished data. Also in U.S. Social Security Administration, *Social Security Bulletin*, quarterly.

F4-15. Medicare—Enrollment and Reimbursements by Level of Reimbursement: 1982

HI=Hospital insurance; SMI=Supplementary medical insurance. Enrollees represent persons ever enrolled during calendar year]

TYPE OF COVERAGE	TOTAL				PERCENT DISTRIBUTION BY LEVEL OF REIMBURSEMENT					
	Unit	Amount	Persons with no reimbursement	Persons with reimbursement	Less than $1,000	$1,000-$1,999	$2,000-$4,999	$5,000-$9,999	$10,000-$14,999	$15,000 or more
HI AND/OR SMI										
Aged: [1] Enrollees	1,000	27,986	39.2	60.8	38.3	5.4	8.3	4.9	1.9	1.9
Reimbursements	Mil.dol	41,526	(x)	100.0	6.0	5.3	18.2	23.4	15.7	31.3
Disabled: Enrollees	1,000	3,284	45.2	54.8	31.8	5.5	7.5	4.6	2.0	3.4
Reimbursements	Mil.dol	6,172	(x)	100.0	4.4	4.2	12.9	17.5	12.9	48.1
HOSPITAL INSURANCE										
Aged: [1] Enrollees	1,000	27,541	76.2	23.8	5.7	4.7	6.8	3.9	1.4	1.3
Reimbursements	Mil.dol	29,214	(x)	100.0	2.8	6.4	20.8	26.0	16.1	27.8
Disabled: Enrollees	1,000	3,284	76.9	23.1	5.4	4.4	6.3	3.8	1.5	1.7
Reimbursements	Mil.dol	3,878	(x)	100.0	2.4	5.4	17.5	22.6	15.5	36.7

X Not applicable.   [1] Persons 65 years old and over.
Source: U.S. Health Care Financing Administration, *Medicare Program Statistics*, annual.

F4-16. Medicare and Medicaid—Selected Characteristics of Persons Covered: 1980 to 1982

[In thousands, except percent. Represents number of persons as of March of following year who were enrolled at any time in year shown. Person did not have to receive medical care paid for by Medicare or Medicaid in order to be counted. For Medicare, covers persons 15 years old and over; for Medicaid covers persons of all ages.

POVERTY STATUS	1980, total	1981, total	1982							
			Total [1]	White	Black	Spanish origin [2]	Under 15 years old	15–44 years old	45–64 years old	65 years and over
MEDICARE										
Persons covered, total	26,200	27,208	27,522	24,644	2,482	703	(x)	672	2,219	24,631
Percent of total population	15.1	15.4	15.5	16.0	12.8	7.2	(x)	.6	5.0	96.1
Below poverty level	4,300	4,454	4,187	3,114	978	205	(x)	199	500	3,489
Above poverty level	21,900	22,754	23,335	21,530	1,504	498	(x)	473	1,719	21,142
MEDICAID										
Persons covered, total	18,966	19,407	18,914	12,022	6,166	2,337	7,067	7,093	1,930	2,824
Below poverty level	11,113	11,687	12,629	7,314	4,866	1,717	5,519	4,719	1,180	1,210
Above poverty level	7,854	7,720	6,285	4,708	1,300	620	1,548	2,374	750	1,614
Percent of total population	8.4	8.8	8.3	6.1	22.7	17.6	13.7	6.6	4.4	11.0
Below poverty level	39.1	37.8	37.9	32.3	50.5	42.8	48.3	33.8	27.3	33.2
Above poverty level	4.0	3.9	3.2	2.7	7.4	6.7	3.9	2.5	1.9	7.3

X Not applicable.   [1] Includes other races not shown separately.   [2] Persons of Spanish origin may be of any race.
Source: U.S. Bureau of the Census, *Current Population Reports*, series P-60, No. 143 and earlier reports.

F4–17. Medicare Enrollments and Benefit Payments, 1966–1983

(000,000 omitted)

Calendar year	Hospital and/or medical insurance		Hospital insurance (Part A)		Supplementary medical insurance (Part B)	
	Number of enrolled persons*	Benefit payments	Number of enrolled persons*	Benefit payments	Number of enrolled persons*	Benefit payments
All Enrollees						
1966 (July-Dec.)	19.1	$ 1,019	19.1	$ 891	17.7	$ 128
1967	19.5	4,549	19.5	3,353	17.9	1,197
1968	19.8	5,697	19.8	4,179	18.8	1,518
1969	20.1	6,603	20.0	4,739	19.2	1,865
1970	20.5	7,099	20.4	5,124	19.6	1,975
1971	20.9	7,868	20.7	5,751	20.0	2,117
1972	21.3	8,643	21.1	6,318	20.4	2,325
1973	23.5	9,583	23.3	7,057	22.5	2,526
1974	24.2	12,418	23.9	9,099	23.2	3,318
1975	25.0	15,588	24.6	11,315	23.9	4,273
1976	25.7	18,420	25.3	13,340	24.6	5,080
1977	26.5	21,774	26.1	15,737	25.4	6,038
1978	27.2	24,934	26.8	17,682	26.1	7,252
1979	27.9	29,331	27.5	20,623	26.8	8,708
1980	28.5	35,700	28.1	25,064	27.4	10,635
1981	29.0	43,455	28.6	30,342	27.9	13,113
1982	29.5	48,134	29.1	33,333	28.4	14,801
1983	30.0	N.A.	29.6	N.A.	29.0	N.A.
Enrollees Age 65 and Over						
1966 (July-Dec.)	19.1	$ 1,019	19.1	$ 891	17.7	$ 128
1967	19.5	4,549	19.5	3,353	17.9	1,197
1968	19.8	5,697	19.8	4,179	18.8	1,518
1969	20.1	6,603	20.0	4,739	19.2	1,865
1970	20.5	7,099	20.4	5,124	19.6	1,975
1971	20.9	7,868	20.7	5,751	20.0	2,117
1972	21.3	8,643	21.1	6,318	20.4	2,325
1973**	21.8	9,225	21.6	6,803	20.9	2,422
1974**	22.3	11,275	22.0	8,295	21.4	2,980
1975**	22.8	13,994	22.5	10,250	21.9	3,744
1976**	23.3	16,328	22.9	11,959	22.4	4,369
1977**	23.8	19,131	23.5	14,012	23.0	5,119
1978**	24.4	21,713	24.0	15,612	23.5	6,101
1979**	24.9	25,431	24.5	18,143	24.1	7,288
1980**	25.5	30,958	25.1	22,077	24.7	8,881
1981**	26.0	37,640	25.6	26,696	25.2	10,944
1982	26.5	41,787	26.1	29,360	25.7	12,427
1983	27.1	N.A.	26.7	N.A.	26.3	N.A.

*As of July 1.

**Benefits estimated by the Health Care Financing Administration.

N.A.—Not available.

NOTE: Detail may not add to totals due to rounding.

SOURCE: Department of Health and Human Services, Bureau of Data Management and Strategy, Health Care Financing Administration.

F4–18. Medicare and Medicaid Benefits by State, 1983

State	Medicare Benefits paid** (000,000)	Number of persons enrolled (000)	Medicaid* Benefits paid*** (000,000)	Unduplicated count of recipients (000)
Alabama	$ 905	516	$ 368.7	311.3
Alaska	35	15	51.2	20.0
Arizona	745	373	—	—
Arkansas	606	360	313.2	190.3
California	7,072	2,793	3,557.2	3,499.9
Colorado	563	289	255.3	147.6
Connecticut	849	420	495.4	215.5
Delaware	138	72	62.1	45.6
District of Columbia	245	78	196.5	117.7
Florida	4,128	1,883	681.3	555.2
Georgia	1,082	626	601.4	441.1
Hawaii	167	93	141.7	100.3
Idaho	173	113	67.3	39.2
Illinois	3,194	1,408	1,347.0	1,051.0
Indiana	1,244	677	596.0	271.7
Iowa	712	429	312.0	189.5
Kansas	646	336	254.5	147.2
Kentucky	744	483	411.0	388.0
Louisiana	857	459	674.7	378.0
Maine	303	165	205.1	122.2
Maryland	1,092	457	446.6	328.0
Massachusetts	1,909	808	1,338.2†	579.1
Michigan	2,599	1,093	1,421.7	1,187.6
Minnesota	924	536	868.1	326.4
Mississippi	558	337	299.4	290.5
Missouri	1,379	726	468.5	341.6
Montana	170	101	86.2	44.8
Nebraska	380	225	146.0	84.0
Nevada	209	88	73.7	27.9
New Hampshire	217	120	93.1	41.7
New Jersey	2,273	992	981.5	611.9
New Mexico	257	142	101.8	84.4
New York	5,440	2,399	6,259.5	2,160.6
North Carolina	1,136	735	567.0	349.1
North Dakota	193	91	83.3	31.9
Ohio	2,745	1,369	1,474.3	910.6
Oklahoma	746	412	388.7	232.5
Oregon	655	356	236.2	153.8
Pennsylvania	4,049	1,768	1,718.8	1,167.2
Rhode Island	278	145	221.7	104.6
South Carolina	552	359	278.8	236.2
South Dakota	166	102	77.8	33.5
Tennessee	1,068	609	508.6	341.2
Texas	3,325	1,540	1,316.7	680.1
Utah	184	130	114.5	66.0
Vermont	122	68	84.3	53.6
Virginia	1,085	604	488.2	306.4
Washington	859	507	427.1	257.6
West Virginia	482	285	140.6	177.4
Wisconsin	1,175	648	901.1	480.1
Wyoming	76	44	24.4	14.2
United States	$60,720	29,406	$32,228.2	19,936.0
Puerto Rico	—	—	119.8	1,547.1
Virgin Islands	—	—	2.6	11.1
Grand Total	$60,720	29,406	$32,350.5	21,494.2

*Medicaid figures are preliminary.

**Medicare data exclude retroactive adjustment made at end of accounting year on basis of reasonable costs of operation.

***Medicaid data for some states includes expenditures not computable for federal funding.

†Excludes data for the blind.

NOTE: Details may not add to totals due to rounding.

SOURCE: U.S. Department of Health and Human Services, Health Care Financing Administration.

F4–19. Aggregate and Per Capita Amount and Percentage Distribution of National Health Expenditure by Type of Expenditure, Selected Calendar Years, 1965–1985

Type of expenditure	Historical year						
	1965	1970	1975	1980	1982	1983	1985*
Aggregate Amount (In billions)							
Total	$41.9	$75.0	$132.7	$248.0	$322.3	$355.4	$456.4
Health services and supplies	38.4	69.6	124.3	236.1	308.1	340.1	438.4
Personal health care expenses	35.9	65.4	117.1	219.1	284.7	313.3	408.2
Hospital care	14.0	28.0	52.4	101.3	134.9	147.2	196.7
Physicians' services	8.5	14.3	24.9	46.8	61.8	69.0	87.9
Dentists' services	2.8	4.7	8.2	15.4	19.5	21.8	26.8
Other professional services	1.0	1.6	2.6	5.6	7.1	8.0	10.1
Drugs and medical sundries	5.2	8.0	11.9	18.5	21.8	23.7	30.2
Eyeglasses and appliances	1.2	1.9	3.2	5.1	5.5	6.2	7.3
Nursing home care	2.1	4.7	10.1	20.4	26.5	28.8	38.9
Other health services	1.1	2.1	3.8	5.9	7.6	8.5	10.3
Program administration and net cost of insurance	1.7	2.8	4.0	9.2	13.4	15.6	20.8
Government public health activities	.8	1.4	3.2	7.7	10.0	11.2	9.4
Research and medical facilities construction	3.5	5.4	8.4	11.9	14.2	15.3	18.0
Research	1.5	2.0	3.3	5.4	5.9	6.2	6.5
Construction	2.0	3.4	5.1	6.5	8.3	9.1	11.5
Per Capita Amounts							
Total	$211	$351	$604	$1,049	$1,337	$1,460	$1,882
Health services and supplies	193	325	565	999	1,278	1,397	1,808
Personal health care expenses	181	306	531	927	1,181	1,287	1,683
Hospital care	70	131	237	429	560	605	811
Physicians' services	43	69	113	202	256	284	362
Dentists' services	14	23	37	67	81	90	111
Other professional services	5	8	12	24	29	33	42
Drugs and medical sundries	26	38	54	78	90	97	125
Eyeglasses and appliances	6	9	14	22	23	26	30
Nursing home care	10	23	46	86	110	118	160
Other health services	6	10	17	25	32	35	43
Program administration and net cost of insurance	8	13	20	39	57	64	86
Government public health activities	4	7	14	33	42	46	39
Research and medical facilities construction	18	26	38	50	59	63	74
Research	8	9	15	23	25	26	27
Construction	10	16	23	28	34	37	47

NOTE: Details may not add to totals due to rounding.

*Projected

SOURCE: U.S. Department of Health and Human Services, Health Care Financing Administration, *Health Care Financing Review*, Winter 1984.

F4–20. Per Capita Personal Health Care Expenditures and Rank for Leading Medical Conditions, According to Age and Sex: United States, 1980

Medical condition	Persons under 65 years of age		Persons 65 years of age and over	
	Male	Female	Male	Female
	Per capita amount			
Circulatory diseases	$ 67	$ 61	$674	$848
Digestive diseases	110	143	213	223
Mental disorders	73	69	181	246
Injury and poisoning	86	61	105	203
Respiratory diseases	60	68	192	137
Neoplasms	30	50	244	178
Musculoskeletal system and connective tissue diseases	40	55	91	187
Genitourinary system diseases	21	82	128	70
Nervous system and sense organ diseases	57	69	168	176
Endocrine, nutritional, metabolic diseases	15	31	82	138
	Rank			
Circulatory diseases	4	7	1	1
Digestive diseases	1	1	3	3
Mental disorders	3	4	5	2
Injury and poisoning	2	6	8	4
Respiratory diseases	5	5	4	9
Neoplasms	8	9	2	6
Musculoskeletal system and connective tissue diseases	7	8	9	5
Genitourinary system diseases	9	2	7	10
Nervous system and sense organ diseases	6	3	6	7
Endocrine, nutritional, metabolic diseases	10	10	10	8

NOTE: Conditions are based on the *International Classification of Diseases, 9th Revision, Clinical Modification.*

SOURCE: National Center for Health Statistics: Computed by the Division of Analysis from data compiled by the Health Care Financing Administration, the National Center for Health Statistics, and other organizations.

F4–21. Health Care Expenditures for Institutionalized Elderly Persons, by Type of Expenditure and Source of Payment, 1986 (in billions)

	Public			Out-of-Pocket	Other Private	Total Expenditures
	Medicare	Other Public	Total Public			
Hospital Care	$7.2	$4.0	$11.2	$ 0.5	$1.0	$12.7
Physicians' Services	0.8	0.3	1.1	0.6	0.2	1.9
Dentists' Services	a/	a/	a/	0.5	a/	0.5
Other Professional Services	0.1	0.1	0.2	0.2	0.1	0.5
Drugs and Medical Sundries	a/	0.1	0.1	0.4	a/	0.5
Eyeglasses and Appliances	a/	a/	a/	0.1	a/	0.1
Nursing Home Care	0.6	16.0	16.6	16.0	0.2	32.8
Other Health Services	0.1	0.4	0.5	a/	0.2	0.7
Total Personal Health	$8.8	$20.9	$29.7	$18.3	$1.7	$49.8

a/ Less than $50 million

Source: ICF estimates

F4–22. Health Care Expenditures for All Elderly Persons, by Type of Expenditure and Source of Payment, 1986 (in billions)

	Public			Out-of Pocket	Other Private	Total Expenditures
	Medicare	Other Public	Total Public			
Hospital Inpatient Care	$41.8	$ 9.8	$51.6	$ 3.3	$ 8.1	$ 63.0
Hospital Outpatient Care	3.1	1.0	4.1	0.6	1.1	5.8
Physicians' Services	18.1	1.4	19.5	5.3	3.6	28.5
Dentists' Services	a/	0.1	0.1	2.3	0.2	2.7
Other Professional Services	2.2	0.3	2.5	0.8	0.2	3.6
Drugs and Medical Sundries	0.1	0.8	0.9	7.3	0.8	9.0
Eyeglasses and Appliances	0.9	a/	0.9	1.4	0.1	2.5
Nursing Home Care	0.6	16.0	16.6	16.0	0.2	32.8
Other Health Services	1.0	1.1	2.1	0.1	0.5	2.9
Total Personal Health	$67.9	$30.6	$98.5	$37.3	$14.9	$150.6

a/ Less than $50 million

Source: ICF estimates

F4–23. Comparison of the Distribution of Health Expenditures, by Health Services

Service	1984 (Waldo/Lazenby)	1986 (ICF)
Hospital	45%	42%
Physician	21	19
Nursing Home	21	22
Other	13	17
Total	100%	100%

Source: ICF estimates and Daniel Waldo and Helen C. Lazenby, "Demographic Characteristics and Health Care Use and Expenditures by the Aged in the United States: 1977-84," *Health Care Financing Review*, Fall 1984.

F4–24. Comparison of the Distribution of Health Expenditures, by Source of Payment

Payment Source	1984 (Waldo/Lazenby)	1986 (ICF)
Medicare	49%	45%
Other Public	18	20
Out-of-Pocket	25	25
Other Private	8	10
Total	100%	100%

Source: ICF estimates and Daniel Waldo and Helen C. Lazenby, "Demographic Characteristics and Health Care Use and Expenditures by the Aged in the United States: 1977-84," *Health Care Financing Review*, Fall 1984.

F4–25. Supplementary Medical Insurance Trust Fund: Status, 1966–83

[In thousands. Calendar year and fiscal year data appear in alternate months of the **Bulletin.**]

Period	Receipts			Expenditures		Assets at end of period [1]		
	Premium income [2]	Federal matching contributions [3]	Net interest [4]	Net medical service benefits [5]	Net administrative expenses [6]	Invested in U. S. Government securities [7]	Cash balances	Total assets
Calendar year:								
1966 [8]	$321,557	...	$1,813	$127,872	$73,766	$118,856	$2,875	$121,731
1967	639,651	$933,299	23,622	1,196,536	110,110	408,665	2,993	411,658
1968	832,368	858,349	20,506	1,518,488	183,222	380,208	40,962	421,170
1969	913,943	907,292	18,061	1,864,759	196,362	182,076	17,268	199,344
1970	1,096,360	1,092,573	12,163	1,974,633	237,840	134,278	53,689	187,967
1971	1,301,758	1,312,790	23,973	2,116,995	259,903	406,902	42,687	449,589
1972	1,382,313	1,388,574	37,184	2,324,645	289,793	619,429	23,794	643,223
1973	1,550,086	1,704,526	56,706	2,526,163	317,803	1,093,493	17,082	1,110,575
1974	1,803,950	2,224,950	94,824	3,318,228	410,012	1,455,278	50,785	1,506,063
1975	1,917,847	2,648,371	106,262	4,272,791	462,171	1,442,025	1,556	1,443,581
1976	2,060,289	3,810,029	106,282	5,079,627	541,867	1,847,771	−49,081	1,798,690
1977	2,246,761	5,386,296	171,831	6,038,234	466,707	3,225,563	−126,927	3,098,636
1978	2,469,582	6,287,474	298,527	7,251,684	502,945	4,343,162	56,429	4,399,591
1979	2,718,769	6,645,073	403,890	8,707,596	557,522	4,885,031	17,174	4,902,205
1980	3,010,643	7,455,168	407,711	10,635,262	610,024	4,563,893	−33,452	4,530,441
1981	[9] 3,721,745	[9] 11,290,790	361,612	13,112,937	914,740	5,943,311	−66,399	5,876,912
1982	[9] 3,697,059	[9] 12,283,622	599,445	15,455,316	771,967	6,348,168	−118,412	6,229,756
1982								
November	344,409	1,137,823	5,904	1,445,250	72,613	5,962,011	−113,944	5,848,067
December	363,160	1,274,461	294,014	1,487,083	62,865	6,348,168	−118,412	6,229,756
1983								
January	348,738	1,146,393	5,930	1,434,875	55,553	6,379,471	−139,083	6,240,388
February	352,785	1,170,819	9,822	1,260,754	55,646	6,481,999	−24,586	6,457,413
March	349,377	1,150,996	6,496	1,479,657	53,916	6,394,467	36,242	6,430,709
April	359,683	1,186,164	8,771	1,370,753	68,131	6,575,343	−28,900	6,546,443
May	343,055	1,132,098	5,771	1,505,120	73,901	6,579,576	−131,230	6,448,346
June	362,083	1,230,535	322,284	1,518,865	63,890	6,854,840	−74,347	6,780,493
July	339,677	1,230,503	6,569	1,415,577	65,267	6,975,099	−98,701	6,876,398
August	348,205	1,326,833	1,800	1,640,071	116,068	6,884,731	−87,633	6,797,098
September	361,265	1,102,178	8,529	1,552,437	70,330	6,958,312	−312,009	6,646,303
October	363,996	1,351,754	11,345	1,777,707	72,284	6,512,225	11,182	6,523,407
November	347,469	1,290,816	12,805	1,528,541	81,366	6,513,451	51,139	6,564,590

[1] Includes gifts.

[2] Represents premiums voluntarily assigned from cash benefits of beneficiaries and annuitants on the rolls of OASI, DI, Railroad Retirement, and Federal civil service retirement; premiums paid by eligible persons not in receipt of cash payments under those programs (including OASI or DI beneficiaries with benefits temporarily withheld); and payments under sec. 1843 of the Social Security Act deposited by States for coverage of eligible aged or disabled individuals receiving cash public assistance and SSI payments.

[3] Under sec. 1844(a) of the Social Security Act.

[4] After adjustment for interest on administrative expenses reimbursed among trust funds.

[5] Represents payment vouchers on letters of credit issued to carriers under sec. 1842 of the Social Security Act.

[6] See table M-5, footnote 7.

[7] See table M-5, footnote 8.

[8] Trust fund activated July 1, 1966; data represent only 6 months' operations, but administrative expenses include "tool-up" period from passage of 1965 amendments.

[9] Section 708 of the Social Security Act specified the provisions for the delivery of Social Security benefit checks when the regularly designated delivery day falls on a Saturday, Sunday or legal public holiday. Delivery of benefit checks for January 3, 1982 occurred on December 31, 1981. Consequently, the SMI premiums withheld from the checks ($264 million) and the general revenue matching contributions ($883 million) were added to the SMI Trust Fund on December 31, 1981. These amounts have been excluded from the premium income and general revenue for calendar year 1982.

Source: See table M-5.

F4-26. Hospital Insurance Trust Fund: Status, 1966-85

[In thousands. Calendar year and fiscal year data appear in alternate months of the **Bulletin**.]

Period	Receipts					Expenditures		Assets at end of period [1]		
	Net contribution income [2]	Premiums from voluntarily insured [3]	Transfers from railroad retirement account [4]	Payments from general fund of the Treasury [5]	Net interest [6]	Net hospital and related service benefits [7]	Net administrative expenses [8]	Invested in U.S. Government securities [9]	Cash balances	Total assets [10]
Fiscal year: [11]										
1966	$908,797	...		...	$5,970	...	$63,564	$785,758	$65,446	$851,204
1967	2,688,684	...	$16,305	$337,850	45,798	$2,507,773	88,848	1,298,168	45,053	1,343,221
1968	3,514,049	...	44,049	283,631	60,655	3,736,322	78,647	1,370,276	60,360	1,430,636
1969	4,423,236	...	54,168	770,968	95,671	4,653,976	104,182	2,001,444	15,078	2,016,521
1970	4,784,789	...	63,537	628,262	137,193	4,803,900	149,003	2,653,322	24,079	2,677,401
1971	4,897,979	...	65,945	873,849	180,337	5,442,409	149,996	3,029,856	73,250	3,103,106
1972	5,225,891	...	66,106	551,351	187,781	6,108,314	167,195	2,883,958	-25,233	2,858,725
1973	7,663,119	...	63,238	429,415	195,828	6,647,977	193,681	4,222,365	146,301	4,368,666
1974	10,602,270	$4,281	99,182	498,780	405,254	7,805,980	258,755	7,864,355	49,344	7,913,699
1975	11,291,088	5,685	132,497	530,405	608,189	10,353,011	258,522	9,760,883	109,156	9,870,039
1976	12,031,498	7,696	137,722	658,430	708,926	12,266,757	311,853	10,942,180	-106,466	10,835,714
July-Sept. 1976 (transition quarter)	3,365,693	2,248	142,850	(12)	4,964	3,314,482	89,177	11,009,482	-61,672	10,947,810
1977	13,648,535	10,506	(13)	[12] 944,000	770,966	14,905,842	301,292	10,973,740	140,945	11,114,685
1978	16,677,267	12,094	[13] 213,745	[14] 859,938	779,970	17,410,782	450,886	11,757,306	38,725	11,796,031
1979	19,926,577	16,507	191,149	[14] 907,849	867,609	19,890,562	452,461	13,163,539	199,161	13,362,700
1980	23,243,769	16,566	244,280	[14] 871,156	1,038,953	23,790,365	497,145	14,656,077	-166,164	14,489,913
1981	30,425,221	20,759	276,468	[14] 833,600	1,307,279	28,907,417	352,894	18,191,479	-98,550	18,092,929
1982	34,390,179	24,814	351,392	1,015,000	1,829,249	34,343,378	520,633	20,799,541	40,011	20,839,552
1983	37,269,615	25,835	357,691	2,963,000	3,321,335	38,101,524	519,234	13,432,921	286,079	13,719,000
1984	41,510,574	35,074	350,630	752,000	2,915,208	41,476,365	631,949	16,918,778	255,394	17,174,173
1984										
June	3,916,901	3,306	350,630	...	845,863	3,639,783	42,895	16,039,634	-41,357	15,998,277
July	3,709,613	2,189	...	...	125,960	3,505,517	62,121	16,179,284	88,848	16,268,131
August	3,415,485	2,495	...	...	128,366	3,868,748	47,054	15,797,074	101,601	15,898,674
September	3,472,239	3,103	...	...	120,830	2,274,845	45,828	16,918,778	255,394	17,174,173
October	3,192,449	1,894	...	...	119,387	4,993,664	50,828	15,794,765	-351,355	15,443,411
November	3,279,469	2,804	...	...	147,872	3,585,064	48,970	15,217,584	21,938	15,239,522
December	3,364,646	-25	...	...	945,458	3,794,033	64,437	15,784,263	-93,131	15,691,132
1985										
January	4,098,298	5,385	...	...	125,377	3,940,333	85,017	17,709,479	9,363	17,718,843
February	3,987,093	4,700	...	...	102,755	3,715,484	54,939	18,087,165	-44,197	18,042,968
March	4,036,482	8,692	...	766,000	146,451	3,939,044	80,035	18,933,808	47,707	18,981,515
April	4,710,217	-3,484	...	...	106,235	4,192,666	95,318	19,634,884	-128,386	19,506,499
May	3,895,111	2,158	...	...	96,285	4,246,570	90,279	19,148,824	14,380	19,163,204
June	3,873,488	3,371	371,390	...	1,066,869	3,666,566	41,250	20,328,122	442,385	20,770,507

[1] Includes gifts.

[2] Represents amounts appropriated (estimated tax collections with suitable subsequent adjustments). Fiscal year 1983 includes a net amount of $883 million representing retroactive contributions on deemed wage credits for military service performed in 1966 and later and the annual contributions on 1983 wage credits. Fiscal year 1984 and June 1984 include $68 million representing an adjustment for the retroactive contributions on deemed wage credits for military service in 1966 and later. Fiscal year 1984 and July 1984 include $79 million in annual contributions on 1984 wage credits. Beginning in January 1984, includes payments from the general fund of the Treasury for tax credits on net earnings from self-employment.

[3] Beginning July 1973, aged ineligibles may voluntarily enroll for HI.

[4] Represents receipts with respect to contributions for HI coverage of railroad workers; see table M-4, footnote 7.

[5] Represents Federal Government transfers from general-fund appropriations to meet costs of benefits for persons not insured for cash benefits under OASDI-HI or railroad retirement and for costs of benefits arising from military wage credits. 1978 reflects $2 million in reimbursement from general revenue for costs arising from the granting of noncontributory wage credits to U.S. citizens of Japanese ancestry who were interned during World War II. Fiscal year 1983 reflects $1,878 million, under the provisions of Public Law 98-21, for noncontributory wage credits for military service performed before 1957.

[6] After adjustment for interest on administrative expenses reimbursed among trust funds. Fiscal year 1983 reflects $695 million, fiscal year 1984 and June 1984 reflect $103 million for interest on deemed wage credits for military service performed after 1956. Beginning in fiscal year 1983, net interest includes interest on advance tax transfers and interest on interfund borrowing.

[7] Represents (a) payment vouchers on letters of credit issued to fiscal intermediaries under sec. 1816 and (b) direct payments to providers of service under sec. 1815 of the Social Security Act.

[8] See table M-4, footnote 8.

[9] See table M-4, footnote 9.

[10] Total assets for fiscal years 1983-85 exclude $12,437,270 thousand loaned to the OASI trust fund in December 1982 under the interfund-borrowing provisions of Public Law 97-123. In January 1985, $1,824,000 was paid back.

[11] See table M-4, footnote 11.

[12] The 1977 transfer is for benefits and administrative expenses during the 5-quarter period covering the transition quarter and fiscal year 1977.

[13] The 1978 transfer is for contributions during the 5-quarter period covering the transition quarter and fiscal year 1977.

[14] Reflects reimbursements for Professional Standards Review Organization: 1978, $29.0 million; 1979, $33.0 million; 1980, $33.2 million; 1981, $33.6 million.

Source: See table M-4.

F4–27. Monthly Contributions to State Employee Health Insurance Plans: 1984 and 1985 Employee-Only Coverage

STATE	COST TO EMPLOYEE 1984	1985	COST TO STATE 1984	1985	TOTAL COST 1984	1985	PERCENT OF TOTAL COST PAID BY STATE 1984	1985
ALABAMA	0	0	94.32	100.00	94.32	100.00	100.0%	100.0%
ALASKA	0	0	184.57	184.57	184.57	184.57	100.0	100.0
	0	0	234.84	234.84	234.84	234.84	100.0	100.0
ARIZONA	1.00	1.00	67.90	79.46	68.90	80.46	98.5	98.8
ARKANSAS	20.84	23.64	48.00	55.00	68.84	78.64	69.7	69.9
CALIFORNIA	9.19	11.90	76.00	86.00	85.19	97.90	89.2	87.8
	24.26	37.17	76.00	86.00	100.26	123.17	75.8	69.8
COLORADO	12.00	12.00	53.12	53.12	65.12	65.12	81.6	81.6
CONNECTICUT ...	0	0	79.98	84.69	79.98	84.69	100.0	100.0
DELAWARE	0	0	64.32	77.80	64.32	77.80	100.0	100.0
	16.92	19.52	64.32	77.80	81.24	97.32	79.2	79.9
FLORIDA	13.28	15.18	59.50	65.20	72.78	80.38	81.8	81.1
GEORGIA	13.10	13.60	56.20	62.95	69.30	76.55	81.1	82.2
		26.65		62.95		89.60		70.3
HAWAII	23.58	17.36	15.98	26.04	39.56	43.40	40.4	60.0
IDAHO	0	0	73.10	73.10	73.10	73.10	100.0	100.0
ILLINOIS	0	0	75.56	77.56	75.56	77.56	100.0	100.0
INDIANA	1.58	1.58	62.88	72.45	64.46	74.03	97.5	97.9
IOWA	19.60	23.34	71.32	79.92	90.92	103.26	78.4	77.4
KANSAS	0	0	84.78	83.42	84.78	83.42	100.0	100.0
KENTUCKY	0	0	49.00	53.82	49.00	53.82	100.0	100.0
LOUISIANA	39.52	39.52	39.52	39.52	79.04	79.04	50.0	50.0
MAINE	0	0	58.20	67.08	58.20	67.08	100.0	100.0
MARYLAND	10.20	10.74	57.88	60.86	68.08	71.60	85.0	85.0
	11.12	20.58	63.00	60.86	74.12	81.44	85.0	74.7
MASSACHUSETTS .	9.55	9.87	85.98	88.82	95.53	98.69	90.0	90.0
MICHIGAN	10.38	11.12	93.41	100.14	103.79	111.26	90.0	90.0
MINNESOTA	0	0	69.50	73.00	69.50	73.00	100.0	100.0
MISSISSIPPI ...	0	0	48.80	58.80	48.80	58.80	100.0	100.0
MISSOURI	0	0	64.00	64.00	64.00	64.00	100.0	100.0
MONTANA	0	0	75.00	93.70	75.00	93.70	100.0	100.0

F4–27. Monthly Contributions to State Employee Health Insurance Plans: 1984 and 1985 Employee-Only Coverage (Continued)

STATE	COST TO EMPLOYEE 1984	1985	COST TO STATE 1984	1985	TOTAL COST 1984	1985	PERCENT OF TOTAL COST PAID BY STATE 1984	1985
NEBRASKA	0	0	38.05	41.25	38.05	41.25	100.0%	100.0%
	10.97	11.89	41.02	44.47	51.99	56.36	78.9	78.9
NEVADA	0	0	103.50	124.20	103.50	124.20	100.0	100.0
NEW HAMPSHIRE ..	0	0	56.33	61.03	56.33	61.03	100.0	100.0
NEW JERSEY	0	0	55.38	58.93	55.38	58.93	100.0	100.0
NEW MEXICO	19.57	17.27	29.34	51.79	48.91	69.06	60.0	75.0
	25.29	27.63	37.93	41.43	63.22	69.06	60.0	60.0
NEW YORK	0	0	44.84	74.44	44.84	74.44	100.0	100.0
	7.76	9.28	69.88	83.57	77.64	92.85	90.0	90.0
NORTH CAROLINA .	0.25	0.25	48.05	48.05	48.30	48.30	99.5	99.5
NORTH DAKOTA ...	0	0	50.00	50.00	50.00	50.00	100.0	100.0
OHIO	25.50	12.75 / 25.50	68.95	68.95 / 68.95	94.45	81.70 / 94.45	73.0	84.4 / 73.0
OKLAHOMA	0	0	100.26	115.31	100.26	115.31	100.0	100.0
OREGON	0	0	80.71	89.51	80.71	89.51	100.0	100.0
– BUBB Plan ...	0	0	115.02	136.70	115.02	136.70	100.0	100.0
PENNSYLVANIA ...	0	0	49.17	54.30	49.17	54.30	100.0	100.0
	0	0	64.58	67.05	64.58	67.05	100.0	100.0
RHODE ISLAND ...	0	0	52.28	52.15	52.28	52.15	100.0	100.0
SOUTH CAROLINA .	0	0	50.37	58.21	50.37	58.21	100.0	100.0
	6.56	6.56	50.37	58.21	56.93	64.77	88.5	89.9
SOUTH DAKOTA ...	0	0	49.36	50.72	49.36	50.72	100.0	100.0
TENNESSEE	17.45	20.07	40.71	46.82	58.16	66.89	70.0	70.0
TEXAS	0	0	66.73	66.29	66.73	66.29	100.0	100.0
	7.89	0	72.00	86.27	79.89	86.27	90.1	100.0
UTAH	7.37	8.25	66.30	74.25	73.67	82.50	90.0	90.0
VERMONT	13.41	8.65	40.22	34.58	53.63	43.23	75.0	80.0
VIRGINIA	0	0	77.80	65.52	77.80	65.52	100.0	100.0
WASHINGTON	0	0	130.30	141.65	130.30	141.65	100.0	100.0
WEST VIRGINIA ..	0	0	73.90	79.95	73.90	79.95	100.0	100.0
WISCONSIN a/ ...	7.64	7.91	68.69	71.21	76.33	79.12	90.0	90.0
WYOMING	24.16	5.94	70.00	100.00	94.16	105.94	74.3	94.4
VIRGIN ISLANDS .	9.36	27.41	28.06	27.41	37.42	54.82	75.0	50.0

a/ Effective January 1, 1985, State contribution is lesser of 90% of standard plan rate (shown in table) or 105% of lowest cost HMO in employee's residence area.

F4–28. Monthly Contributions to State Employee Health Insurance Plans: 1984 and 1985 Employee and Family Coverage

STATE	COST TO EMPLOYEE		COST TO STATE		TOTAL COST		PERCENT OF TOTAL COST PAID BY STATE	
	1984	1985	1984	1985	1984	1985	1984	1985
ALABAMA	77.00	82.50	94.32	100.00	171.32	182.50	55.1%	54.8%
ALASKA	0	0	184.57	184.57	184.57	184.57	100.0	100.0
	0	0	234.84	234.84	234.84	234.84	100.0	100.0
ARIZONA	61.44	70.50	128.14	150.98	189.58	221.48	67.6	68.2
ARKANSAS	44.72	47.52	48.00	55.00	92.72	102.52	51.8	53.6
	70.28	73.08	48.00	55.00	118.28	128.08	40.6	42.9
CALIFORNIA	30.97	39.20	185.00	209.00	215.97	248.20	85.7	84.2
	51.79	100.88	185.00	209.00	236.79	309.88	78.1	67.4
COLORADO	121.00	121.00	53.12	53.12	174.12	174.12	30.5	30.5
CONNECTICUT	20.01	27.26	86.68	117.72	106.69	144.98	81.2	81.2
DELAWARE	0	0	158.18	191.98	158.18	191.98	100.0	100.0
	40.74	46.86	158.18	191.98	198.92	238.84	79.5	80.4
FLORIDA	48.46	55.64	111.82	122.80	160.28	178.44	69.8	68.8
GEORGIA	39.30	39.80	101.65	107.15	140.95	146.95	72.1	72.9
		66.00		107.15		173.15		61.9
HAWAII	72.46	53.36	49.14	80.04	121.60	133.40	40.4	60.0
IDAHO	66.74	66.74	73.10	73.10	139.84	139.84	52.3	52.3
ILLINOIS	76.44	67.18	82.56	84.56	159.00	151.74	51.9	55.7
	129.62	123.02	82.56	84.56	212.18	207.58	38.9	40.7
INDIANA	36.66	36.66	150.37	178.01	187.03	214.67	80.4	82.9
IOWA	138.76	149.28	80.14	99.20	218.90	248.48	36.6	39.9
KANSAS	139.71	137.19	84.78	83.42	224.49	220.61	37.8	37.8
KENTUCKY	73.66	80.92	49.00	53.82	122.66	134.74	40.0	39.9
LOUISIANA	90.96	90.96	90.96	90.96	181.92	181.92	50.0	50.0
MAINE	42.24	48.58	104.08	119.66	146.32	168.24	71.1	71.1
MARYLAND	29.08	31.62	164.82	179.18	193.90	210.80	85.0	85.0
	32.80	56.46	185.92	179.18	218.72	235.64	85.0	76.0
MASSACHUSETTS ..	20.06	21.32	180.52	191.83	200.58	213.15	90.0	90.0
MICHIGAN	29.07	31.16	261.67	280.52	290.74	311.68	90.0	90.0
MINNESOTA	8.50	9.34	146.00	157.18	154.50	166.52	94.5	94.4
MISSISSIPPI	65.00	89.70	48.80	58.80	113.80	148.50	42.9	39.6
MISSOURI	109.00	109.00	64.00	64.00	173.00	173.00	37.0	37.0
MONTANA	42.00	40.70	90.00	110.00	132.00	150.70	68.2	73.0

F4-28. Monthly Contributions to State Employee Health Insurance Plans: 1984 and 1985 Employee and Family Coverage (Continued)

STATE	COST TO EMPLOYEE 1984	COST TO EMPLOYEE 1985	COST TO STATE 1984	COST TO STATE 1985	TOTAL COST 1984	TOTAL COST 1985	PERCENT OF TOTAL COST PAID BY STATE 1984	PERCENT OF TOTAL COST PAID BY STATE 1985
NEBRASKA	0	0	136.24	147.68	136.24	147.68	100.0%	100.0%
	39.29	42.58	146.88	159.23	186.17	201.81	78.9	78.9
NEVADA	97.38	87.16	103.50	124.20	200.88	211.36	51.5	58.8
NEW HAMPSHIRE ..	0	0	152.09	169.78	152.09	169.78	100.0	100.0
NEW JERSEY	0	0	135.44	143.83	135.44	143.83	100.0	100.0
NEW MEXICO	35.74	45.23	53.60	135.67	89.34	180.90	60.0	75.0
	65.79	72.36	98.67	108.54	164.46	180.90	60.0	60.0
NEW YORK	0	0	120.54	158.95	120.54	158.95	100.0	100.0
	31.55	35.46	141.25	162.11	172.80	197.57	81.7	82.1
NORTH CAROLINA .	77.23	77.23	48.05	48.05	125.28	125.28	38.4	38.4
NORTH DAKOTA ...	0	0	140.00	140.00	140.00	140.00	100.0	100.0
OHIO	61.13	30.57	165.27	165.27	226.40	195.84	73.0	84.4
		61.13		165.27		226.40		73.0
OKLAHOMA	108.00	108.00	100.26	115.31	208.26	223.31	48.1	51.6
OREGON	0	0	233.83	257.63	233.83	257.63	100.0	100.0
- BUBB Plan ...	0	0	115.02	136.70	115.02	136.70	100.0	100.0
PENNSYLVANIA ...	0	0	126.07	131.35	126.07	131.35	100.0	100.0
	0	0	175.21	179.36	175.21	179.36	100.0	100.0
RHODE ISLAND ...	0	0	137.49	136.88	137.49	136.88	100.0	100.0
SOUTH CAROLINA .	57.12	57.12	50.37	58.21	107.49	115.33	46.9	50.5
	67.38	67.38	50.37	58.21	117.75	125.59	42.8	46.3
SOUTH DAKOTA ...	110.84	122.36	49.36	50.72	160.20	173.08	30.8	29.3
TENNESSEE	43.56	50.09	101.64	116.89	145.20	166.98	70.0	70.0
TEXAS	24.64	88.36	72.00	87.00	96.64	175.36	74.5	49.6
	142.33	144.48	72.00	87.00	214.33	231.48	33.6	37.6
UTAH	19.50	21.82	175.33	196.39	194.83	218.21	90.0	90.0
VERMONT	37.21	23.99	111.64	95.98	148.85	119.97	75.0	80.0
VIRGINIA	62.40	48.30	146.24	118.48	208.64	166.78	70.1	71.0
WASHINGTON	0	0	130.30	141.65	130.30	141.65	100.0	100.0
WEST VIRGINIA ..	0	0	173.95	187.95	173.95	187.95	100.0	100.0
WISCONSIN [a] ...	18.82	19.33	169.34	173.93	188.16	193.26	90.0	90.0
WYOMING	117.92	111.42	70.00	100.00	187.92	211.42	37.2	47.3
VIRGIN ISLANDS .	44.15	74.68	28.06	27.41	72.21	102.09	38.9	26.8

[a] Effective January 1, 1985, State contribution is lesser of 90% of standard plan rate (shown in table) or 105% of lowest cost HMO in employee's residence area.

F4–29. Monthly Contributions to State Employee Health Insurance Plans: 1984 and 1985 Retiree-Only Coverage

STATE	COST TO RETIREE 1984	COST TO RETIREE 1985	COST TO STATE 1984	COST TO STATE 1985	TOTAL COST 1984	TOTAL COST 1985	PERCENT OF TOTAL COST PAID BY STATE 1984	PERCENT OF TOTAL COST PAID BY STATE 1985
ALABAMA	32.00	50.90	0	0	32.00	50.90	0	0
ALASKA	0	0	156.07	191.85	156.07	191.85	100.0%	100.0%
ARIZONA	57.94	67.68	0	0	57.94	67.68	0	0
ARKANSAS	34.00	37.50	0	0	34.00	37.50	0	0
CALIFORNIA	0	0	66.00	67.51	66.00	67.51	100.0	100.0
	0	6.68	66.41	86.00	66.41	92.68	100.0	92.8
COLORADO	0	0	53.12	48.12	53.12	48.12	100.0	100.0
CONNECTICUT	44.59	45.55	13.38	37.36	57.97	82.91	23.1	45.1
DELAWARE	2.84	0	27.68	33.36	30.52	33.36	90.7	100.0
	18.94	21.70	27.68	33.36	46.62	55.06	59.4	60.6
FLORIDA	55.08	80.38	0	0	55.08	80.38	0	0
GEORGIA	13.10	13.60	56.20	62.95	69.30	76.55	81.1	82.2
		26.65		62.95		89.60		70.3
HAWAII	0	0	46.56	51.08	46.56	51.08	100.0	100.0
IDAHO	24.88	24.88	10.66	10.66	35.54	35.54	30.0	30.0
ILLINOIS	0	0	75.56	77.56	75.56	77.56	100.0	100.0
INDIANA	-	-	-	-	-	-	-	-
IOWA	60.98	66.92	0	0	60.98	66.92	0	0
KANSAS	50.34	39.86	0	0	50.34	39.86	0	0
KENTUCKY	45.25	45.25	0	0	45.25	45.25	0	0
LOUISIANA	20.62	20.62	20.62	20.62	41.24	41.24	50.0	50.0
MAINE	0	0	31.36	31.36	31.36	31.36	100.0	100.0
MARYLAND	8.28	9.02	47.00	51.16	55.28	60.18	85.0	85.0
	8.34	21.50	47.34	51.16	55.68	72.66	85.0	70.4
MASSACHUSETTS ..	4.03	5.08	36.30	45.69	40.33	50.77	90.0	90.0
MICHIGAN	0	0	70.49	75.57	70.49	75.57	100.0	100.0
MINNESOTA	48.85	51.28	0	0	48.85	51.28	0	0
MISSISSIPPI	25.00	34.50	0	0	25.00	34.50	0	0
MISSOURI	35.50	35.50	3.00	3.00	38.50	38.50	7.8	7.8
MONTANA	41.00	49.00	0	0	41.00	49.00	0	0

F4-29. Monthly Contributions to State Employee Health Insurance Plans: 1984 and 1985 Retiree-Only Coverage (Continued)

STATE	COST TO RETIREE 1984	COST TO RETIREE 1985	COST TO STATE 1984	COST TO STATE 1985	TOTAL COST 1984	TOTAL COST 1985	PERCENT OF TOTAL COST PAID BY STATE 1984	PERCENT OF TOTAL COST PAID BY STATE 1985
NEBRASKA	-	-	-	-	-	-	-	-
NEVADA	53:39	61.68	24.84	29.81	78.23	91.49	31.8%	32.6%
NEW HAMPSHIRE ..	0	0	37.21	61.03	37.21	61.03	100.0	100.0
NEW JERSEY	55.38	58.93	0	0	55.38	58.93	0	0
NEW MEXICO	42.04	46.50	0	0	42.04	46.50	0	0
NEW YORK [a]	0	0	44.84	74.44	44.84	74.44	100.0	100.0
	7.76	9.28	69.88	83.57	77.64	92.85	90.0	90.0
NORTH CAROLINA .	0	0	36.32	36.32	36.32	36.32	100.0	100.0
NORTH DAKOTA ...	44.00	44.00	0	0	44.00	44.00	0	0
OHIO	0	0	51.10	49.90	51.10	49.90	100.0	100.0
OKLAHOMA	45.90	45.90	0	0	45.90	45.90	0	0
OREGON	31.06	34.98	0	0	31.06	34.98	0	0
- BUBB Plan ...	34.31	43.78	0	0	34.31	43.78	0	0
PENNSYLVANIA ...	0	0	37.21	43.75	37.21	43.75	100.0	100.0
	0	0	47.91	56.45	47.91	56.45	100.0	100.0
RHODE ISLAND ...	30.63	34.60	0	0	30.63	34.60	0	0
SOUTH CAROLINA .	0	0	50.50	50.50	50.50	50.50	100.0	100.0
SOUTH DAKOTA ...	47.84	49.22	0	0	47.84	49.22	0	0
TENNESSEE	35.01	40.26	0	0	35.01	40.26	0	0
TEXAS	0	0	62.93	66.29	62.93	66.29	100.0	100.0
	6.81	0	72.00	85.02	78.81	85.02	91.4	100.0
UTAH	43.00	49.50	0	0	43.00	49.50	0	0
VERMONT	5.49	3.54	16.49	14.17	21.98	17.71	75.0	80.0
VIRGINIA	36.90	30.96	0	0	36.90	30.96	0	0
WASHINGTON	59.35	64.52	0	0	59.35	64.52	0	0
WEST VIRGINIA [a]	23.95	23.95	0	0	23.95	23.95	0	0
WISCONSIN [a] ...	48.79	51.43	0	0	48.79	51.43	0	0
WYOMING	39.22	44.12	0	0	39.22	44.12	0	0
VIRGIN ISLANDS .	14.88	21.19	14.88	21.18	29.76	42.37	50.0	50.0

[a] Sick leave credits may be used by retirees to pay premiums.

F4-30. Medical Care Component of the Consumer Price Index for All Urban Consumers, 1977-85

[1967 = 100; yearly data are annual averages]

Period [1]	All medical care	Medical care commodities		Medical care services					
		All medical care commodities	Prescription drugs	All medical care services	Professional services			Other medical care services	
					All professional services	Physicians	Dentists	All other medical care services	Hospital room
1977	202.4	134.1	122.1	216.7	194.1	206.0	185.1	244.2	299.5
1978	219.4	143.5	131.6	235.4	208.8	223.1	198.1	267.6	332.4
1979	239.7	153.8	141.8	258.8	226.8	243.6	214.8	296.4	370.3
1980	265.9	168.1	154.8	287.4	252.0	269.3	240.2	330.1	418.9
1981	294.5	186.5	172.5	318.2	277.9	299.0	263.3	366.9	481.1
1982	328.7	205.7	192.7	356.0	301.5	327.1	283.6	421.9	556.6
1983	357.3	223.3	213.8	387.0	323.0	352.3	302.7	464.4	619.7
1984	379.5	239.6	234.3	410.3	346.1	376.8	327.2	479.6	670.8
1984									
June	378.0	239.4	233.5	408.4	345.8	377.1	326.2	484.1	662.0
July...........................	380.3	240.7	234.9	410.9	347.0	378.1	327.9	488.3	672.9
August.........................	381.9	241.6	236.6	412.7	348.2	379.5	329.1	490.7	678.1
September......................	383.1	242.4	238.0	413.9	349.8	380.8	331.9	491.5	679.5
October........................	385.5	244.1	240.2	416.5	351.8	382.2	334.8	494.7	687.1
November.......................	387.5	245.6	242.2	418.5	353.1	383.0	336.6	497.7	691.3
December	388.5	247.3	244.4	419.3	354.0	383.8	337.7	498.2	690.8
1985									
January........................	391.1	248.2	245.4	422.4	356.8	386.1	339.7	501.7	697.7
February.......................	393.8	249.8	247.6	425.3	359.3	389.6	340.4	505.2	700.7
March..........................	396.5	251.9	250.9	428.1	361.9	392.6	343.3	508.0	703.6
April..........................	398.0	253.9	. . .	429.4	363.0	. . .	. . .	509.6	. . .
May............................	399.5	255.2	. . .	430.9	364.9	. . .	. . .	511.2	. . .
June	401.7	257.0	. . .	433.0	366.4	. . .	. . .	513.6	. . .

[1] Source for annual data is table 5A and for monthly data table 5 of the **CPI Detailed Report.**

F4–31. Personal Consumption Expenditures for Medical Care in the United States, 1950–1983

(000,000 Omitted)

Calendar year	Total medical care	Hospital services	Physicians' services	Medicines and appliances	Dentists' services	Net cost of health insurance	All other medical care
1950	$ 8.8	$ 2.0	$ 2.6	$ 2.2	$ 1.0	$0.3	$ 0.7
1955	12.8	3.2	3.5	3.0	1.5	0.6	1.0
1960	19.5	5.3	5.2	4.6	2.0	0.8	1.6
1965	29.4	8.4	8.0	6.2	2.8	1.3	2.8
1966	31.8	9.4	8.5	6.5	2.9	1.4	3.1
1967	34.2	10.7	9.4	6.7	3.2	1.4	2.8
1968	37.9	12.3	10.1	7.5	3.5	1.6	2.8
1969	43.7	15.1	11.5	8.4	4.1	1.9	2.7
1970	49.3	17.6	13.1	9.4	4.6	1.8	2.8
1971	54.4	20.5	14.4	9.9	4.9	2.1	2.6
1972	60.6	22.8	15.7	10.8	5.3	3.2	2.7
1973	67.4	25.4	17.5	11.7	6.3	3.5	3.1
1974	75.5	29.7	19.4	12.8	6.9	3.6	3.2
1975	85.4	34.7	22.5	13.9	7.9	2.8	3.6
1976	96.2	40.4	25.3	15.1	8.9	2.4	4.1
1977	110.5	46.3	29.5	16.4	10.0	3.3	5.1
1978	123.0	52.4	30.9	18.0	12.1	3.3	6.3
1979	141.8	60.1	36.6	20.1	12.9	4.5	7.7
1980	163.8	70.6	43.1	21.7	14.8	4.7	8.9
1981	191.4	83.0	48.9	23.8	17.0	6.3	12.4
1982	215.6	95.8	54.6	25.5	18.4	7.6	13.7
1983	234.9	104.1	61.2	28.0	19.5	8.3	13.8

NOTE: Data are revised. The data exclude private expenditures in federal, state, city and other government hospitals and nursing homes. In some cases the sum of the items does not equal the "Total medical care" shown because of rounding.

SOURCES: U.S. Department of Commerce, Bureau of Economic Analysis, *The National Income and Product Accounts of the United States, 1929-76 Statistical Tables* and July 1984 Special Supplement to *Survey of Current Business*.

F4–32. Indexes of Medical Care Prices: 1970 to 1983

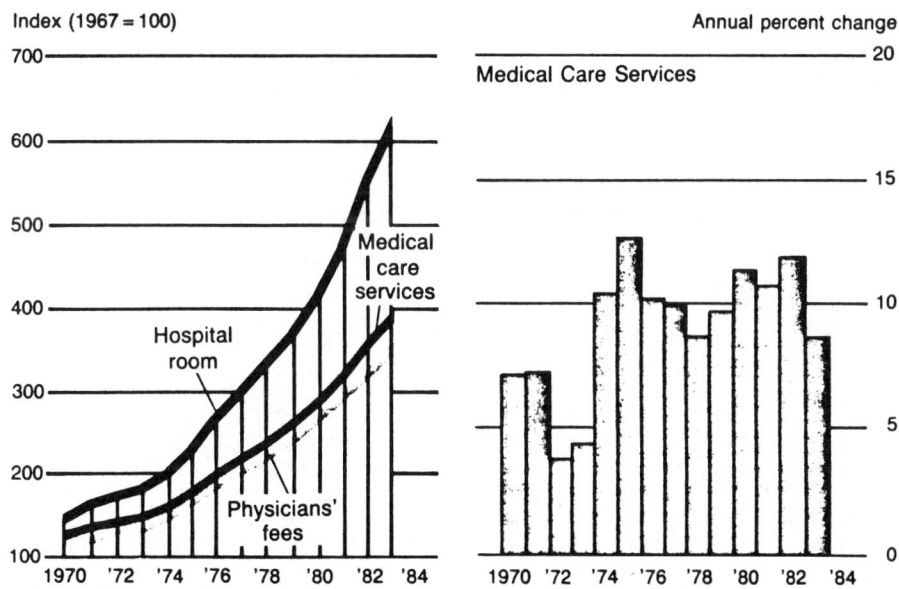

Source: Chart prepared by U.S. Bureau of the Census. For data, see table 151.

F5. PUBLIC AND PRIVATE PENSIONS

F5–1. Federal Pension and Health Programs as a Percentage of GNP and the Budget: 1965 to 2040

	Pension programs as a percent of GNP [1]	Health programs as a percent of GNP [1]	Total as a percent of GNP [1]	Total as a percent of budget [2]
1965	4.1	0.3	4.4	24.9
1970	4.7	1.4	6.1	30.0
1975	6.4	2.0	8.4	37.1
1980	6.5	2.3	8.8	38.2
1982	7.1	2.7	9.7	39.6
1984	7.0	2.8	9.8	39.7
1986	6.6	3.0	9.6	39.4
1988	6.4	3.2	9.6	39.4
1990	[3] 6.6	[3] 3.1	9.7	40.4
1995	6.2	3.7	9.9	41.3
2000	5.8	4.0	9.8	40.8
2005	5.6	4.4	10.0	41.7
2010	6.0	4.7	10.7	44.6
2015	6.0	5.0	11.0	45.8
2020	6.5	5.4	11.9	49.6
2025	7.0	5.9	12.9	53.8
2030	7.1	6.4	13.5	56.3
2035	7.1	7.0	14.1	58.8
2040	7.0	7.5	14.5	60.4

[1] Estimates for 1984 to 1988 are based on CBO baseline assumptions (August 1983); forecasts for 1990 and beyond are based on intermediate assumptions of the Social Security and Medicare actuaries.

[2] Forecasts for 1990 and beyond are based on the assumption that the Budget accounts for 24% of GNP.

[3] The discontinuity in the estimates of pension and health benefits as a percent of GNP between 1988 and 1990 is due to the Social Security trustees assuming that OASDI will grow at a faster rate than CBO in the late 1980's and the Health Insurance trustees assuming that Medicare will grow at a slower rate than CBO assumes.

Source: John L. Palmer and Barbara B. Torrey, "Health Care Financing and Pension Programs," prepared for the Urban Institute Conference on "Federal Budget Policy in the 1980s," Sept. 29 and 30, 1983.

F5–2. Number of Persons Receiving Pensions, by Type of Pension: Monthly Average, Third Quarter 1984

(Numbers in thousands)

Type of pension	Total	Male	Female	Percent receiving Social Security [1] Total	Percent receiving Social Security [1] 65 years and over
Total with pensions	34,165	15,170	18,995	88.5	97.1
Social Security, total	30,233	12,401	17,832	(X)	(X)
Social Security only	20,018	6,570	13,447	(X)	(X)
Private pensions	7,900	5,007	2,893	82.3	95.5
State or local pensions	2,854	1,240	1,614	70.9	87.5
Federal pensions	1,765	1,024	740	51.0	69.3
U.S. military pensions	1,304	1,229	75	19.6	69.5
Federal railroad retirement pensions	781	360	422	(NA)	(NA)

X   Not applicable.
NA   Not available.

[1] The universe for the combination of Social Security with other types of pension income is restricted to persons receiving only two sources of pensions, Social Security and the specified pension type.

F5-3. Percent Distribution of Pension Recipients, by Age and Type of Pension: Monthly Average, Third Quarter 1984

Type of pension	Total	Age				
		Under 55 years	55 to 61 years	62 to 64 years	65 to 69 years	70 years and over
Total with pensions......	100.0	8.2	8.6	12.1	23.2	47.9
Social Security.................	100.0	5.8	4.0	12.2	25.3	52.7
Private pensions................	100.0	3.6	12.5	13.6	27.2	43.1
State or local pensions.........	100.0	4.6	16.1	12.0	23.2	44.1
Federal pensions................	100.0	5.9	16.9	15.1	25.2	36.9
U.S. military pensions..........	100.0	48.8	20.4	7.9	13.5	9.4
Federal railroad retirement pensions......................	100.0	1.4	9.1	12.3	23.0	54.3

F5-4. Benefits and Beneficiaries of Public Employee Retirement Systems, by Level of Government, 1954-80

Calendar year	Benefits (in millions)					Beneficiaries as of June 30 (in thousands)				
	All systems	Federal			State and local	All systems	Federal			State and local
		Total [1]	Civil Service	Armed Forces			Total [1]	Civil Service	Armed Forces	
1954	$1,300.0	$764.5	$337.7	$397.9	$535.0	849.5	450.5	269.3	167.9	399.0
1955	1,463.2	868.2	379.6	456.0	595.0	917.4	490.4	296.9	179.5	427.0
1956	1,664.6	987.6	455.7	495.6	677.0	1,004.2	533.2	327.1	191.3	471.0
1957	1,881.3	1,106.3	535.9	531.1	775.0	1,107.5	584.5	369.3	199.9	523.0
1958	2,155.8	1,280.8	637.4	600.8	875.0	1,222.1	649.1	418.2	215.0	573.0
1959	2,424.1	1,499.1	740.5	663.7	975.0	1,341.2	722.2	475.5	230.3	619.0
1960	2,673.6	1,595.6	816.1	732.2	1,078.0	1,447.9	787.9	514.9	256.0	660.0
1961	3,007.8	1,804.8	908.7	845.3	1,203.0	1,578.3	869.3	559.1	292.6	709.0
1962	3,303.0	2,006.1	999.8	951.7	1,296.0	1,688.1	949.1	601.7	328.8	739.0
1963	3,753.9	2,303.9	1,148.7	1,097.3	1,450.0	1,837.5	1,044.5	643.0	382.2	793.0
1964	4,252.7	2,642.7	1,269.8	1,310.1	1,610.0	1,983.7	1,143.7	688.0	434.7	840.0
1965	4,720.4	2,945.4	1,384.1	1,429.8	1,775.0	2,117.3	1,231.3	728.9	481.0	886.0
1966	5,478.7	3,493.7	1,713.1	1,703.2	1,985.0	2,293.3	1,348.3	795.7	529.8	945.0
1967	6,171.8	3,951.8	1,905.9	1,960.2	2,220.0	2,474.3	1,445.3	831.2	590.1	1,029.0
1968	6,926.5	4,441.5	2,086.8	2,259.6	2,485.0	2,665.6	1,548.6	871.9	651.3	1,117.0
1969	7,919.7	5,084.7	2,346.0	2,631.3	2,835.0	2,853.5	1,650.5	910.4	714.0	1,203.0
1970	9,355.2	6,075.2	2,819.9	2,133.1	3,280.0	3,050.1	1,759.1	958.8	772.8	1,291.0
1971	10,946.8	7,126.8	3,329.4	3,660.2	3,820.0	3,265.0	1,886.0	1,026.3	831.3	1,379.0
1972	12,783.3	8,248.3	3,946.4	4,148.8	4,535.0	3,474.5	2,011.5	1,091.8	890.2	1,463.0
1973	14,974.7	9,659.7	4,808.4	4,679.3	5,315.0	3,796.4	2,171.4	1,192.5	948.2	1,625.0
1974	18,051.7	11,941.7	6,082.5	5,651.0	6,110.0	4,136.3	2,350.3	1,306.2	1,011.5	1,786.0
1975	21,617.3	14,592.3	7,531.5	6,808.0	7,025.0	4,479.7	2,479.7	1,372.1	1,073.0	1,948.0
1976	24,525.6	16,545.6	8,584.4	7,673.6	7,980.0	4,738.7	2,629.7	1,432.0	1,161.0	2,109.0
1977	27,429.0	18,429.0	9,625.8	8,479.2	9,000.0	5,006.3	2,735.3	1,487.9	1,208.3	2,271.0
1978	30,869.0	20,709.0	10,925.2	9,420.2	10,160.0	5,275.3	2,857.3	1,564.5	1,252.1	2,418.0
1979	35,068.2	23,578.2	12,518.7	10,641.6	11,490.0	5,535.4	2,946.4	1,617.3	1,286.3	2,589.0
1980	41,087.5	28,041.5	15,065.3	12,478.1	13,046.0	5,841.6	3,051.6	1,675.3	1,330.3	2,790.0

[1] Includes Federal systems other than Civil Service and Armed Forces not shown separately.

F5–5. Average Annual Benefits, by Reason for Benefit Receipt and Level of Government, 1970 and 1978–80, and Percentage Increase, 1970–80, in Current and Constant (1980) Dollars

Reason for receipt	1970	1978	1979	1980	Percentage increase, 1970–80	1970	1978	1979	1980	Percentage increase, 1970–80
	Current dollars					Constant (1980) dollars				
All public employee retirement systems, total	$3,005	$5,788	$6,269	$6,962	131.7	$5,824	$6,957	$6,912	$6,962	19.5
Age and service	3,271	6,348	6,865	7,583	131.8	6,339	7,630	7,569	7,583	19.6
Disability	3,131	6,009	6,511	7,302	133.2	6,068	7,222	7,179	7,302	20.3
Survivor, monthly benefit	1,510	2,767	3,039	3,462	129.3	2,926	3,326	3,351	3,462	18.3
Federal employee retirement systems, total	3,440	7,238	7,994	9,181	166.9	6,667	8,700	8,814	9,181	37.7
Age and service	4,066	8,343	9,221	10,529	159.0	7,880	10,028	10,166	10,529	33.6
Disability	3,174	6,642	7,273	8,324	162.3	6,151	7,983	8,019	8,324	35.3
Survivor, monthly benefit	1,449	3,390	3,795	4,481	209.2	2,808	4,075	4,184	4,481	59.6
State and local employee retirement systems, total	2,413	4,076	4,305	4,535	87.9	4,676	4,899	4,746	4,535	–3.0
Age and service	2,452	4,408	4,657	4,907	100.1	4,752	5,298	5,134	4,907	3.3
Disability	2,965	4,207	4,442	4,682	57.9	5,746	5,056	4,897	4,682	–18.5
Survivor, monthly benefit	1,667	1,752	1,849	1,946	16.7	3,231	2,106	2,039	1,946	–39.8

F5–6. Benefits and Beneficiaries of Public Employee Retirement Systems, by Reason for Benefit Receipt, 1954–80

Calendar year	Benefits (in millions)					Beneficiaries as of June 30 (in thousands)			
	Total	Age and service	Disability	Survivor Monthly	Survivor Lump-sum	Total	Age and service	Disability	Monthly survivor
1954	$1,300.0	$880.6	$300.8	$68.7	$49.5	849.5	559.3	180.3	109.9
1955	1,463.2	998.0	334.7	80.6	49.8	917.4	606.1	188.8	122.5
1956	1,664.6	1,152.8	359.8	96.3	55.7	1,004.2	671.5	196.7	136.0
1957	1,881.3	1,331.1	377.2	111.6	61.5	1,107.5	756.2	200.8	150.4
1958	2,155.8	1,533.9	419.1	134.7	68.0	1,222.1	834.8	217.2	170.2
1959	2,424.1	1,735.7	459.1	162.1	67.2	1,341.2	906.6	231.5	203.1
1960	2,673.6	1,921.4	491.9	184.6	75.7	1,447.9	977.2	247.2	223.5
1961	3,007.8	2,181.4	530.2	208.3	87.9	1,578.3	1,072.3	262.9	243.1
1962	3,303.0	2,406.8	570.6	228.6	96.9	1,688.1	1,149.5	279.9	258.7
1963	3,753.9	2,762.8	624.9	265.6	100.7	1,837.5	1,263.4	293.7	280.4
1964	4,252.7	3,151.0	692.8	295.8	113.1	1,983.7	1,372.4	310.3	301.0
1965	4,720.4	3,520.1	751.3	324.4	124.6	2,117.3	1,472.2	326.1	318.8
1966	5,478.7	4,104.5	856.7	382.3	135.3	2,293.3	1,607.1	346.1	340.0
1967	6,171.8	4,636.2	942.5	448.0	145.1	2,474.3	1,743.6	364.4	366.3
1968	6,926.5	5,250.1	1,022.5	491.8	162.0	2,665.6	1,889.8	378.1	387.7
1969	7,919.7	6,052.3	1,134.9	553.6	178.9	2,853.5	2,049.0	398.1	406.3
1970	9,355.2	7,209.5	1,311.8	644.7	189.2	3,050.1	2,204.3	418.8	426.9
1971	10,946.8	8,552.7	1,490.7	733.9	199.5	3,265.0	2,375.1	438.7	451.3
1972	12,783.3	10,038.8	1,687.4	837.1	220.0	3,474.5	2,542.7	456.3	475.6
1973	14,974.7	11,866.8	1,906.7	965.1	236.1	3,796.4	2,784.9	486.7	524.7
1974	18,051.7	14,381.7	2,240.6	1,171.1	258.4	4,136.3	3,035.4	517.7	583.2
1975	21,617.3	17,199.7	2,707.3	1,438.9	271.4	4,427.7	3,243.1	549.1	635.5
1976	24,525.6	19,505.8	3,095.9	1,641.4	282.5	4,738.7	3,747.0	576.8	688.0
1977	27,429.0	21,795.1	3,499.6	1,842.2	292.0	5,006.3	3,660.0	611.4	734.9
1978	30,869.0	24,520.3	3,903.5	2,110.8	334.4	5,275.3	3,862.8	649.6	762.8
1979	35,068.2	27,890.9	4,375.9	2,433.8	367.5	5,535.4	4,062.6	672.1	800.8
1980	41,087.5	32,713.1	5,073.1	2,883.6	417.6	5,841.6	4,313.8	694.8	833.0

F5-7. Federal Civil Service Retirement: 1970 to 1983

[As of **June 30** or for years ending **June 30** except, beginning **1978**, as of **Sept. 30** or for year ending **Sept. 30**. See also *Historical Statistics, Colonial Times to 1970*, series H 262-270]

ITEM	Unit	1970	1975	1978	1979	1980	1981	1982	1983
Annuitants, total	1,000	958	1,372	1,564	1,617	1,675	1,779	1,828	1,870
Age and service	1,000	477	732	825	857	905	973	1,010	1,045
Disability	1,000	185	258	323	333	343	348	348	343
Survivors	1,000	296	382	416	427	427	458	470	482
Receipts, total [1]	Mil. dol	4,683	11,377	17,640	20,548	24,389	28,529	31,858	34,711
Employee contributions	Mil. dol	1,740	2,554	3,194	3,447	3,686	4,006	4,171	4,399
Federal government contributions	Mil. dol	1,952	6,707	11,035	12,865	15,562	18,193	19,443	20,615
Disbursements, total [2]	Mil. dol	2,752	7,207	11,014	12,593	14,977	17,779	19,656	20,889
Age and service annuitants [3]	Mil. dol	2,129	6,052	9,246	10,571	12,639	15,010	16,406	17,602
Survivors	Mil. dol	389	908	1,423	1,618	1,912	2,265	2,533	2,783
Average monthly benefit:									
Age and service	Dollars	362	620	827	924	992	1,036	1,117	1,150
Disability	Dollars	221	406	562	629	723	756	820	851
Survivors	Dollars	116	209	296	336	392	419	463	486
Cash and security holdings	Bil. dol	22.4	38.4	56.3	64.3	73.7	84.4	96.6	110.5

[1] Includes interest on investments. [2] Includes refunds, death claims, and administration. [3] Includes disability annuitants.

Source: U.S. Office of Personnel Management, *Compensation Report*, annual.

F5-8. State and Local Government Retirement Systems—Finances: 1970 to 1983

[**In millions of dollars**. For fiscal years closed during the 12 months ending June 30]

YEAR AND LEVEL OF GOVERNMENT	RECEIPTS					BENEFITS AND WITHDRAWALS			Cash and security holdings
	Total	Employee contributions	Government contributions State	Local	Earnings on investments	Total	Benefits	Withdrawals	
1970: All systems	9,848	2,788	2,046	2,554	2,460	3,638	3,037	601	54,918
State-administered	7,184	2,149	1,978	1,237	1,821	2,382	1,913	469	39,966
Locally administered	2,664	639	67	1,318	639	1,256	1,124	132	14,952
1975: All systems	18,898	4,488	4,093	5,023	5,294	7,490	6,540	950	98,064
State-administered	14,208	3,552	3,974	2,623	4,059	5,207	4,480	727	74,703
Locally administered	4,690	936	119	2,400	1,236	2,283	2,060	223	23,361
1980: All systems	37,313	6,466	7,581	9,951	13,315	14,008	12,207	1,801	185,226
State-administered	28,603	5,285	7,399	5,611	10,308	10,257	8,809	1,448	144,682
Locally administered	8,710	1,180	181	4,340	3,008	3,752	3,399	353	40,544
1983: All systems	57,906	8,699	9,862	13,074	26,271	19,254	17,484	1,770	289,731
State-administered	45,127	7,196	9,611	7,585	20,734	14,204	12,757	1,447	229,685
Locally administered	12,779	1,503	251	5,489	5,537	5,050	4,727	323	60,046

Source: U.S. Bureau of the Census, *Finances of Employee-Retirement Systems of State and Local Governments*, series GF, No. 2, annual.

F5-9. Individual Retirement Account (IRA), Keogh Account and Pension Plan Coverage of Employed Persons: 1983

[In thousands, **except percent. As of May.** Covers only persons employed for pay. Data based on supplement to Current Population Survey conducted for U.S. Dept. of Health and Human Service and Employee Benefit Research Institute]

| SEX, AGE, AND CLASS OF WORKER | Employed persons | IRA AND KEOGH ACCOUNT | | | | PENSION PLAN COVERAGE | | | | |
| | | Persons with an IRA | | Persons with spousal IRA | Persons with Keogh account [2] | Wage and salary workers [3] | Persons covered | | Persons participating in plan | Persons with vesting [4] |
		Number	Percent of employed [1]				Number	Percent of wage and salary workers [1]		
Total	**98,964**	**16,713**	**17.1**	**1,954**	**988**	**90,117**	**49,792**	**60.5**	**40,873**	**22,295**
Male	56,028	10,224	18.4	1,812	769	49,753	28,715	63.1	24,948	14,273
Female	42,936	6,489	15.2	142	218	40,364	21,077	57.3	15,924	8,022
16–20 yr. old	7,953	80	1.0	–	–	7,774	1,724	26.6	423	94
21–24 yr. old	11,174	365	3.3	5	24	10,813	4,705	49.7	2,813	843
25–34 yr. old	28,773	3,108	10.9	113	127	26,624	15,306	62.4	12,437	5,148
35–44 yr. old	21,484	3,967	18.7	279	214	19,284	12,285	68.2	10,961	6,432
45–54 yr. old	15,493	4,532	29.6	580	279	13,760	8,779	68.7	8,024	5,252
55–64 yr. old	11,218	4,169	37.5	854	284	9,835	6,295	68.5	5,744	4,174
65 yr. old and over	2,870	491	17.3	124	58	2,027	697	38.5	471	353
Private	74,134	12,041	16.4	1,475	479	74,134	36,690	54.8	29,336	14,799
Federal government	3,226	778	24.4	64	14	3,226	2,800	89.8	2,552	1,737
State government	3,775	648	17.3	81	28	3,775	3,196	88.2	2,774	1,849
Local government	8,665	1,592	18.5	104	28	8,665	7,005	84.7	6,140	3,878
Self-employed	9,165	1,654	18.3	229	439	318	101	33.2	71	32

– Represents zero.
[1] Based on number of persons who responded "yes" or "no" to question of coverage.
[2] A retirement plan similar to IRAs which is available to self-employed persons and unincorporated partnerships.
[3] Includes self-employed persons who also held a wage and salary job.
[4] Persons with pension plan coverage that is irrevocable on the part of the employer. When an employee is vested in a plan, he can draw the expected benefits at retirement age, even if that employment was terminated earlier.

Source: Employee Benefit Research Institute, Washington, DC, *Individual Retirement Accounts: Characteristics and Policy Implications,"* Issue Brief #32, 1984, and *New Survey Findings on Pension Coverage and Benefit Entitlement,"* Issue Brief #33, 1984.

F5-10. Pension Plan Coverage of Civilian Workers by Wage or Salary Income: 1982

| RACE, SPANISH ORIGIN, SEX, AND AGE | NUMBER WITH COVERAGE (1,000) | | | | | PERCENT OF TOTAL CIVILIAN WORKERS | | | | |
	Total [1]	$5,000–$9,999	$10,000–$14,999	$15,000–$19,999	$20,000 and over	Total [1]	$5,000–$9,999	$10,000–$14,999	$15,000–$19,999	$20,000 and over
Total [2]	**46,799**	**5,447**	**9,368**	**9,172**	**20,669**	**43.8**	**28.5**	**51.0**	**66.8**	**75.9**
White	41,084	4,508	7,838	7,935	19,004	44.0	28.0	50.0	66.4	75.8
Black	4,637	822	1,315	1,018	1,189	42.6	33.0	59.2	72.2	80.1
Spanish origin [3]	1,973	351	533	361	619	34.0	24.2	44.3	60.4	70.9
Male [4]	28,372	1,822	3,780	5,078	16,903	48.9	24.1	44.4	62.6	75.4
15–24 yr. old	2,058	466	578	396	392	15.2	17.0	30.2	46.0	54.7
25–34 yr. old	8,087	526	1,304	1,886	4,182	50.0	23.3	43.4	58.6	68.7
35–44 yr. old	7,473	256	696	1,153	5,271	64.7	27.1	49.0	66.7	77.5
45–64 yr. old	10,225	471	1,111	1,572	6,850	68.3	37.1	56.0	71.8	81.2
Female [4]	18,427	3,625	5,588	4,094	3,766	37.7	31.5	56.7	73.0	78.1
15–24 yr. old	1,982	633	715	251	123	15.9	23.2	43.4	58.2	67.2
25–34 yr. old	5,813	972	1,911	1,452	1,143	42.2	30.3	56.5	69.4	72.5
35–44 yr. old	4,548	773	1,211	1,095	1,138	47.3	33.6	58.6	77.1	80.7
45–64 yr. old	5,778	1,161	1,694	1,255	1,307	49.5	38.9	63.7	78.3	83.0

[1] Includes workers with income under $5,000, not shown separately.   [2] Includes other races, not shown separately.
[3] Persons of Spanish origin may be of any race.   [4] Includes persons 65 years old and over, not shown separately.
Source: U.S. Bureau of the Census, *Current Population Reports*, series P-60, No. 143.

F5–11. Retirement Pensions and Income from Assets by Marital Status:[1] Number of Aged Units 65 or Older, and Median Total Money Income, 1982

Retirement pension	All units			Married couples			Nonmarried person		
		Income from assets			Income from assets			Income from assets	
	Total	Yes	No	Total	Yes	No	Total	Yes	No
	Number of recipients (in thousands)								
Total	19,880	13,466	6,413	8,097	6,275	1,822	11,783	7,192	4,591
No benefit	1,340	598	743	417	295	122	923	303	620
One benefit	12,015	7,422	4,594	3,953	2,754	1,199	8,063	4,668	3,395
Social security only [2]	11,492	7,033	4,458	3,750	2,578	1,172	7,741	4,455	3,287
Private pension or annuity only	114	69	45	54	40	13	60	28	31
Government employee pension only [3]	247	208	39	85	79	6	162	129	33
Railroad retirement only	163	112	51	64	56	8	99	56	43
More than one benefit [4]	6,524	5,447	1,077	3,727	3,226	501	2,797	2,221	576
Social security and Federal pension	540	437	102	263	231	32	277	206	71
Social security and railroad retirement, State/local, or military pension	1,546	1,243	303	754	641	113	792	601	191
Social security and private pension or annuity	4,040	3,389	651	2,428	2,082	346	1,612	1,307	305
	Median total money income								
Total	$8,790	$12,040	$4,940	$15,130	$17,810	$8,410	$5,880	$7,950	$4,220
No benefit	4,010	18,260	3,120	19,790	25,650	5,840	3,280	10,420	3,080
One benefit	6,460	8,870	4,670	11,380	14,490	7,360	5,260	6,600	4,140
Social security only [2]	6,310	8,620	4,650	11,060	14,060	7,340	5,190	6,470	4,120
Private pension or annuity only	6,800	(5)	(5)	(5)	(5)	(5)	(5)	(5)	(5)
Government employee pension only [3]	17,640	20,940	(5)	30,550	31,240	(5)	10,850	12,980	(5)
Railroad retirement only	8,120	10,450	(5)	(5)	(5)	(5)	6,670	(5)	(5)
More than one benefit [4]	14,480	16,010	8,670	18,470	19,780	11,680	9,970	11,310	6,810
Social security and Federal pension	17,200	18,760	9,450	21,960	22,740	(5)	11,970	14,530	(5)
Social security and railroad retirement, State/local, or military pension	13,450	15,900	7,920	19,230	20,860	11,450	10,050	11,520	6,820
Social security and private pension or annuity	13,870	15,100	8,910	16,960	18,540	11,570	9,440	10,450	6,450

[1] Receipt of sources is ascertained by response to a yes/no question imputed by the Current Population Survey of the Bureau of the Census. A married couple receives a source if one or both persons are recipients of that source.
[2] Social security beneficiaries may be receiving retired-worker, dependent's or survivors', transitionally insured, or special age-72 benefits.
[3] Includes Federal, State, local, and military pensions.

[4] Includes a small number with combinations of pensions not listed below.
[5] Fewer than 75,000 weighted cases.

Source: Adapted from Susan Grad, **Income of the Population 55 and Over, 1982**, Office of Retirement and Survivors Insurance and Office of Policy, Social Security Administration, 1984.

F5–12. Social Security Dependence: Illustrative Income Potential from Home Equity Conversion Plans, by Marital Status, 1982

Item	Percent of total income made up of social security benefits for—											
	Married men			Unmarried men			Unmarried women			Surviving spouses		
	Less than 50	50–79	80 or more	Less than 50	50–79	80 or more	Less than 50	50–79	80 or more	Less than 50	50–79	80 or more
Total number [1]	1,622	1,050	549	273	242	166	637	515	539	350	189	255
Percent with no home equity	13	16	25	42	57	63	53	52	62	23	30	42
Number with home equity	1,330	834	372	152	98	58	276	222	184	242	113	123
Mean home equity	$55,460	$38,040	$31,420	$43,480	$35,420	$23,920	$38,710	$34,280	$25,230	$46,780	$36,030	$26,130
Mean age	70	70	71	70	70	71	70	70	71	65	68	68
Mean income	$13,630	$6,890	$4,530	$8,790	$5,240	$3,080	$8,450	$4,180	$2,690	$9,750	$5,190	$3,170
10-year RAM annual income	$2,939	$2,016	$1,665	$2,304	$1,877	$1,268	$2,051	$1,816	$1,337	$2,479	$1,909	$1,385
Lifetime sale-leaseback annual income	$3,384	$2,321	$1,963	$2,653	$2,213	$1,495	$2,107	$1,866	$1,405	$2,274	$1,877	$1,361
Reverse SAM annual income	$2,576	$1,767	$1,538	$2,019	$1,734	$1,171	$1,798	$1,592	$1,235	$1,628	$1,505	$1,091
Percent with home equity of $80,000 or more	17	5	5	12	6	2	7	6	0	10	6	1
Mean home equity	$143,080	$126,190	(2)	(2)	(2)	(2)	(2)	(2)	...	(2)	(2)	(2)

[1] Excludes cases in which home equity amount, social security benefits, or total income were unknown.
[2] Sample too small to estimate mean.

F5–13. Railroad Retirement System, 1930–1983

(Thousands of persons and millions of dollars)

Year	Number of Persons — Not Yet Receiving Benefits	Number of Persons — Retired or Disabled	Number of Persons — Survivors and Dependents	Number of Persons — Total	Contributions in Year† — Employers	Contributions in Year† — Employees	Contributions in Year† — Total	Benefits Paid in Year — Retired or Disabled	Benefits Paid in Year — Survivors and Dependents	Benefits Paid in Year — Total	Assets
1930	*	*	–	1,400	$ 30	–	$ 30	NA	–	NA	–
1940	1,205	141	3	1,349	65	$ 65	130	$ 114	–	$ 114	$ 136
1950	1,494	251	136	1,881	273	273	546	254	NA	NA	2,553
1960	862	384	408	1,654	298	298	596	626	$ 336	962	3,740
1970	650	444	539	1,633	493	467	960	1,108	663	1,771	4,398
1971	595	440	543	1,578	475	450	925	1,200	802	2,002	4,300
1972	586	447	542	1,575	525	475	1,000	1,350	825	2,175	4,100
1973	589	443	550	1,582	540	500	1,040	1,550	1,015	2,565	3,800
1974	585	457	546**	1,588	1,201	421	1,622	1,710	1,098	2,808	3,600
1975	532	469	563**	1,564	1,209	423	1,632	1,970	1,313	3,283	3,100
1976	541	466	565**	1,572	1,325	465	1,790	2,102	1,469	3,571	3,065
1977	534	464	569**	1,567	1,457	507	1,964	2,245	1,579	3,824	2,584
1978	553	459	568**	1,580	1,520	546	2,066	2,353	1,668	4,021	2,787
1979	545	455	567**	1,567	1,732	682	2,414	2,552	1,810	4,362	2,611
1980	517	451	564**	1,533	1,845	717	2,562	2,839	2,027	4,866	2,086
1981	477	447	559**	1,483	1,971	838	2,809	3,128	2,243	5,371	1,126
1982	404	443	557**	1,404	2,193	1,015	3,208	3,421	2,422	5,843	460
1983	396	438	552**	1,386	2,169	1,004	3,173	3,565	2,489	6,054	601

NOTE: Details may not add to totals due to rounding.

NA = Not Available.

*Not available separately.

**Figure includes employee annuitants also receiving benefits as dependents of survivors.

†Excludes financial interchange transfers from Social Security trust funds.

SOURCE: U.S. Railroad Retirement Board.

F5–14. State and Local Government Retirement Plans, 1950–1983

(Thousands of persons and millions of dollars)

Year	Number of Persons — Not Yet Receiving Benefits	Number of Persons — Retired or Disabled	Number of Persons — Survivors and Dependents	Number of Persons — Total	Contributions in Year — Employers	Contributions in Year — Employees	Contributions in Year — Total	Benefits Paid in Year — Retired or Disabled	Benefits Paid in Year — Survivors and Dependents	Benefits Paid in Year — Total	Assets
1950	2,600	254	40	2,894	$ 510	$ 395	$ 905	$ 274	$ 26	$ 300	$ 5,154
1960	4,500	590	70	5,160	1,725	1,170	2,895	940	75	1,015	19,600
1970	7,300	1,171	120	8,591	4,920	2,975	7,895	2,905	215	3,120	58,200
1971	7,700	1,254	125	9,079	5,495	3,280	8,775	3,372	248	3,620	64,800
1972	8,100	1,333	130	9,563	6,050	3,570	9,620	4,085	250	4,335	73,400
1973	8,300	1,415	135	9,850	6,649	4,166	10,815	4,785	290	5,075	82,700
1974	9,000	1,495	140	10,635	7,821	4,207	12,028	5,495	340	5,835	92,400
1975	9,500	1,585	145	11,230	9,116	4,488	13,604	6,335	390	6,725	103,700
1976	10,450	1,690	150	12,290	10,502	4,808	15,310	7,250	450	7,700	117,300
1977	10,951	1,989	184	13,124	12,369	5,233	17,602	7,965	490	8,455	130,800
1978	11,080*	2,120*	200*	13,400*	13,621	5,688	19,309	8,945*	605*	9,550	142,573
1979	11,210*	2,260*	210*	13,680*	15,336	6,069	21,405	10,035*	735*	10,770	161,649
1980	11,340*	2,390*	220*	13,950*	17,532	6,466	23,998	11,310*	900*	12,210	185,226
1981	11,480*	2,520*	230*	14,230*	20,020	7,289	27,309	12,740*	1,090*	13,830	209,444
1982	11,607	2,654	244	14,504	21,808	8,123	29,931	14,362	1,318	15,680	245,252
1983	11,430	2,873	221	14,524	22,956	8,699	31,655	16,235	1,249	17,484	289,731

NOTE: Beneficiaries are as of June 30. Financial data is on a calendar year basis prior to 1977, and on a June 30 fiscal year basis thereafter.

*Estimated.

SOURCE: Bureau of the Census, U.S. Department of Commerce.

F4-15. [OASDI Awards:] Average Primary Insurance Amount for Retired Workers and Average Monthly Benefit Amount for Retired Workers, Disabled Workers, and Widows, 1940–83

Year [1]	Retired workers Average primary insurance amounts Total	Men	Women	Retired workers Average monthly amount Total	Men	Women	Average monthly benefit amounts Disabled workers Total	Men	Women	Nondisabled widows
1940	$22.71	$23.26	$18.38	$22.71	$23.26	$18.38				$20.36
1941	22.72	23.29	18.51	22.72	23.29	18.51				20.18
1942	23.64	24.31	19.18	23.64	24.31	19.18				20.05
1943	24.50	25.23	19.96	24.50	25.23	19.96				20.11
1944	24.61	25.21	20.26	24.61	25.21	20.26				20.10
1945	25.11	25.71	19.99	25.11	25.71	19.99				20.17
1946	25.42	26.08	19.89	25.42	26.08	19.89				20.21
1947	26.21	27.05	20.69	26.21	27.05	20.69				20.74
1948	27.14	28.13	21.22	27.14	28.13	21.22				21.04
1949	28.39	29.41	22.27	28.39	29.41	22.27				21.39
1950 (Jan.-Aug.)	29.03	30.16	22.98	29.03	30.16	22.98				21.65
1950 (Sept.-Dec.)	33.24	35.32	26.85	33.24	35.32	26.85				36.89
1951	37.54	40.34	29.49	37.54	40.34	29.49				34.90
1952 (Jan.-Aug.)	39.65	42.81	31.09	39.65	42.81	31.09				35.09
1952 (Sept.-Dec.)	58.11	63.51	44.77	58.11	63.51	44.77				40.77
1953	56.76	61.69	44.62	56.76	61.69	44.62				41.47
1954 (Jan.-Aug.)	56.98	62.03	44.23	56.98	62.03	44.23				41.64
1954 (Sept.-Dec.)	66.36	72.88	51.04	66.36	72.88	51.04				45.79
1955	69.74	75.86	56.05	69.74	75.86	56.05				49.68
1956	68.03	75.76	56.26	67.36	75.76	54.53				53.71
1957	68.91	75.57	57.64	67.59	75.57	54.06				53.92
1958	76.06	83.14	63.13	74.47	83.14	58.59	$84.64	$87.53	$71.95	55.54
1959	83.48	91.31	69.31	81.46	91.31	63.65	91.84	94.86	77.69	60.94
1960	83.87	92.03	69.23	81.73	92.03	63.26	91.16	94.02	78.91	62.12
1961 (Jan.-July)	82.31	90.69	67.49	80.17	90.69	61.70	90.76	93.36	79.65	62.16
1961 (Aug.-Dec.)	80.36	85.06	67.38	75.33	80.41	61.31	91.95	94.94	79.70	69.21
1962	83.83	90.37	70.52	78.80	85.88	64.37	92.71	96.36	79.90	70.49
1963	86.09	93.67	72.48	80.30	88.43	65.71	94.40	98.35	81.27	71.61
1964	87.61	95.57	74.32	81.24	89.78	66.96	94.98	99.27	81.41	73.08
1965 (Jan.-Aug.)	88.57	96.56	74.99	82.69	90.89	68.78	93.26	97.89	80.27	73.81
1965 (Sept.-Dec.)	99.36	108.79	82.34	89.20	99.90	71.26	101.30	106.51	86.75	75.37
1966	100.57	108.82	85.06	93.75	102.85	77.34	101.41	106.40	86.92	74.16
1967	96.62	105.83	81.66	89.74	99.05	74.63	101.84	106.95	87.04	77.68
1968 (Mar.-Dec.) [2]	111.82	122.00	95.49	103.82	114.15	87.25	115.67	121.77	98.35	90.02
1969	114.51	125.37	97.29	106.13	117.09	88.80	118.35	125.11	99.37	91.55
1970	133.94	146.99	113.69	123.82	136.80	103.67	139.79	148.39	115.74	106.95
1971	150.11	165.13	127.23	138.29	152.96	115.93	156.91	167.21	128.56	119.19
1972 (Jan.-Aug.)	152.62	168.24	129.34	140.15	155.23	117.71	159.69	170.69	130.44	120.47
1972 (Sept.-Dec.)	182.87	202.98	153.10	168.88	188.35	140.08	192.52	206.69	156.14	145.25
1973	185.30	206.60	155.10	169.80	189.90	141.40	196.70	212.20	158.30	161.40
1974 (Jan.-Feb.)	192.92	214.65	159.61	174.88	195.17	143.78	197.29	214.21	157.42	166.62
1974 (Mar.-May)	200.62	224.76	166.15	182.46	205.06	150.18	211.41	229.99	168.75	175.60
1974 (June-Dec.)	211.12	236.33	175.29	192.33	216.23	158.33	217.22	237.61	173.23	182.85
1975 (Jan.-May)	216.56	242.76	176.76	196.42	220.35	160.50	220.60	241.48	175.27	185.34
1975 (June-Dec.)	235.13	264.67	191.56	213.68	241.05	173.31	243.47	266.08	192.13	198.88
1976 (Jan.-May)	241.19	273.43	193.03	218.40	247.46	174.99	247.32	270.78	193.97	201.05
1976 (June-Dec.)	257.95	293.96	206.65	233.72	266.64	186.84	271.19	297.10	213.29	214.22
1977 (Jan.-May)	264.80	301.70	209.90	239.60	272.80	190.30	273.20	299.30	214.10	216.90
1977 (June-Dec.)	280.20	322.30	221.50	254.90	293.20	201.40	294.80	323.20	230.00	227.40
1978 (Jan.-May)	288.50	332.60	225.30	262.20	301.80	205.50	300.20	329.30	233.80	233.60
1978 (June-Dec.)	305.00	356.00	237.60	278.40	324.70	217.10	328.80	360.70	254.70	246.50
1979 (June-May)	318.00	368.50	246.50	289.30	335.30	224.40	333.60	366.60	259.10	241.50
1979 (June-Dec.)	348.50	406.00	269.10	317.00	370.80	242.80	360.30	396.50	278.30	275.60
1980 (Jan.-May)	353.80	411.70	270.50	321.10	374.00	244.90	352.10	388.80	269.70	277.50
1980 (June-Dec.)	396.30	465.50	301.00	359.80	422.90	272.90	396.50	437.90	301.00	312.80
1981 (Jan.-May)	400.10	467.50	302.60	363.60	424.20	276.00	389.80	431.40	295.00	313.00
1981 (June-Dec.)	438.80	514.50	332.60	400.10	468.00	304.80	425.60	471.30	320.70	346.30
1982 (Jan.-May)	425.60	504.20	315.10	388.40	457.50	291.40	416.90	462.40	312.70	350.80
1982 (June-Dec.)	447.10	532.70	328.50	408.60	483.00	305.50	441.10	489.50	328.00	375.30
1983 (Jan.-Nov.)	448.00	531.60	330.00	408.20	480.30	306.50	432.40	480.30	317.90	385.10
1983 (Dec.)	451.20	546.40	325.50	410.20	491.80	302.50	445.30	496.80	333.20	400.50

[1] Some years shown in several parts to reflect effects of amendments that change the benefit rates during the year; see the historical summary, beginning on page 2.

[2] Incorporates effects of the 1967 Amendments.

F5–16. [OASDI Awards: Retired Workers] Number, Average Age, and Percentage Distribution, by Age and Sex, 1940–80

Year	Total number (in thousands)	Average age	Percent of retired workers, by age [1]							
			Total	62	63	64	65-69	70-74	75-79	80 or older
Men										
1940	99	68.8	100.0	....	....	....	74.4	17.4	6.4	1.8
1945	166	69.6	100.0	....	....	....	59.2	28.1	10.4	2.3
1950	444	68.7	100.0	....	....	....	69.2	21.0	7.4	2.3
1955	629	68.4	100.0	....	....	....	67.5	24.7	6.8	1.1
1960	630	66.8	100.0	....	....	....	84.7	13.2	1.3	.7
1961	942	65.7	100.0	7.2	9.1	8.6	63.9	9.7	1.0	.5
1962	904	65.7	100.0	11.9	8.8	9.2	58.0	10.4	1.1	.6
1963	736	65.5	100.0	14.2	10.4	7.1	56.6	10.1	1.0	.6
1964	652	65.3	100.0	17.5	10.5	7.6	54.3	9.0	.7	.4
1965	743	65.8	100.0	14.7	9.6	5.9	57.5	8.3	1.8	2.2
1966	1,060	66.0	100.0	10.2	7.4	5.1	63.9	9.4	1.8	2.2
1967	719	64.8	100.0	16.4	11.6	7.7	61.1	2.1	.6	.4
1968	766	64.4	100.0	19.4	10.5	9.4	58.1	2.0	.4	.2
1969	779	64.5	100.0	17.2	11.6	8.3	60.5	1.8	.4	.2
1970	814	64.4	100.0	18.4	12.6	8.4	58.8	1.4	.3	.1
1971	840	64.3	100.0	19.4	13.1	9.2	56.5	1.4	.3	.1
1972	874	64.2	100.0	21.0	13.0	8.7	55.7	1.2	.2	.1
1973	875	64.2	100.0	22.4	12.9	9.3	54.0	1.1	.2	.1
1974	835	64.0	100.0	24.8	13.2	8.7	52.0	1.0	.2	.1
1975	902	64.0	100.0	25.8	14.1	9.0	50.2	.7	.2	(2)
1976	875	64.0	100.0	27.4	13.8	8.6	49.3	.7	.1	(2)
1977	940	64.0	100.0	26.6	14.0	8.5	50.0	.7	.1	(2)
1978	852	63.9	100.0	28.6	13.1	7.8	49.6	.7	.1	(2)
1979	926	64.0	100.0	27.7	12.8	7.8	51.0	.6	.1	(2)
1980	942	63.9	100.0	30.1	13.1	8.5	47.6	.6	.1	(2)
Women										
1940	13	68.1	100.0	....	....	....	82.6	12.8	3.9	0.6
1945	20	73.3	100.0	....	....	....	69.1	23.6	6.2	1.2
1950	123	68.0	100.0	....	....	....	75.9	19.6	3.7	.8
1955	281	67.8	100.0	....	....	....	75.4	18.1	5.5	1.1
1960	351	65.2	100.0	....	....	....	40.6	8.2	1.9	.8
1961	420	65.0	100.0	25.3	13.9	8.9	41.7	7.7	1.7	.8
1962	444	65.1	100.0	28.7	11.6	7.5	40.2	8.8	2.1	1.1
1963	410	64.9	100.0	30.6	13.6	7.0	38.2	7.7	1.9	1.0
1964	390	64.4	100.0	35.8	13.0	7.2	36.0	6.2	1.2	.6
1965	440	66.2	100.0	30.9	11.6	5.9	37.6	7.4	3.5	3.1
1966	588	66.0	100.0	22.8	10.1	5.4	43.9	8.8	4.7	4.3
1967	442	64.1	100.0	19.4	10.5	9.4	58.1	2.0	.4	.2
1968	474	64.0	100.0	36.9	11.7	7.9	39.8	2.4	.8	.4
1969	493	64.0	100.0	33.7	13.8	7.4	42.0	2.2	.6	.3
1970	524	63.9	100.0	34.7	14.1	7.2	41.4	1.9	.5	.2
1971	551	63.9	100.0	34.7	13.9	7.6	41.3	1.8	.5	.2
1972	588	63.9	100.0	36.4	13.6	7.0	40.5	1.8	.5	.2
1973	618	64.0	100.0	36.9	12.5	7.7	38.8	2.4	1.1	.6
1974	578	63.7	100.0	41.3	12.7	7.0	36.3	1.7	.7	.3
1975	603	63.7	100.0	41.6	13.7	7.0	36.1	1.2	.3	.1
1976	601	63.6	100.0	43.3	13.4	6.6	35.2	1.1	.2	.1
1977	654	63.6	100.0	41.6	13.8	6.9	36.3	1.1	.2	.1
1978	620	63.6	100.0	44.1	12.3	6.3	36.0	1.0	.2	(2)
1979	665	63.6	100.0	43.5	12.2	6.4	36.7	.9	.2	.1
1980	671	63.5	100.0	45.9	11.5	6.5	34.9	.9	.2	.1

[1] Age in year of award.

[2] Less than 0.05 percent.

F5-17. Social Insurance and Veterans' Programs: Cash Benefits and Beneficiaries, 1950–82

[In thousands]

Risk and program	1950	1960	1965	1970	1975	1979 [1]	1980	1981	1982
	Amount of benefits								
Total	$6,321,476	$22,610,138	$32,571,492	$55,304,158	$123,235,153	$163,910,141	$187,696,334	$231,368,692	[3]$245,105,453
Retirement [2]	1,423,471	10,754,614	16,786,783	29,096,292	61,543,254	97,465,535	113,548,745	132,731,987	[3]135,330,469
OASDHI	651,409	8,196,131	12,541,519	20,770,000	42,432,000	66,947,000	77,905,000	92,478,000	104,884,000
Railroad Retirement	176,925	594,446	705,311	1,112,850	1,965,707	2,627,617	2,930,619	3,234,175	3,530,582
Public employee retirement [3]	536,929	1,921,382	3,520,054	7,209,454	17,144,748	27,890,918	32,713,126	37,019,812	
Federal civil service	135,267	547,367	896,649	1,849,412	5,228,969	8,459,256	10,227,491	11,880,662	13,074,484
Other Federal employees [4]	151,662	529,015	1,233,405	2,700,042	6,070,779	9,665,662	11,396,635	12,574,875	13,840,403
State and local government	250,000	845,000	1,390,000	2,660,000	5,845,000	9,766,000	11,089,000	12,564,275	
Veterans' programs [5]	58,208	42,655	19,899	3,988	799	(5)	(5)	(5)	(5)
Disability [2][6]	2,441,925	4,859,643	7,041,066	11,000,847	21,883,477	34,858,906	39,244,550	43,831,336	[3]44,750,057
OASDHI		568,167	1,573,237	3,067,000	8,413,941	13,708,000	15,437,000	17,199,000	17,338,000
Railroad Retirement	77,313	146,748	149,431	219,336	402,982	510,847	564,360	610,075	668,281
Public employee retirement [3]	213,250	491,857	751,311	1,311,819	2,702,273	4,375,877	5,073,116	5,718,361	
Federal civil service	40,520	152,466	278,806	518,472	1,307,242	2,413,824	2,884,677	3,329,389	3,663,941
Other Federal employees [4]	148,730	244,392	317,505	538,347	905,031	1,158,053	1,275,439	1,354,267	1,428,158
State and local government	24,000	95,000	155,000	255,000	490,000	804,000	913,000	1,034,705	
Veterans' programs [5]	1,674,000	2,529,673	3,026,384	3,930,903	5,583,240	7,905,294	8,602,174	9,524,400	10,203,177
Workers' compensation	360,000	755,000	1,074,000	1,674,000	3,248,000	6,199,000	7,245,000	8,166,000	8,909,000
State temporary disability insurance [7]	89,261	311,324	425,948	664,551	890,429	1,161,000	1,299,800	1,525,100	1,567,900
Railroad temporary disability insurance	28,099	56,874	40,755	56,236	47,582	60,888	63,200	58,400	55,600
Black Lung benefit program				77,000	595,000	1,033,000	1,077,000	1,030,000	916,000
Survivor (monthly benefits)	901,817	3,671,637	5,871,545	10,271,503	20,716,057	30,712,005	34,899,067	40,130,388	[3]42,799,640
OASDHI	276,945	2,316,211	3,978,990	7,427,558	15,544,000	23,140,000	26,654,000	30,875,000	33,612,000
Railroad Retirement	43,884	201,251	278,442	424,025	914,003	1,223,654	1,371,570	1,527,142	1,644,074
Public employee retirement	34,409	184,620	324,434	644,715	1,448,905	2,433,846	2,883,576	3,375,942	
Federal civil service	8,409	104,707	190,575	428,671	974,968	1,624,796	1,930,252	2,278,003	2,506,907
Other Federal employees [4]		4,913	8,858	16,044	83,937	234,050	301,324	358,864	423,577
State and local government	26,000	75,000	125,000	200,000	390,000	575,000	652,000	739,075	
Veterans' programs [5]	491,579	864,555	1,149,679	1,545,205	2,084,149	2,649,505	2,754,921	2,952,304	3,113,082
Workers' compensation [8]	55,000	105,000	140,000	197,000	365,000	610,000	675,000	730,000	795,000
Black Lung benefit program				33,000	360,000	665,000	635,000	670,000	705,000
Lump-sum payments	86,693	299,503	420,540	582,173	807,830	873,695	1,003,972	928,701	372,944
OASDHI	32,740	164,286	216,930	293,613	337,030	340,000	395,000	332,000	203,000
Railroad Retirement	12,722	19,989	22,158	26,372	25,015	15,363	13,624	13,004	10,963
Public employee retirement	28,522	75,713	124,605	189,204	321,382	367,533	417,648	480,422	
Federal civil service	8,147	11,586	18,106	23,390	20,342	20,852	22,890	35,046	38,568
Other Federal employees	375	1,127	1,499	814	1,040	1,681	2,758	1,931	2,231
State and local government	20,000	63,000	105,000	165,000	300,000	345,000	392,000	443,445	
Veterans' programs [5]	12,709	39,515	56,847	72,984	124,403	150,799	177,700	103,275	118,182
Unemployment	1,467,570	3,024,741	2,451,558	4,353,343	18,284,565	10,294,499	18,935,900	13,746,280	21,852,343
State unemployment insurance [9]	1,373,114	2,866,650	2,283,433	4,183,702	18,188,127	10,212,000	18,756,500	13,538,500	21,513,600
Railroad unemployment insurance	59,804	157,690	60,493	38,710	89,478	82,499	179,400	207,780	338,743
Veterans' unemployment allowances [10]	34,652	401							
Training and related allowances [11]			107,632	130,931	6,960				
	Beneficiaries [12]								
Retirement: [2]									
OASDI	1,918.1	10,309.7	13,918.2	16,869.6	20,014.5	22,421.1	22,267.3	23,612.3	24,148.2
Railroad Retirement	174.8	440.0	498.4	552.5	579.4	591.7	589.4	576.7	574.4
Public employee retirement	406.3	977.2	1,472.4	2,204.3	3,124.1	4,418.0	4,322.0	4,573.4	
Federal civil service	111.0	263.3	359.4	477.1	732.0	856.7	912.8	963.0	989.0
Other Federal employees [4]	73.3	178.9	387.9	642.3	912.1	1,194.3	1,149.2	1,173.9	1,201.7
State and local government	222.0	535.0	725.0	1,085.0	1,480.0	2,097.0	2,260.0	2,436.5	
Veterans' programs [5]	54.1	33.2	14.0	3.1	.6	(5)	(5)	(5)	(5)
Disability: [2]									
OASDI		542.6	1,653.9	2,572.7	4,142.1	4,822.7	4,728.7	4,599.2	4,173.8
Railroad Retirement	76.0	96.6	102.5	95.1	101.7	95.8	95.2	93.6	91.6
Public employee retirement	131.0	247.2	326.1	418.8	526.1	668.9	706.5	732.0	
Federal civil service	43.0	102.1	149.3	185.2	257.8	332.2	354.9	375.0	384.0
Other Federal employees [4]	56.0	90.1	107.8	147.6	163.4	154.7	156.6	146.5	144.5
State and local government	32.0	55.0	69.0	86.0	105.0	181.0	195.0	210.5	
Veterans' programs [5]	2,314.1	2,976.0	3,202.9	3,178.0	3,226.1	3,241.6	3,193.9	3,145.0	3,088.0
State temporary disability insurance [7]	55.2	121.1	148.9	180.9	175.7	189.3	199.2	224.2	216.4
Railroad temporary disability insurance	31.2	28.0	23.5	24.9	14.0	14.4	14.5	13.7	13.5
Black Lung benefit program				25.1	333.2	268.6	252.5	162.7	146.7
Survivor:									
OASDI	1,093.9	3,446.0	4,680.8	6,369.3	7,301.8	7,591.0	8,259.7	7,635.2	7,434.5
Railroad Retirement	136.3	251.3	288.4	324.3	337.6	332.8	330.1	326.1	324.1
Public employee retirement [13]	58.3	223.4	318.8	426.9	559.5	821.8	844.9	902.4	
Federal civil service	18.3	149.5	220.2	296.6	382.3	427.3	439.3	467.0	485.0
Other Federal employees [4]		3.9	6.6	10.3	32.2	83.5	70.6	74.4	82.6
State and local government	40.0	70.0	92.0	120.0	145.0	311.0	335.0	361.0	
Veterans' programs [5]	991.2	1,262.0	1,899.7	2,284.1	2,257.5	1,982.9	1,464.9	1,374.0	1,300.0
Black Lung benefit program				1.5	151.6	161.2	157.8	213.8	207.8

F5–17. Social Insurance and Veterans' Programs: Cash Benefits and Beneficiaries, 1950–82 (Continued)

Risk and program	1950	1960	1965	1970	1975	1979 [1]	1980	1981	1982
	Beneficiaries [12]								
Unemployment:									
State unemployment insurance [14]	1,305.0	1,723.0	1,188.5	1,620.3	3,514.7	2,112.0	2,830.0	3,191.0	3,897.0
Railroad unemployment insurance	76.4	74.0	31.1	17.7	25.9	18.0	38.0	52.0	77.0
Veterans' unemployment allowances [10]	32.1	1.6	....	....	....	....	....	....	....
Training and related allowances [11]	....	....	74.8	60.0	....	....	....	....	....

[1] For some programs, 1979 data are preliminary.
[2] Includes benefits to spouses and children where applicable.
[3] Excludes refunds of contributions to employees who leave service. State and local data not available for 1982.
[4] Included under retirement is a small but unknown amount of disability and survivor payments for 1950.
[5] Retirement data are for veterans of the Civil War, the Indian Wars, the Spanish-American War, the Boxer Rebellion, and the Philippine Insurrection; beginning October 1951, includes all service pensions. Disability data include pensions and compensation, clothing allowance (beginning 1973), and subsistence payments to disabled veterans undergoing training (1944–73). Survivor data includes special allowances for survivors of veterans who did not qualify under OASDHI (Servicemen's and Veterans' Survivor Benefit Act of 1956). Lump-sum payments are for burial of deceased veterans. Beginning 1978, retirement data no longer available separately.
[6] Excludes payments for medical care.
[7] Benefits payable in California, New Jersey, New York, Puerto Rico, and Rhode Island under public and private plans. Beneficiary data for private-plan beneficiaries in New Jersey not available. Beginning in 1980, includes data for Hawaii.
[8] Small but unknown amount of lump-sum death payments included with monthly survivor payments.
[9] Includes payments made by the States as agents of the Federal Government under the Federal employees' unemployment compensation program and under the Ex-Servicemen's Compensation Act of 1958 and payments under the temporary and permanent extended unemployment insurance programs, the Trade Expansion Act of 1962, the Disaster Relief Act of 1970, and the Trade Act of 1974. Beginning 1961, includes program in Puerto Rico.
[10] Under the Servicemen's Readjustment Act of 1944 (terminated July 1949) and the Veterans' Readjustment Assistance Act of 1952 (terminated January 1960). Amount (but not number) includes self-employment allowances.
[11] Under the Area Redevelopment Act of 1961 (November 1961–June 1966) and the Manpower Development and Training Act of 1962 (August 1962–June 1975).
[12] For OASDHI, average monthly number, for the Railroad Retirement program, the public employee retirement systems, the veterans' programs, and the Black Lung benefit program, number on rolls June 30; for State unemployment and temporary disability insurance and for veterans' unemployment allowances, average weekly number; for railroad unemployment and temporary disability insurance, average number during 14-day registration period; for Area Redevelopment Act and Manpower Development and Training Act, number on rolls December 31. Beneficiary data for workers' compensation not available.
[13] For Federal programs under the Uniformed Services Contingency Option Act of 1953 and for State and local government retirement systems, number represents families.
[14] Regular State unemployment insurance, Federal employee, and ex-servicemen programs only.

Source: Based on reports of administrative agencies.

F5–18. Income from Private Pensions or Annuities by Sex and Marital Status: Percentage Distribution of Units and Persons Aged 65 and Older, 1982

Income (recipients only)[1]	Men			Women		
	Total	Married	Nonmarried	Total	Married	Nonmarried
Number(in thousands)	2,976	2,415	561	1,539	416	1,123
Total percent	100	100	100	100	100	100
$1–$499	6	5	9	13	12	13
$500–$999	10	9	14	18	21	17
$1,000–$1,499	12	11	13	19	22	18
$1,500–$1,999	7	7	5	8	9	8
$2,000–$2,499	9	8	10	9	8	9
$2,500–$2,999	6	6	7	6	3	7
$3,000–$3,499	7	7	6	6	6	5
$3,500–$3,999	7	7	6	5	5	5
$4,000–$4,499	5	5	3	2	2	2
$4,500–$4,999	5	5	4	2	2	3
$5,000–$9,999	20	21	17	8	4	9
$10,000 or more	7	8	5	4	5	4
Median income[2]	$2,980	$3,140	$2,400	$1,520	$1,320	$1,680

[1] Units with a person reporting receipt of both a government employee pension and a private pension or annuity are excluded. This is 4 percent of private pension recipients aged 55–61, 5 percent aged 62–64, and 6 percent aged 65 and older.
[2] Rounded to the nearest $10. Medians for 1982 are calculated more precisely than those for previous years in this data series. See technical appendix for further detail.

List of Sources

Figure No.   Source

A1-1 *Demographic and Socioeconomic Aspects of Aging in the US: 1920–2040.* US Department of Commerce, Bureau of the Census, Aug. 1984, p. 32.

A1-2 *Statistical Abstract of the United States, 1985.* US Department of Commerce, Bureau of the Census, 1985, p. xvii.

A1-3 *Aging America: Trends and Projections, 1985–86 Edition.* US Senate, Special Committee on Aging, American Association of Retired Persons, Federal Council on the Aging, and Administration on Aging, 1986, p. 12.

A1-4 *Handbook of Labor Statistics.* US Department of Labor, Bureau of Labor Statistics, Jun. 1985, p. 9.

A1-5 *America in Transition: An Aging Society, 1984–85 Edition.* US Senate, Special Committee on Aging, Aug. 1985. 99th Congress, 1st Session, Committee Print 99–13, p. 8.

A1-6 *America in Transition: An Aging Society, 1984–85 Edition,* US Senate, Special Committee on Aging, Aug. 1985. 99th Congress, 1st Session, Committee Print 99–13, p. 11.

A1-7 *Tomorrow's Elderly: A Report Prepared by the Congressional Clearinghouse of the Future.* US House of Representatives, Select Committee on Aging, Oct. 1984. 98th Congress, 2nd Session, Pub. No. 98–457, p. xiv.

A1-8 *Tomorrow's Elderly: A Report Prepared by the Congressional Clearinghouse of the Future.* US House of Representatives, Select Committee on Aging, Oct. 1984. 98th Congress, 2nd Session, Pub. No. 98–457, p. xiv.

A1-9 *Tomorrow's Elderly: A Report Prepared by the Congressional Clearinghouse of the Future.* US House of Representatives, Select Committee on Aging, Oct. 1984. 98th Congress, 2nd Session, Pub. No. 98–457, p. 2.

A1-10 *Handbook of Labor Statistics.* US Department of Labor, Bureau of Labor Statistics, Jun. 1985, p. 11.

A1-11 Projections of Population Growth at the Older Ages. Metropolitan Life Insurance Company. *Statistical Bulletin,* Jun. 1984, 65:2, p. 10. Reprinted by permission.

A1-12 *Estimates of the Population of the US by Age, Sex and Race, 1980–84.* US Department of Commerce, Bureau of the Census, Mar. 1985. Series P–25, No. 965, p. 5.

A2-1 *Projections of Education Statistics to 1992–93.* (Gerald, Debra E.) US Department of Education, National Center for Education Statistics, Jul. 1985, p. 33.

A2-2 *Estimates of the Population of the US by Age, Sex and Race, 1980–84.* US Department of Commerce, Bureau of the Census. Series P–25, No. 965, Mar. 1985, p. 3.

A2-3 *Aging America: Trends and Projections, 1985–86 Edition.* US Senate Special Committee on Aging, American Association of Retired Persons, Federal Council on the Aging, and Administration on Aging, 1986, p. 23.

A2-4 *Demographic and Socioeconomic Aspects of Aging in the US: 1920–2040.* US Department of Commerce, Bureau of the Census, Aug. 1984, p. 45.

A2-5 *Transportation of Older Americans: Issues and Options for the Decade of the 1980's.* US Department of Transportation, Apr. 1983, p. 24.

A2-6 *Health, United States, 1984.* US Department of Health and Human Services, Public Health Service, 1985, p. 58.

A3-1 *Estimates of the Population of the US by Age, Sex and Race, 1980–84.* US Department of Commerce, Bureau of the Census. Series P–25, No. 965, Mar. 1985, p. 5.

Note: Those figures from government sources are in the public domain.

A3–2 *Demographic and Socioeconomic Aspects of Aging in the US: 1920-2040.* US Department of Commerce, Bureau of the Census, Aug. 1984, p. 41.

A3–3 *Estimates of the Population of the US by Age, Sex and Race, 1980-84.* US Department of Commerce, Bureau of the Census. Series P–25, No. 965, Mar. 1985, p. 2.

A3–4 *Handbook of Labor Statistics.* US Department of Labor, Bureau of Labor Statistics, Jun. 1985, p. 12.

A3–5 *Transportation of Older Americans: Issues and Options for the Decade of the 1980's.* US Department of Transportation, Apr. 1983, p. 25.

A3–6 *Chartbook on Aging in America.* 1981 White House Conference on Aging, 1982, p. 23.

A3–7 *Chartbook on Aging in America.* 1981 White House Conference on Aging, 1982, p. 23.

A3–8 *Profile of Elderly Black Americans.* National Caucus and Center on Black Aged, Feb. 1985, p. 2.

A3–9 *Profile of Elderly Black Americans.* National Caucus and Center on Black Aged, Feb. 1985, p. 2.

A3–10 Trends: All Americans. (Robey, Bryant; Russell, Cheryl) *American Demographics,* Feb. 1984, 6:2, p. 34–35. Reprinted by permission.

A3–11 Trends: All Americans. (Robey, Bryant; Russell, Cheryl) *American Demographics,* Feb. 1984, 6:2, p. 34–35. Reprinted by permission.

A3–12 Trends: All Americans. (Robey, Bryant; Russell, Cheryl) *American Demographics,* Feb. 1984, 6:2, p. 35. Reprinted by permission.

A4–1 *Aging America: Trends and Projections, 1985-86 Edition.* US Senate Special Committee on Aging, American Association of Retired Persons, Federal Council on the Aging, and Administration on Aging, 1986, p. 31.

A4–2 *State Population Estimates, by Age and Components of Change: 1980 to 1984.* US Department of Commerce, Bureau of the Census, 1985. Series P–25, No. 970, p. 9.

A4–3 *State Population Estimates, by Age and Components of Change: 1980 to 1984.* US Department of Commerce, Bureau of the Census, 1985. Series P–25, No. 970, p. 2.

A4–4 *State Population Estimates, by Age and Components of Change: 1980 to 1984.* US Department of Commerce, Bureau of the Census, 1985. Series P–25, No. 970, p. 5.

A4–5 *Every Ninth American.* (Brotman, Herman B.) private print, 1982, p. 30.

A5–1 *State Population Estimates, by Age and Components of Change: 1980 to 1984.* US Department of Commerce, Bureau of the Census, 1985. Series P–25, No. 970, p. 3.

A5–2 *State Population Estimates, by Age and Components of Change: 1980 to 1984.* US Department of Commerce, Bureau of the Census, 1985. Series P–25, No. 970, p. 3.

A5–3 *Statistical Abstract of the United States, 1985.* US Department of Commerce, Bureau of the Census, 1985, p. 15.

A5–4 *Retirement Migration Project: Final Report to the National Institute on Aging.* (Longino, Charles F.; Biggar, Jeanne C.; Flynn, Cynthia B.; Wiseman, Robert F.) Center for Social Research in Aging, University of Miami, Coral Gables, FL, Sep. 1984, p. 3.

A5–5 *Every Ninth American.* (Brotman, Herman B.) private print, 1982, p. 37.

A5–6 *Every Ninth American.* (Brotman, Herman B.) private print, 1982, p. 38.

A5–7 *Retirement Migration Project: Final Report to the National Institute on Aging.* (Longino, Charles F.; Biggar, Jeanne C.; Flynn, Cynthia B.; Wiseman, Robert F.) Center for Social Research in Aging, University of Miami, Coral Gables, FL, Sep. 1985, p. 14.

A5–8 *Retirement Migration Project: Final Report to the National Institute on Aging.* (Longino, Charles F.; Biggar, Jeanne C.; Flynn, Cynthia B.; Wiseman, Robert F.) Center for Social Research in Aging, University of Miami, Coral Gables, FL, Sep. 1985, p. 15.

A5–9 *Retirement Migration Project: Final Report to the National Institute on Aging.* (Longino, Charles F.; Biggar, Jeanne C.; Flynn, Cynthia B.; Wiseman, Robert F.) Center for Social Research in Aging, University of Miami, Coral Gables, FL, Sep. 1985, p. 16.

A6–1 *Caring for Older Veterans.* US Veterans Administration, Apr. 1975, p. 12.

A6–2 *Aging America: Trends and Projections.* American Association of Retired Persons, 1984, p. 22.

A6–3 *Caring for Older Veterans.* US Veterans Administration, Apr. 1975, p. 16.

A6–4 *Caring for Older Veterans.* US Veterans Administration, Apr. 1975, p. 15.

A6–5 *Caring for Older Veterans.* US Veterans Administration, Apr. 1975, p. 14.

A6–6 *Caring for Older Veterans.* US Veterans Administration, Apr. 1975, p. 14.

A6–7 *Caring for Older Veterans.* US Veterans Administration, Apr. 1975, p. 25.

A6–8 *Caring for Older Veterans.* US Veterans Administration, Apr. 1975, p. 15.

A6–9 *Caring for Older Veterans.* US Veterans Administration, Apr. 1975, p. 17.

A7–1 By 2000, the Elderly Will Be the Fastest Growing Age Group Almost Everywhere in the World. *Ageing International,* Summer 1981, p. 15. Reprinted by permission.

A7–2 By 2000, the Elderly Will Be the Fastest Growing Age Group Almost Everywhere in the World. *Ageing International,* Summer 1981, p. 14. Reprinted by permission.

A7–3 Recent Changes in the US: Age at Death Distribution: Further Observations (Meyers, George C.; Manton, Kenneth G.) *Gerontologist,* Dec. 1984, 24:6, p. 573. Reprinted with permission from *Gerontologist,* vol. 24, no. 6, Dec. 1984.

A7–4 *Demographic and Socioeconomic Aspects of Aging in the US: 1920–2040.* US Department of Commerce, Bureau of the Census, Aug. 1984, p. 69.

A7–5 *Demographic and Socioeconomic Aspects of Aging in the US: 1920–2040.* US Department of Commerce, Bureau of the Census, Aug. 1984, p. 30.

A7–6 *Demographic and Socioeconomic Aspects of Aging in the US: 1920–2040.* US Department of Commerce, Bureau of the Census, Aug. 1984, p. 30.

A7–7 *Statistical Abstract of the United States, 1985.* US Department of Commerce, Bureau of the Census, 1985, p. 33.

A7–8 Asian Americans. *The Washington Post,* Oct. 10, 1985, p. A19. Copyright by *The Washington Post.* From material provided by the Population Reference Bureau. Reprinted with permission from *The Washington Post* and the Population Reference Bureau.

B1–1 *Statistical Abstract of the United States, 1985.* US Department of Commerce, Bureau of the Census, 1985, p. 32.

B1–2 *Statistical Abstract of the United States, 1985.* US Department of Commerce, Bureau of the Census, 1985, p. 32.

B1–3 *Demographic and Socioeconomic Aspects of Aging in the US: 1920–2040.* US Department of Commerce, Bureau of the Census, Aug. 1984, p. 87.

B1–4 *Aging America: Trends and Projections, 1985–86 Edition.* US Senate Special Committee on Aging, American Association of Retired Persons, Federal Council on the Aging, and Administration on Aging, 1986, p. 111.

B1–5 *Demographic and Socioeconomic Aspects of Aging in the US: 1920–2040.* US Department of Commerce, Bureau of the Census, Aug. 1984, p. 96.

B1–6 *Demographic and Socioeconomic Aspects of Aging in the US: 1920–2040.* US Department of Commerce, Bureau of the Census, Aug. 1984, p. 96.

B1–7 *Demographic and Socioeconomic Aspects of Aging in the US: 1920–2040.* US Department of Commerce, Bureau of the Census, Aug. 1984, p. 95.

B1–8 *Demographic and Socioeconomic Aspects of Aging in the US: 1920–2040.* US Department of Commerce, Bureau of the Census, Aug. 1984, p. 85.

B1–9 *Statistical Abstract of the United States, 1985.* US Department of Commerce, Bureau of the Census, 1985, p. 57.

B1–10 *American Women: Three Decades of Change.* (Bianchi, Suzanne M.; Spain, Daphne) US Department of Commerce, Bureau of the Census, Washington, DC, Jun. 1984, p. 30.

B1–11 *American Women: Three Decades of Change.* (Bianchi, Suzanne M., Spain, Daphne). US Department of Commerce, Bureau of the Census, Washington, DC, Jun. 1984, p. 28.

B1–12 *America in Transition: An Aging Society, 1984–85 Edition.* US Senate, Special Committee on Aging, Aug. 1985. 99th Congress, 1st Session, Committee Print 99–13, p. 86.

B1–13 *Aging America: Trends and Projections, 1985–86 Edition.* US Senate Special Committee on Aging, American Association of Retired Persons, Federal Council on the Aging, and Administration on Aging, 1986, p. 111.

B1–14 *Vital Statistics of the United States, 1981: Volume III Marriage and Divorce.* US Department of Health and Human Services, National Center for Health Statistics, 1985, p. I-10.

B2–1 *Aging America: Trends and Projections.* American Association of Retired Persons, 1984, p. 88.

B2–2 *Demographic and Socioeconomic Aspects of Aging in the US: 1920–2040.* US Department of Commerce, Bureau of the Census, Aug. 1984, p. 99.

B2–3 *Chartbook on Aging in America.* 1981 White House Conference on Aging, 1982, p. 129.

B2–4 *Chartbook on Aging in America.* 1981 White House Conference on Aging, 1982, p. 129.

B2–5 *Transportation of Older Americans: Issues and Options for the Decade of the 1980's.* US Department of Transportation, Apr. 1983, p. 17.

B2–6 *Demographic and Socioeconomic Aspects of Aging in the US: 1920–2040.* US Department of Commerce, Bureau of the Census, Aug. 1984, p. 99.

B2–7   *Participants in Postsecondary Education, Oct. 1982.* US Department of Education, National Center for Education Statistics, Nov. 1984, p. 14.

B2–8   *Participants in Postsecondary Education, Oct. 1982.* US Department of Education, National Center for Education Statistics, Nov. 1984, p. 8.

B3–1   *Every Ninth American* (Brotman, Herman B.) private print, 1982, p. 18.

B3–2   *Housing Characteristics of Recent Movers.* US Department of Housing and Urban Development, Office of Policy Development and Research. Current Housing Reports, Annual Housing Survey: 1981. Series H–150–81, p. 13.

B3–3   *Housing Characteristics of Recent Movers.* US Department of Housing and Urban Development, Office of Policy Development and Research. Current Housing Reports, Annual Housing Survey: 1981. Series H–150–81, p. 9.

B3–4   *American Women: Three Decades of Change.* (Bianchi, Suzanne M.; Spain, Daphne) US Department of Commerce, Bureau of the Census, Washington, DC, Jun. 1984, p. 10.

B3–5   *Aging America: Trends and Projections, 1985–86 Edition.* US Senate Special Committee on Aging, American Association of Retired Persons, Federal Council on the Aging, and Administration on Aging, 1986, p. 115.

B3–6   *Every Ninth American.* (Brotman, Herman B.) private print, 1982, p. 17.

B3–7   *Developments in Aging: 1984,* vol. 2 *Appendixes.* US Senate, Special Committee on Aging, Feb. 1985. Senate Resolution 354, p. 238.

B3–8   *Need for Long Term Care, Information and Issues. A Chartbook of the Federal Council on the Aging.* US Department of Health and Human Services, Federal Council on the Aging, 1981, p. 69.

B3–9   *Need for Long Term Care, Information and Issues. A Chartbook of the Federal Council on the Aging.* US Department of Health and Human Services, Federal Council on the Aging, 1981, p. 31.

B3–10 *Chartbook on Aging in America.* 1981 White House Conference on Aging, 1982, p. 107.

B3–11 *America in Transition: An Aging Society, 1984–85 Edition.* US Senate, Special Committee on Aging, Aug. 1985. 99th Congress, 1st Session, Committee Print 99–13, p. 73.

B3–12 *National Survey of the Aged.* (Shanas, Ethel) US Department of Health and Human Services, Administration on Aging, Dec. 1982. DHHS Publication (OHDS) 83–20425, p. 260.

B3–13 *National Survey of the Aged.* (Shanas, Ethel) US Department of Health and Human Services, Administration on Aging, Dec. 1982. DHHS Publication (OHDS) 83–20425, p. 168.

B3–14 *National Survey of the Aged.* (Shanas, Ethel) US Department of Health and Human Services, Administration on Aging, Dec. 1982. DHHS Publication (OHDS) 83–20425, p. 183.

B4–1   *Chartbook on Aging in America.* 1981 White House Conference on Aging, 1982, p. 141.

B4–2   *Aging America: Trends and Projections.* American Association of Retired Persons, 1984, p. 97.

B4–3   *Population of the United States: Historical Trends and Future Projections.* (Bogue, Donald J.) Free Press, New York, 1985, p. 653. Reprinted with permission of The Free Press, a Division of Macmillan, Inc. from *Population of the United States: Historical Trends and Future Projections* by Donald J. Bogue. Copyright ©1985 by The Free Press.

B4–4   *Aging America: Trends and Projections, 1985–86.* US Senate Special Committee on Aging, American Association of Retired Persons, Federal Council on the Aging, and Administration on Aging, 1986, p. 118.

B4–5   *Statistical Abstract of the United States, 1985.* US Department of Commerce, Bureau of the Census, 1985, p. 252.

B4–6   *Every Ninth American* (Brotman, Herman B.) private print, 1982, p. 32.

B4–7   *Chartbook on Aging in America.* 1981 White House Conference on Aging, 1982, p. 135.

B4–8   *Chartbook on Aging in America.* 1981 White House Conference on Aging, 1982, p. 135.

B4–9   *Chartbook on Aging in America.* 1981 White House Conference on Aging, 1982, p. 139.

B4–10 *Aging in the Eighties: America in Transition.* (Louis Harris and Associates) National Council on Aging, 1981, p. 17.

B4–11 *Aging in the Eighties: America in Transition.* (Louis Harris and Associates) National Council on Aging, 1981, p. 24.

B4–12 *Aging in the Eighties: America in Transition.* (Louis Harris and Associates) National Council on Aging, 1981, p. 26.

B4–13 *Aging in the Eighties: America in Transition.* (Louis Harris and Associates) National Council on Aging, 1981, p. 30.

B4–14 *Aging in the Eighties: America in Transition.* (Louis Harris and Associates) National Council on Aging, 1981, p. 22.

B5–1 *Aging in the Eighties: America in Transition.* (Louis Harris and Associates) National Council on Aging, 1981, p. 64.

B5–2 *Aging America: Trends and Projections.* American Association of Retired Persons, 1984, p. 95.

B5–3 *Sourcebook of Criminal Justice Statistics–-1982.* (Flanigan, Timothy J.; McLeod, Maureen) US Department of Justice, Bureau of Justice Statistics, 1983, pp. 296–97.

B5–4 Criminals. (Aday, Ronald H.) In Erdman Palmore, *Handbook on the Aged in the United States.* Greenwood Press, Westport, CT, 1984, tables 18.2 and 18.3, p. 297. Copyright © 1984 by Erdman B. Palmore. Reprinted by permission of the publisher.

B5–5 Criminals. (Aday, Ronald H.) In Erdman Palmore, *Handbook on the Aged in the United States.* Greenwood Press, Westport, CT, 1984, tables 18.2 and 18.3, p. 297. Copyright © 1984 by Erdman B. Palmore. Reprinted by permission of the publisher.

B5–6 *Handbook on the Aged in the United States.* (Palmore, Erdman B., ed.) Greenwood Press, 1984, p. 396. Reprinted with permission from G.E. Atunes, et al., "Patterns of Personal Crime against the Elderly," *Gerontologist,* vol. 17, 1977, p. 323.

B5–7 *Key Issues Affecting Low-Income Elderly, Part I: Issue Development Study.* National Senior Citizens Education and Research Center, Washington, DC, 1982, p. 193. Reprinted by permission.

B5–8 *Key Issues Affecting Low-Income Elderly, Part I: Issue Development Study.* National Senior Citizens Education and Research Center, Washington, DC, 1982, p. 193. Reprinted by permission.

B5–9 *Alcohol and Health, Monograph No. 4.* US Department of Health and Human Services, National Institute on Alcohol Abuse and Alcoholism. Special Population Issues, 1982, p. 267.

B5–10 *Alcohol and Health, Monograph No. 4.* US Department of Health and Human Services, National Institute on Alcohol Abuse and Alcoholism. Special Population Issues, 1982, p. 264.

B5–11 *Health, United States, 1984.* US Department of Health and Human Services, Public Health Service, 1985, p. 86–87.

B5–12 Serving Transportation Needs of the Elderly: An Overview. (Polonsky, Stanford I. Jr.) *Traffic Quarterly,* Oct. 1978, p. 624.

B5–13 Travel Behavior among Elderly Nonusers of Reduced-Rate Transit Service. (Cohen, Stanley H.; Hyde, Jeffrey L.) *Traffic Quarterly,* Apr. 1980, 34:2, p. 278.

C1–1 *Aging America: Trends and Projections.* American Association for Retired Persons, 1984, p. 53.

C1–2 *Aging America: Trends and Projections.* American Association for Retired Persons, 1984, p. 53.

C1–3 *Chartbook on Aging in America.* 1981 White House Conference on Aging, 1982, p. 75.

C1–4 *Aging in the Eighties: America in Transition.* (Louis Harris and Associates) National Council on Aging, 1981, p. 135.

C1–5 *Aging in the Eighties: America in Transition.* (Louis Harris and Associates) National Council on Aging, 1981, p. 139.

C1–6 *Aging in the Eighties: America in Transition.* (Louis Harris and Associates) National Council on Aging, 1981, p. 14.

C2–1 *Aging America: Trends and Projections.* American Association for Retired Persons, 1984, p. 65.

C2–2 *Aging America: Trends and Projections.* American Association for Retired Persons, 1984, p. 58.

C2–3 *Aging America: Trends and Projections.* American Association for Retired Persons, 1984, p. 61.

C2–4 *Tomorrow's Elderly: A Report Prepared by the Congressional Clearinghouse of the Future.* US House of Representatives, Select Committee on Aging, Oct. 1984. 98th Congress, 2nd Session, Pub. No. 98–457, p. 41.

C2–5 *Statistical Abstract of the United States, 1985.* US Department of Commerce, Bureau of the Census, 1985, p. 378.

C2–6 *America in Transition: An Aging Society, 1984–85 Edition.* US Senate, Special Committee on Aging, Aug. 1985. 99th Congress, 1st Session, Committee Print 99–13, p. 65.

C2–7 *Caring for Older Veterans.* US Veterans Administration, Apr. 1975, p. 73.

C2–8 *Aging America: Trends and Projections, 1985–86 Edition.* US Senate, Special Committee on Aging, American Association of Retired Persons, Federal Council on the Aging, and Administration on Aging, 1986, p. 88.

C2–9 *Preliminary Review of Injury Data Pertaining to 65 Years and Older.* US Consumer Product Safety Commission, Apr. 1985.

C2–10 *Preliminary Review of Injury Data Pertaining to 65 Years and Older.* US Consumer Product Safety Commission, Apr. 1985.

C3–1   *Need for Long Term Care, Information and Issues. A Chartbook of the Federal Council on the Aging.* US Department of Health and Human Services, Federal Council on the Aging, 1981, p. 47.

C3–2   *Need for Long Term Care, Information and Issues. A Chartbook of the Federal Council on the Aging.* US Department of Health and Human Services, Federal Council on the Aging, 1981, p. 33.

C3–3   *Health, United States, 1984.* US Department of Health and Human Services, Public Health Service, p. 118.

C3–4   *Health, United States, 1984.* US Department of Health and Human Services, Public Health Service, 1985, p. 119.

C3–5   *Caring for Older Veterans.* US Veterans Administration, Apr. 1975, p. 33.

C4–1   *Aging America: Trends and Projections.* American Association for Retired Persons, 1984, p. 56.

C4–2   *Health, United States, 1984.* US Department of Health and Human Services, Public Health Service, 1985, p. 51.

C4–3   *Health, United States, 1984.* US Department of Health and Human Services, Public Health Service, 1985, pp. 59–60.

C4–4   *Health, United States, 1984.* US Department of Health and Human Services, Public Health Service, 1985, pp. 61–62.

C4–5   *Health, United States, 1984.* US Department of Health and Human Services, Public Health Service, 1985, pp. 74–75.

C4–6   Contrasts in the Health of Elderly Men and Women: An Analysis of Recent Data for Whites in the United States. (Wylie, Charles M.) *The Journal of the American Geriatrics Society,* Sep. 1984, 32:9, p. 670. Reprinted with permission from the American Geriatrics Society.

C4–7   *Demographic and Socioeconomic Aspects of Aging in the US: 1920–2040.* US Department of Commerce, Bureau of the Census, Aug. 1984, p. 62.

C5–1   *Health, United States, 1984.* US Department of Health and Human Services, Public Health Service, 1985, p. 98.

C5–2   *Health, United States, 1984.* US Department of Health and Human Services, Public Health Service, 1985, p. 97.

C5–3   Use of Health Care Services by Older Hispanics. (Lopez-Aqueres, W.; Kemp, Bryan; Staples, Fred; Brummel-Smith, Kenneth) *The Journal of the American Geriatrics Society,* Jun. 1984, 32:6, pp. 438–39. Reprinted with permission from the American Geriatrics Society.

C5–4   *Statistical Abstract of the United States, 1985.* US Department of Commerce, Bureau of the Census, 1985, p. 95.

C5–5   *America in Transition: An Aging Society, 1984–85 Edition.* US Senate, Special Committee on Aging, Aug. 1985. 99th Congress, 1st Session, Committee Print 99–13, pp. 77–78.

C5–6   *America in Transition: An Aging Society, 1984–85 Edition.* US Senate, Special Committee on Aging, Aug. 1985. 99th Congress, 1st Session, Committee Print 99–13, p. 78.

C5–7   Contrasts in the Health of Elderly Men and Women: An Analysis of Recent Data for Whites in the United States. (Wylie, Charles M.) *The Journal of the American Geriatrics Society,* Sep. 1984, 32:9, p. 674. Reprinted with permission from the American Geriatrics Society.

C5–8   Contrasts in the Health of Elderly Men and Women: An Analysis of Recent Data for Whites in the United States. (Wylie, Charles M.) *The Journal of the American Geriatrics Society,* Sep. 1984, 32:9, p. 674. Reprinted with permission from the American Geriatrics Society.

C5–9   *Source Book of Health Insurance Data, 1984–1985.* Health Insurance Association of America, 1985, p. 42. Taken from US Department of Health and Human Services, *Changing Mortality Patterns, Health Services Utilization, and Health Care Expenditures: United States 1973–2003.*

C5–10 *Source Book of Health Insurance Data, 1984–1985.* Health Insurance Association of America, 1985, p. 62. Reprinted by permission of Medical Economics Company, Oradell, NJ 07649.

C6–1   *Health, United States, 1984.* US Department of Health and Human Services, Public Health Service, 1985, p. 28.

C6–2   *Health, United States, 1984.* US Department of Health and Human Services, Public Health Service, 1985, p. 103.

C6–3   *America in Transition: An Aging Society, 1984–85 Edition.* US Senate, Special Committee on Aging, Aug. 1985. 99th Congress, 1st Session, Committee Print 99–13, p. 77.

C6–4   *Source Book of Health Insurance Data, 1984–1985.* Health Insurance Association of America, 1985, p. 43. Reprinted by permission.

C6–5   *America in Transition.* (Taeuber, Cynthia) US Department of Commerce, Bureau of the Census, Sep. 1983. Current Population Reports, Special Studies Series P–23, No. 128, p. 16.

C6–6   *Developments in Aging: 1984,* vol 1, *Report.* US Senate, Special Committee on Aging, Feb. 1985, p. 189.

D1–1   *Employment and Earnings.* US Department of Labor, Bureau of Labor Statistics, Sep. 1985, p. 8.

D1-2 *Employment and Earnings.* US Department of Labor, Bureau of Labor Statistics, Sep. 1985, pp. 9-11 .

D1-3 *Handbook of Labor Statistics.* US Department of Labor, Bureau of Labor Statistics, Jun. 1985, p. 18.

D1-4 Current Operating Statistics, Monthly Tables. US Department of Health and Human Services, Social Security Administration. *Social Security Bulletin,* Oct. 1985, 48:10, p. 63.

D1-5 *America in Transition: An Aging Society, 1984-85 Edition.* US Senate, Special Committee on Aging, Aug. 1985. 99th Congress, 1st Session, Committee Print 99-13, p. 56.

D1-6 *America in Transition: An Aging Society, 1984-85 Edition.* US Senate, Special Committee on Aging, Aug. 1985. 99th Congress, 1st Session, Committee Print 99-13, p. 59.

D1-7 *America in Transition: An Aging Society, 1984-85 Edition.* US Senate, Special Committee on Aging, Aug. 1985. 99th Congress, 1st Session, Committee Print 99-13, p. 59.

D1-8 *Economic Characteristics of Households in the United States: Third Quarter 1984.* US Department of Commerce, Bureau of the Census. Current Population Reports, Household Economic Studies, Series P-70, No. 5, 1985, p. 6.

D2-1 Sex-Specific Equivalent Retirement Ages: 1940-2050. (McMillen, Marilyn M.) US Department of Health and Human Services, Social Security Administration. *Social Security Bulletin,* Mar. 1984, 47:3, p. 8.

D2-2 *Economics of Aging: The Future of Retirement.* (Morrison, Malcolm H., ed.) Van Nostrand Reinhold Company, 1982, p. 91. Reprinted by permission.

D2-3 Sex-Specific Equivalent Retirement Ages: 1940-2050. (McMillen, Marilyn M.) US Department of Health and Human Services, Social Security Administration. *Social Security Bulletin,* Mar. 1984, 47:3, p. 9.

D2-4 Sex-Specific Equivalent Retirement Ages: 1940-2050. (McMillen, Marilyn M.) US Department of Health and Human Services, Social Security Administration. *Social Security Bulletin,* Mar. 1984, 47:3, p. 9.

D2-5 *Annual Statistical Supplement, 1983.* US Department of Health and Human Services, Social Security Administration. Social Security Bulletin, p. 139.

D2-6 Effects of OASDI Benefit Increase, December 1983. (Bondar, Joseph) US Department of Health and Human Services, Social Security Administration. *Social Security Bulletin,* Mar. 1984, 47:3, p. 12.

D2-7 Effects of OASDI Benefit Increase, December 1983. (Bondar, Joseph) US Department of Health and Human Services, Social Security Administration. *Social Security Bulletin,* Mar. 1984, 47:3, p. 13.

D2-8 Effects of OASDI Benefit Increase, December 1983. (Bondar, Joseph) US Department of Health and Human Services, Social Security Administration. *Social Security Bulletin,* Mar. 1984, 47:3, p. 13.

D2-9 *Statistical Abstract of the United States, 1985.* US Department of Commerce, Bureau of the Census, 1985, p. 369.

D2-10 *Statistical Abstract of the United States, 1985.* US Department of Commerce, Bureau of the Census, 1985, p. 369.

D2-11 *Aging in the Eighties: America in Transition.* (Louis Harris and Associates) National Council on Aging, 1981, p. 55.

D3-1 *Every Ninth American.* (Brotman, Herman B.) private print, 1982, p. 42.

D3-2 *Aging America: Trends and Projections, 1985-86 Edition.* US Senate Special Committee on Aging, American Association of Retired Persons, Federal Council on the Aging, and Administration on Aging, 1986, p. 79.

D3-3 *Handbook of Labor Statistics.* US Department of Labor, Bureau of Labor Statistics, Jun. 1985, p. 58.

D3-4 *Aging in the Eighties: America in Transition.* (Louis Harris and Associates) National Council on Aging, 1981, p. 100.

D4-1 *Chartbook on Aging in America.* 1981 White House Conference on Aging, 1982, p. 47.

D4-2 *Handbook of Labor Statistics.* US Department of Labor, Bureau of Labor Statistics, Jun. 1985, pp. 82-83.

D4-3 *Handbook of Labor Statistics.* US Department of Labor, Bureau of Labor Statistics, Jun. 1985, p. 88.

E1-1 *Annual Statistical Supplement, 1983.* US Department of Health and Human Services, Social Security Administration. *Social Security Bulletin,* p. v.

E1-2 *Income of the Population, 55 and Over, 1982.* US Department of Health and Human Services, Social Security Administration. SSA Publication No. 13-11871, Mar. 1984, p. 11.

E1-3 *Income of the Population, 55 and Over, 1982.* US Department of Health and Human Services, Social Security Administration. SSA Publication No. 13-11871, Mar. 1984, p. 12.

E1-4 *Income of the Population, 55 and Over, 1982.* US Department of Health and Human Services, Social Security Administration. SSA Publication No. 13-11871, Mar. 1984, p. 13.

E1-5 *Income of the Population, 55 and Over, 1982.* US Department of Health and Human Services, Social Security Administration. SSA Publication No. 13-11871, Mar. 1984, p. 47.

E1-6 *Income of the Population, 55 and Over, 1982.* US Department of Health and Human Services, Social Security Administration. SSA Publication No. 13-11871, Mar. 1984, p. 49.

E1-7 *America in Transition: An Aging Society, 1984-85 Edition.* US Senate, Special Committee on Aging, Aug. 1985. 99th Congress, 1st Session, Committee Print 99-13, p. 47.

E1-8 Incomes of the Aged and Nonaged, 1950-82. (Grad, Susan) US Department of Health and Human Services, Social Security Administration. *Social Security Bulletin,* 47:6, Jun. 1984, p. 9.

E1-9 Incomes of the Aged and Nonaged, 1950-82. (Grad, Susan) US Department of Health and Human Services, Social Security Administration. *Social Security Bulletin,* Jun. 1984, 47:6, p. 9.

E1-10 Current Operating Statistics: Monthly Tables. US Department of Health and Human Services, Social Security Administration. *Social Security Bulletin,* Mar. 1984, 47:3, p. 25.

E1-11 Annual Statistical Supplement, 1984-85. US Department of Health and Human Services, Social Security Administration. *Social Security Bulletin,* p. v.

E1-12 Annual Statistical Supplement, 1983. US Department of Health and Human Services, Social Security Administration. *Social Security Bulletin,* p. 61.

E1-13 *Statistical Abstract of the United States, 1985.* US Department of Commerce, Bureau of the Census, 1985, p. 353.

E1-14 *Key Issues Affecting Low-Income Elderly, Part I: Issue Development Study.* National Senior Citizens Education and Research Center, Washington, DC, 1982, p. 44. Reprinted by permission.

E2-1 Current Operating Statistics, Monthly Tables. US Department of Health and Human Services, Social Security Administration. *Social Security Bulletin,* Oct. 1985, 48:10, p. 49.

E2-2 Current Operating Statistics, Monthly Tables. US Department of Health and Human Services, Social Security Administration. *Social Security Bulletin,* Oct. 1985, 48:10, p. 49.

E2-3 Current Operating Statistics, Monthly Tables. US Department of Health and Human Services, Social Security Administration. *Social Security Bulletin,* Oct. 1985, 48:10, p. 46.

E2-4 *Income of the Population, 55 and Over, 1982.* US Department of Health and Human Services, Social Security Administration. SSA Publication No. 13-11871, Mar. 1984, p. 35.

E2-5 *America in Transition: An Aging Society, 1984-85 Edition.* US Senate, Special Committee on Aging, Aug. 1985. 99th Congress, 1st Session, Committee Print 99-13, p. 38.

E2-6 Measurements of Family Income. (Schwenk, Nancy E.) US Department of Agriculture, Family Economics Research Group. *Family Economics Review,* Jul. 1985, No. 3., p. 2.

E2-7 *Time of Change: 1983 Handbook on Women Workers.* US Department of Labor, Women's Bureau, 1983. Bulletin 298, p. 84.

E2-8 *Income of the Population, 55 and Over, 1982.* US Department of Health and Human Services, Social Security Administration. SSA Publication No. 13-11871, Mar. 1984, p. 30.

E2-9 *Income of the Population, 55 and Over, 1982.* US Department of Health and Human Services, Social Security Administration. SSA Publication No. 13-11871, Mar. 1984, p. 20.

E2-10 *Economic Report of the President, Together with the Annual Report of the Council of Economic Advisers.* Office of the President, Feb. 1985, p. 162.

E2-11 *Economic Report of the President, Together with the Annual Report of the Council of Economic Advisers.* Office of the President, Feb. 1985, p. 163.

E2-12 *America in Transition: An Aging Society, 1984-85 Edition.* US Senate, Special Committee on Aging, Aug. 1985. 99th Congress, 1st Session, Committee Print 99-13, p. 35.

E2-13 *Aging America: Trends and Projections, 1985-86 Edition.* US Senate Special Committee on Aging, American Association of Retired Persons, Federal Council on the Aging, and Administration on Aging, 1986, p. 41.

E2-14 *Income of the Population, 55 and Over, 1982.* US Department of Health and Human Services, Social Security Administration. SSA Publication No. 13-11871, Mar. 1984, p. 52.

E2-15 *Income of the Population, 55 and Over, 1982.* US Department of Health and Human Services, Social Security Administration. SSA Publication No. 13-11871, Mar. 1984, p. 54.

E2–16 *Economic Characteristics of Households in the United States: Third Quarter 1984.* US Department of Commerce, Bureau of the Census. Current Population Reports, Household Economic Studies, 1985. Series P–70, No. 5, p. 1.

E2–17 *Economic Characteristics of Households in the United States: Third Quarter 1984.* US Department of Commerce, Bureau of the Census. Current Population Reports, Household Economic Studies, 1985. Series P–70, No. 5, p. 6.

E2–18 *Statistical Abstract of the United States, 1985,* US Department of Commerce, Bureau of the Census, 1985, p. 373.

E3–1 *Medicare's Role in Financing the Health Care of Older Women.* (ICF Incorporated) American Association of Retired Persons, Jul. 1985, p. 26. Reprinted by permission.

E3–2 *CPI Detailed Report, August 1985.* US Department of Labor, Bureau of Labor Statistics, 1985, p. 4.

E3–3 *CPI Detailed Report, August 1985.* US Department of Labor, Bureau of Labor Statistics, 1985, p. 5.

E3–4 *CPI Detailed Report, August 1985.* US Department of Labor, Bureau of Labor Statistics, 1985, p. 7.

E3–5 *CPI Detailed Report, August 1985.* US Department of Labor, Bureau of Labor Statistics, 1985, p. 6.

E3–6 Current Operating Statistics, Monthly Tables. US Department of Health and Human Services, Social Security Administration. *Social Security Bulletin,* Oct. 1985, 48:10, p. 65.

E3–7 *Health, United States, 1984.* US Department of Health and Human Services, Public Health Service, 1985, p. 141.

E3–8 *Health, United States, 1984.* US Department of Health and Human Services, Public Health Service, 1985, p. 142.

E3–9 *Health, United States, 1984.* US Department of Health and Human Services, Public Health Service, 1985, p. 143.

E3–10 *Economic Report of the President, Together with the Annual Report of the Council of Economic Advisers.* Office of the President, Feb. 1985, p. 165.

E3–11 *Individual Income Tax Returns, 1982 Statistics of Income.* US Department of the Treasury, Internal Revenue Service, 1984, p. 69.

E3–12 Counting What You Keep. (Green, Gordon; Coder, John) *American Demographics,* Feb. 1984, 6:2, p. 24. Reprinted by permission.

E3–13 Measurements of Family Income. (Schwenk, Nancy E.) US Department of Agriculture, Family Economics Research Group. *Family Economics Review,* Jul. 1985, No. 3, p. 3.

E3–14 Where Your Tax Dollars Go. *The Washington Post,* Nov. 19, 1985, p. A15. Copyright by *The Washington Post..* From material provided by the Associated Press. Reprinted with permission from *The Washington Post* and the Associated Press.

E3–15 Counting What You Keep. (Green, Gordon; Coder, John) *American Demographics,* Feb. 1984, 6:2, p. 27. Reprinted by permission.

E3–16 Cost of Food at Home. US Department of Agriculture, Family Economics Research Group. *Family Economics Review,* Jul. 1985, No. 3, p. 26.

E3–17 *Medicare's Role in Financing the Health Care of Older Women.* (ICF Incorporated) American Association of Retired Persons, Jul. 1985, p. 19. Reprinted by permission.

E3–18 *Medicare's Role in Financing the Health Care of Older Women.* (ICF Incorporated) American Association of Retired Persons, Jul. 1985, p. 19. Reprinted by permission.

E3–19 *Developments in Aging: 1984,* vol. 1 *Report.* US Senate, Special Committee on Aging, Feb. 1985. Senate Resolution 354, p. 244.

E3–20 *Developments in Aging: 1984,* vol. 1 *Report.* US Senate, Special Committee on Aging, Feb. 1985. Senate Resolution 354, p. 241.

E4–1 Poverty and Plenty: A Paradox? (Fowles, Donald) *Aging,* Jun.–Jul. 1984, No. 345, p. 47. Reprinted by permission.

E4–2 *Aging America: Trends and Projections.* American Association for Retired Persons, 1984, p. 38.

E4–3 Incomes of the Aged and Nonaged, 1950–82. (Grad, Susan) US Department of Health and Human Services, Social Security Administration. *Social Security Bulletin,* Jun. 1984, 47:6, p. 7.

E4–4 *Aging America: Trends and Projections, 1985-86 Edition.* US Senate Special Committee on Aging, American Association of Retired Persons, Federal Council on the Aging, and Administration on Aging, 1986, p. 53.

E4–5 *Medicare's Role in Financing the Health Care of Older Women.* (ICF Incorporated) American Association of Retired Persons, Jul. 1985, p. 15. Reprinted by permission.

E4–6 *Characteristics of the Population below the Poverty Level: 1983.* US Department of Commerce, Bureau of the Census, Mar. 1984. Current Population Reports, Consumer Income, Series P–60, No. 147, pp. 63–68.

E4–7 *Money Income and Poverty Status of Families and Persons in the United States: 1983.* US Department of Commerce, Bureau of the Census, Aug. 1984. Current Population Reports, Consumer Income, Series P–60, No. 145, pp. 25–26.

F1-1 *Budget of the United States Government: Historical Tables, Fiscal Year 1986.* Executive Office of the President, Office of Management and Budget, 1985, p. C3.

F1-2 *Statistical Abstract of the United States, 1985.* US Department of Commerce, Bureau of the Census, 1985, p. 303.

F1-3 *Statistical Abstract of the United States, 1985.* US Department of Commerce, Bureau of the Census, 1985, p. 303.

F1-4 *Aging America: Trends and Projections, 1985–86 Edition.* US Senate Special Committee on Aging, American Association of Retired Persons, Federal Council on the Aging, and Administration on Aging, 1986, p. 123.

F1-5 *Statistical Abstract of the United States, 1985.* US Department of Commerce, Bureau of the Census, 1985, p. 353.

F1-6 *Statistical Abstract of the United States, 1985.* US Department of Commerce, Bureau of the Census, 1985, p. 361.

F1-7 *Statistical Abstract of the United States, 1985.* US Department of Commerce, Bureau of the Census, 1985, p. 378.

F1-8 Current Operating Statistics, Monthly Tables. US Department of Health and Human Services, Social Security Administration. *Social Security Bulletin,* Nov. 1985, 48:11, p. 25.

F1-9 Current Operating Statistics, Monthly Tables. US Department of Health and Human Services, Social Security Administration. *Social Security Bulletin,* Oct. 1985, 48:10, p. 55.

F1-10 *Program and Demographic Characteristics of Supplemental Security Income Beneficiaries, December 1983.* (Kahn, Arthur L.) US Department of Health and Human Services, Social Security Administration, Office of Policy, Office of Research, Statistics and International Policy. SSA Publication 13–11977, 1984, p. 7.

F1-11 *Program and Demographic Characteristics of Supplemental Security Income Beneficiaries, December 1983.* (Kahn, Arthur L.) US Department of Health and Human Services, Social Security Administration, Office of Policy, Office of Research, Statistics and International Policy. SSA Publication 13–11977, 1984, p. 7.

F1-12 *Program and Demographic Characteristics of Supplemental Security Income Beneficiaries, December 1983.* (Kahn, Arthur L.) US Department of Health and Human Services, Social Security Administration, Office of Policy, Office of Research, Statistics and International Policy. SSA Publication 13–11977, 1984, p. 6.

F1-13 *Program and Demographic Characteristics of Supplemental Security Income Beneficiaries, December 1983.* (Kahn, Arthur L.) US Department of Health and Human Services, Social Security Administration, Office of Policy, Office of Research, Statistics and International Policy. SSA Publication 13–11977, 1984, p. 3.

F1-14 *Program and Demographic Characteristics of Supplemental Security Income Beneficiaries, December 1983.* (Kahn, Arthur L.) US Department of Health and Human Services, Social Security Administration, Office of Policy, Office of Research, Statistics and International Policy. SSA Publication 13–11977, 1984, p. 3.

F1-15 *Developments in Aging: 1984, A Report of the Special Committee on Aging, United States Senate, Pursuant to S. Res. 354, March 2, 1984.* vol. 2, *Appendixes.* US Senate, Special Committee on Aging, Feb. 1985. pp. 252–53.

F1-16 *Developments in Aging: 1984, A Report of the Special Committee on Aging, United States Senate, Pursuant to S. Res. 354, March 2, 1984.* vol. 2, *Appendixes.* US Senate, Special Committee on Aging, Feb. 1985. p. 253.

F2-1 *US Budget in Brief, FY 1986.* Executive Office of the President, Office of Management and Budget, 1985, p. 46.

F2-2 Annual Statistical Supplement, 1983. US Department of Health and Human Services, Social Security Administration. *Social Security Bulletin,* p. iii.

F2-3 Adult Assistance Programs under the Social Security Act. US Department of Health and Human Services, Social Security Administration. *Social Security Bulletin,* Oct. 1985, 48:10, p. 18.

F2-4 Adult Assistance Programs under the Social Security Act. US Department of Health and Human Services, Social Security Administration. *Social Security Bulletin,* Oct. 1985, 48:10, p. 17.

F2-5 *Statistical Abstract of the United States, 1985.* US Department of Commerce, Bureau of the Census, 1985, p. 361.

F2-6 Current Operating Statistics, Monthly Tables. US Department of Health and Human Services, Social Security Administration. *Social Security Bulletin,* Oct. 1985, p. 37.

F2-7 Annual Statistical Supplement, 1983. US Department of Health and Human Services, Social Security Administration. *Social Security Bulletin,* p. iv.

F2–8   Adult Assistance Programs under the Social Security Act. US Department of Health and Human Services, Social Security Administration. *Social Security Bulletin,* Oct. 1985, 48:10, p. 19.

F2–9   *Program and Demographic Characteristics of Supplemental Security Income Beneficiaries, December 1983.* (Kahn, Arthur L.) US Department of Health and Human Services, Social Security Administration, Office of Policy, Office of Research, Statistics and International Policy. SSA Publication 13–11977, 1984, p. 4.

F2–10   *Program and Demographic Characteristics of Supplemental Security Income Beneficiaries, December 1983.* (Kahn, Arthur L.) US Department of Health and Human Services, Social Security Administration, Office of Policy, Office of Research, Statistics and International Policy. SSA Publication 13–11977, 1984, p. 4.

F2–11   Adult Assistance Programs under the Social Security Act. US Department of Health and Human Services, Social Security Administration. *Social Security Bulletin,* Oct. 1985, 48:10, p. 20.

F2–12   *Macroeconomic Demographic Model.* US Department of Health and Human Services, National Institute on Aging, Jun. 1984, p. 82.

F3–1   *US Budget in Brief, FY 1986.* Executive Office of the President, Office of Management and Budget, 1985, p. 50.

F3–2   *Caring for Older Veterans.* US Veterans Administration, Apr. 1975, p. 19.

F3–3   *Caring for Older Veterans.* US Veterans Administration, Apr. 1975, p. 19.

F3–4   *Caring for Older Veterans.* US Veterans Administration, Apr. 1975, p. 34.

F3–5   *Caring for Older Veterans.* US Veterans Administration, Apr. 1975, p. 32.

F3–6   *Health Insurance Coverage among Veterans Aged 55 and Over. Follow Up Analysis.* (Petersen, Nancy J.) US Veterans Administration, Jan. 1985, p. 2.

F4–1   *Statistical Abstract of the United States, 1985,* US Department of Commerce, Bureau of the Census, 1985. p. 94.

F4–2   *Source Book of Health Insurance Data, 1984–1985.* Health Insurance Association of America, 1985, p. 40. Taken from government sources.

F4–3   *Tomorrow's Elderly: A Report Prepared by the Congressional Clearinghouse of the Future.* US House of Representatives, Select Committee on Aging, Oct. 1984. 98th Congress, 2nd Session, Pub. No. 98–457, p. 27.

F4–4   *US Budget in Brief, FY 1986.* Executive Office of the President, Office of Management and Budget, 1985, p. 45.

F4–5   *Statistical Abstract of the United States, 1985.* US Department of Commerce, Bureau of the Census, 1985, p. 97.

F4–6   *Statistical Abstract of the United States, 1985.* US Department of Commerce, Bureau of the Census, 1985, p. 97.

F4–7   *Health, United States, 1984.* US Department of Health and Human Services, Public Health Service, 1985, p. 147.

F4–8   *Aging America: Trends and Projections, 1985–86 Edition.* US Senate Special Committee on Aging, American Association of Retired Persons, Federal Council on the Aging, and Administration on Aging, 1986, p. 107.

F4–9   *Aging America: Trends and Projections, 1985–86 Edition.* US Senate Special Committee on Aging, American Association of Retired Persons, Federal Council on the Aging, and Administration on Aging, 1986, p. 106.

F4–10   *America in Transition: An Aging Society, 1984–85 Edition.* US Senate, Special Committee on Aging, Aug. 1985. 99th Congress, 1st Session, Committee Print 99–13, p. 80.

F4–11   *America in Transition: An Aging Society, 1984–85 Edition.* US Senate, Special Committee on Aging, Aug. 1985. 99th Congress, 1st Session, Committee Print 99–13, p. 80.

F4–12   *America in Transition: An Aging Society, 1984–85 Edition.* US Senate, Special Committee on Aging, Aug. 1985. 99th Congress, 1st Session, Committee Print 99–13, p. 80.

F4–13   *Statistical Abstract of the United States, 1985.* US Department of Commerce, Bureau of the Census, 1985, p. 371.

F4–14   *Statistical Abstract of the United States, 1985.* US Department of Commerce, Bureau of the Census, 1985, p. 372.

F4–15   *Statistical Abstract of the United States, 1985.* US Department of Commerce, Bureau of the Census, 1985, p. 372.

F4–16   *Statistical Abstract of the United States, 1985.* US Department of Commerce, Bureau of the Census, 1985, p. 372.

F4–17   *Source Book of Health Insurance Data, 1984–1985.* Health Insurance Association of America, 1985, p. 34. Taken from US Department of Health and Human Services, Health Care Financing Administration.

F4–18   *Source Book of Health Insurance Data, 1984–1985.* Health Insurance Association of America, 1985, p. 35. Taken from US Department of Health and Human Services, Health Care Financing Administration.

F4–19   *Source Book of Health Insurance Data, 1984–1985.* Health Insurance Association of America, 1985, p. 46. Taken from US Department of Health and Human Services, Health Care Financing Administration, *Health Care Financing Review,* Winter 1984.

F4–20   *Health United States and Prevention Profile, 1983.* US Department of Health and Human Services, National Center for Health Statistics, Dec. 1983, p. 82.

F4–21   *Pension Coverage and Expected Retirement Benefits, Final Report.* (ICF Incorporated) American Council of Life Insurance, Oct. 1982, p. 19. Reprinted by permission.

F4–22   *Pension Coverage and Expected Retirement Benefits, Final Report.* (ICF Incorporated) American Council of Life Insurance, Oct. 1982, p. 21. Reprinted by permission.

F4–23   *Pension Coverage and Expected Retirement Benefits, Final Report.* (ICF Incorporated) American Council of Life Insurance, Oct. 1982, p. 22. Reprinted by permission.

F4–24   *Pension Coverage and Expected Retirement Benefits, Final Report.* (ICF Incorporated) American Council of Life Insurance, Oct. 1982, p. 22. Reprinted by permission.

F4–25   Current Operating Statistics: Monthly Tables. US Department of Health and Human Services, Social Security Administration. *Social Security Bulletin,* Mar. 1984, 47:3, p. 22.

F4–26   Current Operating Statistics, Monthly Tables. US Department of Health and Human Services, Social Security Administration. *Social Security Bulletin,* Oct. 1985, 48:10, p. 39.

F4–27   From *Survey of State Employee Health Insurance Plans.* 1985 Update of Contribution Data, Martin E. Segal Company, New York. Reprinted by permission.

F4–28   From *Survey of State Employee Health Insurance Plans.* 1985 Update of Contribution Data, Martin E. Segal Company, New York. Reprinted by permission.

F4–29   From *Survey of State Employee Health Insurance Plans.* 1985 Update of Contribution Data, Martin E. Segal Company, New York. Reprinted by permission.

F4–30   Current Operating Statistics, Monthly Tables. US Department of Health and Human Services, Social Security Administration. *Social Security Bulletin,* Oct. 1985, 48:10, p. 67.

F4–31   *Source Book of Health Insurance Data, 1984–1985.* Health Insurance Association of America, 1985, p. 53. Taken from US Department of Commerce, Bureau of Economic Analysis, *The National Income and Product Accounts of the United States, 1929–76 Statistical Tables* and July 1984 Special Supplement to *Survey of Current Business.*

F4–32   *Statistical Abstract of the United States, 1985.* US Department of Commerce, Bureau of the Census, 1985, p. 94

F5–1   *America in Transition: An Aging Society, 1984–85 Edition.* US Senate, Special Committee on Aging, Aug. 1985. 99th Congress, 1st Session, Committee Print 99–13, p. 97.

F5–2   *Economic Characteristics of Households in the United States: Third Quarter 1984.* US Department of Commerce, Bureau of the Census, 1985. Current Population Reports, Household Economic Studies, Series P–70, No. 5, p. 4.

F5–3   *Economic Characteristics of Households in the United States: Third Quarter 1984.* US Department of Commerce, Bureau of the Census, 1985. Current Population Reports, Household Economic Studies, Series P–70, No. 5, p. 4.

F5–4   Benefits and Beneficiaries under Public Employee Retirement Programs, 1980. (Bixby, Ann K.) US Department of Health and Human Services, Social Security Administration. *Social Security Bulletin,* Jan. 1984, 47:1, p. 28.

F5–5   Benefits and Beneficiaries under Public Employee Retirement Programs, 1980. (Bixby, Ann K.) US Department of Health and Human Services, Social Security Administration. *Social Security Bulletin,* Jan. 1984, 47:1, p. 27.

F5–6   Benefits and Beneficiaries under Public Employee Retirement Programs, 1980. (Bixby, Ann K.) US Department of Health and Human Services, Social Security Administration. *Social Security Bulletin,* Jan. 1984, 47:1, p. 27.

F5–7   *Statistical Abstract of the United States, 1985.* US Department of Commerce, Bureau of the Census, 1985, p. 370.

F5–8   *Statistical Abstract of the United States, 1985.* US Department of Commerce, Bureau of the Census, 1985, p. 370.

F5–9   *Statistical Abstract of the United States, 1985.* US Department of Commerce, Bureau of the Census, 1985, p. 368.

F5–10   *Statistical Abstract of the United States, 1985.* US Department of Commerce, Bureau of the Census, 1985, p. 368.

F5–11 Home Equity Conversion Plans as a Source of Retirement Income. (Springer, Philip B.) US Department of Health and Human Services, Social Security Administration. *Social Security Bulletin,* Sep. 1985, 48:9, p. 11.

F5–12 Home Equity Conversion Plans as a Source of Retirement Income. (Springer, Philip B.) US Department of Health and Human Services, Social Security Administration. *Social Security Bulletin,* Sep. 1985, 48:9, p. 18.

F5–13 *Pension Facts, 1984/1985.* American Council of Life Insurance, 1985, p. 28. Taken from government sources.

F5–14 *Pension Facts, 1984/1985.* American Council of Life Insurance, 1985, p. 28. Taken from government sources.

F5–15 *Annual Statistical Supplement, 1983.* US Department of Health and Human Services, Social Security Administration. *Social Security Bulletin,* p. 95.

F5–16 *Annual Statistical Supplement, 1983.* US Department of Health and Human Services, Social Security Administration. *Social Security Bulletin,* p. 106.

F5–17 *Annual Statistical Supplement, 1983.* US Department of Health and Human Services, Social Security Administration. *Social Security Bulletin,* p. 218.

F5–18 *Income of the Population, 55 and Over, 1982.* US Department of Health and Human Services, Social Security Administration. SSA Publication No. 13–11871. Mar. 1984, p. 59.

Guide to Relevant Information Sources

JOURNAL ARTICLES

AARP Data Gram

Employment and Retirement among Older Americans. American Association of Retired Persons. *AARP Data Gram,* Jun. 1983.

Housing Satisfaction and Older Americans. American Association of Retired Persons. *AARP Data Gram,* Jul. 1984.

Technology and Older Americans: Attitudes, Uses and Needs. American Association of Retired Persons. *AARP Data Gram,* Oct. 1984.

AARP Public Opinion Highlights

Medicare and Social Security Issues. American Association of Retired Persons. *AARP Public Opinion Highlights,* Apr. 1985.

Social Security Issues. American Association of Retired Persons. *AARP Public Opinion Highlights,* Jun. 1985.

Aging

Poverty and Plenty: A Paradox? (Fowles, Donald) *Aging,* Jun.–Jul. 1984, no. 345, 46–47.

American Demographics

Counting What You Keep. (Green, Gordon; Coder, John) *American Demographics,* Feb. 1984, 6:2, 22–27.

Trends: All Americans. (Robey, Bryant; Russell, Cheryl) *American Demographics,* Feb. 1984, 6:2, 38–42.

Brookings Review

Sectoral Shifts and the Size of the Middle Class. (Lawrence, Robert Z.) *Brookings Review,* Fall 1984, 3–11.

Employee Benefits Journal

Postretirement Health and Welfare Programs. International Foundation of Employee Benefit Plans. *Employee Benefits Journal,* Mar. 1985 10:1, 4–10.

Family Economics Review

Cost of Food at Home. US Department of Agriculture, Family Economics Research Group. *Family Economics Review,* Jul. 1985, no. 3.

Measurements of Family Income. (Schwenk, Nancy E.) US Department of Agriculture, Family Economics Research Group. *Family Economics Review,* Jul. 1985, no. 3, 1–7.

Federal Reserve Bulletin

Survey of Consumer Finances, 1983: A Second Report. US Federal Reserve Bank. *Federal Reserve Bulletin,* Dec. 1983, 70:12.

Geriatric Consultant

Declining Mortality of Older Americans. (Barker, Sally) *Geriatric Consultant,* Jan.–Feb. 1984, 2:4, 25.

Geriatrics

The Aging Alcoholic. (Champlin, Leslie) *Geriatrics,* May 1983, 38:5, 31–95.

Gerontologist

Compression of Mortality: Myth or Reality? (Myers, George C.; Manton, Kenneth G.) *Gerontologist,* Aug. 1984, 24:4, 346–53.

Recent Changes in the US: Age at Death Distribution: Further Observations. (Myers, George C.; Manton, Kenneth G.) *Gerontologist,* Dec. 1984, 24:6, 572–75.

The Journal of the American Geriatrics Society

Use of Health Care Services by Older Hispanics. (Lopez-Aqueres, W.; Kemp, Brian; Staples, Fred; Brummel-Smith, Kenneth) *The Journal of the American Geriatrics Society,* Jun. 1984, 32:6, 435–40.

Contrasts in the Health of Elderly Men and Women: An Analysis of Recent Data for Whites in the United States. (Wylie, Charles M.) *The Journal of the American Geriatrics Society,* Sep. 1984, 32:9, 670–75.

Quality of Ambulatory Care of the Elderly. (Heller, Thomas A.; Larson, Eric B.; Logerfo, James P.) *The*

Editor's Note: All sources are arranged chronologically.

Journal of the American Geriatrics Society, Nov. 1984, 32:11, 782–88.

Social Security Bulletin

Annual Statistical Supplement. US Department of Health and Human Services, Social Security Administration. *Social Security Bulletin.*

Current Operating Statistics, Monthly Tables. US Department of Health and Human Services, Social Security Administration. *Social Security Bulletin.*

Low-Income Energy Assistance Program. (Rigby, Donald E.; Scott, Charles) US Department of Health and Human Services, Social Security Administration. *Social Security Bulletin,* Jan. 1983, 46:1, 11–21.

Relative Importance of Various Income Sources of the Aged, 1980. (Upp, Melinda). US Department of Health and Human Services, Social Security Administration. *Social Security Bulletin,* Jan. 1983, 46:1, 3–10.

SSI: Characteristics of Recipients of Federally Administered State Supplementation Only. US Department of Health and Human Services, Social Security Administration. *Social Security Bulletin,* Apr. 1983. 46:4.

Benefits and Beneficiaries under Public Employee Retirement Programs, 1980. (Bixby, Ann K.) US Department of Health and Human Services, Social Security Administration. *Social Security Bulletin,* Jan. 1984, 47:1, 25–28.

Effects of OASDI Benefit Increase, December 1983. (Bondar, Joseph) US Department of Health and Human Services, Social Security Administration. *Social Security Bulletin,* Mar. 1984, 47:3, 11–13.

Sex-Specific Equivalent Retirement Ages: 1940–2050. (McMillen, Marilyn M.) US Department of Health and Human Services, Social Security Administration. *Social Security Bulletin,* Mar. 1984, 47:3, 3–10.

Incomes of the Aged and Nonaged, 1950–82. (Grad, Susan) US Department of Health and Human Services, Social Security Administration. *Social Security Bulletin,* Jun. 1984, 47:6, 3–17.

Home Equity Conversion Plans as a Source of Retirement Income. (Springer, Philip B.) US Department of Health and Human Services, Social Security Administration. *Social Security Bulletin,* Sep. 1985, 48:9, 10–19.

Adult Assistance Programs under the Social Security Act. US Department of Health and Human Services, Social Security Administration. *Social Security Bulletin,* Oct. 1985, 48:10, 10–21.

Unemployment Insurance, Then and Now, 1935–85. (Price, Daniel P.). US Department of Health and Human Services, Social Security Administration. *Social Security Bulletin,* Oct. 1985, 48:10, 22–32.

Statistical Bulletin

Projections of Populations Growth at the Older Ages. Metropolitan Life Insurance Company. *Statistical Bulletin,* Jun. 1984, 65:2, 8–12.

UN Bulletin on Aging

Population Projections. UN Department of International Economic and Social Affairs, Center for Social Development. *UN Bulletin on Aging,* 1980, V:2.

BOOKS, PAMPHLETS AND REPORTS

1981 White House Conference on Aging

1981 White House Conference on Aging, Final Report, vol. 3, Recommendations, Post Conference Survey of Delegates. 1981 White House Conference on Aging.

Chartbook on Aging in America. 1981 White House Conference on Aging, 1982.

Chartbook on Aging in America—Supplement. (Brotman, Herman B.) 1981 White House Conference on Aging, 1982.

American Association of Retired Persons

Medicare's Role in Financing the Health Care of Older Women. (ICF Incorporated) American Association of Retired Persons, Jul. 1985.

Planning for Retirement: A Bibliography of Retirement Planning Literature. American Association of Retired Persons, 1984.

American Council of Life Insurance

Pension Coverage and Expected Retirement Benefits, Final Report. (ICF Incorporated) American Council of Life Insurance, Oct. 1982.

Pension Facts 1984/1985. American Council of Life Insurance, 1985.

American Hospital Association

Hospital Statistics, 1984. American Hospital Association, Chicago, IL, 1984.

Herman B. Brotman

Every Ninth American. (Brotman, Herman B.) private print, 1982.

Ancestry, Nativity and Language of the Older Population. (Brotman, Herman B.) private print, Jun. 1982.

Care Reports

1982-83 Chartbook of Federal Programs on Aging. (Schechter, Irma; Oriol, William) Care Reports, Bethesda, MD, 1982.

Center for Social Research in Aging, University of Miami

Retirement Migration Project: Final Report to the National Institute on Aging. (Longino, Charles F.; Biggar, Jeanne C.; Flynn, Cynthia B.; Wiseman,

Robert F.) Center for Social Research in Aging, University of Miami, Coral Gables, FL, Sep. 1984.

Executive Office of the President, Office of Management and Budget

Budget of the United States Government: Historical Tables, Fiscal Year 1986. Executive Office of the President, Office of Management and Budget, 1985.

US Budget in Brief, FY 1986. Executive Office of the President, Office of Management and Budget, 1985.

The Free Press

Population of the United States: Historical Trends and Future Projections. (Bogue, Donald J.) The Free Press, New York, 1985.

Greenwood Press

Aging and Public Policy: The Politics of Growing Old in America. (Browne, William P.; Olson, Laura K., eds.) Contributions in Political Science, Number 83, Greenwood Press, Westport, CT, 1983.

Handbook on the Aged in the United States. (Palmore, Erdman B., ed.) Greenwood Press, Westport, CT, 1984.

Health Insurance Association of America

Source Book of Health Insurance Data, 1984–1985. Health Insurance Association of America, 1985.

National Caucus and Center on Black Aged

Profile of Elderly Black Americans. National Caucus and Center on Black Aged, Feb. 1985.

National Council on Aging

Aging in the Eighties: America in Transition. (Louis Harris and Associates) National Council on Aging, 1981.

National Data Base on Aging, National Association of State Units on Aging

Funding Sources and Expenditure Patterns of State and Area Agencies. National Data Base on Aging, National Association of State Units on Aging, Washington, DC, Jul. 1983.

National Senior Citizens Education and Research Center

Key Issues Affecting Low-Income Elderly, Part I: Issue Development Study. National Senior Citizens Education and Research Center, Washington, DC, 1982.

University of California, Ethel Percy Andrus Gerontology Center

Transportation and the Diverse Aged. University of California, Ethel Percy Andrus Gerontology Center. Brochure, 1980.

US Consumer Product Safety Commission

Injury Reports, 1982, 1983, 1984. US Consumer Product Safety Commission.

Preliminary Review of Injury Data Pertaining to 65 Years and Older. US Consumer Product Safety Commission, Apr. 1985.

US Department of Commerce, Bureau of the Census

Social and Economic Characteristics of the Older Population: 1978; Housing. US Department of Commerce, Bureau of the Census. Current Population Reports, P–23, No. 85, 1979.

America in Transition. (Taeuber, Cynthia) US Department of Commerce, Bureau of the Census. Current Population Reports, Special Studies Series P–23, No. 128, Sep. 1983.

Characteristics of the Population below the Poverty Level: 1983. US Department of Commerce, Bureau of the Census. Current Population Reports, Consumer Income, Series P–60, No. 147, Mar. 1984.

Census Projections of the Population 1983–2080. US Department of Commerce, Bureau of the Census. Current Population Reports, Series P–25, No. 952, May 1984.

American Women: Three Decades of Change. (Bianchi, Suzanne M.; Spain, Daphne) US Department of Commerce, Bureau of the Census, Jun. 1984.

Demographic and Socioeconomic Aspects of Aging in the US: 1920–2040. US Department of Commerce, Bureau of the Census, Aug. 1984.

Money Income and Poverty Status of Families and Persons in the United States: 1983. US Department of Commerce, Bureau of the Census. Current Population Reports, Consumer Income, Series P–60, No. 145, Aug. 1984.

Economic Characteristics of Households in the United States: Third Quarter 1984. US Department of Commerce, Bureau of the Census. Current Population Reports, Household Economic Studies, Series P–70, No. 5, 1985.

State Population Estimates, by Age and Components of Change: 1980 to 1984. US Department of Commerce, Bureau of the Census. Series P–25, No. 970, 1985.

Statistical Abstract of the United States, 1985. US Department of Commerce, Bureau of the Census, 1985.

Estimates of the Population of the US by Age, Sex and Race, 1980–84. US Department of Commerce, Bureau of the Census. Series P–25, No. 965, Mar. 1985.

US Department of Education, National Center for Education Statistics

Participants in Postsecondary Education, Oct. 1982. US Department of Education, National Center for Education Statistics, Nov. 1984.

Projections of Education Statistics to 1992–93. (Gerald, Debra E.) US Department of Education, National Center for Education Statistics, Jul. 1985.

US Department of Health and Human Services, Federal Council on Aging

Need for Long Term Care, Information and Issues. A Chartbook of the Federal Council on the Aging. US Department of Health and Human Services, Federal Council on the Aging, 1981.

US Department of Health and Human Services, National Center for Health Statistics

Health, United States, and Prevention Profile, 1983. US Department of Health and Human Services, National Center for Health Statistics, Dec. 1983.

Vital Statistics of the United States, 1981: Volume III Marriage and Divorce. US Department of Health and Human Services, National Center for Health Statistics, 1985.

US Department of Health and Human Services, National Institute on Aging

Macroeconomic Demographic Model. US Department of Health and Human Services, National Institute on Aging, Jun. 1984.

US Department of Health and Human Services, National Institute on Alcohol Abuse and Alcoholism

Alcohol and Health, Monograph No. 4. US Department of Health and Human Services, National Institute on Alcohol Abuse and Alcoholism. Special Population Issues, 1982.

US Department of Health and Human Services, Social Security Administration

National Survey of the Aged. (Shanas, Ethel) US Department of Health and Human Services, Administration on Aging. DHHS Publication (OHDS) 83-20425, Dec. 1982.

Medicare and Medicaid Data Book, 1983. US Department of Health and Human Services, Social Security Administration.

Program and Demographic Characteristics of Supplemental Security Income Beneficiaries, December 1983. (Kahn, Arthur L.) US Department of Health and Human Services, Social Security Administration, Office of Policy, Office of Research, Statistics and International Policy. SSA Publication 13–11977, 1984.

History of Social Security. US Department of Health and Human Services, Social Security Administration, Jan. 1984.

Income of the Population, 55 and Over, 1982. US Department of Health and Human Services, Social Security Administration. SSA Publication No. 13–11871, Mar. 1984.

Joint Distribution of Wealth and Income. (Radner, Daniel B.; Vaughan, Denton R.) US Department of Health and Human Services, Social Security Administration, Office of Research, Statistics and Internal Policy, Mar. 1984.

Medicare Program Statistics, Selected Data, 1978–1982. US Department of Health and Human Services, Social Security Administration, Health Care Financing Administration, May 1984.

Wealth and Income of Aged Households. (Radner, Daniel B.) US Department of Health and Human Services, Social Security Administration. American Statistical Association, 1984 Proceedings, Aug. 1984.

Health, United States, 1984. US Department of Health and Human Services, Public Health Service, 1985.

US Department of Housing and Urban Development

Housing Characteristics of Recent Movers. US Department of Housing and Urban Development, Office of Policy Development and Research. Current Housing Reports, Annual Housing Survey: 1981, Series H–150–81.

US Department of Justice

Sourcebook of Criminal Justice Statistics–1982. (Flanigan, Timothy J.; McLeod, Maureen) US Department of Justice, Bureau of Justice Statistics, 1983.

US Department of Labor

Time of Change: 1983 Handbook on Women Workers. US Department of Labor, Women's Bureau. Bulletin 298, 1983.

CPI Detailed Report, August 1985. US Department of Labor, Bureau of Labor Statistics, 1985.

Employment in Perspective: Women in the Labor Force. US Department of Labor, Bureau of Labor Statistics. Report 721, 1985.

Handbook of Labor Statistics. US Department of Labor, Bureau of Labor Statistics, Jun. 1985.

Employment and Earnings. US Department of Labor, Bureau of Labor Statistics, Sep. 1985.

US Department of the Treasury, Internal Revenue Service

Individual Income Tax Returns, 1982 Statistics of Income. US Department of the Treasury, Internal Revenue Service, 1984.

US Department of Transportation

Transportation of Older Americans: Issues and Options for the Decade of the 1980's. US Department of Transportation, Apr. 1983.

US House of Representatives

Tomorrow's Elderly: A Report Prepared by the Congressional Clearinghouse of the Future. US House of Representatives, Select Committee on Aging. 98th Congress, 2nd Session, Pub. No. 98–457, Oct. 1984.

US Senate

Aging America: Trends and Projections. US Senate, Special Committee on Aging, American Association of Retired Persons, 1984.

Developments in Aging: 1984, A Report of the Special Committee on Aging, United States Senate, Pursuant to S. Res. 354, March 2, 1984. Vol. 1 *Report*; Vol. 2 *Appendixes.* US Senate, Special Committee on Aging, Feb. 1985.

America in Transition: An Aging Society, 1984–85 Edition. US Senate, Special Committee on Aging. 99th Congress, 1st Session, Committee Print 99–13, Aug. 1985.

How Older Americans Live: An Analysis of Census Data. US Senate, Special Committee on Aging. 99th Congress, 1st Session, Committee Print 99–91, Oct. 1985.

Aging America: Trends and Projections, 1985–86 Edition. US Senate, Special Committee on Aging, American Association of Retired Persons, Federal Council on the Aging, and Administration on Aging, 1986.

US Veterans Administration

Caring for Older Veterans. US Veterans Administration, Apr. 1975.

Survey of Aging Veterans. US Veterans Administration, Dec. 1983.

The Aging Female Veteran: Follow Up Analysis from the Survey of Aging Veterans. US Veterans Administration, Nov. 1984.

Health Insurance Coverage among Veterans Aged 55 and Over. Follow Up Analysis. (Petersen, Nancy J.) US Veterans Administration, Jan. 1985.

Current Health Status and the Future Demand for Health Care Programs and Social Support Services. US Veterans Administration, Mar. 1985.

Van Nostrand Reinhold Company

Economics of Aging: The Future of Retirement. (Morrison, Malcolm H., ed.) Van Nostrand Reinhold Company, New York, 1982.

World Priorities

Women: A World Survey. World Priorities, Washington, DC, 1985.

ONLINE DATABASES

AgeLine. Produced by American Association of Retired Persons and National Gerontology Resource Center. Online Service: BRS.

ASI® (American Statistics Index). Produced by Congressional Information Service, Inc. (CIS). Online Service: DIALOG Information Services, Inc.; SDC Information Services.

HEALTH PLANNING AND ADMINISTRATION. Produced by National Library of Medicine (NLM). Online Service: Australian Medline Network; BRS (HEALTH CARE AND ADMINISTRATION); BRS After Dark (HEALTH CARE AND ADMINISTRATION); BRS/Saunders Colleague (HEALTH CARE AND ADMINISTRATION); DIALOG Information Services, Inc.; DIMDI; National Library of Medicine (no longer available through MIC-KIBIC).

MEDLINE. Produced by National Library of Medicine (NLM). Online Service: Australian Medline Network; BRS; BRS After Dark; BRS/BRKTHRU; BRS/Saunders Colleague; DATA-STAR; DIALOG Information Services, Inc.; DIMDI (MEDLARS); INSERM; The Japan Information Center of Science and Technology (JICST); Knowledge Index; MIC-KIBIC; National Library of Medicine; TECH DATA.

NTIS® (National Technical Information Service). Produced by National Technical Information Service. Online Service: BRS; BRS After Dark; BRS/BRKTHRU; BRS/Saunders Colleague; Centre de Documentation de l'Armement (CEDOCAR); CISTI, Canadian Online Enquiry Service (CAN/OLE); DATA-STAR; DIALOG Information Services, Inc.; ESA-IRS; INKA Karlsruhe; The Japan Information Center of Science and Technology (JICST); Knowledge Index; Mead Data Central, REFERENCE Service; SDC Information Services; STN International; TECH DATA.

SOCIOLOGICAL ABSTRACTS. Produced by Sociological Abstracts, Inc. Online Service: BRS; BRS After Dark; BRS/BRKTHRU; BRS/Saunders Colleague; DATA-STAR; DIALOG Information Services, Inc.; TECH DATA.

SOCIAL SCISEARCH® (Online database for *Social Science Citation Index*). Produced by Institute for Scientific Information (ISI). Online Service: BRS; BRS After Dark; BRS/BRKTHRU; BRS/Saunders Colleague; DIALOG Information Services, Inc.; DIMDI; TECH DATA.

Index

by Linda Webster